PRICES, PRODUCTS, AND PEOPLE

PRICES, PRODUCTS, AND PEOPLE

Analyzing Agricultural Markets in Developing Countries

Gregory J. Scott, editor

Published in cooperation with the
INTERNATIONAL POTATO CENTER (CIP)
Address: Apartado 1558 - Lima, Peru. Telex: 25672 PE. Cable: CIPAPA, Lima
Phones: 366920; 354354. FAX: 351570. E-Mail: cip@cgnet.com or cip@cipa.org.pe

LYNNE
RIENNER
PUBLISHERS

BOULDER
LONDON

Cover photograph by Gregory J. Scott

Published in the United States of America in 1995 by
Lynne Rienner Publishers, Inc.
1800 30th Street, Boulder, Colorado 80301

and in the United Kingdom by
Lynne Rienner Publishers, Inc.
3 Henrietta Street, Covent Garden, London WC2E 8LU

© 1995 by the International Potato Center. All rights reserved
by the publisher.

Library of Congress Cataloging-in-Publication Data
Prices, products, and people : analyzing agricultural markets in
   developing countries / Gregory J. Scott, editor.
         p.   cm.
      Includes bibliographical references and index.
      ISBN 1-55587-609-9 (pbk.)
      1. Produce trade—Developing countries. 2. Farm produce—
Developing countries—Marketing—Cases studies. 3. Agricultural
prices—Developing countries. 4. Food industry and trade—
Developing countries. 5. Agriculture—Economic aspects—Developing
countries. I. Scott, Gregory J.
HD9018.D44P74 1995
381'.41'091724—dc20   95-21262
                                                                    CIP

British Cataloguing in Publication Data
A Cataloguing in Publication record for this book
is available from the British Library.

Printed and bound in the United States of America

The paper used in this publication meets the requirements
∞ of the American National Standard for Permanence of
Paper for Printed Library Materials Z39.48-1984.

5 4 3 2 1

Contents

Tables and Figures ix
Foreword, Hubert Zandstra xvii
Foreword, Mike Collinson xix
Acknowledgments xxi

Introduction
    Agricultural Marketing Research in Developing Countries:
    Old Tasks and New Challenges 1
    Gregory J. Scott

Part 1 Field Methods
■ Sub-Sector Analysis

1   Rapid Reconnaissance Methods for Diagnosis
    of Sub-Sector Limitations: Maize in Paraguay 21
    Michael L. Morris

2   Using Rapid Appraisal to Examine Coarse Grain
    Processing and Utilization in Mali 43
    John S. Holtzman, John A. Lichte,
    and James F. Tefft

3   The Policy Analysis Matrix Applied to Agricultural
    Commodity Markets 73
    Barry I. Shapiro and Steven J. Staal

4   A Multi-Product Sub-Sector Study in Rwanda 99
    Scott Loveridge

5   Methods for Evaluating the Market Potential of
    Processed Products 115
    Gregory J. Scott

Part 2 Field Methods
■ Market Analysis

6 Field Methods for Exploring the Role of Indigenous
   Rural Periodic Markets in Developing Countries.......................... 143
   Gina Porter

7 Wall-to-Wall Fieldwork: Secondary Data Collection
   for Food Systems Research 167
   Gregory J. Scott

8 Field and Analytical Methods for Agricultural
   Commercialization Studies: Guatemala... 187
   Maarten D.C. Immink, Ricardo Sibrián, Jorge A. Alarcón,
   and Herwig Hahn

9 Industrial Organization and Market Analysis:
   Fish Marketing.. 217
   R.S. Pomeroy and A.C. Trinidad

10 Socioeconomic Methods for the Study of Input Markets:
   Seed Potato in Argentina... 239
   Olga Della Vedova and Susana Brieva

Part 3 Analytical Methods
■ Price Analysis

11 A Primer on Marketing Channels and Margins........................... 257
   Gilberto Mendoza

12 Using Microcomputer Spreadsheets for Spatial and
   Temporal Price Analysis: An Application to Rice
   and Maize in Ecuador 277
   David L. Tschirley

13 Efficiency and Complexity: Distributive Margins and the
   Profits of Market Enterprises 301
   Barbara Harriss-White

14 Analyzing Market Integration..325
   Francesco Goletti and Eleni Christina-Tsigas

15 Pricing Conduct of Spatially Differentiated Markets 343
   Meyra Sebello Mendoza and Mark W. Rosegrant

Part 4 Analytical Methods
■ Models for Market Analysis

16 A Financial Model for the Implementation and
   Evaluation of Small-Scale Agro-Enterprises............................361
   Carlos Ostertag and Christopher Wheatley

17 Markets, Transaction Costs, and Selectivity Models
   in Economic Development...383
   Stephan J. Goetz

18 Measuring Welfare Benefits from Marketing
   Improvements: Potato Storage in Tunisia................................403
   Keith Owen Fuglie

19 Spatial Equilibrium Models in Agricultural Marketing
   Research: A Simplified Exposition...421
   J. Krishnaiah

20 Programming Models: Potential Applications to
   Agricultural Marketing Research 439
   Scott R. Jeffrey and Merle D. Faminow

21 Equilibrium Displacement Modelling: An Application
   to Indonesian Food Price Policy 461
   Roley Piggott

Index..481
About the Book and Editor 495

Tables and Figures

Introduction

Table 1	Trends in food production and foreign trade in developing countries, 1961-91	3
Table 2	Methods for agricultural marketing research	7

Chapter 1

Table 1	Food system matrix	25
Figure 1	Distribution of maize production in Paraguay, 1986-87	27
Figure 2	Production indices of main crops, Paraguay, 1978-89	30
Figure 3	Trends in nominal and real producer prices for maize in Paraguay, 1972-88	31
Figure 4	Trends in relative producer prices of maize and alternative crops, Paraguay, 1972-88	32
Table 2	Coefficients of variation around trend (CV) of real producer prices of principal crops in Paraguay, 1977-88	32
Figure 5	Seasonal fluctuations in the prices of yellow maize in Paraguay, 1972-88	33
Figure 6	Principal marketing channels for yellow maize in Paraguay	35
Table 3	Estimated marketing margins for yellow maize, 1989	36
Table 4	Profitability of the principal crops in Paraguay	36
Table 5	Sensitivity of maize profitability to changes in maize producer prices	37
Table 6	Sensitivity of maize profitability to changes in maize yield	37
Table 7	Estimated export parity price of maize, Paraguay, 1989	38

Chapter 2

Table 1	Cereal production in Mali by region, 1989-90	49
Figure 1	Grand seasonal indices of retail prices in Bamako, Mali, January 1982-May 1990 (excluding 1988)	50
Figure 2	Wholesale grain prices in Bamako for cereals at comparable stages of processing	51
Table 2	Price analysis and potential problems	52

Chapter 3

Table 1	The policy analysis matrix	77
Table 2	Expanded policy analysis matrix	79
Figure 1	Structure of an activity budget	83
Table 3	A representative zero-grazing farm at Nyeri, Kenya	87
Table 4	Structure of activity budget—farm level	88

Table 5	Structure of activity budget—farm gate to processor: costs incurred by the dairy cooperative	89
Table 6	Structure of activity budget—processing: costs incurred by KCC in milk processing	90
Table 7	Calculations of import-parity milk price	90
Table 8	Summary of milk prices	91
Table 9	System summary: Nyeri dairy market	94
Table 10	Policy analysis matrix—farm level	94
Table 11	Policy analysis matrix—post-farm	94
Table 12	Policy analysis matrix system	94
Table 13	Sensitivity analysis	95
Table 14	Private and social indicators	95

Chapter 4

Table 1	Pair regressions of detrended urban retail dry bean prices before and after hard surface paving of an interurban road link	102
Figure 1	Kigali dry beans: urban-rural price differences and rural grain flows, December 1985-December 1986	107
Table 2	Rural use and degree of rural self-sufficiency, 12 crops, Rwanda 1990	108
Table 3	Conversion factors for calculating AE	110
Table 4	Net rural purchases by household revenue category	111
Table 5	Objectives, strengths, and weaknesses of various methods	112

Chapter 6

Figure 1	Nigeria, showing the two survey areas (map)	147
Table 1	Procedures for rural periodic market field research	157
Figure 2	Maps illustrating aspects of spatio-temporal change in the Jos Plateau survey area	160

Chapter 7

Figure 1	Percentage of potato production in the principal districts of Bangladesh, 1960-85	171
Figure 2	An agricultural calendar for potato in Thailand	172
Table 1	Prices and sales margins for potato sold in Dhaka, Bangladesh, 1981-85	174
Figure 3	Real versus nominal prices for potato in Lima, Peru, 1960-79	175
Table 2	Daily per capita consumption of calories and proteins by principal food groups in Zaire 1979-80	176
Table 3	Guide to the use of secondary information	180

Chapter 8

Table 1	Summary of methodological aspects of three agricultural commercialization studies in Guatemala, 1985, 1987, and 1991	192
Figure 1	Causal model of household and individual effects of the transformation of farm production towards non-traditional export crops	197
Table 2	Operationalizing the conceptual framework: variables and indicators	200
Table 3	Factor analysis of water, housing, and sanitation variables with the Varimax Rotation Method; rural households (n = 376), Central Highlands, Guatemala, 1991	203
Table 4	Probit models to estimate determinants of adoption of market-oriented crop patterns among smallholder farmers, Western Highlands, Guatemala, 1987	204
Table 5	Per capita total income (in constant 1985 prices), co-op and non-co-op households, by community location, 1985 and 1991. Analysis of variance of repeated measures	206
Table 6	Decomposition analysis of income inequality among smallholder farm households (n = 416), Central Highlands, Guatemala, 1991	207
Table 7	Cluster analysis for stratification of rural households according to household output mix, Central Highlands, Guatemala, 1991	210

Chapter 9

Table 1	Alternative market analysis methodologies	218
Table 2	Summary of information on the four fisheries analyzed	220
Table 3	Data requirements for application of the industrial organization framework and price efficiency techniques in fish marketing	221
Table 4	Structural, conduct, and performance characteristics of fish markets at the primary buyer level	223
Table 5	Market structure characteristics and analytical techniques used in four marketing studies	225
Figure 1	Some benchmarks suggested to evaluate whether concentration results in imperfect competition	226
Table 6	Pricing behavior and analytical techniques used in four marketing studies	231

Chapter 10

Figure 1	Table potato and pathogen-tested seed potato production	241
Table 1	Production (000 t) by planting zone and season	243

Table 2	Surveyed area by zone and producer strata	245
Table 3	Current and potential demand for semi-late production in the southeastern region of Buenos Aires Province	249
Table 4	Seed demand	249

Chapter 11

Figure 1	Principal stages of the marketing process in a traditional centralized system	260
Figure 2	Avocado marketing chain in Region V's network of associated producers, Santiago, Chile	260
Figure 3	Vegetable supply flow for Greater Santiago (Chile)	263
Figure 4	Marketing channels for potatoes in Santo Domingo, Dominican Republic	264
Table 1	Prices for potatoes in the marketing channel grown in the North of Chuquisaca, Bolivia	269
Figure 5	Marketing channels for some vegetables in the province of Arica and distributed in the northern and central Chilean markets	271
Table 2	Marketing margins for grade one tomatoes in Chile's Central region, December 1981 to March 1982	272

Chapter 12

Figure 1	Monthly nominal price for wholesale milled rice in Quito, Ecuador, 1971-82	282
Figure 2	An example of a temporal price series and its various components decomposed	284
Table 1	Results of temporal analysis for nominal milled rice prices in Quito, Ecuador, 1971-89	286
Table 2	Formulae in Lotus 1-2-3 for computing the temporal components of the milled rice price	287
Figure 3	Monthly deflated price for milled rice at the wholesale level in Quito, Ecuador, 1971-89	288
Table 3	Analysis of seasonal indices for rice in Quito, 1971-89	289
Figure 4	The Grand Seasonal Index for milled rice in Quito, Ecuador, calculated over 1971-89	290
Figure 5	Monthly seasonal index for milled rice in Ecuador, 1971-89	291
Figure 6	Grand Seasonal Indices, 1971-82 and 1983-89	292
Figure 7	GSI and standard deviations, 1971-82 and 1983-89	292
Table 4	Simple price correlation coefficients for pairs of feed maize markets in Ecuador, 1985-87	294
Table 5	Results of the ICM test, prices for maize, Ecuador, 1987-89	296

Tables and Figures

Chapter 13

Figure 1	Uncertainty in price relations, two examples (a and b)	306
Figure 2	Model of price relations, N.A. Dt. South India	307
Table 1	Returns from flexible, maximizing trade: coarse rice wholesale, 1976-77, one quintal per week (Rps)	309
Table 2	Rigid trading—profit and loss totalled for year: one quintal (Rps) of coarse rice traded weekly, 1976-77	311
Table 3	Returns from rigid trade of one quintal/week at annual average prices (Rps/q) coarse grain wholesale, 1976-77	313
Figure 3a	Combinations of activity in marketing firms in Coimbatore District, India	319
Figure 3b	Least common, most simple patterns of marketing behavior	319
Figure 4	Rates of return and combinatorial complexity in groundnut marketing, South India	321
Figure 5	Rates of return and combinatorial complexity in cotton marketing, South India	322

Chapter 14

Table 1	Comparison of various measures of integration in Bangladesh rice market and in Malawi maize market	337
Table 2	Summary effects of structural factors on measures of integration in Bangladesh	338

Chapter 15

Table 1	Price instability, measured by the coefficient of variation, in the Philippine copra market over three policy regimes, 1971 to 1988	351
Table 2	Validation of the bivariate autoregressive model representation of the spatial pricing conduct in the Philippine copra market, January 1, 1971, to September 30, 1988	352
Table 3	Tests of spatial pricing conduct in Philippine copra markets, January 1, 1971, to September 30, 1988	353
Table 4	Contemporaneous and historical price effects on price response in Philippine copra markets, January 1, 1971, to September 30, 1988	354

Chapter 16

Figure 1	Interpretation of the definition for Internal Rate of Return	364
Table 1	Some differences between the Economic Rate of Return (ERR) and the Financial Rate of Return (FRR)	364

Table 2	Parameters of the cassava flour production process used in the model	369
Figure 2	Sensitivity of Financial Rate of Return (FRR) to amount of initial investment	369
Figure 3	Sensitivity of FRR to capacity utilization	370
Figure 4	Sensitivity of FRR to price of cassava roots	370
Figure 5	Sensitivity of FRR to the root-to-dry-chip conversion factor	371
Figure 6	Sensitivity of FRR to first-grade flour extraction rate	371
Figure 7	Sensitivity of FRR to sales price of first-grade flour	372
Figure 8	Price structure of cassava flour; weighted average price: $201,000	372
Figure 9	Financial Rate of Return (FRR) maximization strategy for the pilot cassava flour plant	374

Chapter 17

Figure 1	Censored versus truncated samples (shooting range example)	386
Figure 2	Illustration of Tobit and OLS lines for censored samples	387
Figure 3	Cumulative and marginal standard normal distribution functions and an illustration of censoring	391
Table 1	Maximum likelihood estimates for factors affecting the use of fertilizer by Senegalese farm households (absolute t-statistic)	392
Table 2	Selectivity model for coarse grain market participation by Senegalese farm households (absolute t-statistics)	396

Chapter 18

Figure 1	An economic model of seasonal crop storage	408
Figure 2	Welfare effects from a reduction in storage costs	412
Figure 3	Welfare effects from a reduction in storage losses	413
Table 1	Welfare effects from a reduction in potato storage costs	416

Chapter 19

Figure 1	A graphical approach to spatial equilibrium	426
Figure 2	Two-region model	426
Table 1	Optimal demand, supply, and commodity flows of rice, sorghum, and pulses (000 t) in different regions of Andhra Pradesh in relation to rest of India	433

Table 2	Optimal allocation of area and production and equilibrium prices of rice, sorghum, and pulses in different regions of Andhra Pradesh under optimal and existing situations.............434
Table 3	Producers' surplus, consumers' surplus, and economic surplus (million Rps) under an optimal situation in different regions of Andra Pradesh..435

Chapter 20

Figure 1	Graphical representation of resource sensitivity analysis..........444
Figure 2	Graphical representation of objective function coefficient sensitivity analysis 445
Figure 3	Graphical representation of MGA 446
Table 1	Initial solution for the least-cost dairy ration problem (initial prices)..450
Table 2	Alternative solutions for the least-cost dairy ration problem—basic MGA approach (adjusted prices) 451
Table 3	Alternative solutions for the least-cost dairy ration problem—MGA approach with specific objectives (adjusted prices)..453

Chapter 21

Figure 1	Matrix R (15 x 15) of equation (13)....................................470
Figure 2	Matrix S (15 x 1) of equation (13)......................................470
Figure 3	Matrix T (15 x 8) of equation (13).....................................471
Figure 4	Matrix U (8 x 1) of equation (13) 471
Figure 5	Matrix V (1 x 8) 471
Table 1	Demand elasticities used for the Indonesian model..................472
Table 2	Supply elasticities used for the Indonesian model...................472
Table 3	Percentage changes in the producer price of rice consistent with maintaining the rice self-sufficiency ratio following a 5% increase in the price of fertilizer....................474
Table 4	Percentage changes in the price of fertilizer consistent with maintaining the rice self-sufficiency ratio following 1% increases in incomes and producer rice prices 475
Figure 6	General equilibrium elasticities matrix G (15 x 8) for the Indonesian model...477

Foreword

Hubert Zandstra

Market phenomena and marketing systems are growing in importance as key factors influencing the success or failure of efforts to improve food production and consumption in developing countries. The rise in importance of commercial agriculture is the product of various converging tendencies. Farmers are no longer interested just in higher yields, or even in higher prices per se, but in more remunerative commercial outlets. Direct public intervention in marketing activities has steadily declined. The role of private entrepreneurs and non-governmental organizations in helping to meet the needs of urban consumers and rural producers is increasingly apparent.

Given these developments, there is a variety of marketing issues for developing countries to address in the years ahead. A few examples of the most noteworthy include overcoming commercial bottlenecks due to inadequate production or postharvest technology, seizing market opportunities resulting from income and demographic changes, and resolving market-related policy problems.

Postharvest research, training, and information have long been an integral part of the work of the International Potato Center (CIP). Marketing research has figured prominently in this regard, with training through collaborative marketing research an ongoing activity. In response to a growing number of requests from our developing country partners, this effort has been extended in recent years to include an assortment of training materials, of which this volume is a part.

Marketing problems and opportunities are by no means peculiar to roots and tubers. Farmers, consumers, and traders as well as national agricultural research institutes typically work with a variety of crop and livestock marketing systems. Therefore, I am pleased that scientists at other centers have joined with us in a common initiative to address the need for appropriate methodologies to analyze agricultural marketing in developing countries. All these researchers have years of experience in this field. As a result of this volume, their acquired knowledge can now be more effectively utilized by colleagues in developing countries.

Hubert Zandstra
Director General
International Potato Center
Lima, Peru

Foreword

Mike Collinson

When the social sciences were brought to bear on African agriculture at the beginning of the 1960s, it was clear that the methods in universities were too data-intensive to be practical on any but the most parochial scale in developing countries. Farmers did not keep records and professionals were thin on the ground. There was a massive trade-off between intensity of data needs for any one study and for coverage studies. While some research objectives could be satisfied by selective case studies, operational objectives demanded coverage.

Through the 1970s, the evolution of rapid appraisal provided a level of understanding of production and systems that was adequate for many purposes. Beyond this, when detailed quantitative analysis was required, the understanding gained from rapid appraisal allowed better researcher decisions on the parameters, the sample needed for reliable capture, and the use of appropriate data collection methods. It made quantitative analysis more efficient.

It was the start of the widening of options in research process that continues today and that finds strong expression in these chapters.

As a devotee of systems approaches to research, I see this collection as particularly timely. The interrelated issues of food security, poverty alleviation, natural resource degredation, and global environmental integrity have increased research complexity. It has become important to relate farmers' decisions to other decisions at the local, regional, national, and global levels. Markets are information links between these levels and the key to understanding their interactions.

Having experienced the "have tool will travel" mentality of academia in the 1960s, one of my own watchwords has remained "horses for courses"— choose the technique that will do the job at hand. This approach is used in these valuable case studies compiled by Greg Scott and his colleagues.

The book records a huge professional effort to understand market foibles. It offers an inventory of approaches to equip research teams in diverse circumstances. In the spirit of horses for courses, it will be invaluable both to teachers and to research practitioners reviewing the field and picking the winner.

Mike Collinson
Washington, D.C.

Acknowledgments

This book would not have been possible without the active support of many individuals and institutions. During some 15 years of work with the International Potato Center (CIP) in more than 20 different developing countries, I have had the opportunity to engage in agricultural marketing research with colleagues in Africa, Asia, and Latin America. Much of that work was greatly facilitated by their support and assistance. This volume represents my attempt to repay them with some tools of the trade so that they might do more marketing research independently.

In paying back that debt, I am extremely grateful to all the other authors in this volume and the institutions that they represent for sharing their ideas and experience on agricultural marketing research in developing countries. I am particularly grateful to Francesco Goletti, Meyra Sabello Mendoza, and Mark Rosegrant from the International Food Policy Research Institute (IFPRI); Barry Shapiro from the International Livestock Center for Africa (ILCA); Michael Morris from the International Center for Maize and Wheat Improvement (CIMMYT); Carlos Ostertag from the International Center for Tropical Agriculture (CIAT); Christopher Wheatley, formerly of CIAT and now with CIP; and Richard Pomeroy and A.C. Trinidad from the International Center for Living Aquatic Resources Management (ICLARM).

Many of the chapters were first prepared for a workshop on agricultural marketing research in developing countries held in March 1993 at the Indian Agricultural Research Institute (IARI), on the outskirts of Delhi. I am grateful to the staff in the Department of Agricultural Economics for co-hosting this event with CIP and providing a collegial atmosphere for debating a wide range of methodological issues. I am also grateful to members of CIP's Delhi office for the tremendous effort required to facilitate such an event. In this regard, special thanks are due Mahesh Upadhya, former head of this office, as well as to M. Kadian and V.S. Khatana.

Transforming the various manuscripts into book chapters was a job that required the support of various people based at CIP-Lima. I am particularly indebted to Patricia Chiroque for handling all the messages to and from the contributors as well as acting as a general secretary for all matters related to the book. Rosario Basay was great at proofreading and helping to put together the index. Sidney Evans steadily translated a number of chapters. My thanks to Julia Wright for help with proofreading. Anselmo Morales was masterful at preparing the figures and maps. I truly appreciate the work of Cecilia LaFosse in helping to design the cover. My special thanks to Princess Ferguson for so carefully checking all the manuscripts for missing citations, figures, or maps. I am particularly grateful to Princess for her incredible persistence in helping me with the text editing and the truly remarkable job she performed in word processing, formatting, and preparing the manuscript for publication.

Gregory J. Scott
International Potato Center
Lima, Peru

Introduction

Agricultural Marketing Research in Developing Countries: Old Tasks and New Challenges

Gregory J. Scott[1]

The purpose of this book is to provide a collection of methods on how to analyze agricultural marketing in developing countries. The methods presented involve applied social science research, but emphasize agricultural economics. The focus is on domestic or internal marketing as opposed to foreign trade. Some procedures stress more data collection (field methods), others data analysis (analytical methods). Most contributions combine elements of both methodological perspectives.

The publication is intended as a source book for those interested in analyzing agricultural marketing in a developing-country context. Foremost in this group would be researchers working in National Agricultural Research Systems (NARS) in Africa, Asia, and Latin America. Many of the papers presented are authored, co-authored, or greatly facilitated by these scientists. The book should also prove useful to, among others, teaching professionals and students, as well as development policy analysts concerned with agricultural marketing issues.

Importance of Agricultural Marketing

The performance of agricultural markets has long been recognized by economists, planners, and policy makers as a critical component in the development process. Hence, analysis of these markets has been an on-going assignment for decades. Particular emphasis beginning in the 1950s was on the perceived imperfections in international commodity markets (Prebisch 1950). So much so, in fact, that by the 1960s policy makers were nearly always unwilling to leave decisions about prices and distribution of agricultural goods solely to the workings of the Invisible Hand, but opted instead for active government participation in, if not control of, marketing activities. By the early 1980s, five emerging trends heightened interest in and concern over future

---

[1] Economist, Social Science Department, International Potato Center, P. O. Box 1558, Lima, Peru.

directions in domestic agricultural marketing on the part of not only economists and policy makers but also producers, consumers, and more recently environmentalists.

Structural adjustment in the form of trade liberalization became standard government policy throughout much of the developing world, but particularly in Sub-Saharan Africa, in the early 1980s. As the record on economic—and especially agricultural—growth became increasingly more disappointing in Africa in the late 1970s, many economists became disillusioned with government intervention in the marketplace as an effective strategy to spur faster development. Comparisons between the rapid expansion in East Asia and the dismal record in Latin America also fueled the reassessment of the role of the state versus that of markets in fomenting economic development (Dutt, Kim, and Singh 1994). A consensus therefore emerged that saw deregulating markets as the cornerstone of reforms needed to accelerate economic growth (Scarborough and Kydd 1992). Domestic agricultural markets were often a focal point of these initiatives. In addition to economy-wide considerations, this policy shift also reflected fundamental changes within the agricultural sector itself.

Farmers in Africa, Asia, and Latin America have made use of agricultural markets, but this use has intensified over the last three decades as agriculture has become more market-oriented in virtually all developing countries. Subsistence production has declined in relative importance in part because technological improvements mean producers have more output to sell. Expansion of road, rail and water networks, as well as telecommunication systems, have made growers more accessible and more vulnerable to market forces (Santos-Villanueva 1966). Population pressure in the countryside resulting in declining farm size has induced many small farmers to explore alternative crop and livestock production patterns linked to non-traditional market outlets to maintain, if not improve, household living standards (Kennedy and Cogill 1987; von Braun et al. 1989).

Over half the developing world's population will reside in cities by the year 2025 (Bongarts 1995). Mushrooming urban areas— particularly in Sub-Saharan Africa—mean that more and more consumers depend on agricultural marketing for their daily food requirements. Furthermore, in much of South Asia the growing numbers of rural landless look to agricultural marketing activities such as storage, processing, transport, and trading as a source of employment. Without income from these occupations, many of these consumers would not have access to food.

Environmentalists have even shown a growing interest in agricultural marketing. For example, if bio-diversity is to be economically viable, commercial outlets need to be found for crops heretofore cultivated only for subsistence use. If particular ecologies (e.g., mountains) are to remain vital sources of sustenance and culture, then agricultural marketing systems linking such ecologies to adjoining environments need to be better understood, potential benefits from marketing activities more effectively exploited, and negative aspects of commercialization minimized.

Most importantly, population growth, increased per capita income, and improvements in infrastructure have meant the sheer volume of goods traded in domestic agricultural markets has increased tremendously (Table 1). Hence, the potential rewards to society and individuals from improvements in domestic agricultural marketing have multiplied in a corresponding fashion.

A variety of forces—political, economic, technological, demographic, environmental, historic—will continue to converge and thereby generate pressure to improve domestic agricultural marketing practices and procedures to satisfy the demands of the people that such activities are intended to serve. The impact of these pressures is compounded by the relative scarcity of information and accelerating pace of change regarding domestic agricultural marketing in developing countries.

Limitations of Previous Research

The last three decades have witnessed a dramatic increase in the amount of research on food problems in developing countries. A growing body of literature therefore exists on topics related to food production, consumption and nutrition. Alternatively, various authors have examined issues of food aid, international trade in agricultural commodities or food security. There is also a growing interest in the marketing of industrial and financial goods (Kindra 1984; Kayak 1986; Kinsey 1988; Roemer and Jones 1991). Studies on the internal distribution and sale of locally produced plant, livestock, and fish products—domestic agricultural marketing— have tended to receive less attention for an assortment of reasons.

Table 1. Trends in food production and foreign trade in developing countries, 1961-91.

Country	Commodity	Production (000 t)		Trade (%)[1]	
		1961	1991	1961	1991
Philippines	rice	3,910	9,673	4.8	0.1
India	wheat	10,997	55,134	28.1	1.2
Kenya	maize	940	2,340	11.2	0.8
Colombia	potato	551	2,225	0.1	1.4

[1] Exports plus imports divided by production.
Source: FAO, PC-Agrostat, unpublished statistics, 1993.

In most developing countries, collection and analysis of statistics on output and use of locally produced agricultural commodities has become fairly routine. Data on agricultural marketing —with the possible exception of prices for urban staples and export crops—are not so regularly monitored. In some instances, data that may exist are hard to gain access to for political or proprietary reasons. Furthermore, those studies on domestic agricultural marketing that are completed, often suffer from restricted publication and dissemination. The shortage of research on domestic agricultural marketing in developing countries is also partly attributable to the scarcity of methodological materials in this specific field of endeavor.

Much of the literature on agricultural marketing in developing countries can be categorized into one of three types. One type consists of compilations of basic principles or concepts regarding agricultural marketing. Often these ideas are presented in the context of a more general treatment of agricultural development issues (see, e.g., Timmer et al. 1983; Stevens and Jabara 1988; Colman and Young 1989; Abbott and Makeham 1990). Given the conceptual nature of these publications, the ideas presented are academic or hypothetical in nature. Such materials provide an extremely useful theoretical background for the analysis of agricultural markets. Their weakness is that other than the reference to specific examples presented to illustrate particular concepts they provide limited operational guidelines for actually applying economic theory in conducting marketing research.

A second type consists of reviews, syntheses, or concept papers regarding the agricultural marketing literature. The literature the authors refer to focuses on developing countries, either in whole or in part (see Breimyer 1973; Bateman 1976; Riley and Staatz 1981; Riley and Weber 1983; ICRISAT 1985; Abbott 1986; Young and MacCormac 1987; Fleming 1990; Abbott 1993; Sellen et al. 1993); or, focusing on particular regions, for example, Africa (Jones 1974; Eicher and Baker 1982), Latin America (Bromley and Symanski 1974; Harrison et al. 1974), or Asia (Bucklin 1977). These publications are often extremely useful guides to the studies available in terms of issues and findings. They also provide provocative insights into relevant research agendas for the future and how these have evolved over time. But, given their often synthetic nature, their emphasis on the overall focus of particular studies and/or their due measure to findings as well as methods, they offer only limited information about the particular procedures referred to.

A third type consists of case studies of particular agricultural markets, marketing systems, or agricultural marketing enterprises (see Elz 1985, 1987; Elz and Hoisington 1985; Abbott 1987; EDI 1987; APO 1989; World Bank 1990). These publications offer the interested reader a wealth of information about specific markets in a particular country for a given product in a given month or year. In so doing, end results of the application of economic analysis to the study of agricultural marketing often abound in such studies. Nevertheless, here what is often lacking is a step-by-step explanation of the procedures on how such location-, time- and product-specific research might be carried out in another place for some other commodity on a future occasion. It is this gap between the conceptual and case study literature on domestic agricultural marketing in developing countries that this book aims to help breach.

In recent years, a select number of publications have focused on conducting applied social science research in developing countries (Nichols 1991; Pratt and Loizos 1992; Bulmer and Warwick 1993). The limited number of previously published studies on applied methods for analyzing domestic agricultural marketing in developing countries merit mention here. This volume tries to go beyond the ad hoc working papers by Holtzman (1986) and Goetz and Weber (1987) on specific marketing topics in two respects (see also Reeves 1986; Fleming 1990; Magrath 1992; Trotter 1992). It provides the reader with up-dated versions of these documents (see the chapters by Holtzman et al. and Tschirley, respectively). Moreover, these revised papers—when taken together with the other papers included in this volume— are intended to present a broader set of methodological guidelines than previous publications set out to achieve. Growing recognition of the importance of the informal sector in terms of its contribution to output, employment and growth (see de Soto 1982) have made plain the necessity for alternative methods to those focusing on agroindustry (see Austin 1992) and more appropriate to the study of small- and medium-scale agricultural marketing enterprises. The present book also differs from the hands-on methods manual by Scarborough and Kydd (1992) in that it tries to offer the reader a series of fairly self-contained papers on particular marketing topics. Given the frequent need for prompt attention to particular policy-related marketing issues, the emphasis in this volume is on practical and rapid research procedures as well as simplified substitutes for more complicated approaches.

Methods for agricultural marketing research cover a potentially vast number of topics. This volume does not pretend to offer an exhaustive compendium of approaches and procedures in this field. Rather, it attempts to set out a collection of methods to help practitioners address the types of marketing questions that analysts are most frequently confronted with in developing countries. It also aims at providing a cross-section of techniques. While the methods presented are not new, bringing them together provides the researcher a better appreciation of the array that are available and, in so doing, a flexibility to call upon those which appear most appropriate for the task at hand. The methods themselves differ in technical complexity because the needs of the intended readership may vary from personal and professional to didactic. The research capabilities of the NARS also vary. With this in mind, many contributions include appendices where guidelines about survey procedures or analytical techniques are spelled out in greater detail.

In addition to the presentation of a particular method, nearly all the chapters include examples of the application of these techniques to specific commodities based on research in different developing countries around the world. The intent here is to enrich the general exposition of a series of methods with an array of commodity-specific experiences involving their use. Those readers with a working knowledge of agricultural marketing research in Africa, for example, may well find the procedures based on studies in Latin America or Asia thought-provoking. In this regard, many of the authors also include an assessment of the strengths and weaknesses of the methods described and/or some all-too-rare reflections on the methodological lessons learned from marketing research in a developing-country context based on their years of experience.

Organization of the Book

The methods for agricultural marketing research presented in this volume cover both field and analytical procedures (Table 2). The field methods have a stronger bent towards data collection procedures, whereas the analytical methods are more focused on interpretation of quantitative information. In actual practice, this arbitrary distinction between the two types breaks down. Fieldwork also requires analytical procedures, if not to analyze data, then to systematically organize their collection as well as to ensure congruence between the theoretical concepts employed and the empirical measures being used to quantify them. In the same way, data analysis of marketing phenomena that is not grounded in a firm understanding of how and why the figures were collected in the first place is subject to some serious errors of interpretation. With that caveat and given that typically agricultural marketing research requires first data collection and then data analysis, the first part of this book concentrates on field methods and the second on analytical methods.

Field Methods covers two areas of research: sub-sector (or food system) analysis and market analysis. Much of the earliest marketing research was influenced by the framework developed by Bressler and King (1970) for assessing competition between firms operating in different locations in the USA but at the same level (e.g., wholesale) in the marketing chain. Following Shaffer (1968), a number of marketing studies were carried out in Latin America that emphasized analysis of the vertical linkages between participants in agricultural marketing activities (see, e.g., Slater et al. 1969) and often had been overlooked in previous research because of the limitations of the then prevailing analytical framework. These studies emphasized analyzing marketing activities from the producer through to the consumer for a particular commodity (see, e.g., Shwedel 1977), thereby proceeding vertically through the marketing process from harvesting to rural assembly, to wholesaling, to retailing utilizing a systems-analysis framework. Hence, there emerged the commodity "sub-sector" or "food system" approach to research on agricultural marketing in developing countries (see Shaffer 1973, 1980; Shaffer et al. 1985).

Table 2. Methods for agricultural marketing research.

Author	Framework	Commodity	Country
Morris	Sub-sector	Maize	Paraguay
Holtzman et al.	Sub-sector	Sorghum, maize	Mali
Shapiro & Staal	PAM	Dairy marketing	Kenya
Loveridge	Sub-sector	Beans	Rwanda
Scott	Food system	Table potatoes	Peru, Bangladesh, Burundi
Porter	Geography/ economic anthropology	Various	Nigeria
Pomeroy & Trinidad	Industrial organization	Fish	Costa Rica, Philippines, Malaysia
Immink et al.	Household models	Vegetables	Guatemala
Scott	Institutional	Processed products	India, Colombia, Peru
Della Vedova & Brieva	Input demand	Seed potato	Argentina
Mendoza	Marketing margin analysis	Potatoes, tomatoes	Dominican Rep., Bolivia, Chile
Tschirley	Time-series price analysis	Rice, maize	Ecuador
Harriss	Static and dynamic margin analysis	Cotton, groundnuts, rice	India
Goletti	Horizontal price integration	Rice, maize	Bangladesh, Malawi
Mendoza & Rosegrant	Bivariate auto-regressive model	Copra	Philippines
Ostertag & Wheatley	Financial accounting	Cassava	Colombia
Goetz	Selectivity models	Coarse grains	Senegal
Fuglie	Partial equilibrium model	Potatoes	Tunisia
Krishnaiah	Spatial equilibrium models	Rice, sorghum, pulses	India
Jeffrey and Faminow	Linear programming	Wheat	Canada
Piggot	Equilibrium displacement model	Rice	Indonesia

One criticism of the sub-sector approach was that such studies required collection of enormous quantities of primary (in lieu of secondary) data that took inordinate amounts of time and cost far too much money. Another was that such an approach paid too much attention to the food requirements of poor, urban consumers and in so doing overlooked the production and marketing constraints of small farmers (Bromley and Symanski 1974). A third criticism was that the food systems approach lacked a formal, quantitative framework so as to be able to measure the effects of several proposed policy changes simultaneously. Partly for these reasons, methods were developed to carry out rapid appraisals of food marketing systems; to gear the outcome of such studies to biological scientists (e.g., plant breeders) as well as policy makers; to formalize the sub-sector perspective for policy analysis; and to facilitate the collection and use of secondary data.

In the first field methods section, Sub-Sector Analysis, **Morris** shows how sub-sector research in the form of rapid reconnaissance guidelines can provide a quick and effective means of understanding complex interactions between production and marketing activities. It also shows how such an approach facilitates marketing research by non-specialists, in this case biological scientists, and generates an agenda for more narrowly focused research initiatives in the future. Most importantly, it illustrates how marketing research can identify the need for new production solutions to overcome what heretofore had been perceived to be a marketing problem, i.e., farmer adoption of new maize technology in Paraguay was low not because of high marketing margins, but because such technology was simply unprofitable.

Holtzman, Lichte, and **Tefft** explain how sub-sector research can provide, at relatively low cost, insights into the linkages between consumer preferences, proposed changes in post-harvest practices, and the market prospects for different commodities. The authors' recommendations on new processing technology emphasize alternatives to the innovations that had been actively considered until their study of sorghum and maize in Mali was completed. Appendix 1 of their paper offers a synthetic overview of the key procedural issues in rapid appraisal of marketing systems using the sub-sector framework.

Shapiro and **Staal** provide a primer on how to use the Policy Analysis Matrix (PAM) to study policy effects at each level of the commodity chain. As a more formal, quantitative variant of sub-sector studies, the PAM facilitates sensitivity analysis of multiple policy changes and a rapid quantitative assessment of the impacts of the proposed policy shifts on different marketing participants. The PAM also allows for international effects on domestic agricultural markets to be readily incorporated into the analysis. As the PAM can be a complex methodological tool for the less experienced researcher, Shapiro and Staal provide a concise guide to its essential elements by presenting results from their analysis of dairy marketing in Kenya to illustrate the PAM's strengths and weaknesses.

Sub-sector studies call upon the use of multiple methodological procedures such as combining the analysis of secondary statistics with that of primary data collected through both formal and informal surveys. **Loveridge** explains how to carry out a national farm household survey using a stratified random sample, how to conduct informal interviews with urban traders, and how to utilize the results to analyze the interface of production and marketing activities. Based on his work in Rwanda, he also provides a retrospective assessment of the objectives, strengths, and weaknesses of these various procedures. An Appendix contains a suggested list of questions for urban traders.

Nearly every applied research methodology related to agricultural marketing in developing countries stresses the need to make effective use of secondary data. Virtually none provides an indication of what this actually entails. **Scott** offers the interested researcher a set of guidelines for data collection in offices, libraries, and labs. These include: what types of data are available; where they most likely can be found; how they can be efficiently procured; and, how such information can be effectively presented.

The second field methods section, Market Analysis, consists of methods that focus on particular locations, products, or marketing issues (e.g., nutrition).

Rural periodic markets are perhaps the most typical location for agricultural marketing activities in developing countries. **Porter** provides a brief historical account of research by geographers and economic anthropologists on periodic markets in developing countries. She then sets out a series of procedures to analyze trading activities at these sites. These include pre-survey work in both libraries and the field; field survey activities at the preliminary and operational stage of data collection; and post-survey tasks such as debriefing field assistants and writing up field notes. Porter makes plain the use of these techniques by providing examples from her field research in Nigeria.

Commodity marketing research in developing countries most often has concentrated on crop or livestock products. **Pomeroy** and **Trinidad** focus instead on fish marketing utilizing a modified industrial organization (IO) framework. They begin with a concise review of alternative methodologies, contrasting the IO approach with descriptive and price efficiency analysis. The authors then provide guidelines on data requirements for a series of analytical techniques related to key IO concepts such as market structure, conduct, and performance. Research results from studies done in Costa Rica, Malaysia, and the Philippines serve to illustrate the use of these procedures.

Is there a life-cycle for agricultural marketing research? By the time the questionnaire forms are designed, the data collected and analyzed, and the final report written up, most researchers are too busy or too tired to give serious thought to making sense of the entire experience. **Immink et al.** provide just such an unusual perspective by setting out the methodological lessons learned from three studies done on vegetable marketing in Guatemala. These include the importance of involving clients in formulating the research agenda and making explicit the conceptual-analytical framework from the outset. The authors also provide detailed suggestions on operationalizing key marketing concepts and the use of particular statistical techniques, e.g., cluster analysis.

One by-product of rapid urbanization in Africa, Asia, and Latin America is a growing interest in the production of processed products, particularly by small- and medium-scale enterprises. Years of research in this field has repeatedly shown the importance of assessing the market potential of such products prior to embarking upon costly and time-consuming research and development efforts (see, e.g., Scott et al. 1993). **Scott** presents an overall framework and a series of five practical research steps to carry out such assessments. Use of the techniques described is then illustrated by examples based on research in India, Colombia, and Peru. Appendix tables provide a checklist for screening prospective products and a tabular framework for analyzing ex-ante estimates of costs and returns.

Marketing and demand for agricultural inputs is the subject of the paper by **Della Vedova** and **Brieva**. The commodity focus is on seed potato in Argentina. The authors present an analytical model followed by the procedures used to quantitatively estimate the variables indicated. These techniques cover survey design, conducting interviews, and data processing. After concluding with a brief description of the lessons learned, the authors provide a sample list of questions for growers.

In the second two parts of this volume, **Analytical Methods**, the first section covers price analysis and the second consists of a series of papers devoted to models for analyzing a wider array of marketing issues.

Price analysis has occupied a central place in agricultural marketing research in developing countries for several reasons. Prices constitute essential economic signals to buyers and sellers regarding current supply and demand. Price data are often the most common—if not unique—form of market information to be found in developing countries. Prices are seen by some market analysts as reflecting all relevant aspects of market conditions such that other variables (e.g., numbers of buyers and sellers, barriers to entry) need not be explicitly examined. In this sense, a study of food marketing, for example, is essentially a study of food prices. Prices have often been the focus, as well as the mechanism, of policy interventions in agricultural marketing. Price analysis has also provided some fertile ground for methodological disputes in the field of agricultural marketing research (see Harriss 1979).

The section on Price Analysis begins with a concise review of how to compare and analyze prices at different levels in the marketing chain, e.g., producer versus consumer. Marketing channels and their participants must first be identified in order to then calculate marketing margins. **Mendoza** initially defines the basic terminology. He next describes procedures so as to estimate empirically these concepts. This presentation is interspersed with a series of examples—based on his research on potatoes in Bolivia and the Dominican Republic, and on tomatoes in Chile—that demonstrate the use of these techniques. In an Appendix, Mendoza includes a list of questions intended to help the interested researcher prepare a survey questionnaire aimed at analyzing growers' marketing practices.

Current prices in a given market are sometimes most readily understood when analyzed in a broader geographical and historical context. **Tschirley** presents the basic descriptive techniques for temporal and spatial price analysis drawing on results from research on rice and maize markets in Ecuador. These include the measurement of cyclical, seasonal, and trend components in time-series price data. They also involve calculating simple correlation coefficients for prices for pairs of markets for a particular time period. Tschirley concludes his paper by indicating how producers and policy makers can make use of the results from this type of price analysis.

Having considered the conventional approaches for analyzing prices and margins, **Harriss-White** stresses the limitations in estimation and aggregation associated with such procedures. She argues that the combinations of activities engaged in by most marketing firms are sufficiently unique to defy grouping such enterprises into categories as so often is done in agricultural marketing research for the purpose of making generalizations. Partly for that reason, Harriss-White presents analytical procedures that serve to capture the true complexity of marketing enterprises and the systems in which they operate—in her view systems arguably more complex than production systems. She offers various examples in the use of such techniques based on her research on cotton, groundnut, and rice marketing in South India.

Goletti and **Christina-Tsigas** approach the complexity of marketing activities from a different perspective. They present a three-stage approach intended to help systematize sequencing of the analysis. This includes a descriptive analysis of the prevailing marketing system; estimation of correlation coefficients using time-series data; and use of a model to measure the magnitude, speed, and symmetry of price adjustments over time. The authors present results from their research on maize (Malawi) and rice (Bangladesh) marketing to illustrate the use of this approach before suggesting possible uses of such findings by policy makers.

The paper by **Mendoza** and **Rosegrant** includes a time-series model that directly tests for pricing conduct. The authors consider this model appropriate for developing countries because of its minimum data requirements. It also enables researchers to test empirically for non-competitive pricing behavior, whereas static structural analysis relies more on subjective inferences about pricing conduct. Findings from an analysis of the Philippine copra market demonstrate the use of the model.

The second section, Models for Market Analysis, covers a broad range of marketing issues. These vary from ex-ante analysis of market profitability to ex-post measurement of the impact of marketing improvements to more user-friendly versions of more complex modelling techniques.

Marketing alternatives for many perishable agricultural commodities can often be expanded through identification of commercial outlets for these products in processed form. However, launching even small-scale processing enterprises entails assessing not only the commercial viability of such endeavors but also determining the most profitable marketing options. **Ostertag** and **Wheatley** present a model to assist such enterprises in decision-making about prices, rates of return on investment, and different processing alternatives. They then illustrate the use of the model with results from their work on cassava in Colombia.

Transaction costs are often a key marketing constraint facing buyers and sellers in developing countries. **Goetz** explains in a step-by-step fashion methods to analyze this limitation to market participation. He begins with a brief problem statement regarding transaction costs and the decision to engage or not in a given economic activity. Goetz then presents a series of statistical models to analyze such situations demonstrating their use with research findings on Senegalese coarse grain marketing.

Marketing studies typically set out to identify potential improvements in existing practices and include recommendations on how these might be achieved. The actual economic impact from implementation of such recommendations is rarely, if ever, discussed. **Fuglie** presents a framework for measuring the social welfare benefits to be derived from policies aimed at improving productivity in agricultural marketing. Equity considerations are also addressed by procedures to calculate the distribution of these benefits among producers and consumers. Fuglie presents research results from his work on potato storage in Tunisia to illustrate the application of this approach.

As marketing activities expand in developing countries, issues related to their spatial dimensions take on increasing importance. **Krishnaiah** presents a primer on spatial equilibrium models in agricultural marketing research. After defining some key concepts, his exposition includes geometric and arithmetic models before turning to linear programming techniques. Studies of rice, sorghum, and pulses marketing in South India provide examples of the use of these models.

Jeffrey and **Faminow** extend the discussion of mathematical programming procedures to include those that can be used to evaluate "nearly optimal" solutions for marketing problems. They focus specifically on the technique Modelling to Generate Alternatives (MGA). They consider this technique to be appropriate for developing countries because it allows for the fact that in such settings important marketing objectives cannot be fully reflected mathematically. Furthermore, the technique that they propose can be utilized using any commercially available mathematical programming software package and requires no special computer skills.

In a similar spirit, **Piggot** presents a modelling procedure to get around the limitations (e.g., scarce time and resources) associated with econometric analysis of marketing phenomena in developing countries. After concisely reviewing the intellectual origins of this approach, Piggot presents the essential features of the model. He then applies the model to the Indonesian food crop sector to demonstrate its potential use. In subsequent sections, he first uses the model to quantify the effects of different policies and then summarizes its strengths and weaknesses.

References

Abbott, J.C. 1986. *Marketing improvement in the developing world*. Food and Agricultural Organization of the United Nations, Rome, Italy.

_____. 1987. *Agricultural marketing enterprises for the developing world*. Cambridge, UK: Cambridge University Press.

_____. (ed.) 1993. *Agricultural and food marketing in developing countries: Selected readings*. Technical Centre for Agricultural and Rural Co-operation (CTA); Wallingford, UK: CAB International.

Abbott, J.C. and J.P. Makeham. 1990. *Agricultural economics and marketing in the tropics*. 2nd edition. Intermediate Tropical Agriculture Series. London, UK: Longman Group UK Limited.

APO (Asian Productivity Organization). 1989. *Marketing farm products in Asia and the Pacific*. Tokyo, Japan: Nordica International Limited.

Austin, J.E. 1992. *Agroindustrial project analysis: Critical design factors*. 2nd edition. Baltimore, MD, USA: The Johns Hopkins University Press.

Bateman, D.I. 1976. Agricultural marketing: A review of the literature of marketing theory and applications. *Journal of Agricultural Economics* 27(2):171-226.

Bongarts, J. 1995. Global and regional population projections to 2025. In *Population and food in the early Twenty-first Century: Meeting future food demand of an increasing population* (N. Islam, ed.). International Food Policy Research Institute (IFPRI), Washington, DC, USA.

Breimyer, H.F. 1973. The economics of agricultural marketing: A survey. *Review of Marketing and Agricultural Economics* 41, Vol. 4.

Bressler, R.G. and R.A. King. 1970. *Markets, prices and interregional trade.* New York, NY, USA: John Wiley and Sons.

Bromley, R.J. and R. Symanski. 1974. Marketplace trade in Latin America. *Latin American Research Review* 9(3):3-38.

Bucklin, L. 1977. Improving food marketing in developing Asian countries. *Food Policy* 2:114-22.

Bulmer, M. and D. P. Warwick (eds.). 1993. *Social research in developing countries. Surveys and censures in the Third World.* London, UK: University College of London Press.

Colman, D. and T. Young. 1989. *Principles of agricultural economics: Markets and prices in less developed countries.* Wye Studies in Agricultural and Rural Development. Cambridge, UK: Cambridge University Press.

de Soto, H. 1989. *The other path: The invisible revolution in the Third World.* New York, NY, USA: Harper and Row.

Dutt, A.K., K.S. Kim, and A. Singh. 1994. The state, markets and development. In *The state, markets and development: Beyond the neoclassical dichotomy* (A. Dutt, K.Kim and A.Singh, eds.). Aldershot, UK: Edward Elgar Publishing Limited.

EDI (Economic Development Institute of the World Bank). 1987. *Seminar on agricultural marketing policy.* Country papers. Document No.065/001. Washington, D.C., USA: The International Bank for Reconstruction and Development.

Eicher, C. and D. Baker. 1982. *Research on agricultural development in Sub-Saharan Africa: A critical survey.* MSU International Development Papers No. 1 . Department of Agricultural Economics, Michigan State University, East Lansing, MI, USA.

Elz, D. (collector). 1985. *Agricultural marketing policy.* Vol. III. Background readings. Washington, D.C., USA: Economic Development Institute of the World Bank.

_____ (ed.). 1987. *Agricultural marketing strategy and pricing policy.* Washington, D.C., USA: The World Bank.

Elz, D. and C. Hoisington (collectors). 1985. *Agricultural marketing policy* Vol. I. Background readings. Washington, D.C., USA: Economic Development Institute of the World Bank.

Fleming, E.M. 1990. Proposal for a marketing systems research approach in agricultural development planning. *Agicultural Systems* 32:97-111.

Goetz, S. and M.T. Weber. 1987. *Fundamentals of price analysis in developing countries' food systems: A training manual to accompany the microcomputer software program "MSTAT".* MSU International Development Working Paper No. 29. Department of Agricultural Economics, Michigan State University, East Lansing, MI, USA.

Harrison, K., D. Henley, H. Riley, and J. Shaffer. 1974. *Improving food marketing systems in developing countries: Experiences from Latin America.* Marketing in Developing Communities Series. Research Report No. 6. Latin American Studies Center, Michigan State University, East Lansing, MI, USA.

Harriss, B. 1979. There is method in my madness: Or is it vice-versa? *Food Research Institute Studies* 17(2):197-218.

Holtzman, J.S. 1986. *Rapid reconnaissance guidelines for agricultural marketing and food system research in developing countries.* MSU International Development Working Paper No. 30. Department of Agricultural Economics, Michigan State University, East Lansing, MI, USA.

ICRISAT (International Crops Research Institute for the Semi-Arid Tropics) (ed.). 1985. In *Agricultural markets in the semi-arid tropics* (ICRISAT, ed.). Proceedings of the international workshop. 24-28 October 1983, ICRISAT Centre, India. International Crops Research Institute for the Semi-Arid Tropics, Patancheru, Andhra Pradesh, India.

Jones, W.O. 1974. Regional analysis and agricultural marketing research in tropical Africa: Concepts and experience. *Food Research Institute Studies* 1(1):112-144.

Kaynak, E. 1986. *Marketing and economic development.* New York, NY, USA: Praeger Publishers.

Kennedy, E. and B. Cogill. 1987. *Income and nutritional effects of the commercialization of agriculture in Southwestern Kenya.* Research Report No. 63. Washington, D.C., USA: International Food Policy Research Institute.

Kindra. G.S. (ed.). 1984. *Marketing in developing countries.* New York, NY, USA: St. Martin's Press.

Kinsey, J. 1988. *Marketing in developing countries.* London, UK: Macmillan Education Limited.

Magrath, P. 1992. *Methodologies for studying agricultural markets in developing countries.* Marketing Series 2. Chatham, UK: Natural Resources Institute.

Monke, E.A. and S.R. Pearson. 1989. *The policy analysis matrix for agricultural development.* Ithaca, NY, USA: Cornell University Press.

Nichols, P. 1991. *Social survey methods: A field guide for development workers.* Development guidelines, vol. 6. Oxford, UK: Oxfam.

Pratt, B. and P. Loizos. 1992. *Choosing research methods: Data collection for development workers.* Development guidelines, vol. 7. Oxford, UK: Oxfam.

Prebisch, R. 1950. *The economic development of Latin America and its principal problems.* Economic Committee for Latin America, United Nations, New York, NY, USA.

Pritchard, N. 1969. A framework for analysis of agricultural marketing systems in developing countries. *Agricultural Economics Research* 21:78-85.

Reeves, E. 1986. Getting marketing into farming systems research: A case study from Western Sudan. In *Social sciences and farming systems research: Methodological perspectives on agricultural development* (J.R. Jones and B.Wallace, eds.). Boulder, CO, USA: Westview Press.

Riley, H.M. and J.Staatz. 1981. *Food system organization problems in developing countries.* Agricultural Development Council (ADC) Report No. 23. New York, USA: ADC.

Riley, H.M. and M.T. Weber. 1983. Marketing in developing countries. In *Future frontiers in agricultural marketing research* (P. L. Farris, ed.). Ames, IA, USA: Iowa State University Press.

Roemer, M. and C. Jones (eds.). 1991. *Markets in developing countries; Parallel, fragmented and black.* Based on a workshop sponsored by the Harvard Institute for International Development, Cambridge, MA, USA, November 1988. San Francisco, CA, USA: International Centre of Economic Growth.

Santos-Villanueva, P. 1966. The value of rural roads. In *Selected readings to accompany getting agriculture moving* (R.E. Borton, ed.). New York, NY, USA: Agricultural Development Council.

Scarborough, V. and J. Kydd. 1992. *Economic analysis of agricultural markets: A manual.* Marketing Series 5. Chatham, UK: Natural Resources Institute.

Scott, G., D. Wong, and M. Alvarez. 1992. Improving village-level processing in developing countries: The case of potatoes. *Ecology of Food and Nutrition* 30:145-163.

Sellen, D., W. Howard, and E. Goddard. 1993. *Production to consumption systems research: A review of methods and approaches.* Report prepared for the International Development Research Centre (IDRC). Department of Agricultural Economics and Business, University of Guelph, Guelph, Canada.

Shaffer, J.D. 1968. *A working paper concerning publicly supported economic research in agricultural marketing.* Economic Research Service, Department of Agriculture, Washington, D.C., USA.

_____. 1973. On the concept of sub-sector studies. *American Journal of Agricultural Economics* 55:333-335.

_____. 1980. Food system organization and performance: Toward a conceptual framework. *American Journal of Agricultural Economics* 62:333-335.

Shaffer, J.D., M.T. Weber, H.M. Riley, and J. Staatz. 1985. Designing marketing systems to promote development in the Third World countries.

In *Agricultural markets in the semi-arid tropics* (ICRISAT, ed.). Proceedings of the international workshop. 24-28 October 1983, ICRISAT Centre, India. International Crops Research Institute for the Semi-Arid Tropics, Patancheru, Andhra Pradesh, India.

Shwedel, K.J. 1977. *Marketing problems of small farm agriculture: A case study of the Costa Rican potato market*. Ph.D. Diss., Department of Agricultural Economics, Michigan State University, East Lansing, MI, USA.

Slater, C., H.M. Riley, V. Farace, K. Harrison, F. Neves, A. Bogatay, M. Doctoroff, D. Larson, R. Nason, and T. Webb. 1969. *Market processes in the Recife area of Northeast Brazil*. Research Report No. 2. Latin American Studies Center, Michigan State University, East Lansing, MI, USA.

Stevens, R.D. and C.L. Jabara. 1988. *Agricultural development principles: Economic theory and empirical evidence.* Baltimore, MD, USA: The Johns Hopkins University Press.

Timmer, P.C., W.P. Falcon, and S.R. Pearson. 1983. *Food policy analysis.* Published for the World Bank. Washington, D.C., USA: The Johns Hopkins University Press.

Trotter, B.W. 1992. *Applying price analysis to marketing systems: Methods and examples from the Indonesian rice market.* Marketing Series 3. Chatham, UK: Natural Resources Institute.

von Braun, J., D. Hotchkiss, and M. Immink. 1989. *Nontraditional export crops in Guatemala: Effects on production, income, and nutrition.* Research Report No 73. Washington, D.C., USA: International Food Policy Research Institute.

World Bank. 1990. *Agricultural marketing: The World Bank's experience, 1974-85.* Washington, D.C., USA: The World Bank.

Young, R.H. and C.W. MacCormac. 1987. Market research and food technology in developing countries. In *Market research for food products and processes* (R.H. Young and C.W. MacCormac, eds.). Ottawa, Ontario, Canada: International Development Research Centre.

Part 1

Field Methods

■ **Sub-Sector Analysis**

1

Rapid Reconnaissance Methods for Diagnosis of Sub-Sector Limitations: Maize in Paraguay[1]

Michael L. Morris[2]

Abstract

Rapid reconnaissance methods were used to conduct a diagnostic study of the maize sub-sector in Paraguay. This chapter reviews the background of the study, describes the design and implementation of data collection activities, discusses simple analytical procedures used to diagnose sub-sector constraints, and identifies issues for follow-up research. Rapid reconnaissance methods provide a quick and effective means of learning about key relationships within a commodity sub-sector, identifying economic constraints, and generating information that can be used to inform research planning.

Key words: Commodity sub-sector, rapid reconnaissance, informal interviews, marketing margins, production technology, input-output parameters, net returns per hectare.

Introduction

During the initial design stages of applied food systems research, one way to increase the likelihood that research issues are correctly identified and prioritized is to use a conceptual framework that permits systematic consideration of potential topics. The sub-sector approach is one such conceptual framework. A sub-sector is an economic unit of analysis specific to a particular commodity or commodity group (e.g., maize, feed grains, cereals). The sub-sector approach differs from more traditional industry-oriented approaches to the study of food systems principally in scope and emphasis. It encompasses a meaningful grouping of economic activities linked horizontally

---

[1] This chapter was previously published in Spanish in Scott and Herrera (1991).

[2] Economics Program, International Maize and Wheat Improvement Center (CIMMYT), P.O. Box 9-188, Bangkok, 10900, Thailand.

and vertically by market relationships (for example, assembly, transportation, and storage). Inclusion of the vertical dimension is important, because problems in the food system can frequently be attributed to poor coordination between successive stages of economic activity.[3]

The sub-sector approach can be particularly useful for the study of agricultural marketing issues, because it ensures that problem diagnosis is undertaken in a comprehensive, system-wide context. Armed with a view of the big picture, researchers can more easily distinguish between factors which decisively influence market performance and those that may be interesting but perhaps not essential. In addition to its theoretical advantages, the sub-sector approach can be very practical. When research resources are limited, sub-sector studies can be carried out using rapid reconnaissance methods, meaning that they need not be excessively demanding in terms of resource requirements.[4]

Rapid reconnaissance methods were used in conducting a diagnostic study of the maize sub-sector in Paraguay. This chapter briefly reviews the background of the Paraguay study, describes the planning and implementation of data collection activities, illustrates selected data analysis techniques, and summarizes the study's findings. The Paraguay maize study illustrates how rapid reconnaissance methods can provide a quick and effective means of learning about complex food system interrelationships, understanding constraints and opportunities, and generating information which can be used in designing follow-up research.

Maize in Paraguay

Maize in Paraguay is grown by small-scale semi-subsistence farmers and by large-scale commercial producers. Production technologies, cropping systems, types of germplasm, and maize utilization patterns vary considerably between these two groups of producers. Smallholders plant maize mainly as a subsistence crop, either monocropped or in association with cotton, cassava, or beans. Land preparation and other cropping operations are performed by hand or using animal traction, and few purchased inputs are used. Most small-scale farmers prefer local maize varieties because of their suitability for traditional dishes, so use of improved germplasm is uncommon. In contrast, large-scale commercial producers grow maize mainly for use as animal feed. Land preparation and other cropping operations are usually mechanized, and high levels of fertilizer and crop chemical are often used. Large-scale producers

---

[3] See, for example, Shaffer (1973; 1980).

[4] For an excellent introduction to rapid appraisal methods as applied to marketing systems, see Holtzman (1986).

tend to prefer hybrids because of their high yield potential and superior feed qualities, and use of improved germplasm is extensive.

In recent years, the maize sub-sector in Paraguay has experienced a great deal of change. Since 1980, area planted to maize has increased more than 200% as growers have moved into fertile regions along the southeastern border of the country, and yields have increased by 25% due to the adoption of improved germplasm and improved management practices. Yet in spite of the tripling of production, agricultural policy makers in Paraguay remain concerned about the performance of the maize sub-sector. Even with favorable agro-climatic conditions, average maize yields remain well below the levels which could be achieved with relatively simple changes in management practices and wider use of currently available improved germplasm. The situation is puzzling, because the large gap between farmers' yields and experiment station yields cannot be explained by the usual factors. Most Paraguayan farmers possess the knowledge to increase their maize yields, yet they deliberately choose not to raise yields, citing high input costs, low producer prices for maize, and market uncertainty. Consequently, most farmers produce only enough maize for home consumption (food and feed), plant a limited area, and use few or no purchased inputs.

The fact that most farmers in Paraguay appear unwilling to make the modest additional investment needed to adopt improved maize production technologies has called into question the traditional assumption that the low productivity of maize in Paraguay is essentially technical in nature. This has emphasized the need to unravel the complex set of technical, economic, and institutional constraints which may be depressing production.

Objectives of the Study

This chapter describes a study launched in 1989 by researchers from Paraguay's Ministry of Agriculture (MAG) and the International Maize and Wheat Improvement Center (CIMMYT). The goal of the study was to identify the principal factors contributing to low levels of maize productivity in Paraguay, with the ultimate objective of helping to improve research planning.

Before a functional work plan could be developed, the broad overall goal of the study had to be translated into specific research objectives. Defining specific research objectives meant first identifying the clients for whom the study was being performed. Early identification of the potential users of a sub-sector study is of great importance, because the interests of the potential users will tend to affect the focus of the research. Meetings were held with officials from the Ministry of Agriculture, researchers from the Research and Extension unit within the Ministry (DIEAF), and senior scientists from the national maize program. It soon became evident that the principal clients of the study would be research administrators—specifically, managers of the national maize program who were interested in developing a long-term research plan. Following extensive discussions, it was possible to identify three key issues facing these research managers: (1) allocation of research resources between maize and other crops; (2) allocation of research resources between different kinds of maize research (e.g., breeding vs. crop management); and (3) allocation of research resources between different kinds of maize breeding activities.

With the clients of the study thus identified and their information needs tentatively prioritized, specific research objectives were agreed upon. The study would:

- Review recent developments in Paraguay's agricultural economy in general and in the maize sub-sector in particular.
- Identify inefficiencies or bottlenecks in the marketing system for maize which may be lowering economic incentives for producers.
- Distinguish between technical constraints to maize production (which can be solved through research) and economic and/or institutional constraints (which must be solved through policy reforms).
- Analyze the implications for the DIEAF Maize Program and, in particular, spell out the critical research resource allocation issues facing administrators.

Data Collection Activities

Developing a data collection strategy

A simple food system matrix was constructed to help organize existing data, identify missing information, and plan data collection activities (Table 1). Economic activities made up the rows of the matrix, while individual commodities appeared as columns. The columns and rows formed individual cells representing combinations of economic activities and specific commodities (e.g., soybean production, cotton processing, maize consumption).

By systematically considering each cell in the matrix, the researchers were able to reduce the risk of prematurely restricting the focus of the study without considering all potentially important issues. Several "priority cells" were identified as potentially important in understanding the organization and performance of the maize sub-sector. Thus, it was possible to design data collection activities so as to focus on information relevant to those cells.

Table 1. Food system matrix.

	Commodities				
Economic activities	Yellow maize	White maize	Soybean	Cotton	Cassava
Inputs distribution	important		important		
Production	important	important	important	important	important
Assembly	important		important		
Transport	important		important		
Storage	important		important		
Processing	important				
Wholesaling	important				
Exporting	important		important		
Retailing	important				
Utilization	important	important			important

Review of secondary data sources

A list of data requirements was drawn up to help guide the search for data from secondary sources (see Appendix 1). With the help of the list, available secondary data sources were carefully reviewed.

Two factors undermine the accuracy of official statistics in Paraguay. First, the national crop reporting service lacks sufficient resources to carry out comprehensive data collection activities. The problem is somewhat less serious in the case of cash crops (e.g., soybean, cotton, and wheat), which tend to be marketed through closely monitored official channels. In contrast, subsistence crops such as maize, cassava, and beans tend to be retained for home consumption, and the relatively small quantities that are sold are usually marketed through informal channels which are rarely subjected to official scrutiny. Second, even if the crop reporting service had more resources, data collection would still be hampered by the large volume of unrecorded trade with Argentina and Brazil. In recognition of these potential problems, the review of secondary information involved not only determining what data were available, but also evaluating their reliability.

Based on the results of this review, two topics were dropped from the agenda: evaluation of the potential export demand for maize, and the assessment of the potential demand for feed maize. Although these topics are clearly important, during the review of secondary data it became evident that very little previous work had been done on them, so that an extensive data collection effort would be necessary to do them justice. This highlights an important advantage of using the sub-sector framework during the initial design phases of research: by identifying gaps in the existing knowledge base, the sub-sector framework can help ensure that proposed research activities are feasible given available time and resources.

Primary data collection activities

In view of the short time available for the study, the decision was taken to rely whenever possible on rapid reconnaissance techniques, i.e., informal interviews with key informants, direct observation of critical stages in the production-transformation-distribution sequence, and reliance on secondary data sources whenever possible.

Reconnaissance survey. Field data collection activities began with an informal reconnaissance survey. Itineraries were prepared for teams made up of 2-3 researchers. Whenever possible, social scientists were paired with technical scientists, and more experienced researchers were paired with less experienced researchers. The composition of the teams was frequently changed, so that all researchers had opportunities to work with all other researchers.

The purpose of the reconnaissance survey was to gain familiarity with important maize production zones, principal categories of farmers and types of maize-based cropping systems, input distribution networks, maize production technologies, and maize utilization patterns. In addition, since marketing was of particular interest, an effort was made to directly observe the various components of the maize marketing system.

The reconnaissance survey was designed to answer the following questions:

- What are the principal maize production zones in Paraguay?
- What are the predominant categories of maize producers?
- What types of maize are produced in Paraguay, and by whom?
- What are the most common maize production technologies?
- What are the principal cropping patterns that include maize?
- What are the principal uses of maize?
- Is maize planted as a food crop, as a cash crop, or both?
- What do farmers consider the advantages and disadvantages of maize?
- Where and to whom do farmers sell their maize?
- What are the principal marketing channels for maize?
- What types of marketing agents (intermediaries) buy and sell maize?
- What types of maize are marketed?

One week was spent on the reconnaissance survey. No attempt was made to cover the entire country; instead, the teams concentrated on zones in which maize is a major crop, e.g., the states of Paraguarí, Itapúa, Alto Paraná and Caaguazú (Figure 1).

Diagnosis of sub-sector limitations: Maize in Paraguay 27

Figure 1. Distribution of maize production in Paraguay, 1986-1987.

During the reconnaissance survey, informal interviews were conducted with input distributors, small-scale semi-subsistence farmers, large-scale commercial growers, producer cooperatives, rural assemblers, elevator operators, transporters, wholesalers, retailers, feed manufacturers, poultry farmers, consumers, researchers, private seed companies, and extension agents.

Frequently one interview led to the next as researchers followed the flow of maize down the marketing channel.

Most respondents were contacted at their places of work. Researchers were very careful to identify themselves and to explain the purpose of their visit. Interviews were unstructured, although researchers carried a checklist of questions to make sure that important points would not be overlooked. To speed the interviews and minimize interruptions, answers were not recorded in writing. Important data were recorded in summary form in field notebooks, sometimes during interviews, but more often afterwards. This effort to keep the interviews informal seemed to encourage frankness on the part of the respondents.

Following the completion of the reconnaissance survey, the decision was taken to focus on two priority topics: (1) the organization and performance of the yellow maize marketing system, and (2) the profitability of maize vs. alternative crops. The second topic normally would not have been considered important in a marketing study. However, the fact that the question of the profitability of principal crops came to be included as a priority research topic demonstrates how the sub-sector approach, by forcing researchers to consider the entire food system, can direct the focus of inquiry into areas different from those contemplated at the beginning of the study.

Interviews with maize traders. Somewhat disappointingly, the review of secondary data failed to turn up potentially important information on maize marketing in Paraguay (e.g., numbers and types of market participants, numbers and types of marketing channels, size and seasonal distribution of grain flows, levels and seasonal movements of prices). This lack of information was considered important, because one hypothesis was that the performance of the marketing system was likely to affect the attractiveness of maize as a commercial crop. Therefore, the research team decided to gather information on the maize marketing system, with the hope that this might shed light on the apparent low profitability of maize.

A list of questions focusing on marketing activities was developed and used to guide informal interviews with 25 maize buyers (Appendix 2). The sample was purposively selected to include at least three respondents from each of the following categories: rural assemblers, itinerant traders, grain elevator operators, producer cooperatives, feed millers, poultry producers, and exporters.

Although the sample characteristics did not allow for rigorous statistical analysis, it was possible to produce descriptive statistics from the stratified data providing preliminary indicators of certain variables of interest. Furthermore, the remarkable consistency in the responses offered strong circumstantial evidence of the existence of a well integrated market, characterized by satisfactory flows of information.

Verification survey of maize production practices. The reconnaissance survey raised strong doubts about the profitability of maize as a commercial crop. Many producers, both large-scale commercial growers and small-scale semi-subsistence farmers, stated that maize is not profitable due to low and variable producer prices, as well as limited marketing opportunities. Scientists from the national maize program questioned these claims, arguing that maize should be profitable at prevailing producer prices, even when produced with low levels of inputs at very low yields.

In an attempt to resolve this controversy, the decision was taken to construct representative crop budgets to determine the profitability of maize relative to alternative crops. Since it was not possible to conduct a formal producer survey in order to develop crop budgets from scratch, the decision was taken to adapt crop budgets previously published by the country's largest producer cooperative and by the national extension service.

Meetings were scheduled with representatives of the producer cooperative and of the extension service in order to discuss the sources of the data used in constructing these budgets. It was learned that the two sets of budgets had been compiled using input-output parameters obtained from extensive farm-level surveys conducted during the two previous years. Although these surveys seemed methodologically sound, the decision was taken to verify selected input-output parameters (e.g., input use, yields) to make sure that they had not changed significantly since the original surveys were conducted.

The crop budgets were verified through interviews held with 15 maize producers in the states of Itapúa, Alto Paraná, and Caaguazú. Key input-output parameters appearing in the budgets were compared with the actual practices of the respondents. Several modifications were made to the budgets, since a number of management practices appeared to have changed during recent years (for example, a reduced number of plowings, substitution of chemical weed control for mechanical weeding). On the whole, farmers' practices were found to be very similar to the parameters used in the published budgets, indicating that the budgets were reasonable.

Survey of input prices. In order to update the crop budgets, the research team collected current input prices by visiting input distributors in important maize producing zones. (Land and labor prices had already been collected during the reconnaissance and budget verification surveys.) Attention focused on prices of major variable inputs such as machinery, fertilizer, seed, and chemical products. Due to the open nature of the Paraguayan economy and the competitiveness of the agricultural input supply industry, prices were found to be remarkably consistent within each zone. The slight price variations between zones corresponded to differences in transportation costs.

Data Analysis Techniques

Selected data analysis techniques are described in this section. The aim is not so much to dwell on specific results, but rather to demonstrate that many useful insights can be drawn from a modest amount of data using relatively simple analytical techniques.

Analysis of historical production and price data

Historical production and price data were analyzed in order to determine how maize has fared over time compared with alternative crops. Figure 2 presents production indexes of Paraguay's major crops, calculated for the period 1972-88. During this period, production of the main commercial crops (soybean, cotton, wheat) experienced strong growth, whereas production of most subsistence crops (cassava, beans) stagnated. Among the subsistence crops, only maize production increased, growing at an average rate of 10% per year.

To what extent was the growth in maize production stimulated by increases in maize producer prices? Figure 3 illustrates long-term movements in nominal and real producer prices of maize during the period 1972-88. Although nominal prices to producers increased considerably, real prices actually declined slightly.

Interpretation of the trends in maize prices is difficult without knowledge of changes in the prices of competing crops. Figure 4 shows

Figure 2. Production indices of main crops, Paraguay, 1978-89.

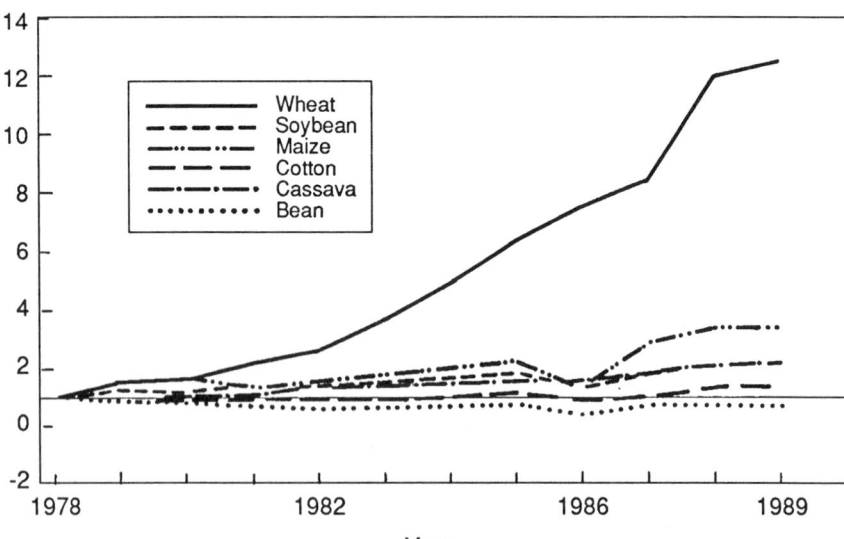

Source: Based on data provided by the Ministry of Agriculture and Livestock (MAG).

Figure 3. Trends in nominal and real producer prices for maize in Paraguay, 1972-88.

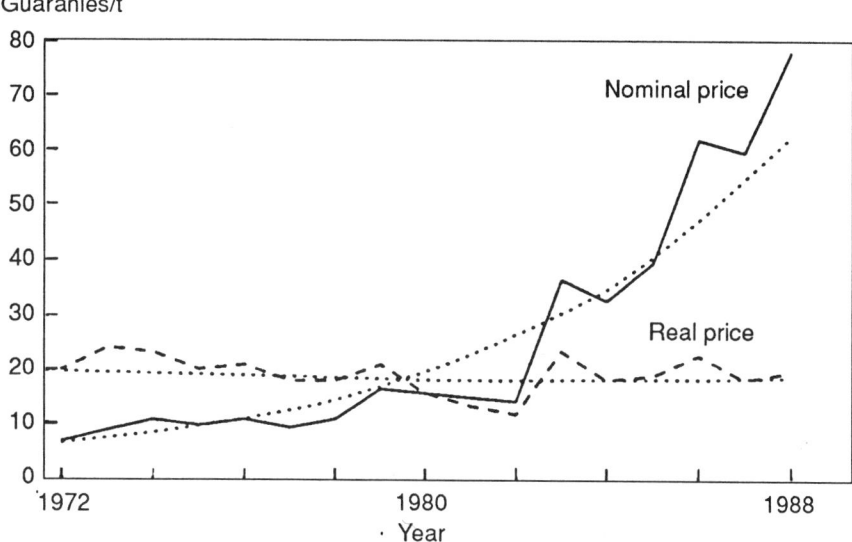

Source: Based on data provided by the Ministry of Agriculture and Livestock (MAG)

movements in the ratio of maize producer prices to producer prices of principal alternative crops during the period 1972-88. Price ratios varied from year to year, but the overall trends were flat, suggesting that changes in relative producer prices neither encouraged nor discouraged maize production. However, maize yields increased more slowly than yields of soybean and cotton, so the relative profitability of maize may have declined despite the lack of change in relative producer prices.

Next, an effort was made to evaluate the claim made by many producers that maize prices in Paraguay are not only low, but highly variable. Coefficients of variation around trend (CV) were calculated for the annual average producer prices of maize and other crops. Surprisingly, the CV around trend for the maize producer price was lower than the CVs for the producer prices of soybean, wheat, cotton, and cassava (Table 2). It was also lower than the main international reference price of maize during the same period.

The low CV of maize producer prices appeared to contradict the claim made by many farmers that maize prices in Paraguay are highly variable. To verify that a mistake had not been made in diagnosing this problem, return visits were made to a number of producers in an effort to determine what lay behind this unanticipated result. Further investigation revealed that the problem of price instability is more a problem of excessive seasonal variability

Figure 4. Trends in relative producer prices of maize and alternative crops, Paraguay, 1972-88.

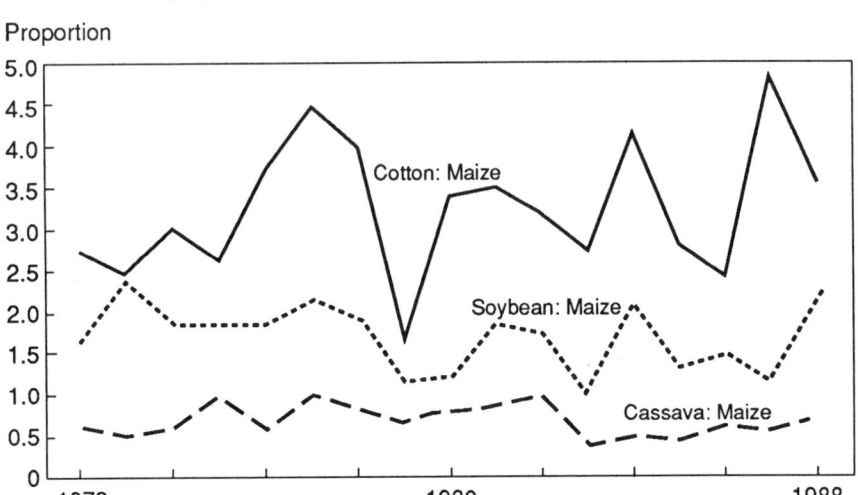

Table 2. Coefficients of variation around trend (CV) of real producer prices of principal crops in Paraguay, 1977-88.

	Soybean	Wheat	Maize	Cotton	Cassava
CV	28	20	18	25	23

Source: Based on data provided by the Ministry of Agriculture and Livestock (MAG).

(i.e., fluctuations within the same year), rather than of variability from one year to the next.

This conclusion was confirmed through additional analysis of maize price data. Monthly prices for maize (both producer and consumer prices) are characterized by a marked seasonal pattern (Figure 5). This pattern is consistent with the normal production cycle. Maize prices typically drop during the course of the harvest, reaching their lowest level in the months following the main soybean harvest (July and August), when most of the maize crop that has been left standing in the field is harvested and brought to market. Maize prices then rise throughout the rest of the year as supplies become more scarce, reaching their highest level in the months just prior to the next harvest

Figure 5. Seasonal fluctuations in the prices of yellow maize in Paraguay, 1972-88.

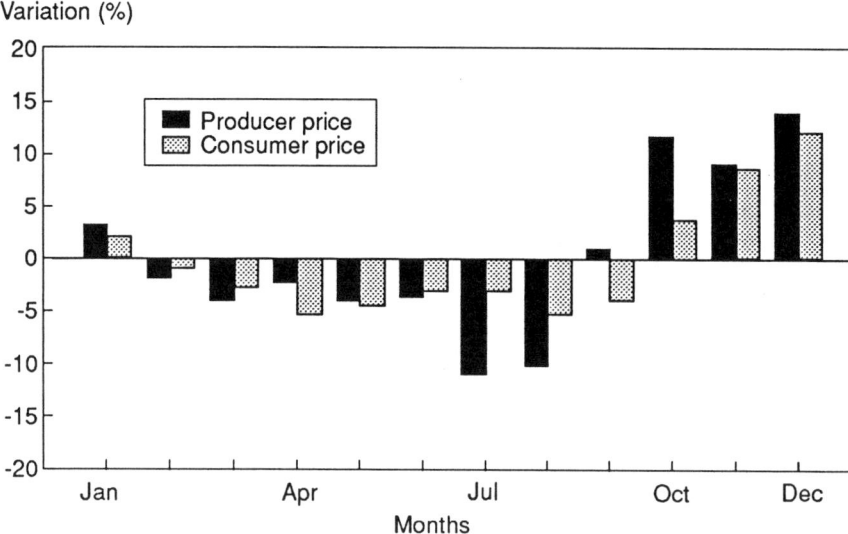

(December and January).[5] Price variability of this order of magnitude is not unusual by global standards. In many tropical developing countries, seasonal variations in maize prices of 40% or more are common. However, in Paraguay the variability in maize prices is large compared to the variability in prices of other crops (especially soybean and cotton), since prices of these other crops are based on international prices and therefore exhibit little short-term variability.

Description of Maize Marketing Channels

The reconnaissance survey revealed that the maize marketing system in Paraguay is much more extensive than is generally believed. One reason Paraguay's maize markets remain poorly understood may be that most maize marketing activities take place outside the formal marketing channels which handle the country's main commercial crops. However, just because the grain elevators that purchase soybean, cotton, and wheat do not handle much maize does not mean that maize marketing does not take place. The survey revealed the existence of a complex, well-developed marketing system for maize involving a large number of intermediaries and comprising many distinct marketing channels.

---

[5] Seasonal variability in producer prices (25% difference between the highest and lowest prices) is greater than in consumer prices (18% difference). This suggests that traders smooth prices by storing grain and selling between harvests.

Based on information generated during the reconnaissance survey, as well as on data collected through the survey of maize marketing agents, a fairly accurate picture was developed of the structure and conduct of Paraguay's maize marketing system. The main market participants were identified, and their standard operating procedures were described. Principal marketing channels were depicted diagrammatically to facilitate interpretation (Figure 6).

Additional information on the organization and performance of Paraguay's rural maize markets emerged during the survey. Marketing agents within each region gave remarkably consistent estimates of farm-gate prices, transport costs between various production and consumption points, and wholesale prices in Asunción (the capital). According to most respondents, buying prices, selling prices, and transport costs are well known to all market participants, with truckers serving as the main brokers of information. This testimony, together with the highly consistent estimates of prices and costs, provided strong circumstantial evidence of a well-integrated maize marketing system characterized by the free flow of information and adequate transportation infrastructure.

Estimated marketing margins for yellow maize were calculated based on data collected from traders (Table 3). The modest returns earned by traders suggest that the maize market is reasonably competitive, since it does not appear to be characterized by concentrations of market power leading to excessive profits.

Profitability Analysis

Given the widely held view that the main constraint to increased maize production in Paraguay is the lack of economic incentives to adopt improved technologies, the decision was taken to study the profitability issue in greater detail. The crop budgets were used to calculate the net returns to maize and alternative crops (Table 4). At current prices and yields, soybean is by far the most attractive crop for commercial growers, generating net returns of G 148,131/ha. Maize generates much lower net returns of G 96,357/ha. Maize is hardly unprofitable; however, since maize must compete with soybean for land and other resources, it remains *relatively* unattractive to commercial farmers. For small-scale farmers, cotton is the most remunerative crop, generating net returns of G 169,278/ha. Cassava follows in profitability, generating net returns of G 142,367/ha. Maize produced using animal traction technology (the most common production technology among small-scale producers) generates negative net returns of G −19,882/ha. This explains why so few small-scale farmers grow maize as a cash crop.

Figure 6. Principal marketing channels for yellow maize in Paraguay.

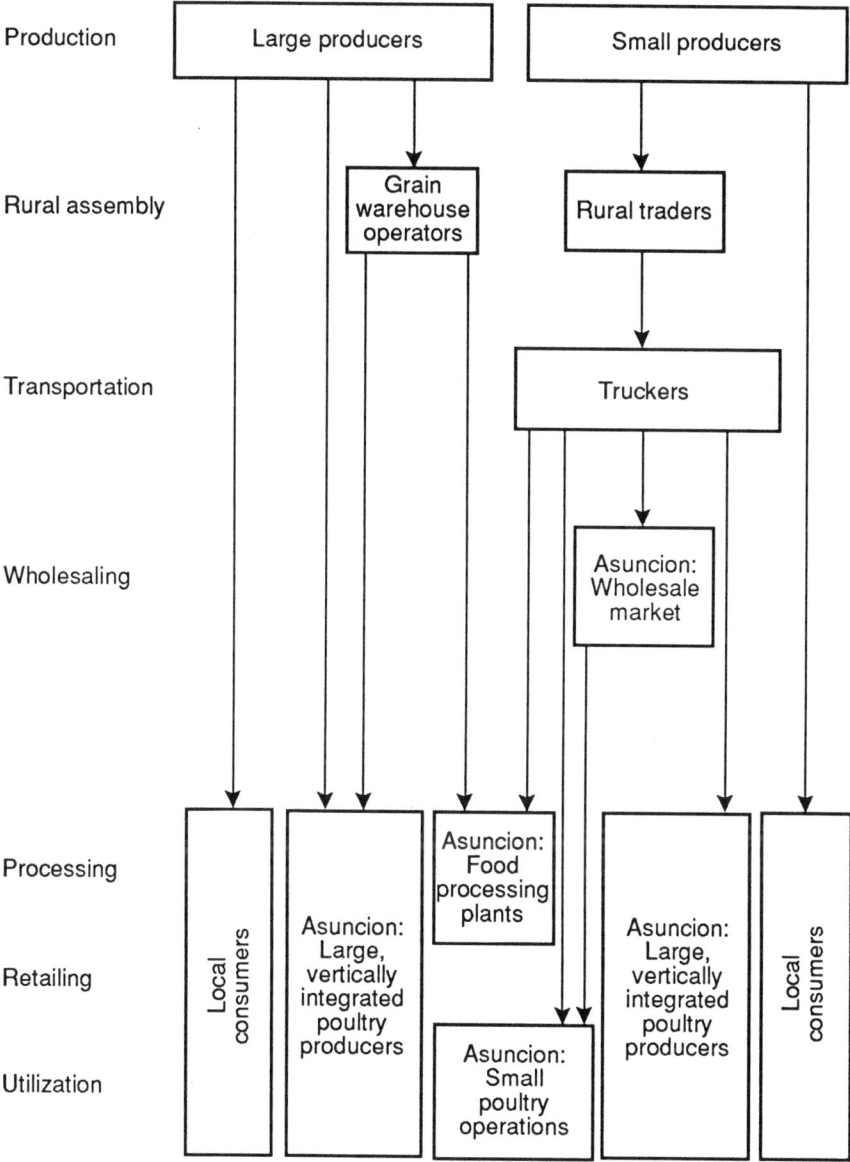

Table 3. Estimated marketing margins for yellow maize, 1989 (Guaraní [a]/kg)

	Alto Paraná	Itapúa
Farm gate price of maize	60	70
Transport to Asunción	+22	+15
Assembler's margin	+18	+15
Wholesale price (Asunción)	100	100
Wholesaler's margin	+10	+10
Retailer's buying price (Asunción)	110	110
Retailer's margin	+10	+10
Retailer price	120	120

a US$1 = 1,000 Guaraní in 1989.
Source: Field surveys done in 1989.

Table 4. Profitability of the principal crops in Paraguay (Guaraní/ha).

Crop	Farmer's net return (per ha)
Large-scale commercial growers	
Soybean	148,131
Maize	96,357
Small-scale producers	
Cotton	169,278
Cassava	142,367
Maize	-19,882

Source: Estimated from crop budgets.

Would output prices have to change before the current profitability rankings were altered? Table 5 depicts net returns per hectare for maize, soybean, cotton, and cassava assuming a range of percentage changes in maize producer prices. Maize being a low-value crop, its price would have to increase significantly in percentage terms in order for maize to overtake competing crops in profitability.

Sensitivity analysis was also carried out to test for the likely effects on the profitability rankings of future technological changes leading to increased productivity in maize. Technological change was modelled by increasing maize yields at current levels of production costs. Table 6 shows relative profitability of maize vs. competing crops, assuming a range of percentage changes in maize yields. As expected, maize yields would have to increase substantially in percentage terms in order for maize to overtake competing crops.

Diagnosis of sub-sector limitations: Maize in Paraguay

Table 5. Sensitivity of maize profitability to changes in maize producer prices.

Large-scale producers	Maize[a]	Soybean	
Net returns with maize (producer price)			
25% lower	21,358		
10% lower	66,358		
5% lower	81,358		
Current Price	96,358	148,310	
5% higher	111,358		
15% higher	126,358		
25% higher	171,358		
Small-scale producers	**Maize[b]**	**Cotton**	**Cassava**
Net returns with maize(producer price)			
25% lower	-48,007		
10% lower	-31,132		
5% lower	-25,507		
Current price	-19,882	169,278	142,368
5% higher	-14,257		
15% higher	-8,632		
25% higher	-8,243		

[a] Maize price would have to increase 17.5% for maize net returns to equal soybean net returns.
[b] Maize price would have to increase 245% for maize net returns to equal cassava net returns and 270% to equal cotton net returns.

Table 6. Sensitivity of maize profitability to changes in maize yield.

Large-scale producers	Maize[a]	Soybean	
Current yield	4 t/ha	25 t/ha	
Net returns with maize yield			
Current yield	96,358	148,310	
5% higher	106,228		
10% higher	116,098		
15% higher	125,959		
20% higher	135,836		
25% higher	145,693		
Small-scale producers	**Maize[b]**	**Cotton**	**Cassava**
Current net returns with maize	1.5 t/ha	1.8 t/ha	18.0 t/ha
Net returns with maize yield	-19,882	169,278	142,368
5% higher	-15,485		
10% higher	-11,088		
15% higher	-6,691		
20% higher	-2,294		
25% higher	-2,103		

[a] Maize yields would have to increase 27% for maize net returns to equal soybean net returns.
[b] Maize yields would have to increase 285% for maize net returns to equal cassava net returns.

Evaluation of Maize Export Possibilities

Many large-scale commercial producers said they would be willing to grow maize as a cash crop if market outlets were assured. Believing that the domestic market is not capable of absorbing significant production increases, many producers suggested that the government undertake market development activities to create export opportunities (as was done for soybean). To help evaluate the export potential of Paraguayan maize (Table 7), an export parity price was estimated based on the international reference price for maize prevailing in Rosario, Argentina, the nearest export point. [6] Although the estimated export parity price appears marginally remunerative, these rough calculations do not take into account the improvements in grain quality which would be needed in order for Paraguayan maize to compete in world markets.

Table 7. Estimated export parity price of maize, Paraguay, 1989.

	US$/t	Guaraní/t
FOB price of maize, Rosario	115	115,000
Transport and handling, Asunción to Rosario	-35	-35,000
Export parity price, Asunción	80	80,000
Wholesaler's margin	-7.5	-7,500
Storing (including fumigation)	-5.0	-5,000
Drying	-5.0	-5,000
Transport and handling, farm gate to Asunción	<u>-2.5</u>	<u>-2,500</u>
Export parity price (farm gate)	60	-60,000

Proposed Follow-up Activities

Originally it was hoped that the preliminary diagnostic study would generate sufficient information to permit the identification and prioritization of research topics for the national maize program. However, it gradually became evident that additional information would be needed before a detailed, long-term research plan could be formulated. The study turned up a number of gaps in the existing knowledge base which would have to be addressed before research priorities could be ranked with any degree of confidence. Three specific activities were identified as leading candidates for follow-up research:

---

[6] The export parity price is the price which Paraguayan producers would receive were they to begin exporting grain.

Survey of maize producers. The review of secondary data made clear that a great deal of basic descriptive information about the maize sub-sector in Paraguay is still lacking. Reliable data are not available on the numbers and distribution of maize producers, area planted to different types of germplasm, sources of maize seed and farmers' seed management practices, maize production practices, maize yields, and maize utilization practices. Much of this information could be collected through a comprehensive national survey of maize producers.

Maize marketing survey. Despite turning up considerable evidence that the maize marketing system in Paraguay is extensive, the preliminary diagnostic study was not able to generate reliable estimates of the quantities of grain moving through the various marketing channels. Important questions about the characteristics of the maize market could be answered through a postharvest marketing survey. This could help resolve the critical question of whether the main constraints to maize production are technical or economic.

Economic analysis of experimental data. Although researchers from the national maize program have demonstrated that a number of currently available improved technologies can bring about significant increases in maize yields, many of the experimental data have not been subjected to rigorous economic analysis. Such analysis is needed to establish whether adoption of improved technologies would actually be profitable. If detailed input-output data are already available, it may be possible to perform economic analysis using the results of past trials. If not, it will be necessary to collect such data during several additional cycles of trials.

Conclusions

From a methodological point of view, the Paraguay maize study was noteworthy in at least two respects.

First, the conceptual framework used to identify key research issues and to organize data collection activities was extremely broad. Instead of restricting the field of inquiry to a narrowly-defined set of marketing problems, the sub-sector approach was adopted to force consideration of a wide range of production, marketing, and consumption issues. Although researchers initially believed that marketing constraints were responsible for farmers' apparent lack of interest in improved production technologies, little empirical evidence was available to support this hypothesis. Consequently, before undertaking a marketing study, it seemed wise to strengthen the case that the main production constraints were indeed being caused by bottlenecks in the marketing system. In the end, it was found that marketing factors were only partly to blame; low profitability also proved to be important, and equally deserving of researchers' attention.

Second, because the conceptual framework was extremely broad, the research methods were necessarily extensive rather than intensive. Notably absent were many familiar elements of the marketing researcher's usual tool kit, e.g., probabilistic sampling, formal interviewing, and longitudinal cost-route surveying. These conventional research methods were replaced by an eclectic set of more ad-hoc approaches to acquiring information, including informal interviewing of key informants, direct observation of marketing activities, participant observation, and extensive reliance on secondary data sources. Use of rapid reconnaissance methods was deemed appropriate considering the brief time frame and limited resources available for the study.

No attempt will be made here to claim that sub-sector studies carried out using rapid reconnaissance techniques will always be appropriate. On the contrary, in many cases where problems are already well understood, narrowly focused studies based on more formal research methods will often be preferable. But as this study in Paraguay made clear, sub-sector studies based on rapid reconnaissance methods can be useful when researchers want to gain a broad understanding of a commodity sub-sector in a relatively short time, with the goal of identifying system constraints in order to better target follow-up research. This is particularly true when research resources are limited. Therefore, before summarily dismissing the sub-sector framework as too broad, or rapid reconnaissance methods as "unscientific," applied researchers would do well to consider adding these tools to their working kit.

References

Holtzman, J. 1986. *Rapid reconnaissance guidelines for agricultural marketing and food systems research in developing countries*. MSU International Development 0, Working Paper No. 30. Department of Agricultural Economics, Michigan State University, East Lansing, MI, USA.

Morris, M. 1991. Diagnóstico de las limitaciones del sub-sector mediante métodos de sondeo rápido: El caso del maíz en Paraguay. In *Mercadeo agricola: Metodologias de investigacion* (G. Scott and J.E. Herrera, eds.). IICA and CIP, Lima, Peru.

Shaffer, J. 1973. On the concept of sub-sector studies. *American Journal of Agricultural Economics* 55:310-318.

———. 1980 Food system organization and performance: Toward a conceptual framework. *American Journal of Agricultural Economics* 62:333-335.

Appendix 1
List of data requirements (used during the review of secondary data)

Historical production data:
- Area, yield, production of maize
- Area, yield, production of alternative crops (soybean, cotton, cassava)
- Livestock production (poultry, beef, pork)

Macroeconomic indicators:
- Demographic statistics (population)
- National accounts data (GNP, GDP)
- Trade flows (imports, exports)
- Exchange rates

Financial data and prices:
- Producer prices for main crops
- Wholesale prices for main crops
- Consumer prices for main crops
- Prices of purchased inputs
- Labor costs
- Land costs
- Import and export prices
- International reference prices
- Price indexes (producer, consumer)

Farm-level data:
- Production systems and crop rotations
- Types of producers
- Management practices used by maize producers
- Technology indicators (use of fertilizer, use of hybrid varieties, use of chemical inputs, use of machinery)

Experimental data on maize production technologies
- Varietal yield trial results
- Agronomic trial results
- Economic analysis of improved technologies

Appendix 2
Questions used during informal interviews with maize market intermediaries

General information: Enterprise name and address, interviewer, date.

1. What percentage of your business (in terms of value) does each of the following products represent? Soybean, maize, cotton, others.
2. Approximately how many tons of maize have you handled during the last three years?
3. Who are the main buyers (domestic and foreign) of the maize you sell?
4. Where is the maize you buy produced?
5. What kind of maize do you buy (white, yellow, both)?
6. What prices have you paid during each of the last three years for average quality maize?
7. How do you decide which price to offer to producers for their maize? Is there always a well-known standard price that is paid by all assemblers, or does each assembler set his own buying price?
8. How would you characterize the maize market in this area (always a lot of competition among assemblers, rarely competition among assemblers, competition among assemblers varies according to supply)?
9. Are there problems with the quality of maize? What are they? What is the approximate amount of maize affected by humidity, impurity, damage (e.g., burnt or broken), mixing of varieties.
10. Do you dry maize? Do you have a drier here?
11. Do you pay for maize transport? From the farm gate to here? From here to the place of sale?
12. Do you use rented vehicles or your own vehicles to transport maize?
13. Current transport costs (specify routes):

    Asunción → Encarnación

    Asunción → Stroessner City

    Asunción → Paraguana

    Stroessner City → Paraguana

    Asunción → Buenos Aires
14. How long (on average) does maize remain in your warehouse before you sell it?
15. Do you sometimes store maize expecting a rise in price before selling it?
16. Any comments on informal maize marketing channels?

2

Using Rapid Appraisal to Examine Coarse Grain Processing and Utilization in Mali

John S. Holtzman, John A. Lichte, and James F. Tefft[1]

Abstract

This paper describes rapid appraisal (RA) methods used in analyzing coarse grain processing, marketing, and utilization in Mali. Topics covered include the research context; team composition and strengths; study focus; and key informants, as well as devising structured informal interview guidelines. Problems encountered in conducting rapid appraisal are also discussed. One key finding of this appraisal was the extent to which the need for processing discourages greater consumption of coarse grains. A pilot innovation in grain dehulling was proposed to overcome this constraint.

Key words: Agricultural marketing, rapid appraisal, informal interviews, coarse grains, processing, utilization, consumption, Mali.

Introduction

This paper describes rapid appraisal methods used in examining coarse grain processing and utilization in Mali. The field work was carried out during a six-week period in November-December 1990 by a team of three American agricultural economists and two Malian analysts. USAID/Mali and the Women in Development Office of USAID/Washington co-funded this research through the Agricultural Marketing Improvement Strategies Project (AMIS), partially funded and managed by the Bureau for Research and Development of USAID/Washington. This research led to the writing of a monograph entitled *Expanding coarse grain utilization in Mali: Current situation, constraints,*

---

[1] Senior Agricultural Economist, Abt Associates, Inc., 4800 Montgomery Lane, Bethesda, MD 20814 USA; Agricultural Economist, 2121 N.W. 20th Street, Gainesville, FL, USA; and Visiting Specialist, Dept. of Agricultural Economics, Michigan State University, East Lansing, MI 48824-1039 USA.

opportunities, and program options (Holtzman et al. 1991). It also generated demand for further in-depth research on coarse grain processing and the maize sub-sector (see Fischer et al. 1992; Boughton 1993; Témé and Boughton 1993; IER/DPAER 1993a-d, 1994; Boughton and Staatz 1993).

The methods described in this paper were methods used to conduct structured informal interviews with coarse grain processors, traders, small-scale commercial food preparers, and consumers. The rapid appraisal (RA) benefitted from five years of applied research on coarse grain production, marketing, and household transactions behavior, which had been carried out by a team of researchers from the CESA (*Commission nationale d'évaluation et de suivi de la stratégie alimentaire*) and the Department of Agricultural Economics of Michigan State University (MSU). Researchers at Tufts University (see Lowdermilk 1991; Rogers and Lowdermilk 1991) were also doing econometric analyses of household food consumption patterns, using data from a national urban household sample survey. A rich empirical base had been established, although relatively little applied research had been done on coarse grain processing and utilization.

The Research Context and Objectives of the Rapid Appraisal Study

The coarse grain processing and utilization rapid appraisal (CGPU-RA) in Mali was undertaken during the harvest period of a quite good agricultural production season, which followed on four years of excellent grain production. OPAM (*Office des produits alimentaires du Mali*), the cereals board, had abandoned supporting coarse grain prices in late 1987, as it lacked the resources to defend a floor price above the import parity price. The board was no longer the monopsony buyer of coarse grain, which had been the only entity to legally transport grain across provincial lines until the mid-1980s. OPAM was in the process of redefining its role from one of a monopsony buyer of grain to a provider of market information and other services to grain producers and traders. It had also created a food grain reserve of 50,000 tons, which could be used to dampen sudden or rapid grain price hikes or to shore up supplies in deficit zones.

Following successive years of good harvests, coarse grain prices were relatively low and demand was saturated by late 1990. Mali also produces and consumes significant quantities of rice. The *Office du Niger* scheme of irrigated rice production in the Niger River valley had stimulated paddy production over several decades, although irrigation efficiency and the operational efficiency of the *Office*'s larger-scale rice mills were low. Mali also imported white, polished rice, shipped from Southeast Asia to the West African coastal ports. Although this Asian rice commanded a premium compared to

Malian rice, consumers prefer it; and it competed well in the Malian market.[2] Rice consumption is significant in urban areas, given its convenience in food preparation relative to coarse grain.

Given this research context of strong harvests and dampened demand for coarse grain, and increasing demand for polished rice, the RA study team sought to examine the general issues of why coarse grain consumption was seemingly limited and what donor agencies and researchers could do to expand demand for coarse grain products. Processing had been identified as a key constraint to coarse grain consumption, particularly in urban areas. Most coarse grains in Mali are processed manually, using an arduous, time-consuming process. Increasingly in urban areas, small mills, powered by diesel fuel or electricity, have been established by entrepreneurs to process coarse grain into grits and flour, which can then be prepared by urban households. These mills process coarse grain on a custom basis in small lots for urban consumers who must bring their grain to the mill for processing, sometimes wait in line, and finally pay a milling fee to the mill operator. Hence, urban households incur additional time and monetary costs in getting coarse grain to a ready-to-cook form, as is processed rice.

Work on coarse grain utilization was being led by the National Food Laboratory and supported by both USAID's Millet and Sorghum CRSP (Collaborative Research Support Program) and the French Government. The food laboratory had developed and was testing a number of millet and sorghum processing techniques and food preparations. It had done virtually nothing on maize processing and preparations, however, even though maize area cultivated and output were growing faster than millet and sorghum area and output had been, and several donors—most notably the World Bank—were planning to promote maize production vigorously in the higher rainfall, higher potential belts of southern Mali. The RA study team examined alternative millet, sorghum, and maize preparations, consumers' familiarity with these preparations and their preferences, and the effectiveness of Malian Government and donor promotion of coarse grain consumption.

Team composition and strengths

Not everyone can successfully conduct a rapid appraisal (RA). Effective RA requires intellectual flexibility, excellent listening skills, an ability to think on one's feet and follow up vague or unclear responses with appropriate, probing

---

[2] Note that the January 1994 devaluation of the CFA franc in Francophone Africa has enhanced the competitiveness of locally grown cereals in domestic markets. While provisional estimates of the Malian rice harvest in 1993-94 indicate that local production will only satisfy 71% of Mali's needs, there is hope that Mali will become a rice exporter to neighboring West African countries in the medium term.

questions, and a willingness to pursue cross-disciplinary issues and themes. The RA team that carried out the Mali CPU-RA possessed these attributes. The researchers had participated in the design and management of both formal surveys of rural households, traders, and markets in Sub-Saharan Africa, and they had conducted rapid appraisals on related problems and issues.

The Mali RA team was comprised of three expatriate agricultural economists (John Holtzman, John Lichte and James Tefft), and two Malian analysts (Bagotigui Bagayoko and Fanta Mantchiny Diarra). Two interviewing teams were formed and each paired an expatriate analyst with a Malian counterpart. One team conducted rapid appraisal surveys of urban processors and sellers of coarse grain, while the other concentrated on urban women as the chief food preparers in urban households.

Study Focus and Key Informants

Given the scope and complexity of the study issues, the RA team had to delimit the study geographically and focus on several groups of key informants. The team decided to focus on urban processing and utilization of coarse grain, because the most significant changes and innovations were taking place in urban Mali. Although the preponderance of coarse grain is processed (manually) and consumed in rural Mali, rice consumption had made the most significant inroads in urban Mali and small mills had expanded more in urban than in rural areas. Most of the fieldwork concentrated on Bamako, by far the largest city and market in Mali. An area of secondary focus was Koutiala, a significant market town in southern Mali, located in a zone of high production potential, increasing maize production, and cotton parastatal (*Compagnie malienne pour le développement des textiles* or CMDT) programs to promote semi-industrial coarse grain processing.

The RA team conducted interviews with policy makers, representatives of donor agencies, Malian and other researchers and analysts (agricultural economists, food technologists), CMDT officials, and many other public and private sector actors. The team concentrated its informal interviews with coarse grain subsystem participants on processors, especially small commercial millers, and urban households or consumers. Structured informal interview guidelines were developed and refined for these two major groups of key informants. These rapid appraisal surveys generated valuable quantitative information about processing machinery and costs of operation, as well as coarse grain consumption by income quartile (using a proxy for income). Less structured informal interviews were conducted with wholesale and retail coarse grain traders, sellers of processed coarse grain products, restauranteurs, producer groups managing semi-industrial mills (in Southern Mali), and fabricators and salesmen of processing equipment.

Information Gathering in Rapid Appraisal

Holtzman (1986) argues that there are four ways to gather information during rapid appraisal studies. These include (1) systematic review of the literature and available secondary data sets, (2) examination of firm or parastatal records, (3) inspection and observation of agricultural marketing facilities and functions, and (4) informal interviews with marketing system informants. Information gathering method 1 is standard, although it is surprising how often analysts do not read available documentation or analyze secondary data before undertaking RA field work. Information gathering method 2 is often not possible in developing countries, as firms and individual marketing agents do not keep detailed records or they may be unwilling to share them with researchers.[3] Information gathering method 3 is a normal part of any field research, although it is not always done very skillfully and researchers may observe marketplaces and transactions in ways which influence the behavior of traders and other marketing system participants. The next section discusses how secondary production and price data were analyzed in Mali. A later section will focus on information gathering method 4, which generates many of the valuable insights and rich details obtained during RA studies. For further information about rapid appraisal methods for marketing research the interested reader should consult Holtzman (1993).

Analyzing Secondary Data

Secondary data sources, collection methods, and data reliability must be reviewed carefully in most developing country contexts. Even when there are problems with secondary data, researchers conducting a rapid appraisal are strongly encouraged to exploit readily accessible secondary data on commodity production and supply, consumption patterns, international trade, commodity subsystem organization, government marketing institutions and their operations, and price relationships. Appendix 1 shows key areas of investigation in undertaking rapid appraisals of food marketing systems in developing countries. For most of these key areas, the method of inquiry requires consulting and analyzing secondary data sources.

Fortunately, the RA team had access to good-quality secondary production data in time-series, compiled with assistance from a European Community (EC)-funded agricultural and economic statistics project. Price data were provided by Michigan State University's Food Security in Africa Cooperative Agreement researchers, who had been conducting formal farm and

---

[3] In Senegal, Wolof-speaking grain traders keep two sets of records. One set is in French and is designed for government tax collectors. The second set is written in Arabic script and kept as a personal record.

market surveys for five years prior to this RA study.[4] Cereals production data by region were examined in depth for two recent agricultural years, 1988-89 and 1989-90. As shown in Table 1, total production figures are adjusted for seed, postharvest losses, and processing losses to arrive at *net production* estimates. Secondary production data, based on estimates of biological yield and area harvested, are adjusted downward significantly to yield more realistic estimates of grain available for consumption. Note that grain that spoils (part of postharvest losses) and hulls removed through processing do have an economic value as animal feed. They are not suitable for human consumption, however.

In 1988, OPAM established a market information unit (SIM or *Système d'information sur les marchés céréaliers*) which began collecting producer and consumer (retail) prices at key urban and selected rural markets. Retail prices had been collected at Bamako for major agricultural products since the early 1980s. In the second half of 1993, the SIM began to collect and report wholesale prices for trader-to-trader transactions.

The RA team used the retail price data to examine seasonal and relative price behavior for major grains. Seasonal price indices, using seven years of retail price data, were generated for maize, sorghum, and millet, illustrating a pronounced price seasonality as would be expected with a storable commodity grown during one long growing season (Figure 1). Relative coarse grain to rice prices were also calculated, showing that maize had the lowest average price relative to rice. This maize price advantage relative to millet and sorghum could be strengthened through maize production increases that make maize the cheapest coarse grain and most abundant calorie source.

Another price analysis involved comparing adjusted coarse grain prices to polished rice prices. Unlike rice, coarse grains are not ready to cook when purchased and approximately 20% of the coarse grain weight is lost during dehulling. As a result, coarse grain prices were adjusted upward to compare all grains at similar stages of processing.[5] While polished rice remained the most expensive grain in most months during the 1988-1989 period (as shown in Figure 2), the difference between coarse grain and rice prices was reduced following these adjustments. The rice-coarse grain price

---

[4] Special thanks go to Philip Steffen for providing time-series price data for Mali. Steffen was the USAID representative to the PRMC (*Programme de restructuration des marchés céréaliers*) Technical Committee in 1987-88 and an analyst on Michigan State University's Food Security in Africa Cooperative Agreement in Mali from 1988 to 1989.

[5] The coarse grain prices were adjusted as follows:

Adjusted CG Price = {(Whole Grain Price) + (12 + 0.8*(10)) + 10}/0.8.

Table 1. Cereal production in Mali by region, 1989-90.[1]

Region	Millet (000 t (%))		Sorghum (000 t (%))		Maize (000 t (%))		Total coarse grains (000 t (%))		Fonio (000 t (%))		Paddy (000 t (%))		Total cereals (000 t (%))	
Kayes	21.1	(2.5)	115.9	(15.9)	23.9	(10.6)	370.2	(20.6)	3.7	(19.3)	2.3	(0.7)	164.6	(7.6)
Koulikoro	116.2	(13.8)	225.1	(30.8)	28.9	(12.8)	160.9	(8.9)	0.4	(2.0)	24.5	(7.3)	372.9	(17.3)
Sikasso	147.3	(17.5)	204.0	(27.9)	154.4	(68.5)	505.8	(28.1)	5.4	(28.3)	160.0	(47.4)	535.7	(24.9)
Segou	386.1	(45.9)	105.4	(14.4)	17.4	(7.7)	508.8	(28.3)	6.8	(35.7)	91.5	(27.1)	675.6	(31.4)
Mopti	132.2	(15.7)	11.6	(1.6)	0.8	(0.4)	144.7	(8.0)	2.8	(14.7)	27.0	(8.0)	239.0	(11.1)
Tombouctou	39.0	(4.6)	68.0	(9.3)			106.9	(5.9)			32.2	(9.5)	134.0	(6.2)
Gao			0.8	(0.1)			0.8	(0.0)					33.0	(1.5)
Total production	**841.8**		**730.9**		**225.4**		**1,798.1**		**19.0**		**337.6**		**2,154.6**	
Less seed/postharvest losses	84.2		73.1		22.5		179.8		1.9		33.8		215.5	
Adjusted production	757.6		657.8		202.9		1,618.2		17.0		303.9		1,939.2	
Less hulls	113.6		98.7		40.6		252.9		1.7		121.6		376.1	
Net production	644.0		559.1		162.3		1,365.4		15.3		182.3		1,563.0	
Difference between net production & conventional estimate	71.6		62.1		18.0		151.7		1.7		(10.1)		376.1	

[1] Totals may not sum exactly due to rounding.
Source: *République du Mali, Ministère du plan, Direction nationale de la statistique et de l'informatique; Ministère de l'agriculture, Direction nationale de l'agriculture. Enquêtes agricoles de conjoncture,* several years.

Figure 1. Grand seasonal indices of retail prices in Bamako, Mali, January 1982-May 1990 (excluding 1988).

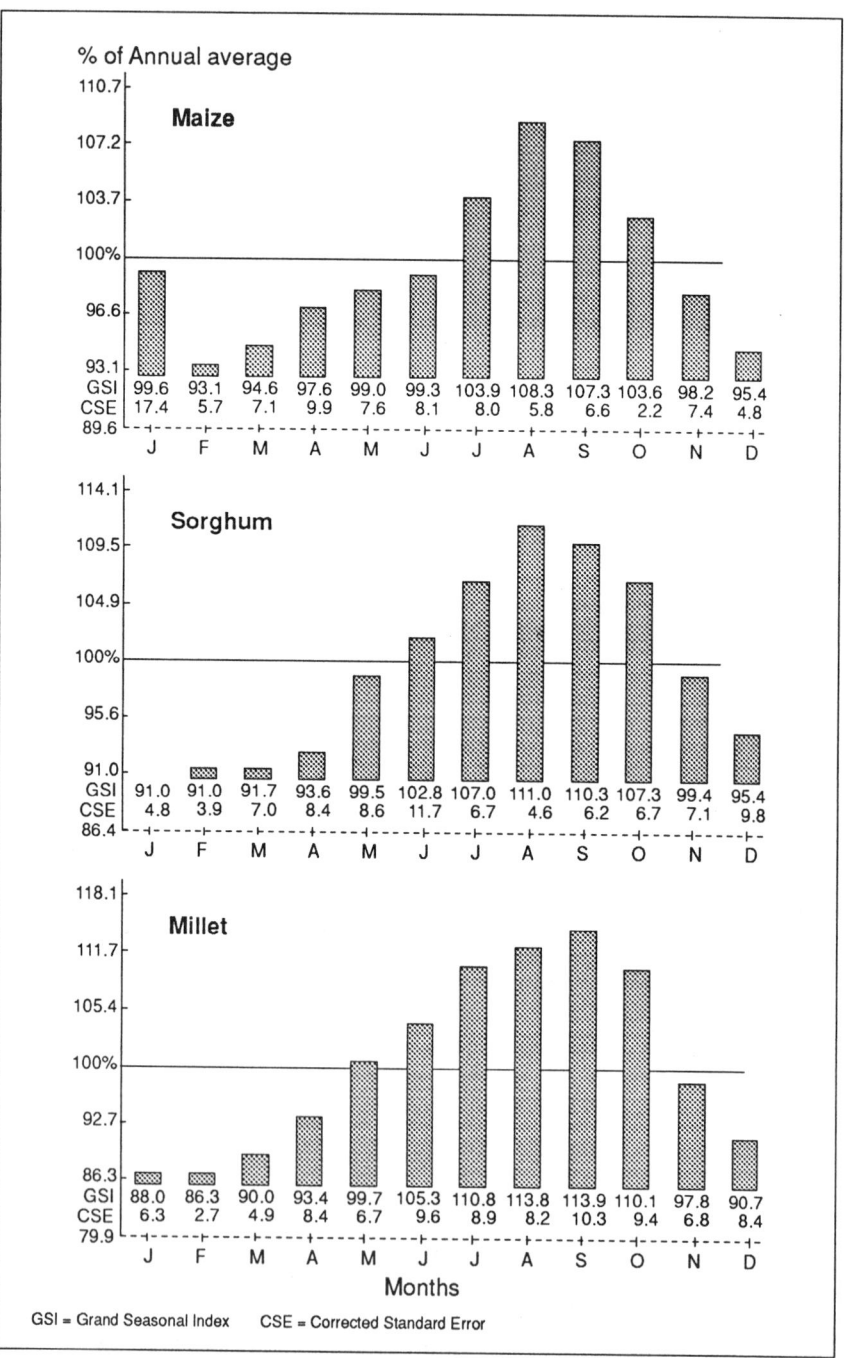

Figure 2. Wholesale grain prices in Bamako for cereals at comparable stages of processing.

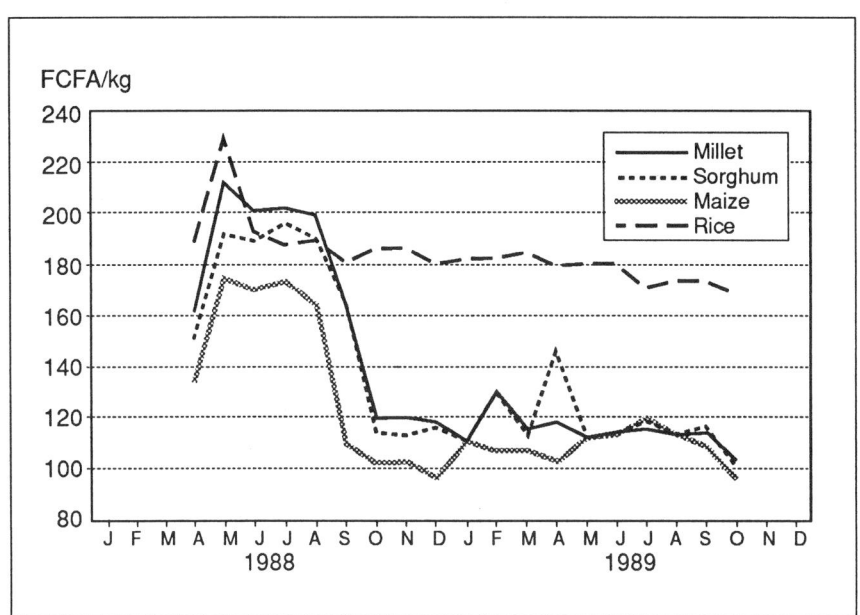

gap would decline further if time spent and distance traveled to and from a processing unit were included in the adjustment calculation.

In addition to the above price analyses, others can be performed using secondary price data. Table 2 lists eight types of price analysis, secondary data sources, data collection pitfalls, and potential analysis problems. Before rigorously analyzing price data, researchers need to identify who collects the price data, the transaction levels of the marketing system at which prices are collected, where, when, and how price data are collected, and how the data are compiled, aggregated, and analyzed. With an understanding of these methodological issues and potential problems, researchers can proceed to various price analyses appreciating what the price data represent and likely orders of magnitude of data error.

Note that poor secondary data recording or storage may constrain access. If price data have been verified, compiled, and entered into a computerized data base, a surprising amount of analysis can be attempted in a short period. If data are not readily accessible, analysts doing rapid appraisal need to make judgements as to the importance of analyzing different types of price data, which in turn will influence their data collection and compilation strategies.

Table 2. Price analysis and potential problems.

Type of price analysis	Data requirements	Data collection pitfalls*	Potential analysis problems
Trends in real prices	Farmgate prices Wholesale prices Retail prices Deflator	- Definition of farmgate price. - Which side of wholesale transaction (buyer, seller). - Reported vs. transacted prices. *These points apply to other types of price analysis as well.	- Change in nature and characteristics of product over time. - Deflator only available for urban area (consumer price index). - Representativeness of basket of goods, accuracy of weights in constructing deflator.
Relative price relationships	Prices for key substitutes and compliments.	- Are data available for key substitutes?	
International/ domestic price comparison	Import parity prices, including international transport costs. Export parity prices, including domestic transport costs. Exchange rates.	- Are domestically produced and internationally traded goods close substitutes? - Which international price? - Quality differences. - Are actual transport costs known (e.g., if trans-shipment)? - Official exchange rate may diverge greatly from shadow exchange rate.	- Assumes domestically produced commodity traded or potentially tradeable. - Poor comparability of domestic and international product can confuse analysis. - May be no direct transport between international exporter and country.
Seasonal price variation	Average monthly, daily, or weekly prices at same level of marketing system.	- If commodity moisture levels, grades and quality vary across seasons, this may affect comparability of data across seasons. - It may not be possible to obtain observations for all commodities through the year.	- Price data are typically only available for urban areas. Price seasonality facing urban consumers may differ from variation facing rural households. - Missing observations and gaps in time series will make it difficult to generate seasonal indices.

(Table 2. continued)

Interspatial price variation	Detailed price data for at least several locations, collected at same points in time, preferably for same level of the marketing system.	- Multilocational prices are not often available in time-series. - Data may be available for major towns and not for rural markets.	- High inter-market correlations may be evidence of effective competition or collusion/oligopoly. Need more information for determining which is the case. - Correlation may be spurious and not evidence of causality.
Marketing margins	Prices at different levels of the food system for the same commodity. Data on marketing costs if wish to analyze net margins.	- Prices at different levels of system must be collected during the same period for the same regions and comparable market channels. - Cost data difficult to collect; may be misrepresented. - May fail to enumerate key cost components.	- Marketing costs vary by scale of enterprise, resulting in different net margins for different firm sizes. - Size of margin and percent of return to producer may vary by commodity, reflecting degree of value added and marketing costs. - Net market margins may reflect differing time periods and degree of value added through storage, transport, handling, grading, processing, and location of distribution.
Commodity/ input price ratio	Consistent series of commodity prices and input prices or cost index series.	- Need to identify relevant input (fertilizer, insecticide, pesticide type).	- Cash inputs (fertilizers, pesticides) may only be used by large farmers. - Importance of input may vary considerably over length of time-series. - If input combinations are used, input costs need to be weighted to reflect relative importance.
Processed product/raw material price ratio	Prices of processed product. Consistent prices of raw material.	- Nature and quality of processed product may change over time. - Quality differences in raw material.	- Comparing ratios with other countries with different processing techniques and costs, nature of processed product, and relative prices may be misleading.

Devising Structured Informal Interview Guidelines

Structured informal interviews can generate valuable information about food system participants' behavior, motivations, intentions, and planned future behavior. Two common misperceptions about rapid appraisal methods of applied research will be discussed in this section. The first is that RA can only generate qualitative information. The second is that informal interviews should be loosely structured, or not at all structured. This paper will argue that RA can generate very precise quantitative data, albeit for small samples, and that the most effective informal interviews are carefully structured rather than extemporized.

Agricultural marketing researchers know how difficult it is to design a formal questionnaire which captures precisely and in a reliable way quantitative information. The more complex and heterogeneous the marketing system, the greater the extent to which this applies. Formal survey instruments are typically administered by enumerators, who may not be professionals or adequately trained, or who may be government employees who face other responsibilities, such as agricultural extension or revenue collection. Data collection, using a formal questionnaire, is a tedious undertaking which leads to both enumerator and respondent fatigue. In most cases, individuals can only do data collection well for 2-3 years; after that point (or sometimes far earlier) they go through the motions or may even fill in questionnaires without actually conducting interviews. Most social scientists who have worked in developing countries and designed formal surveys can recall numerous cases of poor enumerator performance, questions which get garbled in translation, and respondent fatigue with questionnaires that are highly detailed and take more than 1-1.5 hours to administer.

Rapid appraisal and other informal information gathering methods (e.g., case studies) give the researcher more control than a formal survey administered by an enumerator, because the researcher himself or a well-trained research assistant actually does the interviews. In addition, the higher up the marketing chain one interviews system participants, the harder it is to obtain useful and reliable information. It is difficult to match wits with wholesale traders, who are cagey and ever on the lookout for government tax collectors or economic police disguised as impartial researchers. In quite a few cases agro-processors refuse to be interviewed, especially if they are approached by enumerators or young, junior analysts.

Structured informal interview guidelines can and should be devised for conducting interviews with key marketing system participants. Such guidelines should provide a set of questions which are posed to all informants at a particular level or stage of the marketing system, for purposes of consistency and uniformity. Optional questions or sequences of questions should also be formulated so that the analyst can pursue additional or promising areas of inquiry. Structured informal interview guidelines should not be written up in the form of a formal questionnaire. Rather, they can be drawn up as a checklist or an outline of key issues and topics. The more skilled and practiced the analyst, the briefer and more summary a list of questions or topics will likely be. Despite the need for structure, a well-designed informal interview guide will allow analysts to probe, follow-up on unexpected or unclear responses, and pursue promising lines of inquiry (see Holtzman et al. 1993).

In the CGPU-RA, structured informal interview guidelines were devised, initially in the USA, for coarse grain processors and urban households. The guidelines were, of course, revised in the course of the RA field work. Abbreviated versions of these guidelines are attached as Appendix 2. The guidelines were designed based on previous work on the same topic in Senegal (Holtzman 1989), previous related RA and survey research experience in West Africa of all three analysts, and a thorough literature review.

The structured informal interview guidelines were designed to generate both qualitative and quantitative information about coarse grain processing and utilization. Based on the informal interviews, the team generated quantitative estimates of processing costs for a widely used and representative hammermill technology, as well as for urban household coarse grain consumption, purchases, and milling practices. Representative monthly budgets for both diesel- and electric-powered plate mills are presented in Appendix 3. The urban household survey findings are available in Holtzman, Lichte, Tefft, et al. (1991).

Many analysts who have little experience with conducting formal or informal surveys in developing countries assume that collecting quantitative data is a simple matter of asking a straightforward question. This is only the case if the question refers to behavior for a very specific period (e.g., How much rice did you buy in the past two days?). When reference periods are longer, extending a week or so in the past, obtaining reliable quantitative data often requires a series of carefully sequenced questions, as well as a cross-check. For example, in the West African context, several household members might have to respond to a question regarding grain purchases during the past week. Furthermore, grain may have been bought in different, non-standardized retail units. In order to obtain an accurate estimate of household grain purchases, the analyst would have to ask several questions of each household member; in what form was the grain purchased (whole grain, dehulled grain, or grits or flour of different grades); what was the sale/purchase unit; how many units were purchased at each transaction; and how much was paid per unit. Household purchases for the week would be the aggregation of discrete, often heterogeneous purchases of several family members. To ask for a global purchase estimate without careful disaggregation of individual purchases and aggregation of the responses is a recipe for inaccuracy and unreliability.

Informal interviews, if designed properly, are also a useful vehicle for collecting information on flow variables, such as volumes, prices, or throughput, which vary significantly in magnitude within or across seasons or other reference periods. While many researchers may feel that they know reference periods well during which behavior is relatively homogeneous, it is surprising in practice to learn about variability or nuances which were unsuspected at the outset, even when a survey instrument is pre-tested.

Structured informal interviews can generate precise, reliable information on marketing costs, purchase and sale prices, transacted volumes, processed throughput, and other continuous variables over relatively short recall periods. The drawback of rapid appraisal is that sample characteristics may not be well known at the time of sampling or after the RA is completed. The common criticisms of sample bias and small samples which do not permit statistical analysis are valid for rapid appraisal. Quantitative findings have to be presented as indicative or illustrative, not as authoritative or having known statistical properties. Most practitioners of rapid appraisal construct synthetic enterprise budgets for marketing system participant types, which are representative of marketing costs faced by agents of similar scale, technology, and sophistication.

Problems in Conducting the Rapid Appraisal

Anyone who reports that a RA was conducted without any problems is probably not being candid. Effective RA is often just as valuable in highlighting what is not known or what information is difficult to obtain as it is in acquiring valuable, detailed information about households' or firms' behaviors, motivations, and perceptions obtained in probing interviews. A well-conducted RA should help researchers formulate hypotheses or more precise questions for follow-up, in-depth investigation, typically requiring a combination of formal surveys and careful observation.

In conducting the rapid appraisal survey of grain mills and dehullers, the team discovered several types of equipment powered by diesel or electric units of different capacity, and having diverse operating practices and costs. This heterogeneity complicated the task of identifying representative processing costs and returns. In cases where such heterogeneity yields a good deal of variability in estimates, analysts are recommended to identify one or more major, representative technology and operating combinations. In interpreting the results of enterprise budgets, researchers need to emphasize the preliminary, yet illustrative nature of the findings. The enterprise type should be carefully specified, and all the participating analysts gathering data should focus on the chosen, representative enterprise type.

Problems arise in asking processing unit managers to provide detailed cost and throughput data for different periods of the year when there is significant variability in throughput. Retrospective questions can usually generate valid information about cost and throughput data during well-recalled periods of maximum or minimum processing activity (or other economic activity with well-defined seasonality). However, asking informants, during RA, to provide estimates of marketing or processing costs, processed throughput or quantities in storage, and sales/purchases month-by-month over a year period is ill-advised. The same caution in avoiding taxing a respondent's limited recall capacity is advised in carrying out interviews of household food purchase and consumption practices over a long recall period. Given the potential for incomplete recall or telescoping of buying/consumption patterns from a rather long period into a shorter period, researchers inquiring about household transactions are urged to delimit the recall period to one which is well-defined and set off by clear boundaries (in time). Recall periods should be limited to a day, week or month, depending upon the variable in question, the reliability of responses as judged by analysts (and informants themselves), and the nature and frequency of transactions.

Asking households about their consumption patterns and preferences can be a tricky undertaking. Since households in the developing world spend a far higher proportion of their income on food than households in industrial countries, food expenditures can serve as a proxy for households' income, particularly for lower-income households. By reporting low expenditures on food, urban households admit that they are poor, which is not what people care to admit to strangers. A skillful analyst-cum-interviewer can overcome some households' resistance to reporting accurately expenditures on food, but some over-reporting of expenditures may remain.

Another potential problem arises when a male urban household head wishes to respond to questions about household food purchases, preparation, and processing. In Sub-Saharan Africa, male household heads often provide their wives with cash to buy food, constituting an allowance of sorts. This allowance is quite often supplemented by the wives' own income, earned from small enterprises or services. Furthermore, while a male household head may have a general idea about how much money is being spent on food, he is unlikely to do the purchasing and processing, so he cannot accurately report on the level of expenditures for specific items and services, such as custom processing at a mill. The RA team insisted on interviewing the wife or woman who did or was responsible for food purchasing. In a few cases, male household heads were humored by the analysts' asking them a few general, opening questions, where they insisted on being interviewed before their wives. The Malian female analyst conducted the structured informal interviews with the chief woman charged with food purchasing and preparation in the urban household. In cases where several women shared this responsibility, they were all invited to respond to the questions. In this way, a reliable and complete picture of the household's food consumption, processing, and preparation practices emerged.

As a general rule in survey research—whether formal or informal—hypothetical questions are likely to yield ambiguous or dubious responses. As the old adage goes: "If you ask a hypothetical question, you get a hypothetical answer." This statement applies strongly to questions about willingness to pay for new products or improved services, how consumption patterns would change if a household had more income, and how traders or processors would invest increased profits if business revenues expanded. People in many parts of the developing world will respond to these questions based on what they think the investigator wants to hear. Hypothetical, what-if questions generate less reliable information than simply observing how household or firm behavior differs at different levels of purchases, sales, revenues, throughput, technology, and scale.

The Mali CPU-RA was limited in time and geographic scope. As such, the findings of the processing unit and urban household surveys are snapshots of behavior at the time of the surveys, although some effort is made to place "current" behavior in a longer term, cross-seasonal perspective. If the RA team had had more time and resources, it would have expanded the RA surveys to towns other than Bamako and production zones other than the CMDT zone surrounding Koutiala.

Key Findings of the Rapid Appraisal

Coarse grains are the chief source of calories among rural and lower-income urban consumers in Mali. At higher levels of per capita income, urban consumers substitute rice, bread, tubers, fruits, and vegetables for coarse grain. Processing is a significant constraint to expanding coarse grain consumption, since it requires either arduous hand labor or cash outlays for mechanized processing. In contrast, rice is sold already dehulled and ready to cook.

The rapid appraisal survey of urban consumers uncovered nuances in coarse grain consumption patterns and preferences that were not revealed in earlier formal surveys. Key findings were that:

• Urban women place a high priority on the appearance and cleanliness of processed coarse grain, so they prefer to buy unprocessed grain and supervise the mechanical processing themselves. In this way, they are assured of an acceptable product. Hence, any efforts to promote mechanized processing of coarse grain, with the objective of increasing sales of processed grain products, must pay careful attention to product packaging, cleanliness, and presentation.

• Maize consumption is not widespread in most urban areas of Mali. This is driven less by consumer preferences, and more by the unavailability of maize during certain periods and consumer unfamiliarity with maize. However, maize preparations do exist in southern Mali (where maize production is concentrated), which are similar to sorghum preparations and also to rice-based dishes. As maize supply expands, active promotion and extension of maize-based dishes will be required to inform urban consumers of maize attributes.

- The lowest-income households in urban Mali consume the cheapest source of calories, which is sorghum. As incomes rise, households diversify their diets by consuming more rice, bread, and tubers. Traditional forms of sorghum preparation carry the stigma of being poor people's food. Increased availability of maize and knowledge of maize-based dishes could give lower-income consumers the option of diversifying their diets by consuming more maize-based dishes. As maize prices decline relative to prices of other grains with new production coming on-stream, the economic incentive to consume maize will become stronger. Active promotion and extension of maize-based dishes will be necessary in urban areas where consumers are not familiar with maize preparations.

The RA also examined the economic viability of a technologically promising innovation in grain processing, parboiling of sorghum. Parboiling enhances the nutrition and shelf life of sorghum, but it increases the costs of final sorghum products. With USAID/Mali funding, the Millet and Sorghum CRSP, in collaboration with a Malian National Food Laboratory, had undertaken research on sorghum parboiling and hired a private consulting firm to conduct market tests. The mini-survey findings showed that urban households prefer to consume coarse grain processed directly into fine and medium-sized grits rather than the flour or grits produced from parboiled sorghum. Since lower-income consumers are the principal consumers of sorghum, their consumption patterns are very sensitive to price. They cannot afford to buy parboiled sorghum products due to the added processing cost.

Based on their cross-country comparative knowledge of grain processing technologies that were not well known in Mali but were used in other African countries, the RA team members proposed a pilot innovation in grain dehulling. Senegalese dehulling machines are better adapted to dehulling of coarse grain than the currently used Engleberg-type dehuller, which is better suited to rice processing. USAID provided follow-up funding to Abt Associates and Appropriate Technology International in 1991-92 to test and monitor the performance of alternative dehullers, as well as to carry out further applied research in grain-surplus rural areas (see Fischer et al. 1992).

The RA report also recommended that food technology research begin to examine maize processing, utilization, and consumption in addition to concentrating on sorghum, the currently more widely consumed grain. Identification of maize dishes, popular in maize-growing areas of Mali, for promotion in urban areas (which lie mainly in the sorghum belt) is one strategy for expanding human maize consumption and diversifying urban diets.

Conclusions

Rapid appraisal was selected as the research method for examining coarse grain processing and utilization in Mali for several reasons: funding limitations; prior formal survey research which did not directly address processing and utilization issues (but generated hypotheses about how processing costs and inconvenience constrained coarse grain consumption); a generally strong secondary data base (by Sub-Saharan African standards); and the need to address a broad set of policy, institutional, microeconomic and technology issues in an integrated way under tight time constraints. The findings of the Mali CGPU-RA were provocative and stimulated further applied economic research (see Boughton 1993; Témé and Boughton 1993; IER/DPAER various 1993a-d and 1994; Fischer et al. 1992). The examination of maize production, processing, preparation, and consumption issues proved to be timely, as the World Bank and other donors were planning to stimulate maize production but had not considered maize's market potential.

Acknowledgments

The basis for this paper was an AMIS rapid appraisal in November-December 1990, where Holtzman, Lichte, Tefft, and two Malian analysts examined coarse grain processing and utilization in Mali. The funding for the field research was provided by USAID/Mali and the Women in Development Office of the Agency for International Development, Washington, DC. The views expressed in this chapter should not, however, be attributed to the Agency for International Development, Abt Associates, or Michigan State University.

References

Boughton, D. 1993. *The relevance of a commodity sub-sector approach to the design of agricultural research: The case of maize in Mali.* Paper presented to USAID/Mali on May 26, 1993. Bamako, Mali.

Boughton, D. and J.M. Staatz. 1993. *Using the commodity sub-sector approach to design agricultural research: The case of maize in Mali.* Paper submitted to the Selected Paper competition for the 1994 meetings of the International Association of Agricultural Economists in Harare, Zimbabwe.

Fischer, D., K. Schoonmaker, C.B. Freudenberger, and M. Ashraf. 1992. *Coarse grain processing in Mali: Opportunities for improvement.* Appropriate Technology International in cooperation with the Agricultural Marketing Improvement Strategies Project. Washington, D.C., USA.

Holtzman, J. S. 1993. *Assessing the AMIS project experience in using rapid appraisal and future RA directions.* Agricultural Marketing Improvement Strategies Project, Abt Associates, Bethesda, Maryland, USA.

_____ 1989. *Coarse grain processing in Senegal: Issues, constraints and policy and program options.* Agricultural Marketing Improvement Strategies Project, Abt Associates, Bethesda, MD, USA. (French version, *Transformation des céréales locales au Sénégal: Problèmes, contraintes et choix de politiques et programmes*.)

_____ 1986. *Rapid reconnaissance guidelines for agricultural marketing and food system research in developing countries.* MSU International Development Working Paper No. 30. Department of Agricultural Economics, Michigan State University, East Lansing, MI, USA.

Holtzman, J.S., J.A. Lichte, J.F. Tefft, B. Bagayoko, and Mme. F. Mantchiny Diarra. 1991. *Expanding coarse grain utilization in Mali: Current situation, constraints, opportunities, and program options.* Agricultural Marketing Improvement Strategies Project, Abt Associates, Bethesda, MD, USA. (French version, *Pour une plus grande utilisation des céréales locales au Mali: Situation actuelle, contraintes, possibilités et choix de programme.*)

Holtzman, J.S., J. Martin, and R. Abbott. 1993. *Operational guidelines: Rapid appraisal of agricultural marketing systems.* Agricultural Marketing Improvement Strategies Project, Abt Associates, Bethesda, Maryland, USA.

IER/DPAER (Institut de l'économie rurale/Département de planification agricole et économie rurale). 1993a. *Etude filière maïs: Déroulement de l'enquête sur les caractéristiques et les habitudes de consommation des unités alimentaires du District de Bamako et organisation du suivi et des testes de produits à base de maïs.* (Maize sub-sector study: Progress of the survey on consumption characteristics and practices of food consumption units in Bamako District, and the organization of monitoring and consumer tests of maize-based products.) Information Note No. 1. Bamako, Mali.

_____. 1993b. *Etude filière maïs: Stratégie pour la composante technologie alimentaire.* (Maize sub-sector study: Strategy for the food technology component.) Information Note No. 2. Bamako, Mali.

_____. 1993c. *Etude filière maïs: Composante technologie alimentaire et perspectives sur la transformation des céréales sèches.* (Maize sub-sector study: Food technology component and prospects for coarse grain processing.) Information Note No. 3. Bamako, Mali.

_____. 1993d. *Etude filière maïs: Composante technologie alimentaire et l'extension des enquêtes de consommation des céréales sèches.* (Maize sub-sector study: Food technology component and expansion of surveys on coarse grain consumption.) Information Note No. 4. Bamako, Mali.

_____. 1994. Maize sub-sector study: Analysis of household cereal procurement in Bamako: Implications of the devaluation of the FCFA for urban food security *(Etude filière maïs: Analyse de la consommation céréalière à Bamako: Effets éventuels de la dévaluation du FCFA).* (English version.) Information Note No. 5. Bamako, Mali.

Lowdermilk, M.L. 1991. *The characteristics and determinants of food consumption of poor households in urban Mali.* Ph.D. Diss., Tufts University, The Fletcher School of Law and Diplomacy, Medford, MS, USA.

République du Mali, Ministère du plan, Direction nationale de la statistique et de l'informatique and Ministère de l'agriculture, Direction nationale de l'agriculture. 1990. *Enquête agricole de conjoncture.* Bamako, Mali.

Rogers, B.L. and M. Lowdermilk. 1991. Price and non-price determinants of food consumption in urban Mali. *Food Policy* 16(6):461-473.

Témé, B. and D. Boughton. 1993. *Caractéristiques des unités alimentaires du District de Bamako et place du maïs dans les habitudes de consommation.* (Characteristics of food consumption units in Bamako District and the role of Maize in consumption practices.) Bamako, Mali: IER/DPAER, Ministère du développement rural et de l'environnement.

Appendix 1. Key areas of investigation in rapid appraisal of marketing systems.

Areas of investigation	Components	Methods of inquiry	Reasons for investigating
Commodity characteristics	- Different grades, end uses. - Degree of bulkiness, perishability. - Physical/handling requirements. - Degree/type of processing. - Types and magnitude of postharvest losses. - Packaging methods and materials for shipment and sale.	- Review commodity manuals, studies. - Develop commodity calendars showing periods of production and transformation. - Observation of handling, processing, storage, any sorting or grading, and packaging. - Roughly assess nature and degree of postharvest losses.	- Commodity characteristics can influence operation of the subsystem, which functions are performed, how they are performed, and the relative cost at which they are performed. - The nature of the production process influences the timing and magnitude of producer sales and marketed flows. - Postharvest losses are high in many countries. Identification of causes and means of reducing losses can expand food availability.
Consumption patterns	- Seasonal and secular trends in domestic and export markets. - Disaggregated consumption patterns by socioeconomic and ethnic group. - Future market prospects.	- Review consumption studies, food balance sheets, and demand projections. - Construct food balance sheets if data are available. - Interview nutrition/consumption researchers, selected commodity importers, exporters, institutional buyers, and rural and urban consumers.	- Demand drives (or pulls commodities through) subsystems. - The strength and seasonality of demand affect production and storage incentives, as well as the direction and magnitude of marketed flows. Longer run trends and opportunities affect investment decisions of participants in the subsystem.
Supply situation	- Production by year and by region for recent years, noting trends and variability. - Stocks for transformation and consumption by season and region. - Flows from major supply areas to major markets, including imports and exports.	- Review commodity studies. - Interview large wholesalers, parastatal managers, crop production researchers, importers, exporters, processors, and cooperative and trade association officials. - Use map to show flows and apparent surplus and deficit areas. - Describe seasonal variation in stocks and flows.	- Supply and demand are basic elements of economic analysis. - Production levels and variability affect prices (depending on elasticities), returns via the price mechanism, and risk perceptions of producers. - The level of stocks during different periods affects seasonal variation in prices and commodity availability. - Shifts in supply over time may indicate response to policies, technological change, the institutional environment, and alternative institutional arrangements.

Appendix 1. (continued)

Price relationships and seasonality	- Secular trends in real prices at the farmgate, wholesale and retail levels. - Seasonal and cyclical trends in prices. - Changes over time in relative price relationships. - Changes over time in input-output price and (product) value/(input) cost relationships.	- Gather secondary price data for the commodity and close substitutes/complements for a ten or more year period. - Deflate prices or express prices in constant price terms. - Analyze secular, cyclical and seasonal price trends, and changes in relative price relationships over time. - Estimate supply and demand relationships if data permit. - Calculate input-product price ratios, and/or value-cost ratios over several years.	- Relative prices are a measure of the structure of incentives facing food system participants. - Changing relative price relationships may indicate shifts in production and marketing incentives, especially if coupled with accurate production and marketing cost data. - The domestic pricing structure relative to international prices provides insight into regional and national comparative advantage. - Input-product price and value-cost ratios are proxies for the profitability of agricultural production.
Marketing system participants and organization	- Marketing channels and commodity sub-sector stages. - Important assembly, redistribution, and terminal markets. - Types, numbers, and geographical distribution of firms at key subsector stages. - Prevalence and importance of alternative institutional arrangements, such as contracts, vertical integration, direct marketing, cooperatives, and spot markets.	- Review previous commodity studies. - Check for existing enumerations or sample frames in government agencies (e.g., licensing offices). - Interview knowledgeable observers of sub-sectors and selected participants. - Draw a sub-sector map (flow chart) showing principal stages and marketing channels. - Use a geographic map to show important market places. - Identify firms using alternative coordination mechanisms and do case studies.	- Marketing system organization (or structure) influences the conduct of participants, which in turn affects performance. - High levels of concentration of firms at particular stages of the marketing system may lead to higher production/marketing costs than under conditions of lower concentration. - Prevalence of myriad small firms which fail to specialize at one or more levels of the marketing system may lead to scale diseconomies and high costs. - Analysts need to examine the benefits and costs of alternative institutional arrangements as the marketing system evolves.
Sub-sector and marketing system operation or behavior	- Practices and strategies of subsystem participants (individuals, firms, organizations for procuring inputs, processing, storage, and marketing of outputs).	- Identify key stages and participants. - Develop informal interview guidelines. - Sample purposively based upon knowledge of the population of potential respondents from previous records or studies, or from the above characterization of subsystem.	- Operation and behavior in the aggregate affect marketing system performance. - Information is costly to gather and process, and access is unequal. This affects the ability of different size firms to respond to changing market conditions.

Appendix 1. (continued)		
Sub-sector and marketing system operation or behavior (continued)	- Vertical coordination mechanisms: exchange arrangements, risk-reduction/sharing, information dissemination. - Sources, uses and distribution (equity) of production, and marketing information. - Adaptability and responsiveness of subsystem to shifting supply/demand, exogenous shocks, policy changes and uncertainty. - Evidence of market power.	- Conduct selected in-depth informal interviews. - Cross check findings with other subsystem participants and knowledgeable observers.	- The adaptability and responsiveness of commodity subsystems to changing conditions and uncertainty affect levels of output and performance, as well as the continued viability of the subsystem in a particular country. - Better vertical coordination can improve the matching of supply and demand at successive stages of the marketing system and reduce risk. It is important to determine if this is associated with limited entry, unequal access to information, and unequal sharing of risks and rewards.
Marketing system infrastructure	- Physical infrastructure (transport, including roads, ports, airports, and waterways; market places; storage and processing facilities; communications; electricity; water supply). - Infrastructure adequacy and bottlenecks. Evidence of excess or unutilized capacity.	- Review studies of transportation and communication infrastructure, storage/processing capacity and utilization, and market places. - Inspect and assess the adequacy of a sample of the above. - Use map to show key infrastructure. - Identify bottlenecks and constraints, uneconomic excess capacity (or inappropriate scale).	- In some developing countries infrastructural constraints constitute severe bottlenecks that slow food system development and penalize isolated areas and regions. - Excess, underutilized capacity suggests uneconomic investments and resource misallocation.
Government marketing institutions and policies	- Regulatory environment: rules; input and product regulations; laws affecting marketing and trading activities; property rights. - Public marketing institutions (parastatals, cooperatives, joint ventures): the extent and nature of their participation in marketing; effect on the behavior and performance of private participants in the food system. - Macroeconomic policies: price policies; exchange, interest, wage rate policies; fiscal and monetary policies. - Banking and credit policies.	- Regulations: use informal interviews with subsector participants to identify vexing or constraining regulations. Do follow-up interviews with selected policymakers. - Institutions: interview managers, determine the organizational mandate, outline its functions, estimate its market share, examine its pricing policies, assess the effectiveness of distribution and marketing services, and assess the impact of its participation on system performance. - Policies: review macroeconomic assessments of the World Bank, IMF, etc. Assess impact of policies.	- Regulatory environment generally and specific regulations in particular affect behavior and incentives of system actors. - Public marketing institutions dominate food systems in some countries, influence the organization, operation and performance of food systems in many countries, and generally affect the behavior of system participants. - Macroeconomic policies condition and shape the environment in which system participants make decisions about investments and operations. - All above contribute to system stability and/or uncertainty, which greatly influence participant behavior.

Appendix 1. (continued)		
Government marketing institutions and policies (continued)		- Interview bank and credit agency officers. Determine whether credit is subsidized, how it is rationed, who gains access, and the sectoral distribution of credit.	- Banking and credit policies determine who gains access to formal credit, which is often subsidized.
International trade and commodity competitiveness	- Commodity exports and world market situation. - Imports of the commodity or substitutes and their impact on domestic production, markets, and prices. - Trends in exports and imports. - Likely changes in exports and imports, and emerging market opportunities or dependencies. - The competitiveness of exports in particular foreign markets.	- Analyze trade quantity and price data available in statistical abstracts or outside assessments. - Review international commodity production, price, and trade forecasts. - Compare prices of domestically produced commodities with international prices. - Analyze the competitive position of a specific export commodity in key markets. Examine trends in export levels, market shares and prices, and ascertain reasons for changes. - Interview exporters and importers and major domestic buyers in the foreign markets. - Visit export-staging and import-receiving facilities. Inspect exported produce in terminal markets and compare with that of competing suppliers.	- Few, if any, developing country marketing systems are autarkic. International trade in agricultural commodities affects production and marketing incentives, consumption patterns and preferences, and the behavior and opportunities of system participants. - International market conditions influence developing countries' comparative advantage in production and export (import) of agricultural commodities. - In assessing export competitiveness, site visits to markets and buyers' premises and in-depth interviews with importers and end users in foreign markets provide a good picture of how a country's exports compare with those of other suppliers. Such visits to foreign markets often yield concrete input and insights into what needs to be done to meet international grades and standards generally and the requirements of particular buyers and end users.
Representativeness of the period under study	- Timing of the RA relative to the annual commodity production and marketing cycle. - Agricultural and economic characteristics of the year of the RA study relative to earlier years or climatic cycles.	- Compare rainfall data and production estimates with earlier years. - Compare economic data: GDP, balance of payments, inflation rates, trade patterns, exchange rates. - Assess political factors: any change of government, policy changes, movements towards (or away from) democracy.	- The period of observation may be unusual with respect to climate, agricultural production, economic and political conditions, and the effects of recent changes. - Marketing system development is an ongoing process. Historical perspective of long-run patterns of change in basic economic, institutional, political, and environmental conditions is valuable in understanding marketing system development.

Appendix 2

Structured Informal Interview Guidelines

Informal interview guide: urban households

Neighborhood
Name of woman interviewed
Her region of origin and ethnic group
Name of household head
His age and occupation
His region of origin and ethnic group

Number of years resident in Bamako
Religion
Size/composition of family/household
Does the household have a maid?

Food preparations

1. What do you eat for breakfast? How many times per week? Which cereal serves as the base of this meal? Always or during which seasons? Is anything special served on Sundays?

2. What dishes do you prepare for the mid-day meal? How many times per week? Which cereal serves as the base of this meal? Always or during which seasons? What quantity of rice do you prepare? Is anything special served on Sundays?

3. What sauces do you prepare with these different dishes: rice; *Toh*; couscous, etc.?

4. What dishes do you prepare for the evening meal? How many times per week? Which cereal serves as the base of this meal? Always or during which seasons? Is anything special served on Sundays?

5. Do you prepare other dishes using the following foods as the base: Millet; sorghum; maize; rice; fonio; red meat; fish; lettuce/vegetables; bouillon cube; bread; plantain; yam; cassava; sweetpotato; potato; cowpea; bambara groundnuts? Which dishes? How many times per week?

6. What sauces do you prepare with these different dishes served during the evening meal?

7. What quantity of red meat do you need in order to make a good sauce? What quantity of fish? How many times per week do you prepare sauce with red meat or fish?

8. How much do you spend on condiments each day? (Is the price of meat included?) How much do you spend for firewood?
9. Do you prepare special dishes for the children? Which ones?
10. What special dishes do you prepare for holidays?
11. What dishes do you prepare during the Moslem month of fasting (Ramadan)?
12. Do certain family members take meals outside the household? Describe which meals they take and where. Do the children buy snacks at school?
13. Yesterday, what dishes did you prepare for breakfast, the mid-day meal, and the evening meal?

Purchasing patterns and use of processing machines

1. Where do you purchase your cereals (market, village, co-op)? Do you buy in large quantities (by the 90-100 kg bag) or once a week in smaller quantities?
2. Could you estimate how many months during the year you eat sorghum, millet, and maize?
3. How do you dehull your cereals? Manually or by machine? Do you dehull large quantities periodically or do you dehull cereals weekly? What quantity do you typically have dehulled and how much do you pay for the dehulling?
4. How do you grind your cereals into flour? Manually or by machine? Do you mill large quantities periodically or do you mill cereals daily? What quantity do you typically have milled and how much do you pay for the milling?
5. Are there women in your neighborhood who process cereals manually? For which dishes? Is this a common practice? What do they charge for this preparation? Have such women food preparers become more or less numerous recently?

Comparisons

1. Could you compare the following cereals: rice, sorghum, millet, maize, fonio? Which is the easiest to prepare? Make a list which begins with the easiest and ends with the most difficult.
2. Could you compare these different dishes from the standpoint of time required for cooking? Make a list which begins with the most rapidly prepared and ends with the dishes that take the longest time to prepare

(*toh*, couscous, rice, moni, seri, broken rice, broken fonio grains). How much time is required to prepare each dish?

3. Do you buy or use any of the following processed products: already dehulled grain; broken maize grains; broken sorghum grains (prepared in a manner similar to rice); broken sorghum grains (prepared in a manner similar to fonio), grain flour (available in the marketplace); parboiled rice; various dried pasta products such as macaroni, vermicelli; Arab couscous; grain-based porridge?

4. Do you prefer broken sorghum grains prepared in a manner similar to rice or prepared in a manner similar to fonio?

5. Are there products (especially processed products) that you would like to find in the marketplace which are not presently available or are of poor quality?

6. What can help people vary the dishes they eat? What measures in particular can help household to diversify their dishes?

Informal Interview Guide: Millers

City/village

Neighborhood

Name of mill operator

Name of owner/manager

Number of years of operation

1. Equipment inventory: engine, plate mill or hammermill, dehuller, other: type; make, year of manufacture; year of purchase; purchase price; current use.

2. Other investment costs: building or lean-to, storage, scale, packaging equipment, other.

3. Services rendered: Batch processing for particular clients? What are the typical gross (initial) weights and net yields of grain processed for clients? Continuous processing for packaging/sale to households? To institutional buyers? Milling only, or dehulling plus milling?

4. Cost of milling and dehulling grain by kilogram of processed grain (net yield): Grain; Processing operation; Cost/kg; Does miller keep the bran?

5. What are the prices of processed grain products sold by typical sales quantity?

6. Quantities processed by month (or day or week):

Period	Length	Grain	Quantity	Revenues
Post-harvest				
Dry season				
Beginning of rainy season				
Rainy season				

7. Have the quantities processed and the number of clients increased in recent years? Why or why not?

8. Operating costs (indicate the reference period):

Category	Subcategory	Cost	Period or other reference point
Electricity			
Gasoline/diesel fuel			
Oil change			
Lubrication			
Labor costs			
Repairs	(spare parts) sieve, belt		
Taxes	operating license municipal taxes other		
Rent (for structure)			

9. Does the owner intend to invest in or expand his operation? Invest in other processing units? Integrate vertically backward or forward (purchase grain for processing and sale; operate other sales outlets such as restaurants)?
10. Other enterprises (sources of revenue) of the owner/manager?
11. What are the major constraints, and suggestions for alleviating these?
12. Are there too many/enough/too few mills in this town/neighborhood?
13. Are spare parts readily available? Mechanics to do repairs?
14. Do you supply processed grain or do you process grain in large quantities for certain clients?
15. In addition to grain, what other agricultural products do you process (groundnuts, cowpeas, other)?

Appendix 3

Representative mill enterprise budgets

Exhibit A2-1. Monthly budget for diesel-powered plate mill (in FCFA).

Investment costs		
Mill and diesel motor	775,000	
Installation	40,000	
Total	815,000	Not factored into the calculation
Other fixed costs		
Rent	1,500	
Operator salary/food	14,000	
Taxes	9,500	
Total	25,000	
Variable costs		
Lubricant	4,250	5 liters of oil @ 850 FCFA/liter
Disk repair	3,000	2 changes/month
New disk	1,460	1 set of new disks per year
Diesel fuel	13,500	1,000 FCFA in revenue/liter; 2,000 FCFA/day average gross revenue; 2 liters fuel at 225 FCFA/liter = 450 FCFA/day
Other repair/ replacement costs	1,500	Annual and biannual contingency costs to replace belt, bearings, bushings, and parts for motor
Total	23,710	
Total costs	48,710	
Revenues	60,000	2,000 FCFA/day * 30
Net profit	11,290	
Kg milled	7,500	2,000 FCFA day/8 FCFA = 250 kg. * 30 days
Cost per kg	6.49	
Net profit per kg	1.51	

Exhibit A2-2 Monthly budget for electric-powered plate mill (in FCFA)

Investment costs		
Mill and electric motor	675,000	
Installation	125,000	
Total	800,000	Not factored into the calculation
Other fixed costs		
Rent	1,500	
Operator salary/food	14,000	
Taxes	9,500	
Total	25,000	
Variable costs		
Lubricant	850	1 liter @ 850 FCFA/liter
Disk repair	3,000	2 changes/month
New disk	1,460	1 set of new disks per year
Electricity	11,673	1 kilowatt of electricity generates 375 FCFA; 2,000 FCFA/day average gross revenue uses 5.33 kw @ 73 FCFA/kw = 362 FCFA/day * 30
Other repair/ replacement costs	1,000	Annual and biannual contingency costs to replace belt, bearings, bushings, and parts for motor
Total	17,983	
Total costs	42,983	
Revenues	60,000	2,000 FCFA/day x 30
Net profit	17,017	
Kg milled	7,500	2,000 FCFA day/8 FCFA,=,250 kg * 30 days
Cost per kg	5.73	
Net profit per kg	2.27	

3

The Policy Analysis Matrix Applied to Agricultural Commodity Markets

Barry I. Shapiro and Steven J. Staal[1]

Abstract

The critical role of policy in the functioning of agricultural commodity markets is being increasingly recognized. Governments often intervene in commodity markets through prices, regulations, and macro-policies. Policies affect financial returns and comparative advantage. The Policy Analysis Matrix (PAM) can be used to study policy effects at each level of the commodity chain, as well as their effects on alternative technologies. The PAM methodology identifies the cost and revenue structure of marketing activities to evaluate the effects of policy. Non-price factors, including institutional forms of market failure, are often as important as price factors in explaining market functioning. Causes of market failure and effects of investments to improve market performance can also be studied. This chapter presents the PAM methodology and illustrates its use applied to a dairy marketing system at Nyeri, Kenya.

Key words: Dairy marketing, developing countries, Kenya, domestic resources costs, social values, sensitivity analysis.

The Problem

In the past, marketing has often been ignored both by governments of developing countries and donors. The importance of marketing, however, is now more apparent, especially marketing policy and its effects on domestic and international trade. It is being increasingly recognized that marketing research should take place in an international context to increase its relevance. Thus, the critical role of policy in the functioning of commodity markets is being increasingly acknowledged and studied. Developing country governments often intervene in commodity markets to achieve various policy objectives. Frequently-pursued objectives include ensuring food self-sufficiency or food security; providing cheap food to urban consumers, sometimes including the

---

[1] Agricultural Economist, and Graduate Associate, International Livestock Centre for Africa (ILCA), P.O. Box 5689, Addis Ababa, Ethiopia.

poor; stabilizing producer and/or consumer prices; increasing government revenues; increasing marketing efficiency; and controlling inflation. To achieve these objectives, governments often change the prices producers and marketing agents face, causing domestic prices to differ from the world market price.

Empirical evidence points to improvement in price, trade, and macro policy in most developing regions, including Sub-Saharan Africa (Williams 1993). There is still a need, however, to carry out research on all aspects of policies affecting commodity markets. Price policy studies often rely on an aggregate approach which uses Nominal Protection Coefficients (NPC) to assess the effects of public price interventions on the discrepancies between domestic and international prices and the resulting effect on producer and consumer welfare (Bale and Lutz 1981; Jaeger and Humphreys 1988; Williams 1993). Westlake (1987) addresses some of the limitations of the NPC approach, and stresses the importance of incorporating input costs and of thus relying on *effective* protection coefficients. Williams (1993) recently examined livestock pricing policies in a group of Sub-Saharan African countries by tracking changes in NPC based on farm-gate prices. While this approach closely reflects real changes to producer welfare, it does not account for differing production costs under technological alternatives, nor does it separate the changes at the farm and post-farm levels. High domestic marketing costs can distort NPC-based price policy evaluation. While Williams' results show that price incentives to producers have been improving in the countries studied, it is possible that farm-level producers are not benefitting as much as shown. The benefits of price de-control would be captured at the post-farm level if wholesalers, processors, and retailers continue to enjoy market power. The empirical example provided later in this paper illustrates this point.

The Policy Analysis Matrix (PAM) methodology developed by Monke and Pearson provides a systematic framework to identify patterns of incentives for economic agents at each level of the commodity chain, and to analyze the impact of direct policy on these patterns at each level. Besides analyzing policy effects on private profitability, the PAM also examines the relative social optimality of alternative economic activities, thus incorporating the protection coefficient approach. Inclusion of production costs at each level allows effective protection coefficient estimation under technological alternatives. Furthermore, since the PAM evaluates each level of a commodity marketing chain, comparisons between farm and post-farm welfare changes can be made.

Governments usually implement several policies whose effects can be overlapping and even contradictory. Policy makers are thus often unaware of the magnitude of policy effects on individual commodities and levels in the commodity chain. Presenting policy issues and options in a manner understandable to decision makers is another problem faced by policy analysts. The simple and convenient manner in which PAM results can be presented to policy makers is one of the principal motivations for the development of PAM (Monke and Pearson 1989). Furthermore, instead of requiring time-series data of prices and marketed quantities—often difficult to obtain in the developing country setting—the PAM uses simple budget data from representative farms/firms.

This chapter presents the PAM methodology. The economic principles and concepts that provide the rationale for the analysis are introduced. Then the data requirements and steps in the analysis are explained and advantages and limitations of the methodology are discussed. Finally, an example illustrates how the PAM can be applied to dairy agricultural commodity markets.

Policy and Marketing Agricultural Commodities

Policy in the context of the marketing of agricultural commodities can be defined as those government decisions (market interventions) which alter the prices economic agents (such as farmers, traders, processors, wholesalers, retailers, and consumers) face and that affect their incomes and welfare. By intervening in commodity markets, governments alter economic incentives to producers and consumers. Analyses of policy usually concentrate on price and macro-economic factors. In the context of developing countries, however, non-price factors affecting elements of sectoral policies and services are often as important. All of the following types of policies are relevant.

- Price incentives: commodity, factor, and input markets
- Macro-economic and trade policies: taxes, subsidies, quotas, regulations, and licenses
- Sectoral policies: institutions, markets, infrastructure, investment, rural development, capital, labor, land, and livestock
- Services: credit, research, extension, and market information

Studying the effects of policy on commodity markets is essential for evaluating existing policies and prescribing policy changes to develop efficiently functioning markets. Policy objectives often involve tradeoffs and the policies pursued to achieve them can be conflicting, thus policy effects need to be separated out to ensure desired impact. Important marketing policy issues include:

- the various effects of policies on the private profitability of marketing activities, channels, or systems;
- the long-term economic viability/sustainability of marketing activities, channels, or systems;
- the effects of policies on the viability of alternative marketing technologies, channels, or systems;

- the effects of market failures[2] on profitability; and
- the effects of public investments (i.e., infrastructure and services) on improving marketing efficiency.

The PAM methodology provides a means to carry out such an analysis to answer the questions posed above. In order to achieve objectives such as these, a detailed understanding of the cost and revenue structures of each economic activity in each marketing channel in a commodity system is required. An evaluation of the impact of government interventions comes from an understanding of how policy, including regulations, programs and investments, affect those costs and revenues. By affecting profits, policies create incentives or disincentives for market activity and the long-term environment for the development and sustainability of the market.

The Policy Analysis Matrix

Monke and Pearson describe the PAM as an organizational framework to present the effects of policies and policy changes on incentives, applied to production or marketing alternatives (Monke and Pearson 1989). The PAM methodology provides a systems perspective of the commodity chain. The PAM methodology looks at the patterns of incentives for all economic actors in the commodity chain at the microeconomic level and evaluates the impact of policy on these patterns. Central to these incentives are competitive advantages in costs and revenues and how these shift with policy. PAM also examines the relative social profitability of alternative economic activities, the efficiency of resource use in the pursuit of maximizing national income. Socially-optimal activities at all market levels can be identified.

Economic concepts used in the PAM

Costs, revenues, and profits. PAM uses the concept of profit, the difference between costs and revenues, as its point of analysis. The basis of the PAM analysis is the identification of divergences between existing market (private) values and socially optimal values. Estimates of the magnitude of policy transfers to and from all economic actors in the commodity chain are obtained. These transfers are estimated for each input and output relevant to the activity, and their aggregate effect on profits is derived. Such results can provide policy

---

[2] Market failures fall into three categories: imperfect competition, in which a small number of sellers or buyers is able to influence aggregate supply or demand and therefore affect market prices; externalities, in which producers are unable to capture the full benefits for the goods or services they produce, or producers do not pay all the costs associated with production; and "institutional" market failures, situations in which markets do not function efficiently or do not exist because of inadequate development due a lack of infrastructure and institutions, or rent-seeking takes place due to a lack of regulations to prevent cheating.

makers with indicators of the quantitative importance of individual policies as well as a clear sense of the aggregate effect of policies on representative agricultural activities. These cost and revenue structures, presented in the matrix (the PAM), make easy interpretation of results possible.

Private values. The construction of the PAM begins with the estimation of costs and revenues at observed market prices. Budgets based on observed market costs and revenues provide the basis for figures included in the first row of the PAM (Table 1). These are the "private" values that determine "private" or financial profitability. They include the effects of all policy interventions, including both direct and indirect subsidies and taxes. Market prices also reflect the effects of market failure.[3] Private profit, subject to these policy interventions and market conditions, is then calculated. This private profitability shows the actual competitiveness of the agricultural activity.

Social values. Private values differ from "economic" or social values, the costs, revenues, and profits which would occur in the absence of any policy intervention and in the presence of efficiently functioning competitive markets. Economic profit is the difference between social costs and revenues. Social values are the standard by which the policy effects inherent in private values are measured, and are shown in the second row of the PAM matrix. They often cannot be measured from observed domestic market values which may include distortions due to government intervention or market failure. Instead, they are estimated in one of two ways.

Table 1. The policy analysis matrix.

	Revenues	Costs		Profits
		Tradable Inputs	Domestic Factors	
Private values	A	B	C	D[1]
Social values	E	F	G	H[2]
Divergences	I[3]	J[4]	K[5]	L[6]

[1] Private profits (D) = A - (B+C).
[2] Social profits (H) = E - (F+G).
[3] Output transfers (1) = A - E.
[4] Input transfers (J) = B - F.
[5] Factor transfers (K) = C - G.
[6] Net transfers (L) = D - H = I - (J+K).
Source: Adapted from Monke and Pearson (1989).

---

[3] Market failure must be considered if socially efficient prices are to be consistent with the maximization of national income. Like policies, market failures alter costs and revenues and prevent the economy from realizing potential income gains. Identifying institutional forms of market failure and their effects are far more difficult than other types of policies (Monke and Pearson 1989).

For tradable goods, the value of resources and products on the world market best reflect social costs and revenues because world prices would prevail in the economy if there were efficient markets and no domestic policy interventions. As well, valuing resources at world prices is consistent with exhausting potential gains from trade and maximizing national income. For tradable inputs, whether produced domestically or not, social values can thus be obtained from observed world market values net of transfer costs to the market being studied. Exported goods are measured at f.o.b. (free on board) world market prices and imported goods at c.i.f. (costs, insurance, freight) world market prices. World market prices may, however, sometimes be inappropriate for social opportunity values due to imperfect competition, etc. They then can be adjusted to arrive at appropriate social opportunity values.

The social value of domestic factors cannot be measured by world prices since they are not traded. However, they should still reflect underlying scarcity and the most efficient opportunities for domestic use. They are thus measured as the value of those resources when used in the alternative domestic economic activity with the highest return, subject to practicality. Social values of domestic factors are then still the prices that would prevail if the factors were employed so as to maximize national income. The difference between social costs and revenues or social profits illustrate the potential long-run competitiveness or comparative advantage of the economic activity. Such comparative advantage is an indication of the long-term viability of the activity, particularly if policy support of the market is unsustainable.

Policy divergences. The differences between social and private values, shown in row 3 of the PAM, represent the divergences between efficient (free) market results and the observed market results. An important contribution of the PAM analysis is the ability to disaggregate the divergences to identify the specific impact on the market of each policy intervention or market failure. While the basic PAM matrix (Table 1) shows only the aggregated results of these divergences, the expanded PAM matrix (Table 2) identifies each group of divergence separately even when they are off-setting. Thus the effects of policy changes and targets for investments can be identified.

Use of PAM for policy analysis

PAM analysis of systems. The matrix as described above can be applied to any productive activity which entails costs and revenues, for example the farm-to-processor activity in a formal milk marketing system. It can also be applied to a related group of activities. An example is the sequence of activities which take place in the production and marketing of dairy products: farm production, farm-to-processing, processing, wholesaling, and further marketing including retailing. PAM matrices can be constructed for alternative technologies at each level of activity, and aggregated to form marketing channels or a system. In this case, the analysis would be of a commodity system. Such an analysis

Table 2. Expanded policy analysis matrix.

	Revenues	Costs		Profits
		Tradable inputs	Domestic factors	
Private values	A	B	C	D[1]
Social values	E	F	G	H[2]
Effects of all divergences	I[3]	J[4]	K[5]	L[6]
Effects of subsidies	M1	N1	O1	P1
Effects of taxes, duties	M2	N2	O2	P2
Effects of rent-seeking	M3	N3	O3	P3
Effects of market failures	M4	N4	O4	P4

[1] Private profits (D) = A - (B+C).
[2] Social profits (H) = E - (F+G).
[3] Output transfers (I) = A - E and = M1 + M2 + M3 + M4.
[4] Input transfers (J) = B - F and = N1 + N2 + N3 + N4.
[5] Factor transfers (K) = C - G and = O1 + O2 + O3 + O4.
[6] Net transfers (L) = D - H + I - (J+K) and = P1 + P2 + P3 + P4.
Source: Adapted from Monke and Pearson (1989).

allows insights into the aggregate policy effects on an entire commodity system, from producer to consumer. The evaluation of the results of such a system analysis remains similar to that of the single activity PAM.

Comparisons. Comparisons between different systems are also possible through a further extension of the PAM analysis. Policy-impact ratios are produced which cancel all units of measure corresponding to the specific commodity system being studied. The resulting "pure numbers" can be used as a basis of comparison between different commodity systems or between similar systems in different countries or settings. Using the indicator letters in Table 1, these ratio indicators for comparison of unlike outputs are (Monke and Pearson 1989):

(1)   Private Cost Ratio = PCR = C/(A-B)

The Private Cost Ratio is the private cost of domestic resources required to produce a unit of value added, the latter defined as the difference between revenues and tradable input costs. Excess profits, those in excess of normal returns to domestic resources, are indicated by PCR less than 1.

(2)   Domestic Resource Cost Ratio = DRC = G/(E-F)

Similarly, the Domestic Resource Cost Ratio assesses social returns to domestic resources, or social profits. In cross-country comparison, this indicator can serve as a measure of the relative efficiency of domestic resource use (Fox et al. 1990). Ratios 1 and 2 compare private and social profitability with respect to use of domestic resources.

(3)   Nominal Protection Coefficient (NPC)

on tradable outputs = NPCO = A/E

on tradable inputs = NPCI = B/F

The Nominal Protection Coefficients on tradable outputs and inputs essentially serve as alternatives to I and J in Table 1, by expressing divergences between social and private values as ratios rather than absolute values, thus facilitating cross-system comparisons.

(4)   Effective Protection Coefficient = EPC = $(A-B)/(E-F)$

The Effective Protection Coefficient similarly indicates divergences on tradable outputs and inputs combined.

(5)   Profitability Coefficient = PC = D/H

The Profitability Coefficient is an alternative to L, the divergence between private and social profits, and so is a measure of overall subsidy or tax on the system.

(6)   Subsidy (or tax) Ratio to Producers = SRP = L/E

The Subsidy (or tax) Ratio to Producers (SRP) expresses the same measure as a proportion of the total social value of the system output.

These comparison indicators allow the PAM analysis much greater applicability and flexibility than is available given the original activity matrix. If alternative marketing channels exist for a commodity, these indicators can be used to evaluate not only the relative desirability of each channel, but also the relative impacts of existing and potential policy interventions. Similarly, the relative impacts of different policies between national systems can be evaluated.

Sensitivity analysis. The comparison indicators can also be used to determine the sensitivity of private and social incentives to changes in parameters, in this case those affected by policy interventions and investments. Particularly useful are the Private Cost Ratio (PRC) and the Domestic Cost Ratio (DCR), which relate private and social profitability to the use of domestic resources. The ability of policy interventions to improve profit incentives can also be measured by sensitivity analysis; the effects of changes in such parameters as tradable input costs (due to changes in import duties) or market price (such as producer milk price). This would be done by increasing the cost coefficients in the PAM matrix in turn by 1 percentage point and measuring the percent change in PRC and DCR (Sellen et al. 1990). Such analysis evaluates the degree of impact policy changes can have.

Advantages of the PAM. The advantage of the PAM analysis over traditional cost-benefit analyses, is that it is focused on policy impacts on production technologies. Traditional analyses, considering supply and demand characteristics, often produce only the overall effect of policies on the welfare of all producers, consumers, and the economy. The PAM analysis, however, is able to separate out the individual effects of deliberate micro- and macro-policies, as well as market failures and other distortions, and evaluates the impacts of these factors on productive activities at each level in the commodity chain. The implications of policy for the development of alternative technologies become clear. Furthermore, instead of requiring supply and demand estimates dependent on time-series data of prices and marketed quantities—often difficult to obtain in the developing country setting—the PAM uses simple budget data from representative farms/firms.

Limitations of the PAM. The PAM does not provide insights into all the issues relevant to marketing policy. This is because it only deals with issues that affect prices or economic returns at the margin. Not considered are some non-price factors as well as such intangibles as the effects of risk-aversion behavior. These require data and analysis supplementary to that provided by PAM (Monke and Pearson 1989).

The primary methodological shortcoming of the PAM analysis is the use of fixed input-output coefficients, thus ignoring potential economies of scale or costs associated with changes in scale of the productive activity. These fixed coefficients are implicit in the single values for input costs shown in each cell of the matrix. For given levels of market activity, this assumption may not be a problem. Linear programming models of productive activities rely on the same assumption. If policy changes that would lead to changes in the level of activities are expected, however, the fixed coefficients impair the PAM's reliability.

In the market context, PAM does not consider supply and demand interactions which can involve changes in prices of inputs or products. In order to be used effectively, the PAM analysis should be done in a context where these factors are unlikely to have significant impact, for example considering small policy changes in the context of relatively elastic supply and large demand.

A limitation to system-wide PAM analyses lies in the assumption that market prices are given. This assumption also relates to changes in scale, as it assumes that such changes have no effect on either prices received or paid. For a single activity this assumption is reasonable. For aggregated PAM analyses that consider a large share of a national market, however, changes in the scale of that system are more likely to change both input and output prices. For projections of this sort, use of supply and demand elasticities must be made.

Calculation of PAM Coefficients

Activity budgets

To create the PAM matrices needed to carry out the policy analysis, quantity and price information for each alternative activity at the level of the commodity marketing chain is needed. These data are organized into activity budgets which begin to allocate the costs into the categories used by the PAM. These detailed budgets are assembled using both private values and social values for all inputs and outputs, based on detailed knowledge of the productive technologies, and thus the input mixes. The organization of data for both private and social values in an activity budget is illustrated in Figure 1.

An essential aspect of the activity budget is the allocation of costs into domestic resources and tradable inputs. This is necessary due to the different methods of determining the social values of each of these cost categories, which was discussed above. Figure 1 illustrates this allocation by differentiating fixed inputs, labor, and intermediate inputs (on the left-hand column) into labor types (skilled and unskilled), land, capital and tradables inputs. It should be recognized that many inputs have both domestic factor and tradable components, which must be reflected in the cost allocation in Figure 1. For example, the cost of transport to market, an intermediate input, can be differentiated into the cost of fuel and parts (tradables) and the cost of labor and depreciation (domestic factors).

This allocation of costs is based on knowledge of the cost structures of each input type, which may require further budgeting of the input supply activity. Once the proportions of domestic factors and tradables which contribute to each input are established satisfactorily, these proportions can be assumed to remain constant for all further applications of that input type. The elements of the completed activity budgets are then aggregated for inclusion in the PAM matrix.

The concepts behind and measurement of the private and social values of the activity budgets are arrived at in the same manner as in the case of the PAM itself. As discussed previously, the calculation of the elements of the private value row is straightforward, from observed prices and observed output in the case of revenue, and observed input prices and quantities for the cost coefficients. Social prices for domestic factors result from the opportunity cost of those factors in their next best alternative use. For instance, the value of

Policy analysis matrix applied to agricultural commodity markets

Figure 1. Structure of an activity budget.

Costs	Unit of measure	Unskilled	Skilled	Land	Capital	Tradable inputs	Total	Unskilled	Skilled	Land	Capital	Tradable inputs	Total
Fixed inputs													
Direct labor													
Intermediate inputs													
Commodity in process							Z_1						Z_2
Totals		C_1	C_2	C_3	C_4	B		G_1	G_2	G_3	G_4	F	

Revenues			
Outputs	A		E
Profits	D		H
	(D=A-[B+C1+C2+C3+C4]-Z1)		(H=E-[F+G1+G2+G3+G4]-Z2)

agricultural land may be derived from the value of that land under the primary crop or crop mix. Where this is impossible to determine, social prices may be achieved in a reverse manner, by explicitly identifying the quantitative effects of divergences, and then appropriately adjusting the private prices to arrive at an estimate of social prices (Monke and Pearson 1989). Such a technique, however, is unable to identify divergences due to market failure or other non-policy factors.

Social quantities are also problematic, because a large divergence between social and private prices could lead to different supply and demand responses at those price levels. Observed quantities at market prices may not be indicative of quantities under social prices. Where supply and demand elasticities are unavailable, alternative sets of input-output coefficients representing different technologies could be estimated. The technology with the largest social profit would then be used for the social value row (Monke and Pearson 1989). This technique, however, does not allow for changes in output demand due to price changes.

Budget data requirements.[4] Earlier in this chapter it was mentioned that one of the advantages of the PAM over other methodologies dependent upon time-series data is that the data requirements of the PAM are less since the PAM is built from simple activity budgets. This factor is especially important in developing countries where data are limited. To further minimize the time and expense of data collection, several proven techniques can be followed that still ensure data reliability and accuracy.

These time-saving techniques include careful use of secondary data and purposive sampling to obtain primary data. Purposive sampling is widely used in budgeting and in whole-farm modelling using linear programming. Available secondary source data is fully exploited when it is representative and reliable. Secondary data sources readily provide world market price data and some domestic prices. For information on input use and output quantities, as well as farm-gate prices, however, secondary source data is first collected, but then needs to be validated for correctness and representativeness. If the secondary survey information is of sufficient quality, fieldwork efforts can focus on verification, updating, and collection of details about input-output relationships. Validation or filling of remaining data gaps can be accomplished through primary surveys based on the purposive sampling of field-level expert informers for the representative activities to be budgeted. Purposive sampling avoids the problem of unreliable respondents often associated with random samples in field surveys. In random samples, there are often inadequate means

---

[4] This section is based on ideas elucidated in "Notes on Field Research Methods for the PAM" by Monke and Pearson (1990), with modifications based on the field experiences of the authors.

of ensuring the reliability of respondents and of cross-checking questionable answers.

Useful sources of secondary data are documents and expert observers. Documents are usually available from ministries, libraries, NGOs, and donors. To ensure relevance and reliability, secondary data is put in budget format (quantities and prices) for each input and output (documenting data sources, survey dates, and methodologies used). Synthetic budgets are thus generated, and by comparing these budgets with a list of representative activities, the researchers can begin to identify and plan required fieldwork to validate this data and fill in gaps.

Expert observers, the other source of secondary information, are individuals knowledgeable about policies, marketing channels and activities, and technologies at the various levels in the marketing chain, including farming practices. Experts include ministry professionals or commodity experts, international or national agricultural research institute scientists, extension service professionals, technical assistance staff in donor-funded projects, university researchers, enumerators for recent or ongoing surveys, and knowledgeable farmers. The interviews with experts, other than farmers and enumerators, cover such topics as technologies, crop calendars, input-output coefficients, and the organization and functioning of markets, including market failures in the commodity, input, and factor markets.

Identifying expert observers is not difficult, except for expert farmers. For expert farmers, extension and NGO or donor project supervisors can be helpful. From the supervisors or enumerators, we can identify the expert farmers who would provide reliable information and would be willing and able to supply the needed data. Enumerators are not usually a good source for input-output coefficients needed for the budgets, but do know the technologies, crop calendar, and perhaps the local markets. Expert farmers can usually provide a description of technologies, input-output coefficients, prices, and the operation of markets for inputs and outputs.

Interviews with expert farmers have the goal of trying to describe practices that are used by most of the farmers in the region and not necessarily themselves. Asking expert farmers questions about other farmers' practices avoids the motivation to hide personal resources, income, and wealth. If trust can be established, interviews about practices of the expert farmer himself, however, would likely be especially useful for the assessment of more advanced technologies.

As the interviews progress, a consensus should emerge about input requirements and output levels. Information gaps will continue to be identified. One important gap may involve the functioning of markets. Supplementary interviews with ministry professionals, international or national agricultural research institute scientists, extension service professionals, technical assistance staff in donor-funded projects, university researchers, bankers, merchants, and moneylenders may be required.

Even though input-output relations are simple, problems arise with respect to proper calculation procedures. Common complications are the treatments of non-marketed outputs and inputs, such as farm family labor. Non-marketed items can be evaluated at their market-equivalent values, implying that their value to the household or firm is the same as their value in the market. Family labor, for example, is valued at the market wage for hired labor, adjusted for sex, age, and skill level. In many situations, however, family labor may not be able to obtain employment as an alternative to working on their home farm, and the analyst may feel that the opportunity cost for family labor is less than the market wage. But such perspectives are readily incorporated within the market-equivalent approach to pricing. When private profitability calculations turn out to be negative, the result can be interpreted as showing acceptance of rates of return (to family labor, for example) that are less than the market value (Monke and Pearson 1989).

An Application of the Policy Analysis Matrix

Dairy production and marketing in Nyeri, Kenya

The Nyeri district, 200 km north of Nairobi, is a major supplier of milk to the Nairobi milk market. The relatively high altitude of the area (1500-2000 m) and volcanic soils provide appropriate agroecological conditions for an important dairy producing region. Further, as the area is densely populated, land holdings are small, providing incentives for intensive zero-grazing dairy production in addition to the traditional cash crops, coffee and tea. Typical zero-grazing farms have two cows, and include about 1 ha of coffee or tea, with additional small parcels of land devoted to sweetpotato, napier grass (a dairy fodder), and, in some cases, pasture.

Most milk is sold to official dairy cooperatives, which in turn sell to individuals, institutions, and the Kenya Cooperative Creameries (KCC). The KCC is arge private company that is favored by government licenses and regulations that restrict competition. The dairy cooperatives simply collect the raw milk and deliver it without chilling to buyers or the KCC. The KCC either chills the milk and sends it to Nairobi for pasteurization and homogenization, or dries it to be reconstituted during periods of shortage. Although all farms sell some milk locally, in areas closer to urban centers producers tend to sell more raw milk informally and directly to individuals. Prices from local milk sales are higher than from sales to the KCC, which thus serves as a buyer of last resort. The dairy portion of a representative zero-grazing dairy farm at Nyeri is summarized in Table 3.

Table 3. A representative zero-grazing farm at Nyeri, Kenya.

Milk sold to KCC (lt/yr/farm)	5,101
Milk sold locally (lt/yr/farm)	1,496
Cull cows sold annually	0.29
Bull calves sold annually	0.79
Heifer calves sold annually	0.51
Cows held	2
Acres of land	1.35
Family labor used for dairy (mandays/yr/farm)	255.5

Source: Sellen et al. (1990).

Data used in the example

The PAM budgets used in this example are based on work carried out by the USAID-funded Research and Training in Agricultural Policy Analysis Project (RTAPAP) of Egerton University, Njoro, Kenya, in collaboration with Stanford University and the University of Arizona (Sellen et al. 1990). Farm-level budget data were gathered by RTAPAP from July 1988 to September 1990 from dairy producers in several regions of the Kenyan highlands. These data were subsequently updated by the authors to reflect input/output coefficients, prices, and policies of mid-1992. Market-level data were obtained from the dairy cooperatives who handle the milk, as well as from the processor, KCC.

Activity budgets

In order to make use of the PAM methodology, detailed budgets are needed for all productive activities in the commodity marketing chain being studied. In this example we consider three levels of the commodity marketing chain: farm-level, farm-to-processing, and processing. The dairy cooperatives fill the farm-to-processing role by collecting milk and delivering it to the KCC, which carries out the processing. The activity budgets use the same units as the PAM matrices, which are cost and revenue per unit of commodity traded per year. The units are tons of milk per year.

In an activity budget for the farm level, Table 4 shows that the essential aspect of such budgeting is allocating costs between domestic factors and tradable inputs. In these calculations, the ultimate source of each input must be determined, and the proportions of domestic factors and tradables which make up each input must be estimated. In this example, it was found that the costs of farm-level dairy activities average about two-fifths capital, two-fifths labor, and one-fifth tradable inputs (Sellen et al. 1990) The cost of dairy meal, for example, is distributed between skilled labor, capital, and tradable inputs. These proportions are based on estimates of the input proportions used to manufacture dairy meal. Although not illustrated in this example, simple

Table 4. Structure of activity budget-farm level.

Farm level	Unskilled labor		Skilled labor		Capital		Tradable inputs		Cost	
	P	S	P	S	P	S	P	S	P	S
Fixed inputs										
- Livestock					473	553			473	553
- Zero-graze					368	460			368	460
- Equipment					25	28			25	28
- Land					205	306			205	306
Labor										
- Family labor	1549	1549							1549	1549
- Vet. service			76	114					76	114
- AI service			5	9					5	9
Intermediate Inputs										
- Napier	346	346							346	346
- Dairy meal			1	1	26	22	85	83	112	106
- Dipping			85	5	8	8	8	8	24	21
- Other							151	148	151	148
Working capital					14	14			14	14
Total Costs	1895	1895	90	129	1119	1391	244	239	3348	3654
Outputs									**Value**	
- Milk dairy Co-op									4253	8270
- Milk local sale									1701	1701
- Culls, calves sold									506	506
Total Revenues									6460	10477
Profit									3112	6823

budgets may also be necessary for such domestically-manufactured or supplied inputs. The fixed input figures are annualized costs of the capital inputs.[5]

The allocation of resources to veterinary and artificial insemination (AI) services reflects that these services use skilled labor. Under outputs, three sources of revenue are shown. Local milk sales and sales of culled animals are completed and accounted for at the farm level, because these sales are carried out by the farmer directly. The PAM matrices will thus be able to reflect these subsidiary market channels in the analysis.

The activity budget for the farm-to-processor level activity carried out by the dairy cooperative also shows that the intermediate inputs are allocated between the resources used (Table 5).

The fixed inputs costs reflect the annual depreciation of capital equipment, in this case the vehicles used by the dairy cooperative to transport the milk. The allocation of costs the KCC incurs to process the milk is shown in Table 6.

---

[5] Methods to handle depreciation costs of capital goods (i.e., milk coolers and trucks) are not shown. This information can be gotten from any intermediate finance or budgeting text such as Brown (1979).

Table 5. Structure of activity budget, farm gate to processor: costs incurred by the dairy cooperative.

Farm gate to processor	Unskilled labor		Skilled labor		Capital		Tradable inputs		Cost	
	P	S	P	S	P	S	P	S	P	S
Fixed inputs										
- Depreciation					93	92			93	92
Labor										
- Dairy labor	8	8	32	32					40	40
- Co-op labor			17	17					17	17
- Nat. Sec. Payments			1	0					1	0
Intermediate inputs									1549	1549
- Repairs, main			17	17	13	12	34	19	64	48
- Fuel, oil			1	1	2	1	55	48	58	50
- Other			19	19	49	49	10	6	78	74
Commodity in process										
- Raw milk									5500	9360
Total costs	8	8	87	87	157	154	99	73	5851	9681
Outputs									**Value**	
- Milk at KCC									4032	6833
- Milk local sale									2658	2848
Total revenues									6690	9681
Taxes									347	0
Profit after taxes									492	0

Post-farm costs comprise a higher proportion of tradable inputs, about three-fifths of total costs. In both Tables 5 and 6, all outputs follow a single market channel for this example.

Divergences

The divergences between social and private values in the activity budgets are the result of various factors which are described below. It should be noted that some simplifying assumptions must be made in order to arrive at the social values, such as the value of an "efficient" "socially optional" interest rate.

Milk prices. The valuation of social milk prices is critical to determining social returns to dairy. This is done primarily by calculating an import-parity price for processed, packaged milk. Such a price reflects the cost of importing milk powder, and then transporting, reconstituting, and packaging it for sale. Calculations for the cost of imported milk powder are shown in Table 7.

Table 6. Structure of activity budget, processing: costs incurred by KCC in milk processing.

Farm level	Unskilled labor		Skilled labor		Capital		Tradable inputs		Cost	
Fixed inputs	P	S	P	S	P	S	P	S	P	S
Depreciation					203	304			203	304
Labor										
- Salaries			103	98					103	98
- Wages	417	398							417	398
Intermediate Inputs										
- Factory overheads			36	36			143	143	179	179
- Factory repairs			61	61			244	244	305	305
- Machine rentals							7	6	7	6
- Detergents							193	103	193	103
- Water/sewer			11	11	9	7	3	3	23	21
- Electricity			17	16	45	39	32	23	94	78
- Steam costs			10	10	20	10	467	407	497	427
- Refrigeration							45	22	45	22
- Packing			1	1	1	1	572	381	574	283
- Commodity in process										
- Raw milk at factory									4032	6833
Total Costs	417	398	239	233	278	361	1706	1332	6672	9157
Outputs										Value
- Dairy products									13500	13339
Total Revenues									13500	13339
Profit									6828	4282

Table 7. Calculations of import-parity milk price.

Year	A. Average milk powder price, Europe, $/t	B. Approximate informal exchange rate, KS/$	C. c.i.f./ f.o.b. factor	D. CPI, 1992 = 100	E. Milk powder import price, KS/kg in 1992 prices = (A x B x C x D)/1000	F. Average milk import price, 1991-92, KS/kg
1991	1,488	40	1.163	1.12	77.84	
1992	1,712	50	1.163	1.00	99.99	88.92

The average whole milk powder price in Europe is multiplied by the informal exchange rate, the c.i.f./f.o.b. factor, the CPI, and then divided by 1,000 and averaged to obtain the import price of 1 kg of milk powder. The informal market exchange rate is used as a better measure than the official rate of the social value of the local currency, the Kenyan Shilling (KS). The c.i.f./f.o.b. factor, obtained from FAO statistics, is an average markup factor which reflects the cost of handling and transport of agricultural commodities from the world market to Kenya. The Consumer Price Index (CPI) allows all prices to reflect a single based year, thus allowing averaging. To the resulting average price of KS 88.92/kg for milk powder, are added the port costs, inland transport costs, and the costs of reconstitution and packaging. The processing conversion ratio of 8.26 kg milk/kg powder is used. A final wholesale social price (import-parity price) of KS 13.34 /kg of milk is obtained. This is compared to KS 13.50 charged by the KCC to wholesalers.

The same social milk price cannot be used, however, at all levels of the marketing chain. The social price of raw milk paid to producers, for example, must reflect the additional costs of collection and processing. Thus the farm-level social milk price of KS 10.70/kg is obtained by subtracting the KCC processing costs and the cooperative collection costs from the import-parity price calculated above. Similarly, the cooperative-level social milk price of 11.02 is the import-parity price less the KCC processing costs. Finally, the local raw milk market is assumed to be independent of the processed milk market. Since it is subject to little intervention, the observed prices reflect the social values of milk. The price of KS 7.5 /kg is thus used as both the private and social price (plus transport costs) at all levels in the raw milk marketing chain.

Table 8 summarizes the various prices used in the analysis. The private price at the farm-level is the price paid to producers by the dairy cooperative, while the private price at the coop level is the price paid to them by the KCC.

Labor cost divergences. In most cases, the market labor wage reflects the social value of labor; private and social costs of labor are thus the same. Divergences between social and private labor costs at the processing level are a result of taxes on wages. A large divergence in labor costs occurs at the farm level under veterinary and AI services. Such services are heavily subsidized; thus private costs are much lower than social costs. The same is also true for the labor component of dipping services.

Capital cost divergences. Divergences which appear under capital result from two factors: the difference between the interest rate available and an "efficient" interest rate; and taxes on capital equipment. An efficient interest rate reflects

Table 8. Summary of milk prices.

Milk prices in KS/kg	Farm-level observed (private) price	Farm-level social price	Coop-level observed (private price)	Coop-level social price	Wholesale observed (private) price	Wholesale social price
Processed milk channel	5.50	10.70	6.50	11.02	13.50	13.34
Raw milk channel	7.50	7.50	7.50	7.82	n.a.	n.a.

n.a. = not available.

the perceived value of capital in alternative domestic uses, thus, the opportunity cost of capital. At the farm level, taxes on fixed inputs outweigh the existing subsidies on capital, so that private costs are higher than social costs of capital, as is the case at the farm-to-processor level for fixed and intermediate inputs. At the processing level, subsidies on the capital costs of fixed inputs outweigh the taxes.

Tradable input divergences. Social costs of tradable inputs are lower than private costs in most cases at all three activity levels due to import and sales taxes on goods.

Output divergences. The divergences in this category at all three levels result from the social milk prices above private prices.

System Summary

The multiple activity levels of the dairy marketing chain can be combined to form a system analysis which can be summarized to aggregate market level figures (Table 9). The methods of combining farm and post-farm results to produce figures for the whole system depend on the category of values being combined. Because milk is an output at one level but an input at the next, care must be taken not to double-count the value of the milk. Each output and input can be counted only once. If necessary, a conversion factor must be applied between one level and the next (e.g., liters of milk to kgs of butter).

Counting the value of the milk in the main marketing channel only once, the value of output for the system is calculated. This is added to the value of secondary output, local milk sales, and sales of culled animals, which in this case occurs only at the farm level. Thus, the value of the output for the system can be calculated as:

	Private	Social
Final value of main output	13,500	13,339
Plus total value of secondary output	2,206 + 2,848	2,206 + 2,848
Equals system output value	18,554	18,393

Similarly, the input cost of milk at each market level can be counted only once, and this is implicit in the costs of the tradable inputs and domestic factors which have been used to produce that milk. Thus to obtain the system costs, the costs of tradables and domestic factors are summed:

	Private	Social
Tradables, farm level	243	238
Plus tradables, post-farm	1,805	1,405
Plus factors, farm	3,101	3,415
Plus factors, post-farm	1,188	1,239
Equals system cost total	6,337	6,297

Profit for the system as a whole is simply the difference between system revenues and costs. Similarly, divergences are simply the difference between private and social values for each category.

Policy analysis matrices

Based on the structural activity budgets and the system summary, PAMs can be created for each of the market levels and for the system as a whole. Tables 9 through 11 show the resulting matrices.

At the farm level, policy effects on tradables and factors can be seen to be minimal. High social revenues as a result of producer milk prices below the world market price equivalent lead to a large negative policy effect on profits. When compared to social profits, the overall policy effects at the farm level result in a loss to the producers of KS 3,708/t of milk, or 54% of potential profit.

At the post-farm level, the situation is reversed. The large implicit subsidy on tradables is a result of the low milk prices that processors are able to pay to producers. Raw milk is a tradable input at the post-farm level. The result is a substantial increase in private over social profits overall of KS 4,920/t of milk.

For the system as a whole, the divergences between private and social values are less. The largest divergence occurs under tradable inputs, where the tax on tradables increases private costs. These are partially offset by subsidies on domestic factors. The divergence between private and social profits is small, suggesting that the overall effect of public intervention is negligible. The divergences in profits at the farm and post-farm levels, however, show that processors are able to extract a large rent or profit that could have accrued to producers. The analysis suggests that, although milk prices are not officially controlled, the position of the KCC as the dominant raw milk buyer allows it to pay low producer prices, and subsequently increase its profits.

Table 9. System summary: Nyeri dairy market.

Item	Private			Social			Policy and Distortion
	Farm	Post-farm	System	Farm	Post-farm	System	
Value of all outputs	6459	16348	18554	10476	16187	18393	161
- Main	4253	13500	13500	8270	13339	13339	161
- Secondary	2206	2848	5054	2206	2848	5054	0
Total Input costs	3344	7246	6337	3653	12004	6296	40
Tradable inputs	243	1805	2049	238	1405	1643	406
Factors	3101	1188	4289	3415	1239	4654	-365
- Unskilled labor	1895	426	2320	1895	406	2300	20
- Skilled labor	89	327	415	129	320	449	-33
- Capital	1117	435	1553	1391	513	1905	-352
Profit	3115	9102	12217	6823	4183	12097	120

Table 10. Policy analysis matrix-farm level.

KS/t of processed milk	Revenues	Tradables	Factors	Profit
Private	6459	243	3101	3115
Social	10476	238	3415	6823
Effect	-4017	5	-314	-3708

Table 11. Policy analysis matrix-post-farm.

KS/t of processed milk	Revenues	Tradables	Factors	Profit
Private	16348	6058	1188	9102
Social	16187	10765	1239	4183
Effect	161	-4707	-51	4920

Table 12. Policy analysis matrix system.

KS/t of processed milk	Revenues	Tradables	Factors	Profit
Private	18554	2049	4289	12216
Social	18393	1643	4654	12096
Effect	161	406	-365	120

Sensitivity analysis

Table 13 shows the effect (as percent change) on the Domestic Resource Cost (DRC) and Private Cost Ratios (PCR) of a 1% change in cost and revenue parameters. It can be seen that the cost ratios are most sensitive to changes in unskilled labor costs, which make up much of the important domestic factor component of production and marketing. Resource costs are also sensitive to the price of capital.

Indicators

The final table shows indicators of the private and social profitability and cost, and the overall effect of policy intervention (Table 14). A Domestic Cost Ratio of less than one points to large potential social profits for the system. Protection Coefficients of about one indicate the negligible overall public policy effects on the system, as does the small Subsidy Ratio to the system.

This example used actual empirical data to derive the PAM coefficients for formal and informal milk market activities and channels at Nyeri, Kenya. Tables were created showing activity budgets and PAMs. Many other aspects of policy analysis could also be carried out with this data. The effects of exchange rate, producer and retail price control, infrastructure, etc., could also have been disaggregated. Measures to compare the formal and informal market channels, including small-scale processors, could also be set up. Sensitivity analysis of change in variables such as the controlled price and exchange rate could also be carried out. These are left to the reader.

Table 13. Sensitivity analysis.

Parameter	DCR	PCR
Price of unskilled labor	0.49	0.58
Price of skilled labor	0.10	0.16
Price of capital	0.41	0.26
Value of all output for zero profit [DRC or PRC = 1.00]	6297	11193

Table 14. Private and social indicators.

Private cost ratio [C / (A - B)]	0.26
Domestic resource cost ratio [DRC = G / (E - F)]	0.278
Net policy transfer [L = I + J + K]	120.5
Nominal protection coefficient [A / E]	1.1
Effective protection coefficient [(A - B) / (E - F)]	0.99
Profitability coefficient [D / H]	1.01
Subsidy ratio to system [L / E]	0.007

Conclusion

This paper introduced the Policy Analysis Matrix approach to studying policy effects on commodity markets. The economic principles that provide the rationale for the analysis and the concepts that provide the basis for measuring prices and coefficients used to carry out the analysis were explained. The steps in the analysis were presented; and how the PAM can be applied to agricultural commodity markets, such as dairy, was illustrated with an example.

The PAM is an organizational framework to represent the effects of policies and policy changes on the incentives that face economic factors. It is based on an analysis of the cost and revenue structure of productive activities and the effect of policies on profits. It can be applied to all the productive activities of marketing channels or systems. This framework is not only useful for analyzing the effects of price policies. Non-price factors such as market failures that can be especially important in development contexts can also be handled with the PAM methods. Issues related to the prospects for economic growth including the effects of policy on the potential of alternative technologies, the formulation of public investment policy, the allocation of research and development expenditures, and the tradeoffs between efficiency and non-efficiency objectives can be addressed.

An advantage of the PAM over traditional cost-benefit analysis of a market as a whole is that the effects of various policy instruments on the supply-side can be disaggregated. Traditional cost-benefit analysis, considering aggregate supply and demand characteristics, produce only the overall effect of policies on the welfare of all producers and consumers in the economy. Governments usually institute several overlapping policies that can be contradictory. The PAM analysis separates out the individual effects of various micro- and macro-policies, as well as market failures and other distortions, thus helping to identify potential policy and investment targets. PAM also evaluates the impacts of these factors on the alternative technologies used in various marketing activities at each level of the commodity chain. The implications of policy for alternative marketing activities and channels are thus made more clear.

The primary methodological shortcoming is the use of fixed input-output coefficients which makes PAM analysis unable to capture economies of scale due to policy change. In the market context, PAM does not consider supply and demand interactions which can involve changes in prices of inputs or products. Thus, in order to be used effectively, the PAM analysis should consider small policy changes in the context of elastic supply and large demand. A limitation to system-wide PAM analyses lies in the assumption that market prices are exogenously determined. For aggregated PAM analyses that consider a large share of a national market, use of supply and demand elasticities becomes necessary.

The PAM does not treat all marketing policy questions, but treats issues that are critical and complex, and presents them in a simple and understandable manner for policy makers. The PAM thus facilitates communication between economic analysts and policy makers. As well, the PAM provides a useful tool for organizing agricultural data for future research needs (Monke and Pearson 1989). Given the paucity of data that often exists in a developing country setting and the wealth of information and insights obtained with this method, the PAM methodology provides a powerful tool for analysis of the policy and institutional factors that affect the functioning of markets.

References

Bale, M.D. and E. Lutz. 1981. Price distortions in agriculture and their effects: An international comparison. *American Journal of Agricultural Economics* 63(1):8-22.

Brown, M. 1979. *Farm budgets.* World Bank Staff Occasional Paper No. 29. Baltimore, MD, USA: The Johns Hopkins University Press.

Jaeger, W. and C. Humphreys. 1988. The effect of policy reforms on agricultural incentives in Sub-Saharan Africa. *American Journal of Agricultural Economics* 70(5):1036-1043.

Fox, R., T. Finan, S. Pearson, and E. Monke. 1990. Expanding the policy dimensions of farming systems research. *Agricultural Systems* 33: 271-287.

Monke, E. and S. Pearson. 1989. *The policy analysis matrix for agricultural development.* Ithaca, NY,USA: Cornell University Press.

Monke, E. and S. Pearson. 1990. *Notes on field research methods for the PAM (policy analysis for rural development) working paper no. 2.* RATAPAP (Research and Training in Agricultural Policy Analysis Project), Stanford University, University of Arizona, and Egerton University, Egerton, Kenya.

Sellen, D., G. Argwings-Kodhek, et al. 1990. *Dairy in Kenya: Issues in agricultural policy.* RATAPAP (Research and Training in Agricultural Policy Analysis Project). Policy Analysis for Rural Development, Working Paper Series No. 8. Dept. of Agricultural Economics and Business Management, Egerton University, Kenya.

Westlake, M.J. 1987. The measurement of agricultural price distortion in developing countries. *Journal of Development Studies* 35:366-381.

Williams, T.O. 1993. Livestock pricing policy in Sub-Saharan Africa: objectives, instruments and impact in five countries. *Agricultural Economics 8(2):139-159.*

4

A Multi-Product Sub-Sector Study in Rwanda

Scott Loveridge[1]

Abstract

A study in Rwanda illustrates a method for assessing a marketing system in a developing country. The study uses a national stratified random sample of farm households to increase the research scope beyond typical sub-sector studies: national estimates of sales for a broad range of commodities are developed. This method allows estimates of informal imports and exports, as well as providing policy-relevant information about purchase and sales habits of different categories of farm families.

Key words: Market level surveys, sampling methods, farmer food purchases.

Introduction

A sub-sector study examines vertical and horizontal relationships in the production, marketing, distribution, and consumption of a commodity or a group of related commodities. (For a more complete discussion of sub-sector studies, see Shaffer 1973). The advantage of focusing on many aspects of a few commodities is that a framework for tailoring data collection activities with a system-wide perspective is provided. Armed with a system-wide perspective, the analyst is more likely to formulate policy prescriptions that are both realistic and workable. The information in this report reflects the status of Rwanda prior to the social upheavals in 1994.

The rest of this paper is laid out as follows. The second section provides a brief description of the study area and the policy environment to give the reader a sense of the context in which the study was conducted. The next section explains the market-level surveys and analysis that were an integral part of the work. Then follows a discussion of approaches used in collecting and analyzing

---

[1] Associate Professor and Division Director, Community and Economic Development, West Virginia University Extension Service, 404 Knapp Hall, Morgantown, WV 26506-6031 USA.

information about agricultural households. The final section presents arguments for and against adapting the method for use elsewhere.

Study Area and Policy Context

Located in East Africa, and bordered by Tanzania, Uganda, Zaire, and Burundi, Rwanda has the dubious distinction of being the most densely populated country in Africa. The Government of Rwanda (GOR) estimates that over 90% of the population live in the rural areas (*Service National de Recensement* 1991). The major strategy Rwandans have employed to deal with their galloping 3.7% annual population increases has been to expand the amount of land under cultivation. Cultivated area is fast approaching its maximum potential, and the average farm size is dwindling —the current average being roughly 1.2 ha (Loveridge 1989).

Harvests in Rwanda are continuous, with seasonal peaks. Crops that can be stored in the ground (cassava, sweetpotato) or on the tree (banana) tend to be harvested during periods when stocks of more seasonal crops such as beans, sorghum, and maize have run low.

Unlike many African countries, Rwanda has done little to restrict domestic and cross-border food marketing. Movement of basic foodstuffs from one region of the country to another, as well as between rural and urban markets, is essentially unregulated. Beans play a critical role in Rwandan food production and marketing, being the largest source of protein, the third largest source of calories, and among the few easily stored and transported local crops (Loveridge 1989). Beans are thus the most important traded food commodity in Rwanda in terms of national food security. This importance has not been lost on policy makers: most GOR food market policy actions in recent years have centered on beans.

In the 1970s, with assistance from USAID and other donors, the GOR established a parastatal to help manage food aid and stabilize prices. The parastatal focused its activities on beans and sorghum, and tried to improve both consumer and producer prices by appropriately timing its purchase and sales operations. In 1986, frustrated with a lack of success in improving producer prices, the GOR experimented with a pan-territorial mandatory producer price floor for all locally grown food commodities. Given the importance of beans to GOR policy makers, it is natural that much of the work done in the study summarized here focuses on bean markets.

Market Surveys

Market surveys can focus on consumers who come to purchase products at a commercial center, or on producers selling their harvest, but the study here exclusively targeted merchants buying and selling food products. There are several practical advantages to this approach. First, sampling error is likely to be smaller when interviewing merchants than when interviewing consumers or producers. The number of merchants in a market is usually substantially smaller than the number of consumers or producers, so a small number of respondents translates into a high proportion of the population. Second, merchants are much more likely to hold accurate and complete information about market conditions than either producers or consumers. Third, merchants are much more easily identified and approached in a market place than are suppliers or consumers.

Merchants are thus an inexpensive and effective means of obtaining information about markets. Of course there are limitations to using merchants as informants about markets. First, their self-interest may lead them to provide biased information. Second, in developing countries and elsewhere, a considerable percentage of any local product is likely to be produced, marketed, and consumed without coming into contact with merchants in well-established trading centers. Despite the drawbacks associated with merchant surveys, merchants are important sources of information about marketing and should be included in any marketing study. The study in Rwanda used two sources of merchant information in assessing market performance: time-series data and direct questionnaires. Each of these is described below.

Time-series data

Monthly urban price data from the Rwandan Ministry of Planning were used to analyze the effects of road construction on market integration in Rwanda and to examine rural-urban price differences. The effects on market integration are described here, while the rural-urban price differences are illustrated following an explanation of the methods used for estimating rural prices. Tests of market integration are used to determine the degree to which two or more markets for a commodity are jointly influenced by phenomena affecting supply and demand. Market integration is an indicator of market performance. Poor market integration can result from inadequate infrastructure, lack of competition, lack of consistent market information, legal barriers to product movement, or few negotiated transactions per time period. A number of statistical models have been developed to test for market integration (Jones 1974; Harriss 1979; Delgado 1986; Petzel and Monke 1980; Ravallion 1986; Goodwin and Schroeder 1991); the simplest of these is adapted here to illustrate the use of such tests. The more sophisticated models require long data series with no missing observations, which are not available in Rwanda.

Rwanda's road system was consistently upgraded between the 1970s and the late 1980s. To measure the marketing system's reaction to the decreased transport costs resulting from road paving and bridge building activities, tests of market integration were performed prior to and after paving of major highways.

The basic regression model is:

(1) $\quad P_1 = \alpha + \beta P_2 + e$

where P_1 and P_2 are contemporaneous prices in markets 1 and 2, respectively; α and β are estimated parameters; and e is an error term.

The adjusted-r^2 statistic resulting from such market-pair equations is a rough indicator of the linkage between the two markets. The α and β parameters can provide insights into price relationships between the two markets.[2] The α parameter indicates average gains from moving the product between markets. The β parameter measures the extent to which a price change in one market is transmitted to the second market. The model provided by equation (1) was used to test market linkages using Ministry of Planning data collected between 1971 and 1986. The data were detrended by regressing the pooled series from all markets included in the analysis against time. The estimated parameter on time was used as a proxy for inflation in deflating procedures. Table 1 shows adjusted r^2 statistics from dry bean price regressions for market pairs before and after road paving. The reduced transfer costs associated with the new roads appear to have caused price spreads between markets to become narrower due to increased arbitrage between geographically separated markets.

Merchant questionnaires

To gain a better appreciation of how many merchants were handling agricultural commodities and the standard operating procedures of those merchants, a series of merchant interviews were conducted. One survey dealt with merchants' treatment of product. A second survey focused on merchants' suppliers, customers, credit, and reactions to the government's efforts to

Table 1. Pair regressions of detrended urban retail dry bean prices before and after hard surface paving of an interurban road link.

Market pair: Kigali and	Construction years	Before paving		After paving	
		Adj-r^2	Observations	Adj-r^2	Observations
Kibungo	1974-77	0.27	12	0.50	60
Gitarama	1978-83	0.54	48	0.85	33
Butare	1978-83	0.50	47	0.86	29

Source: Ministry of Planning data, 1971-86.

---

[2] A correlation coefficient can be used in place of the adjusted r^2 statistic if the number of observations is the same in all market pairs.

influence prices. A third survey investigated questions regarding cross-border trade in basic agricultural commodities and other items.

Each of these surveys (see Appendix 1 for suggested questions) occupied one analyst for roughly one month from questionnaire design to interviews to data entry, analysis, and report writing. Thus costs were relatively low, but the work yielded important insights. The surveys showed a competitive, if undeveloped, market for most agricultural products. Merchants were focused most heavily on those items that stored well: beans, sorghum, and to a lesser extent, potatoes. Most markets had sufficient numbers of participants to assure a competitive environment, with merchants reacting to, rather than setting, prevailing prices. Results showed that storage by merchants was more accidental than a specific strategy to take advantage of seasonal price fluctuations. Most merchants were simply trying to move product as fast as they could. The merchants were also instrumental in verifying a phenomenon found in the household-level data: large quantities of beans and other products were coming into Rwanda from neighboring countries.

Household Surveys

In contrast to market surveys, household surveys can be expensive and time consuming. In addition, a good deal more attention must be given to methodological issues such as questionnaire and sample design. Yet household surveys are the only way of obtaining certain types of important information about the marketing system. This section describes how to draw a household sample, gives examples of effective data collection methods with such a survey, and provides examples of analysis coming out of the effort.

Sampling method

Where literacy rates are low and modern telecommunications limited, the only reasonable method by which to collect information from households is through personal interviews. A simple random sample of households is typically impractical in developing countries because it would provide a list of households evenly dispersed across the country, making travel to the interview sites difficult and time consuming. A stratified random sample was used to enable clustering of respondents. The sample design for the 1984 survey is discussed here;[3] subsequent survey samples were drawn in a similar fashion.[4] A pilot project yielded an estimate that one enumerator would have time to visit roughly fifteen households for field and production measurements if they were

---

[3] The U.S. Bureau of the Census provided technical assistance for the sample design.
[4] The method for drawing the 1985-1991 sample was slightly more complicated because of the desire to maintain current enumerator housing where possible, while reducing the sample size and dropping the 12 agro-ecological zones.

appropriately clustered. Thus clusters of fourteen households were used as the starting point for sample development. The project budget allowed for 150 enumerators. Project analysts wished to be able to provide statistically valid estimates for the rural areas of the country's ten administrative units (*préfectures*) as well as its twelve agro-ecological zones. Overlaying the two methods of partitioning the country yielded 35 administrative/agro-ecological strata. The number of enumerators allocated to each stratum was roughly proportional to the estimated number of households in the stratum, [5] subject to the requirement that the number of enumerators per stratum be even. [6]

A three-phase procedure was used to select households in each stratum. In the first phase, the rural administrative units (*secteurs*) in each stratum were numbered in a serpentine fashion. A sampling interval for each stratum was determined by dividing the estimated number of households in the stratum by the number of enumerators allocated to the stratum, and a random number table was used to select a starting number for *secteur* selection. In the second phase, the administrative units (*districts de recensement* (DR)) in each selected *secteur* were numbered, and a random number table was used to select sample DRs.

In the third phase, project personnel visited the selected DRs and listed every household. The list was divided into clusters of 10 households each. Each cluster was numbered, and the total number of clusters was divided by two to determine the interval number. A random number table was used to select the first cluster within the DR, and then the interval number was used to select the second cluster. The first seven households within each cluster were selected as survey participants, with the remaining three serving as substitutes in case of refusal to participate, death, or dissolution of the household. The probability of selecting a household was then:

(2) $P_t = P_s * P_d * P_h$

where P_t = probability of household selection; P_s = probability of selecting the *secteur*; = (households in the *secteur*) ÷ (households in the stratum ÷ enumerators allocated to stratum). P_d = probability of selecting a district in the *secteur* = (households in selected district) ÷ (households in the *secteur*); P_h = probability of selecting a household in the selected district = 14 ÷ (households listed in the selected district).

The inverse of P_t is the weight attached to each sample household to estimate national production, purchases, and sales. In cases where households dropped out of the sample mid-year, weights were adjusted by appropriately reducing the number 14 in the calculation of P_h.

---

[5] Estimates of number of households were projections from a 1978 population census.
[6] This facilitates computation of sampling error.

Production estimates

The continuous harvests in Rwanda's production system complicate the life of the researcher, since small continuous harvests are difficult for the enumerator to measure directly or for the farmer to recall accurately over long periods of time. Thus it was necessary for enumerators to visit each household 48 times per year to obtain accurate estimates of the size of the harvest.

Another problem common to many developing countries was the lack of standardized units of measure. Project personnel developed an innovative response to this problem: each household participating in the survey was issued a calibrated bucket with which to measure their harvest. The bucket was roughly ten liters in volume, and was calibrated into fourths. Each time the enumerator visited, the household was asked to report how many buckets of each crop had been harvested since the last visit. The number of buckets harvested was then converted into kilos by means of conversion factors developed by weighing buckets full of each product. The major exception to use of the bucket to measure production was bananas, where households reported the number of pendant bunches harvested. Farmers were asked to specify whether the pendant bunches harvested were small, medium, or large. Conversion factors to kilos for small, medium, and large pendant bunches were established for each prefecture. Another exception to the use of the bucket was for unshelled maize, which were simply counted in ears and converted into kilos.

Production records were kept at each household to facilitate supervision. Every six months a new set of blank records was provided to each household in the survey. The coded sheets were delivered to one of ten field supervisors, who checked for obvious errors, and sent them on to a central office in Kigali for reverification, data entry, and analysis.

Marketing estimates

Once the method for measuring agricultural production was established, it was relatively easy to develop a method to estimate producer marketings. The bucket became the central unit of measure for household purchases and sales of agricultural commodities. The initial survey covered only two crops: beans and sorghum. Enumerators visited each household four times per month for over a year. Each transaction made by every respondent was recorded on separate coding sheets for purchases, gifts received, sales, and gifts given, yielding four sheets per crop. Basic questions asked for each purchase and gift received were:

- form of the product (dry, green, flour, etc.),
- supplier,
- intended use of the product,

- walking time to place of purchase,
- type of measurement unit,
- number of units acquired,
- cash paid for the product,
- value of any in-kind payment for the product, and
- amount of product acquired in buckets.

For sales and gifts given, the questions asked for each transaction were analogous, except that instead of asking the intended use of the product, enumerators asked how the product had been obtained (current season harvest, last season harvest, received as a gift, purchased), and also how they intended to use the money earned through the sale of the product.

As analysis of the pilot study began, it became apparent that the greatest policy interest was generated by estimates of quantities of beans and sorghum bought and sold. This is because the analysis showed that large quantities of beans and sorghum were being brought into Rwanda via informal border trade with neighboring countries. This kind of analysis was possible because the national sampling frame provided weights (see discussion of equation 2) with which one can estimate national rural purchases, gifts, and sales. With these estimates, computation of net rural imports was accomplished with the following identity:

(3) $P + GR - S - GG = NII$

where P = national rural purchases; GR = national rural gifts received; S = national rural sales; GG = national rural gifts given; NII = net informal imports.

Rural utilization of both crops was calculated by adding net informal imports to production. Dividing net informal imports by rural utilization provides an estimate of the percentage of rural utilization that is imported. For dry beans in Rwanda this figure was 14% in 1986. Survey results showed that a majority of rural families were net buyers of beans. Rural prices were estimated by dividing estimates of total quantities purchased by estimates of total amounts paid. By putting monthly estimates of net informal imports to the rural area together with rural-urban price differentials, the study showed a classic rural-urban product flow reversal[7] in Kigali (one of the few regions that was close to self-sufficient in beans) (Figure 1).

All this was a shock to Rwandan policy makers, who had previously assumed that the rural areas were self-sufficient in bean production. By pursuing a policy of trying to raise bean prices, they were making life much

---

[7] See for example, Timmer (1974).

Figure 1. Kigali dry beans: urban-rural price differences and rural grain flows, December 1985-December 1986.

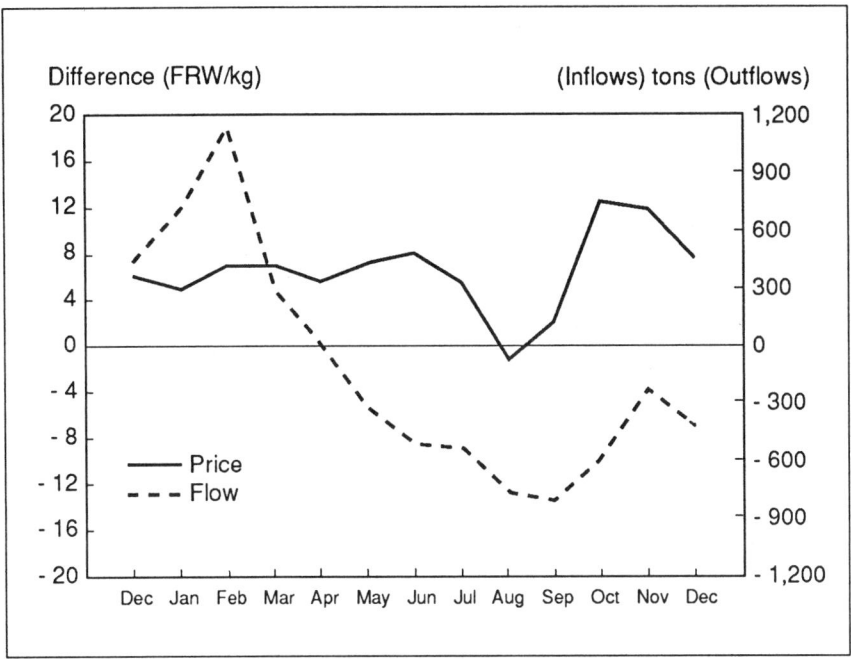

Source: Rural price estimates.

more difficult for the poorest people in their society. Analysis of the data for sorghum provided similar results, and the government's pan-territorial-mandated floor price scheme was scrapped.

The initial debate about the results had to do with their validity. Confirmation from the merchant surveys and from government employees in border towns eventually turned the debate toward questions relating to levels of exports and imports of other crops, and about sources of income for farm families. Faced with a demand for information on imports and exports of other crops, the project turned its energies to developing a new set of questionnaires including all major crops.

Processing the data generated by the ongoing production-related surveys and the bean/sorghum marketing survey had fully occupied the project's data entry team, but few new resources were available to augment the project's capacity in this area. How then to provide information on farmer marketings of all major crops rather than two? Simply replicating the method developed for the bean/sorghum survey could have quadrupled the project's data processing needs. A less intensive data collection system was needed.

Examination of the bean and sorghum data revealed relatively few transactions per family per month, so it was decided to increase the recall period from roughly one week to a month. Recording individual transactions was also dropped; instead, only the quantity exchanged and the value of each form[8] of each of thirty-one major agricultural products or inputs were recorded; all supplemental questions on the nature of the transactions were dropped to reduce data processing costs. Two coding sheets were developed for marketing of agricultural products. The first dealt with acquisitions (purchases and gifts received) and the second with disbursements (sales and gifts given). Similar sheets were developed for livestock transactions. Table 2 reports on production, net imports (calculated using equation (3)), rural utilization (production plus imports), and rural self-sufficiency in major crops. National estimates were obtained by multiplying the survey respondent data by the weighting factors derived from equation (2).

Table 2. Rural use and degree of rural self-sufficiency, 12 crops, Rwanda 1990.

Crop	Production (t)	Net Imports (t)	Rural Use (t)	Degree of self-sufficiency (%)
	(1)	(2)	(1+2)	(1) ÷(1+2)
Beans	205,908	60,537	266,445	77%
Peas	11,036	1,733	12,769	86%
Peanut	8,392	-39	8,353	100%
Soybean	20,675	446	21,121	98%
Sorghum	141,835	25,574	167,409	84%
Maize	95,973	1,995	97,968	98%
Cassava	264,952	20,753	285,705	93%
Potato	285,032	-51,067	233,965	122%
Sweetpotato	819,277	-18,961	800,316	102%
Banana				
- Cooking	602,764	-32,110	570,684	106%
- Beer	1,916,746	-2,505	1,914,242	100%
- Table	256,452	-4,649	251,803	102%

Negative numbers are exports to urban areas or neighboring countries. Sorghum and bananas sold in the form of beer are not included. The unit t stands for tons.

Source: Loveridge (1992).

---

[8] i.e., green, dry, shelled, milled, etc.

One might expect the longer recall period in the more recent survey to translate into forgotten transactions, and therefore lower estimates of marketings. In fact, estimated imports for beans and sorghum were of roughly the same order of magnitude between the two surveys (higher for beans, lower for sorghum).

An understanding of how farmers pay for their food purchases and how farmers at different levels of well-being interact with the market is incomplete unless some measure of non-farm sources of income is available. Similarly, some indication of non-food expenditures can also be useful in understanding a marketing system. Thus the project elected to collect some information on off-farm/non-farm income generating activities and information on farmers' hiring of labor outside the family. Coding sheets similar to those used for transactions were developed, and household revenue was estimated with the following identity:

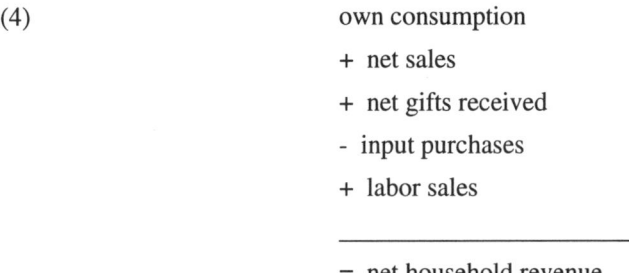

(4)   own consumption
    + net sales
    + net gifts received
    - input purchases
    + labor sales
    ─────────────────
    = net household revenue

Own consumption was computed by estimating the value of agricultural production (kilos produced multiplied by average price during the month of harvest), and subtracting from that figure the value of net agricultural sales. Once a total household revenue was estimated, it was necessary to control for the size and age of the family to facilitate comparisons between households. To account for these differences, the concept of adult-equivalent (AE) was borrowed from the nutritionists to standardize the number of people in the household. Conversion factors presented in Table 3 were used to calculate the number of adult equivalents in each household. Four categories of household revenue per adult-equivalent were established. The categories were chosen so that the cut-off points were at places where the intervals between adjacent households were quite large. Between 20% and 29% of farm families fall into each category.

Once income per adult-equivalent categories were established, it was possible to examine net marketings according to level of family income. Table 4 displays the result of this calculation. Values in the cells are the net quantity of product that families falling into a particular income category purchased (gifts are included in these calculation, but they are small relative to purchases and sales).

Table 3. Conversion factors for calculating AE.

	Sex	
Age	Male	Female
<1	0.41	0.41
1-3	0.56	0.56
4-6	0.76	0.76
7-9	0.91	0.91
10-12	0.97	1.08
13-15	0.97	1.13
16-19	1.02	1.05
20-39	1.00	1.00
40-49	0.95	0.95
50-59	0.90	0.90
60-69	0.90	0.80
>70	0.70	0.70

Source: *Ministère du Plan* (1988).

The estimates presented in Table 4 can help policy makers determine which crops the poorest households are buying and selling. This information can in turn be used to establish marketing and production policies designed to help those households with the greatest needs. For example, the analysis shows that the poorest households are net sellers of beer bananas, while more wealthy households buy beer bananas and sell banana beer. Technical assistance designed to help smallholders develop better ways of producing small batches of banana beer for sale could help poor farmers capture more of the value added associated with the brewing process.

Another important implication of Table 4 is that the poorest households in the rural areas rely heavily on the market to supplement their food supply in nearly every major crop. Thus, improvements in marketing infrastructure (such as the improvements to the road system in conjunction with market integration) are likely to have highly beneficial effects for the poorest farmers by reducing the costs of bringing commodities from neighboring food exporting countries. Efforts should also be made to help policy makers on both sides of Rwanda's frontiers increase their awareness of the potential benefits associated with facilitating these nascent international trade linkages.

Table 4. Net rural purchases by household revenue category (negative numbers are sales).[a]

	Revenue (000 Frw) per adult-equivalent				
	<5	5-7	8-12	>12	Entire country
Beans (t)	16	13	23	8	60
Sorghum (t)	8	5	11	2	26
Cassava (t)	13	10	13	-16	20
Potato (t)	6	-7	-15	-35	-51
Sweetpotato (t)	14	1	-6	-27	-19
Cooking banana (t)	-2	0	1	-31	-32
Beer banana (t)	-15	-4	1	15	-3
Banana beer (l)	-16	-29	-72	-111	-228
Sorghum beer (l)	-12	-14	-27	-8	-61
Cattle (a)	4	-12	-30	-31	-69
Sheep (a)	-37	-37	-76	-46	-196
Goats (a)	-80	-51	-120	-182	-433
Pigs (a)	-3	-28	-51	-31	-113
Poultry (a)	-51	-37	-123	18	-193
Agric. labor (pd)	-4	-3	0	19	12
Unskilled labor (pd)	-3	-2	-4	2	-7
Skilled labor (pd)	-3	-4	-7	-24	-38

[a] Totals include gifts, purchases, and sales.

Units: t = thousands of metric tons; a = thousands of animals; l = millions of liters; pd = millions of person days.

Source: Loveridge (1992).

Strengths and Weaknesses of the Approach

The objectives, strengths, and weaknesses of various research methods touched upon in this chapter are summarized in Table 5. One obvious limitation of the sub-sector study approach is the time lag between initiation of the project and availability of the results. While the methods used for the market-level surveys were quick and effective, the farm-level surveys took much longer to collect, process, and analyze. This is a problem inherent in the farm-level survey method, and has little to do with the efficiency of project personnel in performing the analysis.

A second weakness of the method is the use of highly structured interview formats to collect information on sources of income. Out-of-the-ordinary activities can be missed by such rigid methods. The analyst must choose between analyst-friendly survey formats and more flexible interview schedules that capture every detail of economic activity, but which are much more time consuming and costly to analyze. More flexible interview formats

Table 5. Objectives, strengths, and weaknesses of various methods.

Method	Objective	Drawbacks	Advantages
Statistical tests of market integration	Ability of system to move product efficiently between markets	Indirect measure; data often spotty	Quick and inexpensive
One-shot merchant surveys (non-random sample)	Understanding of current practices and constraints Consistency checks for findings from other markets	Can miss major market channels; random sampling difficult; no national estimates of marketing	Relatively quick and inexpensive Provides opportunity to ask direct questions about system
Multi-visit household surveys (stratified random sample)	Estimates of national marketing, time, and place of producer sales; consumer purchases, imports, self-sufficiency and availability Characteristics of buyer and seller households	Costly Results can take a long time to compile Rigid questionnaire structure needs to reduce data processing needs	Statistically valid results Possible to cross-tabulate marketing variables with other household and regional indicators, leading to a richer set of insights

typically involve much smaller sample sizes, with a concomitant loss of ability to provide statistically valid estimates of national marketing. Rigorous pre-testing may be a way of blending the two alternatives discussed in this paragraph. In Rwanda, the project survey design efforts benefitted from information provided by a household budget/consumption survey (n = 260) conducted in 1983.

The approach discussed in this paper has two major strengths. First, it is comprehensive in that it examines all phases of a commodity's production, marketing, and consumption. Further, the multi-product aspect of the study allows insights into the interactions between products, providing information on which types of products are handled by merchants and which types go through more informal channels, as well as which types of products tend to be sold by the poor, and which provide income for wealthier farmers. Such information about the characteristics of buyers and sellers is critical to the formulation of appropriate marketing policy.

A second strength of the stratified random sample multiple visit farm-level surveys discussed here is the ability to provide national estimates of the volumes of goods traded nationally. Where borders are relatively permeable, as in the case of Rwanda, this may be the only practical way to obtain reasonable estimates of cross-border trade. If Rwanda is typical of other less-developed nations, the importance of trade with neighboring countries has been badly neglected in most studies aimed at improving national marketing systems. When such farm-level surveys can be repeated at regular intervals over a number of years, the availability of national estimates can help policy makers better understand long-term trends in the marketing of agricultural products.

References

Delgado, C. L. 1986. A variance components approach to food grain market integration in Northern Nigeria. *American Journal of Agricultural Economics* 68(4):970-979.

Goodwin, B. K. and T. C. Schroeder 1991. Cointegration tests and spatial price linkages in regional cattle markets. *American Journal of Agricultural Economics* 73(2):452-464.

Harriss, B. 1979. There is method in my madness: Or is it vice versa? Measuring agricultural market performance. *Food Research Institute Studies* 17(2):197-218.

Jones, W. O. 1974. Regional analysis and agricultural marketing research in tropical Africa: Concepts and experience. *Food Research Institute Studies* 13:3-28.

Loveridge, S. 1989. *Uses of farm and market survey to inform food security policy in Rwanda*. Ph.D. Diss., Department of Agricultural Economics, Michigan State University, East Lansing, Michigan, USA.

_____. 1992. *Sources of agricultural household revenue, exports, and their impact on rural food availability*. Agricultural Statistics Division. No. P.24, Ministry of Agriculture and Livestock, Republic of Rwanda.

Ministère du Plan. 1988. *Enquête nationale sur le budget et la consommation des ménages (milieu rural)*. Volume 4: Consommation alimentaire en milieu rural. République Rwandaise.

Petzel, T. E. and E. A. Monke. 1980. The integration of the international rice market. *Food Research Institute Studies* 17(3):307-326.

Ravallion, M. 1986. Testing market integration. *American Journal of Agricultural Economics* 68(1):102-109.

Service National de Recensement. 1991. *Recensement général de la population de l'habitat au 15 Août 1991: Resultats provisoires*. Commission National de Recensement, Ministère du Plan et de la Coopération, République Rwandaise.

Shaffer, J. D. 1973. On the concept of sub-sector studies. *American Journal of Agricultural Economics* 55(2):333-335.

Timmer, C. P. 1974. A model of rice marketing in Indonesia. *Food Research Institute Studies* 13(2):19-74.

Appendix 1

Important questions for urban traders

1. What products do you market (followed by list)?
2. How did you decide which products to market?
3. Have you made changes in the way you treat stocks?
4. How do you obtain stock (farmers, assemblers, truckers)?
5. Are products delivered to you, or do you go get them?
6. What is your current supply (in kilos or tons) of each product you sell?
7. Do you have a truck?
8. Where is your product typically coming from (region of country, or foreign country)?
9. How can you distinguish products from this region from products from other regions?
10. Can your customers usually tell the difference between local products and products coming from somewhere else? Does it make a difference to them if the product is not local?
11. What is your sales strategy (Store, sell as soon as possible, buy at harvest, buy after planting)?
12. How do you decide sales and purchase prices?
13. Are you a wholesaler? A retailer?
14. What are the main problems you encounter in your trade (lack of clients, lack of funds, lack of product, lack of transport, lack of storage capacity, storage losses, taxes)?
15. Have any of your competitors gone out of business? If yes, why?
16. How much would your store cost someone to rent per month?
17. How long have you been in business?
18. If you were in business during the last famine, how did the experience change your business strategy?
19. How long do you typically store your product? What is the longest you would store the product?
20. How do you find out about prices in other parts of the country?

5

Methods for Evaluating the Market Potential of Processed Products

Gregory J. Scott[1]

Abstract

Identifying markets for improved or new processed agricultural products is often considered a critical element in efforts to increase farm incomes, generate additional employment and reduce postharvest losses. Typically, however, the range of potential alternative product markets is often much broader than first realized. Hence, the task of selecting the limited number with the greatest commercial promise can be formidable indeed. Given limited time and resources, it simply is not possible to carry out detailed studies. This chapter presents a practical, low-cost set of procedures to evaluate the various commercial options for small-scale or village enterprise processing.

Key words: formal surveys, informal interviews, market participants, prices, secondary data.

Introduction

Agriculture in developing countries is becoming more and more commercially oriented. And with that trend comes a growing interest in postharvest issues, in particular, processing. There are several reasons for this. Where output is abandoned in the field or underutilized after harvest, processing can increase the usable physical volume and economic value of existing production (Coursey 1982). When seasonal cropping patterns or fixed production cycles restrict availability of agricultural commodities to given time periods, processing can extend their employment. If particular commodities have relatively limited usage, processing can diversify their exploitation and thereby create new markets. In so doing, processing activities can also increase the value-added in rural production through transformation of low-priced raw materials into higher-priced intermediate or finished products. Processing may facilitate transportation and handling of these commodities as well. For those countries facing increasing pressure to expand the availability of locally produced

---

[1] Economist, Social Science Department, International Potato Center, Apdo. Postal 1558, Lima 100, Peru.

foodstuffs (e.g., due to a vanishing agricultural frontier), more effective and efficient processing operations assume even greater importance. Finally, improvements in processing—particularly small-scale or village-level operations—are frequently seen as a way of building on traditional, grass roots expertise in product transformation and as a way to encourage development of entrepreneurial skills by poor or marginal groups, e.g,. small farmers, women, rural landless.

An emerging body of literature on small-scale or village-level processing initiatives (see, e.g., Scott et al. 1993; Wheatley et al. 1995) highlights the importance of a critical assessment of the comparative commercial potential of alternative product markets. The complexity of this exercise is often underestimated by those interested in processing partly because the number of products and corresponding market outlets frequently proves far greater than they initially imagined. Moreover, the prospect of technical improvements in processing procedures frequently brings with it an emphasis that at times borders on fascination with ways to produce a given product, relegating marketing issues to a second generation concern. This development is particularly ironic for small-scale or village-level processing activities, where often the production technology is either known or readily made available and the mechanical skills required to produce such products are either indigenous or easily acquired. Yet, information about market requirements, prices of substitute products, or the size of different market segments is frequently conspicuously absent.

While a wide variety of product market options may be available, identifying those few with the greatest commercial promise in relation to existing (or potential) small-scale processing capabilities requires timely, systematic appraisal. Processing initiatives often emerge in the context of a project with well-defined time limits. Hence, decisions about what markets to aim for need to be made promptly. Local expertise in evaluating markets is also frequently limited. Therefore, the methodology required should be straightforward. This chapter seeks to present a practical, low-cost, and rapid set of procedures to evaluate different commercial processing options for small-scale enterprises.

Although the ideas presented may very well be relevant for any type of processing endeavor, the emphasis here is on methods for small-scale processing.[2] In contrast with industrial (or semi-industrial) processing, small-scale processing relies much more heavily on labor than machinery or equipment. It also utilizes a minimum of sophisticated, hard-to-procure (imported), expensive inputs, e.g., chemicals. The techniques involved are

---

[2] Interested readers may consult Austin (1992) for a treatment of these issues as regards industrial processing; see also Edwardson and MacCormac (1984).

relatively easy to learn and therefore can be—though need not necessarily be—carried out at the village-level.

As in the analysis of farming systems where research activities intended to identify production constraints and potential can be usefully divided into a series of distinct steps (see Byerlee et al. 1982), the methodology presented here for the commercial appraisal of small-scale processing systems consists of a similar, sequential approach. The market research procedures described include those required to decide whether to develop processing beyond the initial, perhaps vague idea, to those appropriate for improving the on-going production and sale of particular products. Together they are intended to address the gamut of market-related issues associated with setting up and running a processing facility for agricultural products. The chapter follows a similar format. After a brief review of the set of methods to be treated, each of the procedures is then explained, one at a time, in greater detail.

Overview of the Approach

Processing—even simple processing—entails a complex set of activities including procurement of inputs, transformation, distribution, and sales. Running a processing facility therefore means addressing the marketing problems associated with each of these tasks. Similarly, going from no processing activities to a fully operational plant involves several different steps. The principal steps involved in evaluating the commercial viability of establishing processing activities all the way to improving their on-going operation can be summarized as follows:

- initial global assessment;
- market and consumer research;
- input market analysis;
- analysis of costs and returns; and
- development of a marketing strategy.

This sequence of steps is not self-perpetuating. For example, if the initial global assessment shows processing to be uneconomical or technically problematic, then the idea should be reconsidered at a minimum or simply abandoned in favor of other possible alternatives (e.g., storage, improved marketing of fresh produce) to achieve the same goals. A similar word of caution applies to the other steps presented. They are by no means all-inclusive, but rather represent the major areas that require marketing research. Furthermore, the steps are not necessarily irreversible. Some work on input supply analysis, for instance, might precede completion of a consumer-oriented market survey. The collection of tasks that these steps represent, however, do build on one another and taken together offer a vision of how commercial prospects for processed products might well be assessed.

Step 1: Initial global assessment

Perhaps the most critical point in any small-scale processing project is the outset, the period of time when market opportunities are analyzed and actual or potential commercial problems assessed. Once the project is underway, the target market(s) have been chosen, and the corresponding processed products to sell in that market selected, mistakes are much harder to correct. Past experience suggests that considering a checklist of issues can facilitate a rapid, but nonetheless systematic consideration of the commercial viability of small-scale processing at the most preliminary level (see also Appendix 1).[3]

Supply. What are the annual quantities of the crop produced in the region? Are there distinct periods of under- or over-supply in the market that generate large fluctuations in prices? How well defined is this cycle?

Demand. Where is the target market located? Who will consume the processed product? How many potential consumers are there? What is the purchasing power of the target group? How traditional are the food preparation habits or consumption patterns of the target group? What quantity of the product will prospective consumers purchase?

Consumer acceptance. Is there a broadly-based acceptance of the crop in the local diet? Are processed products utilizing the same crop already in local diets? Used for animal feed? Or, for industrial use?

Technology. How simple or complex is the processing/marketing technology which is being considered? Can the plant be constructed and maintained locally or will imported parts or equipment be needed?

Labor. Most low-cost technologies substitute labor for capital expenditures on equipment. Is labor plentiful and cheap? Are there seasonal shortages of labor during harvest or planting seasons that would affect plant operation?

Ecology. What are the climatic patterns in the region? Are these adequate for production, harvesting, and storage of the raw material? If solar drying is planned, is there sufficient solar radiation during the period planned for plant operation?

Market orientation. Will the processing facility be a commercial venture or will there be government support? What are the implications for the size and

---

[3] Austin (1992:205-222) provides a detailed set of questions for all aspects of agroindustral processing.

duration of public sector support? If it is to be a commercial operation, what are the capital requirements of such ventures?

Postharvest tradition. How well developed are existing postharvest activities? Does a similar style of processing already exist for other crops?

Institutional factors. Who will be in charge of the processing and marketing? How will this activity be organized: co-op, corporation, partnership? What is the size of the typical local farm? Do some producers' or processors' associations already exist?

Capital requirements. What quantity of capital is required of investors? What type of investor can afford the investment? Is credit available for such investments through existing banking facilities?

The essential feature of the initial global assessment is to synthesize as much of the available information as quickly as possible to consider all the various options. Such a rapid assessment need not include any formal survey work. Rather, maximum use should be made of secondary data, informal surveys involving established processors as well as interviews with knowledgeable individuals in their respective areas of endeavor, e.g., extension agents for answers about crop production.

One, possibly two, weeks' time checking basic statistics, reviewing existing literature, and contacting key informants should usually be sufficient to gather all the information necessary for this preliminary assessment. However, in this expeditious process, it is important not to take short cuts (i.e., to make assumptions based on "common knowledge"). Rather, it is essential to question rationalizations, assumptions, and the basis for optimistic (or pessimistic) appraisals by those interviewed.

A single negative response in the entire checklist may be sufficient to cause cancellation of plans. Likewise, considerable positive feedback on one or two points may outweigh the negative replies to several others. An additional benefit of proceeding through the checklist is the generation of alternatives. For example, by considering each of the items on the list, suggestions or observations may surface that can be useful in modifying or changing the original idea. Alternatively, a totally different product market may come to mind (e.g., crop processing for animal feed rather than for human consumption). Example 1 illustrates the use of an initial assessment.

It should be emphasized that the checklist merely provides a rough and ready appraisal of the prospects for small-scale processing. In that sense, perhaps, it is most useful for inexpensively deciding **not** to process, for quickly identifying major stumbling blocks to this type of activity, or for clarifying which processed products seem most commercially viable. A positive appraisal, based on the checklist, points to the worthwhileness of investing more time in assessing the project's potential. It is not a definitive endorsement of its

> **Example 1: Solar-dried processed potatoes in India.**
>
> In 1984, the idea of solar-dried potato processing was proposed as a means to provide employment for landless laborers and to improve incomes of peasant producers in Uttar Pradesh, India. However, before proceeding, the checklist was utilized to rapidly evaluate the feasibility of this project with the following results.
>
> Uttar Pradesh produces five million tons of potatoes a year. The months of highest production and lowest prices are January to March, when the annual harvest repeats itself year after year (Srivastava 1980).
>
> If only the wealthiest 10% of the population each consumes 0.5 kg of processed products per year, 30,000 t of potatoes are needed for processing. This quantity is not enough to affect (raise) the market price of fresh potatoes.
>
> The dry season in Uttar Pradesh coincides with the major harvesting period, assuring the availability of solar radiation to dehydrate the potatoes.
>
> The technology utilized in the processing is cheap. The procedures involved are relatively easy to learn and operate. There is no need for foreign investment or government grants.
>
> Results of the initial global assessment utilizing the checklist suggested that solar-dried processed potatoes had market potential. With this information, additional work was undertaken to further develop the product and the process (see Nave and Scott 1992; Scott et al. 1993).

technical and economic feasibility. The subsequent steps to be taken simply involve a more in-depth investigation of elements of the original list. The first of these is an evaluation of the market(s) for processed products.

Step 2: Market and consumer research

Processing—particularly a new processing initiative—frequently raises many technical and economic questions concerned with the **production** of particular products. Perhaps for that reason, a tendency often develops to focus on solving these types of problems first and worrying about the marketing and eventual use of processed products later. The danger of this approach is to forget that the commercial success of small-scale processing depends more on what people will buy and how it will be used than whether it can be made. A clear understanding of market/consumer requirements involves two complementary tasks: an inventory of processed products already available in the market; and an assessment of consumer attitudes towards these products.

Market research. Three essential components of market research are:

- identifying the types of processed products for sale and their characteristics including where they are sold (e.g., marketplace, supermarket, shop);

- estimating the most important processed products by the volume and value of products sold; and

- determining what factors impede the expansion of sales.

This information is intended to answer certain basic questions about the proposed processing activity. For example, will the processing create a totally new product (because there are no others like it currently being sold)? Will it be a modified, improved version of existing products (e.g., appearance, package, size of the unit of sale)? Is there already a considerable volume of similar products being sold? Or, is there currently little interest in this type of product? What factors, according to wholesalers, retailers, and consumers, are most important in discouraging greater sale/use of this type of product (e.g., price, appearance, use)?

It is fairly easy to prepare a list of processed products produced from a particular food crop based on visits to representative markets in a given city.[4] Such a list should include information about product characteristics (e.g., color, size, shape, type of package, size of unit of sale, price). "Representative markets" refers to the **types** of places people shop (e.g., store, street market, covered market, supermarket), **not** a particular location where people shop. It is also wise to visit intermediate users (e.g., bakeries, restaurants) as well industrial concerns (e.g., flour mills, confectionary companies) to complete the identification of existing products.

Informal conversations with retailers, wholesalers, and industrial users can serve to clarify opinions about the marketability of different products.[5] For example, could traders sell more, if they could be supplied more? Is **price** the key factor influencing sales? appearance? packaging? Such questions should be posed in a manner that reflects empathy, rather than a sort of aggressive curiosity. The parties interviewed are also less likely to be put off if one notes the key findings elicited in these conversations immediately after leaving the premises, rather than writing down answers in their presence. This exercise can be extremely useful to clarify apparent contradictions, to identify common points of view, and to isolate genuine discrepancies.

---

[4] Coursey (1983) provides a concise review of the types of processed products made from tropical root crops in Africa.

[5] See Young and MacCormac (1987) and Holtzman (this volume) for additional ideas in this area.

While there is no substitute for firsthand information, it may also prove useful to check for additional data in libraries, research institutes or Ministry offices.[6]

A word of caution is in order here about who should collect this type of information. Many food technologists and agricultural engineers (even social scientists) have a certain phobia about information gathering in offices and markets. These locations often require the ritual procedures of appointments; or, they represent a noisy contrast to the tranquillity of a farmer's field or a science lab. Nevertheless, people who work on processing-related agricultural research bring with them their accumulated knowledge about farm commodities and processing techniques. This specialized knowledge puts them in a much better position to evaluate the information offered and, perhaps, probe areas less well-trained interviewers might never have asked about. Results of the market survey provide the basis for conducting interviews with consumers.

Consumer research. Consumer research seeks to establish the level of consumer awareness of processed products; whether they are consumed and if so, with what frequency; how consumers characterize the products, positively and negatively; and what consumers would like in a new product. Product description includes form, flavor, preparation time, storage characteristics, and price. Consumer research aims to distinguish those types of products that have the greatest (or most limited) potential because they are (not) desired on the basis of one or more attributes such as taste, appearance, or use. Similarly, it attempts to discover those that are the most (least) affordable. Such research also seeks to identify those characteristics that are most desirable in existing products or that because of their presence (e.g., poor quality control, unattractive appearance) discourage greater consumption.

Consumer interviews may be carried out in an informal fashion (i.e., without a written questionnaire)—with or without a list of topics to be covered—or utilizing a survey form (see Den Hartog and Staveren 1983). The latter facilitates collection of quantitative responses (e.g., by imposing standard units of measure) and more extensive amounts of information. The former is by definition more flexible. Whether one procedure is more appropriate than the other will depend, among other things, on the number of processed products that questions are to be asked about; the amount of information already available in the literature or through the market survey work; and the experience of researchers in conducting informal interviews.

Both procedures involve considerable advance preparation to specify the questions (or topics) to be asked and the way they should be phrased (to

---

[6] See Scott (this volume) for suggestions on how and where to go about collecting secondary data.

avoid confusing the persons interviewed).[7] It is particularly important to consider how the data will be processed and written up (e.g., are there too many questions to enable ready analysis?) prior to launching the data collection process. Pre-testing of the questions both on actual consumers and on members of the research team can also be extremely useful in minimizing problems of misinterpretation or repetition.

One of the most important aspects of this type of consumer research is to remember that it is a **pilot** survey. In other words, the results gathered are intended to be indicative, rather than definitive. This characteristic is particularly relevant when considering size and composition of the sample of consumers to be contacted. Rough guidelines in this regard would be no more than 200 consumers and no less than 50. Any more than 200 raises a series of questions about the time available to do the interviews, analyze the data, and write-up the results as well as the infrastructure required for processing the data. A sample that is too small raises doubts not only about its representativeness but also preempts much meaningful comparison between the different types of consumers interviewed.

It is essential that the consumer interviews be done with a cross-section of individuals reflecting differences in incomes (or a proxy for incomes such as place of residence). For example, obvious distinctions between low-, middle- and high-income housing areas are easy to identify in most cities in developing countries. By interviewing different types of consumers not only are the current consumption patterns of different groups identified but also some appreciation of the potential for change (e.g., should incomes rise) be detected.

How does one actually select the consumers to interview? One procedure that was used successfully in Lima, Peru was to interview people that were in the act of buying processed products (see Gomez and Wong 1989). In other words, those contacted probably consumed the article in question and hence had some opinions to express about them. Furthermore, if questions are to be asked about several items, then a simple display of the products to be discussed can both arouse curiosity (hence, make consumers eager to be interviewed) and ensure that the names and products that they refer to are not confused. Once the interviews have been conducted, it becomes a question of reporting the results.

Ideally, the same individual(s) who carried out the market survey also undertakes the consumer research. Knowledge they acquired in prior activities is then directly incorporated into this component of the study, sharpening the focus while extending the coverage. The following example illustrates the use of market survey and consumer interviews to evaluate the market potential of processed products.

---

[7] See Appendix 1 and Austin (1992:81-85) for questions related to consumer and market research.

Example 2: Consumer attitudes towards the introduction of sweetpotato bread in Lima, Peru.

To reduce his dependency on imported wheat flour and to lower his costs of production, a local baker in Lima, Peru, came up with the idea of making standard bread rolls by substituting raw, grated sweetpotato for a certain percentage of wheat flour. To evaluate the potential market for this new type of composite bread, a study was carried out to analyze consumers' tastes and preferences as well as buying habits when it comes to bread (Denen 1991). The study also sought to get a sense of consumers' expectations with respect to this new type of bread and their possible response to its regular production and sale.

Utilizing the focus group technique, a cross-section of Lima housewives (as they are the household members who typically make the decisions about bread purchases) were interviewed (Denen 1991). The women selected included those from low-, middle-low, and middle income households.

Initially, the housewives indicated certain negative attitudes towards the new type of bread. They assumed that the sweetpotato bread was sweet tasting. Therefore, it was a category of bread that they associated with consumption: (a) only on special occasions, and (b) by higher income households who could afford such a specialized product. However, once they had a chance to see and taste the sweetpotato bread (that, in fact, has a taste quite similar to the bread they were accustomed to eating daily), the housewives found its flavor quite acceptable. The fact that the sweetpotato bread was intended to be sold at a cheaper price made it particularly attractive and certainly a product that suited their tastes and budgets.

The focus group interviews also generated a number of interesting qualitative findings. The particles of grated sweetpotato readily visible in the bread were perceived by the housewives not as a sign of product imperfections, but rather as clear evidence that it was a natural and nutritious product. The housewives did note that shelf life of the bread was less than the standard wheat bread. This, they felt, needed improvements. They also expressed concerns about the apparent lighter weight of the sweetpotato bread, i.e., were they getting the same volume and value per kilo for this new bread versus the type that they were accustomed to buying. These results were very useful in subsequent efforts aimed at product improvement.

Step 3: Input market analysis

Analysis of input markets and marketing seeks to identify the nature of seasonal supply patterns and whether corresponding price movements would interest growers in selling to a processor, or to consider processing themselves as an alternative outlet for some (or all) of their crop. Such analysis also is intended to assess whether processors can easily procure sufficient quantities of raw material so as to justify establishing a processing facility; taking into consideration here, not only the quality and uniformity of supply, but also assembly and transportation costs.

Depending on operating costs and returns per production unit, processing may be undertaken profitably by operating only a few months a year; or, in other cases, year-round operation may be necessary to earn a profit. Alternatively, growers may already have a ready outlet for their produce even in the peak harvesting period, or may have only occasional difficulty selling their crop.

The reason for analyzing input markets is to determine commodity supply patterns by season, variety planted, experience of producers, and postharvest practices such as grading for size and quality, and the typical uses for these grades. This research also establishes producer preferences for varieties and the reasons why, thus acquiring information from farmers on variety characteristics and performance. The potential processor also has interest in the type of varieties available (or potentially available) in order to obtain desired processing characteristics. Growers' marketing habits are also closely examined: marketing channels and their stability from season to season, typical buyers, and traditional arrangements for payment. Various studies have noted the importance of these marketing considerations in evaluating the potential for small-scale processing (see Abbot 1987:193; Alvarez 1990). Furthermore, major emphasis here is on raw material inputs, rather than labor or capital, because more often than not this represents the critical production factor for small-scale processing.

Once present conditions are mapped out, the research explores the potential for change so as to include (or to expand) processing. Constraints that the producers may have in producing or marketing a processed product themselves may also be analyzed.

In carrying out input supply analysis, it is particularly important to interview different types of representative growers. Small, subsistence growers may have minimal surpluses to sell and hence a limited interest in commercial processing. Just the opposite may apply for growers who seek to maximize profits. The research should aim to measure the interest of both types.

Research procedures. Methods for obtaining this type of information include a synthesis of secondary data; a review of available literature; and primary data collection. Information on the annual volume of crop production in a particular region, department or province can usually be obtained from official data sources. Commodity programs usually have data on planting and harvesting dates. The size of different types of farmers and their importance as a group in accounting for total production can be estimated from agricultural census reports or by synthesizing the results of formal farm surveys. Producer prices for specific crops by calendar year (or month-to-month) are often available

> **Example 3: Potential for potato processing in Northeast Colombia.**[8]
>
> Colombian policy makers concerned with rural development as well as researchers in the National Potato Program are interested in developing alternative uses and markets for potatoes in an effort to stabilize prices and improve grower incomes. They considered small-scale potato processing as one potential means of bringing this about. As a key component in the assessment of the commercial viability of this technology, an attempt was made to determine the needs and interests of local potato producers with respect to this type of processing.
>
> Research methods adopted for this assessment included a review of available studies and secondary data on potato production, prices, and marketing; a gathering of producers to show them the types of dishes that can be prepared with processed potato products (e.g., chips, cakes, soups); and a formal survey of 81 growers. Recent agricultural census data and farm production statistics were consulted to determine the location of potato production in the various localities and the number of potato producers in each. The survey collected information about potential interest in potato processing as well as technical aspects of potato production.
>
> Results of this survey were decidedly mixed. Nearly all growers expressed interest in processed products and a disposition to conduct such activity in cooperation with other farmers. However, they also reported no particular difficulty in selling their harvest at remunerative prices. In fact, the last time prices were disastrously low was several years prior to the survey. Labor shortages at harvest time also raised questions about the feasibility of introducing a labor-intensive technology to operate at a time of year when manpower is already scarce. While these findings did not prompt abandonment of processing, they led to a reconsideration of the economic rationale for this activity.

from government offices. Analyzing this information may be sufficient in itself to identify (or eliminate) certain crops or areas as the most promising commodity or location for processing. For example, perhaps Region "X" produces very few sweetpotatoes and prices for this commodity are always quite high. It therefore seems unlikely that there would be much immediate interest on the part of growers in sweetpotato processing.

In the event that this analysis suggests strong possibilities for particular foodstuffs in particular locations, it is then advisable to check relevant research centers (e.g., university libraries, agro-industrial institutes) to

---

[8] This example is based on ICA (1988).

review the available documentation on previous, farm-level attempts to introduce (or improve) processing activities. This search may well uncover on-going experiments—or, pilot projects that have proven unsuccessful—that merit closer examination to comprehend their operating rationale, track-record, and any major constraints encountered.

A third component of input market analysis research is contact with growers themselves. The purpose of this exercise is to sound out growers' opinions and listen to the reasons for their stated views. Methods for obtaining this type of information may be formal or informal. The larger the number of possible alternatives, and the more precise the quantitative information required, then the more likely that a formal survey may be necessary. The extent to which the range of processing possibilities has been narrowed to one or two specific products from a single commodity in a particular site (e.g., through analysis of secondary data) then informal interviews may be all that is necessary. Rhoades (1982) offers a series of recommendations regarding informal surveys. When the options in terms of commodities, products, or locations are much more numerous, then a formal questionnaire will greatly facilitate data collection. Horton (1982) provides useful guidelines on formal questionnaires. Careful recording of the results of these surveys—be they formal or informal—and contrasting them with the opinions of technical specialists, owner-operators of existing processing facilities can serve as a point of comparison to the views expressed by growers. Example 3 illustrates the use of a formal questionnaire to evaluate processing potential.

Step 4: Analysis of costs and returns

With information on demand (market/consumer research) and supply (analysis of input markets) in hand, the potential processor can then focus on trial production of the product(s) that is best suited for the market. This pilot-type processing serves several purposes. It gives the inexperienced operator an opportunity to practice (learn) the various techniques involved. It allows for technical experimentation such as substituting one procedure for another (e.g., mechanical drying for solar drying), altering the mix (e.g., potatoes and rice, instead of just potatoes) and type (fresh versus stored potatoes) of inputs, as well as the scale of operations. Basic economic considerations that need to be answered here concern estimated costs and returns per unit of output for resulting products. A related issue refers to financial planning, namely **when** these costs and returns occur.

A key question for any processing endeavor is whether such an activity is profitable. Estimates of the costs and returns to processing can provide an indication of this result. More importantly, perhaps, this information indicates which costs have the greatest impact on net returns. It therefore suggests where efforts to improve economic efficiency should be focused in subsequent experimental processing activities. Likewise, these estimates help identify the scale and intensity of operations that are necessary in order to improve profitability. In other words, it is highly conceivable that processing facilities can be expanded or reduced in size depending on the net return to capital and the desire to generate greater employment or process a larger volume of raw material in a fixed amount of time. These estimates provide economic input into that type of decision making. They also represent benchmark data in terms of determining the amount of improvement necessary for the processing in question to become economically operational. For example, it may have so far to go that it seems unrealistic to continue; or major improvements in a short period of time offer the promise that profitability may be more accessible than previously envisioned.

Costs are typically divided into two categories: fixed and variable. Fixed costs are those that occur whether the plant is in operation or not, whether it handles 50 kg of raw material per day or 5000 kg. These costs represent such things as investment in the structure and equipment, interest on any loan to purchase such facilities, and any rent paid for land at the processing site. Fixed costs may also refer to supervisory personnel (e.g., plant manager), a secretary, telephone costs, office supplies, and operating permits or licenses.

Variable costs are those that fluctuate with the intensity of plant operation. These include raw material costs (plus transportation charges to the processing site), labor, supplies (e.g., chemicals), packaging material, fuel, or other expenses associated with producing the processed product itself (e.g., off-site milling charges). Variable costs may also involve such expenses as freight rates for shipping the finished product to market or commission payments to sales agents. Most businesses also include contingencies in their projections of costs to cover unanticipated expense(s).

The fundamental point in calculating costs is to be sure and include **all** expenses associated with processing. Whether a particular cost is included under the fixed or variable category is less important than resisting the temptation to exclude certain items or perhaps overlook others in an effort to make the enterprise appear financially viable. Likewise, this means recording reasonable estimates of the monetary value of non-purchased inputs (e.g., the household's production of raw material).

Revenues are calculated on the basis of estimated (or actual) selling price per unit of sale and the volume of product(s) sold. Revenues may be more difficult to compute because the product in question may never have been sold. Under such circumstances, one can only attempt to generate reasonable estimates based, perhaps, on prices of similar products and/or informal conversations with prospective wholesalers or retailers about what they would likely pay for such a product. Alternatively, one can simulate a range of prices for the product to ascertain the effect on total revenues.

Estimated net returns are simply total revenues less total costs. Estimates of costs (or net returns) per unit of output can be derived by simply dividing total costs (or net returns) by the total number of units produced.

Example 4: Costs and returns to small-scale processing in India.

Results of a rapid appraisal of the prospects for small-scale potato processing in India were extremely positive (see Example 1 above). On that basis and taking into account trial production at a pilot processing facility, it became clear that small-scale potato processing presented a variety of different options. These concerned the scale and intensity of operation of the processing plant, the apparent high costs of certain equipment, and the relative incidence of different inputs on total production costs.

Previous rough-and-ready calculations on these points were inconclusive. The new approach consisted of three procedures: a careful inventory of all structure and equipment needed for simple potato processing; an intensive monitoring of actual processing techniques to account for all inputs employed; and an aggressive, but brief, inquiry into the appropriate price for each of the inputs and outputs (see Nave and Scott 1992). With this information, a personal computer and the program LOTUS 1-2-3, it was possible to construct operating budgets for different scales of plant (see Appendix 2). Simulations subsequently were carried out to calculate the impact on net returns of intensity of yearly operations, the number of years for which financing was obtained to operate the facility and different purchase and selling prices for the products involved.

Using the costs and returns calculations, it was possible to identify at what level of operation the greatest economies of scale took place. The results emphasized as well the importance of extending the processing season, the quantity of raw material processed per day, and the conversion rate from raw material to finished product. Furthermore, the findings focused experimental work much more on ways to improve conversion rates, rationalize the use of labor, and explore avenues for lowering marketing and transportation costs rather than to reduce the expenses associated with fixed costs.

The promising profitability estimates under most scenarios examined generated added interest in costs and returns research. Specifically, in crop processing, there is usually a gap in time between when costs are incurred and revenues received, which creates recurring periods when the cash flow of the business is negative. This cash shortage must be financed from some source. While consideration of such cash flow problems must also be included when analyzing costs and revenues, their solution also depends on the sales and promotion strategy of the processing facility in question. This issue is now addressed in greater detail.

Typically such calculations are all done on a yearly (or seasonal) basis so as to estimate the financial health of the business and in so doing make observations about past performance so as to lower costs, raise revenues, and improve profits in the subsequent time period. Example 4 illustrates these various issues.

Step 5: Development of a marketing strategy

Precisely how the product will enter the market depends in part on a marketing strategy. According to Austin (1992), this involves consideration of four factors: product design, pricing, promotion, and distribution. For example, a decision has to be made on whether to sell the product in bulk, at a steep discount to wholesalers, with little advertising and through established marketing channels versus in a fancy package, in small quantities, to retailers, at a comparatively high price and by way of a distribution network set-up specially for this product. Often research done with marketing agents and consumers in the previous steps can provide some basic information to help make this decision.

Product design. Many marketing initiatives fail because the prospective processing products suffer from poor product design. This concept refers broadly to everything from the particular traits of the package (e.g., quality, material, design), to size of the unit of sale (e.g., individual, family size), to appearance of the product (e.g., color, shape, size) as well as to particular product attributes (e.g., nutritious, easy to prepare). Specifically, a processed product that is marketed in a cheap package, lacks uniform quality, and is considered "poor people's food" (i.e., an inexpensive source of calories) may well be rejected by those target consumers for whom it was intended. They simply may not want to buy something that they perceive as lower status than what they are already eating regardless of supposed benefits. Wholesalers and retailers are likely to be even more sensitive to product design. They are reluctant to share in any financial losses resulting from a product that few people want to buy. The views of these and any other potential clients for processed products must be consulted if the final set of attributes is to approximate desired characteristics.

Pricing. Setting the price for processed products is another crucial marketing decision. Estimates of costs and returns provide some idea of the "break-even" price for these goods, but this may not be equal to what the new facility can/should/must sell its product for. A variety of pricing strategies exist (see Austin 1992:60-61). These include cost-plus, market penetration, loss-leader, market prices, and controlled or subsidized prices (see also Kotler 1986:381-407).

Those undertaking processing initiatives sometimes consider these endeavors as the equivalent of public sector, rural development projects. Under these circumstances, they may base their hopes for financial success largely on efforts to secure contracts with government entities that represent, in effect, a subsidized price for what they produce, i.e., a price that allows them a profit, but that is higher than what they would receive from private firms. While such an arrangement is certainly possible, it may not be the most realistic or sustainable approach, given the often unpredictable behavior of public bureaucracies due to changes in personnel, in policy, or in the availability of public revenues.

Alternatively, a new processing facility may expect to price its products so as to recover its unit production costs plus some percentage mark-up that represents return to management and capital. Cost-plus pricing may appear particularly feasible when the processor sees himself introducing a totally new product. However, new entrants or established firms may be willing and able to sell the same or similar product for a smaller mark-up, for example, due to more efficient production, or even in the short-run for no mark-up at all.

A third pricing strategy aims at market penetration. In other words, the new processor may decide he needs a certain sales volume to achieve a significantly lower level of unit production costs. His pricing policy then aims to capture a sufficiently large number of buyers so as to attain this quantity of sales. This price may be lower than he might be able to charge for a smaller sales volume. When market penetration involves accepting losses on each unit of output sold in one line of products so as to capture another, this is called "loss-leader" pricing.

Market pricing is a more passive strategy than looking for government subsidies or setting your price to weaken rival firms' competition. It says that whatever the market currently charges for this type of product is what one can expect to receive, no more or less. The difficulty here is determining what is the appropriate market to use as a point of reference? A processed product that has a variety of uses may not belong in the same market—in buyers' minds—as one that has relatively few. The situation as regards pricing based on the market price, or as in the other aspects of product development, some other pricing scheme is highly dynamic. Success in large part will depend on a disposition to actively engage oneself in experimenting with different approaches before settling on any one.

Promotion. Promotion refers to such activities as displays in markets and fairs as well as advertising in the local media. Simply making prospective buyers aware that the processed product is available for sale is a task in itself, especially for a new facility with an unknown product. Promotion certainly requires the same degree of imagination and persistence to complement the hard work needed to get the product this far.

Promotion may be directed at final users (e.g., consumers) or the individual or firms that supply these users with the product. Austin (1992:63) refers to promotional efforts aimed at the end-user as a "pull" strategy. Such efforts seek to generate additional demand for the product so that retailers, wholesalers, or commission agents will be compelled to purchase, i.e., pull more from the processor. Austin considers efforts that focus on traders and private firms that sell the processed product in an attempt to convince them to buy more to sell as a "push" strategy. Most processing concerns will probably attempt some of both to maximize their product's chances of success.

The content of promotional schemes also varies. It includes information about one or more product attributes or basic facts about product availability. It may involve as well generating a product image, such as a "convenient" food to prepare (for end-users) or a new, "novel" item to include in your line of goods (for traders or private firms) (see Scott et al. 1993).

Processors can employ either direct or indirect promotional procedures. Direct contact with consumers or shopkeepers has the advantage that the reactions elicited can be noted, analyzed, and when appropriate used to modify on-going production and marketing practices. Indirect contact through the mass media enables the processor to reach many more potential clients in a shorter period of time. The emerging processing facility will have to evaluate which of the strategies (pull or push), contents (facts or image), and procedures (direct or indirect) seem best suited to the prevailing situation.

Distribution. A strategy for distribution must take into account existing marketing channels, the functions performed by the participants, and the possible alternative arrangements that the firm may wish to explore. Mapping out marketing channels serves to clarify the ways that existing products pass from processing facilities to final users. Some may go from processors to wholesalers to retailers to consumers; others may pass from the plant to transporters, to commission agents, to wholesalers, to supermarkets, to consumers. There may very well be several different routes for these products to take. Putting them into perspective, for example by estimating the volumes handled in each, can help single out their respective advantages (e.g., fewer middlemen) and disadvantages (e.g., smaller sales potential).

Functions performed by the participants in these channels is also a key piece of information. Do some traders buy packages of processed product by the truck for distribution wholesale in smaller lots? Is transportation between the processing plant and wholesale market provided by the processor? Do processors or middlemen provide the credit to finance the sales of processed products? Is re-packaging and storage the job of commission agents? By identifying the functions carried out by each of the marketing agents in the principal marketing channels, it becomes clearer what it will take to compete at a given level (e.g., wholesale, retail). Setting one distribution strategy versus another will depend in large part on the success or failure of particular initiatives by the existing processors in question.

> **Example 5: The market for dehydrated french fries in Huancayo, Peru.**[9]
>
> Potatoes are produced all year long in Peru. Nevertheless, production in the highlands is harvested from late November to the end of June and on the coast from early July to about mid-November. As a result, fresh potatoes are expensive and in short supply in highland cities during the off-season (Scott 1985). The possible interest of restaurants and snack bars in Huancayo (pop. 250,000)—located in the central highlands—in purchasing dehydrated french fries became the subject of considerable interest among International Potato Center (CIP) processing personnel during 1987.
>
> Research procedures used to assess the commercial potential for such a product consisted of a short, formal questionnaire and a taste test. The questionnaire was administered in 20 eating establishments including restaurants, snack bars, and mobile food vendors (*ambulantes*). Of those interviewed, 70% reported that they found the dehydrated potatoes "tasty" or "very tasty". None found the product disagreeable. All those contacted reported that they would be interested in purchasing the potatoes. Many respondents (40%) indicated that price would be a key factor in determining the use of the product; 37% reported that the relative ease with which the product could be acquired was also important.
>
> Results of this study confirmed the attractiveness of dehydrated french fries as an alternative to expensive, freshly cut fried potatoes. Questions about the color, quality control, and consistency of the product could then be focused on in subsequent research. In addition, this survey pointed to potential problems in the physical distribution of the product (e.g., the continuous availability of supplies) as well as the credit arrangements that might have to be made to facilitate sale to restaurants and snack bars.

The methods available for finding answers to these questions are similar to those of the earlier steps: a review of the specialized literature; participant observation of existing marketing channels; informal interviews with market participants; or a formal survey to record quantitative information (see, e.g., Gomez and Wong 1989). Much of the information gathered in earlier steps can be built upon to expand available knowledge into more specific areas. Example 5 illustrates how this can be done.

---

[9] This example is based on Mello (1988).

Conclusion

This chapter has focused on the problem of evaluating the market prospects for processed products. The chapter outlined a series of steps to do so. These include assessing the original idea of setting up a processing facility by identifying a particular product market and proceeding through to the marketing of actual output. It explained procedures to assess this endeavor in various stages of development. Examples of these methods were presented in each instance to demonstrate the procedures involved and results obtained. The set of methods offered here is by no means all-inclusive, but rather is intended to suggest the principal types of activities that need to be undertaken. While the emphasis was exclusively on socio-economic methods, the procedures repeatedly call upon the need for information about technical processing procedures and product characteristics for products made by small-scale or village-level enterprises.

References

Abbott, J.C. 1987. *Agricultural marketing enterprises for the developing world*. Cambridge, UK: Cambridge University Press.

Alvarez, M. 1991. *Agroindustria y promoción del desarrollo: los desfíos del mercado. Debate Agrario* 9:69-90.

Austin, J. 1992. *Agro-industrial project analysis.* 2nd Edition. Baltimore, MD, USA: The Johns Hopkins University Press.

Benavides, M. and R. Rhoades. 1987. Socio-economic conditions, food habits and formulated food programs in the pueblos jovenes of Lima, Peru. *Archivos Latinoamericanos de Nutricion XXXVII* (2):259-281.

Byerlee, D., L. Harrington, and D. Winkelmann. 1982. Farming systems research: Issues in research strategy and technology design. *American Journal of Agricultural Economics* 64:897-904.

Coursey, D.G. 1982. Traditional root crop technology: Some interaction with modern science, In Feeding the hungry: A role for post-harvest technology? (M. Greeley, ed.). *IDS Bulletin* 13(3):12-20.

_____. 1983. Potential utilization of major root crops, with special emphasis on human, animal, and industrial uses, in *Tropical root crops: Production and uses in Africa* (E.R. Terry. E.V. Doku, O.B. Arene, and N.M. Mahungu, eds.). International Society for Tropical Root Crops/International Development Research Centre, Ibadan, Nigeria.

Denen, Hetty. 1991. *El mercado potencial de pan de camote: Encuesta a consumidores en Lima Metropolitana y Callao*. Department of Marketing and Market Studies, Agricultural University, Wageningen, Holland/ International Potato Center (CIP), Lima, Peru.

Edwardson, W. and C. MacCormac. 1984. Improving small-scale food industries in developing countries. IDRC, Ottawa, Canada.

Gómez, R. and D. Wong. 1989. *Procesados de papa: Un mercado potencial. Cuadernos de Investigación* No. 11. Centro de Investigaciones de la Universidad del Pacífico (CIUP), Lima, Peru.

Hartog, A.P. den and W.A. van Staveren. 1983. *Manual for social surveys on food habits and consumption in developing countries*. Agricultural University, Wageningen, Holland.

Holtzman, J. 1986. *Rapid reconaissance guidelines for agricultural marketing and food systems research in developing countries*. MSU International Development Papers. Working Paper No. 30. Department of Agricultural Economics, Michigan State University, East Lansing, MI, USA.

Horton, D. 1982. *Tips for planning formal surveys*. Training Document 1982-6. Social Science Department, International Potato Center (CIP), Lima, Peru.

_____. 1988. *Underground crops: Long term trends in production of roots and tuber*. Winrock International, Morrilton, AK, USA.

Instituto Colombiano Agropecuario (ICA). 1988. Proyecto: Comercializacion de Productos Procesados de Papa. In *Informe Anual del Proyecto PRACIPA*. International Potato Center (CIP), Lima, Peru.

Keane, P., R. Booth, and N. Beltran. 1986. *Appropriate techniques for development and manufacture of low cost, potato-based food products in developing countries*. International Potato Center (CIP), Lima, Peru.

Khon Kaen University. 1987. *Proceedings of the 1985 international conference in rapid rural appraisal*. Rural Systems Research and Farming Systems Research Projects, Khon Kaen, Thailand.

Kotler, P. 1986. *Principles of marketing*, 3rd. Edition. Englewood Cliffs. NJ, USA: Prentice Hall International Editions.

Lynam, J. 1989. The evaluation of cassava consumption in Latin America. In *Summary proceedings of a workshop on trends and prospects of casava in the Third World* (J.S. Sarma, ed.). International Food Policy Research Institute (IFPRI),Washington, D.C., USA.

Mello, L.E. 1988. *Estudio tecnológico para la obtención de papas picadas deshidratadas como insumo*. Intermedio National University of Central Peru, Huancayo, Peru.

Nave, R.W. and G.J. Scott. 1992. Village-level potato processing in developing countries: A case study of the SOTEC project in India. In *Product development for roots and tuber crops* (Scott, Wiersema, and Ferguson, eds). Lima, Peru: International Potato Center.

Rhoades, R. 1982. *El arte de la encuesta informal*. (The art of informal inquiry.) Training Document 1982-2. International Potato Center (CIP), Lima, Peru.

Scott, G. 1985. *Markets, myths and middlemen. A case study of potato marketing in central Peru.* Centro de Investigación de la Universidad del Pacífico (CIUP). Lima, Peru.

———. 1988. *Estimates of costs and returns to simple potato processing in India*. Internationa Potato Center (CIP), Lima, Peru.

———. 1990. *Trabajo de campo entre cuatro paredes: recopilación de información secundaria para la investigación sobre sistemas alimentarios*. International Potato Center (CIP), Lima, Peru.

Scott, G.J., D. Wong, and M. Alvarez. 1993. Improving village level processing in developing countries: The case of potatoes. *Ecology of Food and Nutrition* 30:145-163.

Sikka, B. K. 1990. *Marketing of processed potato products in Delhi*. Agro-Economic Research Centre, Himachael Pradesh University. Shimla, India.

Srivastava, B.N. 1980. *Potato in the Indian economy*. Social Science Department Working Paper 1980-2. International Potato Center (CIP), Lima, Peru.

Technical Advisory Committee (TAC). 1987. CGIAR priorities and future strategy. TAC Secretariat, Rome, Italy.

Werge, R. 1979. Potato processing in central highlands of Peru. *Ecology of Food and Nutrition* 7:229-234.

Wheatley, C., G. Scott, R. Best, and S. Wiersema. 1995. Adding value to root and tuber crops: A manual on product development. Cali, Colombia: CIAT.

Wheatley, C. and G. Scott. 1992. Identification of product opportunities. In *Product development for roots and tuber crops* (Scott, Wiersema, and Ferguson, eds.). Lima, Peru: International Potato Center.

Young, R.H. and C.W. MacCormac. 1987. *Market research for food products and processes in developing countries: Proceedings of a workshop*. Singapore, 1-4 April 1986. International Development Research Centre (IDRC), Ottawa, Ontario, Canada.

Appendix 1

Checklist for final screening of products.

Demand

- Define target market (city, region, etc.).
- How many consumers (total, % who could purchase)?
- How much product per person/yr?
- Is purchasing power increasing or not?
- Are consumption, food purchase habits changing?
- Does product fit these changes?
- If product is novel, will acceptance be good?
- If produce is competing against others, will price and quality be better than competitors'?
- For industrial markets: What is the volume of purchases and the price of competing raw materials by industries concerned?

Raw material supply

- Volume of production target region.
- Demand in other markets for this production.
- Seasonality of production and demand in other markets.
- Price fluctuations/cycles.
- Characteristics of both traditional and new varieties (growth cycles, quality, yield).
- Potential for and constraints to increasing production (diseases, erosion, drought, etc.).

Physical factors: determine harvest times and feasibility of natural drying systems.

- Rainfall (dry and wet seasons).
- Does dry season coincide with harvest time?
- Temperature.
- Relative humidity.
- Is there ready access to clean water (for starch extraction especially)?

Organizational aspects

- Are farmers market- or subsistence-oriented?
- Are farmers willing to experiment?
- Has there been a positive experience with co-ops?
- Is institutional support available for co-ops/small businesses?
- Is credit available?
- Are capital requirements manageable?
- Is a separate distribution entity needed?
- Is technical and financial support available for this?

Appendix 1. (continued)

- Will many institutions be involved? Is inter-institutional coordination satisfactory?

Existence of similar activities

- Is small farmer processing novel or a continuation of existing practices?
- What are the strengths and weaknesses of existing operations?
- How can weaknesses be corrected?
- Are there any existing facilities that can be utilized to reduce capital outlay?

Consumer acceptance

- Is this crop accepted in the diet (fresh, processed)?
- Is image good or not?
- Is this product being made already? If not, why not?
- If an existing product, what improvements can be made?
- If a novel product, is this crop accepted in other foods or is it a food accepted with other ingredients?

Capital requirements

- Amount, conditions of loan (interest rate, grace period, etc.).
- Requirement of collateral (land holdings, etc.).
- Standard banking arrangement or special loan scheme for small businesses, co-ops.

Labor

- Costs.
- Availability (seasonality).
- Educational level.
- Gender issues: replacing manual operations by machinery often reduces women's role and can have negative social consequences.

Technology

- Is it already developed, or is further research required; if so, how much and what are the chances of success?
- Imported or local? If imported, are spares, etc., available?
- Can it be managed by farmer group if necessary?
- What training will be required (process operation, business, marketing, etc.); who can provide and finance training activities?
- Can local labor and materials be used in construction?

Benefits

- How well will the product fit project objectives?
- Who will benefit and by how much?
- What is the risk of failure? Who suffers if project fails?
- How much; i.e., economic feasibility.

Source: Wheatley and Scott (1992).

Appendix 2

Estimated costs (Rps.) and returns to small-scale potato processing in India.

	\multicolumn{6}{c}{Quantity of potato processed per day}
	\multicolumn{3}{c}{200 kg}	\multicolumn{3}{c}{1,000 kg}
	Quantity	Unit cost	Total cost	Quantity	Unit cost	Total cost
1. Fixed Costs (A+B+C):			8,368			29,586
A. Equipment			5,568			17,536
Washer-cum-peeler	1	1,800	1,800	2	1,800	3,600
- peeling tubs	1	135	135	3	135	405
- slicing tubs	2	135	270	6	135	810
- rinsing tubs	1	135	135	2	135	270
- post-blanch rinse	1	135	135	2	135	270
- chemical bath	1	135	135	3	135	405
Hand slicer	2	40	80	0	0	0
Mechanical slicer	0	0	0	1	1,800	1,800
Mesh bags	4	22	88	8	22	176
Draining stands	1	50	50	2	50	100
Blancher w/cover (includes masonry work)	1	1,000	1,000	1	1,000	1,000
Drying racks w/nylon nets	12	145	1,740	60	145	8,700
B. Infrastructure			2,300			10,250
Shed for shade & night store	1	1,600	1,600	1	8,000	8,000
Cement & brick work	1	300	300	1	1,500	1,500
Shade for spreaders	1	0	0	1	0	0
Drum & stand	1	150	150	1	250	250
Masonry tank on ground	1	250	250	1	500	500
C. Fresh potato store	1	500	500	1	1,800	1,800

	\multicolumn{2}{c}{200 kg}	\multicolumn{2}{c}{1,000 kg}
	Description	Total	Description	Total
2. Variable Costs		27,385		114,385
A. Potato	120×90	10,800	60×90	54,000
B. Labor for processing	43.5×90	3,915	91.0×90	8,190
Labor for packing	9.5×45×2	855	9.5×45×5	21,375
C. Plastic bags & labels	0.27×128×90	3,110	0.27×640×90	15,552
Outer packing	0.04×128×90	461	0.04×640×90	2,304
D. Chemical products	6×90	540	30×90	2,700
E. Coal	12×90	1,080	32×90	2,880
F. Marketing & transportation	0.325×128×90	3,744	0.295×640×90	16,992
G. Other costs (maintenance, rental, contingency)		2,880		9,630
Number of packages		11,520		57,600
Total variable costs/pack		2.38		1.99

Assumptions: Production of packages of dried potato chips (90 operating days/yr; 5 year loan); labor for processing: 1 supervisor (Rps. 15/day) and 3 and 8 workers (Rps. 9.5/worker/day for 200 and 1,000 kg of fresh potato processed, respectively; ratio chips/fresh potato = 0.16 and 1 package = 0.25 gr; then for 200 kg and 1,000 kg correspond to: 128 and 640 packages, respectively; and every 2 days 210 packages are packed.

Source: Nave and Scott (1992).

Appendix 2 (continued)

	200 kg		1,000 kg	
	1st year	5th year	1st year	5th year
3. Economic feasibility				
A. Annual costs (1+2+3)	**29,798**	**29,011**	**123,676**	**120,898**
1. Fixed costs loan				
- Repayment	1,574	1,574	5,557	5,557
- Equipment	1,114	1,114	3,507	3,507
- Structure	460	460	2,050	2,050
2. Variable costs	27,188	27,188	114,386	114,386
- Potatoes	10,800	10,800	54,000	54,000
- Other variable costs	16,388	16,388	60,386	60,386
3. Interest costs	1,036	249	3,733	955
- Fixed costs 12.5%/yr	984	197	3,473	695
- Operating capital	52	52	260	260
Total annual cost/package	2.59	2.52	2.15	2.10
B. Annual revenues	**28,800**	**28,800**	**144,000**	**144,000**
- Packages produced	11,520	11,520	57,600	57,600
C. Annual net revenues	**-998**	**-211**	**20,324**	**23,102**
- Net revenues/package	-0.09	-0.02	0.35	0.40

Loan repayment for the purchase of the structure and equipment is made in equal installments, annually. For operating capital, the farmer uses his own potatoes for processing using family/household labor, and paying immediately for any marketing and transport costs from sales revenues; hence, the cost of operating capital is assumed to be minimum.

Figures may not sum to totals due to rounding errors.

The selling price for potato chips is Rps. 2.5/250 gram package.

Source: Nave and Sott (1992).

Part 2

Field Methods

■ **Market Analysis**

6

Field Methods for Exploring the Role of Indigenous Rural Periodic Markets in Developing Countries

Gina Porter[1]

Abstract

In developing countries, rural periodic markets frequently represent the first point of sale of agricultural products, particularly for small-scale farmers. This chapter briefly reviews the approaches which have been utilized by geographers and other social scientists in exploring the workings of such markets and the activities of traders operating within them. It then discusses in some detail the approach adopted by the author, a geographer, in two field studies of rural periodic market trade undertaken over varying time scales in different regions of northern Nigeria.

Key words: Geography, survey design, interview procedures, data recording.

Periodic Markets and Research Methods in the Social Sciences: Spatial Perspectives

Periodic markets are public gatherings at an appointed or customary location where people converge to buy, to sell, and to interact socially, at regular intervals less frequently than daily (Bromley 1980). They have a particular fascination for geographers and economic anthropologists, whose differing approaches to the study of rural periodic market trade have been shaped by broad disciplinary perspectives and training. In both cases the focus has usually been on marketplaces and marketplace trade, rather than on marketing of agricultural produce per se.[2] Nonetheless, rural periodic markets play an important role in the agricultural economies of many developing countries.

---

[1] Department of Geography, University of Durham, Science Laboratories, South Road, Durham DH1 3LE, UK.

[2] See Hollier (1986) for a rare geographical analysis of foodstuffs marketing from a commodity perspective.

They are frequently the first point of sale of agricultural products—particularly from small-scale farmers—and often also the point of sale of manufactured durable goods to farmers.

Geographical research on rural periodic markets expanded enormously in the 1960s and 1970s. It tended to reflect the geographer's concern with spatial patterns by focusing on the analysis of spatial structures of marketplace systems on a sub-regional or regional scale. Up to the late 1960s much of this work was descriptive, but throughout the 1970s there was increasing emphasis on analytical approaches, with particular interest in exploring the structure and function of the spatio-temporal integration of market systems (reflecting a long-standing fascination with space/time interrelationships).

Applications of central place theory and other spatial models from the location theory tradition were common at this time, encouraged by the prevailing emphasis on quantitative techniques in social science. Thus the emphasis tended towards measurements of distance between markets and aggregate counts of market traders attending markets across a whole region or country (for example, Thorpe 1978 for Iran), later sometimes coupled with large-scale questionnaire sample surveys of traders. Bromley's study of Ecuador comprised trader counts followed by 1,109 interviews with market traders in 13 large- to medium-sized centers, with subsequent statistical analysis (Bromley 1980). The move to interviewing traders reflected growing awareness of the "deficiency of a substantial amount of recent geographical research on systems of periodic and daily markets... (which) stem largely from an excessive preoccupation with the geometry of spatio-temporal phenomena, from the application of some rather questionable techniques of spatial analysis (such as nearest neighbor analysis), and from a tendency to infer process from patterns rather than to study processes in their own right" (Bromley 1980). In an important review paper, R. H. T. Smith (1980) similarly called for a shift towards investigation of processes which would require, "a more detailed knowledge of the characteristics, values, and spatial behavior of the participants in periodic marketing and periodic marketplaces." There was growing recognition that marketplace networks can only be understood in the context of the social structure of marketplace participants (Trager and Smith 1981); the economic and social elements of the market system are often inextricably intertwined. Unfortunately, this shift in perspective which reflected the growing interest in humanistic and behavioral approaches in geography, was to have only limited impact in the field of rural periodic market study in the 1980s, as geographers became increasingly preoccupied with production and less concerned with marketing and distribution.

In **economic anthropology** much work has focused (through participant observation techniques) on detailed economic behavior in markets, with analyses of individual economic relationships and the nature of transactions (see Plattner 1989: 209-221), though some anthropologists have found larger surveys a useful preliminary or complement to detailed ethnographic research in considering rural economies, as a way of avoiding the danger of generalization from small samples. For example, Handwerker (1979) included interviews with 980 shoppers, in addition to more intensive techniques, in his study of Liberian markets.

Cross disciplinary approaches in periodic market studies are hardly surprising, given the complex interdependence of components in exchange systems. Individual researchers have frequently adopted a mix of techniques and perspectives emanating from their own and neighboring disciplines. In anthropology the work of Carol Smith is particularly notable for its adoption of a mix of geographical and anthropological perspectives in research on periodic market systems (Smith 1975, 1976, 1985). Graham Hollier (1986), a geographer researching spatial patterns in foodstuffs prices in Cameroon, adopted a method from Strickland and Schlesinger (1969) termed "lurking," ("patient unobtrusive observation of market transactions, recording the prices actually agreed by buyers and sellers") which he supplemented with data from key informants and direct questioning to generate apparently accurate price information. Much of his work involved participant observation in a style more commonly associated with ethnography.[3] Occasionally geographers and anthropologists have combined forces to produce useful collaborative research (e.g., Polly Hill and R.H.T. Smith 1972). Recently, there has been renewed appreciation among geographers of the importance of cultural traditions and growing interest in the application of qualitative ethnographic techniques (Eyles and Smith 1988). There seems to be considerable potential for the further combination of geographical and anthropological approaches in field studies of rural periodic markets.

My own work on rural periodic markets, discussed below, though based in geography, and thus essentially spatial in perspective, takes an integrative approach. It combines "in breadth" large-scale survey research with work of a more micro-scale "in depth" nature, attempting to probe linkages between spatial, socio-cultural, economic, and political dimensions of the exchange process at work in marketplaces in order to gain a fuller appreciation of what Siddle and Swindell (1990: 89) so aptly refer to as the "texture" of this "essentially holistic activity". Much of my work in rural markets has centered round three interlinked foci of investigation:

---

[3] Lurking is reviewed (unenthusiastically) by Werner and Schoepfle (1987: 80-81). For an introduction to participant observation techniques, see Burgess (1982: 45-72); Werner and Schoepfle (1987); and Evans in Eyles and Smith (1988: 197-218).

- The dynamics of rural periodic market systems and the specific influence of changing accessibility.

- Gender differences in market trade with particular reference to mobility of participants.

- The impact of change in marketplace systems on gender patterns of trade in specific cultural contexts.

All have implications for the marketing of agricultural produce and its evacuation from rural areas. The development of a field research program which addresses these questions is discussed below, following a brief outline of the two field studies in which the procedure was established.

Markets in Borno and the Jos Plateau: Outline of Two Field Research Programs

My first major field study of rural periodic markets was carried out in Borno, in the remote sudan savanna region of northeast Nigeria in 1977 and 1978, and funded by the University of Maiduguri. I had been resident in the region since 1975. The project consisted of wet and dry season studies of the 35 rural markets of four districts surrounding the state capital, Maiduguri (see Figure 1), and aimed to explore the dynamic nature of the market system and its significance both for market participants and, more widely for the ongoing process of rural development. The fieldwork took place at a time when road construction (funded by Nigeria's oil boom) was proceeding rapidly in the region and the market system was clearly in a state of flux.

In this region the periodic markets have a weekly cycle, meeting once every seven days. The markets possess limited infrastructure; sometimes a few block stalls and a slaughter block, possibly a well. Often the majority of traders, especially women, simply display their wares on a cloth on the ground, or perambulate around the marketplace with their goods on a head tray. In all the rural markets, foodstuffs occupied the greatest area and generally the greater proportion of traders sold agricultural produce. The majority of traders were also farmers and sold agricultural produce and other goods on a very small scale both retail direct to consumers, and in some cases also to wholesale dealers.

The central element of the survey consisted of semi-structured questionnaires to (2,000) male and (700) female traders in the marketplace on market day. These interviews focused on the movement of trade goods and mobility of traders. The trader survey was preceded by semi-structured and group interviews with local government officials, district and village heads and elders, and market officials. It was coupled with interviews with consumers, other market visitors and villagers; informal discussion with some of the major traders (usually male) and some women traders; observation of site access and drainage conditions; and construction of site plans indicating location of stalls and stall types (and appending further notes regarding sex of stall holder, any segregation by ethnic group, etc.). Details of the full schedule of work, refined during the Plateau study, are provided in the following section which highlights some of the specific issues which were addressed in the studies. The data were subsequently analysed using an SPSS cross-tabulation program. Further field visits were made to the Borno survey area between 1978 and July 1984, when another, smaller market study was undertaken to assess the changes in the system over the intervening period.

In January 1991, I undertook a dry season study of rural periodic markets on the Jos Plateau in the Middle Belt of Nigeria, as part of the Jos Plateau Environmental Development Program (a joint project of the universities of Durham and Jos, financed by the European Development Fund) (see Figure 1). This study aimed to provide a broad picture of the condition of rural markets and produce evacuation in the former mining areas of the Plateau,

Figure 1. Nigeria, showing the two survey areas.

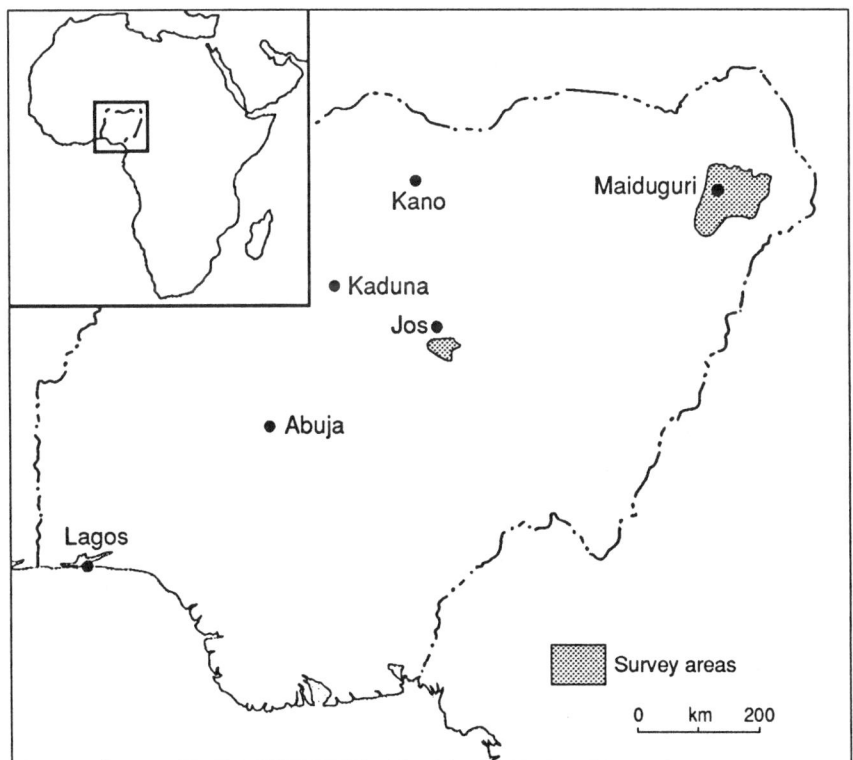

where dry season farming has recently expanded substantially, and to identify issues for further detailed research. It was accompanied by studies of produce evacuation from a sample of small, medium, and large farms (Porter 1992). The approach adopted was based on my earlier Borno experience, but in this case consisted of a study of 23 markets, principally in three contiguous districts. As in Borno, rural periodic markets meet every seven days and most markets have limited infrastructure. Most of the 459 female and 345 male traders interviewed were involved in farming to some degree. Fieldwork included semi-structured individual and group interviews, "guided" interviews, informal free discussion in the markets, and observation; and was followed by cartographic analysis and an SPSS cross-tabulation of trader interviews. A consumer survey was omitted from this study because of time constraints, though traders (who often purchase goods during their market visit) were questioned about purchases.

The Field Program

In the field program outlined below the method adopted is a composite one, utilizing a range of approaches. There is a substantial literature supporting the use of multiple strategies in fieldwork (Burgess 1982: 163-188; Werner and Schoepfle 1987: 68). Much of the procedure discussed is essentially common sense, but may provide a checklist for anyone contemplating field survey work in markets.

Preparative work

Outside the field study region

Library research. Once the selection of the broad regional context for research has been made, much useful background material on rural markets and trade (and associated information concerning production and consumption) in a particular geographic area can be obtained through consultation of relevant published sources: historical background from contemporary travelers' accounts, ethnographic surveys, gazetteers, government reports, etc. In Borno, a great deal of background information on Kanuri culture was gleaned from the writings of the anthropologist Ronald Cohen, who conducted field research in the region in the 1950s and 60s. Unpublished material, including graduate theses and undergraduate dissertations, may also prove illuminating, though in areas like Borno, where universities and research institutions have only been established in recent years, such material is often limited. Obviously, there are dangers of bias in using secondary information which must be borne in mind.

Archives. Consultation of archival material is also often relevant and has been used by some geographers to provide valuable background to studies of contemporary rural market systems (e.g., Gana 1973; Barrett 1988). In Nigeria the national archives offices hold a wealth of material pertaining to colonial markets and trade in agricultural products (district notebooks, assessment and reassessment reports, special district reports, annual, half-yearly and quarterly provincial reports, provincial administrative correspondence, etc.).[4] In the Borno study archival material (together with historical accounts of European travellers to the region and oral testimony) was used to construct a picture of the long-term evolution of rural markets.

Maps. Acquisition of maps at a variety of scales, including ones at as detailed a scale as possible, is vital for any marketing study with a spatial component. A careful examination of maps regarding accessibility, administrative boundaries, and the like should also assist in preliminary decisions concerning the selection of the field survey area. The maps available may well be inaccurate, but it is usually a much simpler task to amend and add to existing maps than to start mapping from scratch. Often maps are only available at national survey offices (Kaduna and Lagos in Nigeria) and, even so, series may well be incomplete. In Nigeria, maps at a scale of 1:50,000 provided detailed (but outdated and possibly inaccurate) coverage. They appear to be unavailable for some areas of the country. In the field, 1:500,000 sheets, showing roads and major settlements, and old provincial maps (at 1:1,000,000) indicating district boundaries, were found to be particularly useful for plotting market locations. In the Borno survey area the propensity of markets and, indeed, whole villages, to move site made mapping extremely difficult. Air photographs may, where available, assist in the location of sites. A useful introduction to the use of maps and air photographs in African fieldwork is provided by Mitchell (in Peil et al. 1982: 61-96).

Research permission. Other preliminaries include obtaining official permission for fieldwork. A range of viewpoints on this sometimes morally difficult matter was expressed by geographers in a series of papers and comments in the journal *Area* in 1987 and 1988. In Nigeria, research permission is generally obtained through association with a local university. Advice concerning restrictions should, if possible, be obtained from researchers in the field. It is usually important to obtain the necessary links before approaching local officials (see below).

In the field study region

Additional pre-survey preparation will be required once the researcher has moved into the fieldwork area.

---

[4] Much material relating to agricultural marketing and markets in British ex-colonies is held at the Public Record Office, Kew, at Rhodes House, Oxford, and (for West Africa) in the Picton Archives, Liverpool, UK.

Local permission. In Nigeria it is important to contact local government officials concerning the project before undertaking any fieldwork. A letter requesting support from the local university registrar's office—assuming affiliation has been negotiated—is generally sufficient to obtain immediate Local Government approval. The secretary to the Local Government Council (LGC) will then prepare letters informing district and village heads in the proposed fieldwork area about the project, and also a letter of permission which the researcher should carry on all field visits. Researchers in rural markets are highly visible and may rapidly become embroiled in confrontational situations if they have not worked through the appropriate channels to inform the relevant authorities. On one occasion the local university insisted on the author obtaining permission from the Nigerian Security Organization before commencing fieldwork in a sensitive border area. Permission was granted by the local branch following an intensive hour-long interview only on the grounds that the researcher was known in the survey area, having carried out previous work there. Conditions change and local markets can be volatile; it is always wise to check on the situation immediately prior to commencing fieldwork, however well the area is known.

Locating markets. For geographers concerned with spatial distributions of rural periodic markets, the location of markets of all kinds is particularly crucial. Discovering the existence and location of rural periodic markets can be a major detection exercise and in Nigeria usually involves some element of trial and error which extends through the survey program. Useful preliminary (inaccurate) lists of markets and market days were obtained in the Borno and Jos surveys from LGC headquarters. In the Borno survey area only 18 of the 48 markets in operation in 1977 were listed in the LGC's printed schedule of markets obtained that year prior to fieldwork, and only 13 of their associated villages were shown by name on published maps of the region. On the Plateau the list of gazetted and non-gazetted markets provided by the LGC Tax Superintendent proved to be similarly incomplete. However, Hill and Smith (1972) mainly used local government records as the basis for their analysis of the spatial and temporal integration of periodic markets in four northern Nigerian emirates; presumably these were more reliable than the Borno and Plateau records. Fuller listings of markets and preliminary information about them were gathered from district heads, but even so, new markets were discovered as the surveys proceeded (generally through interviews with village area heads and traders), and other markets thought still to be in existence were found to be defunct.

On the Jos Plateau the situation was complicated by the existence of *kunnu* markets, where the principal business is the sale of beer and cooked food for immediate consumption, in addition to rural periodic markets of a more conventional type in which mixed retail and wholesale business takes place, though a secondary *kunnu* function may be identified. District and village heads made a clear distinction between the two types, but LGC officials and district heads in some cases were wrong regarding the current status of markets, for sometimes general markets have declined into *kunnu* markets, and sometimes *kunnu* markets have grown into full-scale periodic markets. The existence of neighboring markets with identical names further complicated matters in both the Plateau and Borno, and in Borno the not infrequent migration of villages and markets made published maps particularly inadequate; within living memory a change of site (in one case of 16 km) had been recorded for 16 of the 35 markets surveyed and one bush market had moved site at least four times.

Interview schedules. There is much useful published material concerning the construction of questionnaires/interview schedules (Peil et al. 1982; de Vaus 1990, etc.), but some comments can be made regarding their preparation for use in rural periodic markets.

Given time constraints in fieldwork, it is often necessary, but certainly undesirable (see Chambers 1983: 51), to construct questionnaire and interview schedules prior to entering the fieldwork area. If at all feasible, preliminary visits to local markets should be made first. In the Borno study, familiarity with local markets meant that relatively few amendments were required following the pilot survey.

In the field survey procedure (outlined below under The Survey), it is assumed that assistance with interviewing will be obtained. Interviewers obviously must have fluency in local languages used by traders, but a preliminary decision needs to be taken whether to print interview schedules in the country's official national language (English in Nigeria) or/and in a local language. In Borno, where the ethnic majority are Kanuri, the trader interview schedule was printed in both English and Kanuri. On the Plateau, though the indigenous ethnic group in the survey area are principally Birom, the trader questionnaire was printed only in English because the rural population is very mixed as a result of in-migration during the tin-mining era. Field assistants (carefully briefed in advance about the questions) translated into the relevant local language or the trading *lingua franca*, Hausa; this seems to have resulted in few errors of interpretation, perhaps because some effort was taken to clarify indigenous terminology for types of trade, etc., at the outset. Nonetheless, where only one language will be commonly encountered in the survey area it is advisable to prepare questions in that language, for standardization and to avoid reinterpretation by individual interviewers. The hazards of translation are well described by Briggs (1986) and Werner and Schoepfle (1987: 354-379). For government officials and the like, schedules prepared in the national language will usually be sufficient.

Whatever language is selected, prepared questions should be reviewed where possible with local researchers and with the field assistants who will conduct the interviews. Unseen back translations are a useful cross check to avoid error and ambiguity. Another review of the principal interview schedule(s) following the pilot study is essential, since misinterpretations other than those generated by mistranslation may emerge. In my initial Borno interview schedule, there was an inbuilt assumption—acquired from the periodic markets literature—that many long-distance traders would be encountered in markets, and a series of questions had been designed to establish their movements. The pilot survey suggested that, in fact, most traders returned home every night, and some schedule questions were redesigned to elicit greater information on local travel to markets. The precise content of the interview schedules will depend on the aims of the survey, but a few general points may be suggested. So far as length is concerned, a trader survey cannot be too long if the interview is to be conducted in the marketplace. In the Borno survey a total of 33 short questions were put to traders; this appeared to present no problem regarding length and these were extended to 47 questions in the Plateau survey. Again, few incomplete questionnaires were returned, though this must be approaching the limit; traders were extremely patient despite the interruption to their normal business. Werner and Schoepfle (1987: 344) suggest a maximum of 50 questions.

All discussion concerning financial matters was reserved to the end of the interview schedule; this appears to be the most effective way to deal with such a tricky question. Nonetheless, trader response rates to a question about estimated gross market takings for the day of interview was much lower than for all other questions. In the Plateau survey 21% of men and 19% of women refused to attempt any estimate; "it depends on God" was a common reply. Direct questions to traders to elicit information about profits are unlikely to be satisfactory (see Crow 1988-89 regarding Islam et al.'s Bangladesh survey), hence Hollier's use of more informal methods—participant observation and "lurking"—and Crow's discussions with informants contacted through friends and relations and observation of participants in foodgrain markets (Hollier 1986; Crow 1988-89).

One final practical point. It is advisable to print the interview questions on one side of paper only; even experienced interviewers occasionally miss the back of the sheet, especially when working in the crowded conditions of a busy market.

Recruitment of field assistants. This is probably the most critical element in the pre-survey program. Fieldwork in hot, dusty rural markets is demanding and exhausting. Assistants must be fluent in local languages encountered in the markets and able to communicate proficiently with the researcher. They also need common sense, sensitivity, tact, and courtesy. Peil et al. (1982: 134-136) suggests secondary school students, in preference to university students, as being often less arrogant and more reliable.

In Borno I used first year undergraduate students, and on the Plateau a mix of university students and secondary school leavers, recruited through the university. In both surveys a team of about one dozen local field assistants was found to be sufficient; allowing for absenteeism this usually secured a manageable 8-10 in the field on any day. On balance I found my Borno team more effective, perhaps because I worked with them over a long period and had known some of them prior to their recruitment. In both surveys, a degree of reliability was ensured by being present in every market in which interviewers worked.

In both Borno and the Plateau the participants in marketplace trade are male and female. In many small markets women predominate. One of the beauties of research in rural markets is that it allows interviews with women about their economic activities away from the home where male household heads may obtrude, even inadvertently by their mere presence, and thus restrict exploration of women's trading activities (Hill 1986: 143). It thus seemed important to obtain both male and female assistants for the trader survey. This turned out to be a crucial decision because some women traders, particularly in Borno, clearly preferred to be interviewed by women. In Borno, I was able to secure the assistance of only one woman; in this Moslem area in 1977 it was very difficult to find educated Kanuri women able to travel extensively. My assistant was a young divorcee from the local royal family, one of the university's first Kanuri women students. She travelled round the markets in simple local dress, most successfully interviewing and conversing informally with many poor rural Kanuri and Shuwa women, despite her very different background. My male field assistants, though mainly from urban privileged families, were similarly impressive in their competence, patience, and sensitivity to local courtesies and customs. In the Plateau study assistants had to be recruited very rapidly. They all happened to be Christians (this is a mixed Christian/Moslem area); half the team was female. In this case I had some difficulty at first in persuading female assistants to wear local dress appropriate to the rural markets where they were working; two rapidly dropped out but the remainder subsequently worked fairly effectively. On the Plateau I observed that, when given the opportunity to choose, many of my female assistants preferred to interview male traders, and my male assistants to interview women. Nonetheless, Whitehead and Brown (1986) emphasize the importance of using a team of male and female fieldworkers (for interviewing their own sex) in highly segregated societies where short-term fieldwork is proposed.

The Survey

Fieldwork in Borno and the Plateau can be divided into four phases.

A **preliminary stage** in which each district head in the selected survey area was visited (along with an LGC representative) to obtain formal permission to work in the district, and be interviewed about the district's markets. This interview focused on basic factual information: a list of markets, day(s) held, approximate size and seasonal variations in size, opening times, status regarding wholesale/retail element, location, presence of specialized markets, market closures and reasons for closure, new markets and reasons for establishment, and the role of rural markets (and other outlets) in the evacuation of agricultural produce. Additional questions were asked in the Plateau study about the impact of the recent abolition of the marketing boards, and the value of middlemen in rural marketing (many district heads are involved in trade so not surprisingly responses to the latter question were strongly favorable). The District head normally gave the interview surrounded by members of his entourage, and the response to each question followed consultation with the group. Where disagreement occurred this was recorded and the issue was followed up elsewhere. Preliminary market histories were often elicited from the entourage for individual markets they knew well.

Often village heads were first encountered at the district head's house. District heads generally informed all village heads in the district about the project in advance of the market visits. In cases where markets were particularly remote and difficult to find, district heads often offered to provide a messenger to accompany the field team.

The visits to district heads were followed immediately by a **pilot run** of the main trader survey in one or two small markets. (The procedure followed is described in the Main Survey section below.)

This was followed by **revision** of the trader questionnaire, a **review** and weeding out of field assistants, and the construction of a (flexible) schedule of market visits. The latter had to take into account periodicity of market meetings, vehicle availability (4-wheel drive may be necessary for off-road markets), and access. In the case of a rainy season survey, it is important to bear in mind that markets may be virtually empty on days following heavy rain at the start of the planting season.

In the **main survey** of each rural market, the following structured (but flexible) procedure was adopted. Normally only one market was surveyed each day.

1. On market day proceed to the market with field assistants. In some cases it was necessary to take a representative of the LGC to the market, because of the difficulty of locating markets situated away from the tarred road. (Available maps are inadequate and bush routes change as roads deteriorate.)

2. Locate the village head's house. Often the village head was already in the market. His permission was requested, as a courtesy, before any interviewing

took place. Occasionally, the village head was absent from the village, in which case his deputy was approached.

3. Once permission had been obtained, the field assistants commenced interviewing traders selling in the market. Meanwhile the village head was interviewed. On a few occasions on the Plateau, field assistants attempted to save time by commencing their interviews before I had completed formalities with the village head, and in one of these, markets traders refused to answer questions until the village head had given his approval.

4. Move to the market (usually by this time approaching its peak) and fill in an observation sheet regarding access, site conditions, transport, and lorry/truck parking facilities, etc. Draw a plan of the market site indicating location of stalls and stall types with notes regarding sex of stall holder and goods on sale plus similar notes on perambulating hawkers; essentially a full count of all traders. In many cases the village head insisted on personally conducting a tour round the market, in which case it was necessary to delay drawing up the plan until later.

5. Talk informally (but using check lists of topics) to the market chief, to market committee members where committees existed, to some of the major traders (usually male), and to some of the women traders (if Hausa speakers). In quieter markets the field assistants also chatted informally with villagers and market participants once they had completed their questionnaires.

6. Take photographs.

7. Leave the market. On the Plateau everything had to be accomplished before about 4:30 p.m. Serious drinking tended to become a primary activity after this time among many market visitors and the atmosphere of the market changed. Presumably this is principally a feature of markets in the postharvest period on the Plateau.

8. On the journey back to base, discuss the market and obtain informal feedback from the field assistants (and driver) on their perceptions of the market, their interviews, etc. This debriefing proved very important. On the few occasions when I was unable to travel with the interviewers, I felt I obtained a much less complete picture of the market.

9. Each evening write up field notes and check through all data collected that day including trader interview schedules.

10. Pursue queries from 9 above with assistants on the journey to market the following morning. This was particularly important in the early stages of fieldwork.

Elaboration of some of the above points may be useful. The interview with village heads referred to in point 3 consisted principally of factual questions concerning the village market and the settlement; details of the market's age, functions, trade, seasonal variations in trade (including approximations of average trader numbers), change in trade over the past five years, opening times, age of stalls, facilities, site and changes of site, and fees charged. Questions were also asked about the village economy and history, about trade outside the marketplace, village trade associations, the effects of the abolition of the marketing boards (in the Plateau study), and public transport. Generally, as in the case of the District head interview, this was a group interview with ward heads, elders, and other villagers contributing to the discussion. As in the District head interviews, I found it useful to have an assistant ask questions and note responses, because this allowed me to observe more carefully and pick up nuances in the debate which I might otherwise have missed.

The trader questionnaire, discussed briefly in the pilot run section, was administered by field assistants, as a one-on-one interview, because it dealt with the specific details and experiences of individual traders. Where possible every trader selling in the market was questioned. In large markets this was not feasible, and an on-the-spot sampling strategy had to be devised to obtain as representative a sample for the market as possible. The difficulties of sampling in markets have been observed by others; in the Gambia, for example, Barrett (1988: 14) writes "a rigorous sampling procedure" was "impractical". In rural markets, which frequently take place on open ground with numerous entry and exit points, the problems are particularly great, especially where stalls are few and most traders simply arrange their sale goods on the ground or hawk them round the marketplace on their heads. In another example, Bromley (1980: 154) describes a sampling technique he used in Ecuadorian urban markets.

The trader interview schedule used in Nigeria was designed to explore details of the trader's background, and both trading and non-trading activities. Questions covered residence and place of birth, seasonal occupational variation, type and source of trade goods, pattern of market visitation, transport to market, purchases in the market, storage of goods, links with major regional markets, sales, prices, reasons for marketing, attitude to trading, trade problems, and membership of trade associations. In the Plateau survey, women were asked about restrictions imposed by husbands on their mobility.

Additional details were noted regarding age, sex, ethnic group, trade goods currently on sale, and stall type occupied. The questionnaires were all of a semi-structured type, incorporating a mix of closed and open questions. No precoding of data was attemped (i.e., coding on the questionnaire). The response rate was remarkably high, with very few reported refusals, especially on the Plateau where more women interviewers were available. We did not remunerate traders for interviews (see Whyte 1984: 108) and very few seemed to anticipate remuneration. However, we usually purchased refreshments during the day and some provisions before leaving the market. Sometimes I was given small gifts and reciprocated in kind (colorful postcards are useful for this purpose).

Much useful information was obtained informally (point 5) through conversations with traders toward the end of the market day, as business slackened. On some occasions in Borno, I was invited into compounds to meet the few secluded women (wives of richer men and office holders) who would otherwise have missed the excitement of visiting strangers and learned about compound-based trade. While this kind of information-gathering may appear to lack rigor, it provides a "texture" which cannot be obtained through formal questionnaire interviews, even of the semi-structured kind (Burgess 1982: 107-110).

I found photographs (point 6) a useful mnemonic device, but took them with caution and generally only toward the end of the market day when the market study was finished and traders familiar with the survey team. A second, Polaroid, camera was used to provide an instant photograph as a small gift to those photographed. Permission was always requested from individual traders (and only rarely refused) before proceeding. Photographs can be used as a research technique in markets. A study of 21 market sellers in a Lima marketplace used a photo-interview technique, a structured open-ended questionnaire, and a set of photographs of trading activities, to research women's marketing activities and their perceptions of their role in the marketplace (Bunster 1983).

The "write up" of field notes (point 9) was made in a journal kept at base to record more fully (and legibly) notes taken throughout the day in a separate field notebook. Additional notes reviewed progress, etc. The importance of systematic recording of this type is reviewed, for example, in Burgess (1982: 191-199) and was found to be invaluable.

The field research program discussed above is summarized in the following table.

Table 1. Procedures for rural periodic market field research.

Procedure	Data sought
Pre-survey	
Pre-field preparatory work:	
- library research	Background, especially selection of
- archival research	field study location
- contact local researchers	
- contact local university	(research permission)

Table 1. (continued)

Procedure	Data sought
Field-based preparatory work:	
- visit local government offices	(research permission)
- locate and visit markets	background of study area
- design questionnaires/schedules	
- recruit field assistants	
Field survey	
Preliminary stage:	
- visit district heads	(research permission) Factual information: market days, times, size, characteristics; views on markets and recent change
- pilot survey of trader questionnaire	
- revision of questionnaire	

Main survey: daily procedure (one market per day)

Researcher	Field assistants	
- pursue queries regarding previous day on journey to market		
- visit village head		(survey permission)
	- interview traders	trader background, characteristics, and trading and non-trading activities
- interview village head and elders		Village and market history, economic profile
- fill in observation sheet		Physical conditions: access, site, lorry/truck park
- draw plans of site, stalls, and note perambulating traders		Stall location by type (sex of holder, goods on sale); Full count of all traders
- informal discussion with market committee, major traders, market women	- informal discussion with villagers and traders	Miscellaneous information
- take photographs		Visual record
Post survey		
At market		
- depart market		
- debrief field assistants		

Table 1. (continued)

Researcher	Field assistant	Data sought
- complete field notes At base: - check interview data - write up field notes		Impressions of market

Analysis

This chapter has focused principally on field procedure, but a brief discussion of methods of data analysis may help to clarify the selection of approaches to inquiry in the field. In both the Borno and Plateau studies, a variety of analytical approaches were adopted, including basic cartographic analysis and cross-tabulation of the trader survey data using an SPSS program. These are discussed in turn below, each with reference to a particular research inquiry.

Spatio-temporal change and accessibility

Some indication of the pattern of spatio-temporal change in the market system can be ascertained through simple cartographic analysis of information gathered concerning market size, market establishment, and market closures. District heads, village heads, and elders were asked about change in their markets over the past five years, and traders were asked about their visits (when and how often) to the market in which they were interviewed. In Borno, a resurvey of the four survey districts was made in 1984, six years after the preliminary studies, allowing assessment of interim change in the market system. In both regions, mapping of estimates regarding size of market (in terms of trader attendance) at time of survey, changes in market size over the previous five years, and incidence of recent market establishment emphasized the paramount significance of road construction programs and the expansion of vehicle ownership in reshaping the rural periodic market systems (Porter 1986; 1988; 1993). Examples of maps constructed for the Plateau study are shown in Figure 2.

Gender patterns of trade

While there has been substantial work on women's trade in developing countries, fewer researchers have analyzed gender differences in trade, which can be considerable (Harts-Broekhuis and Verkoren 1987) and are important for understanding patterns of produce evacuation, etc. Analysis of the trader questionnaires in both Borno and the Plateau using an SPSS cross-tabulation program facilitated manipulation of simple gender comparisons for the data set in each study area as a whole, for individual markets, and for groups of markets

Figure 2. Maps illustrating aspects of spatio-temporal change in the Jos Plateau survey area.

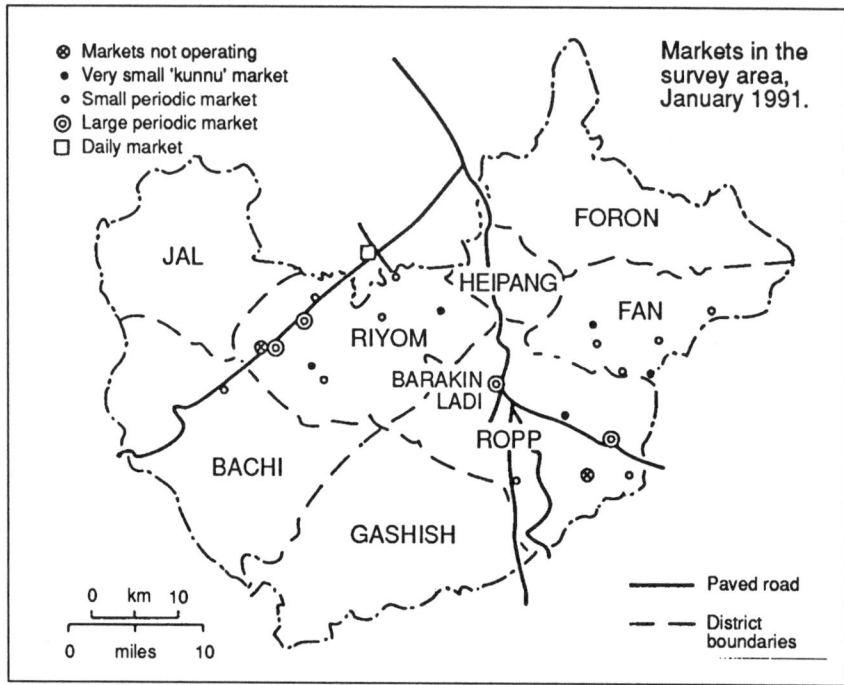

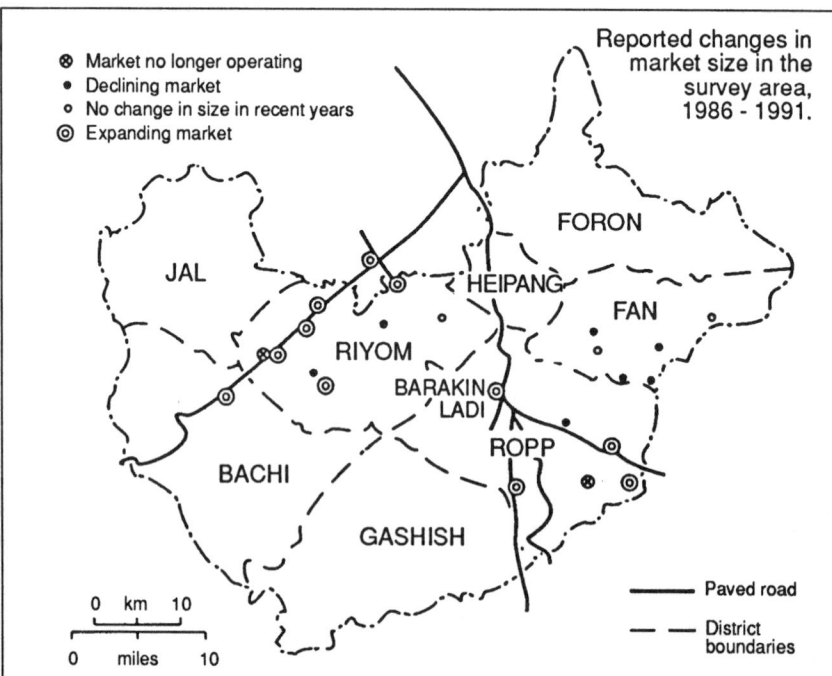

Field methods for exploring the role of indigenous rural periodic markets 161

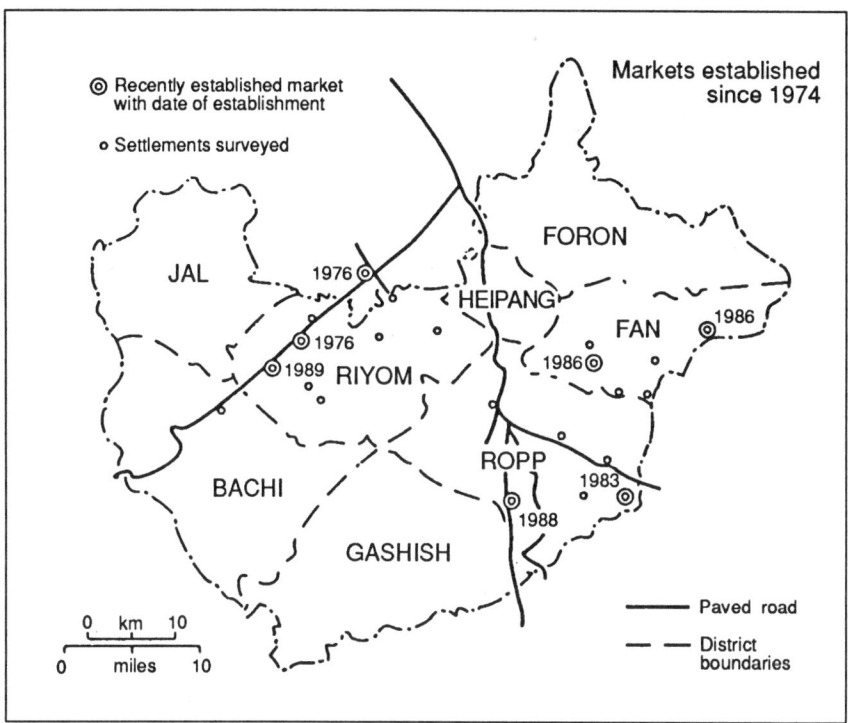

(e.g., roadside vs. bush markets). In the Borno case, additional gender comparisons were constructed for wet and dry season markets and on the Plateau (where the trader population is ethnically diverse) for ethnic groups. Cross-tabulations were computed for sex by a whole range of variables including trade goods, mode of transport to market, distance traveled to market, frequency of market visits, trader types, and size of enterprise, and on the Plateau, reasons for trading and trader problems. The procedure for such analyses is straightforward and well documented. Two brief comments about computer analysis: I found it advisable to code all data myself in order to ensure consistency in categorization; and it is important to commence the exercise as early as possible after returning from the field for maximum recall.

Full details of the analyses are available (Porter 1986; 1988; 1993). In both study areas gender contrasts in mobility were particularly notable in terms of distance traveled to the interview market, mode of transport, frequency of visits to market, and frequency of visits to major regional markets. Females were considerably less mobile than men, though this gender distinction was more marked in Borno where Kanuri cultural conventions restricting female mobility are substantial. In both areas, distinctions in gender mobility have important implications in the context of changes in the market system induced by transport developments. The loss of off-road markets for those resident in associated settlements has more serious implications for women than for men. Even if cultural conventions do not prevent lengthy journeys to distant roadside markets, the multifarious duties undertaken by women in addition to their marketing activities (reflected in the mobility patterns described above) present barriers to future trade.

Conclusion

The orientation of research described in this chapter is distinctly "bottom up", with the principal emphasis on learning from marketplace participants, male and female, many of whom operated on a very small scale indeed in the areas studied. The field method was shaped, inevitably, by resources and time availability. Post-field analysis (and reflection) indicated some of the shortcomings of the studies. In particular it highlighted the need for more research in settlements which have recently lost their markets. Such villages were visited by accident, not design, since the studies reported in this chapter were concerned with rural periodic markets per se.

Additionally, longitudinal studies—rarely carried out—or, at least, resurveys are vital if we are to gain a fuller understanding of the dynamics of rural periodic market systems. The extension of the Borno study over seven years made for a much clearer recognition of the significance of changing accessibility in market system dynamics.

Feedback is another area often inadequately considered and restricted by resource constraints.[5] Yet it is important that those who give their time so freely supplying information be able to obtain some in return, if they want it. In the Plateau study, it was difficult to proceed in one village area because villagers were tired of providing information, and the village head and elders stressed their desire for feedback. In the event, a report on Plateau markets was prepared, together with a gazetteer of all markets and market settlements studied. The latter could be dismembered to provide relevant information for each market village. Copies were sent back to Jos for distribution. They appear to have reached LGC headquarters and district heads. The delay in funding of the next phase of the Jos Plateau Environmental Resource and Development Program has, unfortunately, led to redeployment of staff and it has not been possible to ascertain whether any villages received relevant sections of the report. There may be (should be?) a difficult decision in fieldwork regarding allocation of scarce funds between field study and feedback.

Finally, the critical role of rural periodic markets in the preliminary distribution of products from small scale farmers (and in the distribution of

---

[5] For useful discussion of the difficulties of "returning the research" see Patai (1991) and Wilson (1993).

consumption goods to those farmers) in many developing countries must be reiterated. Over the last decade the perceived failure of state intervention in produce marketing has brought increased reliance on traditional indigenous marketing and distribution systems, following the abolition of state marketing boards, etc. We need to know much more about the dynamics, potentialities, and limitations of rural periodic markets, for the rural marketplace is the point at which many of the poorest farmers in such countries sell their produce. This can only be achieved through careful field research.

References

Barrett, H.R. 1988. *The marketing of foodstuffs in the Gambia, 1400-1980: A geographical analysis*. Aldershot, UK: Avebury.

Briggs, C.L. 1986. *Learning how to ask: A sociolinguistic appraisal of the role of the interview in social science research*. Cambridge, UK: Cambridge University Press.

Bromley, R.J. 1980. Trader mobility in systems of periodic and daily markets. In *Geography and the urban evnironment* (D.T. Herbert and R.J. Johnston, eds.). Chichester, UK: John Wiley & Sons.

Bunster, X.B. 1983. Market sellers in Lima, Peru: Talking about work. In *Women and poverty in the Third World* (M. Buvinic et al.). Baltimore, MD, USA: The Johns Hopkins University Press.

Burgess, R.G. (ed.). 1982. *Field research: A sourcebook and field manual*. London, UK: George Allen and Unwin.

Chambers, R. 1983. *Rural development: Putting the last first*. London, UK: Longman.

Crow, B. 1988-89. Plain tales from the rice trade: Indications of vertical integration in foodgrain markets in Bangaldesh. *Journal of Peasant Studies* 16(2):198-229.

Eyles, J. and D.M. Smith (eds.). 1988. *Qualitative methods in human geography*. Oxford, UK: Polity Press/Basil Blackwell.

Gana, J.A. 1973. *Market centers in Zaria division, Nigeria*. Ph.D. Diss., University of Aberdeen, UK.

Handwerker, W.P. 1979. Daily markets and urban economic development. *Human Organization* 38(4):366-376.

Harts-Broekhuis and O. Verkoren. 1987. Gender differentiation among market traders in central Mali. *Tijdschrift voor Economische en Sociale Geografie* 78(3):214-221.

Hill, P. 1986. *Development economics on trial*. Cambridge, UK: Cambridge University Press.

Hill, P. and R.H.T. Smith. 1972. The spatial and temporal synchronization of periodic markets: evidence from four emirates in northern Nigeria. *Economic Geography* 48:345-355.

Hollier, G. 1986. The marketing of gari in North-West Province, Cameroon. *Geografiska Annaler* 68B(1):59-68.

Patai, D. 1991. U.S. academics and Third World women: Is ethical research possible? In *Women's words: The feminist practice of oral history* (S.B. Gluck and D. Patai, eds.). New York, NY, USA, and London, UK: Routledge.

Peil, M. with P.K. Mitchell and D. Rimmer. 1982. *Social science research methods: An African Handbook*. London, UK: Hodder and Stoughton.

Plattner, S. (ed.). 1989. *Economic anthropology*. Stanford, CA, USA: Stanford University Press.

Porter, G. 1986. Periodic rural markets in Borno, north-east Nigeria. *Annals of Borno* 3:107-125.

———. 1988. Perspectives on trade, mobility and gender in a rural market system: Borno, north-east Nigeria. *Tijdschrift voor economische en sociale geografie* 79(2):82-93.

———. 1992. *Food marketing and urban food supply on the Jos Plateau: A comparison of large and small producer strategies under SAP, Jos Plateau Environmental Resources Development Programme*. Interim Report no. 29, Department of Geography, University of Durham, UK.

———. 1993. Changing accessibility and the reorganisation of rural markets in Nigeria. *Journal of Macromarketing* (Fall):54-63.

Punch, M. 1986. *The politics and ethics of fieldwork*. Beverly Hills, CA, USA: Sage.

Siddle, D.J. and K. Swindell. 1990. *Rural change in tropical Africa*. Oxford, UK: Basil Blackwell.

Smith, C.A. 1975. Examining stratification systems through peasant marketing arrangements: An application of some models from economic geography. *Man* (n.s.)(10):95-122.

———. 1976. Regional economic sytems: Linking geographical models and economic problems. In *Regional analysis*, Vol. 1. New York, NY, USA: Academic Press.

———. 1985. Methods for analysing periodic marketplaces as elements in regional trading systems. *Research in Economic Anthropology* 7:291-338.

Smith, R.H.T. 1979. Periodic marketplaces and periodic marketing: Review and prospect-I. *Progress in Human Geography* 3:471-505.

_____. 1980. Periodic marketplaces and periodic marketing: Review and prospect-II. *Progress in Human Geography* 4:1-31.

Strickland, D.A. and L.E. Schlesinger. 1969. "Lurking" as a research model. *Human Organization* 28:248-250.

Thorpe, J.K. 1978. Periodic markets in the Caspian lowlands of Iran. In *Marketplace trade-periodic markets, hawkers, and traders in Africa, Asia and Latin America* (R.H.T. Smith, ed). Center for Transportation Studies, University of British Colombia, Vancouver, Canada.

Trager, L. and R.H.T. Smith. 1981. Marketplaces in African urban studies: Introduction. *African Urban Studies* 10:1-20.

Vaus, D.A. de. 1990. *Surveys in social research*, 2nd Edition. London, UK: Unwin Hyman.

Werner, O. and G.M. Schoepfle. 1987. *Systematic fieldwork, Volume 1, Foundations of ethnography and interviewing*. Beverly Hills, CA, USA: Sage.

Wilson, K. 1993. Thinking about the ethics of fieldwork. In *Fieldwork in developing countries* (S. Devereux and J. Hoddinot, eds.). Boulder, CO, USA: Lynne Rienner.

Whitehead, T.L. and J. Brown. 1986. Gender-related issues in carrying out rapid team fieldwork in the Cameroon. In *Self, sex and gender in cross-cultural fieldwork* (T.L. Whitehead and M.E. Conway, eds.). Urbana, IL, USA: University of Illinois Press.

Whyte, W.F. 1984. *Learning from the field: a guide from experience*. Beverly Hills, CA, USA: Sage.

7

Wall-to-Wall Fieldwork: Secondary Data Collection for Food Systems Research[1]

Gregory J. Scott[2]

Abstract

Secondary data are often underutilized in research on food systems in developing countries. Reasons for this include incomplete knowledge about types of data available, where such data can most readily be procured, and how to go about collecting and presenting this information in the most efficient manner. This paper presents a series of practical guidelines on secondary data collection in developing countries. The observations should be of particular interest to those researchers engaged in studies of agricultural marketing who often face severe time and resource constraints that limit their capacity to collect primary data.

Key words: Production, marketing, consumption, marketing margins, foreign trade, research methods.

Introduction

Most researchers studying farm and food problems consider fieldwork for understanding these activities as information gathering in farmers' fields, in the market, or among a group of consumers. While several publications have presented procedures for primary data collection for agricultural research (see, e.g., Casley and Lury 1982), much less has been written about "wall-to-wall" fieldwork, i.e., collection of secondary data in offices, libraries, and labs.[3]

---

[1] This is a revised and abbreviated version of a paper presented at the Inaugural Planning Workshop on the User's Perspective with Agricultural Research and Development (UPWARD), Baguio, Philippines, 11-18 Nov., 1990.

[2] Economist, Social Science Department, International Potato Center, P.O. Box 1558, Lima, Peru.

[3] Holtzman (1986:22-30) refers briefly to the types of data utilized for the analysis of prices, marketing costs and margins, as well as the problems associated with this type of secondary data. For a general review of agricultural statistics in developing countries and proposed methods to improve their collection, see Idaikkadar (1979).

Consequently, many researchers tend to underestimate the potential, the process, and the problems associated with this type of data collection.

The underemphasis on secondary data reflects in part the tendency among some agricultural researchers to oversimplify the term "secondary data" itself. They often consider such numbers to be only regularly published government statistics. In fact, secondary data also include: primary data collected and published by other researchers, results of government research with limited circulation, and even unpublished primary data. The neglect of secondary data also indicates a certain lack of familiarity on the part of highly specialized researchers with the range of subjects for which secondary data are available. For example, those scientists who do research on food production problems are likely to be less aware of the information available on food consumption. This paper outlines the broad categories of secondary data that exist on food systems in developing countries as well as suggests how they can be used to answer questions about such systems. It also provides some pointers on where and how to locate this type of information. As will be pointed out throughout the paper and emphasized in a concluding section on how to present secondary data, any data collection exercise should begin with some hard thinking about what type of information is really necessary—be it primary or secondary.[4] Furthermore, once some secondary data are found, then accuracy must be assessed before they can be effectively utilized.

Why Collect Secondary Data?

There are at least three reasons to consider collecting secondary data either in lieu of or in addition to primary information. First, secondary data typically cost less time and money to collect than primary data. As Goetz and Weber (1986) observe, ". . . in many developing countries there are [is] often a surprising wealth of 'hidden' secondary data. . . Because of the substantial costs associated with implementing new primary surveys, researchers are well-advised to make every effort to find and examine existing data before deciding to invest in original data collection activity."

Second, secondary data can help define the scope for collection of primary statistics. Secondary data are frequently assumed to be highly inaccurate and therefore primary data are indispensable to get a reliable picture of the situation. More often than not, the degree of accuracy varies across types of secondary data. Hence, primary data may be necessary for some purposes but by no means all.

---

[4] Scott (1988) includes a list of basic questions about food systems in developing countries (see also Jones 1974).

Third, secondary data may be the only type of information available. Collection of any information is almost by definition restricted to a particular time and place. Clearly, primary data collection cannot go on in the past, nor can it be carried out simultaneously everywhere. In that sense, secondary data can provide knowledge about particular phenomena when it is impossible to collect primary data. This raises questions about types of secondary data found in developing countries.

What Kinds of Secondary Data Are Available?

Many more categories of secondary data can be collected in developing countries than is frequently realized. This situation develops in part because such information may not be continuously published or widely disseminated. It should be emphasized, however, that knowing certain information exists is itself no reason to include it in a research report. One always has to ask "is it relevant?" and "is it reliable?"[5] The following discussion—by no means intended to be exhaustive—focuses on four categories of secondary data.

Policy and development trends

Often one of the most frustrating, if not forgotten, aspects of food systems research relates to policy implications. Frustrating in the sense that researchers frequently can only wonder how their research might address policy concerns. Forgotten because some researchers become so immersed in their own study that they forget to ask themselves how their results might speak to policy issues. Food systems researchers can participate, albeit in absentia, in any number of policy debates to the extent that they are willing to analyze policy papers—written by or for policy makers—that are often quite readily available, e.g., the current Five-Year Plan.[6] A brief review of these documents can sharpen the focus of the study being undertaken. By mentioning the salient facts in the report itself, the researcher helps establish for the policy maker the importance of the findings being presented.

---

[5] Holtzman (1986:24-25) discusses the issue of reliability in the case of price data.

[6] Obviously some policy papers are more candid and accurate than others. Nevertheless, food systems researchers should at least be familiar with the ideas presented in them as part of the information-gathering exercise. If access to documents with this type of information proves difficult, publications found in most major university libraries such as the World Development Report and the Food Production Yearbook contain a wealth of statistics on economic development, agriculture, trade, health, and demography for virtually all developing countries.

Food production

Food systems research typically places major emphasis on understanding the production systems for food crops. Four general areas where secondary data can be useful are: production trends; location and timing of planting; types of farmers; and costs of production.

Detailed data collection on the production of a particular commodity at a particular time and place can often raise questions about its importance relative to other crops, or production this year in comparison with previous years. Collecting primary data on area planted in different crops is one way to estimate their relative importance. Another would be to review available secondary statistics. At a minimum, consulting the secondary data can help alert the researcher as to the types of crops that are grown and therefore that should be considered in primary data collection.

Two key questions associated with understanding cropping systems are: "where are different crops grown?" and "when are these crops produced?" Comparing production statistics for different regions can facilitate identification of major and minor areas of production. Extending the tabulation of secondary data to include several different points in time can provide interesting indications on how the location of output may have shifted over time. Reviewing production trends for the country as a whole or for particular regions need not make clear the emergence of more important growing areas and the decline of others. A simple pie-chart, based on the percentage of national production produced in different districts, illustrates these changes quite sharply (Figure 1).

Planting and harvesting dates are important information for understanding the production system for any food crop. This is especially true where different regions interact with each other (for the exchange of seed) and with the market throughout the year as is the case for potatoes in Thailand. Specifying this complex calendar of activities was made easier by reviewing the literature to define zones of production and the corresponding cropping cycle in each and presenting them in graphic form (Figure 2).

In most developing countries, food crops are grown by more than one type of farmer. Food systems researchers can attempt to develop a typology of farmers based on a formal survey or by comparing results of farm surveys carried out in different parts of the country. Data from such surveys are frequently available in developing countries. By pulling the information in the various survey reports together, one can easily develop a typology for a large group of farmers.

Production costs for a particular food crop—including the share of total costs spent on particular inputs (e.g., seed, fertilizer)—can offer extremely useful insights into production patterns. Deriving estimates of such costs based

Figure 1. Percentage of potato production in the principal districts of Bangladesh, 1960-85.

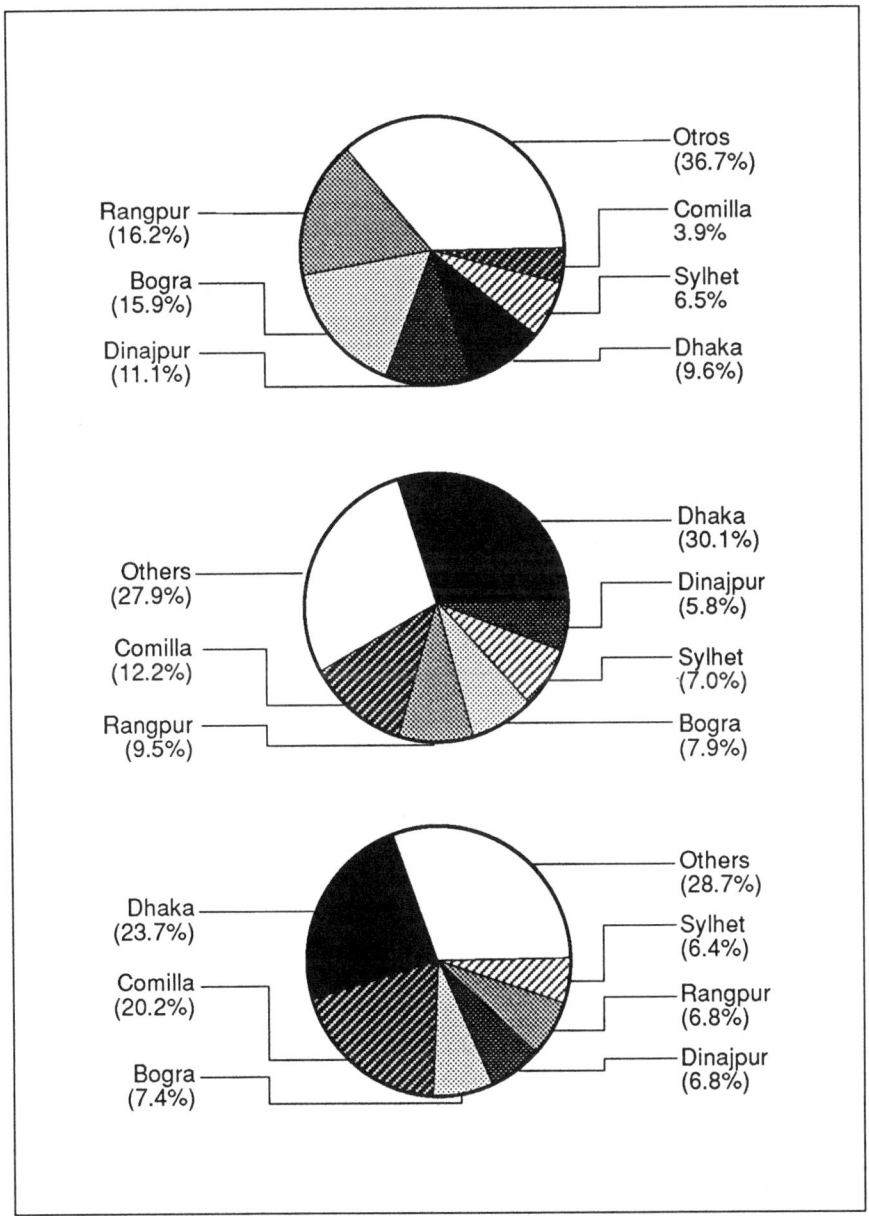

on primary data collection can require a tremendous amount of time and energy. Alternatively, an approximation of these costs can be formulated using results of previously published farm surveys alluded to above. Comparing results from different sites provides a composite of the relative importance of different inputs nationwide.

Food marketing

Food systems research also focuses on marketing activities. The following types of secondary data can be useful for understanding marketing systems in

Figure 2. An agricultural calendar for potato in Thailand.

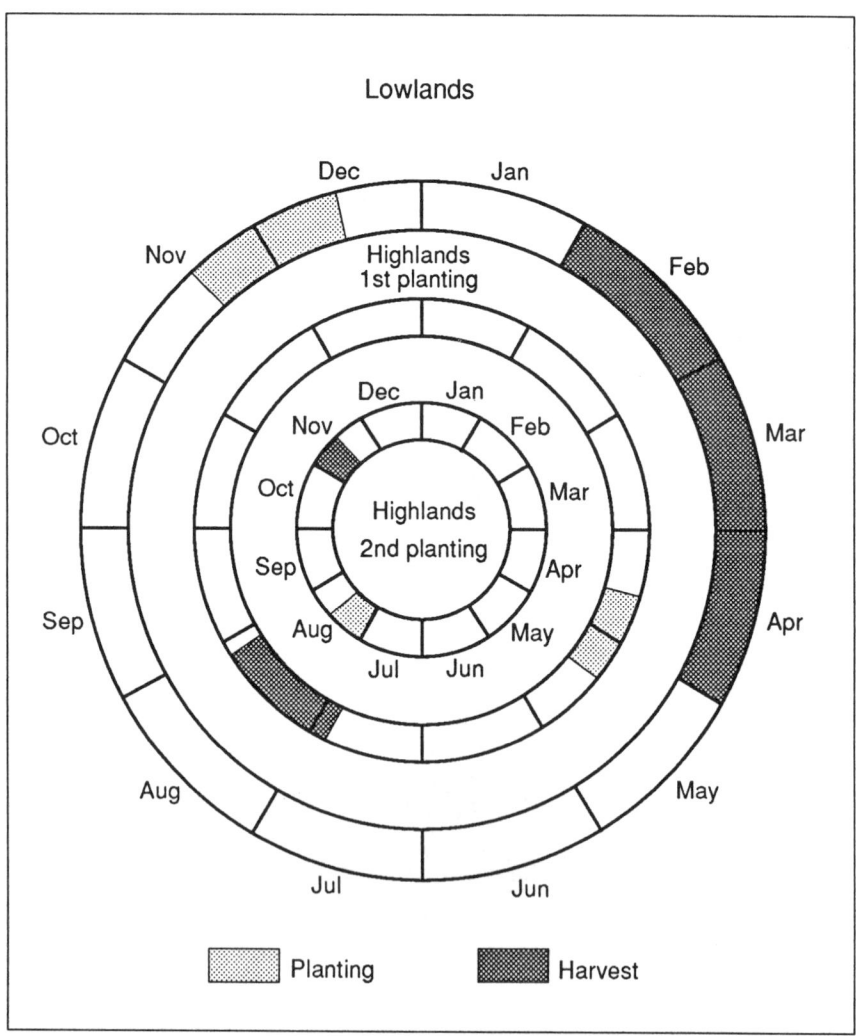

developing countries: foreign trade; percentage of output sold; prices; margins; and volumes sold.

The volume and value of imports plus exports provides one measure of the importance of foreign trade, while there may be concern about the accuracy of official trade statistics. Secondary data nevertheless do provide some indications of the quantities involved. If nothing else, these figures constitute a convenient benchmark against which the results of primary data collection can be compared.

Many marketing studies are concerned with the degree of market integration of producers in a particular region or for a specific crop. Estimates of the quantity of output sold are indispensable for determining this behavior. Secondary data gleaned from farm surveys may well provide indications of the percentage of output sold—even over an extended period of time. At a minimum, one should be familiar with these results before undertaking survey work to estimate this variable directly.

Prices are perhaps the most basic piece of market information. Issues of interest here include the evolution of prices over time, the price of one food crop versus another, differences in prices for distinct varieties, and so on. Food systems researchers are frequently tempted to collect this type of information themselves to be sure of the accuracy of the data. While Holtzman (1986: 22-29) indicates the problems and pitfalls in the use of government price data, he also points out that "researchers need not be paralyzed if data collection methods fall short of the ideal. Rather, analysts need to view prices as approximations which provide insights into the workings of markets, the relative scarcity of resources, and incentives facing food system participants."[7]

Policy makers in most developing countries have a keen interest in the size and evolution of marketing margins for agricultural commodities, particularly those for basic food stuffs. One way to estimate these margins is to conduct a detailed survey of marketing costs and returns. However, a separate survey questionnaire and reasonable sample size for each type of trader requires considerable resources. An analysis of secondary data can provide some general idea of the relative size of the marketing margin of different middlemen (see, e.g., Timmer et al. 1983:171-173, Table 1). In addition, producer prices—gleaned from several years of farm surveys—combined with government statistics on wholesale and retail prices can offer one estimate of the size and evolution of the marketing margins for most food crops in developing countries

---

[7] The questions Holtzman (1986) raises include the training of people who collect such data; definitions of particular statistics and whether they have changed over time; location of data collection and of such information and how it is aggregated; and consistency in who, where, when, and how such data are recorded and analyzed.

(see, e.g., Table 1). In so doing, it can indicate which margin(s) may merit more detailed data collection of a primary nature.

Shipments and price movements for food commodities to major urban markets constitute another marketing topic of widespread concern in developing countries. Policy makers want to know when to expect shortages (or gluts) so as to try and reduce these fluctuations. A first step in this regard is having the necessary information to develop if recurrent supply patterns exist.[8] Typically major urban markets in developing countries do little more than collect this type of information. These numbers can provide the basis for some extremely useful analysis, for example, month-to-month changes in real versus nominal prices over time (Figure 3).

Food consumption

For the food systems researcher, consumption (and utilization) of agricultural commodities is another basic area of inquiry. How production is consumed (or utilized); consumption levels for particular commodities, over time and by different classes of consumers; the relative importance of a particular foodstuff in diets; changes in diets over the years; and the impact of income and/or price changes on food consumption are all issues of vital importance.

Table 1. Prices and sales margins for potato sold in Dhaka, Bangladesh, 1981-85.[a]

	1981	1982	1982-83	1983	1985
Producer's price	1.27	1.07	1.09	1.29	1.33
Margin (%)	67	57	58	69	60
Wholesaler's price	1.43	1.36	1.45	1.55	1.73
Margin (%)	8	15	19	14	18
Retailer's price	1.9	1.88	1.87	1.86	2.2
Margin (%)	25	28	22	17	21

[a] Sources: Producer's price: 1981 (Elías and Islam 1982:36); 1982 (Elías et al. 1982); 1982-83 (Elías et al. 1984a:49); 1983 (Shidker and Rob 1984); 1985 (Maziruddin 1986). Wholesaler's price: 1981, 1982, 1982-83, 1983 (Shidker and Rob 1984); 1985 (Maziruddin 1986). Retailer's price: 1981, 1982, 1982-83 (Economic Indicators of Bangladesh); 1983 (Shidker and Rob 1984); 1985 (Maziruddin 1986).

---

[8] Goetz and Weber (1986:64-97) provide instructions for computerized seasonal analysis of monthly time-series data such as prices and volumes; see also the chapter by Tschirley in this volume.

Figure 3. Real versus nominal prices for potato in Lima, Peru, 1960-79.

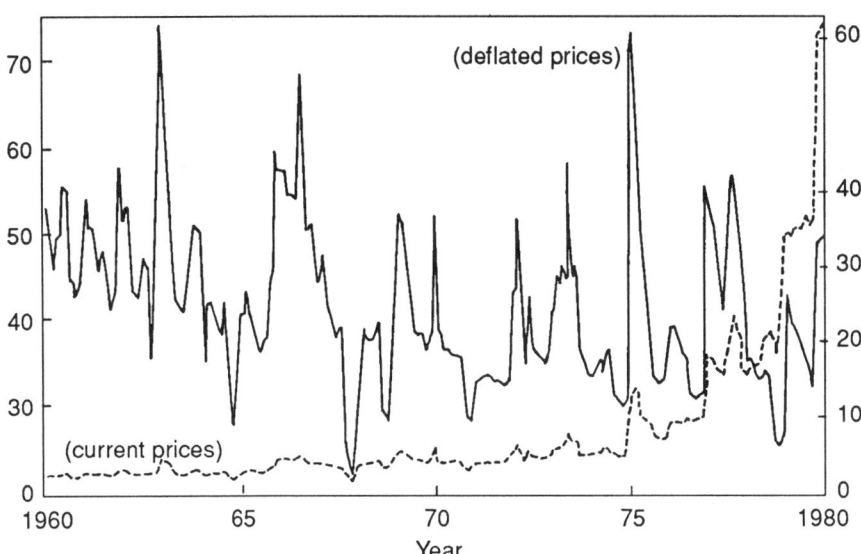

Statistics on the level of annual per capita consumption of a given food commodity provide a benchmark against other consumption indicators. A variety of secondary sources can be consulted to estimate this statistic: published results of household consumption or nutrition surveys; findings based on farmer interviews; figures prepared by the Food and Agricultural Organization of the United Nations (FAO). Furthermore, synthesizing the various results serves as a check on the veracity of any single estimate.

Food systems researchers may be interested in more than just the absolute consumption levels of a particular food commodity, e.g., in its importance in the overall diet. Estimating this importance directly requires a massive amount of primary data. Secondary data are another option. Results of household consumption or nutrition surveys are one source. National (or local) estimates of dietary composition based on production and foreign trade statistics combined with estimates of utilization patterns (for seed, for industrial use, losses) and population are another. FAO also publishes such Food Balance Sheet data (Table 2). These figures can be misleading because they may be based on unreliable production estimates (see, e.g., Horton 1988). They nevertheless are estimates that the interested researcher should be aware of as they are the ones policy makers are often accustomed to utilizing.

Table 2. Daily per capita consumption of calories and proteins by principal food groups in Zaire 1979-80.

Food Groups	Available calories per capita (#/day)	Percent of total	Available protein per capita (g/day)	Percent of total
Roots and Tubers	1,243	59.4	8.0	24.5
Sweetpotato	(23)	(1.1)	(0.3)	(0.9)
Cassava flour	(1,193)	(57.0)	(7.2)	(22.1)
Potato	(8)	(0.4)	(0.2)	(0.6)
Cereals	309	14.8	7.7	23.6
Legumes	39	1.9	2.6	8.0
(dried beans)	(24)	(1.1)	(1.6)	(4.9)
Fruits	131	6.3	1.4	4.3
Oils & fats	163	7.8	0.0	0.0
Meats & meat byproducts	39	1.9	4.2	12.9
Milk	3	0.1	0.3	0.9
Vegetables	31	1.5	2.3	7.1
Seeds and oil products	97	4.6	4.2	12.9
Fish and seafood	12	0.6	1.	5.5
Sugar and honey	24	1.1	0.0	0.0
Eggs	1	0.0	0.1	0.3
Total	2,073[a]	100.0	32.3	100.0

[a] Consumers in Zaire also obtained 33 calories and 0.4 g of protein daily per capita by drinking alcoholic beverages.

Often policy makers and planners are less interested in a detailed descriptive analysis of current consumption patterns than they are concerned about future developments. One essential element in estimating future demand for food involves calculating the effect of possible income changes on consumption. In lieu of collecting massive amounts of primary data, one can combine estimates of income elasticities from secondary sources with government statistics on per capita income trends to calculate increases in the demand for food. Food demand estimates prepared for government documents like the most recent national Five-Year Plan is another way to procure such figures.

The examples cited are by no means exhaustive in terms of the types of data available. Rather, they are intended to suggest the various possibilities that exist. The paper now turns to a discussion of where one finds this type of information.

Where to Find Secondary Data?

Many more institutions have information about food production, consumption, and marketing than may at first be apparent. These include public sector organizations, multilateral and bilateral agencies, and private enterprise sources. As considerable diversity exists, a concise review is appropriate.

Public sector organizations

The public sector in any developing country typically includes administrative/ policy making institutions (APIs) at the national, regional, and local level. National APIs that have data on food systems include government ministries, the office of national planning, national census bureau, and bureau of statistics. Information about particular data can sometimes be found in the central offices of such bureaucracies (e.g., within the Ministry of Agriculture, the Office of Food Crop Production) or in the respective institution's library or documentation center. If local or regional data are what one is after, it may be easier to find it in the provinces.

Libraries at universities or rural development institutes are often overlooked as possible sources of secondary data. Such locations are frequently depositories of student theses, research reports by the teaching staff, and reference documents published by national and international organizations. Most importantly, such libraries often do not throw up the same restrictions on access to data that APIs do.[9]

Central wholesale markets frequently record the only data available on food prices or volumes. Many retail markets also have an administrative section that regularly collects and disseminates prices for the food products sold there. It may even turn out that these prices are more accurate (i.e., by variety, grade) or more complete (types of products monitored) than official figures found elsewhere.

The research department of the Central Bank in many developing countries typically publishes reports assessing the economy's performance. Such publications abound with numeric tables and statistical appendices that include, for example, data on foreign trade and commodity prices. More specialized lending institutions, such as the agrarian bank, produce sector-specific statistical reports. These documents contain a great deal of useful information.

---

[9] In fact, in one country I worked in, I spent several days getting the proper authorization to enter a particular Ministry office only to discover that the exact same data was available to the public at a university library conveniently located nearby.

Multilateral and bilateral agencies

Local offices of the World Bank (and its regional affiliates, the Inter-American Development Bank, the African Development Bank, and the Asian Development Bank) and FAO have copies of reports like the World Development Report (World Bank); the annual Production and Trade Yearbooks (FAO), and Food Balance Sheet Estimates (FAO). Other international organizations that can generate secondary data include the United Nations Development Program (UNDP) and the International Labor Office (ILO). These offices (or missions) also coordinate research by local and international specialists. Results of these studies (e.g., Agricultural Sector Surveys) can be very informative.

The International Agricultural Research Centers (IARCs) such as the International Potato Center (CIP), International Rice Research Institute (IRRI), and the International Center for Wheat and Maize Improvement (CIMMYT) also have offices in different developing countries. The Inter-American Institute for Cooperation in Agriculture (IICA) has one or more offices in nearly every Latin American country. Publications found at these offices can provide specialized data on local agricultural topics.

In many developing countries, foreign governments maintain offices for their foreign aid agencies. These offices frequently have a library/documentation center, files for research/consultancy reports by local or foreign researchers, and some government reports or publications that may be hard to find elsewhere. These publication often include the yearly report by the embassy's agricultural attaches. Such publications typically are jammed with secondary data as well as comments on the government's growth projections and development plans.

Private enterprise sources

Private sector sources for secondary data include non-government organizations (NGOs), and private firms as well as trade associations and banks. Many NGOs combine action-oriented development work—on agricultural production, food marketing, or household nutrition—with research projects in support of these activities. Although the project-specific focus of this research may limit its relevance, the detailed material contained in such documents often can be quite useful.

Many private banks and credit unions in developing countries gather statistics about the local economy. Some of these institutions publish reports or even sponsor research journals. Others keep copies of studies undertaken in their files for reference or to help evaluate possible new lending initiatives. Similarly, input supply firms can offer prices for production inputs. Privately-owned storage facilities may keep records of local prices for agricultural commodities. Trade associations (e.g., producer co-operatives, merchant organizations, cold storage associations, transport cooperatives) often employ staff to keep records of important statistics. These figures often may be made available for consultation by interested researchers.

Given that so many different institutions and locations have some secondary data, and not every organization may have the same statistics, the attached guideline indicates which type of data are most likely to be found where (Table 3). It includes most likely ("best bet") and possible ("worth a try") locations for each sub-set of data indicated.

How to Procure Secondary Data?

Identifying what data you need plus where to find them are often the only easy parts of secondary data collection. Knowing how to actually obtain the statistics in question requires a different set of skills. This component of wall-to-wall fieldwork has to do with persistence, a disposition to give and take, plus investing a professional attitude into interactions with civil servants, foreign specialists, bankers, and development project personnel.

Persistence

One basic tenet of secondary data collection in developing countries is "to get what you want, you just have to keep looking." As Goetz and Weber (1986) observe, "[m]any analysts tend to underinvest in seeking out sources of data because this requires persistence in visiting agencies and finding knowledgeable people who can adequately inform them about data collection activities. Investments in obtaining and utilizing existing data are also not as interesting (and sometimes) not as productive as designing a primary study." A good deal of persistence is required for the following, perfectly understandable, reasons:

- Many offices, libraries, and labs that dispense statistics in developing countries are understaffed, and the data solicited may require considerable extra work. Administrators may want time to verify credentials and to discourage capricious investigators before rounding up the figures requested.
- The office first visited may be in the wrong place (due to inexperience on the researcher's part). The more obscure the statistic, the bigger the institution, then the greater the likelihood that it will require visits to several offices to locate.
- The institution may require that all other possible sources be explored before it agrees to part with the data. Some figures may not be released, prior to publication, simply upon request.

Table 3. Guide to the use of secondary information (● = best bet; ■ = worth a try).

Type of information required	1	2	3	4	5	6	7	8	9	10	11	12	13	14	15	16
Agricultural policy	●		●	■	●					■			■	■		
Strategic planning	●		●	■	●					■			■			
Marketing projects	●				●			●		●	●	●		■		■
Economic indicators	■		●	●	●					●	■					
Production, area & yield	●						●			●			■	■		
Costs of production	●		●		■		●		■				■			
Farm price	●		■		■	■	●	■		■					■	
Farm credit	●		■	■	■	■	●			●			■	■		■
Farm output projections	●				●											
Farm calendar	●				●											
Varieties	●								●					■		
Food balance sheets	●		■			●	●			●		■				
Food expenditures	●	■	●	■			●			●			■			
Food consumption	●						●			■			●	■		■
Nutritional intake	●		■							■			●	■		■
Foreign trade, volume and value	●	●	●	■	■	■				●	■					
Domestic trade, volume and value	●	●					■			■						
Urban prices and price indices	●	●			■	■			●							
Income and price elasticities				●		■				●		■	●			
Marketing infrastructure	●												■			
Marketing margins	●	●	■		■	■	■						■			
Employment patterns				●	■		●			●			■	■		■
Rainfall	●					■			●	■					●	
Maps	●				●			■	●				■			

Where the information can be found: 1. Ministry of Agriculture; 2. Ministry of Commerce; 3. Ministry of Economics and Finance; 4. Central Bank; 5. Planning Office; 6. National Bureau of Statistics; 7. Agrarian Bank; 8. Central Market Administrative Office; 9. Experimental Station; 10. FAO or World Bank offices; 11. Foreign Embassy; 12. Nutritional Institute; 13. University Library; 14. Bilateral Agricultural Project Office; 15. Weather Station; 16. NGO Office.

Being aware of the factors that can influence the amount of effort required to obtain secondary data should help you maintain the persistence necessary to see the job through. It should also make you realize that unrealistically short periods of time allocated to collect secondary data can put you under unnecessary pressure.

Give and take of data collection

As the ultimate goal of any research exercise is to try and put useful information into the hands of a wider audience, this applies as much to the information one has as to the information one hopes to get. Put somewhat differently, most people receive information as well as give it out. Is this the "Catch-22" of secondary data collection? After all, if one had information to share, then presumably one would not be out looking for data. Or, what sort of information does one who is looking for secondary data have to give out? In fact, any researcher should be able to offer several facts.

The first of these is a brief description of the objectives and methodology being employed in the research project itself. This includes institutional affiliation and the potential implications of the research (possibly for the institution being visited, the region's farmers, or consumers). By volunteering this information most people want to respond with something from their side.

Once some data have been collected, one typically has several additional facts to offer to those encountered at a latter stage in the data collection. One can provide people with the figures themselves. In addition, one can also explain the places and publications where such information can be found as advice on where data collection efforts may have been unsuccessful. Furthermore, presenting people with a copy of the final report can also help pay them back for the time invested in providing data.

Being professional

Most administrators responsible for considerable quantities of information tend to treat people in a serious, professional manner who conduct themselves in a similar fashion. One practical suggestion on how to procure secondary data professionally would be a letter of presentation including a shortened version of the research proposal. When meeting someone, offering a professional card also can be a convenient way to say this is not a frivolous request. Furthermore, if one would like to delegate data collection responsibility, one should always accompany the research assistant the first time to introduce oneself and explain the reasons for the visit. Although many libraries and documentation centers are open to the public during regular business hours, it can be very effective to call ahead and make an appointment. An appointment is not only a professional courtesy but it allows people the opportunity to prepare themselves. It also shows that one treats the matter seriously enough and implies that so should they.

A cardinal rule for effective interaction with librarians, data specialists, credit officers is that one defines clearly for them what it is that is being solicited. If these people sense that a particular researcher doesn't know what he/she wants, they are liable to treat requests for information as impulsive or too open-ended and one may wind up with seemingly inexplicable delays. Conversely, if one has read the readily available background material, then people are usually inclined to act more promptly on requests and even volunteer certain data that one may be unaware of. Similarly, when one goes to an office to record particular statistics, be sure and go prepared to record such information. Otherwise, a straightforward exercise becomes burdensome and it prompts people to become uncooperative very quickly.

Researchers typically have greater success in securing secondary data to the extent to which they demonstrate their willingness to do the work themselves. That's not to say that questions about secondary data to the people who publish them, for example, are inappropriate. Rather, it means keeping all questions to a minimum until one has gone through the material carefully and tried to answer as many of these as independently as possible. Let the administrators, librarian or statistician utilize their energy in helping to obtain the information. It's the researcher's job to understand it.

One particular point of caution is also in order. Many the relatively inexperienced researcher who does find his way to a comfortable university library to discover some useful material winds up spending weeks preparing tedious reviews of all the available literature. He would never do this in a cramped government office. If someone plans to spend three weeks scouting out secondary data, he should probably spend 1-2 days in university libraries, get what he needs and move on. However, if you don't take these 1-2 days, you can end up like the research team that dismissed the idea of a literature review as a waste of time only to find at the end of their data collection a nearly identical study had already been done recently.

Here's a quick routine for reviewing the literature. Use the library card file (or computer search) to look for publications by subject matter, then go through the titles noting what looks relevant. Once the document itself has been located, quickly survey the table of contents; then scan the parts on objectives and methods. Next, turn to the conclusions and read them carefully. Finally, check the bibliography for other useful references and run through the data presented to determine if some (or all) should be cited in the on-going study. Avoid getting bogged down by reading reports from cover to cover; or, going in circles for having failed to be systematic. These suggestions should help extract the relevant material in a number of studies quickly and thereby free time to read more thoroughly the most appropriate documents and records.

If someone provides access to certain information with the understanding that it not be distributed to the general public prior to the publication of a first report, respect that understanding. If someone loans public documents **always** return them and make every effort to do so promptly. The same holds true for personal copies of research reports, statistical yearbooks or other reference materials that may have been lent out.

Most people don't insist that they be thanked for their assistance, but they certainly appreciate some recognition of their efforts. Operational ways to do this include exchanging data, offering copies of final reports, providing assistance in their research endeavors. In addition, people generally like to see their names in print. Those that have been particularly helpful deserve mention in the acknowledgements section at the beginning of the final report. If the report includes data or ideas from other publications, the reference should be cited in the text or table and included in the bibliography. Otherwise, future secondary data collection will be quite difficult. Moreover, serious readers may want to know where the original information can be found so they can verify the findings should they so desire.

How to Present Secondary Data?

Perhaps the most useful bit of advice on the presentation of secondary data goes back to the issue of relevance. A draft table of contents of the final research report, thesis, or study prepared in conjunction with the original project proposal can serve at least two useful purposes. First, it can map out prior to data collection the types of data that are absolutely necessary for the research to be successfully completed. This checklist can then keep secondary data collection focused on the essential and help avoid chasing down information that may be interesting, but irrelevant.

Second, it can pinpoint where reference to the secondary data—if not the figures themselves—should be presented in the publication itself. The reader can be greatly assisted in the appreciation of the data available in the document to the extent that the final table of contents includes a complete list of tables, appendix tables, figures, and maps.

If the report includes an abundance of data, it may well prove more useful to the reader to include only summary tables in the main text and place the basic data in an Appendix. This will reduce the chances that the reader will get bogged down in numbers and lose sight of the analysis and its implications for the research issues in question.

Presentation of secondary data can be a great deal more effective when it includes forms other than the standard table involving columns and rows of numbers. Pie charts (Figure 1), graphs (Figure 2), and plotting of time-series data (Figure 3) can be eye-catching, as well as illustrate the otherwise less readily apparent configuration of the numbers, and often facilitate synthesis of massive numbers of statistics. They also break the monotony of tabular presentation. Regardless of the form considered most appropriate, the source of the information presented should always be indicated.

Conclusion

This paper has addressed the problem of collecting secondary data on food systems in developing countries. The paper emphasized at the outset that secondary data refer to much more than simply regularly published government statistics. It went on to suggest that there are at least three reasons for collecting this type of information rather than investing scarce available resources in primary data collection. Subsequent sections offered examples of the broad categories and sub-categories of secondary data that are available on food systems, where they might be located, and how they might be procured.

In the final section, a series of suggestions were made on how presentation of secondary data in research reports might be made more user-friendly and eye-catching. Throughout the paper, researchers were cautioned regarding the importance of assessing the need for particular secondary data (more figures than necessary can obscure rather than enlighten), as well as the accuracy of such figures prior to their collection.

References

Casley, D.J. and D.A. Lury. 1982. *Data collection in developing countries.* New York, NY, USA: Oxford University Press.

Goetz, S. and M. T. Weber. 1986. *Fundamentals of price analysis in developing countries' food systems: A training manual to accompany the microcomputer software program "MSTAT."* MSU International Development Papers. Working Paper No. 29. Department of Agricultural Economics, Michigan State University, East Lansing, MI, USA.

Holtzman, J. S. 1986. *Rapid reconnaissance guidelines for agricultural marketing and food system research in developing countries.* MSU International Development Papers. Working Paper No. 30. Department of Agricultural Economics, Michigan State University, East Lansing, MI, USA.

Horton, D. E. 1988. *Underground crops: Long-term trends in production of roots and tubers.* Winrock International, Morrilton, IL, USA.

Idaikkadar, N.M. 1979. *Agricultural Statistics.* New York, NY, USA: Pergamon Press.

Jones, W.O. 1974. Regional analysis and agricultural marketing research in tropical Africa: Concepts and experience. *Food Research Institute Studies* 13:3-28.

Scott, G. J. 1987. *Marketing Thailand's potatoes: Present patterns and future prospects.* Potatoes in Food Systems Research Series Report No. 3. International Potato Center (CIP). Lima, Peru.

_____. 1988. *Potatoes in Central Africa: A study of Burundi, Rwanda and Zaire.* International Potato Center (CIP). Lima, Peru.

_____. 1988a. *Marketing Bangladesh's potatoes: Present patterns and future prospects.* International Potato Center (CIP) and Australian Development Assistance Bureau (ADAB), Dhaka, Bangladesh.

Timmer, C.P., W.P. Falcon, S.R. Pearson. 1983. *Food policy analysis.* Published for the World Bank. Baltimore, MD, USA: The John Hopkins University Press.

8

Field and Analytical Methods for Agricultural Commercialization Studies: Guatemala

Maarten D.C. Immink, Ricardo Sibrián, Jorge A. Alarcón, and Herwig Hahn [1]

Abstract

Agricultural commercialization coupled with crop diversification has become an important policy instrument for agricultural and rural development in many developing countries. This paper shares methodological insights gained from a number of agricultural commercialization studies conducted in Guatemala. These studies dealt with the short- and long-term impacts among smallholder farmers of crop diversification and commercialization (including for foreign markets) on household resource allocation, farm production, off-farm employment, household income, health, and nutrition. The salient methodological aspects of the three studies are summarized, following a brief discussion of some of the main issues related to agricultural commercialization in developing countries.

Lessons learned from the studies include the need for a closer link between field research and follow-up actions, greater participation by farmers and others in designing the field study, an up-front conceptual-analytical framework to help focus the study on the most relevant research questions and variables to be measured, the inclusion of an operational research component of the commercialization process, and a great deal of sensitivity in applying field methodologies in particular cultural settings. A conceptual framework is presented, and key variables are operationalized in terms of specific indicators. Five different statistical techniques (factor analysis, probit regression

---

[1] Visiting Researcher, International Food Policy Research Institute, Washington, D.C., USA; Statistician, Institute of Nutrition of Central America and Panama, Guatemala City, Guatemala; Freelance Consultant, Lima, Peru; and Researcher, Justus-Liebig University, Giessen, Germany.

analysis, analysis of variance of repeated measures, decomposition analysis, and cluster analysis) to examine specific research questions are applied to the data from the studies.

Key words: Agricultural commercialization, Guatemala, smallholder farmers, research strategies, field methods, analytical frameworks.

Introduction

Agricultural commercialization, particularly in connection with the production of new crops for export, has become an important policy measure in many developing countries. It is seen as a means to generate new sources of foreign exchange, as well as to generate rural development through higher incomes and increased employment. Vertical integration of production, processing, and marketing may well be the key to capturing more of the postharvest value added of the new products. Risk alleviation, particularly for smallholder producers, is another important element, requiring adequate credit schemes and extension services, as well as efficient marketing institutions and infrastructure, timely market information, and effective farmer organizations. Lastly, the national policy environment must be "right", i.e., foreign exchange and external trade policies, fiscal policies, domestic price policies, and agricultural development measures should all be conducive to the expansion in new crop production and provide the right market signals. It is a tall order for all these conditions to be fulfilled at the same time, which may account for the fact that the development impact of these strategies varies significantly from country to country.

The agricultural transformation process in Guatemala is a much-studied phenomenon. Even at present a number of studies are underway—particularly among smallholder farmers—which focus on the expansion in the production, processing, and marketing of new export crops. Much of what follows is based on three studies conducted in Guatemala in which the authors were directly involved.

Field studies are generally undertaken in developing countries to test hypotheses. It is the data and the statistical results that are usually reported (with a brief explanation of the applied methods), to allow peers to evaluate the validity of the reported results. But field studies also generate important methodological lessons from which other researchers can benefit. These are, however, less often shared.

This paper shares some methodological insights from three agricultural commercialization studies conducted in Guatemala. Three methodological elements from these studies are highlighted here: the underlying conceptual framework for the studies and its operationalization in terms of variables and indicators; research strategies and study design; and selected analytical approaches and statistical techniques that were subsequently applied to analyze the data in relation to specific research issues. A description of the three Guatemalan studies follows after a brief discussion of the empirical evidence related to some main issues in agricultural commercialization studies. These issues cast the agricultural commercialization process in a broader development perspective.

Main Issues in Agricultural Commercialization Studies

The Guatemalan studies essentially focused on research issues related to the economic, social, food availability, health, and nutrition outcomes associated with crop diversification and commercialization among smallholder farmers. Both the income and nutritional effects among children of shifts from subsistence to cash crop production are likely to be place- and time-specific, as an early review of several studies has pointed out (von Braun and Kennedy 1986). Structural and other factors may mediate the effects of commercialization of agriculture among smallholder farmers, such as access to high-quality land, ecological conditions, off-farm employment opportunities, market access, and agricultural and price policies (DeWalt et al. 1990). In addition, several potential risk factors can be identified. These include marked price variability over time for cash crops and agricultural inputs, crop failures, weak and inefficient marketing institutions, lack of infrastructure, high input requirements which increase the need for credit and extension services, and lack of timely information about market conditions which may lead to an inefficient allocation of household resources.

A consistent body of empirical evidence from different settings indicates that the income effects from agricultural transformation towards cash cropping in the subsistence sector are generally positive, and can reduce income inequality among farmers adopting new cash crops (Kennedy 1989; von Braun, Puetz, and Webb 1989; Bouis and Haddad 1990; Finlayson et al. 1991; von Braun, de Haen, and Blanken 1991). At least one of the three studies discussed in detail in this paper points to this same conclusion (von Braun, Hotchkiss, and Immink 1989), while another seems to suggest the opposite (Immink and Alarcón 1993). The question of redistributive effects between diversified farmers, and non-diversified farmers and the landless poor have not been investigated. It can be argued, for example, that higher land values and credit costs, higher food prices, and increased rural employment opportunities associated with the agricultural transformation process may produce re-distributive effects.

Household income gains, at least within the observed ranges associated with shifts from subsistence to cash crops among smallholder farm households, are not likely to be sufficient to produce significant improvements in child nutrition in the short-run (Kennedy, Bouis, and von Braun 1992). The nutritional effect from shifts away from subsistence crops and towards cash crops has been a controversial issue. One concern is that the displacement of food crops by cash crops reduces household food availability from a farmer's own production (Lunven 1982; Fleuret and Fleuret 1980; Dewey 1979; Lappe and Collins 1977; Hernández et al. 1974). This reduction in food availability may not be offset by positive income effects in light of a weak income-dietary energy intake relationship (Bouis and Haddad 1992). On the other hand, food crop yields have been shown to increase with some shifts to cash crops, at least partially offsetting the effect of the shift in the land use pattern (von Braun, Hotchkiss, and Immink 1989). Household labor inputs (per unit of land) are likely to be higher in non-traditional crops, thus raising the household's daily dietary energy requirements (Gross and Underwood 1971). Few studies have systematically examined this issue, however. Increased female employment has been hypothesized to reduce child care with detrimental outcomes for child nutrition (Popkin 1980). Lower nutritional quality of the daily diet as a result of changed food intake patterns has also been expressed as a concern (Dewey 1981).

It has been argued that higher real income of farmers adopting cash crops may reduce the incidence of communicable diseases through improved access to curative and preventive health services, and better environmental sanitation (Glover and Kuterer 1990; Netting, Priscilla, and Stone 1989). Yet the high use of agrochemicals in non-traditional crop production has been shown to result in a higher incidence of chronic illnesses and acute diseases, and in negative long-term health effects (Murray and Hoppin 1992; Rosenstock et al. 1991; Vargas, Caballero, and Gutiérrez 1991). Furthermore, high pesticide use associated with non-traditional crops can also pose a serious health and ecological hazard by contaminating water supplies and destroying ecological systems (Murray and Hoppin 1992).

It has also been argued that non-traditional crop production may facilitate entry of women into the labor market or offer women additional employment choices (Alberti 1990; Arizpe and Aranda 1986; Blumberg 1985). This needs to be weighed against any negative effects associated with greater demands on women's time, as indicated above. As cash crops are often more labor intensive relative to traditional crops, a shift toward cash crops may be expected to reduce seasonal migration; this, in turn, may have beneficial effects by preserving family unity and lowering exposure to ethnic tensions for former migrants (Tucker and Castañeda 1991; Glover and Kuterer 1990). One issue that has received little attention relates to the effects of relatively greater competitiveness in cash cropping on social cohesion, cultural values, and traditional organizations. Greater time constraints may also negatively affect people's participation in community development efforts.

Three Agricultural Commercialization Studies in Guatemala

The export-led growth in Guatemala during the 1970s was severely compromised during the first half of the 1980s. The exchange rate policy at the time resulted in an overvalued national currency; exports were implicitly taxed, while domestic prices of imported agricultural inputs rose substantially. But despite erratic trends during the first half of the 1980s, foreign markets for vegetables from Guatemala generally expanded, while domestic production of basic grains, particularly maize, grew little. Between 1980 and 1990, the market value of vegetable exports increased almost fourfold. However, production costs increased sharply during the late 1980s, due to the depreciation in domestic currency. The total land extension in non-traditional export crops increased slightly, but in basic grains decreased significantly during the late 1980s. Market risks increased for smallholder producers, as quality standards related to pesticide and herbicide residues became stricter in foreign markets, resulting more frequently in the rejection of imported produce. The agricultural policy for the second half of the 1980s, as first announced in the 1984-86 National Development Plan, stressed as major goals the diversification of agricultural production for foreign and domestic markets, and increased food production.

For the remainder of this paper we will principally draw on the experiences of three field studies conducted in Guatemala in 1985, 1987, and 1991. These studies dealt with the short- and long-term impacts of agricultural diversification and commercialization among smallholder farmers on household resource allocation (principally labor and land), farm production, household income, health, and nutrition. The 1985 and 1991 studies were conducted in the same population, and entail a partial overlap of the same sample households. This affords an opportunity to compare results over time in the same population, and thus examine some sustainability issues related to agricultural commercialization. Detailed findings have been published elsewhere (Immink and Alarcón 1993; von Braun, Hotchkiss, and Immink 1989). The salient methodological features of the studies are summarized in Table 1.

Export vegetables production and marketing (1985)

Household-level effects of the agricultural commercialization process among smallholder farmers in the central highlands of Guatemala were the main focus of this study. The objective was to trace the linkages starting from the adoption

Table 1. Summary of methodological aspects of three agricultural commercialization studies in Guatemala, 1985, 1987 and 1991.

Methodological characteristics	1985 Study	1987 Study	1991 Study
Basic study design	Cross-sectional; comparison groups	Cross-sectional; comparison groups (created ex post)	Cross-sectional; comparison groups
Commercialization stratifier	Membership in a marketing co-op	Crop mix pattern	- Membership in a marketing co-op - Cluster groups created ex post
Sample selection procedures	Stratified random sampling of households	One-stage cluster sampling method	Stratified random sampling of households
Total sample size (households)	379	906	428
Data collection methods	- Household integrated survey - Anthropometric measurements of children < 10 years	- Farm production and household expenditure survey - Food intake survey (24-hr recall) - Anthropometric measurements of children and adults	- Household integrated survey - Anthropometric measurements of children and women - Macro-contextual study - Ethnographic study
Data processing procedures	Data entry and verification after completion offield surveys	Data entry and verification parallel with data collection	Data entry and verification parallel with data collection

of new vegetable crops for export to re-allocative effects on household resources (i.e., land and labor), household income and expenditures (food and non-food), household food availability, health and sanitation, and nutrition outcomes in children.

The study relied on data generated by an agricultural production and household expenditure survey conducted among smallholder farm households in the Department of Sacatepéquez. The main stratifier for sample selection was membership or not in a cooperative which processes vegetables and markets them mostly abroad. Based on a census conducted in 1983 in six villages where the cooperative's members resided, a sample was drawn at random, consisting of 166 member households and 213 non-member households. During the 1984/85 production cycle, 94% of the sample cooperative households, and 32% of the sample non-cooperative households produced export vegetables. What distinguishes the two subsamples is that cooperative farmers marketed their export crops through a formal, and apparently efficient marketing scheme, whereas non-cooperative farmers had to rely on an informal system of middlemen ("coyotes"). Price setting by the cooperative was related to international prices and the local prices paid by middlemen, maintaining most of the time a small but positive price differential with middlemen.

The household-level survey data included demographics, including occupation and schooling completed; housing conditions and access to basic services; non-farm income, by source and household member; farm production: outputs (including destination), agricultural inputs, labor inputs (household and hired) by gender and age-group, land use and quality; food expenditures and household consumption of self-produced foods, non-food expenditures (by categories); and morbidity during the three days prior to the interview and child feeding practices. In addition, anthropometric measurements (height and weight) of under-ten children were taken.

Crop diversification for local markets (1987)

The study covers a population of farm households in the western highlands of Guatemala, a region characterized by smallholder farming systems, low agricultural productivity, and poor access to major markets. The population is predominantly indigenous. Major staple crops are maize and beans, while wheat is a major cash crop. A crop diversification program was launched in 1982 by the government targeted at smallholder farmers, and promoting the production of cold-weather vegetables, such as broccoli, cauliflower, cabbage, beets, and carrots, as well as potatoes at higher elevations. Credit for mini-irrigation works, soil conservation and farm inputs, and agricultural extension services were the main program instruments. Marketing received little attention under this program.

Data from two different sources were used in the study. In February/March 1987, the Ministry of Agriculture, Livestock and Food (MALF) conducted a farm production and household expenditure survey among a representative sample of 1490 traditional and diversified farm households, selected according to a two-stage sampling procedure (communities, participation in the crop diversification program). In late 1987, the Institute of Nutrition of Central America and Panama (INCAP) conducted a food intake survey among 906 households of the MALF sample. The households in the INCAP subsample were selected by a one-stage cluster sampling method, with communities constituting the clusters. The 24-hour recall method was applied to estimate the food intake of the household as a whole, as well as of any preschool child (6-60 months). The food intake data were converted into daily energy and protein intakes using the Central American food composition table (INCAP 1971), while age- and gender-specific recommended daily allowances for dietary energy and protein were used to calculate adequacy levels for the household as a whole and the preschool child (INCAP 1973) alone. Anthropometric measurements were taken in preschoolers, school-age children (6-15 years), and one male and one female adult per household. These measurements included weight, height, mid-upper arm circumference and skinfolds at four sites: biceps, triceps, subscapular, and suprailiac (UN/ACC/SCN 1990). The field staff for the

INCAP survey was selected from the subregions in which they would conduct interviews, to ensure that they mastered the dominant indigenous language of that region. They were all females, since the survey respondents were women, and body measurements would also be taken in small children.

Data processing of the INCAP survey took place simultaneously with data collection, in order to facilitate the timely identification of inconsistent and missing information, and give the interviewers the opportunity to correct/retrieve information by revisiting the home, if necessary. Since the survey was conducted in a large region, data entry facilities were installed in different places throughout the study area.

Export vegetable production and marketing revisited (1991)

This study was initiated in 1991 as a follow-up to the 1985 study described above. The main aim was to analyze the long-term social and economic sustainability of the transformation of smallholder farming towards the production of export vegetables, under varying market and ecological conditions.

The study involved three methodological components: an integrated household survey, similar to the one in the 1985 study; a macro-contextual study focusing on relevant policy changes during the period 1985-1991, and on trends in macro-level indicators related to export crop production and marketing; and an ethnographic study among community members and smallholder farmers, and members of their households, to gather subjective evaluations of the social, cultural, and material changes that export crop production had created in the household and community.

As in the 1985 study, the main stratifier for sample selection in the 1991 study was cooperative membership. Pure member and non-member cohorts of families were constructed by selecting subsamples of families with unchanged cooperative membership status between 1985 and 1991. In order to increase the statistical power of the 1991 cross-sectional analysis, additional member and non-member families were included in the 1991 sample, using a random selection procedure. Once the household survey got underway, cooperative member families which had retired, died, or had originally been misclassified were eliminated and replaced by other families selected according to the above procedures. Families who were found to live in one house and to share land, income, and expenditures were aggregated into households.

Data were collected on family composition and socio-economic characteristics, infrastructure and basic services, family income by source, food and non-food expenditures, access to health services, on- and off-farm employment by family members, land use, crop production and allocation, and agricultural input use by major crops. Anthropometric measurements (weight, height, and mid-upper arm circumference) were taken from children (up to the age of 13 years) and of adult women in the family, as well as morbidity data for the week prior to the interview. The survey was conducted during the same months of the year as the 1985 survey, to eliminate seasonal factors as confounding variables in the 1985-1991 comparative analysis. Interviews related to farm production were conducted by male interviewers, as much as possible with farmers in their fields. The remaining questions were asked during home visits by female interviewers, who also took the anthropometric measurements.

Data entry took place simultaneously with data collection, to allow for data correction and the retrieval of missing data while the survey was still in progress, and to speed up the process of producing preliminary results once the survey was completed.

The main objective of the macro-contextual study was to provide an understanding of the macroeconomic policy changes during the period 1985-1991 which were relevant to the transformation of smallholder agriculture towards non-traditional export crops. Policy areas which were stressed, included foreign trade liberalization, domestic prices (producer, consumer, and agricultural inputs), taxation and public expenditures, social services, rural infrastructure, rural employment generation, foreign investment, and agricultural technological development. The study methodology consisted of an examination and synthesis of policy documents, research publications, and other relevant reports and studies; an analysis of secondary data of macro-level key indicators, to discern trends and changes; and semi-structured interviews with key informants from private sector trade associations, public institutions, and local-level technical and service agencies (Pinto et al. 1992).

The ethnographic study was to provide a qualitative and subjective evaluation by smallholder farmers and members of their households, as well as by community leaders, of the changes they have experienced as a result of the agricultural transformation process toward export crop production. The basic techniques that were applied included direct observation, semi-structured interviews with key informants—such as community leaders, health center personnel, religious persons, cooperative staff, and others, and focus group discussions with community members, women and men in separate groups, selected at random according to (non-)cooperative membership. These techniques are part of a methodological package for participatory needs assessment, known as RAP (Rapid Assessment Procedures) developed by social anthropologists (Scrimshaw and Hurtado 1987).

Research Strategies and Study Design: Lessons Learned

In this section we want to share some insights that we gained about research strategies and the study design as part of the three field studies. We essentially argue here for a closer link between field research and follow-up actions, greater participation by farmers and others in designing the field study, an upfront conceptual-analytical framework for the study to help focus on the most relevant research questions and variables to be measured, the inclusion of an operational research component of the commercialization process, and a great deal of sensitivity on the part of the researchers in applying field methodologies in particular cultural settings.

Research strategies

In setting the research agenda for a study, it is important to directly involve the intended "clients" of the research output. Field studies are expensive undertakings that utilize scarce human and material resources, which may well be justified if the research results can easily be transformed into action. By inviting potential users of the study results to be partners in the study up front, research issues of direct interest to those partners can be incorporated, thereby greatly increasing the likelihood that findings will be transformed into decision making and action taking. This approach also provides greater opportunity to design the field study with greater relevance to the local setting. It also implies timely prioritizing of the study's outputs, in terms of their timing. The cooperative leadership entered as full partners in the 1991 study and contributed concrete questions for the household survey, e.g., related to land acquisition patterns of the farmers, which reflected a real concern on their part. Commitments were made with participating communities to present findings upon completion of the household survey. Specific issues were subsequently raised in discussions with community groups, and we looked to the household survey data for at least partial answers. All this meant that the initial analysis of the data was geared toward quickly producing mostly descriptive results, and transmitting these in simple forms to these "clients". This also meant that the more academic hypothesis testing had to be delayed somewhat, probably with little damage to the advancement of science given the normal gestation period for academic research.

A conceptual-analytical framework should be the starting point in designing the specific study. Such a framework is presented in Figure 1. The pluses and minuses in the flow diagram indicate the direction of the postulated effects. Some of the variables, such as health and nutrition, for instance, are postulated to be affected positively and negatively through different linkages, and the net effects may thus be uncertain. This points out the complexity of the underlying causality involved, and the need for the measurement of all involved

Figure 1. Causal model of household and individual effects of the transformation of farm production towards non-traditional export crops.

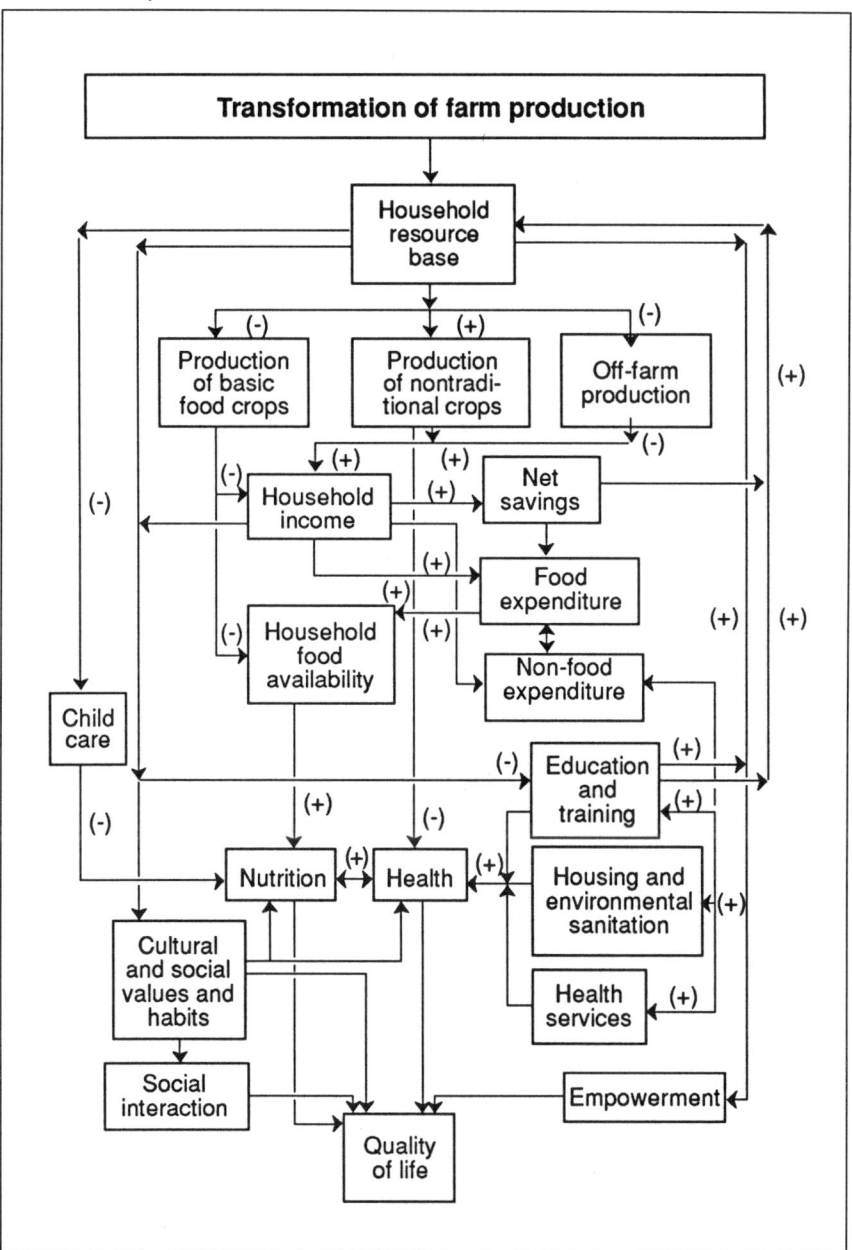

linkages in order to derive valid conclusions about social and economic impacts. As the description of the three studies indicated, none of them covered all of the linkages and outcome variables.

A number of methods can be used to map out a conceptual framework to identify the most important research questions and to ensure that these questions are appropriate and relevant to the specific setting. These methods include:

- synthesizing existing studies, documents, and other relevant materials;

- quick reconnaissance of the study sites or region by the research team; and

- semi-structured interviews with key informants, such as farmers' representatives, personnel of local technical agencies, representatives of processing and marketing firms, and key policy decision makers.

Studies that examine micro-level outcomes of certain processes, such as the transformation of smallholder agriculture towards cash cropping, should provide a macro-context in order to better understand those outcomes. Household and community-level processes interact with macro-level processes to produce specific outcomes. This is particularly relevant for agricultural marketing studies because of continuous interactions between farmers' production decisions, production outcomes, processing and marketing facilities and institutions, political and ecological conditions, domestic and foreign policy outcomes, and national and international market conditions. In more longitudinal studies, many of the factors that either positively or negatively affect the long-term sustainability of the agricultural transformation process are likely to be part of the macro-environment.

Academic researchers usually define the outcome variables to be measured in field studies in accordance with the research hypotheses and with their own interests along disciplinary lines. In these cash cropping studies, the main outcome variables included: crop production levels, household income and expenditures, food availability, health, and nutritional status. The results from the earlier studies were generally positive, yet we kept hearing general comments about adverse effects. This suggested that other outcome variables should be included, particularly outcomes which carry a great deal of weight for the smallholder farmers and members of their households, especially women and children. This prompted the inclusion of the ethnographic component in the 1991 study. The study provided greater insights into the perceived impact of the agricultural transformation process, and thus what other outcomes should be measured in future evaluation studies. It also made clear that these impacts are not the same for everyone. For example, whereas male farmers saw positive outcomes from cash crop production in terms of higher incomes, acquisition of certain assets, and being an independent producer (rather than a day laborer), women saw negative effects in terms of greater allocation of their time (and that of children) to on-farm production, and to marketing of certain crops locally. They also felt harassed by police, were subjected to a daily municipal vendor's fee, and faced poor terms of trade when selling crops in local markets. Thus, measurement of household outcomes hide outcomes with differential weights for different household members.

In evaluation studies such as these described above, it is important to include a study component which focuses on the operational processes of transforming agriculture toward market production. Unless we know how effective and efficient policy, program, and project measures were, whom they reached, and to what degree, we can never evaluate whether such transformations can generally be expected to produce the measured outcomes. For example, in the above studies we cannot disaggregate the outcomes among farmers by different levels of exposure to the commercialization program, either in the case of the government or of the cooperative program. Nor do we know whether or not the programs in the studies were "average" in their mode of operation, effectiveness and efficiency.

Variables and Indicators

The conceptual framework presented in Figure 1 serves as a guide to identify the variables that need to be operationalized by constructing specific indicators (Table 2). These indicators need to be translated into the design of the survey form that will produce the appropriate data for analysis. The list of variables and indicators is included here as a reference for fellow researchers who may be in the process of designing similar studies in the developing world.

Several measures of the degree of commercialization at the household level have been proposed, including the following (von Braun and Kennedy 1994):

- Commercialization of agriculture:

    Output side: value of agricultural market sales/value of total agricultural production;

    Input side: value of purchased agricultural inputs/value of total agricultural production;

- Commercialization of rural economy:

    Value of goods and services acquired through market transactions/total household income.

Table 2. Operationalizing the conceptual framework: variables and indicators.

Variable	Indicators
Household resource base	
- Land	- Farm size, crop extension
- Labor	- Household size - Household age and gender composition
- Human capital	- Literacy of household members over 10 years - Age, years of schooling completed by farmer and spouse - Years in farming, or in non-farm occupations
- Physical capital	- Farm equipment - Animal stock - Farm infrastructure
Farm production	- Percent of land in different crops - Total production of each crop - Allocation of crop production to sales, household consumption, seeds - Yields (total production/total crop area) - Technical coefficients per crop: (1) ag. inputs (fertilizer, herbicides, pesticides) per ha; (2) person-days of household and hired labor per ha
Off-farm production	- Non-farm occupations of household members - Person-days spent in non-farm work (by type of work) by household members
Household income	- Sum of: food expenditures, non-food expenditures, and market value of household-produced and consumed foods and of net food transfers - Sum of: net income from farm production, wage earnings, net business income, property income, and net transfer income.
Household food availability	- Per capita intake of household-produced and consumed foods (kg/year) - Per capita food expenditures plus per capita value of household-produced and consumed foods, plus per capita value of net food transfers - Contribution to total dietary energy availability by different food groups (grains, vegetables, dairy products, etc.)
Health	- Illness (yes/no) during reference period (3, 7 days) - Symptoms and duration of each episode - Use of health care services and diagnosis - Intake of medicines, and source (including traditional medicines)

Table 2 (continued)	
Variable	Indicator
Nutrition	
- Pre-school children (12-60 months)	- Height-for-age - Weight-for-age - Weight-for-height - Mid-upper arm circumference (for age)
- School-age children (5-15 years)	- Same as for pre-school children - Weight/height
- Adults	- Weight/height - Mid-upper arm circumference and arm muscle circumference - Skinfolds at biceps, triceps, suprailiac, and subscapular sites - Percent of body weight in fat and fat-free mass - Weight of fat and fat-free mass (kg)

Field procedures

The experience with the simultaneous data collection and processing in the field, as was done in the last two studies, has generally been positive, particularly in the 1987 study which involved a large, dispersed area with a mountainous topography and poor roads. The need to transport data forms over long distances and difficult roads to a central data processing point was eliminated. In general we feel that this field practice led to a higher quality data set, and most definitely to a quick turn-around in producing first results.

Certain information provided by respondents may have a gender-bias, as when a female respondent is asked to provide certain information about male household members, and vice versa. For example, it appears that men may under-report the number of hours that women spend in on-farm field activities, or women may over-report the amount of money that men provide for household expenses, especially for food. One solution may be to ask those same questions appropriately of both women and men, and compare the responses. In any event, it appears clear that validation studies should be conducted for areas of information which are subject to gender-bias in responses.

In countries where different languages are spoken locally, it is important to recruit and train field staff from the different language areas, as was done in the 1987 study. This will facilitate better communication between interviewee and interviewer, which goes beyond just speaking the same language. In the 1991 study, the field staff was also recruited from the study area (which essentially encompasses only one indigenous language), and communication with the local population was also excellent.

Analytical Approaches and Statistical Procedures: Applications

In this section we highlight some of the complex statistical techniques that were applied in one or more of the three studies described above. More frequently applied statistical techniques, such as univariate statistics (distribution parameters, frequency distributions), analysis of variance and multivariate regression analysis are not discussed though these were also applied. In the case of each of the five statistical techniques (factor analysis, probit regression analysis, analysis of variance of repeated measures, decomposition analysis, and cluster analysis), we link the application with a specific research question. Details of the five techniques can be found in appropriate statistical texts, some of which are referenced below.

Factor analysis of farm household characteristics

Factor analysis (Harman 1967) was applied to water, housing, and sanitation variables in the 1991 study. Preliminary analysis showed that there were significant statistical associations among these variables. This meant that these variables could not individually be included in a regression model of the determinants of morbidity in children. Co-linearity among household characteristics often occurs, since these indicators merely represent different dimensions of the poverty syndrome, and differentiation by poverty level is usually present among the rural poor: some are poorer than others. Factor analysis generates, through data reduction, the linearly independent factors which can then be included as independent variables in regression models (Table 3). The six variables were recoded in ascending order. Other housing and sanitation variables (roofing and floor materials, presence of latrine) were eliminated because there was a high degree of homogeneity among the sample households. The matrices were rotated with the Varimax method (Kaiser 1958). After experimenting with different numbers of specified factors, and examining Eigen values and percents of variation explained by the generated factors, it was determined that the best results were obtained with three factors. The factor loadings after matrix rotation guide the interpretation of the generated factors in Table 3: Factor 1 can be qualified as representing "housing quality", as number of rooms and construction material of the walls have the greatest relative weights; Factor 2, "access to water"; and Factor 3, "sanitation". Together, the three factors explain 69.5% of the total variation in the original variables. The Eigen values are all above or about equal to one. Estimation of the effects of these factors on different outcomes at the household level can then be obtained in subsequent multivariate analysis.

Probit regression analysis: determinants of crop adoption

The 1985 and 1987 studies included an analysis of the determinants of the adoption of new cash crops among the smallholder farmers. In both cases, a Probit model was formulated to examine what farmer and household characteristics were associated with the adoption of certain crop mix patterns. The dependent variable was a truncated (1, 0) indicator, meaning that a farmer had or had not adopted a certain crop pattern. The estimated coefficients in the Probit model can be converted to approximate linear probability estimates, by multiplying them by 0.4 (Amemiya 1981).

The results from the 1987 study are presented here in Table 4. The total sample of farmers had been classified into four groups according to certain crop mixes, three of which (potato farmers, wheat farmers, and vegetable growers) were considered to be more market-oriented than the fourth (maize farmers). The model postulated that adoption of market-oriented crops depends on: farm size, availability of household labor, human capital stock of the heads of household, location of the farm, and access to farm services (credit and extension services). Each of the groups of market-oriented farmers were compared separately to the maize farmers.

Results indicate that access to credit is generally an important factor associated with the adoption of diversified crop patterns, and that household labor supply constraints, alternative employment opportunities, and farm location can play a role, too (Table 4). Farm size and the human capital stock of the heads of household, however, are not associated with any crop adoption pattern.

Table 3. Factor analysis of water, housing and sanitation variables with the Varimax Rotation Method; rural households (n = 376), Central Highlands, Guatemala, 1991.

Water, housing and sanitation variables:	Factor loadings		
	Factor 1: Housing quality	Factor 2: Access to water	Factor 3: Sanitation
Sewage system	.36	.34	.62
Garbage disposal method	-.03	.01	-.93
Walls	.79	-.01	.09
Number of rooms	.76	.13	.12
Sources of water	.37	.71	.10
Water supply sufficiency	-.12	.87	.07
Eigen values	2.16	1.07	0.93
Percent of variation	36.1	17.8	15.6

Source: Immink et al. (1993)

Table 4. Probit models to estimate determinants of adoption of market-oriented crop patterns among smallholder farmers, Western Highlands, Guatemala, 1987.

Independent variables	Potato farmers	Wheat farmers	Vegetable growers
VAR 1	-.069 (1.84)**	-.017 (.91)	-.008 (.62)
VAR 2	.217 (1.23)	.100 (.73)	.317 (2.42)*
VAR 3	.399 (1.24)	-.119 (.48)	-.376 (1.75)**
VAR 4	.008 (.00)	-.127 (.50)	-.542 (2.58)*
VAR 5	-.137 (.56)	-.061 (.29)	.045 (.22)
VAR 6	-.541 (2.25)*	-.019 (.09)	.393 (2.17)*
VAR 7	-.001 (1.18)	.001 (.57)	-.001 (.10)
VAR 8	.306 (1.38)	.005 (.03)	-.126 (.68)
VAR 9	-.782 (2.53)*	.138 (.65)	-.003 (.02)
VAR 10	.536 (2.16)*	1.051 (3.61)*	.748 (3.34)*
VAR 11	.668 (2.57)*	-.006 (.02)	-.174 (.74)
D1	1.910 (1.19)	.151 (.13)	.848 (1.00)
D2	.790 (1.58)	.003 (.01)	-.254 (.51)
D3	-1.308 (2.59)*	.101 (.22)	-.740 (1.80)**
D4	.416 (.89)	-.247 (.49)	.068 (.16)
D5	-1.476 (2.81)*	-5.700 (.02)	.189 (.46)
Constant	-.599 (.51)	.734 (.60)	-.150 (.14)
X^2	171.18	52.49	85.43
$(P < X^2)$	(.0001)	(.0001)	(.0001)

Coefficient = probit estimate; t-ratio in parentheses. VAR 1: cropland extension under cultivation; VAR 2: no. of household members >10 years of age; VAR 3: a household member employed off-farm: business; VAR 4: a household member employed off-farm: permanent salaried work; VAR 5: a household member employed off-farm: cottage industry; VAR 6: a household member employed off-farm: day laborer; VAR 7: age of head of household; VAR 8: literacy status of head of household; VAR 9: literacy status of spouse; VAR 10: received credit last year (1 = yes); VAR 11: received agricultural extension services last year (1 = yes); D1: Totonicapan; D2: Quetzaltenango; D3: San Marcos; D4: Huehuetenango; D5: El Quiché.
*P < .05
**P < .10.
Source: Immink and Alarcon (1993).

Analysis of variance of repeated measures: income changes over time

Analysis of variance of repeated measures (Kirk 1982) was applied in the comparison of certain production, income, and nutrition outcomes in the same cohort of farm households of the 1991 and 1985 studies. Repeated measures designs have the statistical advantage in that they separate the between-subjects variability from the within-subjects variability, i.e., households serve as their own control. It is the second type of variability that is of interest in an analysis that compares results over time. One application, which is presented in Table 5, was to examine whether per capita income in real terms had changed between 1985 and 1991, and whether this change was different according to cooperative membership status, and according to community of residence of the

Field and analytical methods for agricultural commercialization studies 205

farmers. The design in this case is flawed, because farmers were not assigned at random to the treatments (cooperative membership, and community of residence), but so-called "carry-over" effects may have been minimal because of the substantial time interval between observation points.

The results suggests that the positive income differential in 1985 between cooperative and non-cooperative farmers was, on average, confined to farmers residing in Santiago as compared with the non-difference between cooperative and non-cooperative farms in the other villages. Overall, real per capita income declined between 1985 and 1991 ($P<.01$), due to high inflation during the years preceding 1991. The decline in real incomes was smaller among Santiago farmers ($P<.05$), but did not differ according to cooperative membership status ($P>.40$), either among farmers in Santiago or in the other (smaller) communities ($P>.10$). As a result, the 1985 differential in mean per capita income between cooperative and non-cooperative households in Santiago of Q 150 (+42%) was reduced to Q 50 (+13%) in 1991. Whereas the income differential between cooperative and non-cooperative households in the other communities changed from Q -21 (-4%) in 1985 to Q 13 (+4%) in 1991.

Decomposition analysis of income inequality

A decomposition analysis of income inequality was applied to the data for the farm households included in the 1991 study. The basic question that we attempted to answer was whether the production and marketing of export crops significantly contributed to the income inequality among smallholder farmers as compared to other sources of farm and non-farm income. At the same time, we wanted to examine what percent of the overall income inequality was contributed by the net income from export crops. The concern was with the equity effects of the production and marketing of export crops among this group of farmers.

The analysis decomposes the coefficient of variation and the Gini coefficient as measures of income inequality, to examine the contribution of each specified source of income to the overall income inequality (Pyatt, Chen, and Fei 1980; Fei, Ranis, and Kuo 1978). The key parameters which are generated in the analysis are source income weights (W_i), relative concentration coefficients in overall inequality (C_i, g_i), factor inequality weights (W_iC_i, w_ig_i), source income Gini coefficients (G_i; which will exceed one when some farms have negative net incomes), and the correlation ratio between source income inequality and total income inequality (R_i).

Table 5. Per capita total income (in constant 1985 prices), co-op and non-co-op households, by community location, 1985 and 1991. Analysis of variance of repeated measures.

	Co-op households				Non-co-op households			
	Santiago		Other communities		Santiago		Other communities	
	1985	1991	1985	1991	1985	1991	1985	1991
	------Mean (SD)------							
Per capita total income (Q per year)	510 (288)	437 (242)	464 (267)	353 (200)	360 (226)	387 (163)	485 (491)	340 (179)

Analysis of variance of repeated measures

Between-subjects effects

Sources of variation:	DF	Mean sum of squares	F	p
Within cells	229			
- Constant	1	100,894 77,316,064	766.31	.000
- Community (1,0)	1	19,494	0.19	.661
- Co-op membership (1,0)	1	256,361	2.54	.112
- B*C	1	300,286	2.98	.086

Within-subjects effects

Sources of variation:	DF	Mean sum of squares	F	p
Within cells	229			
- 1991-1985 difference	1	49,781 633,571	12.73	.000
- Community *A	1	306,008	6.15	.014
- Co-op membership *A	1	29,612	0.59	.441
- A*community *Co-op membership	1	124,780	2.51	.115

Q = quetzales; DF = degrees of freedom; F = F statistic; p = p statistic.

Table 6. Decomposition analysis of income inequality among smallholder farm households (n = 416), Central Highlands, Guatemala, 1991

Income sources	Source income weight $(W_i) = \mu_i/\mu$	Relative concentration coefficient in overall inequality $(C_i) = \rho_i \sigma_i/\mu_i \over \sigma/\mu$	$(g_i) = {R_i G_i \over G}$	Factor inequality weights $(W_i C_i)$	$(W_i g_i)$	Source Gini co-efficient $(G_i) = {2 \operatorname{Cov}(Y_i,r_i) \over n\mu_i}$	$R_i = {\operatorname{Cov}(Y_i,r) \over \operatorname{Cov}(Y_i,r_i)}$	$\bar{X}$ (SD)
Net crop income:								
- Export crops:								
Snowpeas	.27	1.34	1.23	0.36	0.31	0.99	0.73	248(739)
Others	.03	0.24	0.57	0.01	0.02	1.03	0.33	28(101)
- Maize	.06	0.19	0.22	0.01	0.01	0.84	0.15	53(89)
- Traditional crops	.05	1.29	1.38	0.06	0.06	1.77	0.46	43(276)
Non-farm income:								61(204)
- Off-farm agricultural earnings	.07	0.35	0.55	0.02	0.04	0.92	0.35	
- Off-farm non-agr. earnings	.41	1.05	1.03	0.43	0.43	0.77	0.79	382(790)
- Agricultural and non-agr. sales income	.21	0.93	0.97	0.11	0.11	0.91	0.63	108(361)
Total						0.59		922(1221)

The results in Table 6 generally lead to conclusions such as:

- snowpea production contributed significantly and positively to income inequality because it had a high relative concentration coefficient, a moderately high source Gini coefficient, and a high correlation with overall income inequality, as well as a relatively high source income weight (27%); about 33% to 36% of the overall income inequality was contributed by snowpea production; other export crops played a very minor role in determining overall income inequality;

- maize production reduced income inequality: low concentration coefficients, relatively low source Gini coefficient, and virtually no correlation with overall income inequality; about 1% of overall income inequality was due to maize production;

- traditional vegetables production also enhanced income inequality, but minimally so because of the relative low source income weight (5%), only about 6% of overall income inequality was due to traditional vegetables; and non-farm income, particularly off-farm non-agricultural earnings represented a major share of total income and contributed a major share of the overall income inequality (56-58%); off-farm non-agricultural earnings seem to have enhanced overall income inequality.

Cluster Analysis for Sample Stratification

Cluster analysis (Anderberg 1973; Everitt 1980; Aldenderfer and Bashfield 1984) was applied in the 1991 study in order to create for the household sample an ex post stratifier which was based on the relative importance (or weight) of different types of production—particularly export crop production—in total household production. The objective was to generate clusters of households in such a way as to minimize differences of certain variables within each cluster, and to maximize the differences between clusters. In other words, the procedure analyzes the composition of the total output of each farm, and assigns households to groups whose members are more similar to each other (in terms of output shares in this case) than to members of the other groups. The process involved a sensitivity analysis by varying the variables to be included and the number of clusters to be generated, and then comparing various parameters, to arrive at a decision as to which set of clusters best met the above-stated objective.

Part of the sensitivity analysis is presented in Table 7. The variables that figured in the analysis were expressed as percent contributions to the total value of farm and off-farm household production. In examples 1 (Table 7a) and 2 (Table 7b), the variables are the same, but the number of pre-specified clusters to be generated differ. In example 3 (Table 7c), the variables are varied by combining some of the variables of the first two examples (VAR6=VAR2+VAR3; VAR7=VAR4+VAR5). Presented in the three examples are the final cluster centers, which are the standardized mean values of the variables in each final cluster, and the Euclidean distances between pairs of final clusters.

In example 1, VAR1, VAR2, and VAR4 are different in the three clusters, but VAR3 and VAR5 are not. Extending the analysis to four clusters, the first four variables are different in each cluster, but the fifth is not. The Euclidean distances between clusters 1 and 3 in example 1, and between clusters 1 and 3, and 2 and 3 in example 2, are lower than between remaining pairs. But in example 3, we see that the three variables are different in each cluster, and that the distances between the pairs of clusters are greater than in example 1. The analysis of variance confirms that the variables differ significantly between clusters in all three examples, i.e., the between-cluster variation far exceeds the within-cluster variation, as indicated by the F-ratios.

It was decided to use the three clusters generated with VAR1, VAR6, and VAR7 (example 3) as the main stratifier in the 1991 analysis. Households in cluster one were generally labelled as traditional farm households, since 71.5% of the total value of production stems on average from the production of traditional crops. For those in cluster two the major share results from export crop production (83%) and these households are thus labelled as export farm households. The non-farm households (cluster three) are mainly dependent on off-farm earnings (77.9%).

Final Thoughts

Two-way capacity building. Field studies such as the ones described above, which involved both researchers from developed country institutions as well as researchers and non-researchers from the developing world, often offer significant opportunities for capacity building in designing social research, and in data management and analysis. This capacity building should operate in two directions between partners from the developed and developing countries. A key first step is open dialogue between all research partners to set the research agenda for the collaborative study. The research partners should be fully involved in all stages of the research project, from start to finish. Continuous self-analysis of the project implementation process by the research partners converts the project into a learning-by-doing experience. Even if this diverts some time and energy away from study implementation, the extra costs often represent a good investment, particularly if the collaboration is long-term.

Table 7a. Cluster analysis for stratification of rural house holds according to household output mix, Central Highlands, Guatemala, 1991.

Example 1: VAR1 - VAR5; 3 Clusters

Cluster	Final Cluster Centers				
	VAR1	VAR2	VAR3	VAR4	VAR5
1(n=167)	70.4	14.9	4.7	7.7	2.2
2(n=107)	7.1	10.5	2.2	77.3	2.9
3(n=125)	8.1	51.8	14.1	7.2	18.8

	Analysis of Variance				
	Cluster MS	Df	Error MS	Df	F
VAR1	191,260	2	214	396	896
VAR2	64,509	2	405	396	159
VAR3	4,803	2	259	396	19
VAR4	190,924	2	189	396	1,008
VAR5	11,454	2	369	396	31

Euclidean distances:

Cluster	Cluster		
	1	2	3
1	..		
2	94.2	..	
3	74.8	83.8	..

Table 7b. Cluster analysis for stratification of rural households according to household output mix, Central Highlands, Guatemala, 1991 (Cont'd.).

Example 2: VAR1 - VAR5; 4 Clusters

Cluster	Final Cluster Centers				
	VAR1	VAR2	VAR3	VAR4	VAR5
1(n=164)	71.0	15.0	3.8	7.9	2.3
2(n=107)	8.7	56.8	4.8	7.9	21.8
3(n=22)	9.0	19.8	66.0	4.5	0.8
4(n=106)	7.2	10.5	1.7	77.7	2.9

	Analysis of Variances				
	Cluster MS	Df	Error MS	Df	F
VAR1	127,916	3	211	395	606
VAR2	49,170	3	359	395	137
VAR3	27,230	3	77	395	353
VAR4	127,647	3	187	395	682
VAR5	9,881	3	353	395	28

Euclidean Distances:

Cluster	Cluster			
	1	2	3	4
1	..			
2	77.6	..		
3	88.1	74.6	..	
4	94.8	86.0	97.9	..

Table 7c. Cluster analysis for stratification of rural households according to household output mix, Central Highlands, Guatemala, 1991 (Cont'd.).

Example 3: VAR1, VAR6, VAR7; 3 Clusters

Final Cluster Centers:

Cluster	VAR1	VAR6	VAR7
1 (n=163)	19.4	71.5	9.1
2 (n=90)	83.0	10.3	6.7
3 (n=146)	15.4	6.7	77.9

Analysis of Variance

	Cluster MS	Df	Error MS	Df	F
VAR1	149,749	2	209	396	717
VAR6	194,267	2	197	396	984
VAR7	224,852	2	202	396	1,112

Euclidean Distances

Cluster	Cluster		
	1	2	3
1	..		
2	88.2	..	
3	94.6	98.2	..

Legend: VAR1: Percent - gross value of export crops.
 VAR2: Percent - gross value of maize and beans.
 VAR3: Percent - gross value of traditional vegetables.
 VAR4: Percent - earnings - non-agricultural work.
 VAR5: Percent - earnings of agricutural work.
 VAR6: Percent - gross value of traditional crops.
 VAR7: Percent - off-farm earnings.

New paradigms for field studies. Agricultural marketing studies in developing countries are presumably undertaken to contribute to the development of the rural population. As has been pointed out elsewhere (Edwards 1989), the relationships between scientific research and socio-economic development are complex and certainly not linear. It seems valid to ask: how much does social research contribute to solving socio-economic development problems? Perhaps alternative paradigms of conducting research in developing countries are needed. These should probably give greater weight to creating space for the rural poor to become the subjects of research (and by extension of their own development), and for indigenous knowledge and popular science to become fully integrated with scientific knowledge and methods. At the same time, we as social researchers should carefully reflect on our role in contributing to short- and long-term solutions of development problems, and on how to become effective partners in such new paradigms.

References

Alberti, A. M. 1990. Impact of participation in nontraditional agricultural export production on the employment, income, and quality of life of women in Guatemala, Honduras, and Costa Rica. AID 596-0108-c-00-6060-00. Washington, DC, USA:Chemonics International Consulting Division.

Aldenderfer, M.S. and R.K. Bashfield. 1984. *Cluster analysis.* Beverly Hills, CA, USA: Sage.

Amemiya, T. 1981. Qualitative response models: A survey. *Journal of Economic Literature* 19:1483-1536.

Anderberg, M.R. 1973. *Cluster analysis for applications.* New York, NY, USA: Academic Press.

Arizpe, L. and J. Aranda. 1986. Women workers in the strawberry agribusiness in Mexico. In *Women's work* (E. Leacock and H. I. Safa, ed.). South Hadley, MA, USA: Bergin & Garvey Publishers, Inc.

Blumberg, R.L. 1985. *Following up a Guatemalan "natural experiment on women in development" gender and the Alcosa agribusiness project in 1985 versus 1980.* Washington, DC, USA: USAID/LAC/PPC.

Bouis, H.E. and L.J. Haddad. 1992. Are estimates of calorie-income elasticities too high? A recalibration of the plausible range. *Journal of Development Economics* 39:333-364.

Bouis, H. E. and L.J. Haddad. 1990. *Effects of agricultural commercialization on land tenure, household resource allocation, and nutrition in the Philippines.* Research Report 79. Washington, DC, USA: International Food Policy Research Institute.

von Braun, J. and E. Kennedy (eds.). 1994. *Agricultural commercialization, economic development and nutrition.* Baltimore, MD, USA: The Johns Hopkins University Press.

von Braun, J. and E. Kennedy. 1986. *Commercialization of subsistence agriculture: Income and nutritional effects in developing countries.* Working Papers on Commercialization of Agriculture and Nutrition 1. Washington, DC, USA: International Food Policy Research Institute.

von Braun, J., H. de Haen, and J. Blanken. 1991. *Commercialization of agriculture under population pressure: Sustainability problems and nutritional effects in Rwanda.* Research Report 85. Washington, DC, USA: International Food Policy Research Institute.

von Braun, J., D. Hotchkiss, and M. Immink. 1989. *Nontraditional export crops in Guatemala: Effects on production, income, and nutrition.* Research Report 73. Washington, DC, USA: International Food Policy Research Institute.

von Braun, J., D. Puetz, and P. Webb. 1989. *Irrigation technology and commercialization of rice in The Gambia: Effects on income and nutrition*. Research Report 75. Washington, DC, USA: International Food Policy Research Institute.

DeWalt, K.M., B.R. DeWalt, J.C. Escudero, and D. Barkin. 1990. Shifts from maize to sorghum production. Nutrition effects in four Mexican communities. *Food Policy* 15:395-407.

Dewey, K.G. 1979. Agricultural development, diet, and nutrition. *Ecology of Food Nutrition* 8:265-273.

———. 1981. Nutritional consequences of the transformation from subsistence to commercial agriculture in Tabasco, Mexico. *Human Ecology* 9:151-187.

Edwards, M. 1989. The irrelevance of development studies. *Third World Quarterly* 11:116-135.

Everitt, B. 1980. *Cluster analysis*. London, UK: Heinemann Educational Books.

Fei, J.C.H., G. Ranis, and S.W.Y Kuo. 1978. Growth and the family distribution of income by factor components. *Quarterly Journal of Economics* 92:17-53.

Finlayson, M., J. McComb, B. Hardaker, and P. Heywood. 1991. *Commercialization of agriculture at Karimui, Papua New Guinea: Effects on household production, consumption, and the growth of children*. Department of Agricultural Economics and Business Management, University of New England, Armidale, N.S.W., Australia.

Fleuret, P. and A. Fleuret. 1980. Nutrition, consumption, and agricultural change. *Human Organization* 39:250-260.

Glover, D. and K. Kuterer. 1990. Frozen vegetables in Guatemala: Tapping the small farmer's potential. In *Small farmers, big business; Contract farming and rural development*. New York, NY, USA: St. Martin's Press.

Gross, D. and B. Underwood. 1971. Technological change and caloric costs: Sisal agriculture in northern Brazil. *American Anthropologist* 73:725-740.

Harman, H.H. 1967. *Modern factor analysis*. Chicago, IL, USA: University of Chicago Press.

Hernández, M., C.P. Hidalgo, J.R. Hernández, H. Madrigal, and A. Chavez. 1974. Effect of economic growth on nutrition in a tropical community. *Ecology of Food and Nutrition* 3:283-291.

Immink, M.D.C. and J.A. Alarcón. 1993. Household income, food availability, and commercial crop production by smallholder farmers in the Western Highlands of Guatemala. *Economic Development and Cultural Change* 41:319-342.

Instituto de Nutrición de Centro América y Panamá (INCAP). 1973. *Recomendaciones dietéticas diarias para Centro América y Panamá*. Guatemala City, Guatemala: INCAP.

――――. 1971. *Valor nutritivo de los alimentos para Centro América y Panamá*. Guatemala City, Guatemala: INCAP.

Kaiser, H.F. 1958. The Varimax criterion for analytic rotation in factor analysis. *Psychometrika* 23:187-200.

Kennedy, E. 1989. *The effects of sugarcane production on food security, health, and nutrition in Kenya: A longitudinal analysis*. Research Report 78. Washington, DC, USA: International Food Policy Research Institute.

Kennedy, E., H. Bouis, and J. von Braun. 1992. Health and nutrition effects of cash crop production in developing countries: A comparative analysis. *Social Science and Medicine* 35(5):689-697.

Kirk, R. 1982. *Experimental design: Procedures for the behavioral sciences*. Second edition. Belmont, CA, USA: Wadsworth, Inc.

Lappe, F. M. and J. Collins. 1977. *Food first: Beyond the myth of scarcity*. Boston, MA, USA: Houghton Mifflin Co.

Lunven, P. 1982. The nutritional consequences of agricultural and rural development projects. *Food and Nutrition Bulletin* 4:17-22.

Murray, D. and P. Hoppin. 1992. Recurring contradictions in agrarian development: Pesticide problems in Caribbean Basin nontraditional agriculture. *World Development* 20(4):597-608.

Netting, R.M., M. Priscilla, and G.D. Stone. 1989. Kofyar cash-cropping: Choice and change in indigenous agricultural development. *Human Ecology* 17(3):299-319.

Pinto, I., P. Mejicanos, G. Schell, and M. Rayo. 1992. *Evolution of the macroeconomic policy and its effects on the production and marketing processes of non traditional products*. (mimeo) Guatemala.

Popkin, B. M. 1980. Time allocation of the mother and child nutrition. *Ecology of Food and Nutrition* 9:1-14.

Pyatt, G., C. Chen, and J. Fei. 1980. The distribution of income by factor components. *Quarterly Journal of Economics* 95:451-473.

Rosenstock, L., M. Keifer, W. Daniell, R. McConnell, K. Claypoole, et al. 1991. Chronic central nervous system effects of acute organophosphate pesticide intoxication. *The Lancet* 338 (July 27):223-227.

Scrimshaw, S.C.M. and E. Hurtado. 1987. *Rapid assessment procedures for nutrition and primary health care: Anthropological approaches to improving programme effectiveness*. Tokyo, Japan, and Los Angeles, CA, USA: United Nations University and Latin American Studies Center, University of California.

Tucker, S.K. and J. Castañeda. 1991. *The substitution of cash crops for traditional agriculture: Causes and concerns*. Paper prepared for the Conference on Resource and Environmental Management in an Interdependent World, 1991, San Jose, Costa Rica.

Vargas, F., R. Caballero, and E. Gutiérrez. 1991. *Las exportaciones no tradicionales en Centroamérica: El entorno económico de la producción de melon en el caso de Guatemala. Informe preliminar. Asociación para el Avance de las Ciencias Sociales en Guatemala*. Guatemala City, Guatemala.

UN/ACC/SCN. 1990. *Appropriate uses of anthropometric indices in children*. UNESCO, Geneva, Switzerland.

9

Industrial Organization and Market Analysis: Fish Marketing

R.S. Pomeroy and A.C. Trinidad[1]

Abstract

The traditional framework of industrial organization as a tool for market analysis is illustrated using results from research on fish marketing in Asia and Latin America. As posited in industrial organization theory, a causal flow exits between market structure, conduct, and performance. This theory can be tested using indicators that determine the existence and extent of deviations from the perfectly competitive model.

Market structure is the environment in which the firm operates. It includes the following elements: buyer/seller concentration, product/service differentiation, and entry barriers. The paper explains these concepts in greater detail and shows how they may be used in applied research. Market conduct refers to the patterns of commercial behavior arising from market structure. Practical guidelines for analyzing market conduct such as buying and selling practices and pricing behavior are presented. Market performance indicators discussed include net returns and marketing margins.

Key words: Market structure, barriers to entry, market conduct, market performance, marketing margins.

Introduction

Market analysis studies can be classified using descriptive, price efficiency, and organizational criteria (Table 1). The descriptive approach contains little statistical analysis and reaches conclusions regarding performance and efficiency based on the researcher's subjective assessment. This approach has been used extensively as a basis for studying commodity flows and marketing techniques, but is not deemed as useful for intercommodity comparisons (Smith 1981).

---

[1] International Center for Living Aquatic Resources Management (ICLARM), MC PO Box 1501, Makati, Metro Manila, Philippines.

The price efficiency approach analyzes marketing in its dimensions of space, time, and form (King and Henry 1959; King 1965; Bressler and King 1970). Examination of the efficiency with which the marketing system transmits information among the different producer, wholesale and retail markets is achieved through the application of various pricing criteria.

Table 1. Alternative market analysis methodologies.

Approach	Data requirements	Source
Descriptive		Smith (1981)
Functional		
- Exchange		
- Physical		
- Facilitating		
Institutional		
- Merchants		
- Agents		
- Spectators		
Organizational		Koch (1980)
Structure		
- Industry maturity		
- Governmental participation		
- Product differentiation		
- Concentration index	- number of buyers & sellers at each market level - volume of trade handled by each buyer/seller	
- Barriers to entry		
cost structures	- initial investment cost and components - initial working capital	
scale economies	- average marketing costs per trader - average amount of trade handled per trader	
- Vertical integration		
- Diversification		
Conduct		Koch (1980)
- pricing strategy		
predatory		
exclusionary		
collusive		
- Product strategy		
- Responsiveness to change		
- Research and innovation		
- Advertising		
- Legal tactics		
- Method of selling		

Table 1. (continued)

Performance		Mudiantono (1990)
- Net returns		Pomeroy (1989), Scheid & Sutinen (1981), Torres et al. (n.d.)
- Marketing costs & Margins	- marketing costs & components - prices at all market levels - prices at different markets	Pomeroy (1989), Scheid & Sutinen (1981) Torres et al. (n.d.)
- Producer's share		Mudiantono (1990)
- Value added		Mudiantono (1990)
Price efficiency		
Price differentials		Smith (1981)
- Spatial	- prices in markets i & j	
- Inter-temporal	- time-series price data - time-series storage costs	
- Form	- prices in markets i & j - processing costs	
Market integration	- price movements in markets i & j	Smith (1981)
Location theory		
Regional analysis		
Inter-regional trade analysis	- price movements in markets i & j	

Source: Smith (1981) unless otherwise indicated.

Industrial organization analysis is the focus of this paper. Industrial organization methodology is a standard tool for the analysis of markets in the United States and the United Kingdom (Scherer 1980). This theory tells us that the market structure (the environment) determines market conduct (the behavior of economic agents within the environment) and thereby sets the level of market performance (how close the industry comes to meeting the norm or standard of reference of social welfare) (Caves 1982). If we can uncover reliable links between elements of structure, conduct, and performance, we have a powerful tool for economic analysis. Causation may, however, run both ways, from economic performance to conduct to structure. The relationship may also be dynamic in character and change with time. This issue may limit the predictive and analytical value of the approach and must be considered when interpreting the results of industrial organization analysis.

The industrial organizational approach emerged in the developed country context where industries, often dominated by a few very large firms, represent a prominent sector of the economy (Bain 1968). Its applicability to the more atomistic situation typical of most agricultural factor and product markets in developing countries has been questioned. In addition, Smith (1972) believes that the structure-conduct-performance framework has limited transferability to the developing country scene because of underdeveloped infrastructure, intersectoral relations, and development objectives, as well as the unique social and political structures found in the Third World. Smith proceeds to develop several performance criteria that he considers more relevant to developing countries, although the issue of evaluating departures from the perfectly competitive model remain. Smith, however, states that he sees the necessity for revising only performance dimensions of the industrial organizational approach through price efficiency analysis, while leaving structural and conduct dimensions as described by Bain basically intact (Smith 1972).

Application of the industrial organization framework in fish marketing is illustrated in this chapter (price efficiency is discussed in Part Two of this volume). Results presented here are from four empirical studies (see Table 2): a small-scale fishery in Matalom, Leyte, Philippines (Pomeroy 1989); the Navotas Fish Port Complex, Navotas, Philippines (Torres et al. n.d.); fish marketing in Peninsular Malaysia (Ishak 1988); and the small-scale fishery sector in the Gulf of Nicoya, Costa Rica (Scheid and Sutinen 1981). Furthermore, market analysis will concentrate on the primary buyer level—herein referred to as buyers—and be specified empirically in different ways in the four studies.

Data Requirements

Essential to the analysis of markets is the identification of market participants, channels and arrangements. Sources of data are, as in the four case studies considered in this paper, sample surveys conducted in fishing communities for periods ranging from two months (Torres et al. n.d.) to five months (Scheid and Sutinen 1981) and seven months (Pomeroy 1989). In addition, daily record keeping by middlemen of costs and earnings, volume and direction of trade,

Table 2. Summary of information on the four fisheries analyzed.

Fishery type	Location	1st Buyer	Duration of study (months)	Source
Small-scale	Matalom, Leyte, Philippines	middlemen[1]	7	Pomeroy (1989)
Small-scale & industrial	Peninsular Malaysia	coastal wholesalers	-	Ishak (1988)
Small-scale	Gulf of Nicoya, Costa Rica	buyers	5	Scheid & Sutinen (1981)
Industrial	Navotas, Philippines	brokers	2	Torres et al. (n.d.)

[1] Middlemen, here and in the text may, and in fact, does include women; we are aware that this term is not appropriate.

Industrial organization and market analysis: Fish marketing 221

Table 3. Data requirements for application of the industrial organization framework and price efficiency techniques in fish marketing.

Analytical techniques	Data requirements
Concentration index	- number of buyers & sellers at each market level - volume of trade handled by each buyer/seller
Entry barriers:	
- Capital cost	- initial investment cost and components - initial amount of working capital
- Scale economies	- average marketing costs per trader - average volume of trade handled per trader
Marketing costs & margins	- fixed marketing costs & components - variable marketing costs and components - costs of transportation, storage, & processing - prices at all market levels, i.e., ex-vessel, wholesale, retail, peddling price - prices at different markets
Market integration	- price movements in markets i & j
Price differentials:	
- Time	- time-series price data to reflect seasonality - monthly storage costs
- Space	- prices in markets i & j
- Form	- prices in markets i & j - processing costs

species handled, and prices is essential. Buying and selling prices should, as much as possible, be collected as time-series data. Costs of marketing and prices should be collected at the wholesale and retail levels. While it is possible to enumerate the data requirements to evaluate market structure and performance (Table 3), variables that characterize market conduct are harder to quantify. Experience from these case studies suggests that they have to be gleaned by researcher observation and analysis.

The next three sections present the industrial organization analytical framework. Market structure is discussed first followed by conduct and performance.

Market Structure

Market structure is defined as characteristics of the organization of a market which seem to influence strategically the nature of competition and pricing behavior within the market (Bain 1968). Structural characteristics may be used as a basis for classifying markets. Markets may be perfectly competitive; monopolistic; or oligopolistic.

Perfect competition is an economic model of a market possessing the following characteristics: each economic agent acts as if prices are given, i.e., each acts as a price taker. In other words, no large firm or group of firms dominate buying and selling. The product being sold is considered a homogenous good. Product differentiation does not exist. There is free mobility of all resources, including free entry and exit of business firms. And finally, all economic agents in the market possess complete and perfect knowledge (Scherer 1980).

Pure monopoly exists when there is only one seller (producer) in the market. There are no direct competitors or rivals in either the popular or technical sense. Barriers to entry prevent other potential competitors from selling in this market. However, pure monopoly is undermined if the policies of a monopolist are constrained by the indirect competition of all commodities for the consumer's money and of reasonably adequate substitute goods, and by the threat of potential competition if market entry is possible.

Oligopoly is said to exist when more than one seller is in the market but when the number is not so large as to render negligible the contribution of each. A typical oligopoly exists when, for example, three firms control over 50% of all sales of a particular good in a particular market and certain barriers prevent potential competitors from entering the market. These definitions are likewise applied to monopsonists and oligopsonists who are buyers instead of sellers (Tomek and Robinson 1981).

A characterization of structure, conduct, and performance elements of the three types of industry structure as applied to fish markets at the primary buyer level are presented in Table 4. The four salient aspects of market structure include the degree of seller concentration; the degree of buyer concentration; the degree of product differentiation; and the conditions of entry (Koch 1980). These elements measure the extent of deviations from the perfectly competitive norm. The larger the deviation, the more imperfectly competitive is the market, i.e., an extreme case would be monopoly. Procedures for analyzing market structure are illustrated here for market concentration and entry conditions.

Market Concentration

Market concentration is defined as the number and size distribution of sellers and buyers in the market. Concentration is felt to play a large part in the determination of market behavior within an industry because it affects the interdependence of action among firms. The greater the degree of concentration, the greater the possibility of non-competitive behavior, such as collusion, existing in the market. While empirical relationships between structure and performance are not always fully known, almost all studies of seller concentration suggest a positive, though often weak, association between concentration and profitability. Furthermore, Devine et al. (1984) write that: "buyer concentration is analogous to seller concentration, and in principle a range of absolute and relative measures of buyer concentration corresponding to

Table 4. Structural, conduct, and performance characteristics of fish markets at the primary buyer level.

Structure & concentration index	Structural elements; entry barriers		Conduct variables		Performance variables		
	Capital cost	Scale economies	Price-setting behavior	Price differentiation	Net returns	Marketing margins	Producer's share
Perfect competition (low)	low	none	no personal contact among market participants	none	moderate-fair returns to management, labor, & risk	moderate to fair returns to management labor & risk	high
Oligopoly (medium-high)	medium/ high	present	collusive	specialized product & services	moderate/high	moderate to high	medium
Monopoly (high)	high	present	exclusionary to predatory	specialized product & services	high	high	low

those of seller concentration could be constructed. However, such measures have not been constructed, due largely to the absence of data classifying the total purchases of each type of product by purchasing firms."

These relationships between concentration and market behavior and performance must not, however, be interpreted in isolation. Other factors, such as the firm's objectives, barriers to entry, economies of scale, and assumptions about rival firms' behavior, will all be relevant in determining the degree of concentration and the relationship between concentration and behavior and performance (see Scherer 1980).

Koch (1980) lists two kinds of partial concentration indices: the Gini coefficient and the Herfindahl index. Both utilize market shares to determine the extent of market concentration. The Gini coefficient is based on the Lorenz curve which plots a cumulative distribution of income against a corresponding population group.

Other measures of market power include the Lerner index (Lerner 1934), which measures the deviation of price from marginal cost; the Rothschild index (Rothschild 1942), which is a ratio of the slope of the product-demand curve faced by the firm, divided by the slope of the demand curve for the same product; the Bain profit index (Bain 1941); and Papandreou's index of penetration and insulation (Papandreou 1949).

All four fish market studies utilized the concentration ratio (market share ratio), with Pomeroy (1989) and Scheid and Sutinen (1981) capping the analysis via the Lorenz curve. Market shares are estimated based on the amount of fish handled by each unit, i.e., wholesaler/buyer, as a percentage of total volume handled or:

$$MS_i = \frac{V_i}{\Sigma V_i}$$

where

MS_i = market share of buyer i

V_i = amount of fish handled by buyer i

ΣV_i = total amount of fish handled

The cumulative frequency distribution is devised by ranking the buyers according to market share and cumulating the shares.

In the two districts studied by Pomeroy (1989) in the Philippines, the Lorenz curve indicated that 50% of the industry made 80% of the fish purchases. Scheid and Sutinen (1981) observed the same ratio in Puntarenas, Costa Rica. Ishak (1988) used concentration ratios and Herfindahl indices which yielded similar results, i.e., 8 coastal wholesalers controlled 60% of the total volume of landings. In the other Philippine case, the one broker accounted for more than 57% of total volume handled (Torres et al. n.d.).

The results of market concentration analysis in the four studies are presented in Table 5.

Empirical studies in the field of industrial organization suggest certain levels of concentration at which non-competitive behavior for sellers begins in certain industries. Benchmarks used to evaluate whether concentration indices result in imperfect competition are shown in Figure 1.

Barriers to entry

The concentration index may indicate tacit or explicit collusion and, ultimately, lower prices for fishermen and higher profits for middlemen, but unless there are appreciable barriers to entry, such price collusion is bound to be undermined (Scherer 1980). Bain (1968) contends that a barrier to entry is simply any advantage held by existing firms over those firms that might potentially produce in a given market. Stigler (1968) proposes an alternative definition of an entry barrier, namely, the production cost which must be borne by the potential entrant but not by existing firms.

Table 5. Market structure characteristics and analytical techniques used in four marketing studies.

Study	Market concentration	Technique used	Entry barriers
Pomeroy (1989)	50% of buyers control 80% of fish purchases	Lorenz curve	initial capital cost,[1] loanable funds; scale economies,[2] service differentiation[3]
Ishak (1988)	8 coastal buyers control 60% of total landings	Lorenz curve	institutional aggrupation; scale economies; product differentiation[4]
Scheid & Sutinen (1981)	same as Pomeroy (1988)	concentration ratio; Herfindahl index	initial capital cost,[1] loanable funds; product differentiation[4]
Torres et al. (n.d.)	1 buyer controls 57% of total landings	concentration ratio	initial capital cost; scale economies; product differentiation[4]

[1] In Pomeroy (1989), includes pails, scales, and baskets; in Scheid & Sutinen (1981) includes ice boxes and freezers.
[2] Verified using least squares regression.
[3] *Suki* vs. non-*suki* buyers.
[4] Type of species handled.

Potential entry barriers exist due to demand conditions, including product differentiation and price elasticities; control over input supplies; legal and institutional factors; scale economies; capital requirements; and technological factors. Entry barriers observed in the four studies are also included in Table 5. Two barriers to entry that are often of critical importance in developing countries—given relative factor endowments developing versus developed countries—are capital costs and scale economies.

Capital costs. Capital requirements serve as an entry barrier because only those who can afford such a monetary outlay can enter the market. In fish marketing, initial capital costs include equipment (the type of which may vary from one fishery to another (see Table 5), daily operating capital, and loanable funds. Initial investment costs can be compared to average disposable incomes from other sources of livelihood, i.e., fishing, farming, processing, to determine the prospects of attracting potential entrants (Pomeroy 1989).

Pomeroy (1989) and Scheid and Sutinen (1981) noted that initial capital costs provide a restrictive entry barrier especially for small-scale fishermen. In addition, both studies underscored the importance of having a "long leash" especially during periods of low supply and the availability of funds for emergencies, weddings, fiestas, and the like, which fishermen value as more important than a fair price for their fish (Pomeroy 1989). Ishak (1988) noted that institutional aggrupations with selective membership also functioned as an entry barrier among coastal wholesalers in Malaysia.

Figure 1. Some benchmarks suggested to evaluate whether concentration results in imperfect competition. Note that Rhoades's and Kaysen and Turner's indices are mutually consistent, while Bain's and Mann's criterion are less strict.

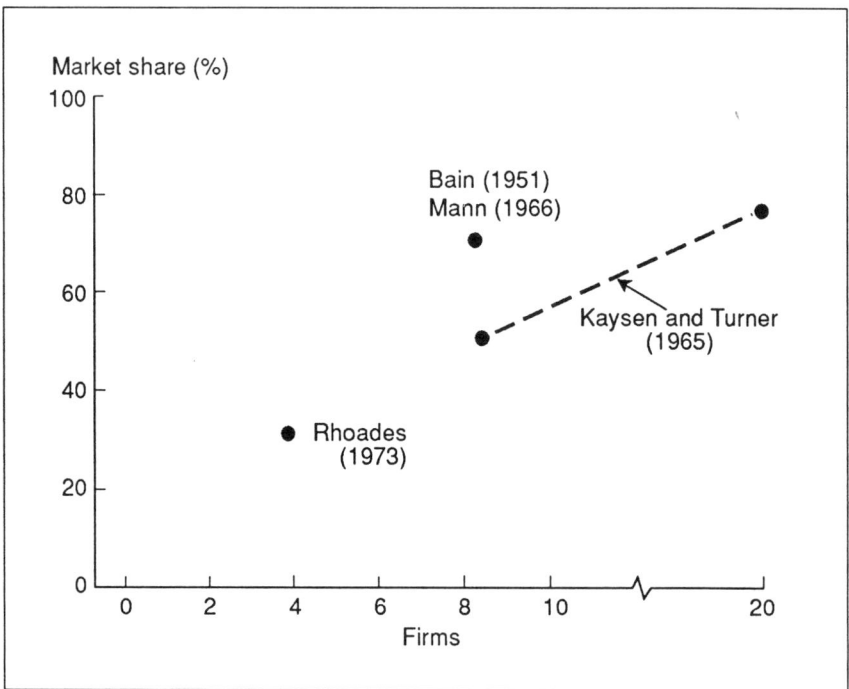

Scale economies. Scale economies are a useful measure for explaining market concentration. Why does one firm monopolize the sale of a particular product when potential rivals might produce something similiar? The existence of economies of scale is a condition permitting relatively large firms to market their products at considerably lower average costs than smaller firms. Simply stated: a firm will attempt to expand its operations in order to lower average unit costs and increase profits. To the extent that unit costs are lower for larger firms, economies of scale are said to prevail. Other firms cannot compete because they are not sufficiently large to capture these economies. It is possible beyond some scale that further firm size brings no additional unit cost savings (Sherer 1980). One cannot, however, assume that profitability is solely a function of scale economies. Other variables affect relationship as Scherer (1980) states, "... profitability reflects the overall suitability of the firm's size in relation to its market environment, and not just production and cost advantages." Ishak (1988) further notes the high degree of market interdependence attached to scale operations among coastal wholesalers in Peninsular Malaysia.

One method used to measure the presence of scale economies is to examine the average cost function associated with the firm's marketing activities. Data requirements include, in addition to volume of fish handled, all marketing costs such as transportation, storage, loading, market fees, and labor. Average costs per middleman are thus estimated by dividing total marketing costs by the volume of fish. Economies of scale is verified in Pomeroy's (1989) study using least squares regression of the form:

$$AMC = \alpha + \text{ß}Q + \varepsilon$$

where AMC is the cost per kilogram of fish handled per middleman; Q is the daily amount of fish handled per middleman; and ε is the error term.

This model when applied to the Matalom fishery indicated that a significant negative relationship existed between fishing costs and the volume of fish handled, thus verifying the existence of scale economies.

Market structure elements found in the four fish market studies are summarized in Table 5. High concentration ratios, high entry barriers, and product/service differentiation at the primary buyer level suggest oligopsonistic structures for the four cases.

Market Conduct

Market conduct refers to the patterns of behavior that firms follow in adapting or adjusting to the markets in which they sell or buy (Bain 1968). Such a definition implies the analysis of human behavioral patterns that are not readily identifiable, obtainable, or quantifiable. Thus, in the absence of a theoretical framework for market analysis, there is a tendency to treat conduct variables in a descriptive manner or as Ishak (1988) points out, as a spill-over in the assessment of market performance.

Bain (1968) names two closely interrelated aspects of market conduct: "the manner in which, and the devices and mechanisms by which, the different sellers coordinate their intrinsically rivalrous decisions and actions, adapt to each other, or succeed in making them mutually consistent as they react to demands for their products in a common market"; and "the character of pricing policies and related market policies that the sellers in the industry adopt; assessed in terms of the individual or collective aims or goals that they pursue as they determine their selling prices, their sales promotion outlays, the designs and qualities of their products and so forth." By examining the relationship between the factors of market structure and these price-setting practices, it may be possible to make some predictions about the consequences of these behavioral patterns for performance.

Given the premise that market structure affects conduct, there is a generalized price-setting behavior that characterizes a perfectly competitive market, a monopoly, and an oligopoly. Perfect competition describes a market in which there is complete absence of direct competition among economic agents (Gould and Ferguson 1980). The price-setting mechanism can be viewed via the *tâtonnement* process in a Walrasian world whereby consumers do not interact directly with producers except by the auctioneer who sets market clearing prices. At the other end of the spectrum is the monopsonist, who may set purchase prices lower than equilibrium levels, thus capturing additional consumer surplus. The oligopsonist is on an intermediate level. His market conduct is characterized by the tendency to influence prices and an awareness that his profits depend upon the actions of his rivals. In the case where the participants cooperate to pursue a common policy to increase their overall profits, the fishers may encounter more than one price, which tends to be lower than it would be given a perfectly competitive market. This price-fixing behavior and long-run profits of monopsonists and oligopsonists can be enhanced by entry barriers combined with information and location factors (Ishak 1988).

Market conduct defines the conditions which make possible exploitative relationships between fishers and buyers. This is done via unfair price-setting practices which Smith (1981) classified as collusive, predatory, or exclusionary. These practices result in a level of profit over and above marketing costs and low or nonexistent profit margins for the producer. While these results are tackled in the section on market performance, analysis of market conduct deals with the conditions which encourage such behavior. This is made possible by organizational patterns that cause artificial restraints on prices, i.e., deviations from the demand-supply functions. A result is the weakening of the bargaining position of fishers. This is aggravated by informational and location factors which limit the options available to fishers.

This condition is exemplified by a socio-economic relationship of patronage, i.e., *suki* in the Philippines (Pomeroy 1989; Smith, Puzon and Libunao 1980; and Librero 1985) and *bertaukeh* in Malaysia (Ishak 1988). Research conducted by Pomeroy (1989) and Ishak (1988) show how this relationship affects price-setting as well as buying and selling practices. Pomeroy notes that fishers engaged in a *suki* relationship receive lower prices which varied according to the size of their outstanding loans. Furthermore, *suki* middlemen have the tendency to agree on a "target" price, i.e., collusive behavior. Ishak (1988) observed that such a relationship dictates to whom the fish should be sold. This patronage further contributes to the perpetuation of an oligopsonistic market structure.

There are no agreed upon procedures for analyzing the elements of market conduct. Rather, previous research points to some guidelines—in the form of questions—that have been culled from the four fish marketing studies to illustrate different approaches. These questions provide a systematic way to detect indications of unfair price-setting practices and the conditions under which such practices are likely to prevail. More specifically, they cover the following topics: the existence of formal and informal marketing groups that perpetuate such practices; formal and informal producer groups that affect bargaining power; the availability of price information and its impact on prevailing prices; the distance from the major market and its impact on prices; and the feasibility of utilizing alternative market outlets. The questions also provide an indication of the type of data needed and data collection procedures.

Buying and selling practices

- What is the source of fish (e.g., commercial fishers, municipal fishers, middlemen who operate fishing boats, inland traders)?
- Are there formal or informal marketing or producer groups that affect bargaining power?
- What buying/selling practices are in place (e.g., auction sale (open or secret bidding), contract sale, first-come/first-serve)?
- What distribution channels are used?
- Are there observed unethical trading practices (e.g., short weights, misleading price quotations, usurious practices, use of chemicals for fish preservation)?
- If credit is provided, what are the frequency and terms of payment?

Pricing behavior

- Who sets prices (e.g., one buyer or many buyers)?
- How are prices set (what is the degree of personal contact among market participants)?
- What factors are considered in price-setting (e.g., basic supply and demand conditions or artificial price restraints)?
- What is the basis for price differentiation?
- How do prices adjust to prevailing market conditions?
- Are there constraints in the use of specific market channels?
- Does the physical location of the market (in relation to other markets) affect prices and marketing arrangements?

Results of market conduct analysis from the four studies are presented in Table 6.

In the Matalom study (Pomeroy 1989), ex-vessel prices paid to *suki* fishers are set by a group of middlemen, the number of which is small relative to the number of fishers. Middlemen base the price on current supply, incoming supply, previous day's prices, number of fishers, season, and weather conditions. Due to the oligopsonistic structure in both cases, there is a likelihood of price collusion among *suki* middlemen and fishers. Price collusion among middlemen was verified through observation of their price-setting behavior. This is manifested via the "target price" which is agreed upon by the middlemen and adjusted according to the strength of the *suki* relationship with the individual fisher. As a result, statistical analysis—in the form of the Duncan's multiple range test—to assess price collusion yielded negative results, i.e., there were observed variances from the "target price".

The same study verified that a negative relationship exits between ex-vessel prices paid to *suki* fishers and the size of the loan still outstanding. Additionally, price differentiation was observed between *suki* and non-*suki* fishers whereby the *suki* fishers received lower prices. The margin was interpreted as an implicit interest charge for loans.

A t-test was also used by Scheid and Sutinen (1981) to verify the difference between ex-vessel prices paid by buyers from Puntarenas and from the outlying villages. The same study noted that ex-vessel prices were also affected by the amount of credit and supply services granted to fishers.

The impetus to adjust prices according to demand and supply conditions is quite clear in the Matalom case. This is reinforced by the possibility to shift *suki*, and the availability of price information among *suki* and non-*suki* fishers. Such is not the case in Navotas wherein pricing is done in "whispered bids" (Torres et al. n.d.) and in Malaysia (Ishak 1988) where shareholders are not well-informed of prevailing prices because transactions are conducted in Chinese and done in utmost secrecy.

Market Performance

Market performance refers to the impact of structure and conduct as measured in terms of variables such as prices, costs, and volume of output (Bressler and King 1970). By analyzing the level of marketing margins and their cost components, it is possible to evaluate the impact of the structure and conduct characteristics on market performance (Bain 1968). For most countries, it is generally acknowledged that a distribution system displaying acceptable performance is one that allows technological progress, has the ability to adapt, innovate, and utilize resources efficiently and to transmit prices that reflect costs (OECD 1982). Prices are thus viewed as a stimulus for an efficient

Table 6. Pricing behavior and analytical techniques used in four marketing studies.

Study	Source of Fish	Buying practices	Price-setting practice	Price determinants/(technique used)	Factors affecting net returns	Factors affecting marketing margins	Major cost components
Pomeroy (1989)	small-scale fishers	contract sale	collusion	- strength of *suki* relationship/ (Duncan's multiple range test) - outstanding loans/ (least-squares regression)	- market share - buyer's experience & skill - low ex-vessel price	- decrease in supply or increase in demand for fish - species handled, i.e., margin is higher for first class species	transportation cost, 41%
Ishak (1988)	commercial fishers; buyers; inland traders	-	whisper bids[1]	- outstanding loans - amount of service	-	-	-
Scheid & Sutinen (1981)	small-scale fishers	contract sale	-	-	-	- quantity of fish handled[2] - level of operating costs[2] - spoilage losses[2]	ice, 44%
Torres et al. (n.d.)	commercial fishers; buyers; inland traders	commission	whisper bids	-	- credit extension - buyer's experience & skill - risk bearing	(same as Pomeroy (1989)	hired labor, market fees, depreciation

[1] Pricing transactions are conducted in Chinese, leaving out the Malay crew members.
[2] With reference to retail level.

allocation of resources. Hence, desirable market performance is directly related to the competitiveness of an industry because distortions thereof tend to impede price efficiency. This section will discuss two major indicators of market performance: net returns and marketing margins (see also the second part, Analytical Methods, of this volume).

Estimates of net returns and market margins provide indications of an exploitative nature when net returns of buyers are much higher than the fair amount, i.e., including all marketing costs and a return to management and risk, and when market margins increase not because of higher real marketing costs but because prices paid to fishers are lower. The analysis of market performance using the industrial organization framework is as follows: collusive pricing (market conduct) becomes possible if (1) market concentration is high (market structure); (2) entry barriers are high (market structure); and (3) market information is not available to all participants (market conduct). This results in net returns and marketing margins that are much higher than the "fair" amount.

Determining the excessiveness of net returns and margins involves subjective elements which will vary between researchers. Pomeroy (1989), for example, used as benchmarks average returns and margins of middlemen for specific products (poultry and vegetables) in the agricultural sector mainly because fishery averages were not estimable, given the paucity of fish marketing studies.

Factors affecting net returns and marketing margins and the major components of marketing costs are summarized in Table 6.

Net returns

Net returns per middleman can be calculated by subtracting from gross returns fixed and variable costs. The mathematical formulation is:

$$NR = \Sigma P_i V_i - (FC + VC)$$

where:

NR	=	Net returns
P_i	=	Price per species/class handled
V_i	=	Amount per species/class handled
FC	=	Fixed costs
VC	=	Variable costs

Analysis of net returns aims to verify (or refute) the existence of above-average profits to middlemen. If the market were perfectly competitive, net returns would roughly equal a "fair" return to the middleman's capital.

However, oligopsonistic market structure would tend to increase returns as manifest price distortions as well as bias buying and selling practices (Table 4).

Marketing margins

In the fish marketing studies, the marketing margin (see also Mendoza this volume) is the difference between the ex-vessel price received by fishermen and the retail price paid by consumers. This amount can be interpreted as the cost of providing a mix of marketing services (Tomek and Robinson 1981). In a perfectly competitive market, the margin should, on the average and in the long run, be equal to the costs of marketing including costs of capital with a competitive return to labor, management, and risk. Of concern is the size of marketing margins, changes in marketing margins, and the incidence of changes in margins. Changes in factor prices, market efficiency, and market services embodied in the product change marketing margins. Marketing margins may fluctuate due to perishability of the product, the number of levels of participants in the marketing channel, the marketing services provided, and the risk and uncertainty borne by each of the market participants. Furthermore, marketing margins provide only one point of reference in the evaluation of performance and should be compared with measures of profits earned by marketing firms to determine whether or not the margins are excessive (Tomek and Robinson 1981).

Out of their respective marketing margins, middlemen pay for labor, equipment, capital, and other incidentals employed in carrying out their marketing functions. These marketing costs also include payments for management, capital, and risk. According to the perfectly competitive model for market behavior, the net margin received by middlemen is not larger, on average, than that needed to keep him or her in that particular business. If residual profits were larger, other firms would be attracted into the industry and profits would be reduced. If, however, entry is limited so that oligopsony or other forms of imperfect competition exist in the market, middlemen may be in a position to obtain larger margins than would be possible if the number of buyers was greater and the competition sharper (Scheid and Sutinen 1981).

Marketing margins can be defined alternatively as the price of a collection of marketing services which is the outcome of the demand for and the supply of such services (Tomek and Robinson 1981). The price of such services is determined by particular primary and derived demand and supply relations. A margin changes because certain of these functions shift relative to others.

Marketing margins can be presented in both absolute and relative terms. Absolute marketing margins may be defined as the difference between the price paid by consumers and that obtained by producers (see also Timmer et al. 1983). These marketing margins are based on absolute levels of prices.

Marketing margins expressed in percentage terms are dependent on the relative level of prices.

Based on the various interpretations, high marketing margins imply either an above-average return on the cost of providing marketing services (including fair returns to labor, management, and risk) or an implicit price that is higher than that resulting from demand and supply for marketing services. The existence of high marketing margins can be detrimental to fishers (in the form of low ex-vessel prices), to consumers (in the form of high retail prices), or both. Such high margins result from imperfectly competitive market conditions. Analysis of marketing margins based on Pomeroy (1989) as well as Scheid and Sutinen (1981) illustrates this (see Table 6).

A 7-month time series of gross margins in Matalom (Pomeroy 1989) yielded the following observations: an increase in gross margins coincided with a decrease in supply of fish (bad weather) and/or an increase in the demand due to holidays and fiestas; and gross margins were higher for first class fish. Similar results were observed by Torres et al. (n.d.) among brokers in Navotas.

Scheid and Sutinen (1981) decomposed the overall marketing margin into primary buyers', transporters' and retailers' margins. The fact that retailers received the highest margin can be attributed to the following: fish are usually sold by retailers in small quantities; higher operating costs prevail at the retail level; and the greatest spoilage and shrinkage losses are often assumed by retailers.

Pomeroy's study highlights the effect of demand and supply forces on marketing margins, while that of Scheid and Sutinen emphasizes marketing costs and risk. Basic economic sense tells us that prices adjust depending on demand and supply forces; however, imperfect market conditions result in artificial restraints on prices. The oligopsonistic structure identified by Pomeroy as well as by Scheid and Sutinen results in collusive price-setting behavior that weakens the position of fishers, as in the case of Pomeroy. This causal relationship implies that equity issues can be resolved by improving market structures.

Another parameter related to marketing margins is the producer's share. The producer's share is the ratio of producer price (ex-vessel) to consumer price (retail) (Mudiantono 1990). Mathematically, the producer's share can be expressed as:

$$PS = \frac{P_x}{P_r} = 1 - \frac{MM}{P_r}$$

where:

PS	=	producer's share
P_x	=	ex-vessel price of fish

P_r = retail price of fish

MM = marketing margin

The above equation tells us that a higher marketing margin diminishes the producer's share and *vice-versa*. It also provides an indication of welfare distribution among production and marketing agents. In the Gulf of Nicoya study, Scheid and Sutinen (1981) report that the fisher's share of retail price is 41%, whereas the wholesale and retail sector received 22% and 37%, respectively.

Fish marketing costs generally include transfer costs, market fees, hired labor, ice, interest on borrowed capital, interest on fixed investment, depreciation, and the cost of family labor. However, the structure and magnitude of costs depend on factors such as time and place of marketing, market conditions, and the marketing channel involved.

In general, components of marketing costs are of interest to policy makers because such knowledge can serve as the basis for reducing inefficiencies or establishing interventions that reduce such costs. A rather simplistic illustration is as follows: where transport is the principal marketing cost, the policy response includes improvement of infrastructure such as roads and rail lines. When labor constitutes the major cost component, the policy response is to induce adoption of labor-saving devices such as machinery. As an example, brokers at the Navotas Fish Port attribute a major portion of their marketing costs to hired labor, market fees, and depreciation (Torres, Pahuayon and Salayo n.d.). In the small-scale fishery of Matalom, at least 41% of total variable costs is accounted for by transportation (Pomeroy 1989); this was even higher for villages farther from the major retail market. In the Gulf of Nicoya, at least 44% of total monthly expenditures by primary buyers is allotted for ice (Scheid and Sutinen 1981).

Conclusions

In this paper, the industrial organization approach to market analysis was presented. The industrial organization framework posits a causal relationship between market structure, conduct, and performance. Operational measurement of these key industrial organization concepts was illustrated with results from four case studies on fish marketing carried out in Costa Rica, Malaysia, and the Philippines.

In the Leyte (Philippines) case, Pomeroy (1989) verified the homogeneity and rationality of small-scale fishers using descriptive and participatory techniques. He then addressed the issue of middleman exploitation using the industrial organization framework. Using techniques to verify market concentration, entry barriers, and product/service differentiation, Pomeroy classified the primary fish-buyer market in Matalom as an oligopsony (few buyers vs. many sellers). As a consequence of this imperfectly competitive structure, Pomeroy went on to find that price-setting practices tended to be collusive. Similar findings were reported with regard to price-setting practices in the case of Malaysia (Ishak 1988) and the Navotas Fish Port Complex (Torres et al. n.d.).

The limitations of the industrial organization approach include, as pointed out earlier, the dynamic rather than causal relationship between market structure, conduct, and performance. The approach also implicitly assumes a fairly substantial amount of data, preferably collected over a fairly long time. Also critical to this approach is the participation and astute observation of the researcher when it comes time to analyze market conduct. While the paper offers some systematic methodological guidelines in this area, it also notes the importance of subjective judgements with regard to the link between market conduct and performance.

References

Bain, J.S. 1941. The profit rate as a measure of monopoly power. *Quarterly Journal of Economics* 55:271-293.

Bain, J.S. 1951. Relation of profit rate to industry concentration, American manufacturing, 1936-1940. *Quarterly Journal of Economics.* 65:293-324.

Bain, J.S. 1968. Industrial organization. 2nd Edition, John Wiley and Sons, New York.

Bressler, R.G. and R.A. King. 1970. *Markets, prices and interregional trade*. NY, NY, USA: John Wiley and Sons.

Caves, R. 1982. *American industry: structure, conduct, performance*. 5th Edition. Englewood Cliffs, NJ, USA: Prentice Hall.

Devine, P.J., N. Lee, R.M. Jones and W.J. Tyson. 1984. *An introduction to industrial organization*. 5th Edition. London, UK: George Allen and Unwin.

Gould, J.P. and C.E. Ferguson. 1980. *Microeconomic theory*. 5th Edition. Homewood, IL, USA: Richard D. Irwin, Inc.

Ishak Haji Omar. 1988. *Market power, vertical linkages and government policy: the Malaysian fish industry*. Ph.D. Diss., University of East Anglia, East Anglia, UK.

Kaysen, C. and D.F. Turner. 1965. *Antitrust policy*. Cambridge, MS, USA: Harvard University Press.

King, R.A. (ed.) 1965. *Interregional competition research methods*. The Agricultural Policy Institute, University of North Carolina, Raleigh, NC, USA.

King, R.A. and W.R. Henry. 1959. Transportation models in studies of interregional competition. *Journal of Farm Economics* 41:997-1011.

Koch, J.V. 1980. *Industrial organization and prices*. 2nd Edition. London, UK: Prentice/Hall International.

Lerner, A.P. 1934. The concept of monopoly and the measurement of monopoly power. *Review of Economic Studies* 1:157-75.

Librero, A.R. 1985. Marketing system for fish in the Philippines. In *Small-scale fisheries in Asia: socioeconomic analysis and policy* (T. Panayotou, ed.). International Development Research Centre (IDRC), Ottawa, Canada.

Mann, H.M. 1966. Seller concentration, barriers to entry, and rates of return in thirty industries, 1950-1960. *Review of Economics and Statistics* 48:296-307.

Mudiantono. 1990. The use of structure, conduct and performance of the market to measure the marketing efficiency (A theoretical framework). *MEB* 2(1):53-59.

Organization for Economic Cooperation and Development (OECD). 1982. *Price formation and the performance of agrofood systems*. OECD, Paris, France.

Papandreou, A.G. 1949. Market structure and monopoly power. *American Economic Review* 39:883-97.

Pomeroy, R.S. 1989. *The economics of production and marketing in a small-scale fishery: Matalom, Leyte, Philippines*. ICLARM.

Rhoades, R. 1973. The theory of imperfect markets reconsidered. *J. Econ. Issues* 12(4):871-891.

Rothschild, K.W. 1942. The degree of monopoly. *Economica* 9:24-40.

Scheid, A.C. and J.G. Sutinen. 1981. The structure and performance of wholesale marketing of finfish in Costa Rica. In *Small scale fisheries in Central America: Acquiring information for decision making* (J.G. Sutinen and R.B. Pollnac, eds.). International Center for Marine Resource Development, University of Rhode Island, RI, USA.

Scherer, F.M. 1980. *Industrial market structure and economic performance*. 2nd Edition. Chicago, IL, USA: Rand McNally College Publishing Co.

Smith, E.D. 1972. Agricultural marketing research for less-developed areas. *Amer. J. Agr. Econ.* 54(4):666-670.

Smith, I.R. 1981. *The economics of the milkfish fry and fingerling industry of the Philippines*. ICLARM Technical Reports 1. International Center for Living Aquatic Resources Management, Manila and Aquaculture Department (ICLARM), Southeast Asian Fisheries Development Center, Iloilo, Philippines.

Smith, I.R., M.Y. Puzon, and C.N. Vidal-Libunao. 1980. *Philippine municipal fisheries: a review of resources, technology and socioeconomics*. ICLARM Studies and Reviews No. 4. International Center for Living Aquatic Resources Management (ICLARM), Manila, Philippines.

Stigler, G.J. 1968. *The organization of industry*. Chicago, IL, USA: Richard D. Irwin, Inc.

Timmer, C. P., W.P. Falcon and S.R. Pearson. 1983. *Food policy analysis*. Baltimore, MD, USA: The Johns Hopkins University Press.

Tomek, W.G. and K.L. Robinson. 1981. *Agricultural product prices*. 2nd Edition, Ithaca, NY, USA: Cornell University Press.

Torres, E.B., I.M. Pabuayon, and N.D. Salayo. Undated. *Market structure analysis of fish distribution channels supplying Metro Manila*. Department of Agricultural Economics, College of Economics and Management, UP Los Baños, College, Laguna, Philippines.

10

Socioeconomic Methods for the Study of Input Markets: Seed Potato in Argentina[1]

Olga Della Vedova and Susana Brieva[2]

Abstract

Production and use of seed potatoes in Latin America has undergone major changes in recent years. At the beginning of the 1980s, Argentina became self-sufficient in basic potato seed, and in so doing overcame the traditional need to import such seed on an annual basis.[3] This achievement resulted from the generation, transfer, and adoption of improved seed technology. Development and diffusion of this technology was a joint effort involving producers, as well as the private and public sectors. Participants included the National Plant Protection Service (*Servicio Nacional de Sanidad Vegetal*), the National Institute of Agricultural Technology *(Instituto Nacional de Tecnologia Agropecuaria*, INTA), the *Universidad Nacional de Mar del Plata* (UNMDP) and the International Potato Center (CIP). With the continued support of these organizations, Argentina seeks to maintain self-sufficiency in the supply of improved quality seed. As part of this overall effort, research was carried out to identify production and utilization patterns for potato seed; and in so doing, estimate demand for this important input. This chapter presents a methodology for characterization of potato seed production and use. It also presents a rapid, informal method to estimate demand for potato seed and demonstrates how it can be used (Monares 1986). Additionally, the design and use of a formal questionnaire as a

---

[1] This chapter was previously published in Spanish in Scott and Herrera (1991).

[2] Economist, Unidad Integrada Balcarce-Facultad de Ciencias Agrarias (Universidad Nacional de Mar del Plata), Estacion Experimental Agropecuaria de Balcarce (Instituto Nacional de Tecnologia Agropecuaria), C.C. 276-7620, Balcarce, Argentina.

[3] Potato seed goes through several generations of production from basic to registered to certified and finally to ordinary seed.

statistical tool to collect data is elaborated upon. Next are the main research results, an evaluation of these, and some final considerations.

Key words: Demand, supply, questionnaire, seed renewal rate, sample design, and selection.

Introduction

Potatoes are produced in a wide variety of agroecologies. In Latin America, different types of growers, potato varieties, and planting seasons give rise to a complex of production systems which has undergone substantial changes in recent years, particularly as regards seed production. This necessitates analysis of new production conditions and estimates of seed supply and demand, so as to prevent seed surpluses or deficits.

In Argentina potatoes are grown in many provinces. However, with time, the resulting pattern of area planted shows locations of intense potato production. The main producing areas are shown in Figure 1. They produce over 80% of the nations' supply of table (ware) potatoes. Production is distributed throughout the year in four seasons: early, semi-early, late, and semi-late. During the eighties, Argentina became self-sufficient in potato seed as a result of initiatives by local seed growers working in collaboration and with support from private and public institutions, including CIP. Among other achievements, Restricted Areas (Figure 1) were established to produce pathogen-tested potato seed.[4]

In light of these developments and to prevent a level of output that might jeopardize investments made or risk shortages that would require a return to imports of basic seed, officials at the National Plant Protection Service realized it was necessary to closely monitor local production. They therefore requested a study to identify the emerging characteristics of potato production and utilization in the most important table potato production areas and to estimate actual and potential demand for seed.

A multidisciplinary team including two economists, a geneticist, and a pathologist from the Balcarce Integrated Research Unit (*Unidad Integrada Balcarce*) Agricultural Experiment Station-National Institute Agricultural Technology Sciences (*Estacion Experimental Agropecuaria-INDA/Facultad de*

---

[4] Pathogen tested potato seed is defined as that which complies with legal requirements—in terms of the low-level of pest (principally virus) infestation present in the seed tubers—and which has been grown under official supervision. A large proportion of seed potato typically does not meet these standards and is therefore called "common seed." Common seed may be labelled as such with or without private laboratory tests.

Figure 1. Table potato and pathogen-tested seed potato production.

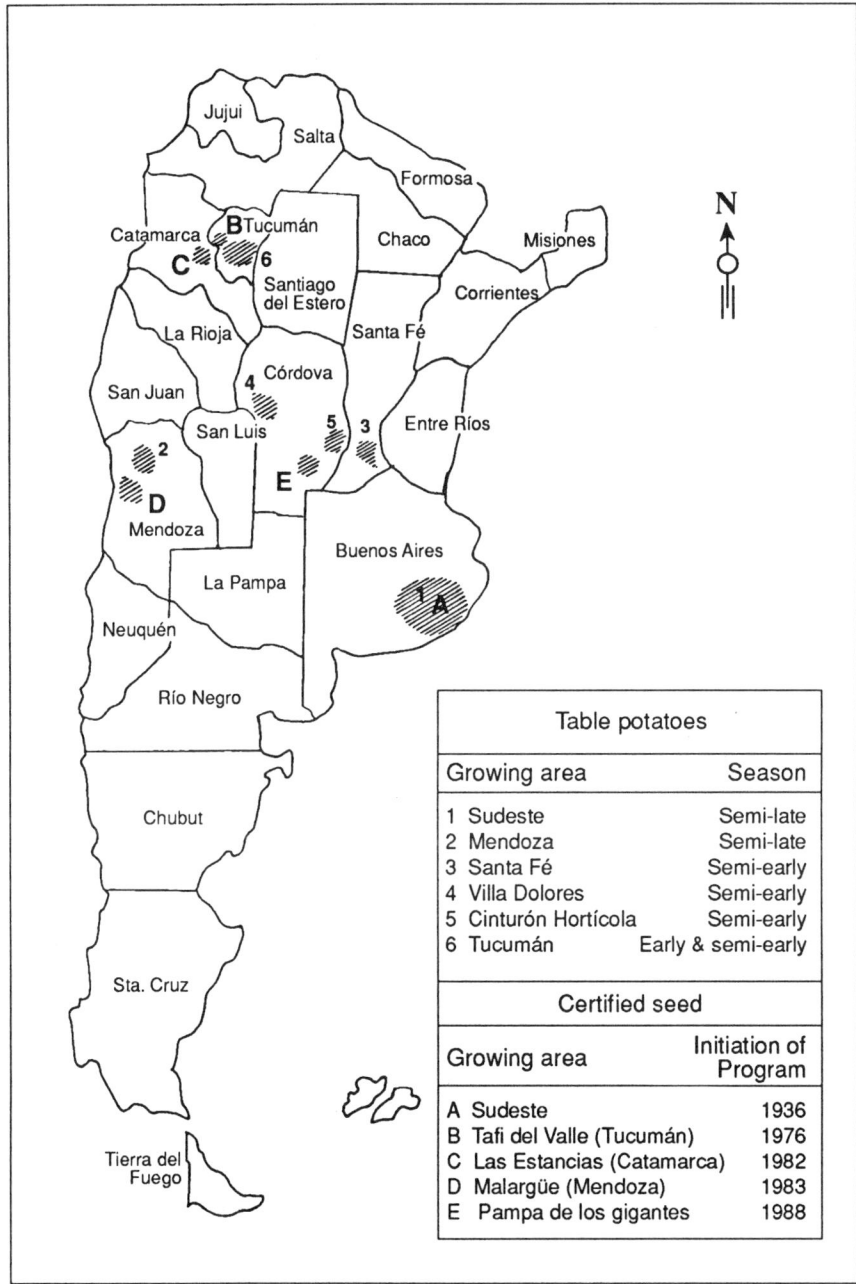

Source: Della Vedova and Brieva (1988).

Ciencias Agrarias-UNMDP), with support from CIP, defined the problem, goals, and methodology.

Due to the lack of prior research on potato cropping systems, the size of the market for seed, and the complex set of areas where tested seed and ware potatoes are grown during various seasons, the study was planned in two stages. In the first stage, the team analyzed production and use, and then demand for seed in each table potato production area. In the second stage, they will conduct a similar study in the Restricted Areas where pathogen-tested seed is produced under program supervision.

In this chapter, we present the methodology used to identify seed production and utilization patterns and to estimate demand for seed. We also explain the design and implementation of a formal survey, data processing procedures, and the implications of main research results. We then suggest some methodological lessons learned, before offering a few final considerations.

Methodology

Characterization of seed production and use requires different types of data. These include figures on total area and its use, land tenure systems, importance of potato cultivation in terms of the investment made, non-farm sources of income, and level of production technology as measured by cultural practices, seed quality, storage, and marketing.

Total seed requirements for a single variety were estimated using the following equation (Monares 1986):

$$Sa = A \times Ts \times Tr \times Pj$$

where:

Sa = Seed demand (sack[5])

A = Potato area planted (ha)

Ts = Amount of seed (sacks/ha)

Tr = Seed renewal rate (%)

Pj = Area planted to variety j (% of total area)

Statistics on total potato area planted were obtained from official sources. The team interviewed potato growers to estimate all the other variables. The amount of seed (Ts) is the average number of sacks used per hectare weighted by the survey area. The percentage of the total area planted to variety j (Pj) is the portion planted in that variety relative to the total survey

---

[5] The commonly used 50 kg sack of potatoes.

area. The renewal rate (Tr) is a key variable in determining or quantifying demand. It is the portion of seed the grower renews every year.

The research team decided to utilize formal surveys to collect information from farmers (see Appendix). Although the team already had some information about table potato production and marketing, they still needed to quantify key variables to estimate demand.

Sample Determination

Selecting the research sites. In order to properly demarcate the area where the survey would be administered, it was necessary to include various production zones and growing seasons (Table 1), as well as to consider their annual contribution to total national supply. The selected areas produce 1.9 million tons of potatoes, or 86% of national table production.

Sample size. The survey was conducted utilizing a stratified random sample. Strata were defined in consultation with extension agents and crop management specialists. Stratification and sampling were based on a list of growers with different corresponding areas under potato cultivation. The list was compiled using information provided by growers' associations and cooperatives, as well as INTA extension agents. This list was subsequently verified by potato rural assemblers in each of the zones to achieve 80-90% representation of the estimated universe.

Table 1. Production (000 t) by planting zone and season.

Planting Zone	Seasons				
	Early	Semi-early	Semi-late	Late	Total
Southeast Buenos Aires	-	-	1,176[a]	-	1,176
Mendoza	-	30	91[a]	-	120
Santa Fé	-	42	-	29	71
Villa Dolores	-	90	-	50	140
C. Hort. Córdoba	-	130	-	58	188
Tucumán	102[a]	18	-	7	128
Subtotal zones	102	311	1,267	144	1,824
Total country	116	335	1,299	165	1,914
Contribution to domestic supply by season (%)	6	17	68	9	100

[a] Total output from the selected areas is 86% of national table production.

Ultimately, the chosen sample included farms that comprised 20% of the total area planted to potato in a given zone. This level of coverage largely reflected the limited resources and operational capabilities of the research team. The selection of growers in the stratified sample was determined at random. The number of growers picked was in proportion to the total area for each stratum.

The team carried out 182 interviews in six zones (Table 2). During the growing season the survey took place, the growers interviewed had planted 18,587 ha of potatoes with the harvest mainly destined for sale or use as table potatoes (as opposed to seed, for example). Except for the production zone in the southeastern part of Buenos Aires Province, the survey's targeted sample size—fixed at 20% of the total area planted in potato—was largely achieved.

Survey Design

The survey (see Appendix) includes 29 pieces of information obtained from growers in a single interview. A pretest of the questionnaire allowed the team to make the necessary corrections, verify the feasibility of administering the survey in a relatively short time, and determine the logical sequence of questions that would keep growers interested and motivated.

The survey form is not organized by topics. Questions were therefore grouped by type: land tenure and land-use patterns; production technologies employed; marketing practices; and estimation of demand. The answers to questions about land tenure and land use reveal that the 182 producers surveyed cultivate a total of 130,000 ha of which 15% are devoted to potato, 18% to other crops, and 57% to raising livestock.[6] The survey responses also show that in most zones land rental is the predominant tenure pattern among potato growers. This reflects a permanent search for parcels where potato has not been grown for at least 3 to 4 seasons. Another group of questions is aimed at identifying the technical level achieved by growers.[7]

Survey answers are sufficiently detailed so as to enable identification of plot location within each zone, reveal the rationality of land use and attest to the growing importance of fallow periods. Technical production information, such as irrigated and rainfed parcels, planting dates, quantity and quality of seed planted per hectare, and marketing information such as prices, site, and origin, allowed the team to make estimates of the total volume traded during the season. The researchers estimate that 98% of seed utilized had been tested

---

[6] See questions 2, 3, 5 and 6 in the Appendix.

[7] See questions 7, 8, 9, 13, 14, and 17 to 24 in the Appendix.

Table 2. Surveyed area by zone and producer strata.

Zone	Season	Strata (ha)	Surveys done	Potato area (ha)	Surveyed area (as % of total)
Southeast Buenos Aires	Semi-late		80	10,321	17
		1-50	22	694	
		51-119	35	2,694	
		120-299	14	2,457	
		>300	9	4,526	
Mendoza	Semi-late		29	2,083	39
		1-20	9	99	
		21-50	6	189	
		>51	14	1,795	
Sante Fé	Semi-early		21	1,486	45
		1-20	5	70	
		21-50	6	235	
		>51	10	1,181	
V. Dolores	Semi-early		17	1,729	38
		1-20	-	-	
		21-50	8	319	
		>51	9	1,410	
C. Hort. Córdoba	Semi-early		14	1,147	21
		1-20	2	35	
		21-50	3	115	
		>51	9	997	
Tucumán	Early and semi-early		21	1,770	24
		1-20	2	26	
		21-50	5	118	
		>51	14	1,626	
Total of surveyed zones			182	18,587	

in "official" (45%) or private (53%) labs. During the season under study, 37% of the total area was planted utilizing purchased seed.

Other questions addressed the importance farmers attach to seed quality, how they verify seed health, and why some growers do not use seed produced under official supervision. The study revealed that whole seed ("*semillon*") is not popular, possibly due to insufficient supply of quality whole seed. Some growers link small seed size to sanitary problems and hold that potato cutting results in the larger-sized tubers preferred by consumers. The research team also identified the technology used by most seed producers as well as their history as seed producers within the survey zones (except one)—either within their own zones (agroecological conditions permitting) or in one of the Restricted Areas. Survey questions about seed storage revealed that refrigerated chambers are widely used for product preservation. Finally, the researchers asked questions about cultivation practices, such as the use of fertilizer, soil analysis, and planting techniques.

An understanding of commercial seed flows based on survey data proved more elusive. For example, the team was unable to identify such flows, nor the types of seed entering the market. In the absence of a centralized seed market and of a related price series, team members wondered how producers found out about the current price of seed. An implicit agreement was found to exist between buyers and sellers regarding price formation; it was agreed that a certain ratio between the price of seed potato versus that of table potato would prevail. The exact size of the ratio depends on whether the seed comes from Restricted Areas or table-producing zones.

Estimates of demand required information about the quantity of seed per hectare (Ts) and the portion of the total area planted to a give variety (Pj). These figures were computed and then weighted for the area in each zone, the production season, and the variety in question. The renewal rate (Tr)—a key variable in quantifying demand—was determined by asking producers to declare how often they renew their seed stock with either local or imported seed. Results were expressed as an annual renewal percentage. This figure reveals what growers consider to be the degeneration rate for the variety used on the basis of their experience as potato farmers. One interpretation of these results is that they indicate implicitly the maximum amount of seed farmers would be willing to buy under normal conditions. However, this interpretation should be qualified to take into consideration such additional factors as farmers' finances, their success in producing their own quality seed, and the market price of seed.

Conducting the Survey

Field work took place in two phases: March-June and September-November (1987) so as to coincide with growing seasons in different production zones (Figure 1). During the first phase, the team covered about 70% of the total targeted survey area corresponding to the semi-late growing season in the production zone in the southeastern part of Buenos Aires Province—the most important production area—and from Mendoza. In the second phase, the team surveyed potato growers (Tables 1 and 2) during the early and semi-early growing seasons in the Santa Fe, Tucumán, and Villa Dolores zones, and in

Córdoba's horticultural belt. This accounts for the remaining 30% of the targeted area.

Data Processing

The data were coded before processing using PC-XT hardware and SYSTAT software (version 1985) by SYSTAT Inc. Pre-coding of data is recommended. However, in this case as their collection and then coding was spread over time, it permitted relatively easy entry and control for accuracy. For purposes of analysis, the data were classified as qualitative and quantitative. Binary classification by attribute was preferred for qualitative data. However, the team occasionally resorted to multiple choice classification and determined frequency distributions for the different responses and the respective totals in each case. Measurement units for the quantitative variable included areas in hectares and 50 kg sacks of potatoes. This enabled the team to compute area planted to a given variety as a percentage of the total planted area, as well as the various types of seed.

The growers' renewal rate was estimated using the following weighted average equation:

$$Tr_j = \frac{P_{ji} \times Sup.\,P_{ji}}{Supt.\,P_j}$$

where:

Tr_j = Renewal rate for variety j

P_{ji} = Producer i renewal rate for variety j

Sup. P_{ji} = Area planted by producer i to variety j

SuptP$_j$ = Total area planted to variety j

The seed rate is the weighted average per area planted for the quantity of seed per hectare each grower plants per variety planted, or:

$$Ts_j = \frac{C_{ji} \times Sup.\,P_{ji}}{Supt.\,P_j}$$

where:

Ts_j = Seed rate per hectare for variety j

C_{ji} = Number of sacks of variety j producer i uses per hectare

Sup. P_{ji} = Number of hectares planted by producer i to variety j

Supt. P_j = Total area planted to variety j

Once the renewal (Tr) and seed (Ts) rates have been quantified and the portion of total area planted to variety j (Pj) is known, this information combined with official statistics on the area planted to potato within each zone are all the data that are needed. The team then used these figures and Monares' (1986) agroeconomic method to estimate seed demand.

Results

Argentina's National Plant Protection Service has supervised potato seed production since 1933. Likewise, INTA's National Potato Program staff includes teams of plant pathologists and geneticists. However, at the time this study was initiated, the Program had no empirical estimates of the size of the seed market, nor the types of producer and seed involved.[8] The program also had little hard data on the rate of adoption of improved potato technology recommended by private and public institutions. Information about survey variables used to determine seed production and use patterns revealed that potato production in Argentina is a commercial operation in which growers seek to maximize profits. As a result, a strong and highly uniform level of technological innovation exists.

Most growers are land owners who also rent land, diversify their production, and utilize soil conservation practices. Since 98% of the seed planted is tested in private labs (53%) or by the National Plant Protection Service (45%), growers are perfectly aware of their seed's quality.

In all zones but one, a large number of growers are making a concerted effort to produce their own seed within the local potato zone—agroecological conditions permitting—or in the Restricted Areas designated for seed production.[9] Growers' own seed accounts for 63% of seed planted. Purchased seed accounts for the remaining 37%.

In the absence of a formal seed market to generate prices, an implicit agreement regarding price formation operates between producers and sellers. This agreement is based on a strong correlation between seed and table potato prices. The type of seed, whether officially certified or "common" tested seed, has a strong influence on the prevailing ratio which fluctuates between 2 to 3 sacks of table potato for every sack of seed potato. The production zone of southeastern Buenos Aires Province plays a crucial role in this market as it consumes 58% of all seed traded; next are Las Estancias, Malargüe (Mendoza), and Tafi del Valle (Tucumán). The team estimated current demand for seed during the 1987-89 survey period for each production zone and growing season by variety (Table 3). The team then estimated potential demand for seed as well. Current demand is calculated by assigning a value for the renewal rate equal to the difference between growers' own seed and purchased seed. An

---

[8] Differentiating between officially-tested seed and common seed, with or without tests.

[9] The Córdoba Horticultural Belt.

estimate of potential demand can be derived from survey results from giving the renewal rate the value estimated by the growers for seed renewal (Table 4). The difference between current and potential demand reflects the impact of agronomic and economic factors.

Research results were presented to the National Seed Commission, an adjunct body of the National Plant Protection Service. The Commission includes representatives from all sectors involved in some aspects of potato production. It counsels government officials on development of Restricted Areas for seed production, classification and quality control standards, table and seed potato import licensing, and other related issues.

Lessons Learned and Conclusions

Limitations of the agro-economic method used to estimate demand include exclusion of some variables such as the price of seed and growers' incomes. However, it is a quick way to assess the size of the market. By using growers' assessments of their seed's degeneration rate, the team was able to approximate the rate of seed renewal. Potential demand can thus be estimated as well as the impact of various factors such as the price of seed, grower's financial status, and success of attempts by growers to produce their own seed.

Table 3. Current and potential demand for semi-late production in the southeastern region of Buenos Aires Province.

	Spunta variety				
	A (ha)	Ts (sacks)[a]	Tr (%)	Pj (%)	Sacks[a]
True	60,100[b]	52.4	0.46[c]	0.487	705,493
Potential	56,649[b]	52.4	0.70[c]	0.487	1,011,930

[a] 50 kg sacks.
[b] Average total area planted in potato for the previous 5 seasons is 56.649 ha. Area planted in potato during the period the survey took place was 60,100 ha.
[c] The estimated value of actual Tr based on responses to survey question 12 is 0.46; estimated potential Tr based on question 13 is 0.70.

Table 4. Seed demand.

	Total planted	Potential demand	True demand
Tons	220,477	137,844	79,379
50 kg sacks	4,409,545	2,756,875	1,587,595
Total (%)	100	63	37

Further analysis of these elements would yield more precise values for potential demand. Additionally, proper planning of the time and human resources required for data processing would permit the research team to carry out alternative or simultaneous analysis of information and thus help prevent delays and difficulties in generating survey results. This can be better achieved by field testing the survey questionnaire, ensuring logistical support for the field work, and hiring survey takers who are not only thoroughly knowledgeable regarding the questionnaire to be used, but also fully committed to the project's objectives.

A multidisciplinary approach to identifying the problem to be studied, the objectives of this particular research project, the methodological tools, and even the design of the survey proved highly positive. However, only social scientists participated in the actual field work and data analysis, thereby limiting the interpretation of the results.

One recommendation derived from the authors' experience in this research project would point to the need for active involvement of all team members at each and every stage of the process so as to insure an optimal outcome.

A list of producers may be a crucial data collection requirement. If no official list is available, several sources of information may be used to compile such a list including cooperatives, producers' associations and extensionists, among others.

Data processing is greatly enhanced by using in-house computing capabilities. If this is not possible, we recommend pre-coding the questionnaire before recording data in the field or inputting the figures into the computer. Furthermore, a software operator (either a statistician or a computer scientist) should be included in the multidisciplinary research team.

Finally, demand for potato seed can be estimated quite efficiently through a formal survey. The methodology used to do this can best be seen as a simple and rapid way of calculating the size of the market. The degree of accuracy in these calculations depends to a great extent on a representative sample chosen to estimate parameters such as seed rate (Ts), renewal rate (Tr), and percentage of the total area planted to a given variety j (Pj). More precise sample design and selection will achieve more precise results. Cross-section analysis demands the use of constant parameters over time. This problem can be overcome by repeating the estimation procedures over several periods, i.e., by combining cross-section and time-series analysis.

References

Della Vedova, O. and S. Brieva. 1988. *Caracterización de la producción y uso de semilla de papa en Argentina: una aproximación al problema* .

Departamento de Economía y Sociología Rural, Unidad Integrada Balcarce (E.E.A. INTA Balcarce, Facultad de Ciencias Agrarias-UNMDP), Argentina.

Monares, A. 1986. *Métodos agroeconómicos para estimar el uso esperado y la demanda de semilla certificada de papa*. (mimeo) Social Science Department, International Potato Center (CIP), Lima, Peru.

Scott, G. and J.E. Herrera (eds.). 1991. *Mercadeo agrícola: Metodologías de investigación*. IICA (International Institute for Cooperation in Agriculture), San Jose, Costa Rica/CIP, Lima, Peru.

Appendix

Survey questionnaire on seed potato in Argentina

General data: interviewer; date of interview; zone (southeastern part of Buenos Aires Province, Pedro Luro, Tucumán, Villa Dolores, Córdoba, Mendoza, southern part of Santa Fé Province); growing season: semi-late, early, semi-early; name of producer.

1. Experience with table potato production (in years).
2. Land use and land tenure during the recent growing season. Indicate total area (in hectares and for each kind of tenure) under cultivation area planted to potato; area planted to other crops; and land for other uses (fallow, pasture).
3. In terms of investment made, what are the main agricultural activities you engage in? Enumerate the production activities from more to less important (potato, cattle, cereals, oilseeds, other).
4. Do you have other sources of income besides agriculture? If the answer is yes, indicate which economic activity your income comes from (agroindustry, finance, trade, others).
5. If you rent land for potato production, describe the general characteristics of your contract. Duration (one or more growing seasons); payment (in cash or a share of the harvest); payment deadlines; production delivery arrangement (in piles in the field, bagged and on the truck, other); technology utilized (irrigation, fertilizer, seed quality, others); condition of the field at the end of rental season (planted, not planted, others).
6. If you rent land for potato production, what does your decision depend on? Rental rates; expectations about potato prices; years of fallow since last use field location; soil testing for nematodes; irrigation possibilities; other reasons (detail).
7. If you plant potatoes on your own land, do you have a pre-established crop rotation (yes, no)? If the answer is yes, which is the most frequent one (detail crops and frequency)?
8. Area planted in potato takes place in how many fields? Name of the field; area (ha); location.
9. Varieties, growing season, and seed utilization during the 87-88 crop year. Variety; area (ha); irrigated, rainfed; planting date; seed quantity (sack per ha): cut, "*semillon*"; source of seed: own, pathogen tested, tested "common" (sacks and virus %), non-tested "common"; price; origin; and supplier.

10. Every how many years do you normally renew or change you seed? Domestic varieties: Huinkul, Ballenera, Serrrana; Imported varieties: Spunta, others.
11. Do you always buy seed from the same supplier (yes, no, why)?
12. Do you usually buy seed in the same zones (yes, no, why)?
13. Do you verify the virus percentage in the seed you buy (yes, no, why)? How do you verify it? Do you require a certificate of (seed) analysis from the seller? Do you perform your own analysis on the purchased seed?
14. In case the producer has not purchased pathogen-tested seed, why haven't you purchased pathogen-tested seed for this growing season? Is it that you never plant pathogen-tested seed? The price is too high? It yields the same as non-tested seed? Your expectation regarding table potato prices are low? Or other (detail)?
15. What do you think of pathogen testing?
16. What are the principal problems you have had with seed? Indicate separately for your own seed and for purchased seed.
17. Keeping question 9 in mind, why do you use "*semillon*"? Why don't you use it?
18. Do you plant certain parcels specifically to produce seed potatoes (yes, no)? If the answer is yes, indicate if this seed is for sale of for on-farm utilization. If the answer is no, why don't you produce it?
19. If the answer to question 18 is yes, detail the additional cultural practices and/or labor that you employ on those parcels planted to produce seed. You plant better quality seed? Do you pull out some plants to maintain purity/uniformity in the field? Do you use more insecticide? Do you have tests done on the plant leaves? Do you burn off the foliage with defoliant or do you grind it up with a grass cutter? Before the vegetative cycle ends: do you have tests done on the seed tubers? Do you separate them from table potatoes? And others (detail).
20. Where do you usually store the seed you use for each growing season? Indicate if it is in cold storage or in the field according to varieties of own or purchased seed.
21. Do you store Spunta produced in the southeastern part of Buenos Aires Province in cold storage (yes, no, why)?
22. Do you perform soil tests to determine the quantity of fertilizer to apply (yes, no)?
23. Do you perform soil tests for nematodes in fields you own (yes, no)?
24. What distance do you allow between plants? Indicate distance between plants in meters and between furrows in centimeters according to intended use of the harvest (seed or table potatoes).

25. In the case of seed producers, how many years have you been producing seed?
26. Have you produced seed every year (yes, no)? If the answer was no, why have you produced seed only in some years?
27. If you are a seed producer, do you sell to producers of your zone (if not, detail in percentage)? Do you sell to producers in other zones (yes, no, detail for each zone in percentage): southeastern Buenos Aires Province, Pedro Luro, Tucumán, Villa Dolores, Córdoba, Mendoza, southern Santa Fé Province?
28. What kind of seed do you usually sell? Express in percentages. Pathogen tested, tested "common", non-tested "common".
29. How do you collect information about prices for seed potatoes (distinguish between buyer and seller)? From producers in your potato production zone, producer associations, visits to other zones, estimates based on the price of table potato, others?

Part 3

Analytical Methods

- **Price Analysis**

11

A Primer on Marketing Channels and Margins[1]

Gilberto Mendoza[2]

Abstract

This chapter presents a methodology for the analysis of marketing channels, margins, and costs for agricultural products. This is a crucial component of an overall methodology to study marketing using a "commodity subsystems approach." The procedures presented are particularly useful in the absence of time or financial resources to carry out more exhaustive marketing research.

Key words: Prices, producer, consumers, physical functions, exchange functions.

Introduction

Marketing is usually seen as a "system" because it comprises several, usually stable, interrelated structures that, along with production, distribution, and consumption, underpin the economic process. Marketing studies adopt different viewpoints and approaches. For instance, the functional or marketing functions (physical, economic, and exchange) approach; the organizational or institutional approach covering all market participants (producer, trader, transporter, wholesaler, retailer, consumer, etc.); the commodity sub-systems approach (which combines the previous two approaches); the postharvest approach which analyzes all harmful or loss-provoking elements and other causes in the transfer of products; and the mixed systems approach.

In a commodity subsystem approach, the institutional analysis is based on the identification of the major marketing channels. This approach includes the analysis of marketing costs and margins.

---

[1] This chapter was previously published in Spanish in Scott and Herrera (1991).

[2] Former marketing specialist, Instituto Interamericano de Cooperación para la Agricultura (IICA), La Paz, Bolivia; currently, private consultant, Apartado Aéreo 477, Popayán, Colombia.

Physical distribution (i.e., functions) and economic activity (i.e., buying, selling) are two dimensions of marketing carried out by institutions or people. An analysis of these two dimensions of agricultural marketing is intimately linked to the institutions created by law or by corporate standards (whether these enterprises are public or privately-run companies) or by custom or simply by established procedure, that have emerged as a result of the social and economic relation between the participants in the marketing process (middlemen, consumers, and producers).

Marketing institutions include market stabilization agencies, boards of foreign trade, supermarket chains, wholesaler/retailer networks, a town's central market, or agreements between producers and rice millers. The effectiveness of marketing institutions depends on the involvement of the relevant people.

The following methodology for analyzing marketing activity combines elements of both the functional and institutional approach alluded to earlier. It consists of several steps. The analysis of marketing channels begins with a review of basic concepts. This is followed by a review of the procedures involved in this type of analysis, including the preparation of the formal (or informal) questionnaires as well as determination of the channel participants, including the procedures needed to determine sample size. Methods for computing marketing margins are then presented. Finally, some methodological guidelines concerning the geographical and temporary limits to this type of research are reviewed.

Marketing Channels

Basic concepts

The analysis of marketing channels is intended to provide a systematic knowledge of the flow of the goods and services from their origin (producer) to their final destination (consumer). This knowledge is acquired by studying the "participants" in the process, i.e., those who perform physical marketing functions in order to obtain economic benefits. In carrying out these functions, marketing agents achieve both personal and social goals. They earn a (personal) financial reward by performing an activity desired by society. They add value to production and in so doing help satisfy consumers' needs. The price the consumer pays for the goods (the physical commodity) and services (e.g., transportation, bulk-breaking, grading) rendered conpensates the marketing agent for his efforts. This price also serves as a signal to all the actors in the marketing channel, i.e., producers, rural assemblers, transporters, wholesalers, and retailers.

The process that links production to consumption can be either centralized or decentralized. The organizational system for marketing agents in a marketing chain may be classified accordingly. The center of centralized systems is typically occupied by a wholesaler. His (her) most important function is to help establish prices. This function has repercussions for the price of goods at various levels—from their origin (the producer level) to their destination (the consumer level). Figure 1 shows the three main stages in a centralized marketing system, i.e., concentration or collection, standardization or preparation (done by the wholesaler), and dispatching through appropriate channels to complete distribution.

In the decentralized system, the focal point of activity at a single location, as evidenced by the wholesaler's traditional overtures towards retailers (and producers), is completely displaced. Instead, producers and rural assemblers take on added responsibilities. In Figure 2, the producer's organization replaces the wholesaler (22% of the harvest) as production moves from its origin to the retailer; the bottom part shows the wholesaler taking over the rest of the marketing process. This approach provides the researcher with a scheme to begin mapping out the various agents involved in the marketing process, including their connections and functions.

Marketing Agents

Some traditionally accepted definitions help to identify and classify participants in the marketing process. In the real world, these classifications are by no means mutually exclusive.

Producer. The first link in the marketing chain. The producer harvests the crop and supplies the product to the second agent. From the moment he chooses what to grow, he is already making a marketing decision (by answering the questions of what, when, and how much to grow).

Rural assembler. Sometimes also known as the transporter or the trader/transporter, he is the first link between the producer and other middlemen. He collects several smaller lots of scattered rural production and combines them into a single load at one location. In so doing, he typically classifies these diverse lots into fewer types. To the extent he arranges for or provides shipping, the key function the rural assembler provides in addition to assembly is transport.

Wholesaler. He concentrates the various, intermediate-sized loads and puts the product into large, uniform units. These activities all contribute to price formation. In so doing, the wholesaler provides information to suppliers (e.g., growers, rural assemblers) and assumes to a varying degree the risks associated with the transfer of property rights attached to the goods and services being bought and sold. He also facilitates mass and specialized storage operations,

Figure 1. Principal stages of the marketing process in a traditional centralized system.

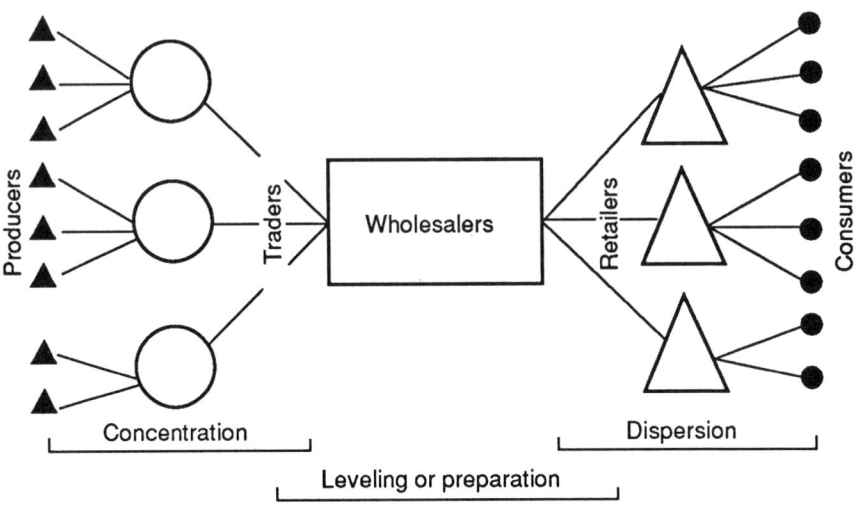

Figure 2. Avocado marketing chain in Region V's network of associated producers, Santiago, Chile.

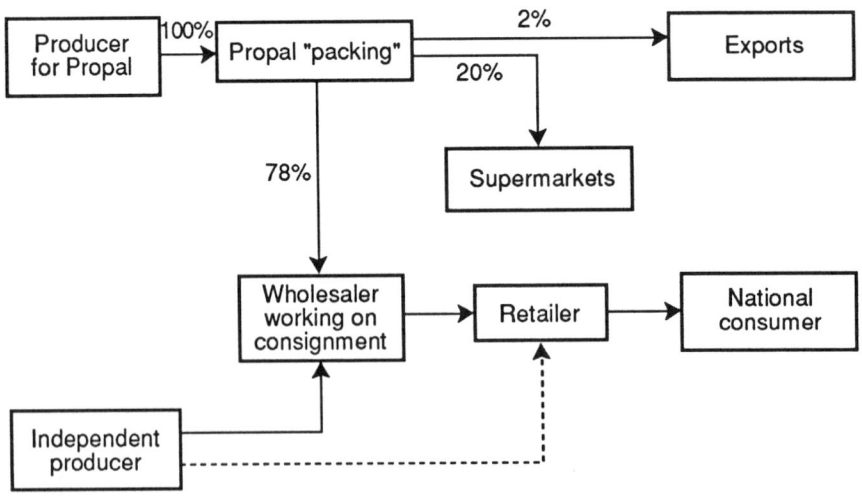

Source: Mendoza et al. (1982).

transportation and, in general, the subsequent distribution operations involving retailers.

Retailers. Middlemen, which includes supermarkets and other large-scale retailers who divide up large shipments of produce and sell it to consumers in small units. The basic function that they provide is bulk-breaking.

Food processing companies. Enterprises that use agricultural commodities as raw material.

Exporters and importers. These are companies that buy and sell agricultural products in foreign markets. These products vary from those freshly harvested to those that have gone through various stages of processing.

Government institutions or agencies. These include all government organizations that guarantee minimum prices to the producers and regular, price-controlled supplies to consumers. In several countries, these organizations no longer exist, or they no longer guarantee minimum prices or supplies. In some cases, their sole role now is to provide food assistance to low-income households.

Producer and consumer associations. These include professional associations and farmer cooperatives that regulate and influence the production and marketing process. They may also be consumer associations that substitute for middlemen and have an impact on marketing margins.

Brokers. These agents work for a commission on behalf of other participants. They operate at all levels of the marketing chain. Typically, they work for either a flat rate or percentage (of the selling price) commission.

Other organizations. Institutions such as "marketing boards", which may be mixed public-private (parastatals) or solely private entities with some semi-monopolistic concessions (private companies, export cartels, etc.).

Consumer. The last link in the marketing chain. Families usually personify the final consumer. However, processing companies may also be considered the user (or consumer), albeit at the intermediate stage.

These participants and their respective functions often may overlap. The most widespread combinations are: traders-wholesalers that collect the commodity and supply it to retailers, wholesalers-retailers (wholesalers that also sell directly to consumers), and wholesalers-exporters.

Methodology

We can identify and analyze the marketing channels for a class of products (e.g., fruits, vegetables) or for a particular item. Figure 3 shows the marketing channels for vegetables in Santiago, Chile. This type of analysis demands a large and systematic research effort aimed at all the horticultural products coming in and out of a particular market. In-depth and more detailed analysis of marketing channels for a single product is more frequent. Figure 4 shows the marketing channels for potatoes in Santo Domingo, Dominican Republic. The procedures involved in this type of analysis include the following.

The first step is to determine the final market for the product(s) in question. Next, its one (or several) supply sources must be identified. The concept of "marketing" summarizes the physical and economic processes whereby the goods are transferred from the producer to the consumer. The "marketing chain" is the path the goods follow from their source of original production to their ultimate destination for final use. As many marketing channels may exist as there are separate sources and/or destinations for each item. A specific analysis must be made in each case in which the objective in every instance is to trace the movement (purchase and sale) of the product from the source of supply through as many steps as exist before it reaches its point of final sale.

Figure 4 shows the chain for commercialization of potatoes produced in San José de Ocoa in the Dominican Republic, which accounts for 90% of national production. The potatoes are mostly sent to Santo Domingo, the main consumption center. While other channels may exist in the same country for the same product, it is sufficient for the researcher to identify and analyze the most important one(s).

Once the product's source(s) and final destination(s) have been determined, the research analysis parameters can be established. These include the volume (or period) of supply, or the time during which the harvest occurs (this may be one week or over a month). The essential component of the analysis is the appropriate unit of measure, i.e., one that accurately represents what it is that is supplied and demanded, bought and sold. The extent of detail portrayed in this unit of measure depends on the statistical information available, and on the accuracy and depth of the study. In the survey carried out in the Dominican Republic (Figure 4), where statistics on potato supply were found to be imprecise, a one-month period during the peak harvesting season was chosen as the time period during which to conduct the research. The procedures actually utilized will be explained in the following section.

The research on vegetable marketing in Santiago (Chile) was to collect the basic information needed to plan the establishment of a wholesale terminal market to improve supply of farming products to Greater Santiago. As a sample frame, the study analyzed secondary data on 100% of the supply of vegetables that went into and out of the city during a six-month period. Figure 3 shows that the findings enabled researchers to determine the origin of supply (by regions), its final destination (consumers in Santiago and regional markets after going through Santiago), and the relative importance of different types of middlemen. In every case, the volume handled is given as a percentage of the total.

Figure 3. Vegetable supply flow for Greater Santiago (Chile).

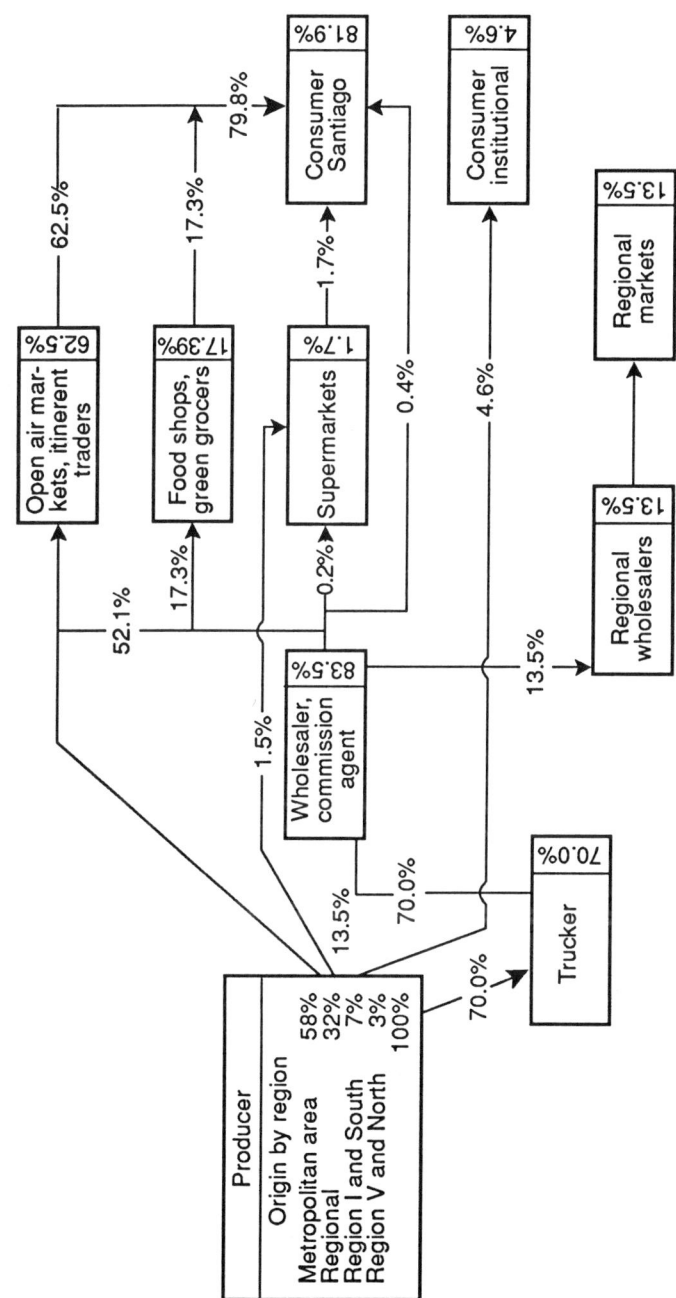

Source: Mendoza (1987).

Figure 4. Marketing channels for potatoes in Santo Domingo, Dominican Republic.[a]

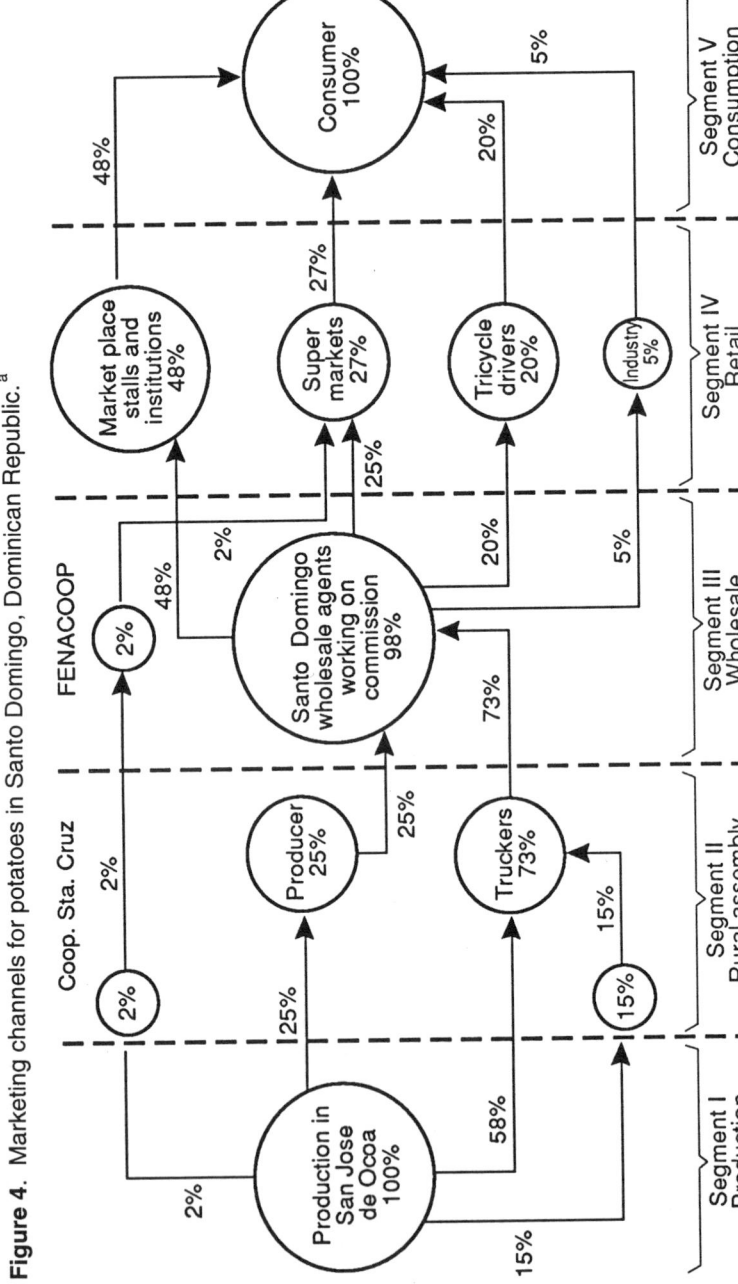

[a] In this study, the various "segments" or levels of the marketing process were identified to facilitate the demarcation of sampling areas for analyzing the marketing channels and margins. Growers themselves assemble and transport 25% of the produce that is transferred from the farm to the wholesalers in Santo Domingo.

The next step consists of a participatory survey of all of the types of marketing agents involved in the marketing chain. By interviewing all types of marketing agents, the researcher can more easily follow the marketing process from its origin to its final destination (this can also be done the other way around: from its final destination to its origin). Sampling is done so as to include and thereby classify the physical functions of all the "segments" or stages in the marketing chain provided by one type of marketing agent against that provided by other types. The "participatory" aspect refers to the in situ interviews so that the researcher can note responses and observe marketing practices simultaneously.

The sequential nature of the survey procedures not only provides a systematic appreciation of the respective roles of the different marketing agents but also facilitates cross-checking information.

Proper sampling and the interviews themselves meant it was possible to determine who acts as the marketing agent who sells (e.g., producer, rural assembler, trader/transporter) and the one who acts as the marketing agent who buys (e.g., wholesaler),[3] where transactions take place, the physical functions carried out (transportation, classification, packaging, and storage), and other functions (financing and price information, for example). Besides information on marketing channels, the survey also generated data on marketing margins, which is why it included questions concerning buying and selling prices, as well as places and dates of where the trades took place. The Appendix includes a survey guide to the kinds of issues to be addressed in a formal questionnaire about marketing procedures administered to producers as part of a study of potato marketing in Bolivia. This survey examined the prices, places, and dates of sale. It also tried to determine the identity of the buyers.

From the answers given to the basic questions in the study ("From whom did you buy?" "To whom did you sell?") one can deduce who is next in the marketing chain to be surveyed. In the case of the Dominican Republic, the answers given by the traders when they were asked "To whom did you sell?" led to the discovery of the third segment of the chain (Figure 4), the urban wholesaler, who answered a survey form specially adapted to his conditions. This form also included the aforementioned basic questions.

The 'retailer' appeared in the wholesaler's answers to the last question: "To whom do you sell?" (but in practice, retailers should be classified into

---

[3] By asking "From whom do you buy? and "To whom do you sell?" each agent in the chain confirms (contradicts or clarifies) what the preceding (or following) one said. For example, if the wholesaler is asked "Who do you buy from?" and he answers "From the rural trader or transporter," he identifies the seller and his answers can be compared. He should have answered "To the wholesaler," to those answers given by the traders when asked "To whom did you sell?"

several different types as shown in Figures 3 and 4). Successive interviews with retailers allowed us to complete the process and to arrive at the "final destination or end-user," the consumer.

Sample size

Researchers do not agree on the sample size and sampling procedures that should be used in each segment of the marketing chain. The decisions involved are partly a function of the information currently known, time and resources available, accessibility to and openness of the marketing participants themselves, as well as the estimated size of the trading population.

Perhaps it is best to begin by determining the different types of agents at each stage of the marketing chain and the possible size (number of stages) of the marketing channel. Then, the sequence or the order of the whole marketing process should be reviewed. This can be done even from the source to the final destination (from the producer to the consumer) or the other way around (beginning with the consumer). The first procedure is often easier, especially for less experienced researchers.

There is no iron-clad rule to help one determine the number of interviews required for each stage or segment of the marketing chain. For the marketing of a single type of agricultural commodity, from one production area (origin) and for one urban market (destination), several hundreds or thousands of producers, thousands and even millions of consumers, one to two dozen rural traders, two to three dozen wholesalers, and five hundred to a thousand and even thousands of retailers, can often be found. Thus, the establishment of a fixed procedure (e.g., a certain percentage of the estimated population of a particular type of participant) could prove excessive for some segments of the study (in particular the consumer segment) and insufficient for others (traders and wholesalers). In some studies of marketing channels and margins, as many as 30% of all traders and wholesalers were surveyed (approximately 12 interviews in each case); between 5% and 8% of producers, 5% of retailers, and less than 1% of consumers.

Sampling by segments without size limits established a priori can simplify things, particularly in rapid appraisals of marketing systems. One rule of thumb to apply in these instances is to reduce or amplify the number of interviews to be conducted in the sample according to the extent of variability in the responses to the questions. The tolerable level of dispersion at which point no further interviews are required can be determined by the interviewer himself (if he has been adequately trained) or by his supervisor.

A trained surveyor typically becomes rapidly aware of the degree of uniformity or variability in the answers. This allows him to determine the appropriate sample size he needs for each type of participant in each market segment.

Sampling is more demanding when the marketing channel and the percentage of production that flows through each circuit are studied. In these cases, the definition of the time period, or sample frame, as well as the definition of the geographical area (from origin to final destination, stages 1 and 2 already mentioned) are more rigorous and should be supported with statistical information or primary data.

Marketing Margins

No other term associated with agricultural marketing is more misunderstood than the concept of a marketing margin. Exchange activities add ownership benefits to products and also generate income for sellers. Not all of this income is pure profit. In fact, a big marketing margin may, in fact, result in little or no profit, or even a loss for the seller involved. That depends on the marketing costs as well as on the selling and buying price. Furthermore, marketing margins are not always earned only by middlemen. Many observers confuse a marketing margin with a trader's margin of profit. This is simply not the case. A marketing margin really measures the share of the final selling price that is captured by a particular agent in the marketing chain. It includes costs and typically, though not necessarily, some additional net income. In the case of agricultural marketing, farmers receive part of the marketing margin as producers per se. To the extent that they also perform marketing activities (e.g., rural assembly, transport), they also earn an additional share of the total marketing margin.

Calculating Margins

When there are several participants in the marketing chain, the margin is calculated by finding the price variations at different segments and then comparing them with the final price to the consumer. The consumer price then is the base or common denominator for all marketing margins. Some errors and misunderstandings result when the margin calculations are done using a different denominator. These relative margins, expressed as a percentage, cannot be compared between themselves as if they belonged to the same chain because they have different bases. That is why margin calculation should be done using a single basis, i.e., the final consumer price. Computing the total gross marketing margin (TGMM) is always related to the final price or the price paid by the end consumer and is expressed as a percentage:

$$TGMM = \frac{\text{Consumer price} - \text{Farmer's price}}{\text{Consumer price}} \times 100$$

It is useful to introduce here the idea of "producer participation," "farmer's portion," or "producer's gross margin" (GMM_P) which is the portion of the price paid by the end consumer that belongs to the farmer as a producer.

It should be emphasized that growers that act as middlemen also receive an additional marketing margin. The producer's margin is calculated as a difference:

$$\text{GMMP} = \frac{\text{Price paid by the consumer} - \text{Marketing gross margin}}{\text{Price paid by the consumer}} \times 100$$

In a marketing chain with only one trader between producer and consumer, the net marketing margin (NMM) is the percentage over the final price earned by the intermediary as his net income once his marketing costs are deducted. The percentage of net income that can be classified as pure profit (i.e., return on capital) depends on the extend to which factors such as the middleman's own, often imputed, salary are included in the calculation of marketing costs.

$$\text{NMM} = \frac{\text{Gross margin - Marketing costs}}{\text{Price paid by the consumer}} \times 100$$

Because precise marketing costs are frequently difficult to determine in many agricultural marketing chains for the reasons alluded to above (i.e., these costs are often both cash costs and imputed costs), the gross and not the net marketing margin is calculated. Thus, the "marketing margin" should be understood as the gross marketing margin. However, this very important consequence is frequently overlooked and for that reason marketing researchers are well advised to emphasize it in reporting their findings.

Margin determination surveys should be conducted parallel to channel surveys. To determine the channels, one asks the questions "From whom did you buy?" and "To whom did you sell?" To obtain information concerning the margins, agents have to answer the questions "What price did you pay?" and "What was the selling price?" Nevertheless, there is a pragmatic difference. When interviewees are asking about the channels, they usually reply without hesitation. They also willingly and quite accurately answer the question "What was the selling price?" The researcher can also easily verify, at any time, the selling prices in the market. However, interviewers frequently are reluctant to answer the question "At what price did you buy?" Under such circumstances (and in an effort to verify the accuracy of the responses that are freely given), the question "How did the sale occur?" aims at obtaining the following information:

- Quantity sold: to derive ultimately the price per unit of sale.
- Price (or payment) received or selling price: to calculate the margin.
- Place of sale: to refine the estimate of gross marketing margin and determine the significance of place embodied in the product sold in a particular location.
- Date of sale: to complete the calculation of the gross marketing margin and the aggregation of utility of time.

A primer on marketing channels and margins

- To whom did you sell: to determine the marketing chain.

Even if the answers available only concern the selling price, one can still calculate accurately the gross marketing margin. The buying price by a marketing agent can be determined with the information on the selling price given by the agent that precedes him in the marketing chain (Table 1). Below is an example of a margin calculation based on data about the selling price of one product (all of the same quality, during one week, in kilograms).

Based on the data concerning the selling and buying prices, one can calculate the marketing margins by applying the gross marketing margin calculation formulas (GMM). The results are as follows:

$$\text{TGMM (complete distribution channel)} = \frac{6.00 - 3.26}{6.00} \times 100 = 46\%$$

$$\text{TGMM}_{RA} \text{ (rural assembler/trucker)} = \frac{4.50 - 3.26}{6.00} \times 100 = 21\%$$

$$\text{GMM}_W \text{ (wholesaler)} = \frac{5.00 - 4.50}{6.00} \times 100 = 8\%$$

$$\text{GMM}_r \text{ (retailer)} = \frac{6.00 - 5.00}{6.00} \times 100 = 17\%$$

$$\text{TGMM (total supply process)} = \text{GMM}_{RN-T} + \text{GMM}_W + \text{GMM}_R = 46\%$$

$$\text{GMM}_P \text{ (producer participation)} = 100\% - 46\% = 54\%$$

Table 1. Prices for potatoes in the marketing channel grown in the North of Chuquisaca, Bolivia.

Marketing chain participant	Selling price ($/11 kg)
Producer on a farm in Sucre	3.26
Rural assembler/trucker in Santa Cruz	4.50
Wholesaler in Santa Cruz	5.00
Retailer in Santa Cruz	6.00
Consumer (not a seller; only a buyer)	6.00

Source: Agricultural Development Project for the North of Chuquisaca - IICA 1989.

Procedures to Estimate Marketing Margins

With respect to the number of interviews per type of marketing participant and other methodological aspects, procedures similar to the ones used for studying marketing channels are suggested, after having taken into account considerations of space, time, and available resources. For the study of channels and margins, an area extending from the point where the product originates to its final destination is determined. Take for instance, the potatoes harvested in San José de Ocoa and distributed in Santo Domingo, Dominican Republic (Figure 4), or the vegetables produced in Arica and consumed in Santiago and other Chilean markets (Figure 5). The time period of interest is the number of days it takes for the produce to go through the marketing channel, i.e., from the moment it leaves the farmer's field to the moment it reaches the consumer.

Previous studies have found that one can typically estimate marketing margins quite accurately through price surveys carried out at all levels in the distribution channel during one week under normal supply conditions. In the case of non-perishable commodities, e.g., for durable grains—frequently stored for a period of months—the procedure of surveying one typical week need not be modified. It only has to be complemented by data collection for prices before and after storage.

Studies of non-perishable agricultural products that are typically traded in international markets, e.g., cereals, cotton, coffee, often have access to reasonably good statistical information recorded and/or published by various official and private sources, as well as earlier research results. This information can be extremely useful to help evaluate/clarify the survey responses elicited from marketing agents. This scenario is much less likely in the case of perishable products, and thus estimating the margins here depends to a much larger extent on primary data collection in the form of surveys carried out over time intervals that reflect the relevant marketing cycle.

Stability of Marketing Margins

Estimating marketing margins is often less demanding as regards the number of interviews and sample size used, than is the effort required to determine marketing channels. In several studies this author was involved with, systematically recording prices at different levels of the marketing chain during a two-to-three-week period was sufficient to calculate quite accurately the relevant marketing margins. This proved to be the case both for yearly marketing cycles and even longer periods.

Some studies have attempted to show that price variations provoke changes in magnitude of the marketing margins. For one such study, they have utilized as the period of study a longer time frame than the one to three weeks suggested above. Table 2 provides information for a 17-week systematic study

A primer on marketing channels and margins   271

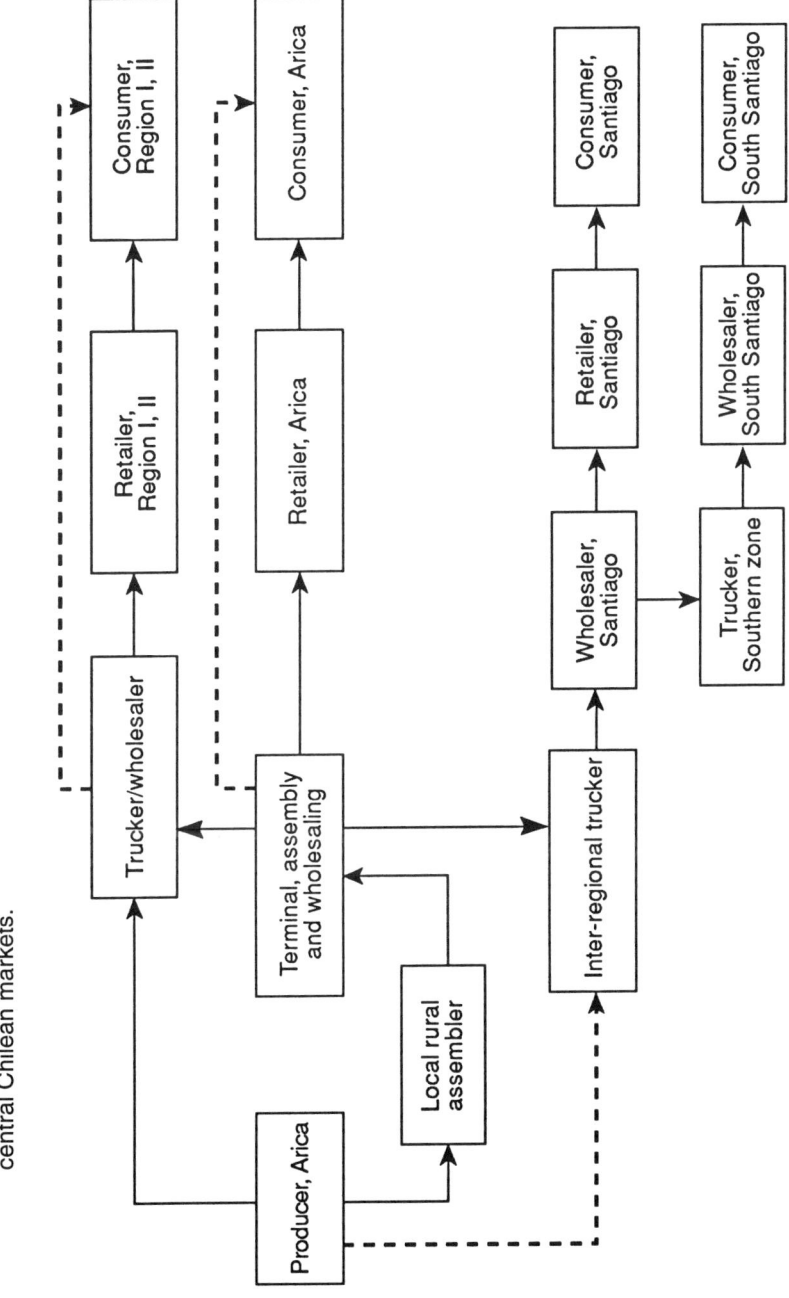

Figure 5. Marketing channels for some vegetables in the province of Arica and distributed in the northern and central Chilean markets.

Table 2. Marketing margins for grade one tomatoes in Chile's Central region, December 1981 to March 1982.

Week	Producer		Wholesaler			Retailer		Consumer	
	Price received ($/kg)	Particip. PGM (%)[a]	Margin ($/kg)	Particip. GMMw (%)[a]		Margin ($/kg)	Particip. GMMr (%)[a]	Price ($/kg)	Particip. (%)[a]
Nov. 30 - Dec. 5	19	38	8	16		23	46	50	100
Dec. 7	19	47	6	15		15	38	40	100
Dec. 14	21	42	10	20		19	38	50	100
Dec. 21	20	37	9	17		25	46	54	100
Dec. 28	15	43	7	20		13	37	35	100
Jan. 4	7	35	5	25		8	40	20	100
Jan. 11	8	36	4	18		10	46	22	100
Jan. 18	8	32	5	20		12	48	25	100
Jan. 25	8	32	6	24		11	44	25	100
Feb. 1st	9	32	8	29		11	39	28	100
Feb. 8	5	25	6	30		9	45	20	100
Feb. 15	7	32	5	23		10	45	22	100
Feb. 22	6	30	6	30		8	40	20	100
Mar. 1st	7.5	34	5.5	25		9.5	41	22.5	100
Mar. 8	8	32	4	16		13	52	25	100
Mar. 15	5.5	22	4.5	18		15.5	60	25.5	100
Mar. 22	7.6	38	5.4	27		7	35	20	100
Average	11	34	6	22		13	44	30	100

[a] The producer's share (GMMp) and each middleman's margin are derived using the consumer price as a basis.

Source: Ministry of Agriculture, Chile; and IICA (1982).

of the marketing margins of greenhouse tomatoes in Chile's central region and sold in Santiago. This information covers the period from the time before the principal harvest (November 30 to January 3) to the peak harvest season in the summer (January 4 to March 28). Besides providing full and much needed information, the importance of this methodology lies in demonstrating that even when there are price variations at all market levels, the marketing margins remain relatively stable.

Thomsen and Foote (1952) hold that, except during periods of definite changes in prices of goods or in the rates of costs, the margin rate percentage remains surprisingly stable throughout the years—even more than product prices—because some of the cost components (e.g., transportation costs, rental of facilities, labor, taxes, etc.) change less rapidly than prices. This can be easily verified even in countries with high inflation rates. Prices may change every day, but marketing costs do not change for weeks or even months (at least in relative terms).

Under conditions of imperfect competition between marketing agents, middlemen can modify the absolute (and relative) marketing margins independently from the marketing costs. These modifications absorb the price fluctuations caused by changes in supply and demand. Plate (1969) holds that, theoretically, an increase in the margin would affect both producers and consumers. Nevertheless, in reality the changes in marketing margins — according to the elasticity in the supply price and the demand for the product—do not affect producers and consumers in the same way. As demand becomes more elastic and the supply more inelastic, the increase in the margin will be weighted more heavily against producers and their selling price will be affected more. But, as demand becomes more inelastic and supply more elastic, increases in the total marketing margin will have a greater impact on consumers. Thus, price changes are not necessarily equally distributed between marketing participants.

It follows that because the short-term supply for food is less elastic than demand, when marketing costs decrease, the producer usually gets an immediate benefit, but in the long term the beneficiary is the consumer (Darrah 1976). Due to the intermediary's ability to control his margin, the decrease in producer's prices is not reflected in immediate price discounts for the consumer. This is an exasperating situation for farmers, who do not understand why the lower prices they get are not reflected in the price paid by the consumer. However, when prices to the consumer fall, most of the resulting impact is on the producer. It is to be noted that increase in prices paid to growers translate immediately into increases in prices paid by consumers.

Generally, over time marketing margins become larger due to increases in the value added by the marketing system. For example, an increase in processing costs is not forced onto the consumer by the marketing system, but is something that the consumer has forced onto the market system for several reasons, among them urban development and working women.

Conclusions

The study of marketing channels and margins is a very important part of the research methodology used to analyze the marketing of either a product or a set of products. If you want to evaluate the costs that make up marketing margins, it is important to determine which participant in the marketing process performs which marketing function, to decide what is the required investment, and to decide what are the net margins generated at each stage or segment of the marketing chain.

The methodology outlined above combines the analysis of channels, margins, and prices at all market levels; market functions, their costs; and the net incomes of the participants. Studies of marketing margins often identify only the gross margins obtained by different middlemen in the marketing process (GMM) and the producer's portion (GMM_p). This constitutes the basic set of information on the subject; and it can be used most effectively in the decision-making process if it is complemented by the analysis of marketing channels.

Depending on the availability of resources and the degree of precision required by the research project, a study of marketing margins may be completed by determining the functions of each intermediary (actor in the process) and the cost of these value-added functions.

This is a low cost, easy-to-use methodology that gives short-term results. However it does have a few limitations. These tend to originate more from procedural errors of the field researchers and from self-imposed conceptual barriers of some practitioners.

References

Darrah, L.B. 1976. *Food marketing*. New York, NY, USA: Ronald Press.

Mendoza, G. 1987. *Compendio de mercadeo de productos agropecuarios*, 2da. Edición. Instituto Interamericano de Cooperación para la Agricultura (IICA), Quillota, Chile.

Mendoza, G. et al. 1982. *Canales de comercialización y precios de la palta*. Ministerio de Agricultura–IICA, San Jose, Costa Rica.

Ministerio de Agricultura de Chile e IICA. 1982. *Estudio sobre comercialización de hortalizas*. (A study of the marketing of horticultural crops.) Ministerio de Agricultural, IICA, Santiago, Chile.

Plate, R. 1969. *Política de mercados agrarios*. Francisco Munoz Escalona (Trad). Academia León, Madrid, Espana.

Proyecto de desarrollo Agrícola Norte de Chuuisaca e IICA. 1989. *Estudio sobre comercialización de papa cultivada en el área del proyecto norte de Chuquisaca*. (A study of the marketing of potatoes harvested in the project area in North Chuquisaca.) IICA, La Paz, Bolivia.

Thomsen, F.L. and R.J. Foote. 1952. *Agricultural prices*, Second Edition. New York, NY, USA: McGraw Hill.

Appendix

Survey research guide on marketing procedures (as applied to growers at the first point of sale)

General information: community, group, producer's name, type of producer.

1. Agricultural production cycle.

   Production cycle referring to information about the last harvest.
2. Area planted and/or amount of seed used.
3. Quantity harvested and month of harvest.
4. Utilization of produce harvested.

   Indicate amounts for sale, on-farm consumption, feed, processing, seed, and other.
5. Description of sale.

   Amount, price, place of sale, date of sale, buyer, method of payment, type of credit (if used).
6. Marketing aspects.

   Indicate if change in buyers and/or sellers from one marketing season to another, the costs, time, and distances of transportation and time spent selling the product.
7. Marketing problems.

   Appraisal of the number of buyers, prices received, payment problems, transportation problems.
8. Storage and processing.

   Quantity stored and for how long, price comparison before and after storage, storage problems, date and place of sale.
9. Processed products.

   Specify the products, quantity processed, reasons for not processing, comparative income between fresh versus processed products.
10. Credit.

    Type of credit available, conditions, expiration date, guarantees, interest rates, problems in obtaining credit, problems in repaying the loan, credit advantages.
11. Technical assistance.

    Specify the type of assistance received, the institutions that provided it; or the activity and conditions under which assistance is provided.
12. Participation in organizations.

    Specify if you belong to an economic organization (e.g., cooperative, marketing board) and what is your activity.

12

Using Microcomputer Spreadsheets for Spatial and Temporal Price Analysis: An Application to Rice and Maize in Ecuador[1]

David L. Tschirley[2]

Abstract

The importance of prices in market economies and the clear trend toward market deregulation point to the need for practical methodologies for analysis of agricultural prices. This chapter presents methodologies for temporal and spatial analysis of agricultural prices using desktop computers available to researchers who have only a basic knowledge of Lotus 1-2-3 or Quattro Pro. This analysis should be complemented with other empirical and historical analyses that will provide the elements for proper interpretation and utilization of price data. Moreover, such studies will help determine the cause and effect of problems identified and thereby contribute to designing their solutions. The cases of rice and yellow maize in Ecuador yield important results that can help in the design of marketing strategies for the private sector and in counteracting some negative attitudes within the public sector that bear little relation to what actually happens in markets. Likewise, the results underline the need to improve the quality of situation and outlook information for agricultural markets in Ecuador.

Key words: Rice, cycle, seasonal index, spatial integration, yellow maize, trend, Ecuador.

Introduction

A clear trend exists toward the liberalization of agricultural markets in the developing and developed world. This points to the importance of analyzing

---

[1] This chapter was previously published in Spanish in Scott and Herrera (1991).

[2] Dept. of Agricultural Economics, Michigan State University, East Lansing, MI 48824 USA.

agricultural prices as factors that greatly influence the pace and direction of agricultural development. As market signals of the relative scarcity or abundance of a given product, prices serve as incentives to direct the allocation of economic resources and to a large extent they determine the structure and rate of economic growth. The liberalization of agricultural markets implies accepting potentially substantial variation in prices across time, space, and product form. This price variation is necessary if the private sector is to perform its marketing functions (e.g., assembly, storage, transport, processing).

However, it is important to identify the nature, as well as the causes, of such changes and determine if they reflect, or not, efficiency in the marketing system. The analysis of agricultural prices—complemented by systematic empirical and historical marketing research —is an essential step in the diagnostic process.

Finally, the knowledge gained through the analysis of prices can help alleviate possible negative attitudes in the public sector toward markets and marketing processes in general. Also, it may help to demonstrate that marketing agents' profits are not as high or as constant as is commonly held. Or, such knowledge can simply serve to identify marketing problems and their causes. In so doing, this information can contribute enormously to the formulation of more rational and sustainable price and marketing policies.

Despite the obvious need, the analysis of agricultural prices is not a commonly used tool among researchers in many developing countries. Some of the reasons are weak systems for collecting price information and insufficient training in analysis methodologies. However, reliable information about basic products is available in most Third World countries, at least at the wholesale level. Moreover, there are practical methodologies for researchers without specialized training. Finally, electronic spreadsheets such as Lotus 1-2-3 and Quattro Pro make such analyses relatively simple and reliable.

Methodology and Results

This chapter presents methodologies for temporal and spatial price analysis. Estimates apply to milled rice and yellow maize, Ecuador's two most important cereal crops.

Temporal analysis

Time-series of either prices or quantities can be analyzed using various methodologies. A simple but useful approach is the graphic analysis of monthly trends in prices or quantities. The analyst should draw three kinds of graphs prior to undertaking more sophisticated analysis. These are single product, single level graphs (producer, wholesaler, or retailer); single product, multilevel graphs; and graphs of at least some products that substitute for and/or complement one another in production or consumption. The first graph will give the researcher an approximate view of the trends, seasonal patterns, and cyclical fluctuations, as well as the degree of instability in the series. The second type of graph will give a sense of the size and evolution (e.g., bigger to smaller) of marketing margins over time. Finally, the third type of graph will permit a first approximation of comparative trends in production or prices.

Other, more sophisticated approaches try to quantify the relations already mentioned. One such approach is to run a regression of a time-series against a time variable and other "dummy" variables to estimate seasonality.[3] Additionally we can use ARIMA models (Goetz and Weber 1986), in particular to quantify seasonal patterns.

The approach we explain here is based on the so-called "classical model" for the decomposition of a time-series into its separate components. It estimates the trend (T), cyclical (C), seasonal (S), and random (E) indices of the series[4]:

(1) $P = T \times C \times S \times E$

where:

T = Trend component
C = Cyclical component
S = Seasonal component
E = Random component

T is expressed as price per unit while C, S, and E are all indices.

This analysis defines price trends as a direct relation between time and price. It does not take into consideration other possible explanatory variables. The causes of a trend include inflation, a sustained increase in demand vis-à-vis stable supply, or technological progress that creates a constantly increasing supply for a stable demand. The two types of trends most commonly identified are linear and logarithmic. The methodology presented here for decomposing a time-series is based only on the linear trend (see Equation 1 in the Appendix for the logarithmic equation). It is calculated as a simple linear regression of price against a time variable:

(2) $P = f(T)$

where

T = 1, 2, 3, ... n; and
P = nominal price.

---

[3] See Tomek and Robinson (1981) and Pindyck and Rubinfield (1981).

[4] This methodology is explained in detail by Goetz and Weber (1986).

To calculate the trend, one uses the constant and the trend coefficient resulting from the regression:

(3) $\quad T_i = a + bt_i$

where

T_i = trend value during period i
a = the constant estimated by the regression
b = the trend coefficient estimated by the regression
t_i = the value of the variable during period i

The constant has no economic significance while the trend coefficient indicates an increase of the variable vis-à-vis a one unit increase in the time variable.

Seasonality is defined as a systematic movement that repeats itself every 12 months. The rather predictable price fluctuations of this type are common among agricultural products, mainly, though not exclusively, among products that may be stored. The most common reason for seasonal price movements is the seasonal fluctuation of supply. For instance, weather determines rice and yellow maize planting and harvesting. Therefore, grain supply will generally fluctuate in accordance with the production cycle. These changes in the availability of grain are typically reflected in seasonal price movements. Demand fluctuations can also cause seasonal price changes. Demand for chicken in Ecuador increases sharply at Christmas and Easter. One would expect seasonal price increases at those times of the year.

To estimate the seasonal index of a time-series, one first has to calculate the centered moving average (CMA) over 12 months (CMA^{12}, equations 2 and 3 in the Appendix). The technique of using the centered moving average (for any given number of periods–n) substitutes the observed value in the time-series with the average of that value and a given number of observations taken immediately before and after it. Consequently, the CMA^n eliminates random variations and systematic movements of a duration equal to n. If one computes a CMA^{12} (for n = 12) with monthly data, one completely eliminates seasonal price movements.

Figure 1 shows nominal prices and CMA^{12} for wholesale milled rice in Quito from January 1971 to December 1982. Three CMA^{12} characteristics are worth mentioning. First, it has the same trend as the price. [5] In the second place, the CMA^{12} will show cyclical fluctuations around the price series.[6]

---

[5] In fact, the CMA for any period will show the same trend as that of the original series.

[6] Tomek and Robinson (1981) hold that the CMA can induce cyclical behavior by introducing an autocorrelation (p.181). However, this problem is not common, and the CMA technique is widely used by researchers throughout the world.

Finally, the CMA^{12} has eliminated very short-term fluctuations appearing in the original series. In terms of equation (1):

(4) $CMA_i^{12} = TC_i$

In other words, the centered moving average represents the trend and cyclical components of the original series, and eliminates seasonality and randomness. Therefore, the seasonal index (SI) can be calculated as a division of the original price by CMA^{12} multiplied by 100:

(5) $SI_i = (TCSE_i/TC_i) = SE_i = (P_i/CMA_i^{12})*100$

Two characteristics of the SI should be underlined here. First, it includes not only seasonal fluctuations (S) but also random ones (E). Second, it makes no sense to talk about a "deflated" or "nominal" SI. As the index is calculated by dividing a nominal series (the original price) by another nominal series (the CMA^{12}), the SI can be considered already deflated.

In the case of a storable product—where seasonality results mainly from seasonal supply variations—it is important to isolate pure seasonality from other random and cyclical price movements. Once seasonality has been isolated, it is possible to use other types of analysis to measure the efficiency of temporal price patterns and to identify likely changes in these patterns. Two of the most relevant analyses are the computing of standard deviations for monthly SIs and calculating the trend in a given month's index over the years. Standard deviations on monthly indices reveal the stability of the seasonal price pattern. If standard deviations as a whole are relatively large vis-à-vis the seasonal pattern, then one may conclude that seasonal price movements cannot be readily predicted. A comparison of 12 standard deviations among themselves would also reveal during which months of the year uncertainty about future supply and demand is greatest.

Calculating trends in the indices of a given month, along with t statistics for the trends, allows one to investigate possible changes in the seasonal pattern. This chapter applies both techniques.

The cycle in a time-series is defined as a systematic movement replicated over a given period.[7] In theory, a cycle could cover any number of years. Explaining the causes of a cyclical pattern is harder than explaining seasonality, as is isolating the true cycle from random movements.

---

[7] The duration of a cycle is measured as the lapse of time between a peak or trough and the next peak or trough. Seasonality can be defined as a 12-month cycle.

Figure 1. Monthly nominal price for wholesale milled rice in Quito, Ecuador, 1971-82.

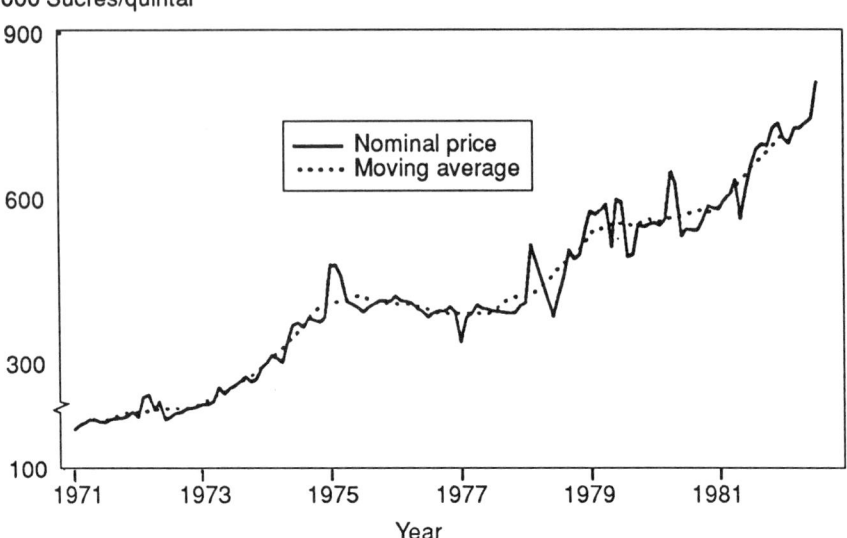

The reasons for a cycle can be endogenous or exogenous. An example of the first type is the hog cycle in the United States market. One explanation for this cycle suggests that it results from erroneous price expectations combined with a lag between the decision to invest in new animals and sending animals to the market for slaughter.

Briefly, high (low) prices would cause the producers to invest even more (less), which, given the delay between investment and slaughter, would decrease (increase) the price of hogs after the production cycle. This low (high) price would eventually provoke a decrease (increase) in investment and the cycle would continue.[8]

Exogenous causes, including weather patterns, could be responsible for the cyclical character of production and agricultural prices. The business cycle is a common phenomenon in many industrialized countries, and appears to be due to exogenous causes.

The cyclical index (CI) of a time-series can be calculated as follows:

(6) $\quad CI_i = TC_i/T_i = C_i = CMA_i/T_i$

---

[8] For further explanations of this phenomenon, see Tomek and Robinson (1981: 178-189).

In other words, one can calculate the cyclical index by dividing the 12-month centered moving average by the trend.

The grand seasonal index (GSI) is useful to summarize the typical seasonal behavior of a time-series. It is calculated by obtaining the average seasonal index for each month of a given year and then adjusting this 12-figure series in such a way that it adds up to 1,200. Specifically:

(7) $$GSI_i = \overline{SI}_i \times \frac{1200}{\sum_i \overline{SI}_i}$$

Where:

$\overline{SI}_i$ = is the average seasonal index for month i.

In theory, the GSI is an average of the seasonal indices (which include random factors, Equation 4) that removes all random movement of the time-series. Consequently, the GSI represents the pure seasonal average of the series during the period under analysis. It shows the real seasonal fluctuation for the prices of the series. The GSI is thus a good starting point for analysis of the feasibility of storage.[9] Finally, Figure 2 shows the trend, cycle, seasonality, and randomness of a hypothetical time-series.

An illustrative case is the analysis of the historical prices of milled rice in Ecuador, where this grain is a staple, provides more calories, and has a greater impact on the Consumer Price Index (CPI) than any other food commodity. Rice is harvested at the end of two production cycles in Ecuador: the large winter harvest in May and June, and the smaller summer harvest, carried out mostly in October and November. Consequently, one would expect to observe low seasonal indices from May to November and higher indices during the rest of the year.

The rice market is relatively open. An average of 90% of production is sold through private marketing channels (Ramos 1989). However, the government buys or sells at official prices when deemed necessary. It also controls imports and exports, and will periodically seize private stocks of rice if traders are considered to be "speculating". Thus, temporal analysis of rice prices combined with historical and empirical knowledge of the rice market would provide interesting results regarding the possible impact of Government policies on the evolution of seasonal price movements, and thereby potentially offer useful guidelines for improving these policies.

---

[9] Analysis not included in this document. For further explanations, see Goetz and Weber (1986).

Figure 2. An example of a temporal price series and its various components decomposed.

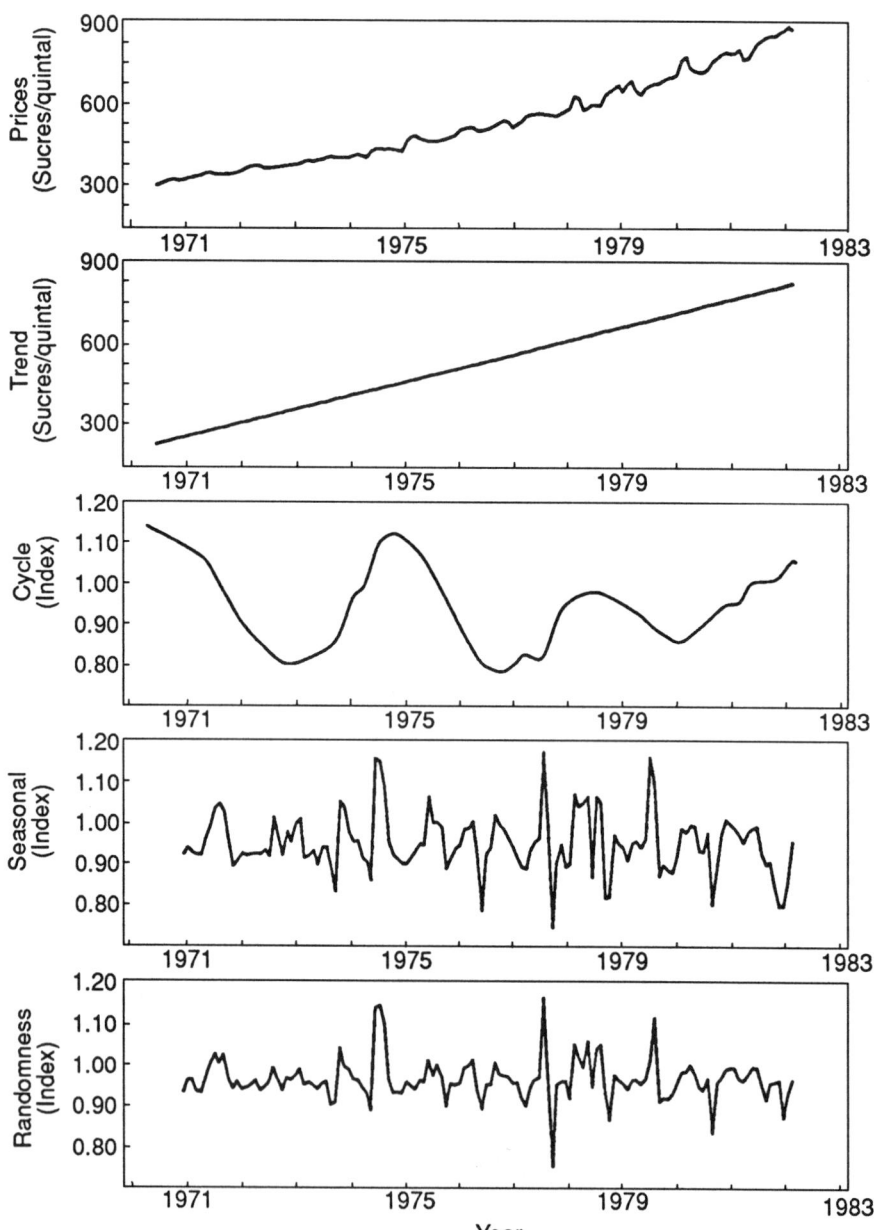

The methodologies explained in this chapter were applied to the wholesale price of milled rice in Quito, Ecuador, between January 1971 and December 1989. The entire analysis was done with Lotus 1-2-3, Version 2.2. First, the year, the month, and the nominal price for the first three columns of the electronic spreadsheet were entered (Table 1). Once the data were reviewed to verify that they had been entered correctly, prices were deflated and expressed graphically, and the first part of the graphical analysis as explained above could precede (Figure 3).[10]

Examination of the graph suggests that seasonal and/or random fluctuations of rice prices have been greater since 1983. Based on this hypothesis, the analysis could then go on by dividing the information into two periods 1971-82 and 1983-89. Nevertheless, and for the didactic purposes of this chapter, the first analysis will be based on the entire period to demonstrate how the methodology can also facilitate the identification of the hypothesis to be tested. The results for the sub-periods mentioned above will then be presented.

Table 2 shows the formulae entered and the linear regression made with Lotus 1-2-3 for the complete analysis of trend, seasonality, and cycle. As indicated in the chart, a number is assigned to every row and a letter is assigned to every column of the spreadsheet. Formulae entered refer to these numbers and letters to identify the cells that go into the calculations. The formulae are identical to those already explained above (the formula for the PCM[12] is Number 3 in the Appendix).

Part of the results of the temporal analysis for prices of milled rice between 1971 and 1989 are presented in Table 1. First, it should be noted that there are no values for the CMA[12] and the seasonal and cyclical indices for the first and last six months of the period under analysis. This is due to the formulae used to compute these series. The second point is that the trend and the cyclical index values were negative in 1971. This result is an anomaly due to accumulated inflation in the nominal prices leading to a logarithmic, instead of a linear, trend. Consequently, if the aim of the analysis is to calculate the current trend of the series, it is logical to start the estimation from the deflated prices and then add inflation. Nevertheless, the classical price decomposition model begins with nominal prices. The same methodology is used in this study. This does not create problems as long as seasonal price analysis remains the main objective of the study.[11]

---

[10] The Lotus 1-2-3 manual explains in detail how to enter data, make graphs, run regressions, write formulae and do all other previous steps necessary for this analysis.

[11] As indicated for the CMA[12] and the seasonal index formulae, trend is excluded in the calculation of these components.

Table 1. Results of temporal analysis for nominal milled rice prices in Quito, Ecuador, 1971-89.[a]

Year	Month	Nominal Price in Quito	Trend	CMA[12]	Seasonal Index	Cyclical Index
1971	Jan	176	-1.341			
	Feb	185	-1.314			
	Mar	189	-1.288			
	Apr	195	-1,262			
	Mav	195	-1.235			
	Jun	191	-1.209			
	Jul	190	-1.183	195	0.973	-0.165
	Aug	196	-1,156	198	0.988	-0.172
	Sep	197	-1,130	202	0.977	-0.178
	Oct	199	-1.103	205	0.973	-0.185
	Nov	201	-1.077	207	0.973	-0.192
	Dec	209	-1.051	208	1.005	-0.198
1980	Jan	550	1.508	550	1.000	0.365
	Feb	545	1.535	553	0.986	0.360
	Mar	555	1.561	553	1.003	0.354
	Apr	645	1,587	555	1.163	0.349
	May	623	1,614	558	1.116	0.346
	Jun	524	1.640	562	0.932	0.343
	Jul	539	1.667	565	0.954	0.339
	Aug	536	1,693	568	0.943	0.336
	Sep	536	1.719	571	0.939	0.332
	Oct	553	1.746	569	0.972	0.326
	Nov	580	1.772	566	1.025	0.319
	Dec	576	1.798	566	1.018	0.315
1989	Jan	9.074	4.357	9.172	0.989	2.105
	Feb	10.209	4.384	9.645	1.058	2.200
	Mar	15.773	4.410	10.129	1.557	2.297
	Apr	12,369	4,437	10,572	1.170	2.383
	May	10,970	4,463	10,842	1.012	2.429
	Jun	10.849	4.489			
	Jul	10.084	4.516			
	Aug	10,540	4,542			
	Sep	10,818	4,568			
	Oct	10.426	4.595			
	Nov	10.424	4.621			

[a] Only data for 1971, 1980 and 1989 are included for lack of space.
Source: Ministry of Agriculture and Livestock, Quito.

Using microcomputer spreadsheets for spatial and temporal price analysis 287

Table 2. Formulae in Lotus 1-2-3 for computing the temporal components of the milled rice price.

	D	F	H	J	L	N
	Nominal price	Trend	12-month centered moving average	Seasonal Index	Cyclical Index	Grand Seasonal Index
10	988	+U$11+C10*T$17				((+J22+J34+J46+J58+J70+J82)/6)*100*N$23
11	1,211	+U$11+C11*T$17				((+J23+J35+J47+J59+J64+J83)/6)*100*N$23
12	939	+U$11+C12*T$17				((+J24+J36+J48+J60+J64+J84)/6)*100*N$23
13	934	+U$11+C13*T$17				((+J25+J37+J49+J61+J64+J85)/6)*100*N$23
14	1,161	+U$11+C14*T$17				((+J26+J38+J50+J62+J64+J86)/6)*100*N$23
15	1,311	+U$11+C15*T$17				((+J27+J39+51 +J63+J75)/5)*100*N$23
16	1,510	+U$11+C16*T$17	(@SUM(D10..D21)+@SUM(D11..D22))/2	+D16/H16	+H16/F16	((+J16+J28+J40+J52+J64+J76)/6)*100*N$23
17	1,637	+U$11+C17*T$17	(@SUM(D11..D22)+@SUM(D12..D23))/2	+D17/H17	+H17/F17	((+J17+J29+J41+J53+J65+J77)/6)*100*N$23
18	2,023	+U$11+C18*T$17	(@SUM(D12..D23)+@SUM(D13..D24))/2	+D18/H18	+H18/F18	((+J18+J30+J42+J54+J66+J78)/6)*100*N$23
19	1,950	+U$11+C19*T$17	(@SUM(D13..D24)+@SUM(D14..D25))/2	+D19/H19	+H19/F19	((+J19+J31+J43+J55+J67+J79)/6)*100*N$23
20	1,882	+U$11+C20*T$17	(@SUM(D14..D25)+@SUM(D15..D26))/2	+D20/H20	+H20F20	((+J20+J32+J44+J56+J68+J80)/6)*100*N$23
21	1,814	+U$11+C21*T$17	(@SUM(D15..D26)+@SUM(D16..D27))/2	+D21/H21	+H21F21	((+J21+J33+J45+J57+J69+J81)/6)*100*N$23
22	1,755	+U$11+C22*T$17	(@SUM(D16..D27)+@SUM(D17..D28))/2	+D22/H22	+H22F22	
23	1,760	+U$11+C23*T47	(@SUM(D17..D28)+@SUM(D18..D29))/2	+D23/H23	+H23F23	
24	1,851	+U$11+C24*T$17	(@SUM(D18..D29)+@SUM(D19..D30))/2	+D24/H24	+H24F24	
25	1,914	+U$11+C25*T$17	(@SUM(D19..D30)+@SUM(D20..D31))/2	+D25/H25	+H25F25	
26	...	...	...	...	...	
27	...	...	...	...	...	
28	...	...	...	...	...	
29	...	...	...	...	...	
30	...	...	...	...	...	

Regression results to calculate the trend in a time-series: price trend 1983-89.

Constant	-542
Regression	2,081
R^2	0.59
Number of observations	83
Degrees of freedom	81
Standard deviation	102.31
t statistic	9.53
	10.73

Source: Prepared by the author, Lotus 1-2-3 output format.

Figure 3. Monthly deflated price for milled rice at the wholesale level in Quito, Ecuador, 1971-89.

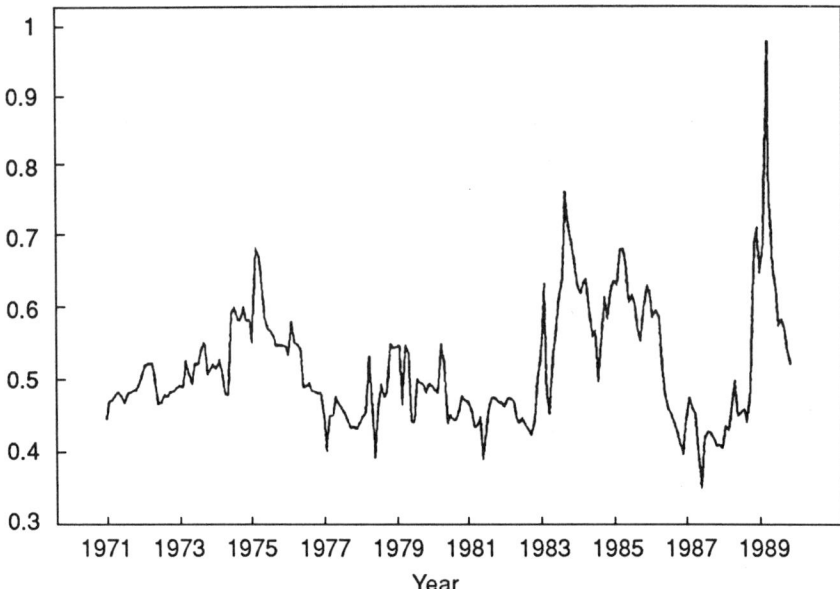

Source: Weekly Bulletin of Agricultural Prices and Market News, Ministry of Agriculture and Livestock; Monthly Statistical Information, Central Bank of Ecuador.

Figure 4 shows the grand seasonal index for this period. It indicates that the trend in seasonal prices is pronounced, but unstable. In real terms, the index increases almost 12% from June—when the seasonal price is at its lowest level—to the seasonal peak in April. However, the lines over and under the GSI indicate that fluctuations are erratic and unpredictable. To calculate the upper line, a standard deviation of every month's seasonal index was added to the GSI. To estimate the lower line, a standard deviation was subtracted. It is important to note that none of the indices for the months December to May exceeds the 100 annual average by more than one standard deviation. Likewise, none of the indices inferior to 100 are more than one standard deviation away from this average.

Table 3 shows a descriptive analysis of the seasonal indices for each month of the period. The mean, standard deviation, maximum and minimum, trend, and t-statistic for the trend of the seasonal indices were calculated for every single month.

The indices' standard deviations measure their variability. They can be interpreted as a measure of the level of uncertainty in the seasonal fluctuations.

Table 3. Analysis of seasonal indices for rice in Quito, 1971-89.

Year	Jan	Feb	Mar	Apr	May	Jun	Jul	Aug	Sep	Oct	Nov	Dec
1971							0.973	0.988	0.977	0.973	0.973	1.005
1972	1.028	1.064	1.072	1.057	1.000	0.949	0.960	0.976	0.972	0.974	0.975	0.974
1973	0.983	0.969	1.045	1.009	0.972	1.019	0.997	1.032	1.043	0.967	0.971	0.982
1974	0.953	0.988	0.988	0.945	0.903	1.076	1.066	1.018	0.999	1.000	0.967	0.959
1975	0.924	1.161	1.155	1.104	0.999	0.971	0.965	0.956	0.956	0.968	0.980	0.995
1976	0.991	1.086	1.034	1.037	1.027	0.945	0.965	0.985	0.991	1.024	1.025	1.038
1977	0.971	0.865	0.975	0.986	1.050	1.031	1.024	1.007	0.988	0.968	0.949	0.945
1978	0.981	0.998	1.005	1.173	1.029	0.832	0.958	0.994	0.950	0.956	1.091	1.066
1979	1.075	1.086	0.930	1.086	1.074	0.890	0.892	1.012	0.995	0.988	0.962	0.996
1980	1.000	0.986	1.003	1.163	1.116	0.932	0.954	0.943	0.939	0.972	1.025	1.018
1981	1.030	1.028	0.980	0.979	1.016	0.877	0.947	1.015	1.042	1.033	1.026	1.013
1982	0.996	1.019	1.026	1.028	0.978	0.953	0.960	0.911	0.875	0.876	0.920	1.000
1983	1.046	1.179	0.838	0.761	0.876	0.930	1.021	1.068	1.269	1.165	1.081	1.017
1984	0.970	0.969	1.026	1.066	1.000	0.936	0.944	0.819	0.915	0.994	0.945	1.002
1985	1.053	1.022	1.093	1.116	1.082	0.987	1.009	0.978	0.916	0.894	0.984	1.060
1986	1.082	1.059	1.104	1.110	0.991	0.946	0.923	0.939	0.936	0.936	0.922	0.907
1987	1.023	1.102	1.109	1.089	0.936	0.838	0.989	1.003	0.983	0.968	0.940	0.918
1988	0.893	0.962	0.943	1.032	1.060	0.883	0.842	0.821	0.742	0.761	1.066	1.092
1989	0.989	1.058	1.557	1.170	1.012							
Mean	0.999	1.033	.049	1.051	1.007	0.941	0.966	0.970	0.972	0.968	0.989	0.999
Standard deviation	0.049	0.076	0.075	0.093	0.061	0.064	0.050	0.066	0.101	0.079	0.052	0.048
Maximum	1.082	1.179	1.155	1.173	1.116	1.076	1.066	1.068	1.269	1.165	1.091	1.092
Minimum	0.893	0.865	0.838	0.761	0.876	0.832	0.842	0.819	0.742	0.761	0.920	0.907
Trend	0.001	0.001	0.008	0.003	0.001	-0.006	-0.004	-0.005	-0.005	-0.004	0.000	0.001
Seasonal t	0.588	0.308	1.263	0.701	0.311	-2.186	-1.634	-1.946	-1.116	-1.253	0.177	0.378

Source: Ministry of Agriculture and Livestock, Quito.

Figure 4. The Grand Seasonal Index for milled rice in Quito, Ecuador, calculated over 1971-89.

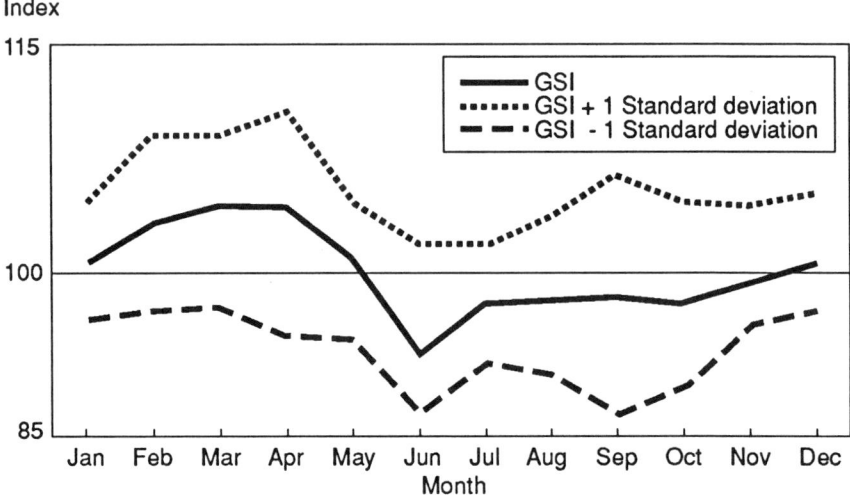

Source: Prepared for this study based on monthly prices for milled rice.

For this interpretation, the standard deviations indicate the usual level of uncertainty for a given month. In view of this, these variables show an interesting pattern. The standard deviations are lowest in July and November through January, when the market's uncertainty is at its minimum level—just after both harvests—and when information on the market's condition is readily available. Likewise, the standard deviations are at their peak just before the harvests in March-April and September. The lack of complete and reliable information on supply and demand conditions creates even more uncertainty during these months. Results demonstrate the importance of having good and timely market information to reduce random fluctuations in prices.

Analysis of the trend and the t-statistics for the principal harvesting months (June-October) highlights a notable difference vis-a-vis other months. While all the trends are negative during June through October, they are positive for the rest of the year. Furthermore, the t-statistics are higher and the absolute values for the means are 2 to 6 times higher, except in March. Apparently, prices are falling more steeply during the harvest and rising higher during the postharvest period (March especially). The seasonal index shown in Figure 5 appears to confirm these observations.

These results are positive, albeit tentative proof in support of the first part of the hypothesis, i.e., prices are showing greater seasonal fluctuation as the years go by. For further analysis of these results and to test whether price randomness has also increased, the two sub-periods, 1971-82 and 1983-89, will be examined by calculating the GSI and standard deviations for each sub-period (Figures 6 and 7). Three points are clear. First, as established in the preceding section, indices from June to October definitively fell during the second period. Second, standard deviations for the seasonal indices increased in the second period. Thus, both parts of the hypothesis proposed at the beginning of this study are accepted: both seasonal and random fluctuations increased during the second period.

Finally, it appears that the pattern of uncertainty changed during the two periods. During the first period, uncertainty was greatest (measured by the standard deviations in Figure 7) during the period of scarcity (from February to April). Uncertainty decreased during the winter harvest, and remained relatively low until the end of the calendar year. Between 1983 and 1989, uncertainty has two well-defined peaks. The first occurs in March, before the winter harvest. Once the harvest begins, standard deviations decrease. However, they immediately begin to increase until they reach another peak in September, before the summer harvest in October and November.

Figure 5. Monthly seasonal index for milled rice in Ecuador, 1971-89.

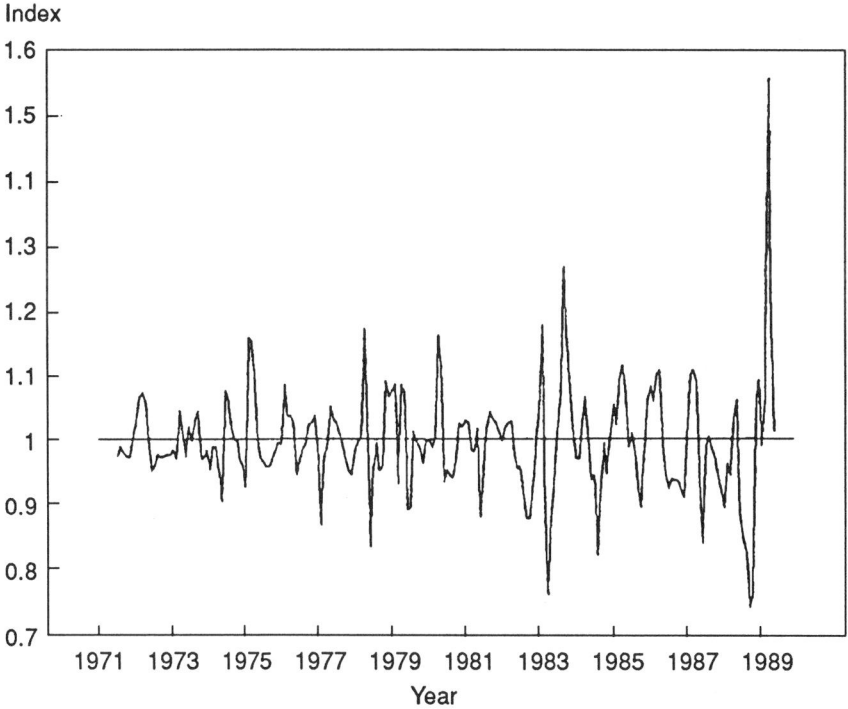

Source: Prepared for this study based on monthly prices of milled rice in Quito, 1971-89.

Figure 6. Grand Seasonal Indices, 1971-82 and 1983-89.

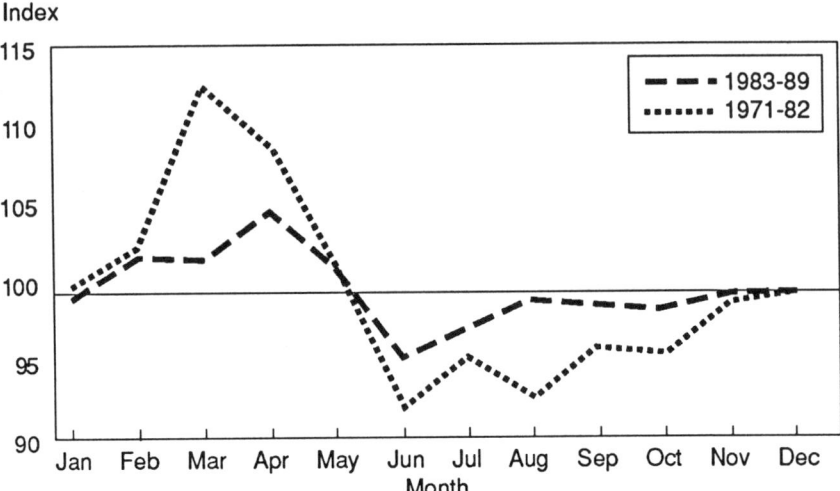

Source: Prepared by the author based on milled rice montly prices in Quito, 1971-89.

Figure 7. GSI and standard deviations, 1971-82 and 1983-89.

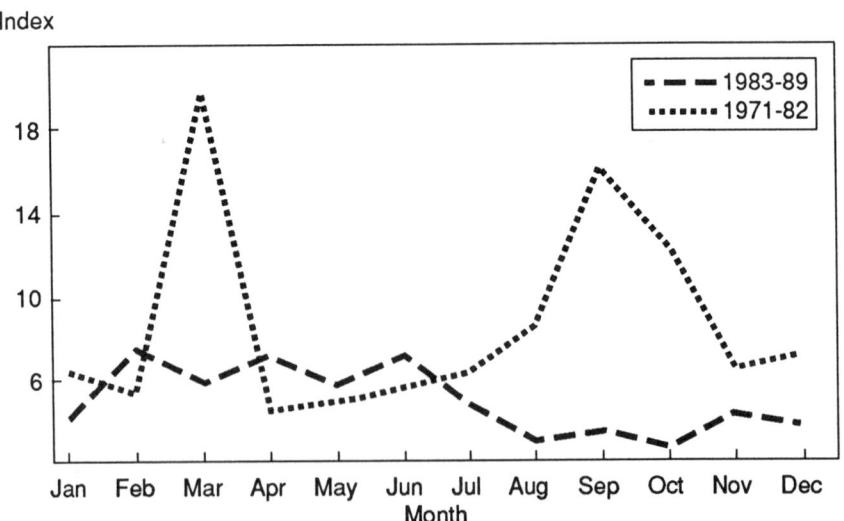

Source: Prepared by the author based on milled rice monthly prices in Quito, 1971-89.

Spatial Analysis

A marketing system is spatially integrated when prices in each individual market respond not only to their own supply and demand, but to the supply and demand of the set of all markets. A corollary is that the structure of each individual market (in the sense of the number of buyers and sellers) is less important in an integrated system than the structure of the system as a whole.

Spatial integration fulfills a very important social function. In short, a local scarcity (surplus) in an integrated system is less prejudicial to local consumers (producers) because it induces the arrival (departure) of products from other locations. It increases supply (demand) and decreases (increases) the price. Consequently, local prices in an integrated system would be more stable than those in a non-integrated system. Spatial arbitrage generates these results. For this type of commercial behavior to work well requires a free and efficient market.

Simple correlation coefficients generated from prices for feed maize in Ecuador serve to illustrate this point. Calculation of simple correlation coefficients (r) between prices in pairs of markets is the most frequently used quantitative approximation to measure markets' spatial integration. The correlation coefficient (r) is a measure of the co-variance between two variables. It takes on values that vary between -1.0 and 1.0. A value of 1.0 (-1.0) indicates that a perfect positive (negative) correlation exists between variables. To calculate the percentage of variation of a variable which is explained by variation in the other one, it is necessary to raise the value of square r. For example, a correlation coefficient of 0.90 shows that 81% of the variation in one variable is explained by the variation in the other. A simple procedure consists of running linear regressions in Lotus 1-2-3 between each pair of markets to be analyzed and then taking the square root of the R^2 from the regressions.

Table 4 contains results of the spatial analysis of maize prices in Ecuador. The correlation coefficients were calculated using nominal prices, deflated prices, and changes in nominal prices. By using nominal prices, two different types of upward bias are introduced in the correlation coefficients. First, two given markets with no possibilities whatsoever of exchanges between them (for example, because of topographical barriers or government prohibition on interregional transport of the products), but affected by the same macro-economic factors, would probably have a high correlation coefficient simply because of inflation. If the seasonality of the commodity in question is similar for each isolated market, the correlation coefficients would also be positive. By calculating the correlation coefficients with deflated prices, one eliminates the first bias, but keeps the second. By calculating the correlation coefficients based on changes in nominal prices, all bias is removed.

Table 4. Simple price correlation coefficients for pairs of feed maize markets in Ecuador, 1985-87.

Pairs	Nominal prices	Deflated prices	Change in prices
Los Ríos-Guayas	0.986	0.923	0.850
Los Ríos-Manabí	0.956	0.781	0.520
Guayas-Manabí	0.968	0.826	0.725

Source: Ministry of Agriculture and Livestock, Quito.

In each case more than 90% of the variation in nominal prices can be explained by prices in the other market. However, only between 52% and 85% of changes in prices can be explained in this way. Note that the coefficients of correlation for nominal prices show slight differences that increase as the calculations are made based on deflated prices, and then on changes in prices. This would mean that the correlation coefficient is not a very sensitive measure of market integration. There are other limitations involved in the use of correlation coefficients: inability to identify the seasonal patterns of integration or to distinguish between short- and long-term integration. [12]

On the basis of these criticisms, we should note that spatial as well as temporal analyses must be complemented with empirical and historical research on the markets being considered. Used in this way, spatial and temporal analysis can significantly increase the researcher's knowledge of the way markets work. However, it must be emphasized that when such analyses are used in isolation they can lead to completely erroneous conclusions.

A more sophisticated assessment of market integration is possible using the index of market correction. This index, developed by Timmer (1987), is used to distinguish between short- and long-term integration. This approach posits a market structure consisting of one principal and several secondary markets. While the principal market controls price formation, secondary markets respond mainly to conditions in the principal market. Relations between each secondary market and the principal market for maize were analyzed for this study.

As a first step, changes in prices in the secondary market are hypothesized to be a function of changes in prices in the principal market, changes in the spatial margin between the principal and the secondary market, price levels in the principal market and a vector for local variables. Specifically, the following relation is estimated:

(8) $S_t - S_{t-1} = a + b(S_{t-1} - P_{t-1}) + c(P_t - P_{t-1}) + dP_{t-1} + eX_{t-1}$

---

[12] For an in-depth discussion, see Timmer (1987: 213-223); Ravaillon (1986); Delgado (1986); and Harriss (1979).

where:

S = Logarithm for the price in the secondary market
P = Logarithm for the price in the principal market
X = Vector for local variables in the secondary market
t = Time

To facilitate interpretation of the coefficients, the equation was reorganized as follows:

(9) $S_t = a + (1 + b)S_{t-1} + c(P_t - P_{t-1}) + (d - b)P_{t-1} + eX_{t-1}$

Coefficient $(1 + b)$ represents the impact of the local price during the prior period on the current local price. Coefficient $(d - b)$ represents the impact of the principal market's price during the preceding period on the secondary market's current price. If markets are integrated in the short term (from one period to the next) and if the structure of primary and secondary markets and the price formation process this structure implies really exist, then value $(d - b)$ should exceed value $(1 + b)$. Timmer's Index of Marketing Connection (ICM) is:

(10) $IMC = (1 + b)/(d - b)$

In keeping with the last paragraph's interpretation, the lower the ICM, the more integrated the markets will be in the short term.

Markets may not be integrated in the short term, but they may be in the long term. That is to say that conditions in the primary market may not influence the secondary price in a definite way from one period to the other. But, during some as yet undefined number of periods, and on average, such conditions may indeed have a determining effect. If such was the case, the changes in the principal market's prices would be proportionally reflected in the secondary market and the 'c' coefficient would approach one.

In short, conditions for integration are: an ICM less than one in the short term and c equal to one in the long term. This analysis was conducted on prices for feed maize in Ecuador. Two rural assembly markets were used as secondary markets. Wholesale markets in Quito and Guayaquil were used as principal markets (Table 5). Results show that maize markets seem to be integrated in the short as well as long term. Portoviejo (Manab Province) constitutes the possible exception. It is worth noting that this observation coincides with previous analysis carried out without using correlation coefficients and after considerable field research. Survey results suggest that traders are well acquainted with the prices in the different markets. Their choice of market (Quito or Guayaquil) to sell their products depends on the most favorable price.

The use of ICM is criticized mainly because it is based on a rather unrealistic assumption: prices in secondary markets are affected only by the

Table 5. Results of the ICM test, prices for maize, Ecuador, 1987-89.

Markets	ICM	c
Quito and Quevedo	0.18	0.80[a]
Quito and Portoviejo	0.60	0.61[b]
Guayaquil and Quevedo	-0.09	0.91[a]
Guayaquil and Portoviejo	0.61	1.06[a]

[a] Value 1.0 is within one standard deviation.
[b] Value 1.0 is within two standard deviations.
Source: Quito and Guayaquil: Ministry of Agriculture and Livestock; Quevedo and Portoviejo: Instituto de Estrategias Agropecuarias, Quito.

principal market. The truth is that many systems of markets are interrelated in such a way that they are all influenced by one another. This implies that the best analysis is a simultaneous one. However, ICM is clearly a more sensitive measure than the correlation coefficients which are so commonly used. In fact, equation 8 equals the regression used to calculate the correlation coefficient with changes in prices, but it adds other variables (the spatial margin, the price itself in the principal market, and local factors) that are definitely important. Consequently, Timmer's approach should yield better results in the analysis of market integration.

Producers' and Policy Makers' Use of the Analysis

The temporal and spatial price analyses presented in this document provide the fundamental descriptive basis for designing private marketing strategies, public sector policies, and further research by market analysts.

Temporal analysis

The GSI and the statistics regarding the monthly and seasonal indices provide a starting point for the design of commercial strategies for rice producers or traders. Specifically, the most relevant results can be summarized briefly as follows: First, and in general, storage is risky. If the product is not stored at least until February, it probably will not be profitable. The risk would be greater for producers because they harvest the greatest part of their production in May when the seasonal index is above its annual average of 100. Secondly, April could be the ideal month to sell the stored product (even though, before definitely establishing this conclusion, further analyses would be required) (1971-72 and 1983-89), from the point of view of possible profits and storage risks. In both periods, April's seasonal index was the highest or the second highest. Furthermore, its standard deviation is much less than in March during both periods. Finally, storage may have become more profitable since 1983, but it has also become more risky.

For policy makers, the value of temporal analysis lies in systematically understanding the markets under study, and thus in the possibility of designing more appropriate policies for their particular circumstances. An essential lesson to be obtained from this analysis is that, notwithstanding the government's intervention in buying and selling rice, seasonal and random fluctuations have increased through the years. It is thus imperative to do further research on the impact of other policies (e.g., controls on foreign trade) that influence prices for rice.

This analysis demonstrates the importance of having reliable and timely information. Besides what has been said about standard deviations in the seasonal indices, it calls attention to the need for better forecasts of harvests. Since the rice harvest begins around mid-April and reaches its peak in May, one would expect a rapid market response with a relatively low seasonal index during May. However, this index remains rather high in May and does not reach its minimum until June. This is why storage is extremely risky for the producer. With better and more timely harvest forecasts, the market could respond more quickly; as a result, better incentives could be created so that the producers store their output, thereby reducing the need for government intervention.[13]

Finally, someone must bear the storage risk identified in this analysis. By assuming some of this risk, the private sector reduces the part that government would have to assume. From this point of view, it may be easier to convince policy makers that an effective policy is to increase the private sector's capacity to assume an even bigger part of the risk. This could be done by increased availability of marketing credit (almost non-existent in Ecuador); by stopping the seizures of private grain stocks; and by providing more and better information on the market's current position, as well as most likely future direction.

Spatial analysis

Spatial integration analysis established that, in the short term, as well as in the long term, the different markets for maize are rather well integrated. These results, along with other empirical research results, are reliable indicators of the existence of healthy competition in the markets under review. Nevertheless, both analyses—computation of correlation coefficients and ICM—suggest that, while markets in Manabí are not independent of those in other markets, they are in fact more isolated (Tables 4 and 5). This is due to the lack of an adequate road between Los Ríos and Manabí provinces. Such a road would permit integration of Manabí's markets not only with those in Los Ríos, but also with

---

[13] Peck (1978) and many other authors have demonstrated that private storage stabilizes annual and seasonal cereal prices.

markets in Quito, since a good road already exists between the last two locations.

Conclusions

The methodologies employed for temporal and spatial analyses of rice and maize prices in Ecuador showed interesting and useful results. Temporal analysis of rice prices managed to identify not only seasonal patterns, but also interesting changes in these patterns over time. Spatial analysis of maize markets showed that the different markets for this grain form a truly integrated system. This result reinforces the tentative observation based on the results of intensive field research.

These methodologies are available to researchers who have only a basic knowledge of programs such as Lotus 1-2-3 and Quattro Pro. As regards temporal analysis, once the electronic spreadsheet for one product has been made, it takes very little time to adjust it to another product. These methods do not require specialized training, but the researcher has to have empirical knowledge about the market to be studied, along with an historical perspective. This type of knowledge is essential to ensure effective application of these methodologies and to correctly interpret their results. Knowledge developed in this way would provide a starting point for the analytical studies required to determine the causes and effects of the problems identified. It would also help design solutions based on the actual as opposed to alleged situation in these markets.

References

Delgado, C.L. 1986. A variance components approach to food grain market integration in northern Nigeria. *American Journal of Agricultural Economics* 68(1):970-979.

Goetz, S. and M. Weber. 1986. *Fundamentals of price analysis in developing countries. Food systems: A training manual to accompany the microcomputer software program MSTAT.* MSU International Development Working Paper No. 29. Dept. of Agricultural Economics, Michigan State University, East Lansing, MI, USA.

Harriss, B. 1979. There is a method in my madness: Or is it vice versa? Measuring agricultural market performance. *Food Research Institute Studies* 17:197-218.

Peck, A.E. 1978. Implications of private storage grains for buffer stock schemes to stabilize prices. *Food Research Institute Studies* 16(3):125-140.

Pindyck, R. and D. Rubinfeld. 1981. *Econometric models and economic forecast.* New York, NY, USA: McGraw Hill.

Ramos. H. 1989. *The financial system supporting rice marketing in Ecuador*. Ph.D. Diss., Michigan State University, East Lansing, MI, USA.

Ravallion, M. 1986. Testing market integration. *American Journal of Agricultural Economics* 68(1):102-109.

Timmer, C.P. 1987. *The corn economy of Indonesia.* Ithaca, NY, USA: Cornell University Press.

Tomek, W.G. and K. Robinson. 1981. *Agricultural product prices.* Second Edition. Ithaca, NY, USA: Cornell University Press.

Appendix

Formulae for the logarithmic trend and CMA

Logarithmic trend

Logarithmic trend is expressed in the following way:

(1) $\quad \text{Log}(T_i) = a + bt_i$

where:

T_i = the value of the trend during period i
b = the trend's coefficient
t_i = the value of the seasonal variable during period i
Log = the natural logarithm

Logarithmic trend represents the trend's grow rate by percent.

Central Moving Average (CMA)

This is the general formula for the CMA in n periods during t:

(2) $\quad CMA_t^n = \sum_{i=t-((n/2)-1/2)}^{i=t+((n/2)-1/2)} P_i \Big/ n$

The specific formula for CMA^{12} is:

(3) $\quad CMA_t^{12} = \left[\sum_{i=t-6}^{i=t+5} P_i + \sum_{i=t-5}^{i=t+6} P_i \right] \Big/ 24$

It should be noted that because of the formula used there are no CMA^{12} values for the first and last 6 periods of the series.

13

Efficiency and Complexity: Distributive Margins and the Profits of Market Enterprises

Barbara Harriss-White[1]

Abstract

This chapter critically examines some methodological attempts to evaluate efficiency using secondary and primary data. It begins with a concise review of the types of data typically utilized to calculate marketing margins, noting the limitations in estimation and aggregation associated with such figures that seriously compromise their usefulness. Static and dynamic analyses of margins are treated next. Problems in comparing profits and costs for different types of firms engaged in trading the same commodity are highlighted. The paper concludes that the conventional approaches for analyzing market phenomena are inadequate and our empirical knowledge of actual marketing systems is still in its infancy. Examples based on research on South Asian grain markets illustrate these various findings.

Key words: Prices, costs, profits, marketing systems, South Asia.

Introduction

A marketing system can be regarded as a multi-layered sequence of physical activities (long stylized as consisting of processing, **transport**, and storage) and of transfers of property rights from the farm-gate to the consumer. Transactions, involving price and contract formation and their necessary transaction costs, cannot be assumed to accord in a neat, layered way with the sequence of physical activities. Furthermore, the operation of the firms which comprise marketing systems can be assumed to accord neither with any given activity nor even with actual transfers of title in conditions where the boundaries of firms are indistinct (as when kin run branches) and when

---

[1] University Lecturer in Agricultural Economics, Queen Elizabeth House, International Development Centre, 21 St Giles, Oxford OX1 3LA, UK.

property rights are not clearly identifiable (as in joint families and/or in conditions of patriarchal precedence).

If a marketing system is allocatively efficient, consumer preferences are transferred without distortion to producers who will use such price information to make production decisions which are allocatively efficient in turn. But the evaluation of the efficiency of an agricultural marketing system is seriously theoretically compromised in two respects: the state of perfect competition does not actually exist, and there is thus no deinstitutionalized means whereby supply is supplied and demand demanded and in relation to which actually existing marketing systems can be evaluated; and the degree of Pareto suboptimality of a market cannot be determined from analysis of single markets alone.

Given this background, it is the purpose of this chapter critically to examine some methodological attempts to evaluate efficiency using secondary and primary data. Reference is made throughout to substantive material from field research on South Asian agricultural markets.

Commonly Available Data

Studies of efficiency require data on prices and costs. The most commonly available secondary data, compiled by statistics departments, is that on open market prices per unit quantity (e.g., a quintal) for a given form (e.g., paddy) and quality (e.g., superfine) of a given commodity (e.g., rice) for a given time period (e.g., a week) for a specified location (e.g., a town) and sometimes for a specified stage in the marketing system (e.g., wholesale). Certain characteristics of such evidently tractable data need noting.

First these data have reduced the entire transactions of a settlement over a period of time into a single price. If this is an average, it is usually an average from an unknown population of transactions. It will also have masked within-period variations in price due to supply and demand, due to changes in competitive conditions, due to systematic price discrimination according to the relative economic power of bargaining parties, and due to variations in contract (particularly price variations reflecting the incidence of interlocked contracts between unequal bargaining parties where disguised interest on earlier loans cannot be separated from the product price). If it is a spot price, this price may result from a form of contract which is rare and unrepresentative. Second, commodity variety, form, and quality are to be presumed to be homogeneous, and stage in the marketing system standardized. Clearly, creation of this stock-in-trade of pricing efficiency analysis has involved heroic acts of aggregation. In addition, the quality of this data may be (and frequently is) impaired by systematic investigator bias, by missing data, and by the absence of cross checking or of scrutiny for error.

In India, flows data cannot be assumed reliable and usually are obtained from estimates. Data on costs may be available (but from State Trading Corporations which monitor the milling and storage costs of private firms to which they may subcontract activity, not from the Statistics Department whose central objective is to compile cost of living indices), but such cost data are not obtained from random or representative samples. The latter kind of data requires field enquiry. Field enquiry then reveals that most of the cost components of marketing are themselves formed through "markets". These have been called derived markets. These costs therefore vary.

Transport costs vary with technology and capacity utilization. Rates are known to be affected by a large number of factors: perishability and mass; volume-weight ratios; weather and road conditions (dramatically affecting wear and tear); loading and unloading rates (which themselves are market-determined and subject to variation depending principally on the mode of transport, the combination of tasks required, bag size and weight, the competitive environment for coolie labor, and its form of organization); the structure of the market in transport brokerage; the existence of collective negotiation; the relation between open market and state-administered rates for transport and the degree of state intervention in transport; seasonal factors affecting aggregate demand for transport; and return load possibilities.

Processing costs normally differ non-trivially with technology. The coexistence of technologies with differing costs may be ascribed to inefficient factor rigidities. Alternatively they may be understood as the outcome of the variety of real-world institutions comprising a marketing system under conditions of social heterogeneity. The cost variation might then be argued to be efficient in the context of a configuration of social institutions which has to be taken as given.

The measurement of storage costs is fraught with practical difficulties (establishing positive and negative quality premia for age; measuring physical loss) and conceptual problems (finding an interest rate to reflect the opportunity cost of capital locked up in inventory; a rate for depreciation on buildings and equipment; a wage rate proxy for family labor; a risk component, etc.). Only a subset of transactions costs (travel, published information, telecommunications, membership of regulating institutions, entertainment) are actually measurable. Costs derived from field enquiry do not relate to the analytical frame of abstract official data. If the two are to be combined, then the field material has to be subjected to a reductionist treatment for which there is no accepted methodology in order to generate cost proxies.

Thus it is hardly surprising that many studies of market efficiency are confined to the use of price data. But given their limitations, it is a monument to human daring that they are used at all.

The Static Analysis of Margins

The very simplest mode of daring to evaluate efficiency consists of the comparison of the shares of a final retail price obtained at (arbitrarily) recorded points in a marketing system. Any evaluation of such data has to be relative and comparative. The shares of one product will be compared with those of the same product at another point in space or time, or sometimes under changed policy conditions. Or they may be compared with those of other products. It is usually hypothesized that if the market is efficient, shares will be identical in different locations. But an identical share is neither a necessary nor a sufficient condition for market efficiency. At the very least, costs of transport and land rental could vary between rural and urban locations in a hypothetically efficient system. Changes in shares over time would also reflect changes in the supply and demand for marketing services (their supply affected by factor prices and technology and their demand by income). Interpretation is compromised by a host of unknown factors (for instance inter-product differences in perishability or risk or in the necessary or actual services rendered by the marketing system; or in inter-regional or temporal variations in factor costs). It is obvious that the inferential evaluation of efficiency by means of prices alone is as dangerous in the simple analysis of co-integration (which is outside the scope of this chapter—see the discussion in Palaskas and Harriss-White 1993 and Goletti, this volume, for examples).

The Dynamic Analysis of Distributive Margins

With cost data available, certain hypotheses about allocative efficiency have been tested. Markets are efficient if (1) postharvest price behavior reflects storage costs; (2) inter-marketplace price differences reflect transport costs; and (3) price differences due to product form reflect processing costs (Lele 1971). In the simplest analyses, the frequency distributions of price differences between observable points in a marketing system are compared with "average" or "representative" costs of transport or storage or processing. It is also possible to simulate combinations of transport, storage and processing between pairs of marketplaces (Harriss 1981). It is difficult however to know how to account for conditions where margins exceed costs, to explain periods of loss, or to make sense of the common case where margins oscillate above or below costs.

In dynamic analyses, a key assumption has been that of unidirectional price formation and physical flows:

(1) $\quad M = Ur - \left(\dfrac{1}{C}\right) R_p$

where:

M = the marketing margin

Ur = urban rice price

Rp = rural paddy price

C = milling conversion ratio

But pan-seasonal unidirectional price formation must not be assumed. In a model landscape with one rural market and a central one, prices may rise postharvest to reflect storage costs to a point where urban prices may plateau. This can happen when a retail ceiling is imposed by government or when goods are imported from elsewhere. Rural prices may be unaffected by the reasons for the urban price plateau. They may then rise to a point where it is profitable to reverse the direction of physical flows. At harvest time, the reverse price relationships return to normal. During periods of transition — when the differences between rural and urban prices are less than transport costs—no physical flows are possible at profit. The difference between rural and central market prices may be negative, zero, or less than the marketing margin for the unidirectional model to be invalidated. Whenever bi- or multi-directional price formation occurs, it is reasonable to infer non-competitive behavior (because of a state imposed intervention such as a price ceiling, or because of monopoly control of the postharvest grain supply in a central location).

Tests using regression analysis of variance require informed local judgement on the appropriate division of agricultural and marketing calendars to reveal the kind of changed price relations described above (Timmer 1974). In the absence of such information, differences between pairs of price series net of relevant costs may be plotted (Harriss 1981) (as in Figures 1 and 2). Figure 1 shows variety specific relationships between prices of paddy and of rice for two sets of pairs of marketplaces, one under conditions of relatively regular but reversed flows and one under highly uncertain conditions of two-way flow.

Empirical studies of paddy and rice markets in Southeast and South Asia (Timmer, op. cit; Harriss, op. cit.) show both systematic seasonal reversals in price formation between central and peripheral marketplaces and pervasive, sporadic price movements which seem to be quite specific to a given variety of an agricultural commodity. These relationships have been generalized in Figure 2 where price relations between paddy in one produce center and rice in three consumer centers are depicted. These are affected by policy changes, the time distribution of harvests, seasonal storage costs, regional monopoly control over storage, the possibility of imports to urban centers from elsewhere, and random fluctuations. It has been concluded that such markets are not allocatively efficient, but the precise reasons for this state are uninterpretable without detailed local knowledge.

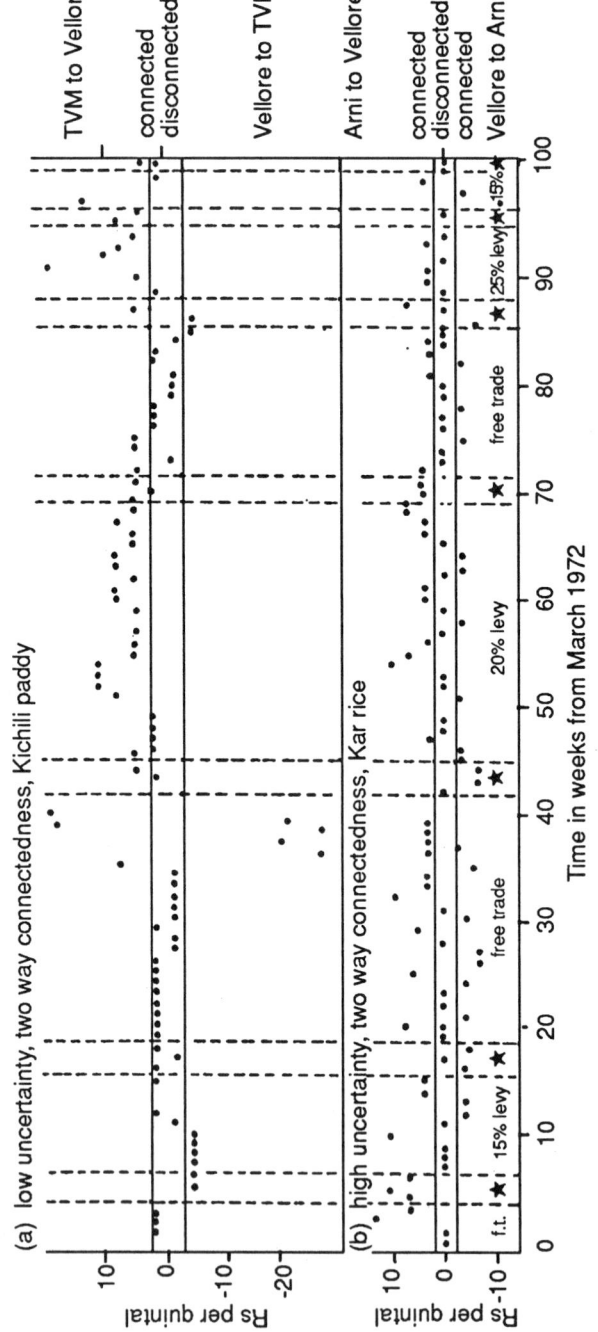

Figure 1. Uncertainty in price relations, two examples (a and b).

Figure 2. Model of price relations, N.A. Dt. South India.

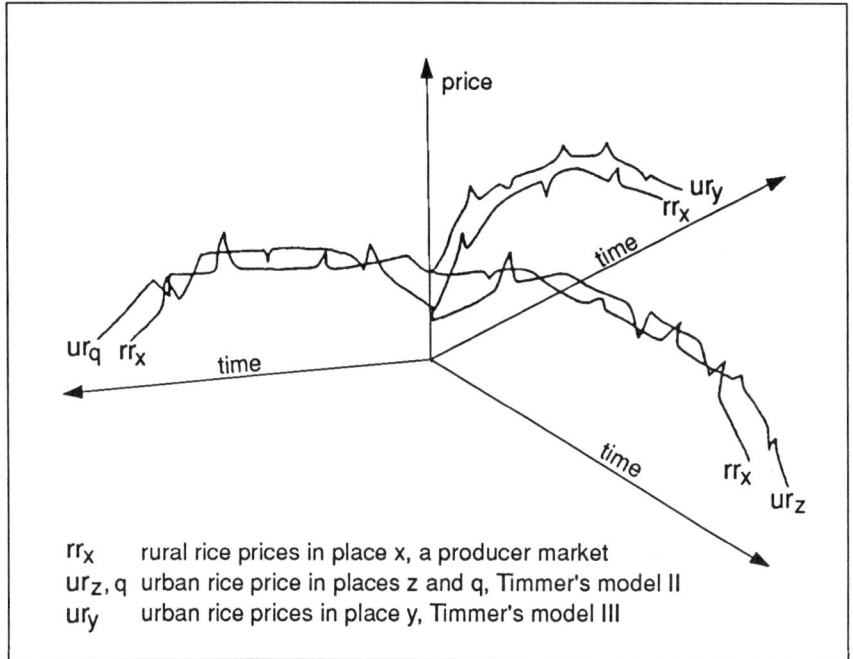

rr_x — rural rice prices in place x, a producer market
$ur_{z,q}$ — urban rice price in places z and q, Timmer's model II
ur_y — urban rice prices in place y, Timmer's model III

These studies also demonstrate the point that the more complex and dynamic (in terms of time, space, and form) are the combinations of marketing activities allowed for in an analysis of the relations between costs and margins between pairs of places, the more frequent and greater the positive differences between price margins and costs—concluded to permit the physical flows between places which are necessary for efficient marketing. Conversely, the more rigid and restricted the possibilities allowed for, the less frequent and lower the price differences and the greater the incidence of negative margins—concluded to inhibit physical flows. Thus evaluations of allocative efficiency tend to depend on the type of method imposed on stylized data.

Dynamic Analysis and the Profit Seeking of Firms

The same relation (that the more flexible the simulation of relation between costs and margins, the greater the possibility of continuous and/or regular physical flows) can be demonstrated for a single productive activity (e.g., transport) in a system of n marketplaces, if it can be assumed that the transfer of a single unit of a given product will not alter prices. In a series of simulations, the returns to flexible trade (2) may be compared with those from repeated or network contracts (3) over a variety of time periods (4).

First the maximum unit price difference net of transport costs between place i and all others in a system of marketplaces is aggregated for a year of 52 weeks:

(2) $\sum_{t=1}^{52}$ Mijt = Max (Pijt + Tijkt - Pikt)

where:

P = unit price
T = transport cost
i = commodity
j.k = places (1-n) where (j=/=k)
t = unit of time (1-m)

Second, annual returns from weekly spatial transfers between rigid pairings such as characterize repeated network trade can be aggregated:

(3) $\sum_{t=1}^{52}$ (Pijt + Tijkt - Pikt)

Third, annual returns from flexible or rigid spatial transfers at seasonal averages of h weeks are aggregated:

(4) $\sum_{t=1}^{h} \frac{(Pijt + Tijkt - Pikt)}{h}$

Greater realism may be achieved by a stylization of the complexities of the transport market. Transport types may depend on the distance to be travelled. Transport costs may rise with inflation. Thus let

Ajk = 0 if < 50 kms; Ajk = 1 if > 50 kms

Bit = cost per unit distance by bullock cart for commodity i in week t

Hit = cost per unit distance by lorry for commodity i for week t

Then:

Tijkt = (1-Ajk) Bit djk + Ajk Hit djk

(5) Bit = B_{io} + 1/52 ($B_{i,52}$ - B_{io})

Hit = H_{io} + 1/52 ($H_{i,52}$ - H_{io})

Efficiency and complexity:Distributive margins & the profits of markets 309

The results of empirical exercises on weekly prices of wholesale coarse rice (obtained from the state Department of Statistics) for a year beginning in 1976 in a system of 22 marketing centers in the South Indian state of Tamil Nadu are presented in Table 1 (for equation 2), Table 2 (for equation 3), and Table 3 (for equation 4). A distance matrix was assembled for this system of places. Segmented transport markets were simulated with coefficients for bullock cart transport for distances under 50 kms and for lorry transport for longer distances, coefficients which were made to rise weekly in accordance with transport cost inflation. During this period the average price of coarse rice was Rs 180 per quintal, but the coefficient of weekly price variation for the set of 22 prices (averaging 22%) was twice that of the period 1977-79 (10.5%) identifying 1976-77 as a period of unusual spatial as well as temporal price turbulence.

Table 1 gives annualized returns for each place on a Rs 180 quintal of coarse rice transported weekly to the place maximizing the price difference minus transport costs. This exercise simulates conditions of full information, fully available transport, and a complete network of intermediary contacts. It is assumed that the simulated transfer of one quintal does not affect market prices. Under these conditions, trade is highly profitable, total returns varying from

Table 1. Returns from flexible, maximizing trade: coarse rice wholesale, 1976-77, one quintal per week (Rps).

Place	Max. profit for years (Rps)	Diff. max. profit places	Most frequent destination
Madras	0.000	0	Kovil
Kanchipuram	821.300	2	Madras
Salem	863.035	6	Madras
Dharmapuri	548.985	4	Madras
Coimbatore	643.170	10	Madras
Erode	369.550	5	Madras
Pollachi	768.115	10	Madras
Tirupur	536.710	6	Madras
Dharapuram	391.555	3	Madras
Mettupalayam	405.820	8	Madras
Gobichettipalayam	402.830	6	Madras
Avinashi	360.335	7	Madras
Bhavani	269.825	2	Madras
Udumalai	547.525	8	Madras
Kodumudi	247.200	1	Madras
Pernamallur	587.615	10	Madras
Trichy	233.915	5	Madras
Madurai	876.310	9	Madras
Dindigul	1,058.825	8	Madras
Ramnad	973.825	8	Madras
Tveli	675.815	7	Madras
Kovilpatti	324.350	4	Madras

120% for the small center of Kokumudi to 600% for the large exporting town of Dindigul. Towns in this simulation traded with a range of other places to maximize returns (2-10 others) averaging six other places, although the state capital of Madras (population 4 million) was the most frequent destination.

Table 2 gives a matrix of returns from a simulation of the cumulative positive and negative returns from trade fixed between all origins and estimations. It simulates generalized conditions of network trade. Under these conditions more trade makes net losses than makes net profits. The majority of towns (10) make profits from repeated trade with three or fewer of the other 21. Seven towns can trade rigidly at profit with four to six other towns and six towns can trade with more than six (the maximum being Dindigul with 14). When Table 1 (equation 2) is compared with Table 2 (Equation 3), maximum returns are always less in the latter case.

Table 3 shows returns if the prices at which trade takes place are computed as annual averages. The point of this simulation is that price data are often analyzed in monthly, seasonal, or annual form. The consequence is that results are radically different from those of Table 2, showing that trading profits are made on short term price fluctuations which are masked by long-term averages. The distribution of profits and losses is less extreme, but more trade is at cumulative net profit than at cumulative net loss. The majority of towns (9) could trade at profit with over 14 other places, eight with 7-13 places, three towns with four to six places, and three towns with three or fewer places. The more disaggregated the analysis, the higher the apparent returns to trade. Micro-level fluctuations in prices and flexibility of response to price levels are proved here to be the keys to the profitability of trade.

All such simulations face the insurmountable problem of reductionism. As industrial organization and agricultural marketing theorists separately concluded over a generation ago, we are left with no method of measuring the efficiency of resources engaged other than in terms of accounting profitability (Bain 1968; Wollen and Turner 1970). To the problems of measuring accounting profitability we now turn.

Table 2. Rigid trading-profit and loss totalled for year: one quintal (Rps) of coarse rice traded weekly, 1976-77.

Madras	Kanchi	Salem	Dharma	Cbe	Erode	Poll	Tpur	Dhara	Mett	Gobi
0.00	820.30	840.20	558.35	585.00	346.90	705.00	495.30	379.75	351.95	365.00
-994.70	0.00	-124.63	-301.07	-360.00	21.70	-250.40	-179.55	24.30	-216.60	-83.68
-1370.60	-309.00	0.00	-325.73	-258.32	49.70	-179.66	-83.10	29.28	-46.99	12.96
-950.85	-50.40	89.47	0.00	-22.38	125.90	3.80	49.96	117.10	134.04	46.76
-1340.40	-311.20	18.08	-265.18	0.00	18.20	42.00	14.14	-9.47	-8.11	-21.60
-586.90	-245.80	-159.50	-339.50	-84.20	0.00	-36.00	-19.11	-62.40	-73.80	-59.24
-1500.60	-455.20	-174.46	-403.40	-229.20	-54.00	0.00	-66.44	-98.38	-150.63	-129.10
-981.30	-288.75	-186.90	-306.64	-218.26	-74.31	-134.44	0.00	-88.90	-213.40	-106.88
-683.45	-347.10	-125.08	-279.70	-94.47	-16.80	-81.18	0.70	0.00	-57.15	-72.68
-844.85	-267.00	-128.79	-240.96	-92.32	-9.90	-58.62	-47.60	-4.95	0.00	-65.66
-726.20	-237.68	-98.64	-228.24	-87.60	-0.44	-22.10	28.92	-37.55	-57.46	0.00
-672.30	-235.50	-165.15	-270.07	-87.75	-45.40	-49.35	-66.24	-23.85	-53.00	-126.40
-412.15	-170.70	-137.63	-199.27	-76.60	12.72	-33.61	-41.70	-48.50	-48.12	-60.26
-1120.80	-362.50	-186.80	-310.24	-113.50	99.60	67.50	161.76	86.84	114.78	45.70
0.00	0.00	0.00	0.00	0.00	0.00	0.00	0.00	0.00	0.00	0.00
-387.00	-166.30	-76.65	-172.00	-69.55	13.92	-82.45	-12.64	-31.82	-60.60	-56.46
-982.45	-284.10	-221.72	-292.85	-254.95	-11.40	-84.05	-58.86	-88.90	-91.00	-116.12
0.00	0.00	0.00	0.00	0.00	0.00	0.00	0.00	0.00	0.00	0.00
-457.00	-34.64	-66.75	-191.27	-23.37	46.70	43.22	110.78	47.45	6.15	36.89
-1491.70	-525.30	-430.67	-531.40	-525.00	-47.71	-366.61	-223.06	-62.06	-201.50	-231.87
-1602.60	-671.80	-515.87	-672.07	-491.50	-135.60	-387.30	-129.05	-155.75	-213.38	-248.80
-1754.50	-731.84	-572.70	-747.16	-506.65	-268.80	-531.91	-410.35	-247.24	-461.60	-354.80
-1540.20	-566.00	-407.96	-576.55	-490.00	-123.30	-247.94	-236.66	-238.93	-280.46	-266.72
-657.90	-311.60	-166.20	-326.41	-142.30	-62.48	-86.60	-52.17	-95.40	-83.52	-99.74

Table 2. (continued)

Avin	Bhav	Udu	Kodu	Pern	Trichy	Mrai	Dind	Ramnad	Tveli	Kovil
327.30	260.05	496.80	247.20	551.95	217.00	843.10	1009.20	958.90	633.00	315.90
-75.72	43.95	-179.14	49.30	-70.26	-180.62	-40.33	176.97	30.56	-206.20	17.54
-7.35	46.37	-296.80	45.75	-27.12	-180.75	95.33	83.93	-34.71	-337.96	-142.20
141.73	141.93	40.96	120.40	158.75	-72.07	160.51	225.13	132.04	-75.35	11.59
-24.75	-17.00	-131.30	29.05	-28.55	-130.37	131.70	284.50	47.65	-208.40	-115.10
-91.40	-30.28	-201.60	-41.28	-21.00	-116.30	-64.75	-1.80	-60.00	-136.50	-166.48
-126.15	-19.82	-211.50	29.95	-52.45	-226.98	47.83	125.10	-5.12	-244.54	-205.00
-99.36	-39.30	-289.44	-13.04	-133.66	-224.62	-33.26	-62.65	-62.15	-370.06	-185.97
-81.45	-9.10	-164.96	-5.62	-24.50	-146.15	-71.86	23.04	-23.04	-190.73	-151.40
-37.00	3.28	-199.02	27.00	-13.40	-187.65	-33.70	52.42	-3.40	-281.26	-83.52
-71.60	1.94	-217.90	7.95	-27.52	-153.71	27.93	34.60	-6.40	-326.32	-95.14
0.00	-19.51	-223.65	-18.36	-36.32	-160.88	-49.45	48.70	-18.15	-144.15	-108.16
-49.51	0.00	-181.12	-12.28	-18.75	-105.95	-49.50	-9.98	-5.12	-110.50	-110.74
66.15	112.87	0.00	92.72	113.02	-49.87	73.42	229.10	42.16	-94.00	-15.20
0.00	0.00	0.00	0.00	0.00	0.00	0.00	0.00	0.00	0.00	0.00
-47.16	-25.88	-124.88	0.00	-12.10	-70.00	-63.45	-39.25	-22.45	-107.40	-82.12
-82.92	-16.35	-275.77	-27.50	0.00	-211.48	-26.74	-36.53	-54.30	-254.60	-190.75
0.00	0.00	0.00	0.00	0.00	0.00	0.00	0.00	0.00	0.00	0.00
27.32	60.05	-99.87	25.00	-5.28	0.00	192.63	96.72	163.00	-2.00	33.60
-132.05	-43.50	-377.38	10.95	-202.94	-277.77	0.00	-53.20	-57.28	-288.09	-70.80
-198.70	-85.18	-486.50	-19.25	-211.33	-301.48	-191.60	0.00	-270.74	-421.39	-193.50
-328.35	-157.12	-569.84	-84.05	-365.70	-350.50	-100.68	-192.94	0.00	-622.44	-299.00
-166.35	-84.50	-309.07	-27.00	-214.60	-208.00	95.31	116.41	-136.44	0.00	-177.40
-100.16	-30.74	-155.20	-4.52	-65.75	-166.40	-58.80	95.10	17.00	16.60	0.00

Table 3. Returns from rigid trade of one quintal/week at annual average prices (Rs/q) coarse grain wholesale, 1976-77.

	Madras	Kanchi	Salem	Dharma	Cbe	Erode	Poll	Tpur
Madras	0.00	-29.90	-26.30	-43.36	-25.95	-126.85	-28.86	-75.99
Kanchi	26.30	0.00	2.42	-14.79	2.64	-98.36	-0.31	-47.83
Salem	16.16	-11.27	0.00	-20.08	0.35	-102.33	-3.36	-51.73
Dharma	34.06	6.42	14.83	0.00	16.91	-87.48	13.06	-34.67
Cbe	11.25	-16.35	-4.97	-23.30	0.00	-103.90	-4.41	-53.47
Erode	114.85	87.15	96.84	76.80	100.60	0.00	97.39	49.01
Poll	13.56	-14.09	-3.45	-21.94	0.81	101.89	0.00	-50.82
Tpur	62.49	34.45	44.23	26.39	47.80	-54.20	45.24	0.00
Dhara	109.94	81.12	92.36	74.52	96.22	-6.03	91.81	45.85
Mett	76.48	48.53	60.34	43.74	64.16	-38.62	59.85	10.69
Gobi	89.05	61.20	72.70	52.83	74.93	-27.12	71.58	24.63
Avin	97.68	70.26	79.87	63.08	83.73	-19.68	79.86	34.63
Bhav	136.50	109.36	117.64	101.50	120.21	20.89	119.15	69.80
Udu	50.25	22.63	30.74	15.26	36.39	-65.35	35.04	-13.47
Kang	175.76	147.32	158.58	140.10	161.18	59.94	157.67	111.62
Kodu	145.39	118.43	129.57	111.09	131.75	29.82	128.54	81.54
Pern	67.75	39.98	49.09	32.96	51.25	-47.76	50.74	1.56
Sathy	175.91	148.28	159.54	140.95	161.53	58.98	158.26	111.44
Trichy	97.38	69.78	75.97	57.20	80.51	-20.84	77.30	30.47
Mrai	36.92	9.58	19.07	0.55	20.57	-80.63	18.67	-29.27
Dind	39.77	12.37	20.26	1.78	25.37	-78.06	22.16	-26.21
Ramnad	21.67	-5.94	2.26	-16.25	4.12	-99.60	3.00	-46.52
Tveli	24.96	-2.27	5.38	-12.25	8.54	-92.93	8.07	-45.81
Kovil	111.25	83.94	90.81	72.32	94.74	-8.22	91.28	43.93

Table 3. (continued)

	Dhara	Mett	Gobi	Avin	Bhav	Udu	Kodu	Pern
Madras	-124.64	-92.38	-101.93	-111.48	-148.26	-65.85	-159.37	-80.05
Kanchi	-97.26	-64.13	-73.56	-82.71	-119.11	-37.27	-130.13	-50.72
Salem	-99.71	-66.01	-75.76	-86.77	-124.66	-42.83	-132.66	-56.20
Dharma	-82.65	-47.70	-60.72	-68.66	-105.91	-23.42	-116.25	-37.43
Cbe	-101.17	-67.40	-78.83	-88.23	-127.41	-47.51	-135.80	-59.35
Erode	1.08	34.44	23.61	12.84	-22.24	60.25	-33.24	46.14
Poll	-100.36	-66.60	-76.98	-86.88	-123.26	-38.64	-133.79	-54.64
Tpur	-50.26	-19.69	-27.87	-36.07	-76.55	8.91	-84.75	-7.77
Dhara	0.00	31.14	18.73	9.79	-27.52	57.39	-37.42	40.70
Mett	-34.59	0.00	-13.62	-21.95	-59.71	24.82	-70.05	8.75
Gobi	-24.87	8.49	0.00	-13.60	-49.36	34.36	-60.36	19.02
Avin	-15.64	18.35	4.60	0.00	-40.48	43.39	-51.89	28.30
Bhav	22.72	56.26	44.50	35.17	0.00	81.74	-12.35	67.16
Udu	-61.11	-27.94	-40.51	-49.69	-86.99	0.00	-96.34	-18.48
Kang	62.26	93.78	84.48	75.56	38.08	122.82	26.10	106.81
Kodu	32.74	65.85	53.43	43.70	7.58	92.32	0.00	76.00
Pern	-46.10	-12.33	-24.15	-33.07	-69.89	13.23	-80.95	0.00
Sathy	61.84	95.14	82.68	76.02	37.77	121.02	25.78	104.62
Trichy	-18.64	14.12	4.04	-5.58	-42.53	40.88	-54.70	23.95
Mrai	-77.51	-44.66	-56.15	-64.74	-103.09	-18.55	-112.16	-33.89
Dind	-74.23	-40.99	-53.09	-61.37	-99.85	-15.13	-109.08	-31.33
Ramnad	-94.26	-62.46	-72.47	-82.04	-119.18	-35.34	-128.23	-50.43
Tveli	-93.11	-60.58	-73.16	-76.38	-115.50	-28.84	-124.69	-46.39
Kovil	-4.01	30.13	18.20	8.68	-28.53	57.47	-38.01	39.13

Table 3. (continued)

	Trichy	Mrai	Dind	Ramnad	Tveli	Kovil
Madras	-106.98	-51.02	-52.67	-37.27	-43.86	-128.33
Kanchi	-78.39	-22.15	-23.86	-8.67	-14.89	-99.42
Salem	-85.87	-26.36	-29.65	-14.17	-20.92	-106.23
Dharma	-69.74	-10.06	-13.24	2.25	-3.65	-89.81
Cbe	-86.66	-29.12	-29.87	-13.12	-23.09	-107.61
Erode	16.49	74.01	71.19	83.16	79.94	-6.09
Poll	-84.65	25.60	-27.86	-13.53	-18.33	-105.86
Tpur	-35.42	21.26	19.82	33.02	26.85	-57.16
Dhara	11.59	69.14	67.93	81.39	72.65	-8.98
Mett	-21.38	36.26	35.44	47.46	42.46	-40.57
Gobi	-9.35	46.88	45.44	59.57	51.98	-30.38
Avin	-0.78	56.49	55.37	68.18	63.96	-21.70
Bhav	37.94	93.79	92.53	106.70	100.50	16.74
Udu	-47.39	9.61	8.53	21.81	18.50	-65.99
Kang	78.46	134.21	133.44	147.40	141.92	57.39
Kodu	45.70	104.66	103.23	117.58	111.25	27.18
Pern	-32.62	25.97	24.04	38.43	32.59	-52.63
Sathy	76.43	134.19	132.56	146.13	141.05	56.18
Trichy	0.00	56.28	51.87	68.81	63.57	21.05
Mrai	-60.15	0.00	-5.31	12.74	7.26	80.13
Dind	-60.06	-0.81	0.00	11.71	8.49	76.02
Ramnad	-76.31	-16.26	-21.79	0.00	-12.85	97.36
Tveli	-71.97	-11.85	-15.12	-2.96	0.00	87.89
Kovil	14.15	71.49	71.10	83.26	82.85	0.00

Returns to Trading Firms

Marketing systems are not only mechanisms of resource allocation, they are also mechanisms of resource extraction and of intersectoral resource transfers. In an integrated economy, intersectoral differences in returns reflect risk. In an unintegrated economy such differences may be accentuated by factor rigidities and by barriers to capital mobility. In the classic empirical studies of agricultural markets in India, returns to trade were proxied by the relation between per unit prices and costs. Price differences net of unit costs were expressed as a proportion of unit sales prices. This concept of returns to trade is the return on variable capital rather than on total capital invested. The latter requires accounting data from individual firms.

Sensitive firsthand data on investments, costs, and profits are notoriously hard to obtain. Successful field methods involve the deployment and reconciliation of a variety of cross-checking means of approach to sensitive questions: via a business historical enquiry, via estimates, via the construction of cost and profit profiles of busy and slack periods, and via cost component proxies (Harriss 1992). Profit (P) is computed as the total gross value of output, including that from byproducts (and at actual prices which may be illegal) (O) less cost (C) (which comprise raw materials, labor, rent and/or depreciation on land, buildings, equipment and machinery, electricity, diesel, maintenance and repair of machinery, and equipment including sacks, cesses, licences, interest on loans (which may actually be taken at a range of rates), and transactions costs, e.g., travel, information, entertainment, bribery where necessary, postage and telecommunications, and the cost of membership of regulating institutions). The rate of profit (r) is (P) expressed as a proportion of capital stock (of land, buildings, equipment, and machinery) (CS) and own working capital (WC) thus:

(6) $$r = \frac{(O - C)}{(CS + WC)}$$

Over and above the practical and psychological problems of obtaining such data, there are a number of conceptual problems with the comparison of (P) and (r) across firms within an agricultural marketing system in a less developed country. First, the proportion of labor which is waged varies significantly. In family firms—the marketing equivalent of peasant production—labor is unwaged and its marginal product cannot be assumed to equal the wage rate, even if "the" wage rate could be identified. "Profit" is used for the consumption of the firm-family, or for firm-families where families are nuclear and firms are jointly owned. In conditions where the major factor of marketing is labor, consumption and investment cannot be distinguished.

Responses to the lack of valorization of labor, or of some labor in trading firms, is to net out of (P) an estimate for the consumption of labor using budget data on household expenditures or using assumptions about consumption such as a local poverty line. (The latter was done for the rates of profit represented in the figures showing returns to combinations of trading activity presented later in this chapter.) The commonly observed rising income elasticity of consumption will mean that the use of a poverty line will overestimate the pure profit of family-firms above the poverty line.

Secondly, ownership arrangements are frequently complex. The evidence on returns presented later (Figures 4 and 5) have been calculated as though the firm were an isolated business. But a marketing firm can be part of a joint family's multiple enterprise combine. In such a case the allocation of profit between consumption and investment across the range of enterprises is made opportunistically and flexibly by trader-owners and the returns from agricultural trading cannot be isolated from those from other family enterprises. Netting out household or worker subsistence from the gross returns of one firm alone will lower the apparent (P) and (r).

Responses to this feature of market firms has involved taking estimates of portfolio investments and returns (and/or imputations from other kinds of evidence) and simulation of returns under a variety of plausible assumptions.

Thirdly, the wage labor component of marketing firms is difficult to cost. Firms cannot be supposed to offer standard contracts at market clearing rates. Instead there will exist a variety of contractual forms, extra-contractual arrangements, and forms of payment. The latter involves cash and kind. The latter may be food or non-food. It may be a routine periodic payment or it may be an optional perk or bonus paid at festivals or annually or at time of need. Many trading firms may also make extremely rudimentary welfare payments to certain types of employees at times of need. All this variety has to be obtained from field enquiry and then plausibly imputed for a cash account (which has been done for the firms whose rates of profit are presented in Figures 4 and 5).

It will be realized that computing the aggregate rate of return to marketing under such circumstances can only be a rough and ready exercise. Attempts to do this have discovered that returns to trade in South Asia are markedly higher than returns to other sectors of the rural economy such as agricultural production (within which returns to one commodity itself may vary by a factor of three) moneylending and agro-industry (Harriss 1985). The hypothesis that trading firms will exhibit constant or increasing rates of return to size is generally not supported (Harriss 1981; 1991).

More on the Comparability of Firms

We have seen that it is generally assumed that markets are price-making institutions on which commodities are bought and sold; made up of firms the efficiency of whose individual economies can be compared, as is conventionally done with respect to units of production. We have begun to appreciate that characteristics of the internal structure of ownership and of labor deployment in marketing firms make such comparisons difficult.

Field surveys also lead to the questioning of the comparability of the activity of trading firms. Commonly there are no firms which simply buy and sell—all trading firms carry out more than pure trading activity and some firms do not buy and sell, being pure brokers. The activities of an agricultural marketing system have been empirically identified for South Asian conditions as follows:

buying (B)	agricultural production (P)
sale of byproducts (BP)	selling (S)
brokerage (BR)	storage (ST)
finance of trade (FTR)	transport (TR)
finance of production (FP)	processing (PC)

and processing is subdivisible such that firms can and do perform subsets of the complete set of activities (e.g., for rice: parboiling, drying, and milling; for cotton: cleaning, averaging, ginning, pressing, and baling) and/or they operate with a variety of co-existing technologies (e.g., for chewing tobacco: pit, sun, or Jaffna curing; for groundnut: cattle operated pestle and mortar (*chekku*), rotary, and expeller).

The unquestioned assumption that firms can be compared with one another is reinforced by linguistic labels, not only in English but also in local vernaculars. Although it is often found that these linguistic classifications are inconsistent (confusing size (e.g., wholesaler), function (e.g., miller), location (e.g., itinerant trader) and although their use as norms is commonly inadequate and incomplete as a description of actual activity, a reasonable hypothesis is:

1. that marketing firms are strongly patterned by activity in ways which correspond to vernacular labels such that even if a marketing system is not to be supposed to consist of comparable firms it is nonetheless composed of subsets of comparable firms.

This can be tested via the combinatorial algorithm of Q-Analysis (Atkins 1977; Chapman 1981) (Figure 3) which searches a multidimensional set of attributes to identify the combinatorial patterns they make and the

Efficiency and complexity:Distributive margins & the profits of markets 319

Figure 3a. Combinations of activity in marketing firms in Coimbatore District, India.

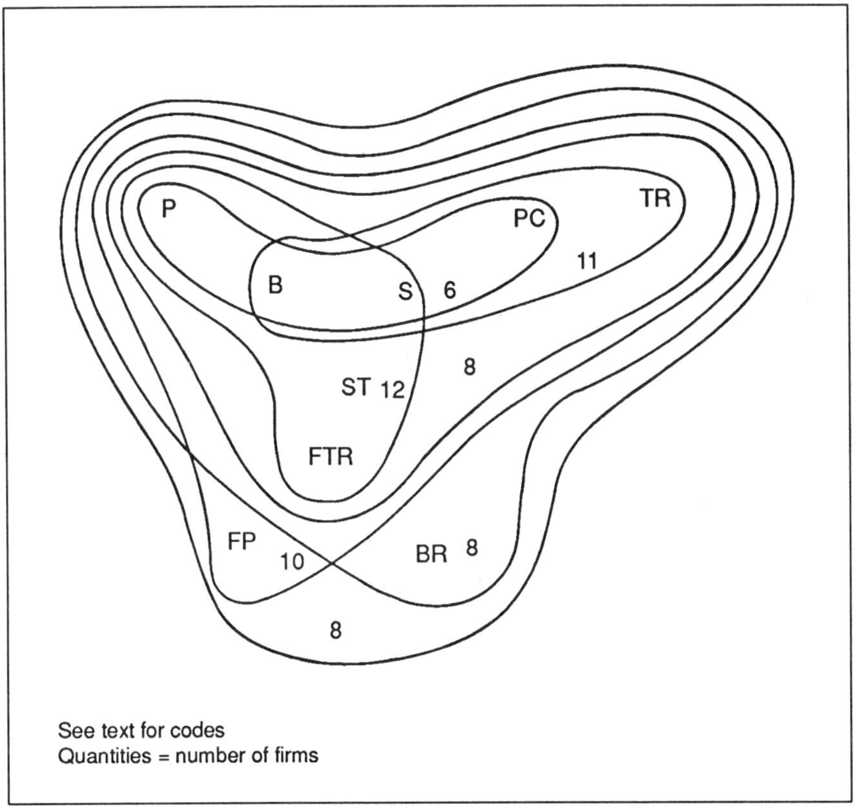

Figure 3b. Least common, most simple patterns of marketing behavior.

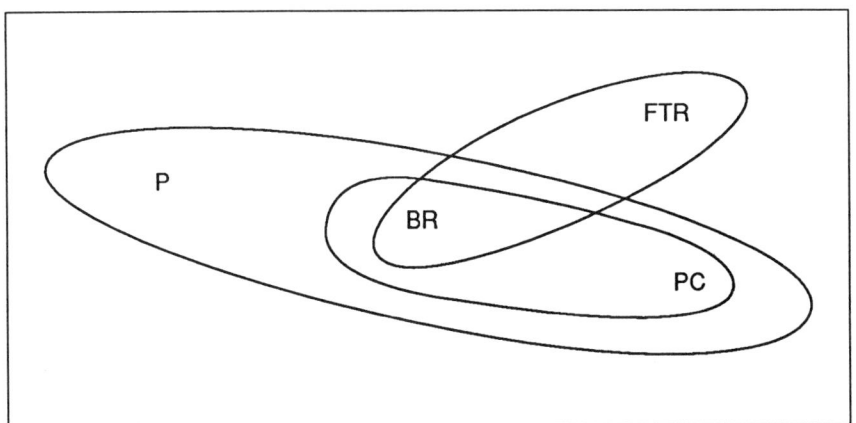

loading of subsets of cases on structures of patterns. Structures revealed using Q-Analysis place cases into sets which might exhibit variation from one end to the other, but in which, along a chain of connection, cases overlap with others in many respects. What then is of analytical significance is the breaks in the chain, breaks which may inhibit flows of various types.

In a set of n activities

(e.g., { B/S/BR/FTR/FP/P/BP/ST/TR/PC })

the theoretical maximum combination of n activities, factorial n or n!, usually greatly exceeds the sample size. The hypothesis (1.) suggests that actual combinations are greatly less than maximum.

Once the distribution of combinations becomes known, not only can the relation of activities of the system of linguistic classification be evaluated but other flow variables (known in Q-Analysis as "traffic") can be related to this structure (known as "backcloth").

Thus it may further be hypothesized:

2. that diversity in activity is risk minimizing rather than profit maximizing, in which case diversity would be negatively associated with the rate of profit.

The statistical analysis of such an hypothesis would require (a) an indicator of diversity, (b) a sample of trading firms of a size sufficient to enable firm size and crop type to be held constant (the former because diminishing returns to size would otherwise confound the results, the latter because crop type independently affects the activity subset), and (c) where other confounding factors such as tax evasion can be identified and controlled. These are ambitious data requirements. The alternative would be a disaggregated combinatorial analysis (as in Figures 4 and 5 which display the relationships between activity combinations and rates of profit in groundnut and cotton processing and trading firms in the marketing system of Coimbatore District in South India).

Empirical research on activity combinations (hypothesis 1 in Figure 3) shows that activity distributions are unrelated to vernacular classifications. One hundred and fifty trading firms reduced by little: to 51 combinations if processing is aggregated and to 107 if processing is classified into its constituent activities. The activities of individual firms are not congruent with the stages of marketing with which this chapter began. Instead marketing systems are composed of firms with (a) complex combinations and (b) extreme diversity of activity. The majority of trading firms mix pure trade with productive activity. { P/B/S/TR } is the commonest core combination. An agricultural marketing system is thus likely to be composed of much less similar entities than is the sphere of agricultural production. Generalization about the firms comprising this sector is not strictly legitimate.

Empirical research on returns to combinations of activities (Figures 4 and 5 and hypothesis 2) shows generally that there is no relation between functional complexity and rates of profit in agricultural marketing systems. The example of cotton reveals a multiplicity of unique combinations with two cores:

{ B/S/TR/GIN/BALE/DRY }

and

{ P/BR/B/S/TR/FTR }

Linked to these two cores are chains of unique firms whose rate of profit declines with increasing complexity. Rather the same appears to be true for rice.

With respect to groundnuts, a core combination of:

{ B/S/TR/DEC/DRY }

with relatively low rates of profit generates chains of firms with forward and backward combinatorial linkages which add to the rate of profit and therefore behave in an opposite way to firms trading in cotton and rice. Positive

Figure 4. Rates of return and combinatorial complexity in groundnut marketing, South India.

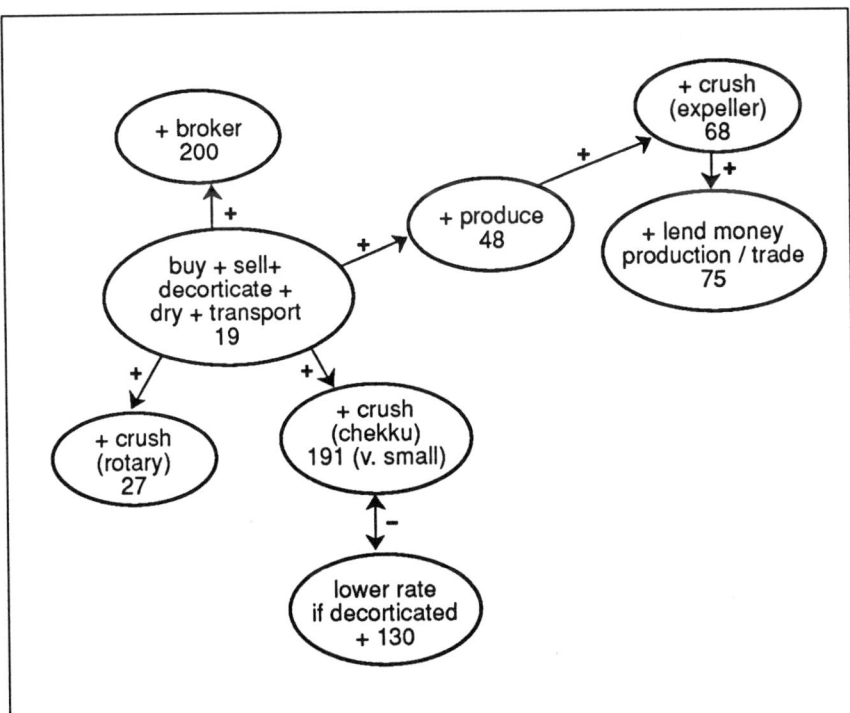

Figure 5. Rates of return and combinatorial complexity in cotton marketing, South India.

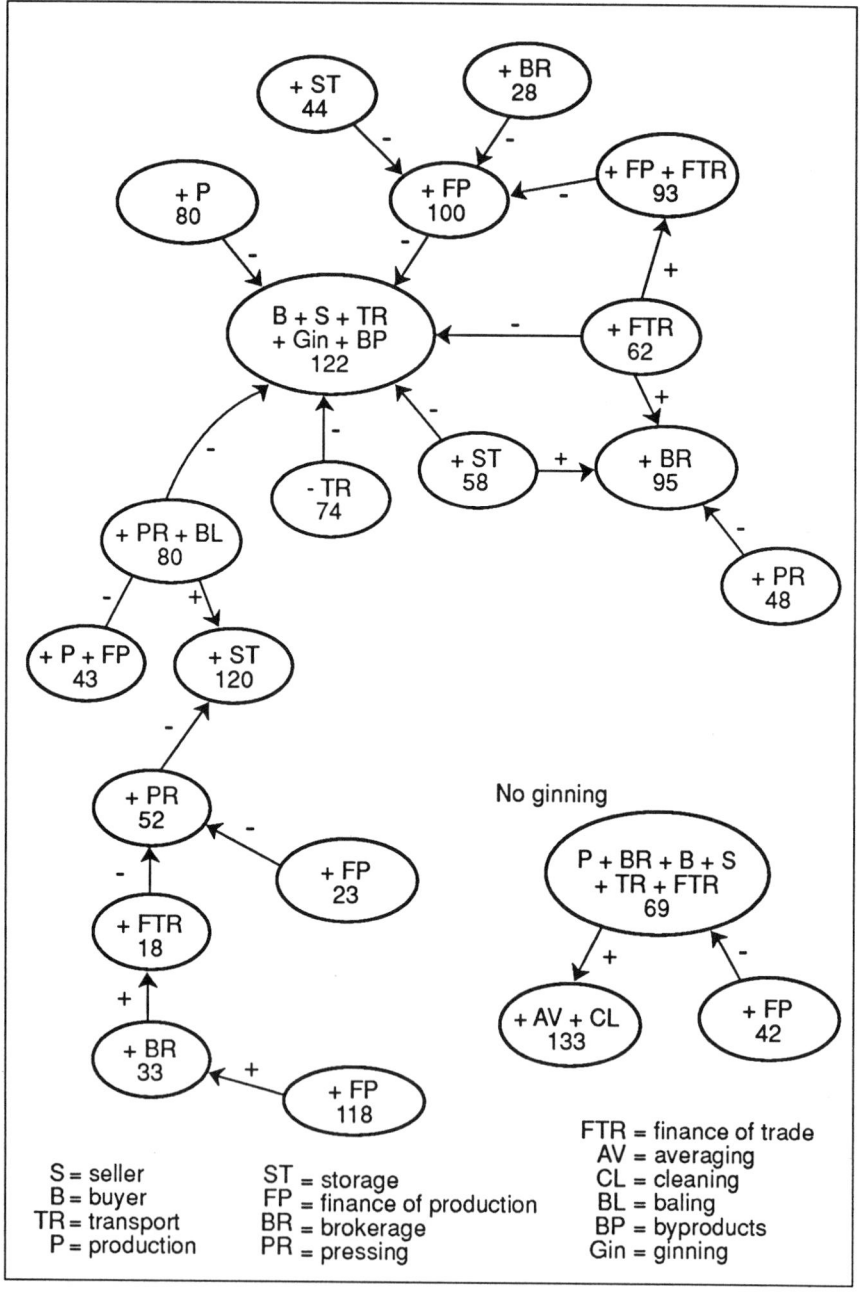

relationships between complexity in activity and rates of profit are also found in the millets and tobacco marketing systems (Harriss 1991). The reasons for these fairly systematic but opposite trends in the relation between complexity and returns are at present unknown. It may be speculated that the reason for the high incidence of unique combinations may be to do with the creation of reputation, but such an hypothesis entails unrestricted information which is far from realistic in marketing systems embedded in social institutions of caste, gender, and locality. The rate of profit is maximized in very small-scale family enterprises (the marketing analogue to petty commodity production) and in larger pure trading and brokerage firms.

Summing Up

It has to be concluded first that the activity combinations of marketing firms are more often than not unique and that non-trivial uniqueness in samples indicates uniqueness in populations of firms. It is therefore not possible to assume that trading firms can be lined up in a production function approach to marketing efficiency (Bateman 1976) or compared along lines of industrial organization (Bain 1968). So, second, we conclude that the comparative efficiency of firms is not evaluable under the kinds of circumstances we have described here. Third, we conclude that evaluations of efficiency using aggregate data on prices and costs which mask over the variation revealed here are themselves dependent upon the type of analytical method imposed upon such data. Fourth, we would emphasize that marketing systems are inherently complex in structure, arguably much more so than is agricultural production. Lastly, we speculate that perhaps they are also chaotic in behavior for some price series are now known to behave in non-random, non-linear, chaotic ways (Savit 1988). Both empirical knowledge of actual marketing systems and methods for their analysis are thus still in their infancy.

Acknowledgments

I am grateful to Prof. George Peters and Dr. T.B. Palaskas of Queen Elizabeth House, Oxford, for their reactions to the original sketch of this paper, to R. Ravichandran, G. Rodrigo, and Prof. S. Guhan for access to the data used in this study, and to Sally Westwood, Liz Phillips, and Margaret Mutch of the University of East Anglia Computing Centre, and Prof. G. Chapman, now of the School of Oriental and African Studies, London University, for program assistance. Remaining errors are my responsibility.

References

Atkin, R. H. 1977. *Combinatorial connectivities in social systems*. Basle, Germany: Birkhause Verlag.

Bain, J. S. 1968. *Industrial organization*. New York, NY, USA: Wiley.

Bateman, D. I. 1976. Agricultural marketing: A review of the literature on marketing theory and of selected applications. *Journal of Agricultural Economics* 27(2):171-226.

Chapman, G. P. 1981. Q analysis. In *Quantitative geography: A British view* (N. Wrigley and R.J. Bennet, eds.).

Harriss, B. 1981. *Transitional trade and rural development*. New Delhi, India: Vikas.

———. 1985. Agricultural markets and intersectoral resource transfers: Cases from the semi-arid tropics of South East India. In *Agricultural markets in the Semi Arid Tropics* (Von Oppen, ed.). ICRISAT, Hyderabad, A.P., India.

———. 1991. *Masters of the countryside: A political economy of agricultural markets in a developed region of South India*. Report to the Overseas Development Administration (UK Govt.); Queen Elizabeth House, Oxford.

———. 1992. Talking to traders about trade. In *Fieldwork in developing countries* (S. Devereux and J. Hoddinott eds.). London, UK: Harvester Wheatsheaf.

Lele, U. J. 1971. *Food grainmarketing in India: Private performance and public policy*. Ithaca, NY, USA: Cornell Unversity Press.

Palaskas, T.B. and B. Harriss-White. 1993. Testing market integration: New methods with material from the West Bengal food economy. *Journal of Development Studies* 30(1):1-57.

Savit, R. 1988. When random is not random: An introduction to chaos in market prices. *Journal of Futures Markets* 8:271-79.

Timmer, C.P. 1974. A model of rice marketing margins in Indonesia. *Food Research Institute Studies* 13(2):145-167.

Wollen G.H. and G. Turner. 1970. The cost of good marketing. *Journal of Agricultural Economics* 21, 63-77.

14

Analyzing Market Integration

Francesco Goletti and Eleni Christina-Tsigas[1]

Abstract

Knowledge about the extent to which markets are integrated is crucial for the success of commercial liberalization policies. This chapter presents an analytical framework for the study of market integration including a descriptive analysis of the market network, time-series analysis, and a model to test the degree of horizontal market integration. The chapter includes applications of this framework to rice markets in Bangladesh and maize markets in Malawi. Results in the latter case show liberalization of markets served as an incentive to private traders to enter the maize trade.

Key words: Prices, government policy, cointegration coefficients, time series analysis, Bangladesh, Malawi.

Introduction

The recent move toward market reform in most developing countries has renewed an interest in the working of agricultural markets as a source of income, employment, and food security. The success of the reform process in promoting equity and efficiency is constrained by numerous structural deficiencies in local markets. One of the main consequences of these structural deficiencies is poor market integration, the difficulty with which information and trade flows among spatially separated markets. Therefore, among other things, the reform process needs to take into account the extent of agricultural market integration.

This chapter presents some methodologies to analyze market integration, because knowledge about the extent to which markets are integrated is important for several reasons. First, by identifying groups of closely integrated markets and by knowing the extent of price transmission across different locations within a country, a government may improve the

---

[1] Research Fellow, Markets and Structural Studies Division, International Food Policy Research Institute, 1200 17th Street, N.W., Washington, DC, 20036, USA; and Agricultural Economist, Purdue University-ERS, USDA, Washington, DC, USA.

design of its market liberalization policies. For example, it avoids duplication of interventions and, as a result, decreases the fiscal burden on the budget. Second, knowledge of market integration allows monitoring of price movements. For example, the knowledge of the speed of adjustment to shocks (e.g., in a country's key commodity sector) arising in different areas of the country is paramount to more effectively managing a price stabilization policy. Third, integration models can be used to forecast prices all over the country. For example, knowing the relationship among prices in neighboring markets facilitates forecasting analysis. Finally, by identifying the structural factors responsible for market integration, investment policy in the marketing infrastructure can be improved, because this allows policy makers to understand which kind of marketing infrastructure is more relevant to the development of agricultural markets in a country. In this chapter, we present the conceptual and analytical framework, then applications of this framework in Bangladesh and Malawi, and close with some conclusions.

Conceptual Framework

Markets are complex institutions encompassing hierarchies and interlinked transactions which may involve simultaneous considerations of various commodities (Palaskas and Harriss 1991). Performance, as well as the integration of markets, is the result of the actions of traders and of the operating environment determined by the infrastructure available for trading and policies affecting the price transmission from one market to another.

This chapter addresses two sets of issues. The first set of issues deals with the concept and measurement of market integration. What does it mean that markets are integrated? How is market integration measured? How do different measures of market integration relate to each other, and what different insights do they give? The second set of issues deals with the relationship between market integration and structural factors. These issues are addressed with a three-stage approach: a study of the marketing network; consideration of the measures of integration; and analysis of the determinants of market integration.

Price correlations measure the co-movements of prices that underlie the intuitive idea of market integration. The problem is that these co-movements sometimes cannot be separated from long-run time trends and seasonality effects. More sophisticated methods aim at discovering if there is a stable long-run linear relationship among prices in different localities. If such a relation is found, then these price series are said to be cointegrated. The presence of **cointegration** between two price series is indicative of interdependence between them.

Assuming that the markets under consideration are integrated, policy makers are interested in knowing the extent of this integration. The degree of integration is then related to the process of price transmission over time. Within this dynamic adjustment process, it is possible to distinguish a short-run and a long-run transmission. This process leads to the computation of magnitude and speed (i.e., how much time is needed for prices to be transmitted from one location to another) of the adjustment.

Data on prices, transaction costs, and trade flows across spatially separated markets are needed to measure the degree of integration between these markets. However, since price data are usually the most readily available and most reliable information on developing countries' marketing systems, market integration is often studied using only price information. This allows measuring the extent, not the causes of integration. In order to understand why (or why not) markets are integrated, we need to consider the factors that affect market integration (Goletti, Ahmed, and Farid 1994). Among the most important of these factors are marketing infrastructure, government policy, dissimilarities in production, and supply shocks.

Marketing infrastructure is the set of transportation, communication, credit, and storage facilities that allow a smooth and reliable functioning of the markets.

Government policy influences market integration in a complex way. There are numerous public interventions that affect the marketing system in addition to the price stabilization policy, such as trade restrictions, credit regulations, and transportation regulations. On one hand, smoothing seasonal fluctuations enhances the co-movement of prices across markets; on the other, this very stabilizing process may hinder the transmission of price signals across markets in a way that long-term multipliers should be able to capture.

Dissimilarities in production affect market integration by dividing markets into those that generally have a surplus in the commodity under consideration, those that have a deficit, and those that are marginally self-sufficient. If a market i is a surplus (net exporting) market and market j is a deficit (net-importing) market, then the likelihood that markets i and j are linked by trade in the examined commodity is higher than if both markets were surplus or deficit.

Supply shocks such as floods, droughts, diseases, and pest attacks affect production directly by creating localized scarcities, whereas other shocks, such as strikes, affect the transportation of goods, making it very difficult for them to reach their final destination.

Analytical Framework

We address the conceptual issues using a three-stage approach. In the first stage, the market network is described using information obtained by a rapid appraisal.[2] In the second stage, time-series analysis of price data is conducted to arrive at a set of measures of market integration, and the issues of seasonality, as well as price rigidities, are examined. In the third stage, the measures of integration computed in the second stage are linked to structural determinants of market integration.

Stage 1: Market network

Basic information about the market network can be obtained by means of rapid appraisal (Goletti 1993a). The objective is to collect data such as (1) number and type of participants in each regional market, as well as the volume of their transactions; (2) trade flows among different markets; (3) access to marketing infrastructure such as trucks, railways, river transportation, and telephones; (4) degree of price information by market participants; (5) degree of information concerning export promotion programs, and structure of marketing costs.

The outcome of these appraisals is a descriptive analysis of the market network and an intuitive notion of the main structural factors affecting market integration.

Stage 2: Time-series analysis

This section considers various measures of integration which are derived from price time-series. The first two measures, namely correlation and cointegration coefficients, explicitly capture the price co-movement aspect of market integration. The last two measures, long-term multipliers and composite indexes, capture the dynamic aspect of price integration.

Correlation coefficients

Correlation of price series at different markets is related to the idea that integrated markets exhibit prices that move together. Due to its simplicity, correlation analysis remains the most common approach to measuring market integration (Farruk 1970; Jones 1972; Lele 1972).[3]

---

[2] By a rapid appraisal we mean a subjective estimate of the environment in which the market network operates. This estimate is obtained mainly by means of questioning the participating agents.

[3] A statistic to test if the correlation coefficient $p_{i,j}$ between prices in markets i and j is different from zero is given by
$$T = \sqrt{(n-1)} \frac{P_{i,j}}{\sqrt{(1 - P_{i,j}^2)}}$$
which has a t distribution with n-2 degrees of freedom, where n is the number of observations on the price series, under the hypothesis that $p_{i,j} = 0$ (Lindgren 1976).

Parallel movements in prices can occur for several reasons other than the integration of markets. For example, they can occur because of the common influence of inflation on both the examined price series, or because the same seasonal influences are present in both markets. This is especially true for agricultural commodities where peak and deficit seasons often take place at the same time. Therefore, in order to eliminate some of these spurious correlations, price differences instead of price levels are sometimes considered in computing correlation coefficients. Besides the problem of spurious correlation, there are other serious problems (Blyn 1973; Harriss 1979; Timmer 1974) related to the often non-stationary nature of the price series involved. For example, correlation analysis cannot help to determine the direction of integration among markets. These problems are taken up by the cointegration analysis.

Cointegration coefficients

The cointegration procedure, which provides more information than the correlation procedure, is an econometric technique that allows the identification of both the degree of integration and its direction between two markets.

Regional prices move over time because of various shocks. If in the long run they exhibit a linear constant relation, then we say that they are cointegrated. To use the cointegration procedure, several steps needed to be carried out on the price series under examination: first, the Augmented Dickey Fuller test and then the Engle Granger Two-Step Procedure. Both of these procedures are easily accessed from standard statistical packages. If the ADF tests prove that the two price series are integrated and cointegrated, then price changes in one market are useful to predict price changes in the other market. The existence of cointegration therefore implies that there is some market integration and it helps to explain its direction.

Let p_{it} denote the price of the commodity under consideration at time t and at location i. In order to study the interdependence of prices between any pair of markets i and j, examination has been suggested (Ardeni 1989; Goodwin and Schroeder 1991; Palaskas and Harriss 1991) if there is any relationship among the price series in the two markets, such as the one expressed by a linear relation:

(1) $$p_{i,t} = \alpha + \beta \cdot p_{j,t} + u_{i,t}$$

Since the price series are generally non-stationary, this relationship has interest only if the error term $u_{i,t}$ is stationary, implying that price changes in market i do not drift far apart in the long run from market j. [4] When $u_{i,t}$ is

---

[4] By stationary, we mean a process in which neither the variance of a current disturbance ε_t nor the autocorrelation between a current disturbance ε_t and one-period lagged disturbance $\varepsilon_{\tau-1}$ depend on t.

stationary, the two series are said to be cointegrated. However, standard statistical techniques do not allow conducting explicit tests of the significance of parameters α and β. Engle and Granger (1987) proposed a two-step procedure for evaluating the properties of a pair of non-stationary economic time-series.

In the first step, each price series is tested for the order of econometric integration, that is, for the number of times the series needs to be differenced before transforming it into a stationary series. The test for integration is the Augmented Dickey Fuller (ADF) test (Dickey and Fuller 1979):

$$(2) \quad \Delta p_{i,t} = \alpha_0 + \alpha_1 p_{1,t-1} + \sum_{k=1}^{k=K} \alpha_{k+1} \Delta p_{i,t-k} + \varepsilon_{i,t}$$

where Δ refers to the difference operator, that is $\Delta x_t = x_t - x_{t-1}$, for each variable x. The null hypothesis is that the series $p_{i,t}$ is integrated of order 1, and the alternative hypothesis is that the series is of order 0. If the t statistics for the coefficient α_1 is greater in absolute value than a critical value given by the ADF critical value, then the null hypothesis is rejected, and the alternative hypothesis of stationarity is accepted. If the null hypothesis is not rejected, then one must test whether the series is of order of integration higher than just 1, possibly of order 2. In this case the same regression equation (1) is applied to the second differences $\Delta^2 p_{i,t} = \Delta (\Delta p_{i \cdot t})$.

In the second step, the residual $u_{i,t}$ of the OLS regression (1) between the two series is again tested for stationarity, with the ADF test.

If the first step results in two nonstationary series, both integrated of order 1, and the second step results in a stationary error term, then the two series are said to be cointegrated of order 1,1.

The presence of cointegration is indicative of interdependence between the two series. In other words, cointegration is indicative of non-segmentation between the two series. Cointegration analysis is a powerful tool to give a clear answer about the existence or not of a relation between two economic time-series.

In the previous section it was seen that two markets i and j are cointegrated when prices exhibit a stable long-term linear relation. Market segmentation refers to the case when the two markets do not exhibit cointegration either in the direction from i to j or from j to i. However, in order to have practical relevance, the definition of market segmentation could be restricted even further.

It makes sense to consider only those pairs of markets that are close. If markets i and j are very far away from each other, the lack of cointegration may be due to transportation costs. It is more interesting to focus on those markets that, in spite of being separated by less than a critical distance, do not exhibit cointegration. A critical distance can be defined as, for example, the maximum distance that could be covered by a one-day trip of a truck loaded with the commodity under consideration. Under these assumptions, segmented markets are those markets that are not cointegrated with each other and that are separated by less than a critical distance.

Dynamic adjustments

In addition to knowing that markets are integrated, we need to know the extent or the degree of integration, which is measured by the magnitude of price transmission. The process of price transmission usually takes time and the immediate impact of price shocks should be distinguished from the impact that is building over time. A short run and a long run can then be distinguished, and dynamic multipliers computed.

The reduced form of a structural model of spatial equilibrium (Takayama and Judge 1971) allows one to compute magnitude and speed of the dynamic adjustment process. The price p_{it} depends on variables, θ_t, affecting both supply and demand. However, the market equilibrium is efficient only under perfect competition and risk neutrality conditions (Newbery and Stiglitz 1981). In reality, imperfect competition, imperfect information, the absence of markets to deal with risk, and many institutional constraints introduce structural rigidities that affect the dynamics of the price transmission process. Moreover, the presence of expectations and storage implies that prices are better described by a dynamic process whereby the current and past value of exogenous variables are taken into account:

(3) $\quad p_{i,t} = f(\theta_t, \theta_{t-1}, \ldots, \theta_0) + \varepsilon_{it}$

Information about the structural variables θ is difficult to obtain. Ravallion (1986) and Boyd and Brorsen (1986) proposed to decompose this dynamic process into a deterministic part, D_t, and a stochastic part, S_t, as follows:

(4) $\quad p_{i,t} = D_t + S_t + \varepsilon_{it}$

The deterministic part includes trend and seasonal dummies, X_{it}. The stochastic part is modelled as an autoregressive process, whereby the values of prices are regressed upon their past. Whereas cointegration analysis offers a method to understand if there is any long-run relationship, the autoregressive process of price changes allows study of the dynamics of price transmission. Price changes, rather than price levels, are the preferred unit of analysis. First differences of logarithm are taken because they offer an immediate interpretation in terms of percentage change. For every pair of market locations i and j, the following bivariate autoregressive process is estimated:

(5) $$p_{i,t} = \sum_{k=1}^{k=m_i} \alpha_{i,k} p_{i,t-k} + \sum_{h=0}^{h=n_j} \beta_{i,h} p_{j,t-h} + X_{i,t} \gamma_i + \varepsilon_{i,t}$$

where $\varepsilon_{i,t}$ is an error term; $\alpha_{i,k}$, $\beta_{i,h}$, and γ_i are coefficients to be estimated; and m_i and n_j are the number of lags of prices in markets i and j, respectively.

In the estimation, problems of simultaneity may be encountered, related to the contemporaneous use of prices in market i and in market j. Since both prices may respond to the same type of shock, it is expected that the error term $\varepsilon_{i,t}$ will be correlated with the price $p_{j,t}$. To overcome this problem, an instrumental variables estimation of $p_{j,t}$ can be used, taking lagged values of the prices of all markets included in the study. The three lags, one for prices in market i, one for prices in market j, and one for the instrumental variables, are determined simultaneously by application of the Akaike information criterion (Akaike 1969).[5]

The **magnitude of price adjustment** is estimated with dynamic multipliers. Dynamic multipliers are interpreted as the effect of a price change due to a random shock or a shift in an exogenous variable. In the context of the model introduced above, the cumulative effect of a shock to price in market j on the price in market i, after k periods is

(6) $$\lambda_k^{ij} = \sum_{h=0}^{k} \frac{\partial E_t p_{i,k+h}}{\partial p_{j,k}}$$

where E_t refers to the expectation operator based on information available at time t. The full adjustment of the dynamic process described by the model is given by the long-run dynamic multiplier, which corresponds to

(7) $$\lambda_\infty^{i,j} = \lim_{k \to \infty} \lambda_k^{i,j}$$

The immediate impact of price $p_{i,t}$ and $p_{j,t}$ on the expected value of $p_{i,t}$ is given by $\partial E_t p_{i,t} / \partial p_{i,t} = 1$, and $\partial E_t p_{i,t} / \partial p_{j,t} = \beta_{i,0}$. For subsequent periods the following recursive formulae are used:

(8) $$\frac{\partial E_t p_{i,t+h}}{\partial p_{i,t}} = \sum_{r=1}^{\min(m_i,h)} \alpha_{i,r} \frac{\partial E_t p_{i,t+h-r}}{\partial p_{i,t}}, \quad h = 1, 2, \ldots$$

and

---

[5] A criterion proposed by Akaike (1969) can be used to estimate the order of an autoregressive process based on an extension of the maximum likelihood principle. The criterion consists of choosing the number q of lags that maximizes the expression given by $AIC = \ln \hat{\sigma}^2 + \frac{2q}{T}$

where T is the number of observations and $\hat{\sigma}^2$ is the estimated residual variance (see Judge et al. 1985: 244-245).

$$\text{(9)} \quad \frac{\partial E_t P_{i,t+k}}{\partial p_{j,t}} = \sum_{s=0}^{\min(n_t,k)} \beta_{i,s} \frac{\partial E_t P_{i,t+k-s}}{\partial p_{i,t}}, \quad k = 1, 2, \ldots$$

Composite index involving both magnitude and speed of adjustment

The analysis of dynamic adjustments allows the study of the **speed** of price transmission. That is, how much time is needed for price changes to be transmitted from one location to another. This is an issue of concern to policy makers for planning food distribution and price stabilization. Sometimes, the speed of price transmission is related to the efficiency of the market system. However, this assumption is not always valid. Rapid adjustment is just an indication of the flexibility of the mechanism. It does not necessarily imply a well-functioning system.

Within the context of this discussion, it is important to consider the speed of adjustment as just another dimension of integration. Considering two markets, A and B, with the same value of the magnitude of price adjustment with respect to a third market, C, the shorter the time to complete this adjustment, the better integrated the market. In other words, this suggests a new indicator of integration which is a combination of the magnitude and speed of adjustment. A ratio of the two is an example of such an indicator, after normalization between 0 and 1. This ratio is denoted by μ, with $\mu = \lambda/\tau$, where λ is the long-term multiplier and τ is the time to adjust to the long run. The closer the number is to one, the more integrated the markets are. There are two advantages in the use of this composite index. The first one is that it combines the information of two measures into one, and the second one is that it can rank market integration across countries. If the components of this measure—the long-term multiplier or magnitude of adjustment (the bigger the better) and the time to adjust (the smaller the better)—happen to be such that in country A the time to adjust is larger than in country B and at the same time the magnitude of adjustment is bigger in country A than in country B, the decision as to which of the two countries has higher market integration will be taken with the help of the ratio of the two, or the composite index.

Price rigidities

Underlying the intuition of a well-integrated marketing system is the capacity to transmit price changes across different localities. One important characteristic of this capacity is its flexibility. Flexibility of the price transmission mechanism can be specifically interpreted in terms of the **symmetry** of price adjustment. It is sometimes claimed that only price increases are transmitted to consumers, whereas traders are the main beneficiaries of price decreases. If the market system were well integrated, then price increases should be transmitted to the same extent as price decreases. This is an issue related to the rigidity of price adjustment in the marketing chain. In order to explore this issue, the framework of market integration can be extended by incorporating asymmetric price responses. The literature on asymmetric price responses, as applied to marketing channels, has been focused on vertical integration, specifically on the relation between farm, wholesale, and retail prices (Kinnucan and Forker 1987). Evidence has been presented that price responses are asymmetric, with the common claim that retail prices reflect cost increases more rapidly than cost decreases.

The Model

In the following model some of the ideas of this literature are applied to study horizontal market integration. The main issue is whether or not price increases are transmitted across markets with the same intensity of price decreases. Starting with the model of equation (5):

(10) $$p_{i,t} = \sum_{k=1}^{k=m_i} \alpha_{i,k} p_{i,t-k} + \sum_{h=0}^{h=n_i} \beta_{i,h} p_{j,t-h} + X_{i,t} \lambda_i + \varepsilon_{i,t}$$

the second term on the right hand side can be decomposed as follows:

(11) $$\sum_{h=0}^{n_i} \beta_{i,h} p_{j,t-h} = \sum_{h=0}^{n_i} \beta_{i,h} (p_{j,o} + p_{j,t-h}^+ + p_{j,t-h}^-)$$

where for any variable x_t, x^+_t is the positive phase, and x^-_t is the negative phase. Intuitively, the positive (negative) phase associated to a time-series is the cumulative sum of the positive (negative) changes of that variable. In order to define the positive and negative phase of x_t precisely, let us proceed as follows.

Let Px_t and Nx_t be the positive and negative increment of variable x_t, namely:

(12) $$Px_t = x_t - x_{t-1} \text{ if } x_t > x_{t-1}$$
$$= 0 \quad \text{otherwise}$$

and (13) $$Nx_t = x_t - x_{t-1} \quad \text{if} \quad x_t < x_{t-1}$$
$$= 0 \quad \text{otherwise}$$

Then, the positive phase is defined recursively as:

(14) $$x_0^+ = 0 \quad \text{and} \quad x_t^+ = x_{t-1}^+ + Px_t$$

The negative phase is similarly defined as:

(15) $$x_0^- = 0 \quad \text{and} \quad x_t^- x_{t-1}^- + Nx_t$$

Equation (5) is then generalized, allowing the coefficients of the positive and negative phases to be different:

(16) $$p_{i,t} = \sum_{k=1}^{n_i} a_{i,k} p_{i,t-k} + \sum_{h=0}^{m_i} \{b'_{i,h} p^+_{j,t-h} + b''_{i,h} p^-_{j,t-h}\} + X_{i,t} c_i + e_{i,t}$$

The symmetry price response hypothesis is then (see Kinnucan and Forker 1987):

(17) $$H_0 : \sum_{k=0}^{m_i} b'_{i,k} = \sum_{k=0}^{m_i} b''_{i,k}$$

Stage 3: Factors of integration

Market integration, however measured, is the result of the action of traders, as well as the operating environment determined by the infrastructure available for trading and policies affecting the price transmission. All the measures of integration considered so far have in common the feature of being computed using only price information available in a specified period of time. Each market link is summarized by just one number. However, markets are complex institutions and their performance as well as their integration is the result of numerous factors.

Among these factors, marketing infrastructure, price stabilization policies, the degree of dissimilarity in production in different areas, as well as supply shocks, are important explanatory factors of market integration.

To estimate how these factors relate to integration of markets, the four measures of market integration introduced in the previous section will be used: the correlation of price differences ρ_{ij}, the cointegration coefficient b_{ij}, the long-term multiplier λ_{ij}, and the composite index μ_{ij} incorporating both long-term multiplier and time to adjust.

To test hypotheses concerning the effect of structural factors on market integration one needs to specify the explanatory variables mentioned above.

Marketing infrastructure includes transportation, communication, and credit. These variables are expected to influence market integration positively.

Price stabilization policy is supposed to influence market integration in a complex manner. On one hand, by smoothing seasonal and inter-year fluctuations it enhances the co-movement of prices across markets. On the other hand, this very stabilizing process may hinder the transmission of price signals across markets in a way that long-term multipliers should be able to capture. In order to test these hypotheses, it is necessary to get an index of the degree of price stabilization policy undertaken by a government in various affected areas. One simple way to do this is to consider the correlation between prices and end-of-period public stocks. This correlation is expected to be negative and its absolute value is taken to be indicative of the degree of price stabilization policy.

Production affects market integration through the degree of dissimilarity in self-sufficiency of various markets. If market i is a surplus market and market j is a deficit market in the commodity under consideration, then the likelihood that i and j are linked by trade is higher than if both markets were surplus or deficit areas. The degree of dissimilarity is usually measured by the absolute value of the percentage difference in production per capita. Another variable related to production is the number of production shocks affecting various districts. These shocks can include days of flooding, drought, cyclone, salted water, pest attack, diseases, or number of deaths (as collected from newspapers). Their effect on market integration is not clear a priori. When the production shocks are of a tremendous magnitude, one would expect market integration to be disrupted. In the case of normal production shocks, they may even positively affect market integration, in so far as they add incentives to trade between affected areas and other areas.

Applications

Monthly price data at different rice markets in Bangladesh and different maize markets in Malawi have been used for the time-series analysis. In the case of Bangladesh, a more comprehensive data set including both weekly prices and structural variables has also been used.

Time-series analysis

As we see in Table 1, markets that appear to be well integrated based on one measure of market integration are not necessarily well integrated according to the other measures. This table provides us with descriptive statistics for these measures of integration, showing that even though the average correlation coefficient of price changes in Bangladesh and Malawi is approximately the same (27%), the correlation is significant only for a small number of market links in Malawi, whereas it is significant over all market links in Bangladesh.

In Malawi the magnitude of the longterm price adjustment in one maize market due to a shock originated in another maize market is on average 58% versus 74% in Bangladesh. Moreover, the adjustment is lower in Malawi taking 5.7 months versus 2.6 months in Bangladesh. The composite index has a value of 0.15 for Malawi, which is less than half the value for Bangladesh, implying again a lower degree of market integration in the former country.

The long-term adjustment of 87% for Bangladesh is relatively high, especially in relation to other developing countries, where average long-term multipliers of less than 0.50 are common (Mendoza and Rosegrant 1991). The 36% of long-term adjustment for Malawian maize markets is low and shows that the markets are not well integrated even in relation to other developing countries.

Table 1. Comparison of various measures of integration in Bangladesh rice market and in Malawi maize market.

Measure of Integration	Significant market links (%)		Average of the measure of integration over the significant market links	
	Bangladesh	Malawi	Bangladesh	Malawi
Correlation coefficient ρ	100	11	0.268	0.274
Long-term multiplier λ	87	36	0.735	0.585
Time to adjust in months τ	87	36	2.6	5.7
Composite measure μ	87	36	0.302	0.147

Cell (i,j) gives the long-term response of price in market i to a shock originating in market j.
Significant market links at the 95% level.
Source: Goletti (1993b) and Goletti and Babu (1994).

Price rigidities

In the case of maize markets in Malawi, the price transmission mechanism in the wholesale market is characterized by symmetry (Goletti and Babu 1994). In 50 of the 56 cases examined, the hypothesis that the response of wholesale prices in market A to downward movements in market B is the same as the response to upward movements could not be rejected. According to this result, the symmetric price response hypothesis could not be rejected, even though some asymmetry in price response may occur at specific lags. Therefore, the result supports the belief that wholesale agents benefit from wholesale price decreases to the same extent as they do from price increases.

Structural factors affecting integration

Goletti and Farid (1993) identified structural factors responsible for the integration of rice markets in Bangladesh. The effect of some structural factors appears to be strong across different specifications of the measure of market integration. As expected, distance negatively affects market (Table 2), but this effect is significant only for correlation and cointegration coefficients.

Road infrastructure, measured by paved road density, has a positive and significant effect on market integration, for both correlation and composite index of integration.

Contrary to expectation, telephone density has a negative effect on market integration. We cannot say anything about the effect of bank services. The unexpected signs of telephone and bank branch densities may be partly explained by the type of data used. First, with respect to telephones, what is relevant to trade is not simply the availability of telephones in an area, but the availability of country-wide telephones, as opposed to local phones that work only through an exchange operator in the district headquarters. Second, with respect to the bank branch density, probably this variable is not a good proxy of credit available to traders. Possibly, the total amount of bank deposits or bank loans by district could be a better indicator.

Railway density also has an unexpected negative effect, especially for long-term multiplier and composite measures of integration. An explanation is that rail transportation is undertaken over very long distances, when prompt delivery is not a major consideration. Moreover, the density of railways is not necessarily related to the location of main trade links. The railway network was built largely in colonial times for considerations independent of rice trade.

Table 2. Summary effects of structural factors on measures of integration in Bangladesh.

Effects	Correlation of price differences	Cointegration coefficients	Long-term multiplier	Composite measure	Congruence among measures
Distance	-	-	0	0	-
Paved road density	+	0	0	+	+
Telephone density	0	-	-	-	-
Bank branch density	-	+	0	+	?
Railway density	0	0	-	-	-
Number of strikes	-	0	-	-	-
Degree of price stabilization	+	+	-	-	+/-
Degree of dissimilarity in production	+	0	+	+	+
Production shocks	+	0	+	0	+
R^2	28.4	13.4	11.7	10.0	

+ = significantly positive effect; - = significantly negative effect; 0 = not significantly different from zero; Congruence refers to the overall conclusion from the different measures of integration; +/- = that it has a positive effect on correlation and cointegration coefficients and a negative effect on long-term multiplier and composite measures.
Source: Goletti and Farid (1993).

Labor conflicts affect rice trade indirectly. For example, strikes were found to have a significant negative effect on market integration, since they disrupt normal trade. The degree of price stabilization policy seems to have an asymmetric effect on correlation and cointegration coefficients, on one hand, and on long-term multiplier and composite measures, on the other. One explanation is that price stabilization is strengthening the degree of price co-movements as measured by correlation and cointegration coefficients, but is hindering the process of price transmission as measured by long-term multiplier and composite indexes. The government maintains foodgrain stocks to stabilize prices. Since the correlation between public stocks and prices is expected to be negative, the higher the absolute value of such a correlation, the higher is the degree of policy intervention.

Dissimilarity in production affects market integration positively. Production shocks also have a positive effect on market integration. This probably has to do with the period considered in the estimation. The three years 1989/90 to 1991/92 were characterized by mild (relative to Bangladesh history) production shocks. On the contrary, Goletti (1993b) considered severe supply shocks, such as major floods in Bangladesh, and it was found that they have a negative effect on integration. This implies that when the production shocks are not normal, their effects on market integration are negative.

By identifying road infrastructure, strikes, and dissimilarities in production as the three most important structural factors affecting the development of rice markets in Bangladesh, a few policy implications emerge as a way of fostering market integration. First, there is an indication toward investing in paved roads. Second, by resolving labor conflicts, the government would improve efficiency not only of the sectors where those conflicts take place, but also the development of rice market integration. Third, there is no need for giving production incentives in the deficit regions, since the country will be better off by trading across regions with production dissimilarities.

Implication for Policy

What are the implications of these results, and how do they help a policy maker to design a more effective policy? The following example will try to answer this question. Let us suppose that it is expected that the price of rice will increase in Bangladesh market A due to an anticipated bad harvest. If it takes 2.5 months for a price change to be transmitted from the central market, where rice stocks are kept, to market A, then the government should plan to release stocks accordingly in order to prevent the expected price increase.

As another example, let us assume that commodity stocks are kept in more than one location, and a drought is expected in, say, location A. If the government knows: (1) that market A is well connected with several other markets in which stocks are kept and (2) the speed of price adjustment among these markets, then the government may try to intervene by sending stocks from the central market to all the other markets. However, resources can be saved by releasing stocks only in the markets which are best integrated with market A.

These analytical techniques to measure market integration can also be used to evaluate the effect of market liberalization on market integration. For example, it has been found (Goletti and Babu 1994) that when market liberalization started in Malawi, the number of maize markets that were cointegrated increased. Market liberalization increased the participation of the private sector in the maize marketing system. This situation was depicted in the new maize prices which reflected this information. This positive effect of market liberalization on market integration was captured by all measures of market integration.

It is also useful to know why certain markets are more integrated with certain other markets. For example, let us suppose that a major food producing region is not well integrated with an urban center due to lack of transportation infrastructure. The government may use this information to prioritize its infrastructure budget and allocate more funds to increase the degree of integration between urban and food producing regions.

Conclusions

This chapter has presented several methods to analyze market integration. The methods have been classified within a three-stage approach that helps to organize the sequencing of the analysis. In the first stage, quick estimates of the environment in which the market network operates can be obtained. In the second stage, time-series of prices are analyzed in order to derive several measures of market integration. In the third stage, the relation between market integration and structural factors is explored. Applications of these methods have been reported and some policy implications have been drawn from these cases. Policy makers may use results from market integration studies to apply policies in a more efficient manner. Decisions about the timing as well as the location of a policy application should take into consideration factors like the degree of market integration and speed of price adjustment.

In the present context of market reforms of both agricultural inputs and outputs, detailed knowledge of the markets and marketing system is extremely relevant. The development of private marketing systems is expected to be accompanied by a growing integration of markets. In one specific application (to Malawi) this was found to be true. However, numerous structural deficiencies may obstruct the enhancement of market integration in other situations. We need to learn much more about the transmission of price signals and information along marketing channels in developing countries. It is hoped that by extending the number of applications of these methods, a better understanding of the working of markets in developing countries can be obtained.

References

Akaike, H. 1969. Fitting autoregressive models for prediction. *Annals of the Institute of Statistical Mathematics* 21:826-839.

Ardeni, P.G. 1989. Does the law of one price really hold for commodity prices? *American Journal of Agricultural Economics* 71(3):661-669.

Blyn, G. 1973. Price series correlation as a measure of market integration. *Indian Journal of Agricultural Economics* 28(2):56-59.

Boyd, M. and B.W. Brorsen. 1986. Dynamic price relationships for US and EC corn gluten feed and related markets. *European Review of Agricultural Economics* 13:199-215.

Dickey, D.A. and Fuller, W.A. 1979. Distribution of the estimators for autoregressive time series with a unit root. *Journal of the American Statistical Association* 74 (366):427-31.

Engle R.F.C. and C.W.J. Granger. 1987. Co-integration and error correction: Representation, estimation, and testing. *Econometrica* 55(2):251-76.

Farruk, M. O. 1970. *The structure and performance of the rice marketing system in East Pakistan*. Occasional Paper no. 31. Department of Agricultural Economics, Cornell University, Ithaca, NY, USA.

Goletti, F. 1993a. *Rapid appraisal of the rice market network in Bangladesh*. International Food Policy Research Institute, Washington, DC, USA.

———. 1993b. *The effects of supply shocks on market integration. An application to Bangladesh rice markets*. International Food Policy Research Institute, Washington, DC, USA.

Goletti, F. and S. Babu. 1994. Market liberalization and integration of maize markets in Malawi. *Agricultural Economics* 11(2,3):311-324.

Goletti, F., R. Ahmed, and N. Farid. 1994. Structural determinants of market integration. The case of rice markets in Bangladesh. *Developing Economies* (forthcoming).

Goodwin, B.K. and T.C. Schroeder. 1991. Cointegration tests and spatial price linkages in regional cattle markets. *American Journal of Agricultural Economics* 73(2):453-64.

Granger, C. 1969. Investigating causal relations by econometric models and cross spectral methods. *Econometrica* 37:424-38.

Harriss, B. 1979. There is a method in my madness: or is it vice versa? Measuring agricultural product performance. *Food Research Institute Studies* 17(2):197-218.

Jones, W.O. 1972. *Marketing staple food crops in tropical Africa*. Ithaca, NY, USA: Cornell University Press.

Judge, G. G., W. E. Griffiths, R. C. Hill, H. Lütkepohl, and T. Lee. 1985. *The theory and practice of econometrics*. New York, NY, USA: John Wiley and Sons.

Kinnucan, H.W. and O.D. Forker. 1987. Asymmetry in farm-retail price transmission for major dairy products. *American Journal of Agricultural Economics* (May):285-292.

Lele, Uma. 1972. *Food marketing in India: Private performance and public policy*. Ithaca, NY, USA: Cornell University Press.

Lindgren B. W. 1976. *Statistical theory*, 3rd edition. New York, NY, USA: MacMillan Publishing Co., Inc.

Mendoza, M. and M. Rosegrant. 1991. Marketing of corn in the Philippines: market integration and the dynamics of price formation. In *The Philippines corn livestock sector: Policy and performance* (Rosegrant and Gonzalez, eds.). International Food Policy Research Institute, Washington, DC, USA (mimeo).

Newbery, D. M.G. and J. Stiglitz. 1981. *The theory of commodity price stabilization: A study in the economics of risk*. Oxford, UK: Oxford University Press.

Palaskas, T.B. and B. Harriss. 1991. *Testing market integration: New approaches with case material from the West Bengal food economy*. Institute of Economic Analysis, Manor Road, Oxford, UK.

Ravallion, M. 1986. Testing market integration. *American Journal of Agricultural Economics* 68(1): 102-109.

Takayama, T. and Judge G. 1971. *Spatial and temporal price and allocation models*. Amsterdam, Holland: North Holland.

Timmer, P.C. 1974. A model of rice marketing margins in Indonesia. *Food Research Institute Studies* 13(2):145-167.

15

Pricing Conduct of Spatially Differentiated Markets

Meyra Sebello Mendoza and Mark W. Rosegrant[1]

Abstract

Noncompetitive pricing behavior in oligopolistic commodity markets is verified using a time-series model. A more realistic representation of the dynamics of the price discovery process, the bivariate autoregressive modelling proposed in this paper is practical for applications in developing countries because of its minimum data requirements.

Collusive, discriminatory, price leadership, or competitive pricing conduct is tested empirically for Philippine copra. Findings disclosed a limited, organized pricing scheme where Manila (an urban market center) leads the other regional markets in discovering copra price locally. No evidence was found to support popular assertions of collusive pricing commonly associated with a concentrated market.

Key words: Collusion, price discrimination, bivariate autoregressive model, dynamic, price discovery, Philippine copra.

Background

In agricultural commodity markets in developing economies, market concentration is a strong indicator of noncompetitive pricing behavior and of inefficient market performance. The presence of few, large market agents within a defined market boundary is sufficient evidence of market power and collusive pricing. This assertion is typically validated in most marketing studies employing the conventional market structure-conduct-performance paradigm. Although such noncompetitive pricing behavior cannot be verified explicitly in the static structural market analysis, the results of these studies provide the most persuasive argument for government intervention in agricultural markets in developing countries. Governmental price control

---

[1] Research Analyst and Research Fellow, International Food Policy Research Institute, 1200 Seventeenth Street, N.W., Washington, DC, 20036-3006 USA.

policies, increased public spending in improved market information services, uniform product grading and standardization, and the organization of farmers into cooperatives have been justified based on the alleged market power possessed by market agents over the farmers.

In this paper, we propose a time-series model which directly tests for pricing conduct. Compared to static methods, this model realistically captures the dynamics of the price adjustment process which characterize real market exchange. The paper proceeds as follows. A generalized spatial marketing system of a typical oligopolistic commodity market is described in the next section. The dynamic vector autoregressive representation developed in that section is then illustrated in the following section for the Philippine copra market case. The procedures employed in the time-series modelling exercise and three hypotheses of oligopolistic pricing behavior are then specified. The two next sections present the data requirements and the sample period covered. Findings of the study and the conclusions are reported in the last two sections.

Modelling Spatial Pricing Behavior

The agricultural marketing system in most developing countries is characterized by a highly atomistic production side, in which there are numerous farmers growing perishable crops on small farms dispersed all over the countryside; and by an oligopolistic market, where there are few traders. Assume that a typical marketing system can be represented by a multiple autoregressive representation:

(1) $$[\Delta P_t^i] = \sum_{p=1}^{m} [A_p][\Delta P_{t-p}^i] + \sum_{q=1}^{n} [B_q][P_{t-q}^j] + [\varepsilon_t^i]$$

where $[\Delta P_t]$ denotes an (N x 1) vector of contemporaneous price changes in N market locations at time t, and the terms ΔP^i_{t-p} and ΔP^j_{t-q} are the historical values of price changes in these markets. The term $[A_p]$ is a (n×p) and $[B_q]$ is a (n×q) vector of the estimated coefficients, and ε_t^i are serially uncorrelated errors. Thus, equation (1) is interpreted as the contemporaneous price changes in each local market located in i (i=1, 2,..., N) as a function of contemporaneous price changes and lagged price changes in all the other markets as well as its own historical prices.

The market boundary covered by a typical trader is generally narrow, being limited by an inadequate transportation system and inherent structural deficiencies, such as naturally occurring geographical barriers. Thus, N in equation (1) may cover 2 or 3 adjacent or non-contiguous villages. Because there is considerable distance between production sites and consumption sites, transportation cost is generally high and there are sizable economies of scale in transportation. For this reason, market service areas covered by traders typically overlap, with several traders operating within the same villages as other traders. Where market boundaries overlap, there is a high degree of price competition between traders buying within the same location so that a price change made by one trader would likely be matched by a price change by its close, rival trader. Traders operating outside this market area would not likely react to a price change unless these competitors intend to penetrate the same market. Thus, a price change in one market would result in a series of price reactions and feedbacks that spread throughout overlapping and contiguous market areas, but such a price change will not have a discernible effect on more distant markets.

The rigor of price competition among rival traders, however, is moderated by added services they render farmers. In addition to providing transportation services, traders are the major sources of credit for farmers. Generally, farmers differentiate among traders on the amount of credit they could obtain from traders and thus, although there are several potential buyers within the village, a farmer's indebtedness to a trader narrows his choice to a single trader. This credit-marketing arrangement has been asserted to allow traders some form of price fixing or price discrimination in each of the market areas in which they operate. However, the importance of mutual trust and the reputation or character of the trader within the community in sustaining a long standing trading relationship between farmers and traders is often sufficient deterrence to price exploitation by traders.

Overall, there are three pricing conducts that characterize an oligopolistic market which are tested in this study: market independence or price discrimination; collusive and organized pricing; and price matching with offsetting lags. The implications of each of these hypotheses in pricing conduct in the time-series model representation in equation (1) are described in greater detail in the following section.

An Empirical Application: Philippine Copra Market

The spatial pricing behavior representation in equation (1) is generalized so that it can be easily replicated to any commodity and country cases. As an illustration, equation (1) is empirically tested for the Philippine copra [2] market.

The Philippine coconut industry: A brief background

Coconut, a principal agricultural commodity in the Philippines, was harvested in 24% of total agricultural area in 1990, ranking third to corn (29%) and rice (25%) (NEDA 1991). Grown in 78% of the 1,551 municipalities and 59 of the 75 provinces in the country, coconut production accounted for 20% of total domestic agricultural supply in 1990, next to sugarcane production which tops

---

[2] Copra is the white kernel or meat of a mature coconut.

the list at 28%. Rice is recorded at 16% of total domestic production and corn at 8% (NEDA 1991).

Coconut is largely produced in four regions: Southern Tagalog region, where 20% of coconut farms are located; Bicol (13%), Eastern Visayas (13%), and the Mindanao regions (44%).[3] Altogether, these regions produced 90% of total coconut supply in 1960-1986 (PHILCOA 1989). About one-third of rural Filipinos grow coconut for livelihood (Santos 1987). Beyond the farm gate, approximately 15,000 Filipinos derived their earnings from buying and selling coconut (mainly copra) and 20,000 from processing coconut into copra, coconut oil, charcoal, and coir (David 1977).

Consumption of coconut products is concentrated in Luzon and Mindanao and the majority of the coconut processing plants are located there. Of the total oil milling capacity, 45% is accounted for by coconut oil mills in Luzon (mainly those in Manila and nearby provinces) and 47% is in Mindanao. Of the 10 coconut desiccators in the country, 7 are in Luzon and 3 in Mindanao. Approximately 96% of the total registered exporters/traders of coconut products listed by the United Coconut Association of the Philippines (UCAP)[4] have their base of operation in or around Manila, and the remaining 4% is in Mindanao (UCAP 1990).

As a major source of income for the Philippine economy, coconut contributed about 10% to gross value added (GVA) in agriculture in 1990 (NEDA 1991). Sales of coconut products in the foreign market generated 54% of national dollar reserves in the same year (PHILCOA 1989). About 85% of domestic coconut production is marketed abroad and 15% is consumed locally. Coconut exports are mostly in the form of coconut oil (81%) earning 64% of total foreign revenues, copra (9%) contributing 5%, and desiccated coconut (6%) generating 11%, with copra cake and non-traditional coconut products such as activated carbon, coconut shell charcoal accounting for the balance. Domestically consumed coconuts are in the form of foodnuts (young, green unhusked coconut), edible and inedible oil, coconut coir, and charcoal (PHILCOA 1989).

---

[3] The Philippines is composed of three major islands, Luzon, Visayas, and Mindanao. For administrative purposes, the country is divided into 12 regions: the Ilocos Region, Cagayan Valley, Central Luzon, Southern Tagalog, and Bicol in Luzon; the Visayas Islands into Western, Central, and Eastern Visayas Regions; and Mindanao into Western, Northern, Southern, and Central Mindanao.

[4] UCAP is the umbrella organization of the public and private sectors of the coconut industry in the country, which consists of coconut farmers, the Philippine Coconut Authority (the government), coconut oil millers, copra exporters, coconut desiccators, coir producers, coconut shell charcoal processors, and soap and detergent manufacturers.

The Empirical Model and Estimation Procedures

Estimating the multiple vector autoregressive formulation represented in equation (1) is impractical. If extended to N number of markets with n lags for each N market, the dimension of the matrix and the number of variables can be unwieldy and, thus, estimating it computationally tedious. Another potentially serious consequence of including too many variables is the problem of multicollinearity, a condition which prevails when there is a high linear correlation between exogenous variables. Multicollinearity would result in biased standard errors and thereby invalidate inferences drawn from conventional statistical tests. That is, one would be more likely to accept a false hypothesis (Type II error).

A more simplified version of equation (1) is used and equation (1) is re-written as:

(2) $$\Delta P_t^i = \sum_{k=1}^{p} \alpha_k \Delta P_{t-k}^i + \sum_{l=0}^{m} \beta_l \Delta P_{t-l}^j + e_t$$

where ΔP_t^i is the contemporaneous price changes in market center i, ΔP_t^j is contemporaneous price changes in market j, i not equal to j, and the subscripts t-k and t-l are the historical price changes in each market.[5] Equation (2) is estimated for pairs of copra markets. In all, there are 10 bivariate autoregressive equations estimated.

The definition of price changes

Weekly changes in copra prices in (2) are calculated by obtaining the first differences of their natural logarithms and then multiplying by 100 to avoid any scaling problem. This specification is appropriate in studying pricing behavior because it represents the intertemporal changes in prices in one market in response to price changes in another market. Compared to price levels, the use of first differences likewise has econometric appeal because the problem of first-order autocorrelation is eliminated (Brorsen 1983). The notations α_k and β_l are the estimated coefficients and e is the error term. For simplicity and following previous modeling efforts, equation (2) is assumed linear in all parameters.

---

[5] This is a weak form test of market efficiency where information on past prices is reflected in contemporaneous prices (Fama 1976). Fama also distinguishes two other market efficiency tests: a semi-strong form efficiency test is one where market agents utilize all publicly available information and the strong form efficiency test where all public and private information is used in forming price expectations.

Procedures for estimation

There are several procedural steps to follow in estimating equation (2). The first step involves the identification of the lag structure for weekly changes in copra prices in each market center. For this purpose, the Akaike Information Criteria (AIC) was employed (Akaike 1974). Compared to the widely used Box and Jenkins method, the choice of the lag lengths based on the AIC procedure is more precise because there is less arbitrariness exercised.

Unlike previous studies where uniform lags were specified, a different lag length is used for each weekly price series. This modification has theoretical appeal because it is a more realistic representation of actual market exchange. For many reasons (Brorsen 1983; Boyd and Brorsen 1986; Heytens 1986; Mendoza and Farris 1992), price adjustments to exogenous shocks seldom occur instantaneously, i.e., some markets would respond quicker to shocks whereas other markets would exhibit delayed response. The AIC-selected lag lengths for each price series are 4 (weeks) lags for Manila, 5 lags for Cebu City, 5 lags for Davao City, and 7 lags each for Legaspi City and Lucena City. To validate the lag specification, the errors are diagnosed for serial correlation using the Durbin-Watson (DW) test statistic. A statistically insignificant DW statistic would confirm that the lags are correctly specified. Otherwise, longer lags should be included.

Hypothesized pricing behavior tested

Based on equation (2), and following Ravallion (1986) and Faminow and Benson (1990), three behavioral pricing relationships are tested:

Hypothesis I: Market Independence

$H_0^1: \beta_l = 0, l=0, 1, 2,..., n$

Hypothesis II: Perfect and Instantaneous Cooperative Pricing

$H_0^2: \beta_0 = 1, \alpha_k=\beta_l=0, k=1, 2,..., m$

Hypothesis III: Price Matching with Delayed Response

$H_0^2: \beta 0 = 1, \sum_{k=1}^{p} \alpha_k + \sum_{l=1}^{m} \beta_l$

Hypothesis I implies that price changes in location j do not affect price changes in market i. Failure to reject this hypothesis would suggest that traders exercise a form of spatial price discrimination. Perfect cooperative pricing with no lags in responses between markets i and j, i not equal to j, in Hypothesis II would indicate an organized, collusive pricing system, where price adjustments occur instantaneously because of some pricing arrangements between market agents. Such collusive pricing behavior is an effective marketing strategy in maintaining a secured share in the market. If Hypothesis II is false, a form of price leadership exists between markets where a price change is first discovered in one market and then after some time, is transmitted as a price change in another market. The pricing scheme postulated in Hypothesis III implies an unorganized market where a tacit collusive arrangement within a group of traders or cartel invokes a response from buyers outside the group, with some delay. This is also consistent with a base-point pricing system, with prices based on a reference or central market or a price leadership pricing system. If all three hypotheses are false, a noncooperative form of pricing arrangement is said to exist and the pricing system could be discerned as competitive. The bivariate specification of equation (2) allows for the testing of each hypothesis for each market pair in both directions, where the hypotheses are verified for the direction of causality originating from Y to X, i.e., X=f'(Y) and the reverse direction, Y=f''(X). Price leadership or unidirectional causality is indicated by a statistically significant test running from Y to X, but not the reverse. In this case, Y is the price leader and X is the follower (Granger 1969).

The Price Series Data

In comparison to structural models typically employed in studies of pricing behavior, the data requirement in estimating bivariate representation in equation (2) is minimal—price data are sufficient. For this reason (among others),[6] time-series modelling has practical appeal, especially in developing countries where the market information system is still relatively undeveloped.

For the study, copra prices at week ending (Friday), when volume of trading is the heaviest, were collected from the Weekly Bulletin published by UCAP. Weekly copra prices were obtained for five principal cities including Manila, Lucena City, Legaspi City, Davao City, and Cebu City, and thus, the bivariate estimation of equation (2) for each of these market pairs would involve 10 combinations.

These 5 major cities are classified by UCAP as consistent price leaders for each reporting week and therefore are expected to dominate the local price

---

[6] Time-series modelling is a parsimonious representation of structural models. As a reduced form representation of structural models which are formulated based on sound economic theory, the time-series model is not entirely devoid of theoretical concepts. Compared to structural models, there is less subjectivity exercised in time-series modelling because the usual zero-one type restrictions are not imposed (Ford 1986). Because economic theory is often ambiguous about the classification of variables which affect price expectations by market agents, whether they are demand- or supply-related variables, the time-series model allows "every variable in the system to affect every other variable" and the data to specify the dynamics of this relationship (Bessler 1984). Thus, there is less "guesswork" in time-series representations.

formation process for copra.[7] Because these are active trading centers, copra prices discovered in these urban centers are accurate and unbiased indicators of local variations in copra supply and demand conditions.

Weekly prices are appropriate for analyzing spatial price behavior because price movements tend to be more frequent and discernible than daily, monthly, and annual data. More complete and continuous series are more readily available for weekly prices. Of the 923 price observations for each of the five major cities included in the study, less than 4% have missing values. Where there are data gaps, missing observations were replaced by simple linear extrapolation.

The price quotations are reported in pesos per kilogram on *resecada* grade basis (copra with 8% or less moisture content). Using price quotations for comparable grades eliminates the problem of price variations that could arise from product heterogeneity, which in turn could affect the dynamics of price relationships.

The Sample Period Covered

The weekly copra price data covered an 18-year period from January 1, 1971, to September 30, 1988, a period over which there were significant shifts in domestic government policies and which eventually led to the creation of a concentrated coconut industry.

Prior to 1971, intervention policy was in the form of exchange rate control, and thereafter a more direct and intense regulation of the coconut industry was instituted until 1986. Aimed to generate more revenues from escalating copra prices resulting from general worldwide instability in the 1970s, several forms of levies were legislated. In June, 1971, for example, the creation of the Coconut Investment Fund, or Cocofund, provided for a levy of P 0.55 (centavos) on every kilogram of copra sold at the farm level. In 1973, copra farmers were charged a levy of P 0.15/kg under the Coconut Consumer Subsidy Fund (CCSF), in addition to the levy under the Cocofund. Although the CCSF was to be repealed after the world oil crisis, the levy became a permanent tax policy and was raised to P 0.20/kg in 1974. This policy resulted in declining farm prices for copra and in support to farm prices. The

---

[7] Copra prices are collected by UCAP for several major provincial ports of loading around the country. Over the years however, the number of sample provincial ports have changed from 18 ports in 1967 to 42 in 1978 and 35 in 1982, primarily because of the disappearance of active trading in copra in some ports. From the total number of ports, 10 trading centers are listed as price leaders for each week of reporting and depending on the volume of copra traded for that week, some ports could drop out of the list and be replaced by other ports. Of these market centers, Manila, Cebu City, Davao City, Legaspi City, and Lucena City are consistent price leaders.

Philippine Coconut Planters Trading, Inc. (PCPTI) was created in 1977, which on behalf of the government, bought copra directly from farmers at highly subsidized prices.

In 1977, the United Coconut Oil Mills (UNICOM) was established, by presidential decree, to revitalize the nation's failing oil milling and refining industry. With its unification under a single entity, UNICOM maintained an unchallenged monopoly control of the coconut oil industry. By 1979, it owned two-thirds of the country's total rated coconut oil milling capacity (Clarete and Roumasset 1983), with their ownership expanding to 93% in 1982 (Habito 1983). Exports of coconut products were also regulated by UNICOM and in 1982 accounted for about 80% of total foreign sales (Habito 1983).

Aside from promoting a more concentrated industry, these intervention policies were also accompanied by highly volatile domestic copra prices. The estimated coefficient of variation of the nominal weekly copra price quotation in the major buying centers ranged from about 18% to over 19% during the 1971-1972 period when government control was minimal (Table 1). Direct government regulation in the 1973-1985 period resulted in greater price instability as exhibited by the coefficients of variation soaring from about 59% (Manila) to nearly 75% (Lucena) over this period, and then slightly tapering from 39% to nearly 42% in 1986-1988 when control was lifted.

Confronted with mounting popular opposition, the government rescinded its monopoly control of the coconut industry in the 1980s. In 1980, the Cocofund and CCSF taxes were repealed. The UNICOM was abolished in 1985, and in 1986, the export restriction imposed in 1983 on copra was lifted.

Table 1. Price instability, measured by the coefficient of variation,[a] in the Philippine copra market over three policy regimes, 1971 to 1988.

Policy regime:	Spatial markets				
	Manila	Cebu	Davao	Legaspi	Lucena
			- (%) -		
1971-72	18.0	58.6	17.5	19.4	19.2
1973-85	58.9	71.2	72.9	74.3	74.7
1986-88	39.0	40.6	40.1	41.5	39.6
All periods	65.4	73.9	7 3.9	74.6	73.1

[a] Coefficient of variation is calculated as: $CV = \left[(\frac{\sigma}{\bar{X}}) * 100 \right]$ where σ is the standard deviation and $\bar{X}$ is the mean.

Empirical Results and Discussion

Table 2 shows that the bivariate autoregressive model is a valid representation of the spatial pricing system for Philippine copra. As indicated by the adjusted R^2s, the overall performance of the 10 estimated equations is reasonably good. Results of the Durbin-Watson statistic indicate no serial correlation, implying that the lag lengths specified by the AIC procedure for each copra market are adequate enough to capture all irregularities in the prices. Overall, these findings suggest that current changes in copra prices in each of the markets considered in the study could be explained by changes in its own past prices as well as current and historical price changes in the other markets.

As summarized in Table 3, three hypothesized pricing conducts were tested using the F test statistic. Independent pricing behavior hypothesized in the second column of Table 3 was rejected for all combinations of market pairs. Hence, there is no evidence to indicate that Filipino traders exercise price discrimination between urban centers, which contradicts the assertion made in many previous studies of market performance in the Philippines.

Results of the F test statistic presented in the third column indicate that there is no organized pricing or cartel agreement between traders in copra pricing, i.e., contemporaneous price adjustments between markets do not occur instantaneously. All F test statistics are highly significant at the 1% level.

Table 2. Validation of the bivariate autoregressive model representation of the spatial pricing conduct in the Philippine copra market, January 1, 1971, to September 30, 1988.

Exogenous Variable	Endogenous variable				
	Manila	Cebu	Davao	Legaspi	Lucena
(Adjusted R^2)[a]					
Manila	-	0.17	0.10	0.12	0.34
Cebu	0.58	-	0.81	0.73	0.63
Davao	0.59	0.57	-	0.87	0.60
Legaspi	0.51	0.46	0.85	-	0.53
Lucena	0.47	0.21	0.35	0.31	-
(Durbin-Watson statistic[b])					
Manila	-	2.01	2.01	1.99	2.01
Cebu	2.07	-	1.98	1.94	2.02
Davao	2.03	2.02	-	2.05	2.00
Legaspi	2.05	2.06	2.05	-	1.98
Lucena	2.06	2.01	2.07	2.01	-

[a] Adjusted coefficient of determination measures the "goodness of fit" or explanatory power of the model.
[b] DW equal or close to 2 indicates the absence of serial correlation.

Pricing conduct of spatially differentiated markets   353

Table 3. Tests of spatial pricing conduct in Philippine copra markets, January 1, 1971, to September 30, 1988.

Spatial market pairs $P_x \Rightarrow P_y$	Hypothesized pricing behavior		
	Independent pricing $\beta_j = 0$	Instantaneous and perfectly cooperative $\beta_0, \beta_j = \alpha_i = 0$	Perfect price matching with offsetting lags $\beta_0 \cdot \sum_{j=1}^{n} \beta_j + \sum_{i=1}^{n} \alpha_i = 0$
Cebu $\Rightarrow$ Manila	26.04*	430.81*	690.59*
Manila $\Rightarrow$ Cebu	56.07*	171.46*	123.31*
Davao $\Rightarrow$ Manila	13.32*	650.21*	1,061.47*
Manila $\Rightarrow$ Davao	75.01*	163.21*	67.48*
Legaspi $\Rightarrow$ Manila	5.60*	527.25*	1,478.52*
Manila $\Rightarrow$ Legaspi	83.16*	81.99*	54.27*
Lucena $\Rightarrow$ Manila	46.73*	474.91*	1,308.17*
Manila $\Rightarrow$ Lucena	101.03*	65.47*	0.84^{ns}
Davao $\Rightarrow$ Cebu	328.99*	573.31*	1,381.80*
Cebu $\Rightarrow$ Davao	23.56*	90.50*	33.48*
Legaspi $\Rightarrow$ Cebu	110.15*	425.81*	1,278.77*
Cebu $\Rightarrow$ Legaspi	30.05*	71.76*	44.01*
Lucena $\Rightarrow$ Cebu	57.82*	391.41*	1,350.51*
Cebu $\Rightarrow$ Lucena	19.95*	104.48*	230.37*
Legaspi $\Rightarrow$ Davao	60.24*	301.21*	182.88*
Davao $\Rightarrow$ Legaspi	155.36*	207.65*	23.96*
Lucena $\Rightarrow$ Davao	26.47*	117.27*	236.68*
Davao $\Rightarrow$ Lucena	31.57*	80.60*	102.14*
Lucena $\Rightarrow$ Legaspi	43.50*	105.57*	185.79*
Legaspi $\Rightarrow$ Lucena	25.22*	139.17*	100.09*

* Highly statistically significant, $|Prob| > |F_t| = 0.001$, where F_t is the critical F value.
ns Not statistically significant.

In general, no evidence of perfect price matching with some lags is found in most of the price series analyzed. As shown in the last column of Table 3, all F test statistics are highly significant, except for the market pair of Manila and Lucena. This finding for Manila and Lucena suggests a price leadership relationship exists between these markets, with price changes discovered first in Manila and then, after some time, in Lucena.

To further verify the results of the third hypothesis, the estimated coefficients of the bivariate autoregressive models are individually examined. In Table 4, the contemporaneous price effects and lagged price effects are separated for each market pair, including the amount of time it takes for the impact of past prices to dissipate. In all cases, results confirm the absence of perfect price matching between markets. The coefficient, β_0, which measures

Table 4. Contemporaneous and historical price effects on price response in Philippine copra markets, January 1, 1971, to September 30, 1988.

Spatial market pairs $P_x \Rightarrow P_y$	Contemporaneous price effect[a]	Lagged price effects Magnitude[b]	Lag length[c]
Cebu $\Rightarrow$ Manila	0.1521*	0.0971	1
Manila $\Rightarrow$ Cebu	0.3035*	0.6500	2
Davao $\Rightarrow$ Manila	0.1192*	0.3677	4
Manila $\Rightarrow$ Davao	0.3453*	1.1897	2
Legaspi $\Rightarrow$ Manila	0.1003*	0.2258	4
Manila $\Rightarrow$ Legaspi	0.3860*	1.5079	2
Lucena $\Rightarrow$ Manila	0.2353*	0.9410	7
Manila $\Rightarrow$ Lucena	0.9253*	1.1940	1
Davao $\Rightarrow$ Cebu	0.1174*	0.4839	1
Cebu $\Rightarrow$ Davao	0.4554*	0.0000	0
Legaspi $\Rightarrow$ Cebu	-0.0499ns	0.3523	1
Cebu $\Rightarrow$ Legaspi	0.4796*	1.1036	4
Legaspi $\Rightarrow$ Davao	0.7540*	1.1360	3
Davao $\Rightarrow$ Legaspi	1.0001*	2.0839	4
Lucena $\Rightarrow$ Davao	0.4330*	1.0610	6
Davao $\Rightarrow$ Lucena	0.5400*	1.6140	5
Lucena $\Rightarrow$ Legaspi	0.4300*	2.1300	6
Legaspi $\Rightarrow$ Lucena	0.4400*	1.6621	6

* Highly significant at 1%.
[a] Contemporaneous price effect of market j on market i, i not equal to j, is measured by β_0.
[b] The lagged price effects of market j on market i, i not equal to j, is $\sum_{l=1}^{m}\beta_l$ where n is the lag length.
[c] Lag lengths, n, of statistically significant and positive coefficients.

the contemporaneous price effects rarely equals unitary. However, it is noteworthy that the impact of Manila on Cebu, Davao, Legaspi, and Lucena tends to be nearly three times larger than the impacts of each of these markets on Manila, suggesting the dominant role of Manila in the discovery of local copra prices. That Cebu is the second most important commercial market seems to be supported by our finding that the contemporaneous price effects of Cebu on Davao, Legaspi, and Lucena exceed the impacts of these markets on Cebu.

Upon closely examining the magnitudes of the β_0, the impact of Manila seems to be larger for markets located close to it than those located farther away. For example, the β_0 coefficient between Manila and Lucena, the city closest to Manila, is 0.93, higher than the distant markets of Davao at 0.35, and Cebu at 0.30. Because of the proximity between Lucena and Legaspi, the finding of a nearly perfect price matching is not very surprising.

The central role of Manila in the price formation process for copra is also supported by the magnitude of the lagged effects it has on the other markets. In all cases, past price changes in Manila exerted a larger influence on contemporaneous price changes in Cebu, Davao, Legaspi, and Lucena, but the impacts of past price changes in these markets on Manila is not as pronounced. Although there are substantial time lags in price responses between markets, the transmission to other markets of new information about price changes in Manila takes a shorter time. On average, it takes about 1 to 2 weeks for prices in Manila to affect prices in Cebu, Davao, Legaspi, and Lucena.

The patterns of lagged price relationships and period of price adjustments among Cebu, Davao, Legaspi, and Lucena is much less discernible. There is no systematic distance-decay observed among these markets. This may be partly explained by the fact that Manila is the most important base market in copra pricing. Thus, while there is some delay and feedback, price changes in Manila will elicit a quicker price response in Cebu, Davao, Legaspi, and Lucena markets. As noted earlier, the reverse impact of price changes in these markets on Manila is moderate and is generally very sluggish. Restrictive government regulation of shipping routes outside Manila and fewer cargo vessels in operation may partly explain the differences in the periods of adjustments. Shipping schedules from Manila to the other major ports are more frequent than route schedules from the other ports to Manila, and thus shipments from the other islands may take some time to reach Manila.

Conclusion

This paper examines pricing behavior using a dynamic, time-series model. Compared to static structural market analysis, this model captures the dynamic price relationship in real market exchange and provides a direct and explicit testing of pricing conduct in an imperfect market. Because there are minimal data requirements and less subjectivity exercised in the model specification, the bivariate time-series model proposed here is practical for use by marketing researchers and can be easily replicated in other country cases.

Our findings suggest a limited, organized pricing for Philippine copra where Manila is the price leader, and the urban markets of Cebu, Davao, Legaspi, and Lucena are followers. Moreover, although these markets are interdependent, our data provide no support for the existence of collusive pricing behavior among traders in these cities. Overall, our results disclose that price responses are non-unitary, suggesting that price changes are not perfectly matched across markets, and that price adjustment to new information originating from another market is commonly delayed.

References

Akaike, H. 1974. A new look at the statistical model identification. *IEEE Transaction on Automatic Control* AC-19:716-723.

Bessler, D. 1984. An analysis of dynamic economic relationships: An application to the U.S. hog market. *Canadian Journal of Agricultural Economics* 32:109-124.

Boyd, M. and B.W. Brorsen. 1986. Dynamic price relationships for U.S. and EC corn gluten feed and related markets. *European Review of Agricultural Economics* 13:199-215.

Brorsen, B.W. 1983. *A study of the efficiency and dynamics of rice prices* . Ph.D. Diss., Texas A&M University, College Station, TX, USA.

Clarete, R. and J.A. Roumasset. 1983. *An analysis of the economic policies affecting the Philippine coconut industry* . Philippine Institute of Development Studies Working Paper, Manila, Philippines.

David, V. 1977. *The barriers in the development of the coconut industry* . MBA Thesis, Ateneo de Manila Graduate School of Business, Manila, Philippines.

Fama, E.F. 1976. *Foundations of finance portfolio decisions and securities prices*. New York, NY, USA: Basic Books, Inc.

Faminow, M. and B. Benson. 1990. Integration of spatial markets. American Journal of Agricultural Economics 72:49-62.

Ford, S. 1986. *A beginner's guide to vector autoregression*. Staff paper P86-28, Department of Agricultural and Applied Economics, University of Minnesota, Minneapolis, MN, USA.

Granger, C.W.J. 1969. Investigating causal relations by econometric models and cross spectral methods. *Econometrica* 37:423-438.

Habito, C. 1983. *Policy issues in the coconut industry: A survey* (unpublished manuscript).

Heytens, P.J. 1986. Testing market integration. *Food Research Institute Studies* 20: 25-41.

Mendoza, M.S. and P.L. Farris. 1992. The impact of changes in government policies on economic performance (the ARCH model). *Journal of Policy Modeling* 14(2):209-220.

National Economic Development Authority (NEDA). 1991. *Philippine statistical yearbook 1991*. Manila, Philippines.

Philippine Coconut Authority (PHILCOA). 1989. *Philippine coconut industry yearbook*. Diliman, Quezon City, Philippines.

Ravallion, M. 1986. Testing market integration. *American Journal of Agricultural Economics* 1:102-109.

Santos, O.F. 1987. The coconut industry: increased exports hike revenues. *Fookien Times* 1986-1987.

United Coconut Asssociation of the Philippines. 1990. *Semi-annual coconut statistics*. Quezon City, Philippines.

_____. *Weekly bulletin* (several issues).

Part 4

Analytical Methods

- **Models for Market Analysis**

16

A Financial Model for the Implementation and Evaluation of Small-Scale Agro-Enterprises

Carlos Ostertag and Christopher Wheatley[1]

Abstract

A computerized financial model of a cassava flour pilot plant in Colombia was developed that calculates the Financial Rate of Return (FRR) profitability parameter. Model components and basic assumptions are presented. The FRR computed, based on actual data, 28%, is slightly less than the opportunity cost of capital, 30%. The model is being used in project decision-making in price determination, establishment of strategies to increase the FRR above 30%, and selecting processing alternatives. Application of this model to other phases of product development and to other crops is discussed.

Key words: Product development, rate of return, cassava, cooperative.

Product Development and Cassava Flour

An important way in which market opportunities for many agricultural crops can be expanded is through the development of commercially viable new or improved products. If this can be achieved using small-scale processing to add value to crop products in or near the farm, valuable welfare benefits can be obtained. However, the difficulties involved in producing marketable products of acceptable quality in continuous supply, and of competitive price at a small scale and often under the management of people with limited education, has led to many failures. In addition, numerous research institutions working in the processing and food science area have concentrated on the technical aspects of product development, without giving due weight to market and economic

---

[1] Associate Scientist, Cassava Utilization Section, Centro Internacional de Agricultura Tropical (CIAT), A.A. 6713, Cali, Colombia and Processing Specialist, International Potato Center (CIP), Bogor, Indonesia (formerly Head, Cassava Utilization Section CIAT), respectively.

considerations. Hence, many novel products are created in the laboratory, with no commercial application.

Cassava is a major root crop in the tropics. In Andean Latin America, demand has been in historical decline as food habits have shifted from consumption of the fresh roots by rural populations to a diversified carbohydrate diet in urban environments. Research efforts in Latin America—by Centro Internacional de Agricultura Tropical (CIAT), national programs, and universities—have been focused on generating novel or improved processed products for food and feed markets to counteract this situation. The objective was to provide farmers with additional income from small-scale processing and the added value thereby obtained. Initial successes were obtained with a methodology developed by CIAT (see Perez-Crespo 1991). This approach had an institutional as well as technical component. The institutional effort focused on small-farmer, cooperative enterprise development. The technology involved producing sun-dried chips for use in national animal feed industries in Colombia, Ecuador, and, more recently, Northeast Brazil (Ospina and Wheatley 1992). These initiatives led to the introduction of a project to develop a commercial cassava flour industry, producing a high-quality product for the food industry on a small scale in farmer-managed and owned enterprises.[2] Experience with the animal feed and other projects suggested a methodology for product development consisting of four phases (Best et al. 1991; Wheatley et al. 1995).

- Opportunity identification
- Experimental research
- Pilot enterprise operation
- Commercial expansion or replication

The opportunity identification and experimental research phases were completed by 1988. A pilot project was initiated the following year with the construction of a pilot flour plant alongside an existing, cassava-drying plant operated by a small-farmer cooperative in Chinu, Cordoba Department, Colombia. This pilot operation involved the farmers in all activities associated with the commercial operation of a flour enterprise, including:

- raw material supply (continuity, quality, price),
- efficient operation of process,
- quality control,
- personnel management,
- sales and marketing, including product promotion, and

---

[2] This project was funded by the International Development Research–Canada (IDRC).

- accounting and financial management.

The pilot plant represented the first occasion in which the experimental process for producing cassava flour had been tested in a commercial environment. This test entailed continuous use of equipment, and less than ideal operating conditions and/or raw material quality, etc. As a result of the initial trial, considerable modifications were made to the process during the pilot operation. From a technical perspective, the pilot plant became, in effect, an applied research site.

On the financial side, it was soon found that the variable costs of flour production were too high. Hence, a means to reduce processing costs had to be found. A financial model—both for the process and the enterprise as a whole—was then developed in order to measure economic viability under different operating conditions. This model soon found many applications in project decision making as a research and management tool. For example, it enabled project personnel to not only monitor processing costs, but also quantify the effect that operational variables had on profitability and thereby determine which were most important. The model also helped enterprise managers fix maximum raw material purchase prices as well as minimum flour sales prices.

This paper presents details of the financial model used. It also gives examples from the cassava flour project of the applications of the model to project and enterprise decision making. Conclusions are drawn as to the usefulness of this model at other phases of the product development process.[3]

The Financial Model

A financial model of the cassava processing plant was developed using Lotus 1-2-3 (CIAT 1992). This program permits rapid updating of the model and instant calculation of several profitability parameters. It also allows prompt observation of the sensitivity of the profitability parameter to the variation of any given cost or quantity.

Selection of profitability parameters

Multiple profitability parameters exist, but one of the most common ones is the Internal Rate of Return (IRR), which has, among many versions, two of interest: the Economic Rate of Return (ERR) and the Financial Rate of Return (FRR) (Gittinger 1982). The definition of these profitability parameters is the following: that rate which discounts a series of annual cash flows in such a way

---

[3] Details of the project itself can be found elsewhere (CIAT 1988; Ostertag and Wheatley 1992; and Wheatley and Best 1991).

that its present value is equal to the initial investment. Figure 1 interprets the previous definition.

The difference between the ERR and the FRR lies in how the annual cash flows are derived. Table 1 contrasts these two parameters. For our case, we have selected the FRR as a profitability parameter because we are more interested in the entrepreneurial point of view.

The minimum FRR value was established as the opportunity cost of capital in Colombia, or nearly 30%. The opportunity cost of capital is the interest given up by the investor by having capital invested in a processing plant. The entrepreneur will be motivated to invest in a processing plant only if he can obtain an FRR above the rate of interest which he can receive in any bank, for example.

Figure 1. Interpretation of the definition for Internal Rate of Return.

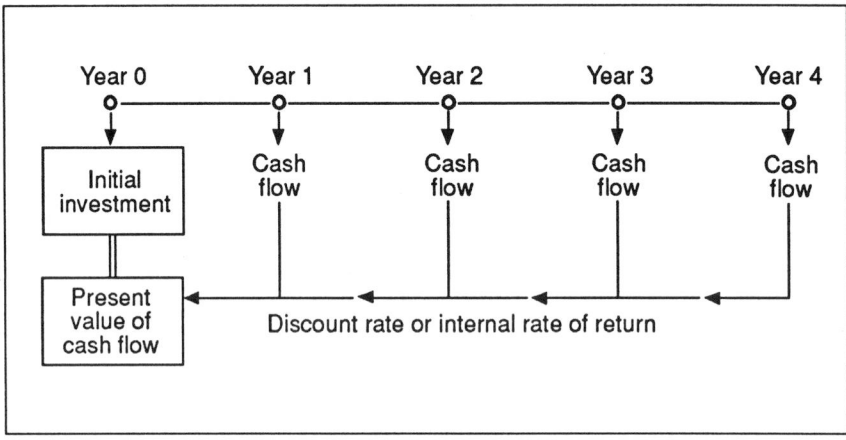

Table 1. Some differences between the Economic Rate of Return (ERR) and the Financial Rate of Return (FRR).

ERR	FRR
Assumes the point of view of society in general	Assumes the point of view of the enterprise
Market costs and prices are not always used	Always uses market costs and prices
Taxes are not considered to be a cost	Taxes are considered as a cost to the firm
Subsidies are regarded as a cost to society	Subsidies are regarded as an income for the firm
Does not take financial costs into account	Financial costs can be taken into account

Source: Gittinger 1982.

It must be noted that to estimate the ERR or FRR one does not take depreciation into account because it does not really represent a cash flow (Davidson et al. 1978). In the case of profitability estimates, depreciation is only considered when calculating the amount of taxes to be paid (Davidson et al. 1978); in the Colombian case, cooperatives are tax-exempt.

The different types of cassava processes can be compared from a profitability perspective by comparing their individual FRRs.

Preliminary Decisions for the Development of the Financial Model

Before developing the model, one must make decisions on the following five topics: project life, plant production capacity, capacity utilization, rate of inflation, and residual value of assets.

Project life. This refers to the economic life of the processing plants. There are no rules that impose a certain number of years for project evaluation. One can say, however, that as incomes and costs are more distant in time, their importance decreases. For example, $100 today has a greater value than $100 in two years. The longer the assumed project life, the greater the FRR and, as the project is more profitable, the project life will have less impact on the FRR. This model assumes a project life of eight years.

Production capacity. Rural cassava processing plants cannot normally operate continuously at certain times of the year due to climatic or root-supply limitations. In this case, one must assume a number of months per year and estimate a theoretical capacity for use in the model. In some cases, the plant operates above theoretical capacity due to optimum conditions. In this particular case, it is assumed that the plant processes roots for 10 months per year with a capacity of 180 tons per year.

Capacity utilization. Here one must choose either to use a constant rate of capacity utilization throughout the project life or to start at a low utilization rate and increase it gradually. In our model, we assume a constant capacity utilization of 80% from year 1 through year 8.

Inflation rate. The first decision one must make is whether inflation will be considered at all. If not, then the minimum FRR should be the opportunity cost of capital minus the annual inflation rate. If inflation is taken into account, then we must decide which rate to use and if it will be the same for income and costs. The model supposes an annual inflation rate of 25% for both.

Residual value of assets. At the end of project life, one must assume that the plant is sold. This model supposes that the sales price is equivalent to 40% of its value in year 0, including the increase in land valuation.

Model components

It is convenient to describe the cassava flour process briefly before presenting the different component of the model. Freshly harvested roots with a moisture content of approximately 65% are transported to the plant in 50-60 kg sisal sacks in the morning, are promptly weighed, and are then selected (small, diseased, and deteriorated roots are rejected) and prepared (the woody stem is removed). Afterwards, the roots are washed with chlorinated water in a cylindrical drum to remove dirt and most of the outer bark. The washed roots are fed directly into a chipping machine, and the chips are deposited in a metal container which is used to carry the chips to the fixed-bed drying chamber. There the chips are placed on a perforated metal-sheet floor and are dried by hot air forced up from below by a fan. The air is heated by a coke-fired burner. Chips are dried at a loading rate of 100-150 kgs/m^2 at a temperature of 60°C taking from 10 to 14 hours to reach the targeted moisture content of 10%. The dry chips are then processed into flour and bran in the in-plant milling system consisting of a simple roller mill and two cylindrical screens. The final product, cassava flour, is packaged in 50-kg polypropylene bags and stored in the warehouse until distribution and sale (CIAT 1988; Ostertag and Viera 1992).

The main elements of the model are described below.

Investment. This item refers to all of the buildings, equipment, and studies necessary for cassava processing. Investments include land, plant design, engineering studies, buildings, roads, transformer, machines and equipment, plant installation, and contingencies.

Working capital. Working capital is part of the initial investment, but is considered a separate element in the model because it involves cash to operate the plant as opposed to funds spent to design, and then build and equip it. Since inflation has been included in this model, the model contains additions to working capital to maintain purchasing power. For this reason, we chose to subtract the initial working capital and subsequent additions from income. The working capital required is a function of production costs, production volume, and credit terms. It must be returned at the end of the project life.

Maintenance costs. This is the annual sum necessary to keep buildings and equipment in good working condition. This amount is divided by the number of tons produced per annum and is considered a fixed cost.

Basic information. The basic assumptions are detailed here, including plant capacity and utilization, fresh-root-to-whole-flour conversion factor, and per ton consumption parameters of the following: man hours, polypropylene bags, kw-hours, fuel, water, etc. Along with unit prices, this data is the basis for estimating variable costs per ton.

Variable costs per ton. Variable costs are those process costs which vary directly with production volume. These costs include raw material, labor, packaging, electricity, fuel, water, etc. Transportation costs and commissions can also be included here.

Fixed costs per ton. Fixed costs are those costs which do not vary with the production volume. The salaries of managers, foremen, or watchmen, as well as miscellaneous expenses, are all fixed costs.

Sales price and margins. The sales price used in this case is a weighted average of the prices of first-grade flour and bran. The weights used are based on extraction rates (%). Losses during the milling process are also considered. This allows the calculation of several margins, such as gross margin (sales price minus variable costs) and net margin (sales price minus variable costs and fixed costs).

Outputs from the model

Annual cash flow matrix and FRR. In year 0 the initial investment is made and, therefore, the cash flow for that year is negative. Starting in year 1, the annual income generated by the sales of the cassava-based product is estimated. Variable costs, fixed costs, and initial working capital and annual additions are subtracted from this amount. The result is a series of nine cash flows, from year 0 to year 8. This series is processed to obtain the FRR.

Net present value. This model includes another profitability parameter called net present value (NPV). It consists of the discount of the series of cash flows using the opportunity cost of capital as the discount rate. The minimum acceptable NPV is 0 (Van Horne 1980).

Use of the Model

The model is not only useful for profitability estimation, but also for sensitivity and cost structure analysis. The objective of sensitivity analysis is to determine which variables (for example, cost of raw material) have a greater impact on the FRR. Also, one can establish the maximum and minimum values of those variables that will enable the FRR to be greater or equal to the opportunity cost of capital. This permits, for example, the institution of purchasing policies for raw materials and the establishment of purchasing price ceilings.

The model also allows the analysis of price composition per ton; in other words, to estimate the relative importance of the different input costs, and profit margins. Price composition can also be compared across processes.

Results

At the start of the pilot phase, the model was constructed using assumptions for most of the data required. Since the plant was not yet in operation, most of the operating variables were based on experiences with the experimental plant at CIAT. Raw material costs and flour and bran sales prices were similarly estimated as no production had yet taken place on site. Only some of the unit costs (e.g., electricity and coal prices) used real data. As the pilot project progressed, assumptions were systematically replaced with real data obtained from the operation of the processing plant and the enterprise. However, at the time this paper was written, one important assumption still remained: capacity utilization. It is set at 80%.

Data and/or parameters fed to the model must be updated regularly because of inflation and according to the latest findings and experiences of the pilot plant. The results presented below correspond to December 1992.

Table 2 shows the process parameters used in the model. These figures also appear in Appendix 1, the financial profitability analysis model.

Profitability. The model indicates that if the pilot plant operates at 80% capacity, the FRR will be 28%. The opportunity cost of capital in Colombia is 30% and, hence, some improvements are required to make investing in this business attractive.

The required investment in buildings and equipment is US$63,174. The average sales price is Col$201 per ton (Col$700 = US$1), the variable costs amount to Col$160/t, and the fixed costs add up to Col$15/t, and therefore the net margin is Col$41/t.

Sensitivity of the FRR. Figures 2 to 7 present a sensitivity analysis of the FRR to several parameters such as initial investment, capacity utilization, cost of cassava roots, root-to-dry-chip conversion factor, first-grade flour extraction rate, and sales price of first-grade cassava flour. The FRR is quite sensitive to all of the latter variables but is especially responsive to the sales price of first-grade flour and cost of fresh roots.

Cost structure. The model is also helpful in identifying price composition and the relative importance of the different costs (See Figure 8). As already mentioned, the price used is a weighted average of both the first-grade flour and the bran. This information also appears in page 2 of Appendix 1.

The most salient characteristics of the price structure are the importance of the raw material cost, the high costs of coke (the fuel used for drying), and the relatively minor weight of fixed costs.

Table 2. Parameters of the cassava flour production process used in the model.

Plant capacity	180 t
Capacity utilization rate	80%
Root-to-dry chip-conversion factor	2,8:1
Man hours per ton of whole flour	70
Bags per ton of flour	40
Kilowatt hour per ton of whole flour	150
Coke (kg) per ton of chips	550
Water (m^3) per ton of chips	7
First grade flour extraction rate	85%
Bran extraction rate	14%
Milling losses	1%

Figure 2. Sensitivity of Financial Rate of Return (FRR) to amount of initial investment.

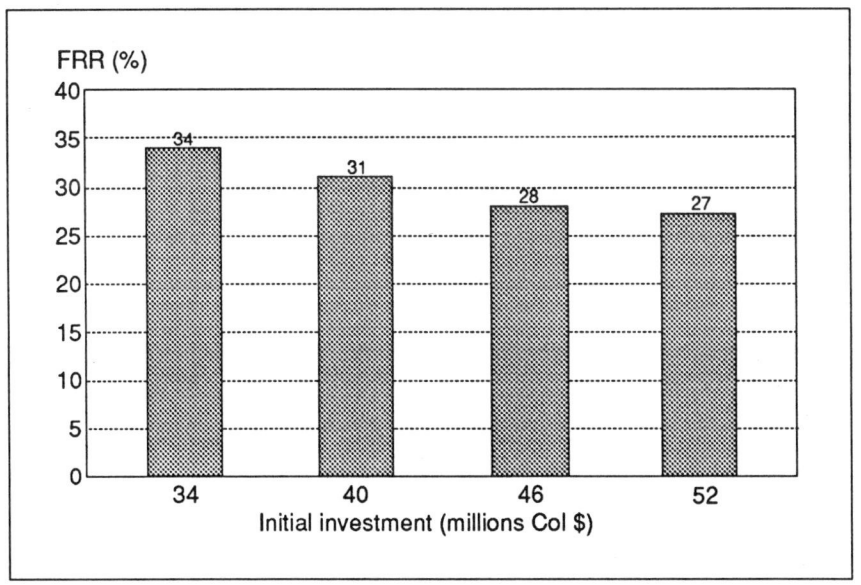

Figure 3. Sensitivity of FRR to capacity utilization.

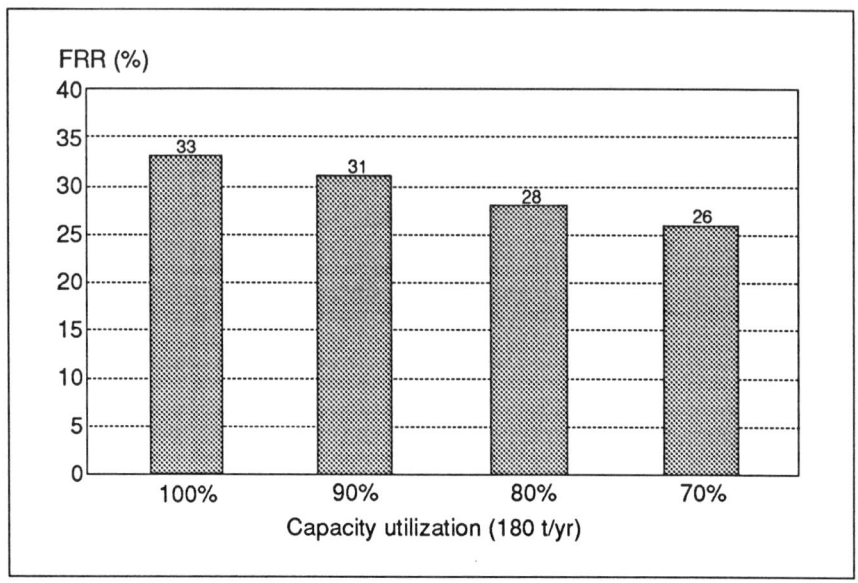

Figure 4. Sensitivity of FRR to price of cassava roots.

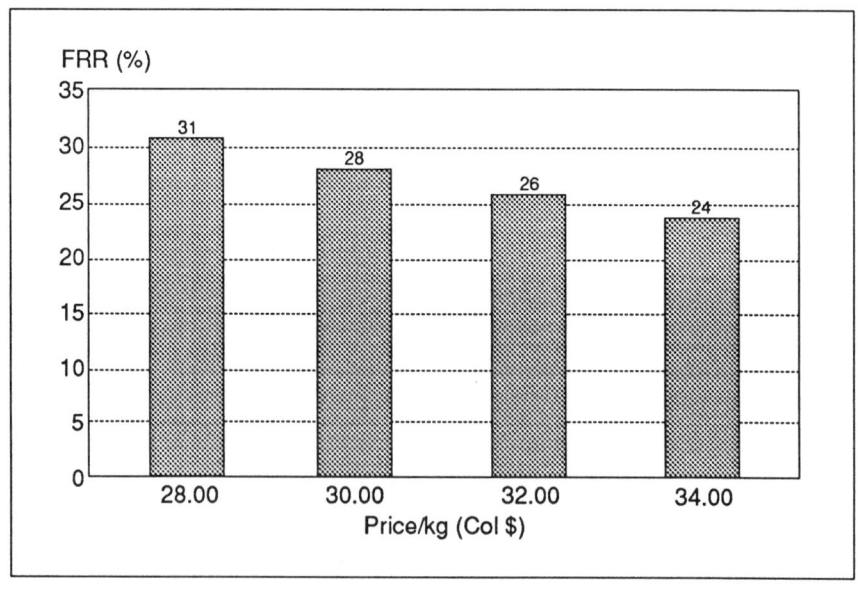

Figure 5. Sensitivity of FRR to the root-to-dry-chip conversion factor.

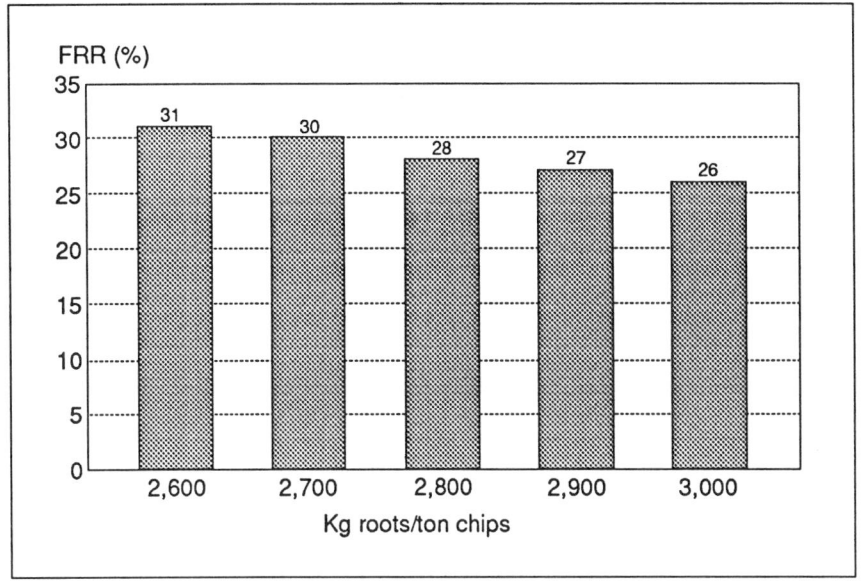

Figure 6. Sensitivity of FRR to first-grade flour extraction rate.

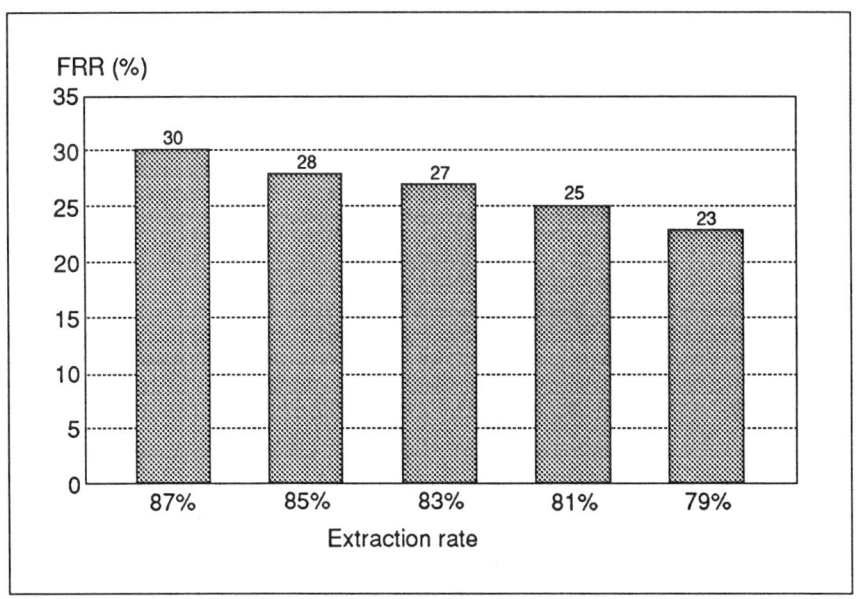

Figure 7. Sensitivity of FRR to sales price of first-grade flour.

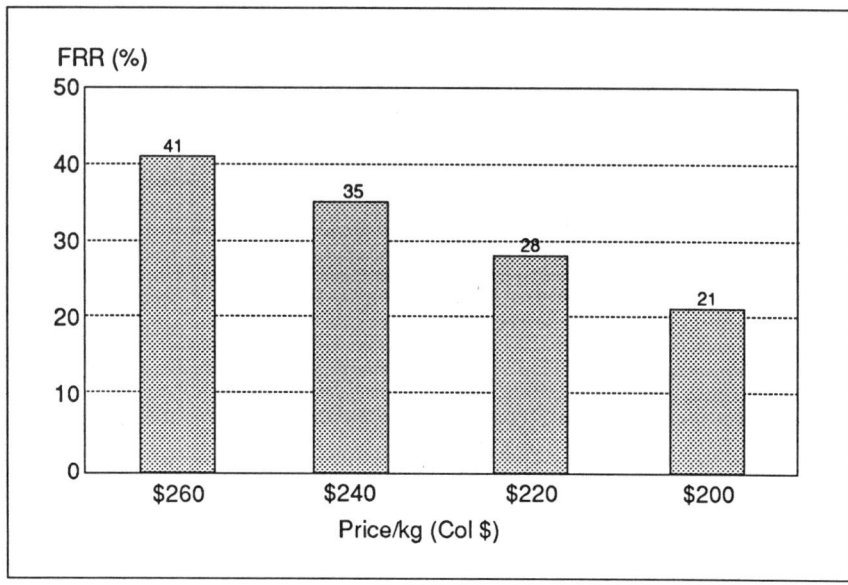

Figure 8. Price structure of cassava flour; weighted average price: $201,000.

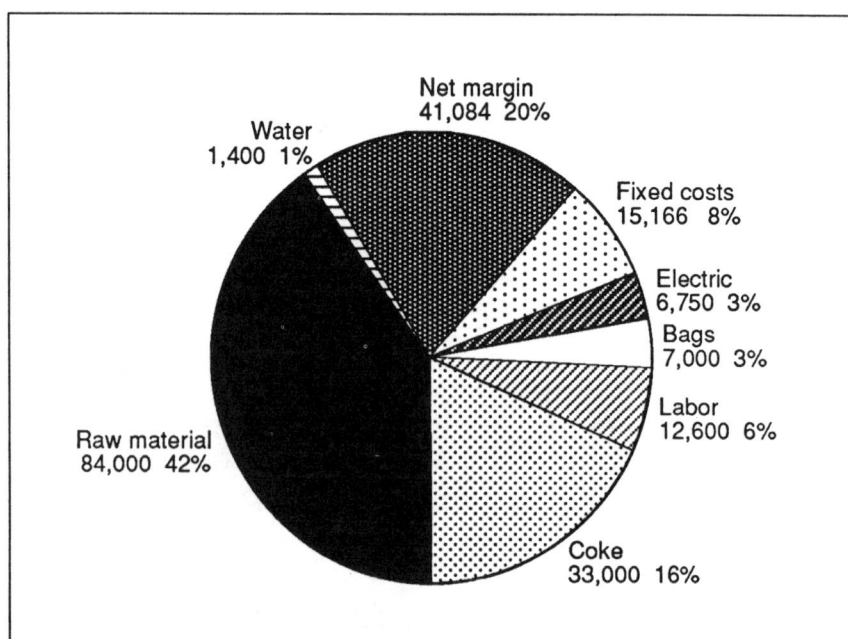

The Model and Decision-Making

This model can be used to support decision-making when the financial perspective is important. Some examples are given below.

Design of an appropriate credit arrangement for processing plants. With a few modifications, the model can be converted into a tool for analyzing liquidity. This simply requires subtracting the cost of capital amortization and interest payments from income when calculating annual cash flows. Liquidity analysis is especially appropriate when a plant is financed with borrowed money that must be repaid, along with interest. In this case, it is useful for identifying years with negative cash flows, thus aiding the design of a realistic financing system for processing plants. This type of system encompasses such aspects as the proper amount to be lent, interest to be charged, and grace period required.

Information to banks, donors, project personnel, cooperatives, and private entrepreneurs. It is evident that all of these actors in the development process require information on financial parameters, some to judge the convenience of lending money or of investing, and others to evaluate their ability to pay their debts.

Price determination. The development of this financial model not only gives us a clear idea of cost composition—which alone is an insufficient basis for making price decisions—but also allows us to visualize the relationship between price level and profitability. This information, combined with data on prices of competitive products, is a good foundation for making pricing decisions.

Identification of strategies to improve profitability. In the Results section, it was mentioned that the current profitability of the pilot plant, assuming a capacity utilization rate of 80%, was 28%. Since this parameter is slightly below the opportunity cost of capital, there is a profitability problem. However, if we analyze the efficiency of the various process operations and complement it with the application of the model for (a) simulating the impact on the FRR of several processing and marketing alternatives, and for (b) conducting sensitivity analyses, including factors such as initial investment and capacity expansion, a viable strategy can be proposed for raising the FRR to acceptable levels.

Point (a) can be better illustrated with the following examples. The model easily demonstrated that it was more profitable to sell cassava flour than cassava chips. The profitability of three different chip-milling systems was then compared. The most profitable milling option was in-plant, small-scale roller milling. This was followed by subcontracting of milling in a commercial wheat mill. In-plant milling with a hammer mill was shown to be the least

Figure 9. Financial Rate of Return (FRR) maximization strategy for the pilot cassava flour plant.

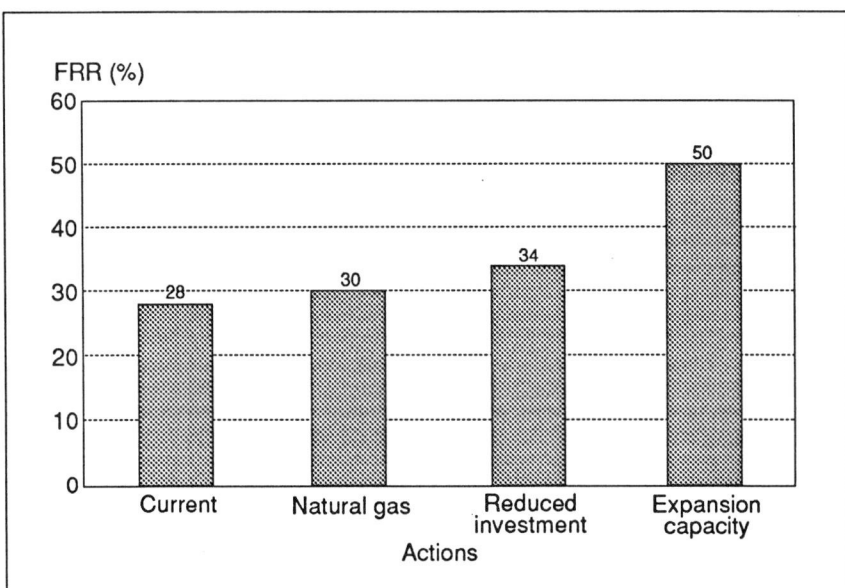

profitable. This latter analysis led the project to initiate the development of a small-scale roller mill for in-plant production of flour.

The current project strategy to maximize the FRR includes the following components.

- Increase capacity utilization to the 80% level assumed in the model. This will require promotional activities to achieve market penetration.
- Improve drying efficiency through use of alternative fuels (natural gas). This option will also reduce labor costs.
- Make a 25% reduction in the cost of future plant buildings. This can be achieved by means of a more inexpensive design built with different, cost-efficient materials. Another option is to eliminate the milling operation in plants and instead execute it at a central site. This could generate a 50% saving in plant building costs.
- Expand capacity of the pilot plant. Once capacity utilization of the pilot plant reaches 80%, a small additional investment will double capacity.

Figure 9 shows the cumulative effect of the last three components on the FRR. As can be seen, the effect of capacity expansion on FRR is very pronounced.

Conclusions

This model was originally developed to determine the financial viability of a cassava flour production and marketing enterprise. As the project progressed, it was increasingly used as a research tool to assist in determining where efforts should concentrate in order, for example, to produce the greatest reduction in variable costs. It also helped to determine the operational specifications developed for the different items of equipment used (washer, chipper, drier, etc.). From the managerial perspective, the model proved useful in setting the quality and price specifications for fresh cassava raw material (dry matter content as reflected in fresh-root-to-dry-chip conversion ratios).

Based on this experience, the authors consider that this type of model can be useful at other phases of product development as well, including the following.

Experimental research phase. Scientists often have to select between different process options, which may have different investment operational costs involved, and perhaps produce products with different qualities suitable for different markets at different prices. Using a model approach with assumed data for each process/product option, the most profitable alternative can be selected as the focus for further research. It should be borne in mind also that many small farmers and enterprises are risk adverse, and that they may be more interested in products/processes involving low capital investment and producing less than optimal profits, if the alternative is higher capital investment with higher profitability. However, when using the model, decisions on this basis can be made with the participation of potential users of the technology. Finally, the research phase terminates with a pre-feasibility study which justifies (or not) the continuation of the project at the pilot phase. The outputs of the financial model will be essential for this pre-feasibility study, especially if there is a choice to be made between process and/or product options. The model at this stage can also be used to help design the pilot operation, by comparing (for example) different scales of operation of a pilot plant, determining the minimum number of months/years in which the plant must be operational, levels of capacity utilization, etc.

Pilot enterprise phase. As seen in this paper, the model can become an essential tool for researchers carrying out adaptive research to improve pilot commercial operations. It can also serve managers of the enterprise. They need information to determine maximum and minimum acceptable raw material and product prices/costs as well as to monitor the operation of the process. At the conclusion of the pilot phase a feasibility study is completed, which will be used to justify (or not) the expansion or replication of the pilot enterprise. The outputs of this model form an important component of this feasibility study.

Commercial expansion and replication phase. At this stage, the pilot enterprise will have been evaluated as successful. The model can be used to help plan the expansion stage, by providing inputs to such questions as:

- Is it better to expand the pilot plant or build new, small-scale plants in other areas?
- How will transport and other marketing costs affect ability to sell products in more distant markets (determine size of market)?
- What is the maximum rate of interest we can pay on any loan for capital investment?
- What other new products/markets can be explored?

As the new enterprises become self-managing, they will need to become familiar with the use of the model. It will also be useful for monitoring and evaluation of the project during this phase.

This paper has presented the use of a financial model in one project in Colombia involving the pilot production of cassava flour for the food industry by a small-farmer cooperative enterprise. This model will be relevant to similar projects involving cassava, other root and tuber crops, and indeed almost any product development activity undertaken in developing countries with agricultural raw materials and a small-farmer/user focus. Further details of the product development methodology, in which this model was used, can be found in Wheatley et al. 1994.

Acknowledgments

The authors would like to thank the members of the COOPROALGA, the small-farmer cooperative of Chinú, Cordoba, and Ing. Miguel A. Viera, project advisor to the cooperative, for their cooperation in generating the data presented in this model.

References

Best, R., C.C. Wheatley, and G. Chuzel. 1991. A product development approach to cassava utilization. *Journal of Root Crops* 17:237-248.

Centro Internacional de Agricultura Tropical (CIAT). 1988. *Final report of the project production and use of cassava flour for human consumption*. Centro Internacional de Agricultura Tropical (CIAT), Cali, Colombia.

Centro Internacional de Agricultura Tropical (CIAT). 1992. *Cassava Program: Annual Report 1992*. CIAT, Cali, Colombia.

Davidson, S., J. S. Schindler, C. P. Stickney, and R. Weil. 1978. *Managerial accounting*. Hinsdale, Il, USA: The Dryden Press.

Gittinger, J. P. 1982. *Economic analysis of agricultural projects*. 2nd Edition. Baltimore, ML, USA: The Johns Hopkins University Press.

Ospina, B. and C.C. Wheatley. 1992. Processing of cassava tuber meal and chips. In *Roots, tubers, plantains and bananas in animal feeding* (D. Machin and S. Nyvold, eds.). Proceedings of the FAO expert consultation held Jan 21-25 1991 at CIAT, Cali, Colombia. FAO, Rome, Italy.

Ostertag, C. and M.A. Viera. 1992. *Establecimiento de la planta piloto*. In *Informe final de la fase de proyecto piloto: Proyecto de producción y comercialización de harina de yuca para consumo humano* (C. Ostertag and C. Wheatley, eds.). CIAT, Cali, Colombia.

Ostertag, C. 1992. *Aspectos de mercadeo*. In *informe final de la fase de proyecto piloto: proyecto de producción y comercialización de harina de yuca para consumo humano* (C. Ostertag and C. Wheatley, eds.). CIAT, Cali, Colombia.

Ostertag, C. and C. Wheatley (eds.). 1992. *Informe final de la fase de proyecto piloto: proyecto de producción y comercialización de harina de yuca para consumo humano*. CIAT, Cali, Colombia.

Pérez-Crespo, C. A. 1991. *Integrated cassava projects: a methodology for rural development. in integrated cassava projects* (C.A. Perez-Crespo, ed.). CIAT, Cali, Colombia.

Van Horne, J. C. 1980. *Financial management and policy*. Fifth Edition. Englewood Cliffs, NJ, USA: Prentice-Hall, Inc.

Wheatley, C. and R.A. Best. 1991. How can traditional forms of nutrition be maintained in urban centers: The case of cassava. *Entwicklung + Landlicher Raum*. 1/91:13-16

Wheatley, C.C., G.J. Scott, S. Wiersma, and R.A. Best. 1994. *Adding value to root and tuber crops: A manual for product development*. CIAT, Cali, Colombia.

Appendix 1

Model of Financial Profitability Analysis

Cassava Flour Project in the Atlantic Coast of Colombia; final products: cassava flour and bran; date: Dec. 1992 (exchange rate: Col$730 = US$1.00).

A. Estimated investment * maintenance cost (Col$, Dec 1992).

Construction (based on the assumption that the land is donated by the farmer coop)	Cost	Maintenance coefficient	Cost of maintenance
Soil Survey	133,000		
Surveying	133,000		
Construction	25,000,000	0.005	125,000
Transport of equipment	1,000,000		
Equipment installation	500,000		
Supervision	800,000		
Admin. & contingencies	3,750,000		
Subtotal	31,316,000		
Equipment and supplies			
Scale (500 kg)	180,000	0.010	1,800
Root seletion table	300,000	0.005	1,500
Water pump	180,000	0.020	3,600
Washing machine	1,000,000	0.020	20,000
Chipping machine	420,000	0.100	42,000
Hopper	55,000	0.050	2,750
Motor for chipping machine	200,000	0.020	4,000
Motor starter	145,000	0.020	2,900
Fan	700,000	0.010	7,000
Fan motor	430,000	0.020	8,600
Motor starter	140,000	0.020	2,800
Coal burners (2) w/duct	1,500,000	0.050	75,000
Drying chamber	680,000	0.050	34,000
Drying chamber covers	120,000		
Metal shovels (6)	23,000	0.200	4,600
Wooden rammers (6)	100,000	0.005	500
Carts (2)	200,000	0.005	1,000
Funnels (2)	120,000	0.005	600
Transformer 50 kva	3,000,000	0.010	30,000
Sisal bags (4)	18,000	1.000	18,000
Premilling machine	750,000	0.050	37,500
Motor for premilling machine	100,000	0.050	5,000
Motor starter	45,000	0.050	2,250
Small-scale milling system	2,800,000	0.050	140,000
Bag-closing machine	350,000	0.050	17,500
Furniture	350,000	0.020	7,000
Supplies	200,000		
Contingencies (5%)	695,300		
Subtotal	14,801,300		
Total (Col$)	46,117,300	Total	587,900
US$	63,174		

B. Basic capacity and cost information (COL$ 1992).

Annual plant capacity (t) (assumes that plant operates during 10 months)		180
Annual plant production (t)		144
Capacity utilization rate		80%

Item	Unit	Unit cost	Number of units/t of whole flour
Fresh roots in plant	kg	30	2,800[a]
Labor	man hour	180	70
Poly bags	bag	175	40
Electricity	kilowatt hour	45	150
Coke	kg	60	550
Water	M^3	200	7

[a] Assumes that selected and prepared cassava is used and that reject is purchased at market prices by chip plant.

	Variable costs/t of whole flour	Cost weight (%)
Raw material (roots)	84,000	52.53
Coke	33,000	20.64
Labor (4 workers)	12,600	7.88
Electricity	6,750	4.22
Poly bags	7,000	4.38
Water	1,400	0.88
Total variable costs	144,750	90.52
	Fixed costs/t of whole flour	
Manager (80,000/month)[a]	2,778	1.74
Foreman (50,000/month)	3,472	2.17
Watchman (46,000/month)	3,833	2.40
Plant maintenance	4,083	2.55
Other expenses (200,000)	1,000	0.63
Total	15,166	9.48
Total production cost/t whole flour	159,916	100.00

[a] This amount is shared by chip and flour plants.

C. Sales price and margins.

				Price/t (Col$)	Extraction rate (%)
Price/t placed at Chinú[a]	201,000	First grade flour		220,000	85.00
Net margin (%)	0.20	Bran		100,000	14.00
Net margin/t ($)	41,084	Loss			1.00
Gross margin (%)	0.28				
Gross margin/t ($)	56,250				

[a] Weighted average of first grade and bran sales prices.

D. Cash flow matrix.

	1992	1993	1994	1995	1996	1997	1998	1999	2000
Inflation rate		0.250	0.250	0.250	0.250	0.250	0.250	0.250	0.250
Initial investment	46,117,300								
Working capital[a]		2,302,790	575,698	719,622	899,527	1,124,409	1,405,511	1,756,889	2,196,112
Income:									
Sales		28,944,000	36,180,000	45,225,000	56,531,250	70,664,063	88,330,078	110,412,598	138,015,747
Salvage value[b]									109,952,211
Working capital									10,980,558
Less:									
Variable cost		20,844,000	26,055,000	32,563,750	40,710,938	50,888,672	63,610,840	79,513,550	99,291,937
Fixed cost		2,183,900	2,729,875	3,412,344	4,265,430	5,331,787	6,664,734	8,330,917	10,413,647
Total production cost		23,027,900	28,784,875	35,981,094	44,976,367	56,220,459	70,275,574	87,844,467	109,805,584
Net cash flow	-46,117,300	3,613,310	6,819,428	8,524,284	10,655,355	13,319,194	16,648,993	20,811,241	146,946,821

[a] Working capital is increased annually according to inflation rate to maintain purchasing power.
[b] Assumed to be 40% of initial investment; includes land valuation.

E. Calculation of profitability parameters.

Financial Rate of Return (FRR)	28%
Minimum acceptable FRR or opportunity cost of capital[a]	30%
Net present value using a 30% discount rate	-2,557,461

[a] Actually, the current opportunity cost of capital is lower than the inflation rate, but the 30% floor used is more realistic because the investor will want to beat the inflation rate by at least 3 percentage points.

17

Markets, Transaction Costs, and Selectivity Models in Economic Development

Stephan J. Goetz[1]

Abstract

Markets fail in their role of allocating scarce resources to alternative ends when transaction costs become so high as to preclude exchange. An important step toward improving the functioning of markets in this case is to understand the nature and effects of transaction costs facing input suppliers, farmers, food retailers, and/or consumers. This paper presents statistical methods for analyzing constraints to market participation faced by buyers and sellers. The decision to participate in the market is separated from the decision of how much to buy or sell, conditional on participation.

Key words: Statistical methods, conditional market participation, censored variables, Tobit, Probit.

Introduction

When the cost of executing an otherwise advantageous exchange between two parties exceeds the net benefit realized, the exchange fails to take place. The market in this case is unable to coordinate the supply of and demand for the good or service in question, that is, to allocate scarce resources to conflicting ends. The gains that could have been realized from trading are lost forever to the economy. "Economic development" can be defined as enabling mutually beneficial exchange to take place between two or more parties where there previously was none, by reducing transaction costs.

Market failure can be complete for a certain commodity in a particular region or country. For example, New Zealand kiwi fruits are not sold in rural

---

[1] Associate Professor, Department of Agricultural Economics, 317 Agricultural Engineering Building, University of Kentucky, Lexington, KY 40546-0276, USA.

Senegal, West Africa, because the cost of shipping the fruit is prohibitive relative to effective local demand. In other cases, market failure is only partial in the sense that some economic agents (households, producers, or consumers) are able to participate in an exchange while others are not. For example, some farmers in Senegal may consume fish while others do not. In the latter case, which is examined in this paper, market failure is specific to individuals or households rather than the community as a whole.

The purpose of this paper is to present statistical methods for analyzing and modelling the effects of transaction costs on economic activity. Transaction costs are broadly defined to include ex ante costs of determining whether an exchange is advantageous, costs of actually carrying out the exchange (such as finding buyers or sellers and transportation costs) and—where applicable—ex post costs of ensuring that all provisions of the exchange were met. By better understanding these costs and identifying ways of reducing their impact, policy prescriptions can be derived which directly contribute to economic development by making the benefits of trade available to a broader set of individuals. The potential applicability of the methods presented is very large. They may be relevant for market exchange between participants at all levels of the food system, starting with input suppliers, farmers, and traders and ending with consumers. The results of the analysis can thus be used to design policies that can improve coordination in the food system be removing bottlenecks and more subtle barriers to trading. All of the statistical models presented can be estimated using commercially available software, as discussed below.

The paper begins by discussing censored variables. This is followed by a review of the Tobit estimation method along with an extension of that method. Unlike the ordinary least squares method, the Tobit method yields unbiased coefficient estimates for regressions in which the dependent variable is censored. A selectivity model is subsequently discussed. This method improves on the Tobit model in cases where the decision of an individual to carry out an activity (such as buying fertilizer) is influenced by non-random and unobservable factors such as the willingness to bear risk. Additional information can be elicited from the data to distinguish between those variables which influence the probability of an individual using fertilizer and those which affect the quantity of fertilizer used once the individual has decided to use fertilizer. If the decision to use fertilizer is affected by a different set of variables than is the decision about the quantity of fertilizer used, then different policy prescriptions will have to be made depending on whether the goal is to increase fertilizer use among existing fertilizer users or to increase the proportion of farmers using fertilizer. For example, high transaction costs involved in obtaining fertilizer may be preventing some farmers from using fertilizer. Removing or reducing these costs may be more cost effective than changing relative input/output prices in stimulating fertilizer use.

Censored Variables

Applied researchers often encounter data samples in which only a certain percentage of survey respondents participate in a particular activity, while others do not. One plausible explanation for this behavior is that non-participants face higher transaction costs, all other things being equal, so that they do not realize a net benefit by participating. In other words, they face a threshold which can only be surmounted at a cost that exceeds the net benefit realized by trading or participating in the activity. Examples include hiring non-family laborers; growing a certain crop such as tobacco or tea; using fertilizer or other improved inputs such as irrigation; participating in government-sponsored production or marketing programs; selling a certain food such as rice; or consuming a certain food such as fish.

An important distinction is that between *censored* as opposed to *truncated* samples. Judge et al. (1985: 779) provide the example of a shooting range, where shots are fired at a circular target with a given radius, r (Figure 1). Suppose that whenever the target is hit an observer records the distance of the shot from the center of the target, while r is recorded every time the target is missed. No information is recorded on how far off from the target the shot lies. Then the data are censored in the sense that they lie in the range [0,r]. We also know the number of shots that missed the target. The difference in a truncated sample is that the number of times the target is missed is not recorded. Two questions of economic interest are, first of all, what determines whether or not the target was hit—and was that a random or a systematic process—and second, what determines the proximity to the center of the target.

Suppose a researcher finds that only 47.5% of the farmers in a random (censored) sample use fertilizer. Then the variable $FERTLIZR_i$, kilograms of fertilizer used by farmer i, is *censored* in the sense that some farmers are "censored" to use 0 kgs of fertilizer (in the analogy of the target, these people miss the target altogether, but we do not know how "close" they may have come to hitting it, i.e., to using fertilizer). In this situation there is more information in the data than is obvious on the surface. First of all, looking at all N farmers in the sample, we can separate the fertilizer users from the non-users. Empirically, this means the zero or limit observations are separated from the non-zero (continuous) or non-limit observations. Second, among the users (non-limit observations) there will be differences in the amount of fertilizer used.

Farmers in fact face a two-step decision process. The first decision is whether or not to use fertilizer. The second is how much fertilizer to use, conditional on having decided to use fertilizer in the first place. There is no reason to expect that the variables affecting the decision of whether or not to use fertilizer are the same as those affecting the amount of fertilizer used. Also, a given variable may *increase the probability* of fertilizer use, but *reduce the*

Figure 1. Censored versus truncated samples (shooting range example).

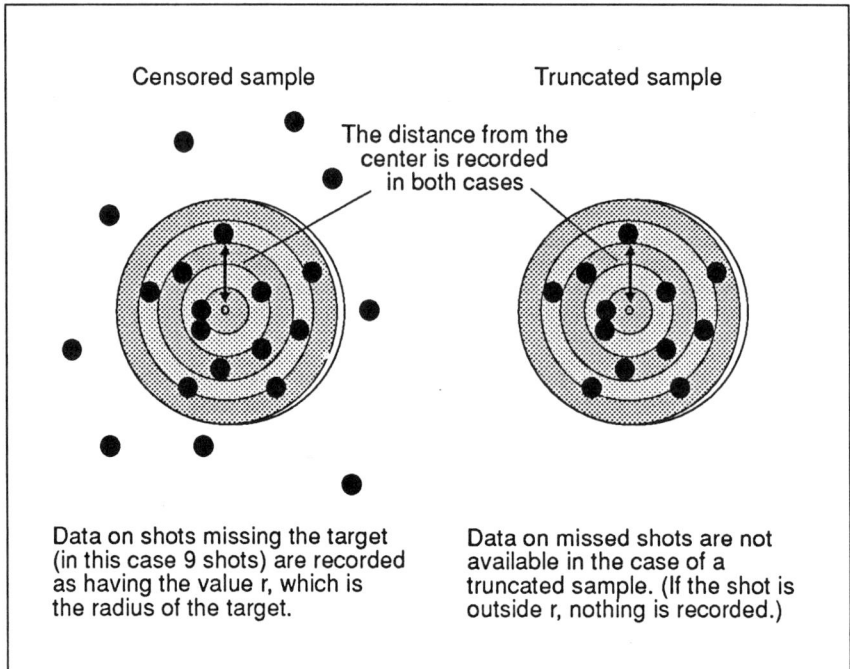

amount used once it has been decided to use fertilizer, and vice versa. Thus, a variable can have opposite effects on the level and the probability with which a given activity is carried out. Alternatively, a variable may affect only the probability, or the level, but not both.

Suppose one were interested in estimating an equation that relates fertilizer use to various explanatory variables such as the price of fertilizer facing the i-th farmer or farm household ($PFERT_i$); the price of an output such as corn ($PCORN_i$); and farm household characteristics ($HHCHAR_i$), with error term u_i:

(1a) $FERTLIZR_i = b_o + b_1 PFERT_i + b_2 PCORN_i + b_3 HHCHAR_i + u_i.$

Here $FERTLIZR_i$ is defined as actual expenditures on fertilizer by the i-th farmer. In addition, we define:

(1b) $FERTLIZR_i^* = b_o^* + b_1^* PFERT + b_2^* PCORN + b_3^* HHCHAR + u_i^*$

where $FERTLIZR_i^*$ denotes the *desired* expenditure on fertilizer, which may differ from the actual amount because of credit (income) constraints or some other reason (including high transaction costs). All we know about the i-th farmer is that measured or *observed* expenditure on fertilizer is FERTLIZR$_i$ whenever FERTLIZR$_i$>FERTLIZR$_i$* (i.e., actual exceeds the desired expenditure), and FERTLIZR$_i$ is zero otherwise. Among those who did not purchase fertilizer, we do not know how far away individual farmers were from buying fertilizer, only that they did not buy any. Some farmers may have been *almost* prepared to buy fertilizer, while others would have needed considerable additional "convincing."

These relationships are shown in Figure 2 for hypothetical data relating fertilizer use to the number of workers available. The upward slope in the data reflects the fact that fertilizer use increases only if more workers are available because of the increased labor requirements at harvest brought about by higher yields. One can imagine that among the non-users some (such as B) would have been less likely to use fertilizer than others (such as A), given the same number of workers. Another way of interpreting this problem is that observations on the dependent variable over the negative range of fertilizer use have been transformed or collapsed into a single number (in this case zero), since it is not possible to observe negative quantities of fertilizer.

If a non-negligible proportion of farmers (say 5% or more) do not use fertilizer, ordinary least squares (OLS) estimation of (1a) yields biased

Figure 2. Illustration of Tobit and OLS lines for censored samples.

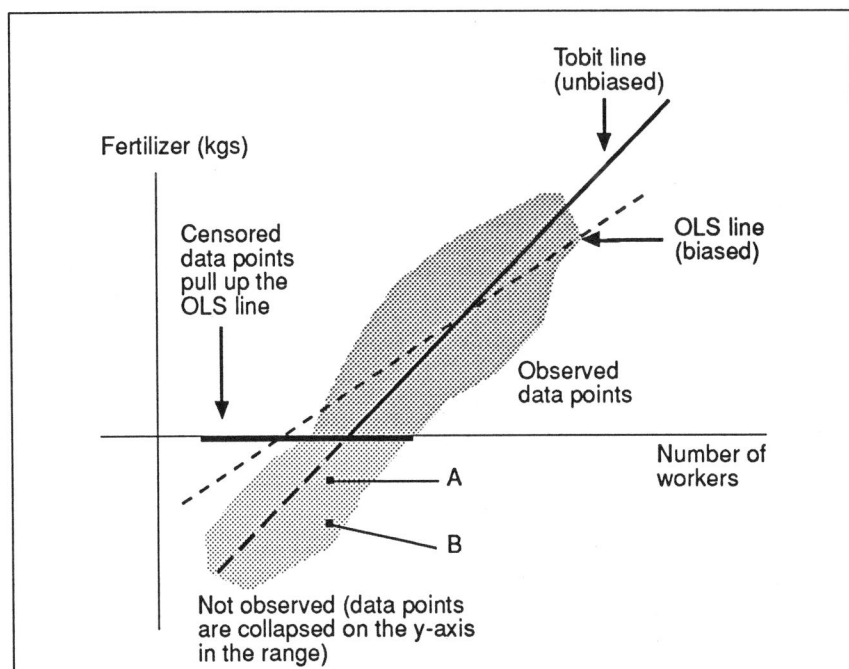

parameter estimates for β. More specifically, OLS underestimates the true effect of the parameters, as shown in Figure 2 (this is referred to as *attenuation of the slope*). Simply dropping households not using fertilizer will produce biased parameter estimates if the decision to use fertilizer is not a random process (as discussed in more detail below). References on the topic of censoring include Maddala (1988), Greene (1990), and Tobin (1958).

Tobit and Truncated Estimation

Consistent estimates of β are obtained by using the Tobit estimator. The estimation can be done in two steps, or by using maximum likelihood methods; we begin with the two-step method. To save space, the following abbreviations will be used: f = FERTLIZR, X = (PFERT, PCORN, HHCHAR) and β = (b_0, b_1, b_2, b_3). For our sample data we know the following:

(2a) $f_i = X_i \beta + u_i > 0$ if $f_i > 0$, $u_i \sim N(0, \sigma_u)$,

(2b) $f_i = 0$ otherwise.

For farmers using fertilizer (2a), the error term u_i is assumed to be normally distributed with mean zero and standard deviation σ_u.

The condition $f_i > 0$ can also be written as $X_i \beta > -u_i$. This provides additional information which can be used in the estimation to circumvent the attenuation bias mentioned above. More specifically, the condition can be thought of as implying that the respondents for whom it holds have a stronger (unobserved) desire or ability to pay for the fertilizer. It is possible to calculate the probability that farmer i uses fertilizer; that probability depends on relative prices and the farmer's characteristics, X_i:

(3) $\text{Prob}(f_i > 0) = \Phi(X_i \beta / \sigma)$

Here, σ is the standard deviation associated with error term u_i in equation (2a) and Φ is the cumulative standard normal distribution function, which is associated with the familiar bell curve shown in Figure 3:

(4) $F = F(X_i \beta, \sigma^2) = \int_{-\infty}^{X_i \beta / \sigma} \frac{1}{(2\pi)^{1/2}} e^{-k^2/2} dk$

It is necessary to estimate β/σ jointly because there is insufficient information in the data to estimate both parameters separately (a common assumption is that $\sigma = 1$). Thus, for each farmer i the independent variables X_i are plugged into equation (3), parameters β and σ are estimated, and the probability of purchasing fertilizer is then calculated. Computer software is available for calculating the values of this function, and its marginal functions, as discussed below.

An important variable needed to correct for the bias associated with a censored model estimated by means of OLS is the inverse *Mill's ratio*, λ_i (or Hazard function). It is calculated for each observation and defined as the marginal (ϕ or mdf) divided by the cumulative (Φ or cdf) normal distribution function:

(5) $\quad \lambda_i = \dfrac{\varnothing(X_i\beta)}{\Phi(X_i\beta)} = \dfrac{\varnothing_i}{\Phi_i} \qquad$ where $\qquad \varnothing = \dfrac{\partial \Phi(X_i\beta)}{\partial X_i\beta}$

This is the ratio of the *marginal* to the *cumulative* probability of a household buying fertilizer, or being in the "fertilizer purchasing state." The mdf traces out how the cumulative (cdf) probability of fertilizer use changes as the independent variables change. The term λ_i corrects for the bias associated with omitting households not buying fertilizer when it is included in an OLS regression of non-zero values of f_i on $X_i\beta$ (i.e., including only households which used fertilizer).

The regression on the subsample buying fertilizer is:

(6) $\quad E(f_i|f_i > 0) = X_i\beta + E(u_i|X_i\beta > -u_i) = X_i\beta + \sigma \dfrac{\phi_i}{\Phi_i}$

The parameter on regressor λ_i provides an estimate of σ. By convention, the subscripts on ϕ_i and Φ_i mean we are dealing with a specific value estimated for a given household. When the subscripts are not given, we are dealing with a function. If the intent is to estimate an equation using the entire sample, an additional step is necessary. To verify this, use the fact that the expected value of f_i, i.e., $E(f_i)$ is the probability-weighted sum of the expected value of f_i for those who buy fertilizer, $E(f_i|f_i>0)$, and those who do not (which is $E(f_i|f_i=0) = 0$, so that the second term in the sum can be ignored). The probability of buying fertilizer is $\text{Prob}(f_i>0) = \Phi_i(X_i\beta/\sigma)$, so we can estimate equation (7) by OLS (ϕ_i and Φ_i are numbers, just like those in vector X_{ii}):

(7) $\quad E(f_i) = \Phi_i \left[X_i\beta + \sigma \dfrac{\phi_i}{\Phi_i} \right] = X_i\Phi_i\beta + \sigma\phi_i$

This two-step method closely simulates the decision maker's problem: first, whether or not to buy fertilizer and, second, if fertilizer is bought, how much of it to buy. Equation (3) is actually a Probit model, in which the parameter estimates show which variables determine whether or not a farmer buys fertilizer. Equations (6) or (7) then show which variables affect purchases of fertilizer, conditional on the decision to buy fertilizer having already been made.

As indicated above, different variables may affect the probability of purchasing fertilizer as opposed to the amount purchased. In fact, the Tobit model is rather restrictive because a positive (negative) parameter increases (decreases) both the probability of an individual using (in our example) fertilizer, as well as the quantity used. This obviously need not always be the case. Lin and Schmidt (1984) present a specification test for the Tobit model which detects whether or not the same process affects both the probability of the dependent variable being non-zero and its level.

Tobit parameters can also be estimated using maximum likelihood methods. For example, the econometric software package LIMDEP© (for *Lim*ited *Dep*endent variable) by Bill Greene offers this option (Greene 1990); the program also calculates the Mill's ratio and associated quantities (mdf and cdf), as well as a variety of other maximum likelihood estimators (including Probit and Logit models). After taking logs, the Tobit function is:

$$(8) \quad \log L = \sum_{f_i = 0} \log(1 - \Phi_i) + \sum_{f_i > 0} \log\left[\frac{1}{(2\pi\sigma^2)^{1/2}}\right] - \sum_{f_i > 0} \frac{1}{2\sigma^2}(f_i - X_i\beta)^2$$

The first summation, over farmers who do not use fertilizer, corresponds to the probability mass that is in the left-hand tail of the mdf in Figure 3. Intuitively, in the Tobit method this mass is reallocated to the point of censoring, 0 in this case, and yields the quantity $\Phi(0)$. The point of censoring can be any number, not only zero. The second summation term accounts for the remainder of the mdf. With a *truncated* estimator, on the other hand, the mass from the censored tail is reallocated evenly over the remainder of the existing distribution to the left of the truncation point.

LIMDEP© also includes a *truncated* maximum likelihood estimator, which is based on the assumption of an explicit truncation of the dependent variable at zero (or any other value specified by the user). This can be used to directly estimate parameters of an equation for farmers using fertilizer, without having to worry about the bias arising from exclusion of part of the sample (assuming the distributional assumption holds). In general, LIMDEP© probably has the most complete set of built-in commands of any currently available package. A recent review of econometric software can be found in MacKie-Mason (1992).

Table 1 shows Tobit, Probit, and truncated models for fertilizer use in a sample of 198 Senegalese farm households. Ideally, fertilizer prices would have been included in the equations, but there was insufficient variation in prices over space. An example of a selectivity model is provided in the next section.

Figure 3. Cumulative and marginal standard normal distribution functions and an illustration of censoring.

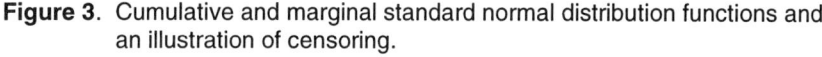

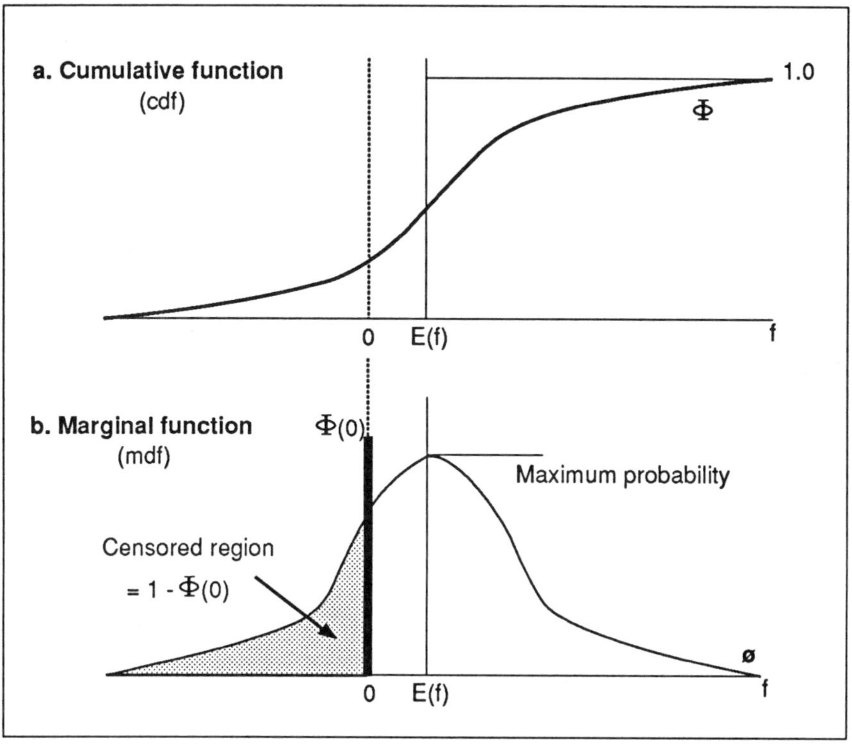

Especially noteworthy in Table 1 is the fact that the probability of using fertilizer decreases with a household head's age, but the amount used—conditional on using fertilizer—increases with age. The more rigid Tobit estimator is unable to pick up this subtlety, and the estimated parameter for age is in fact not significantly different from zero in this case. The Tobit coefficients for participation in the SODEFITEX cotton and maize production programs are both positive and statistically different from zero. However, while participation in the cotton program increases the probability of using fertilizer, it does not affect the quantity used, conditional on participation. The opposite is true for the maize program. At the same time, the estimate for core female labor differs significantly from zero in the Tobit model, but not in either of the other two models. The implication is that this variable *jointly* affects both the probability *and* level of fertilizer use, and it is not possible to discern separate effects. Consequently, both the single- and two-step methods have limitations, and it may be useful to employ both to gain the greatest amount of insight possible.

In summary, the model for censored data discussed in this section can be estimated using the following four steps. With a package such as LIMDEP©, the difference between estimating a Tobit as opposed to an OLS model is as simple as entering the command:

"TOBIT; LHS=f; RHS=X $" instead of

"CRMODEL; LHS=f; RHS=X $".

Table 1. Maximum likelihood estimates for factors affecting the use of fertilizer by Senegalese farm households (absolute t-statistic).

Independent variable	Estimator		
	Tobit	Probit	Truncated
Constant	−1,384	−.2582	−51,412
	(1.38)	(.483)	(1.87)*
VI labor (Vert. integrated)[a]	3,068	.1743	1,103
	(1.93)*	(1.92)*	(.390)
HI labor (Concession)[a]	54.2	.180	−10,165
	(.012)	(.722)	(.964)
Interaction (HI*VI)	−3,738	−.342	267
	(1.48)*	(2.19)*	(.071)
Core labor: male	1,605	.103	428
	(.865)	(.967)	(.111)
Core labor: female	2,978	.141	2,233
	(1.61)*	(1.37)	(.593)
Household head age	−61.2	−.0126	732
	(.411)	(1.58)*	(2.02)*
Equipment value/worker	520	.0137	1.09
	(1.44)*	(.678)	(1.48)*
SODEFITEX cotton[b]	27,730	1.62	19,402
	(3.68)*	(3.20)*	(1.38)
SODEFITEX maize[b]	18,974	.514	37,113
	(1.81)*	(.768)	(2.19)*
Number of households	198	198	94
Log-likelihood value	1,131	118	1,002
Prediction success: p = 0 [p = 1]		71% [57%]	

* = significant at 15% or lower.

[a] VI and HI refer to labor from vertically and horizontally integrated or extended families, respectively. Vertical integration occurs when married sons remain in their father's household instead of forming their own production and consumption unit, while horizontal integration involves groupings of households of married sons who have the same father. Core labor is that of household heads and their spouses as well as unmarried sons and daughters. See Goetz(1993) for further details.

[b] Predicted values of the variables which denote participation in parastatal crop production programs.

Source: Adapted from Goetz (1990).

1. Develop an empirical model relating the dependent variable to predetermined regressors (right-hand side variables): $f = X_i \beta$.

2. Estimate a Tobit model using the entire sample. The coefficient estimates (β^{TOBIT}) show the joint effect of each regressor on both the probability of the dependent variable being non-zero, and the level of the dependent variable. A Tobit parameter, therefore, cannot be directly compared with an OLS parameter. Appendix 1 shows how marginal effects are calculated for the Tobit model.

3. Estimate a Probit model using the entire sample and all the variables included previously. The dependent variable (f) has to be recoded to "1" for all non-limit observations (f>0), using a new variable name (e.g., "fprobit"), and leaving all the limit observations as they were (at zero). This is easily done in virtually all software packages. The parameter estimates (β^{PROBIT}) then show the effect of different variables on the probability that the dependent variable is non-zero (i.e., that farmers purchase fertilizer), but not on the amount of that variable (quantity purchased). The interpretation of probit parameters is also discussed in Appendix 1.

4. Estimate a truncated model using only non-limit (non-zero) observations; this yields parameter estimates β^{TRUNC}. The interpretation of marginal effects in this model is also non-standard, and identical to a special case of the Tobit model (see Appendix 1). The Tobit or censored model is in fact an extension of the truncated model.

Selectivity Models

The next step is to consider more formally the *process* whereby individuals *select* themselves into alternative programs or states. As discussed earlier, examples of states may include the state of growing tea as opposed to not growing tea; the state of hiring non-family labor vs. using only family labor; the state of selling coarse grains vs. not selling any; or the state of consuming fish vs. not consuming fish. The decision as to whether or not to be in a certain state is a *discrete* one. In contrast, the decision regarding *how much* of an activity to pursue conditional on being in a state is *continuous*—that is, how much tea to grow; how much non-family labor to hire; or how much fish to consume. Conceivably, different variables will affect the discrete and the continuous decisions, but the decisions may still be statistically interdependent (i.e., related).

If the process that switches an individual into a certain state is not a random one, but affected by both observable and unobservable variables, then ignoring information about the switching mechanism may lead not only to less efficient but also to biased parameter estimates in the equation related to the continuous decision. Individuals may differ in their propensity to switch into a certain state, such as using fertilizer or consuming fish, for a number of reasons. Some of these may be observable while others are not. They include factors such as special education about or skill in using fertilizer; a special taste for fish; different preferences towards risk; or lower transaction costs because of transportation equipment available (carts or trucks), special language skills required to trade with certain ethnic groups, an inherent preference for interacting with strangers, strong interpersonal skills, or access to radios and newspapers with market price information. All of these factors may affect the discrete participation decision in a systematic fashion, so that ignoring them would lead to serious estimation bias.

After discussing the two-step Tobit method above, the way of correcting for these biases by using a *selectivity* model is fairly straightforward. A key difference is that the equation modelling the discrete decision about switching into a given state is expanded to allow these additional factors—at least those that are observable—to come into play explicitly. Also included in this YES/NO equation, that has values 0 or 1 as the dependent variable, are the variables reflecting transaction costs involved in switching into the state. Some variables will affect both the discrete and continuous decisions, while others belong in the discrete equation, but not the continuous equation. For example, certain fixed transaction costs will not be relevant in the continuous equation.

We start again with a censored random sample of survey respondents, such as farm households. Suppose the intent is to "explain" the coarse grain marketing behavior of households, and in particular the fact that some households sell coarse grains while others do not. A reasonable hypothesis is that at least some households are prevented from selling (all other things being equal) because they face high transaction costs, which are household-specific. Define $S_i=1$ for households which sell coarse grains and $S_i=0$ otherwise, and let S_i^* denote the (unobserved) desired propensity to sell. Similarly, let Q_i represent the actual quantity of coarse grains sold and Q_i^* the desired quantity. Then Q_i is equal to 0 or Q_i^*, depending on which is greater. We assume that the non-random (systematic) process which switches households into a selling state is given by the selectivity model in equation (9a), which can be estimated using (9b) as a discrete process (0-1). The regression equation for kilograms of coarse grains sold is represented by (9c):

(9a) $S_i^* = Z_i \gamma + v_i$ where v_i is distributed as $N(0,\sigma_v)$

(9b) $\text{Prob}(S_i=1) = \Phi(Z_i \gamma)$ for those with $S_i^* > 0$ or $Z_i \gamma > -v_i$

(9c) $Q_i = W_i \alpha + \varepsilon_i$, $[Q_i = \max(0, Q_i^*)]$

(9d) $(Q_i | S_i=1) = W_i \alpha - \rho \sigma_\varepsilon \phi_i / \Phi_i + \omega_i$

The true Q_i which a given household wants to sell is observed only for those who participate in the market (i.e., $S_i^*>0$). Other households may want to sell coarse grains but they are prevented from doing so because of transaction costs and for other reasons, so that we do not observe their true Q_i; all we know for these households is that the actual quantity is zero. An important assumption about the error terms $[v,\varepsilon]$ in equation system (9) is that they are jointly distributed as bivariate normals with means 0, standard deviations of 1 and σ_ε, respectively, and with covariance ρ.

Regressors in W_i include input-output prices and other socioeconomic variables affecting the quantity of coarse grains sold. Regressors in Z_i include not only the variables in W_i but also variables measuring transaction costs (such as access to market information, etc.). These variables influence the discrete participation decision but not the decision about the (continuous) amount to be sold. Once the estimate of γ has been obtained, the predicted value of $S_i = Z_i\gamma$ is plugged into the formula for the Mill's ratio to calculate a λ_i value for each household.

Equation (9d) has as a dependent variable the quantity of coarse grains sold by the ith household, conditional on the fact that it has decided to sell something (that is, it excludes households not selling coarse grains). While it is true that $E(\omega_i | S_i=1)=0$ so that equation (9d) yields unbiased estimates, the estimates are not efficient because the error term is heteroscedastic: $\text{var}(\omega_i) = \sigma_\varepsilon^2(1-\rho^2\xi_i)$, where:

$$(10) \quad \xi_i = \frac{\phi((Z_i\gamma))}{\Phi(Z_i\gamma)}\left[\frac{\phi(Z_i\gamma)}{\Phi(Z_i\gamma)} + Z_i\gamma\right] = \lambda_i(\lambda_i + Z_i\lambda)$$

The heteroscedasticity arises because the variance of ω_i is observation-dependent rather than a constant number.

Lee and Trost (1978) suggested a correction procedure for this problem (see Appendix 2). There is another issue in that the selectivity term in equation (9d) is estimated, and therefore has a variance associated with it. This means the other standard error estimates for all parameters in the equation are biased; they are in fact downward biased. Lee, Maddala, and Trost (1980) have proposed a method for dealing with this problem (see Appendix 2). In practice many researchers ignore the latter bias and simply report their results as being "conditional" on the selectivity term.

Empirical results for a selectivity model are presented in Table 2. The first equation corresponds to the mechanism or process which switches farmers into the "coarse grain selling state": $\text{Prob}(S_i=1) = \Phi(Z_i\gamma)$. The second equation relates to the quantity sold, conditional on having chosen to sell coarse grains: $(Q_i|S_i=1) = W_i\alpha - \rho\sigma_\varepsilon\phi_i/\Phi_i + \omega_i$. The first set of variables (up to age-squared) are common to both equations, while the last three reflect fixed transaction cost variables which affect only the participation decision. It is noteworthy that prices of coarse grains and rice affect the quantity of coarse grains sold, but

Table 2. Selectivity model for coarse grain market participation by Senegalese farm households (absolute t-statistics)[a].

Independent variable	Probit Eqn. (9b)	2-stage OLS Eqn. (9d)
Constant	5.463 (1.41)	892. (1.69)* [1.27]
Price of course grains	.000750 (.056)	7.96 (3.06)* [2.26]*
Price of rice	-.0246 (.980)	-6.47 (2.53)* [1.91]*
Transformation technology (=1)	.224 (.500)	189. (3.28)* [2.21]*
Consumer/producer ratio	-.581 (1.50)	-138. (2.65)* [1.24]
Age of head	-.0944 (1.78)*	6.07 (.74) [.47]
Age-squared	.000944 (1.94)*	-.0501 (.63) [.36]
Market information	1.750 (2.41)*	
Cart ownership	.195 (.370)	
Market information x cart ownership	-0.975 (1.61)*	
Selectivity term		155. (2.08)* [1.85]*
Likelihood ratio test	62.6*	
Adjusted R-square		43.4

[a] t-statistics in parentheses are calculated using regular standard errors; those in square brackets are based on corrected standard errors.

* = significant at 10% or lower;

Source: Adapted from Goetz (1992); because of space limitations, only a subset of variables included in the equations is shown.

not the probability of market participation. Conversely, the age of the household head affects the probability of participation but not the amount sold. The selectivity term in the continuous equation is statistically different from zero.

The positive parameter estimate indicates a selling household in the sample sells more than a household selected at random from the sample.

The three steps for estimating a selectivity model can be summarized as follows.

1. Estimate a Probit model which has as its dependent variable a "1" for households selling coarse grains (or engaging in the activity being examined) and a zero otherwise. This yields an estimate of parameter γ in equation (9b).
2. For each observation, calculate the selectivity term $\lambda_i = \phi(Z_i\gamma)/\Phi(Z_i\gamma)$, using predicted values from the Probit equation in step 1. As indicated earlier, this is easily done with a program such as LIMDEP©.
3. Estimate an OLS regression using only the non-limit household s or units, adding λ_i to the regressors (equation 9d). Use the procedures discussed in Appendix 2 to obtain heteroscedasticity-corrected parameters as well as parameters that are not conditioned on the selectivity term.

Summary and Conclusion

The statistical models presented here can be applied to a wide class of economic development problems. In Goetz (1992) a selectivity model is estimated which switches households into alternative market participation states of being only buyers of coarse grains, only sellers, both buyers and sellers, or non-participants in the coarse grain markets (i.e., autarkic).

Many further extensions are possible, involving increasingly complex probability equations. For example, farmers may have the choice of switching into the states of not selling coarse grains, selling to the market, selling to a parastatal, or to a combination of the latter, combined with the option of purchasing from each of these sources. The decision to sell in (buy from) a particular market outlet is likely to be a systematic (i.e., non-random) one, so that this type of problem should be analyzed using a selectivity model. Similarly, farmers may have the option of participating in a variety of public or parastatal production programs for specific crops. Whenever a decision is made as to whether or not to participate in a program, and to what extent to participate (e.g., how much fertilizer to use or how much land to allocate to a particular crop), a potential selectivity problem arises.

Finally, it is hoped that as researchers focus more closely on economic agents' discrete decisions about whether or not to participate in an activity (or switch into a certain state), the costs which prevent participation will become more clearly identified. As a result, policies can be formulated to reduce these costs and in turn stimulate economic development by improving the articulation of supply and demand between two or more parties.

References

Goetz, S.J. 1990. *Market reforms, food security, and the cash crop-food crop debate in Southeastern Senegal*. Ph.D. Diss., Department of Agricultural Economics, Michigan State University, East Lansing, MI, USA.

———. 1992. A selectivity model of household food and marketing behavior in Sub-Saharan Africa. *American Journal of Agricultural Economics* 74:444-452.

———. 1993. Interlinked markets and the cash crop-food crop debate in land-abundant tropical agriculture. *Economic Development and Cultural Change* 41:343-61.

Greene, W.H. 1990. *Econometric analysis*. New York, NY, USA: Macmillan. (Information on LIMDEP© is available from Econometric Software, Inc., 43 Maple Ave., Bellport, NY 11713, USA; Phone (515) 286-7049; FAX: 938-2395).

Judge, G., C. Hill, W. Griffiths, T. Lee, and H. Lutkepohl. 1985. *The theory and practice of econometrics*. New York, NY, USA: Wiley.

Lee, L.F. and R.P. Trost. 1978. Estimation of some limited dependent variable models with application to housing demand. *Journal of Econometrics* 8:357-82.

Lee, L.F., G.S. Maddala, and R.P. Trost. 1980. Asymptotic covariance matrices of two-stage Probit and two-stage Tobit models for simultaneous equations models and selectivity. *Econometrica* 48:491-503.

Lin, T.F. and P. Schmidt. 1984. A test of the Tobit specification against an alternative suggested by Cragg. *Review of Economics and Statistics* 65:174-77.

MacKie-Mason, J.K. 1992. Econometric software: a user's view. *Journal of Economic Literature* 6:165-87.

Maddala, G.S. 1988. *Limited-dependent and qualitative variables in econometrics*. Econometric Society Monograph No. 3. Cambridge, UK: Cambridge University Press.

McDonald, J.F. and R.A. Moffitt. 1980. The use of Tobit analysis. *Review of Economics and Statistics* 60:318-21.

Murphy, K.M. and R.H. Topel. 1985. Estimation and inference in two-step econometric models. *Journal of Business Econometric Statistics* 3:370-79.

Tobin, J. 1958. Estimation of relationships for limited dependent variables. *Econometrica* 26:24-36.

Appendix 1

Calculation of marginal effects

1.   Tobit Model

a. $\dfrac{\partial E(f^*)}{\partial X_j} = \beta_j$

b. $\dfrac{\partial E(f)}{\partial X_j} = \beta_j \Phi\left(\dfrac{X_i \beta}{\sigma}\right) = \beta_j \Phi_i$

c. $\dfrac{\partial E(f \setminus f^* > 0)}{X_j} = \beta_j \left(1 - \dfrac{X_i \beta}{\sigma} \lambda_i \lambda_i^2\right) = \beta_j (1 - \xi_i)$

See McDonald and Moffit (1980). In 1b and 1c parameter estimate β_j is adjusted to reflect the fact that a probability is associated with the switch into the non-limit state. The quantities Φ_i and ϕ_i (or λ_i) are easily calculated with a program such as LIMDEP©.

2.   Probit Model

$$\partial \dfrac{E(f)}{X_j} = \beta_j \phi\left[\dfrac{X_i \beta}{\sigma}\right] = \beta_j \phi_i$$

It can be shown that $\beta^{OLS} \cong 0.4 \beta^{PROBIT} = (1/\phi(0)) \beta^{PROBIT}$.

3.   Truncated Model (c.f. with 1c above).

$$\dfrac{\partial E(f|f > 0)}{\partial X_j} = \beta_j \left[\dfrac{X_i \beta}{\sigma} \lambda_i - \lambda_i^2\right]$$

Appendix 2

Correction of the parameter estimates

The following procedure yields parameter estimates that are both heteroscedasticity-corrected and that take into account the fact that the selectivity term is estimated (i.e., stochastic).

Using OLS, estimate equation (9d) provides consistent (unbiased) parameter estimates for α and $a = \rho\sigma_e$. To correct for heteroscedasticity, first estimate the variance of ω_i, as follows:

$$\text{var}(\omega_i | S_i = 1) = \hat{\sigma}_v^2 - \hat{\sigma}_\varepsilon^2 \frac{\phi_i}{\Phi_i}\left[Z_i\hat{\gamma} + \frac{\phi_i}{\Phi_i}\right] = \hat{\sigma}_v^2 - \hat{\sigma}_\varepsilon^2 \hat{\xi}_i$$

where an estimate of σ_v^2 is obtained from:

$$\hat{\sigma}_v^2 = \frac{1}{N_1}\sum_{i=1}^{N_1}\left[\hat{v}_i^2 + \hat{\sigma}_\varepsilon^2\left[Z_i\hat{\gamma}\frac{\phi Z_i\hat{\gamma}}{\Phi Z_i\hat{\gamma}}\right]\right]$$

and N_1 is the number of households selling coarse grains (i.e., the number of non-limit observations). Once the variance has been estimated, standard weighting procedures to correct for heterescedasticity can be applied.

A problem with this calculation is that the variance is not always positive. Lee and Trost (1978) suggested an alternative calculation for situations where that is the case:

$$\hat{\sigma}_v^2 = \frac{1}{N_1}\sum_{i=1}^{N_1}\left[\hat{\omega}^2 + \hat{\sigma}_\varepsilon^2 Z_i\hat{\gamma}\frac{\phi(Z_i\hat{\gamma})}{\Phi(Z_i\hat{\gamma})} + \hat{\sigma}_\varepsilon^2 \frac{\phi^2(Z_i\hat{\gamma})}{\Phi^2(Z_i\hat{\gamma})}\right]$$

which is always positive.

Unfortunately, this is not the only correction needed. It is also necessary to account for the fact that the selectivity term is an estimated quantity (in the first-step equation), and therefore has an associated distribution. If this is not corrected for, the estimated variances will underestimate the true variances.

The following procedure can be used (see, e.g., Maddala 1988; also Lee, Maddala, and Trost 1980; or Murphy and Topel 1985); the matrices can be programmed in certain statistical packages (such as LIMDEP ©), so that the calculations are simpler than they may first appear. Define Z as consisting of observations (Z_1, Z_2), which correspond to households selling coarse grains (Z_1) and those not selling any, respectively (Z_2). Define D_i as a N_1 by N_1 diagonal matrix which has at its i-th diagonal term the quantity ξ_1, and zero everywhere else (an example of a diagonal matrix follows). Define $G_i = (W_{1i}, \lambda_i)$ as the regressors of the household selling coarse grains (including the selectivity term), and similarly for Q_i. Lastly, define the N×N diagonal matrix $\Lambda = \text{diag}$ (λ_{1i}, λ_{2i}) as:

$$\begin{bmatrix} \lambda_{11}\lambda_{21} & 0 & \cdots & 0 \\ 0 & \lambda_{12}\lambda_{22} & \cdots & 0 \\ \vdots & \ddots & \ddots & \cdots \\ 0 & \cdots & \cdots & \lambda_{1N}\lambda_{2N} \end{bmatrix}$$

then the two-stage estimates are:

$$\begin{bmatrix} \hat{\alpha} \\ \hat{a} \end{bmatrix} = (\hat{G}'\hat{G})^{-1}\hat{G}'Q_1$$

with variance-covariance matrix:

$$\text{Var}\begin{bmatrix} \hat{\alpha} \\ \hat{a} \end{bmatrix} = \hat{\sigma}_\varepsilon^2 (G'G)^{-1} - \hat{\sigma}_v^2 (G'G)^{-1} G'[D - DZ_1(Z'\Lambda Z)^{-1}Z'D]G(G'G)^{-1}.$$

18

Measuring Welfare Benefits from Marketing Improvements: Potato Storage in Tunisia

Keith Owen Fuglie[1]

Abstract

Agricultural marketing is an essential component of a food system, adding transportation, storage, and processing services to food products. New technologies which reduce the costs of marketing can lower marketing margins between farm-gate and retail markets and affect the welfare of both farmers and consumers. The equilibrium quantity and price effects and the economic welfare implications of technical change in agricultural marketing are examined in a partial equilibrium model. An application of the model is made to potato storage in Tunisia. Improved pest control in rustic potato stores has reduced storage losses and lowered seasonal price margins. The economic and welfare effects of improved potato storage in Tunisia are estimated.

Key words: Agricultural marketing, economic welfare, storage, potatoes, technical change, Tunisia.

Introduction

High marketing margins can persist either because of monopolistic elements in the marketing chain or because the real costs of marketing are high. Empirical studies of agricultural marketing efficiency in developing countries have generally supported the competitive market paradigm (Ruttan 1969; Jones 1972; Scott 1985), which suggests that the real cause of high margins may be low productivity of marketing services. However, there have been few formal economic studies evaluating policies aimed at improving the technical efficiency of agricultural marketing in developing countries. This chapter develops a framework for investigating the social welfare implications of

---

[1] Agricultural Economist, Economic Research Service, U.S. Department of Agriculture, Washington, DC, USA.

improving productivity in the marketing sector and applies the model to potato storage in Tunisia.

Improving the productivity of agricultural marketing services will increase social welfare by reducing the cost of transforming agricultural commodities through space, time, or form, and thereby extend the market for agricultural products. Methods for quantifying the welfare effects of agricultural technical change are reviewed by Norton and Davis (1981) and are extended to a multi-market framework in Alston (1991). One approach is to model technological change in the marketing sector as an outward shift in the supply of marketing services. The effect of the supply shift on equilibrium prices and quantities and on producer and consumer surpluses at each market level (farm, marketing, and retail) can then be determined (Alston 1991).

This approach is used below to estimate the welfare benefits from improvements in crop storage, a marketing service which transforms a product through time. A feature of crop storage is that the commodity is consumed in both its "raw" and "processed" forms (i.e., both with and without marketing services added). A change in marketing behavior will affect consumers at both ends of the marketing chain. Previous models of technical change in agricultural marketing have assumed that consumers only demand the final product (for a review of empirical studies, see Alston 1991). However, for a broad range of marketing services (including storage, transportation, and food processing) consumer demand exists at multiple stages of the marketing chain. This feature carries important implications for how welfare gains from marketing improvements are distributed among the various economic agents.

In the next section an analytical framework is developed for analyzing the effects of a technical change which reduces storage costs. Farmers choose optimal production and storage, taking prices as given. A market-level model solves for output prices endogenously. In this framework, changes in storage costs will affect both quantity produced and stored.[2] The distribution of welfare benefits among producers and consumers depends critically on how the storage supply function shifts and on the elasticities of supply and demand. Following this is an empirical application of the model to potato storage in Tunisia. The adoption of improved pest management in rustic potato stores by farmers in the 1980s led to a reduction in storage losses (Fuglie et al. 1993). Farm survey data and time series trends in marketing margins provide evidence on the size of the shift in the storage supply function. Estimates of total welfare benefits and the distribution of these benefits among producers and consumers are estimated.

---

[2] If increased storage merely redistributed fixed supplies among periods, then consumers would be necessarily worse off, which is the classic Waugh-Oi-Massel result of commodity price stabilization (Massel 1969). With supply responses, consumers may benefit along with producers.

Conceptual Model of Crop Storage and Food Supply

Seasonal prices and the supply of output and storage

Most economic studies of crop storage have assumed that different agents carry out production and storage activities (Working 1949; Brennen 1958; Wohlgenant 1985) and do not consider how changes in storage costs may affect production. While some studies have considered production and marketing decisions jointly, such as the literature on agricultural household models (Singh, Squire, and Strauss 1986), these models have ignored storage costs (for an exception, see Renkow 1990).

A two-period model is developed below to describe farm production and storage decisions. Production takes place only in the first period. In the second period all market supplies come from farm storage. Farmers have the option of selling their crop at harvest (the first period) or storing all or a part of their crop in the hope of securing a better price in the non-production season. Stores are liquidated by the end of the second period.

Prices and technology are assumed to be known. In period 1, a farmer purchases a vector of inputs x at price w and combines them to produce output $q(x)$. Production technology $q(x)$ is increasing and quasiconcave in x. All, a part, or none of the crop can be sold at harvest at the market price p_1 or placed in storage in order to receive a higher price (p_2) in the second period. Let q_t be the quantity marketed in each period t (t = 1,2).

There are two components to storage costs. One component is storage losses due to shrinkage, rotting, and pest damage. Let δ be the proportion of a store that is lost to these factors ($0 \leq \delta \leq 1$).[3] If q_s is the quantity stored, then $q_2 = (1-\delta)q_s$. Another component of storage costs includes the costs of marketing inputs such as labor, materials, and depreciation. Let $C(q_s)$ be the storage cost function for marketing inputs which is increasing in and convex q_s.[4]

---

[3] The proportion of losses typically increases with the length of storage and may be stochastic in nature, particularly if losses are caused by pests. In this two-period model, however, it is assumed that δ is constant and known

[4] Some studies have also assumed a "convenience yield" as a component of storage costs (Working 1949; Wohlgenant 1985; Renkow 1990). "Convenience yield" refers to the value of being able to meet future needs for the commodity from one's own inventory (for example, "pipeline stocks" in the case of a food processing company, or food security needs on the part of a semi-subsistence household). In the model below, convenience yield is not considered explicitly but could be viewed as a component of marketing input costs $C(q_s)$.

The farmer's joint production, storage, and marketing decision is to chose x, q_1, and q_2 in order to maximize

(1) $\quad \pi(x, q_1, q_2) = p_1 q_1 = (1-r)p_2 q_2 - wx - C(q_s)$

subject to $\quad$ (1a) $\quad q(x) = q_1 + q_s$

and $\quad$ (1b) $\quad q_2 = (1-\delta)q_s$

where r is the appropriate time discount rate. (1a) is the production constraint and (1b) takes into account storage losses.

To solve the constrained optimization problem in (1), we substitute $(1-\delta)q_s$ for q_2 and set up the following Lagrangian equation:

(2) $\quad$ Maximize $L(x, q_1, q_s) = p_1 q_1 + (1-r)p_2(1-\delta)q_s - wx - c(q_s)$

$$+ \theta * [q(x) - q_1 - q_s]$$

where θ is the Lagrangian multiplier.

Quasiconcavity of the production function $q(x)$ and convexity of the storage cost function $C(q_s)$ are sufficient for the first order conditions to describe a unique, global maximum:

(3a) $\quad -w + \theta q_x = 0$

(3b) $\quad q_1 (p_1 - \theta) = 0$

(3c) $\quad q_s [(1-r)(1-\delta)p_2 - C_s - \theta] = 0$

where q_x and C_s are partial derivatives. (3a) is the familiar input decision rule (marginal revenue = marginal cost) where the Lagrangian multiplier is the marginal value of production. In (3b) and (3c), q_1 and q_s serve the role as "slack" variables in a linear programming sense. The marginal value of production (the value of θ) is given by p_1 if at least some of the crop is sold in period 1 (i.e., if $q_1 > 0$). If at least some of the crop is stored ($q_s > 0$) then the marginal value of production equals $(1-r)(1-\delta)p_2 - C_s$. If a portion of the crop is marketed in both periods, then $p_1 = (1-r)(1-\delta)p_2 - C_s$.

The first order conditions tell us which price determines a farmer's supply decision. Even in the absence of any price uncertainty, the price upon which a farmer bases his production decision may not be accurately reflected in observed market prices or the price received for the crop. If a portion of the crop is sold at harvest, then the relevant supply price is p_1. But if all of the crop is stored, then production is based on $(1-r)(1-\delta)p_2 - C_s$, which in this case is greater than p_1 (since $\theta > p_1$ when $q_1 = 0$) but less than p_2. This implies that a farmer who stores all of his or her crop is likely to use inputs more intensively than a farmer who sells at harvest.

The model also describes the equilibrium price relationship that is likely to prevail between periods. In a market in which deliveries are forthcoming in both periods, the seasonal price relationship is given by

$$(4) \quad p_2 = \frac{p_1 + C_x}{(1-r)(1-\delta)}$$

Although some farms may have access to better storage technology or cheaper credit, (4) describes the price relationship expected to prevail when r, δ, and C_s characterize the average conditions faced by a representative farm. For such a farm, output decisions are based on p_1, the price that prevails at harvest. Another implication of (4) is that seasonal price differences are determined solely by storage technology and interest rates. Anticipated shifts in consumer demand or crop production technology don't enter into the seasonal price relationship (although they may affect quantities delivered in each period). This was the principal insight of Working's (1949) seminal article on the interpretation of futures prices: that the basis (the difference between future and spot prices) reflects solely the carrying costs of stocks, and that the spot price carries as much information about the price that is expected to prevail in the future as the future price itself.

Figure 1 illustrates seasonal price formation graphically. The two periods are represented back-to-back in the diagram. Production takes place only in the first period and according to supply schedule S. D_1 and D_2 are the demand functions for each period. The storage supply curve in the second period is the excess supply (ES) from period 1 (ES equals S minus D_1 minus storage losses), plus the marginal cost of marketing inputs C_s, and is denoted StS in the figure. The intersection of the storage supply and the demand curve in period 2 establishes the market equilibrium price p_2 and quantity demanded Q_2 that prevail in that period. The period 1 price p_1 is determined by the intersection between Q_2 and the excess supply curve (given by point A in the diagram). Q_T is the total quantity produced and Q_1 is the quantity demanded in period 1, given p_1. $Q_s = Q_T - Q_1$ is put into storage. The difference between quantity stored and quantity demanded in period 2 is the quantity lost in storage.

Welfare benefits from improving marketing productivity

An improvement in storage technology will reduce the storage margin between periods by reducing either the marginal storage costs C_s or the rate of storage losses δ. If we assume that C_s is constant for all Q_s, then a reduction in C_s will result in a downward parallel shift in the storage supply function StS in Figure 1. A change in δ, on the other hand, will cause a pivotal shift in StS. Both types of supply shifts will be explored below. It turns out the nature of the storage supply shift is important in determining the distribution of welfare benefits between consumers and producers. Lindner and Jarrett (1978) reported a similar result for shifts in the agricultural supply function in a one-period model.

The framework used below to analyze the welfare effects of a change in storage technology is based on the model developed by Muth (1964) (see also Alston and Scobie 1983). However, Muth only considered one source of consumer demand: for a single retail food product involving farm and marketing inputs. In our model, consumers demand both the "raw" farm product and a "processed" product which has marketing services added.

Supply and demand conditions in the two-period model are described in equations (5) to (8). The capital Q's indicate aggregate market quantities.

(5) $\quad Q_1 = Q_1(p_1)$

(6) $\quad Q_2 = Q_2(p_2)$

Figure 1. An economic model of seasonal crop storage.

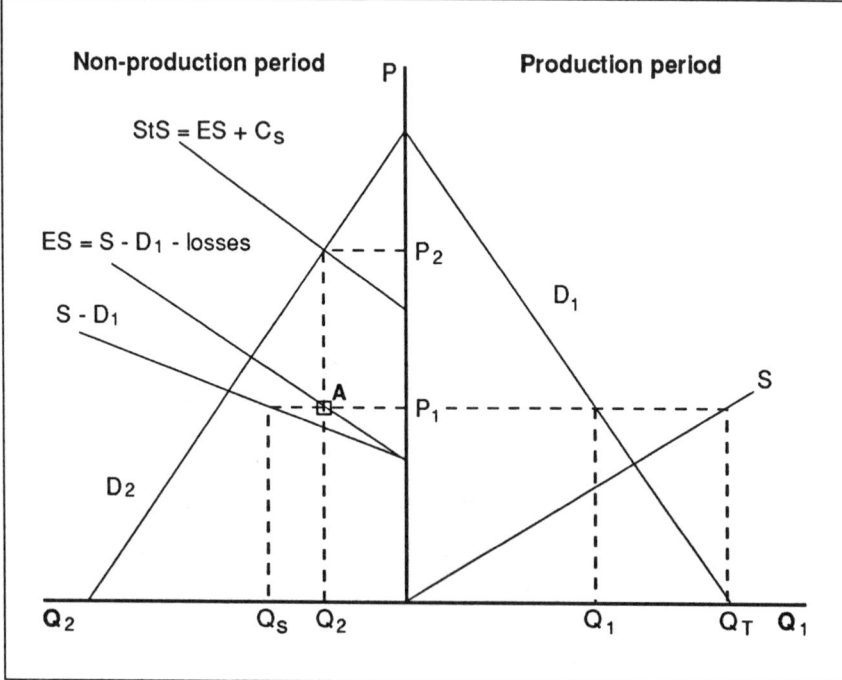

Measuring welfare benefits from marketing improvements

(7) $\quad Q_T = Q_T(p_1)$

(8) $\quad Q_T = Q_1 + Q_s$ where $Q_2 = (1-\delta)Q_s$.

Q_1 and Q_2 are consumer demand in each period. Q_T is total crop production which takes place only in period one. Equation (8) is the market equilibrium condition, where Q_s is total quantity stored.

Solving equations (5) to (8), using also the seasonal price relationship in (4), yields an equilibrium solution for prices and quantities in each period as a function of technology and demand parameters. Changes in storage technology parameters will lead to a new equilibrium solution. Welfare analysis is based on comparing producer and consumer surpluses under each equilibrium.

To simplify the notation it is convenient to represent storage losses by $\phi \equiv 1/(1-\delta)$ and the market interest rate by $\rho \equiv 1/(1-r)$ (note that $\phi \geq 1$ and $\rho \geq 1$). Then (4) becomes

(4′) $\quad p_2 = \rho\phi \, (p_1 - C_s)$

With the new notation, the market equilibrium condition can be written

(8′) $\quad Q_T = Q_1 + \phi \, Q_2$

Improvements in storage technology are represented by the parameters α and β. A reduction in the marginal cost of marketing inputs holding storage losses constant is given by $(C_s-\beta)$ and a reduction in storage losses holding marginal storage costs constant is ($\phi-\alpha$). With improved storage technology, the seasonal price relationship becomes

(4″) $\quad p_2 = \rho(\phi-\alpha) \, (p_1 + C_s - \beta)$

A change in storage technology causes market prices and quantities to adjust to a new equilibrium. These effects can be determined by expressing the market model in derivative form:

(9) $\quad dQ_1^* = -\eta_1 dp_1^*$

(10) $\quad dQ_2^* = -\eta_2 dp_2^*$

(11) $\quad dQ_T^* = \varepsilon dp_1^*$

(12) $\quad Q_T dq_T^* = Q_1 dQ_1^* + Q_2(\phi dQ_2^* - \alpha)$

(13) $\quad p_2 dp_2^* = \rho\phi(p_1 dp_1^* - \beta) - \rho\alpha(p_1 + C_s - \beta)$

where $dX^* = dX/X$. η_t is the absolute value of the demand elasticity in period t and ϵ is the elasticity of supply, with $\eta_t > 0$ and $\epsilon \geq 0$.

It is now a straightforward exercise to solve for the displacements caused by technical change. Solving (9) to (13) for dp gives

(14) $\quad dp_i^* = \dfrac{Q_2\eta_2\rho\Phi^2\beta + Q_2\eta_2\rho\Phi\alpha(p_1 + C_s - \beta) - p_2 Q_2 \alpha}{p_2 Q_t \epsilon + p_2 Q_1 \eta_1 + p_1 Q_2 \eta_2 \rho \Phi^2}$

The solution to the other displacements in endogenous variables can be found directly by substituting the solution to (14) into (9) to (13).

The changes in social welfare resulting from the shift in the storage supply curve can be measured by the following:

(15) $\quad \Delta CS_1 = -p_1 Q_1 dp_1^* (1 - 0.5 dQ_1^*)$

(16) $\quad \Delta CS_2 = -p_2 Q_2 dp_2^* (1 - 0.5 dQ_2^*)$

(17) $\quad \Delta PS = p_1 Q_t dp_1^* (1 - 0.5 dQ_t^*)$

CS_1 is consumer welfare from consumption in period 1 and CS_2 is the present value of consumer welfare in period 2. The total change in the consumer surplus is $\Delta CS = \Delta CS_1 + (1-r) \Delta CS_2$. The effect on producer surplus is ΔPS. The total social value of the improvement in storage technology is given by $\Delta TS = \Delta CS + \Delta PS$.

Inspection of (13) shows that p_2 will always fall when storage technology is improved (the second term on the right hand side of (13), which is negative, will dominate the first term regardless of the sign of dp_1). In other words, when storage costs or losses are reduced, more supplies are delivered to the non-production period.

The effect of technical change on p_1, however, is ambiguous. In (14), the first two terms of the numerator are positive while the third term is negative (the denominator is always positive). Which terms dominate depends, among other things, on the relative strengths of the technical change parameters.

The effect on p_1 becomes clearer when we consider each type of technical change separately. When technical change is modelled by a change in the marginal cost of marketing inputs (i.e. $\beta > 0$ and $\alpha = 0$), dp_i simplifies to:

(18) $\quad dp_1^* = \dfrac{Q_2 \eta_2 \rho \phi^2 \beta}{p_2 Q_T \epsilon + p_2 Q_1 \eta_1 + p_1 Q_2 \eta_2 \rho \phi^2}$

which is unambiguously positive. A reduction in the marginal cost of storage (with no change in storage losses) increases the period 1 price and causes an increase in both the quantity stored and quantity produced. The average price received by farmers also increases.

This situation is depicted in Figure 2. The storage supply curve shifts downward in a parallel fashion from StS to StS'. Farmers respond by increasing the quantity stored and period 2 prices fall from p_2 to p_2'. The increase in storage comes about from an increase in production and a decline in consumption in period 1. Period 1 price increases from p_1 to p_1'.

The shaded areas indicate the effects of the marketing improvement on welfare surpluses. Consumers gain A in period 2 but lose B in period 1. Producers gain B + C. Region B is transferred from consumers to producers and C is a net welfare gain. Producers will always benefit from this type of technical change although the effect on consumers is ambiguous. Total welfare surplus increases by A + C.

When new technology reduces storage losses ($\alpha>0$ and $\beta=0$), dp_i becomes

$$(19) \quad dp_1^* = \frac{Q_2 \alpha [\eta_2 \rho \phi (p_1 + C_s) - p_2]}{p_2 Q_T \varepsilon + p_2 Q_1 \eta_1 + p_1 Q_2 \eta_2 \rho \phi^2}$$

The sign of (19) cannot be determined without additional information. However, note that $p_2 \approx \rho\phi(p_1 + C_s)$. Substituting this into (19) yields

$$(20) \quad dp_1^* = \frac{Q_2 \alpha p_2 (\eta_2 - 1)}{p_2 Q_T \varepsilon + p_2 Q_1 \eta_1 + p_1 Q_2 \eta_2 \rho \phi^2}$$

Equation (20) shows that when technical change is modelled as a reduction in storage losses, p_1 is likely to fall, except when $\eta_2 > 1$. Since the demand elasticity for most agricultural products is significantly less than 1, there is a strong likelihood that prices in both periods will fall when storage losses are reduced.

In this situation the additional food made available from the reduction in storage losses is being allocated to consumption in both periods. This is illustrated in Figure 3, where a new storage technology eliminates storage losses. This shifts the storage supply curve downward (in a pivotal fashion) from StS to StS', and the excess supply curve from ES to ES'. Prior to the introduction of the new technology, Q_s is stored but only Q_2 reaches the market in the non-production period. The difference, $Q_s - Q_2$, is the amount lost in storage. With the new technology, farmers are able to reduce production and increase market deliveries in both periods. Consumers gain area A in period 2 and B in period 1. Producers lose B + C in quasi-rents. Region C is the welfare loss resulting from withdrawing resources from production or from transferring resources to other uses with lower social value. Total welfare changes by A - C.

Figure 2. Welfare effects from a reduction in storage costs.

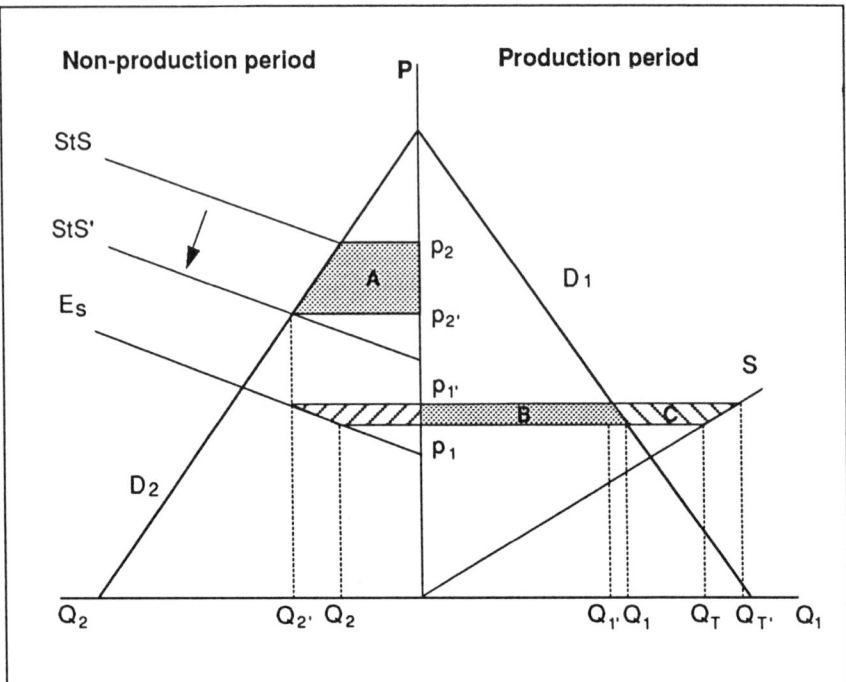

In the situation shown in Figure 3, producers lose and consumers gain from technical change. This is quite different from the case depicted in Figure 2. This demonstrates the importance of the nature of the supply shift in determining the distribution of welfare benefits among producers and consumers. The model also suggests which type of supply shift is appropriate. A reduction in marginal storage costs implies a parallel shift in supply of storage while a reduction in the rate of storage losses implies a pivotal shift.

Welfare Benefits from Improved Potato Storage in Tunisia

In Tunisia, total annual potato production between 1987 and 1990 averaged 191,000 tons per year. Three potato crops are harvested annually: the *Saison* crop between May and July (95,000 t), and *Arrière-Saison* crop from November to February (77,000 t), and the *Primeur* crop in March and April (19,000 t) (Ministry of Agriculture 1990). Potatoes can be produced year-round except during the hot summer months. From August to October, market supplies of potatoes come entirely from storage of a part of the *Saison* crop. According to data on monthly potato sales in the Tunis wholesale vegetable market (the main farm-to-retail transaction point for the Tunisian potato crop), it appears that

Figure 3. Welfare effects from a reduction in storage losses.

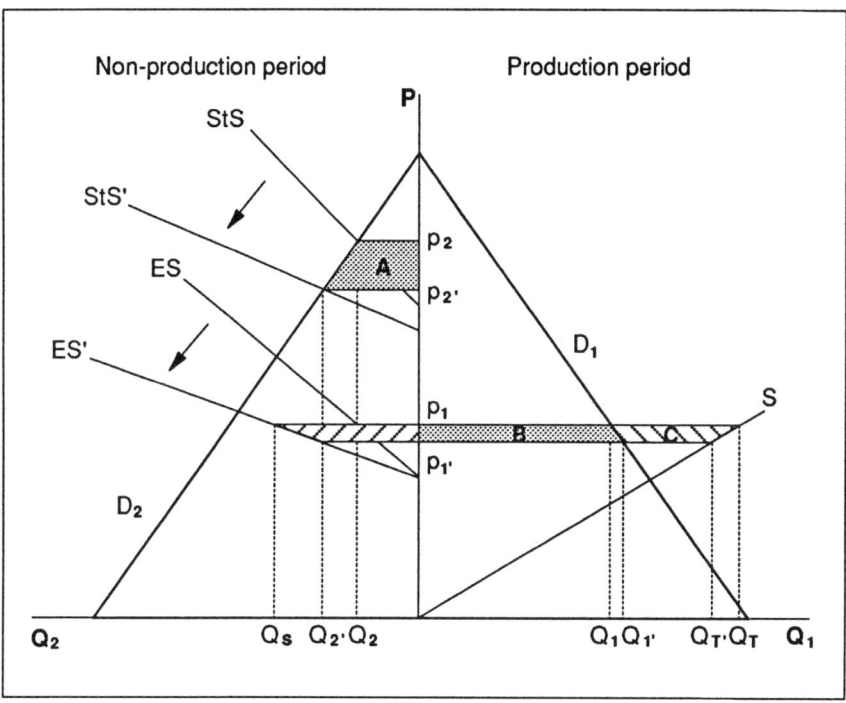

about 40% of the *Saison* crop is kept in farm stores for later sale during the summer months (Interprofessional Vegetable Group n.d.). Potato prices follow the seasonal supply of potatoes. Retail potato prices in Tunis averaged 335 Tunisian Dinars per ton (TD/t)[5] during the May-July harvest period and rose to 430 TD/t during August-October (1986-1990 average prices). Prices fell again to around 270 TD/t in November-January when the *Arrière-Saison* crop reached the market (National Statistics Institute monthly series, 1975 onward).

Farm potato stores are unrefrigerated and are vulnerable to a high rate of loss from transpiration and shrinkage, insect pests, and other pathogens (von Arx et al. 1988). On-farm storage trials conducted in 1990 showed that transpiration and shrinkage accounted for about 11% weight loss over three months of storage from June to September (Ben Salah et al. forthcoming). Infestation by the potato tuber moth (*Phthorimaea Operculella, Zeller*) is a major threat to potato stores. In fact, the potato tuber moth is the principal insect pest of potato in North Africa and is primarily a storage pest (Raman et

---

[5] All prices are in 1990 values, having been deflated by the monthly consumer price index (National Statistics Institute). One Tunisian Dinar is about $1.10.

al. 1987). Farm surveys have observed potato stores that have been completely lost after three months of storage due to insect infestation (von Arx et al. 1988).

Research on improving potato storage management in Tunisia began in the late 1970s. During the 1980s, several improved methods of pest control were disseminated to farmers, including new chemical treatments, biological controls, and improved cultural practices. Farm surveys conducted over this period have documented the diffusion of improved pest and storage management methods (von Arx et al. 1987; Fuglie et al. 1993). These efforts have been highly successful at disseminating improved methods of potato tuber moth control, especially the use of cultural practices and insecticides. Samples taken from 40 farm stores during the summer of 1990 did not find any stores in which pest damage exceeded an economic threshold (CIP 1992). However, estimates of storage losses based on storage sampling must be interpreted cautiously. Actually measuring the impact of insect infestation through sampling faces both practical and conceptual limitations. Farmers may be reluctant to have their stores disturbed in order to accurately sample their stores for damages. Furthermore, farmers can often avoid outright quantity losses by liquidating their stores upon observing signs of infestation. Potato farmers in Tunisia clearly follow this strategy. They may sell their stores upon noticing a buildup of insect damage. Since the market tolerates a low level of infestation, farmers can avoid most quantity losses by selling early. In this case, storage "losses" are in terms of lower prices received rather than in quantities discarded (von Arx et al. 1988).

An indirect way of measuring the effect of improvements in storage technology is to analyze trends in seasonal price movements, or "storage margins." The storage margin is the price rise between production and non-production periods. If an improved storage technology is widely adopted in a competitive market, the storage margin would be expected to fall (Gardner 1975). Lower loss rates would result in increased supplies being delivered in the non-production period, and the seasonal distribution of the crop would be smoothed.

Retail and wholesale potato price data between 1975 and 1990 (National Statistics Institute, monthly series, 1975 onward) were analyzed to determine shifts in storage margins before and after the availability of improved storage technology. The seasonal price spread (storage margin) for each year was calculated by taking the difference between the average price during the storage sale period (August, September, and October) and the harvest period (May, June, and July). Monthly retail and wholesale prices were weighted by monthly potato sales in the Tunis wholesale vegetable market (Interprofessional Vegetable Group n.d.) and deflated by a monthly consumer price index (National Statistics Institute 1975 onward).

This analysis suggests that the storage margin declined significantly over this period. The average value of the seasonal storage margin during

This analysis suggests that the storage margin declined significantly over this period. The average value of the seasonal storage margin during 1975-1979 was 136 TD/t at the retail level. During 1986-1990, the average storage margin was only 95 TD/t, or about two-thirds the level of 11 years earlier. Using wholesale prices, storage margins fell from 134 TD/t to 79 TD/t over the same period, or by about 40%.

The seasonal price relationship derived in (4) can be used to derive the implicit rate of storage losses δ that would account for the observed margins. Solving (4) for the rate of storage loss δ yields

$$(21) \quad \delta = 1 - \frac{(p_1 + C_s)}{p_2(1 - r)}$$

Using retail prices and assuming an opportunity cost of farm capital of 2% per month, the observed storage margins are consistent with storage losses of 20% in the late 1970s and 11% in the late 1980s. The 1980s rate is consistent with the rate of losses from transpiration and shrinkage alone, without additional losses from pest damages. The 1970s' rate of 20% includes losses due to pest damage prior to the availability of improved pest control methods. The corresponding rate of losses implied by the wholesale price margins are 26% in the 1970s and 12% in the 1980s. Both retail and wholesale price data strongly support the hypothesis that significant improvements have taken place in storage technology.

These storage loss rates are consistent with storage losses observed for root and tuber crops in developing countries but are higher than loss rates observed for grains. Youdeowei (1989) estimated that storage losses from insect pests in Sub-Saharan Africa range from 5% to 70%, depending on the crop and environmental conditions. Horton (1988) reported that for root and tuber crops, storage losses from shrinkage, rot, and pest damage range from 10% to 30% over a typical storage season; while Lipton (1972) reported average storage losses for grains in the tropics to range from 4% to 8%.

The storage margin analysis suggests that the loss rate for potato storage in Tunisia declined by about 10% or more between the late 1970s and the late 1980s. However, there is a significant margin of error in this estimation. In the empirical analysis, the reduction in storage losses is varied to determine the sensitivity of the results to this estimate. In sensitivity analysis, alternative loss rates of 5%, 10%, and 15% were assumed.

Changes in the marginal cost of storage inputs might also affect storage margins. The adoption of new pest control inputs would increase these costs if insecticide application increased. However, an assessment of potato storage costs from a farm survey in Tunisia showed that insecticide application costs make up only a small fraction of storage costs (Fuglie 1993). Furthermore, better application methods have resulted in more thorough coverage while keeping application rates to a minimum (Fuglie et al. 1993). In the empirical analysis, the marginal cost of storage C_s is assumed to have remained constant while the rate of storage losses δ fell, through the application of improved pest control technology.

To complete the model, estimates of demand and supply elasticities are drawn from other studies. An analysis of seasonal potato demand in Tunisia (Fuglie 1991) estimated the own-price demand elasticity of potatoes to be 0.4 during the *Saison* harvest period and 0.8 during the storage months. Chavas (1984) estimated the short- and long-run supply elasticities for horticultural crops in Tunisia to be 0.17 and 0.37, respectively. Since potatoes are grown on irrigated farms which also produce other horticultural crops which compete for the same land and water resources, these estimates probably represent the lower bounds of potato supply elasticity.

Table 1 gives the effects of the marketing improvement on total economic welfare and the surpluses going to consumers and producers. Sensitivity analysis shows the welfare effects under different sets of assumptions about the parameter values. Assuming that improved pest management reduced the rate of storage losses by 10%, the total change in welfare benefits ranged between 2.171 million TD and 2.987 million TD

Table 1. Welfare effects from a reduction in potato storage costs.

Elasticities			Welfare effects (figures in 000 Dinars/yr)		
Demand		Supply			
η_1	η_2	σ	ΔTS	ΔCS	ΔPS
0.1	0.2	0.0	2,987	13,336	-10,349
0.4	0.8	0.0	2,250	2,888	-638
0.7	1.4	0.0	2,171	1,423	748
0.1	0.2	0.2	2,458	6,612	-4,154
0.4	0.8	0.2	2,171	1,423	748
0.7	1.4	0.2	2,187	1,567	620
0.1	0.2	0.4	2,325	4,924	-2,598
0.4	0.7	0.4	2,222	2,590	-368
0.7	1.4	0.4	2,198	1,669	529
5% reduction in losses			1,011	1226	-215
10% reduction in losses			2,233	2,699	-466
15% reduction in losses			3,685	4,442	-757

η_t is the demand elasticity in period t and σ is the supply elasticity.
ΔCS = change in consumer's surplus and ΔPS=change in producer's surplus.
ΔTS = change in total social welfare (may not equal ΔCS+ΔPS due to rounding).
The first nine rows assume 10% reduction in storage losses and vary the elasticities of demand and supply. The last three rows assume $\eta_1 = 0.4$, $\eta_2 = 0.8$ and $\sigma = 0.2$ and vary the rate of loss/reduction.

annually, depending on the values of the supply and demand elasticities. Varying the elasticity values has a much more significant effect on the distribution of benefits among producers and consumers than on total benefits. Improved storage technology of a commodity with inelastic demand tends to transfer welfare surpluses from producers to consumers. When demand is relatively elastic, total benefits are shared between producers and consumers. Producers benefit from higher average prices and consumers benefit from a more evenly distributed supply.

Under what we consider to be the most likely set of parameter values ($\eta_1 = 0.4$, $\eta_2 = 0.8$, $\sigma = 0.2$ and a reduction in the rate of storage losses from 21% to 11%) the total change in welfare surplus equals 2.233 million TD annually, or 10.5% of the gross wholesale value of the *Saison* crop. At the lower and upper ranges of the estimates of loss reduction (5% and 15% reduction in losses) the estimate of the total welfare benefits from improved potato storage ranges from 1.011 million TD to 3.685 million TD.

Summary

Increasing the productivity of marketing services will affect not only the quantity marketed but also the quantity produced through the equilibrium price effects. Total food supply available for consumption may also be increased if new marketing technology reduces the rate of losses.

The distribution of welfare gains among producers and consumers from an improvement in marketing depends on the nature of the storage supply shift and on the response of supply and demand to changes in market prices. New storage technology that reduces the rate of storage losses can increase the quantities delivered to the market in both production and non-production periods. Technology that reduces the marginal cost of storage will reduce market prices in the non-production period but will increase the price at harvest if the increase in the quantity stored exceeds the production response. Consumers benefit the most from improvements in the storage of staple commodities since the seasonal variability in food prices and quantities is reduced. Producers, on the other hand, would prefer improvements in storage technology for price-elastic commodities since the price depression from increased market quantities is less.

The empirical example given in this chapter showed how a relatively modest research program to improve potato storage methods in Tunisia resulted in significant economic gains. Marketing productivity was enhanced by improving the control of the potato tuber moth, a major storage pest, and thereby reducing storage losses. By the early 1990s, social benefits from improved seasonal distribution of the potato crop were estimated to be between 1.0 and 3.7 millions Tunisian Dinars annually, with our "best guess" at 2.2 million Dinars (about 8% of the gross annual market value of the *Saison* crop).

Acknowledgments

This research was conducted while the author was a Rockefeller Foundation Research Fellow with the International Potato Center. The generous support of the Rockefeller Foundation and the International Potato Center for this research is gratefully acknowledged. Tom Walker, Gregory Scott, Roger Cortbaoui, Margriet Caswell, Jet Yee, and George Frisvold made valuable comments on earlier drafts of this chapter. They are not responsible for remaining errors, however. The views expressed are the author's alone, and no official endorsement by the USDA, the Rockefeller Foundation, or the International Potato Center should be inferred.

References

Alston, J. M. 1991. Research benefits in a multimarket setting: A review. *Review of Marketing and Agricultural Economics* 59:23-52.

Alston, J. M. and G. Scobie. 1983. Distribution of research gains in multistage production systems: Comment. *American Journal of Agricultural Economics* 65:353-356.

Ben Salah, H., K. Fuglie, A. Ben Temime, A. Rahmouni and M. Cheikh. *Developpment d'une strategie de lutte integré contre la teigne de la pomme de terre*, Phthorimaea operculelle (Zeller), *dans les exploitations agricoles de Tunisie. An. Inst. Nat. Rech. Agron. Tunisie* (forthcoming, in French).

Brennen, M. J. 1958. The supply of storage. *American Economic Review* 48:50-72.

Chavas, Jean-Paul. 1984. *Un modele econometrique de l'agriculture Tunisienne.* Final Report 90-4, Agricultural Policy Implementation Project. Ministry of Agriculture, Tunis, Tunisia (in French).

CIP. 1992. *1992 Annual report.* International Potato Center, Lima, Peru.

Fuglie, K. O. 1993. *How to get higher prices for your potatoes.* Social Science Training and Extension Bulletin. International Potato Center, Lima, Peru.

_____. 1991. *The demand for potatoes in Tunisia.* Working Paper No. 1991-6. Lima, Peru: Social Science Department, International Potato Center.

Fuglie, K.O., H. Ben Salah, M. Essamet, A. Ben Temime, and A. Rahmouni. 1993. The development and adoption of integrated pest management of the potato tuber moth, *Phthorimaea Operculella* (Zeller), in Tunisia. *Insect Science Applications* 14(4):501-509.

Gardner, B.L. 1975. The farm-retail price spread in a competitive food industry. *American Journal of Agricultural Economics* 57:399-409.

Horton, D. 1988. *Underground crops: Long-term trends in production of roots and tubers*. Morrilton, AR, USA: Winrock International.

Interprofessional Vegetable Group. n.d. *Groupement interprofessional des legumes*. Unpublished data. Ministry of Agriculture, Tunis, Tunisia.

Jones, W.O. 1972. *Marketing food staples in tropical Africa*. Ithaca, NY, USA: Cornell University Press.

Lindner, R.J. and F.G. Jarrett. 1978. Supply shifts and the size of research benefits. *American Journal of Agricultural Economics* 60:48-58.

Lipton, M. 1972. Comment on post-harvest food conservation. In *Nutritional policy implementation: Issues and experience* (N.S. Scrimshaw and M.B. Wallerstein, eds.). New York, NY, USA: Plenum Press.

Massel, B. E. 1969. Price stabilization and welfare. *Quarterly Journal of Economics* 83:284-298.

Ministry of Agriculture. 1990. *Annuaires des statistique agricole*. Tunis, Tunisia: Ministry of Agriculture (in French).

Muth, R.F. 1964. The derived demand curve for a productive factor and the industry supply curve. *Oxford Economic Papers* 16:221-234.

National Statistics Institute. 1975 onward. *Bulletin mensuel de statistique*. Tunis, Tunisia: Ministry of Planning, various issues (in French).

Norton, G.W. and J.S. Davis. 1981. Evaluating returns to agricultural research: A review. *American Journal of Agricultural Economics* 63:685-699.

Raman, K.V., R.H. Booth and M. Palacios. 1987. Control of potato tuber moth *Phthorimaea operculella* (Zeller) in rustic potato stores. *Tropical Science* 27:175-194.

Renkow, M. 1990. Household inventories and marketed surplus in semisubsistence agriculture. *American Journal of Agricultural Economics* 72:664-675.

Ruttan, V.W. 1969. Agricultural product and factor markets in Southeast Asia. *Economic Development Cultural Change* 17:501-519.

Scott, G. 1985. *Markets, myths, and middlemen: A study of potato marketing in Peru*. Lima, Peru: International Potato Center.

Singh, R.P., L. Squire, and J. Strauss, eds. 1986. *Agricultural household models*. Baltimore, MD, USA: The Johns Hopkins University Press.

von Arx, R., J. Goueder, M. Cheikh, and A. Ben Temime. 1987. Integrated control of potato tubermoth *Phthorimaea Operculella* (Zeller). *Insect Science Applications* 8:989-994.

von Arx, R. P. T. Ewell, J. Goueder, M. Essamet, M. Cheikh, and A. Ben Temime. 1988. *Management of the potato tubermoth by Tunisian farmers:*

A report of on-farm monitoring and a socioeconomic survey. Lima, Peru: International Potato Center.

Wohlgenant, M. 1985. Competitive storage, rational expectations, and short-run food price determination. *American Journal of Agricultural Economics* 67:739-48.

Working, H. 1949. The theory of the price of storage. *American Economic Review* 39:1254-1262.

Youdeowei, A. 1989. Major arthropod pests of food and industrial crops of Africa and their economic importance. In *Biological control: A sustainable solution to crop pest problems in Africa* (J.S. Yaninek and H.R. Herren, eds.). International Institute of Tropical Agriculture, Ibadan, Nigeria.

19

Spatial Equilibrium Models in Agricultural Marketing Research: A Simplified Exposition

J. Krishnaiah[1]

Abstract

This chapter provides a simplified exposition of the basic understanding of a spatial equilibrium model (SEM), types of spatial equilibrium models, and purpose of SEM. A geometric and mathematical model with a hypothetical example, the conditions under which a programming approach is required, and the merits and demerits of linear and quadratic programming approaches are discussed. A three-commodity, three-region spatial price equilibrium and area allocation model was developed for empirical application to the food grain sector to determine optimal spatial crop allocation, commodity flows, and prices in Andhra Pradesh.

Key words: Spatial equilibrium model, food grain, India, marketing.

Equilibrium

Equilibrium is characterized by the acquiescence of buyers and sellers, in that no participant in the market has an incentive to modify his behavior. An equilibrium exists when, at a certain positive price, the quantity demanded (qd) is equal to the quantity supplied (qs). The price at which qd = qs is the equilibrium price. At such a price, there is neither excess demand nor excess supply (negatively excess demand). Thus, an equilibrium price can be defined as the price at which there is no excess demand and at which the market is cleared. In conventional terms, equilibrium will exist if the demand and supply curves have at least one point in common in the non-negative quadrant.

---

[1] Associate Professor, Department of Agricultural Economics, College of Agriculture, A.P. Agricultural University, Hyderabad-500 030, A.P., India.

General Competitive Spatial Equilibrium

General competitive spatial equilibrium is said to be attained if conditions are met in four areas.

Market equilibrium

- Homogeneity and uniqueness of commodity prices for all consumers and producers in each country or region. This condition states that each commodity with the same quantity and quality characteristics has only one price throughout the economy; and homogeneity and uniqueness of transport costs or prices of moving any commodity from one country or region to any other country or region by any transportation output generated by any country or region. This condition specifies that unit transport costs between each pair of trading regions are constant irrespective of the distance moved.
- No excess demand for any commodity in any country, and efficient market pricing; and no excess demand for transportation output between any pair of countries, and efficient pricing of transport output. These conditions specify that when the market price for the commodity is positive, there is no excess supply or demand and when there is a positive excess supply, the commodity price must be zero at equilibrium.
- Locational price equilibrium that stipulates the efficient pricing and allocation of commodities over space. This condition states that: (1) the price in the importing country must be exactly equal to the price in the exporting country, plus the unit transportation cost (price) between them and (2) when the latter price is larger than the former, there will be no flows between them.

Consumer equilibrium (consumption efficiency) which stipulates that each consumer maximizes his utility subject to his income constraint.

Producer equilibrium (production efficiency) which stipulates that each producer maximizes his profits, subject to his production, technological, and institutional constraints.

Balance of payments equilibrium which states that the value of exports plus income from export activities plus dividends received from abroad should be equal to the value of imports plus dividend payments to individuals abroad.

Spatial Price Equilibrium

In many practical spatial equilibrium problems, a sector or a part of the economy is handled as the object of investigation for attaining certain localized objectives such as (regional, sectoral, etc.) welfare maximization, profit maximization, cost minimization, etc. Certain unknowns are taken as given and due to this, all things being equal, an economy is treated as facing a partial equilibrium situation or spatial price equilibrium. Thus, an economy is said to be in a spatial price equilibrium if the conditions of "market equilibriums" are met.

The Spatial Equilibrium Model (SEM)

A spatial model is a theoretical construct having space as one of its components. Spatial Equilibrium Model (SEM) characterizes several economic activities: the regional locations of production; the regional levels of consumption and relative level of prices; and the formulation of the equilibrium situation of the economy. In an economy where demands, supplies, and transport costs are known for each geographical area, the model could be used to determine the optimum set of prices and geographical flows. Given two or more locations, the demand and supply functions for a given product in terms of its market price at that location, and unit transport costs for carrying the product between these locations, SEM gives competitive equilibrium prices in each location, the amounts supplied and demanded in each location, and the level of exports and imports. These models include formulations commonly called activity analysis models, inter-regional competition models, transportation models, spatial equilibrium models, plant location models, and simulation models. Although several meaningful classifications could be used, the usual distinction is to group the models into simulation models based on systems of estimation equations (empirical but not for optimization), and activity analysis models involving physical production activities and demand relationships (normative and optimizing). SEM, the subject of this chapter, falls under the second category.

Activity analysis type models

Activity analysis type models usually specify discrete regions representing producing and consuming points, although sometimes market area boundaries are determined by the model itself. Regional consumption might be pre-assigned, or treated as a function of local price. For supply functions, however, production costs for one or more levels in the production process are specified for each region. Under the assumption of profit maximizing behavior at all production levels, net consumer surplus could be maximized to yield equilibrium shipping patterns, regional production, and relative and absolute prices for all levels of activity, as well as final regional consumption. A perfectly competitive market is assumed, but consideration of other types of market behavior is also possible.

Simulation models

These models may use the simultaneous equation approach consisting of linear behavioral and definitional equations and/or bilinear equilibrium conditions, non-stochastic, or dynamic competitive equilibrium conditions. Normally, the effects of hypothetical scenarios like increasing crop productivity and other policy changes on crop production, consumption, prices, and farmer's income could be simulated.

Purpose of SEM

The equilibrium models reflect specifications which permit economic forces over sectors and space to act in unison to determine the optimum price and allocation outcomes. A great variety of situations can be handled by these specifications. In an economy where demands, supplies, and transport costs are known for each geographical area, the SEM could be used to determine the optimum set of geographical flows and prices. Alternatively, if the prices of and the demands for the final commodities are assumed known, along with the primary commodity endowments, technical conditions of production, and transport costs for each geographical area, the SEM could be used to determine the competitive spatial price and allocation scheme. In the activity analysis models, competitive behavior can be specified for all participants and competitive spatial equilibrium could be taken as the norm. The specifications could be altered to accommodate other types of market behavior. The market-oriented models could be changed so that for either a centralized or decentralized decision situation, the behavior of a monopolist or monopsonist would be reflected. For situations involving countries, such things as trade agreements, import tariffs, export subsidies, import quota, or ad valorem tariffs do exist and do alter the pricing and allocation outcomes. Each of these simulations can be handled in the model by introducing additional restrictions or modifying the data used. For instance, in the partial equilibrium market-oriented spatial model, a tariff could be introduced as an addition to the transport cost between countries and an export subsidy could be treated as a negative tariff. In addition, the gains to the society through inter-regional trade, such as producers' surplus, consumers' surplus, and economic surplus can be effectively assessed through SEM. The impact of trade restrictions can also be evaluated.

Simplified Exposition of SEM

For a better understanding of spatial equilibrium, the techniques of spatial equilibrium modelling can be conveniently grouped under two categories: the geometrical model and the mathematical model.

Geometrical model

A graphical approach for the spatial equilibrium problem could be followed when there are two regions and one commodity. For brevity, one can consider situations with and without trade. In the situation without trade, transport costs are assumed to be equal to zero and in the situation with trade there is a specific transport cost. Let the supply and demand functions be S_1 and D_1 and S_2 and D_2 in regions 1 and 2, respectively. If trade were not allowed, each region would reach equilibrium at the intersection of its supply and demand functions. However, if trade were allowed, traders would recognize the opportunity to profit by arbitrating products from region 1 to region 2. The quantity offered for trade in region 1 is the difference between the quantity producers supply and that which consumers demand at prices higher than the equilibrium price (P^e_1). This is treated as excess supply function ES_1 as shown in the center graph of Figure 1. The quantity region 2 offers to purchase is the difference between the quantity consumers demand and producers supply at prices lower than P^e_2. This is treated as ED_2 in the center graph of Figure 1. Equilibrium is reached at the intersection of ED_2 and ES_1. Price is equal in both the markets. Equilibrium production and consumption are q^s_1 and q^d_1 in region 1 and q^s_2 and q^d_2 in region 2, and the equilibrium level of trade is q_{12}. The quantity traded between the two regions is equal to the difference between the quantities supplied and demanded within each region, i.e., $(q^s_1 - q^d_1) = q_{12} = (q^d_2 - q^s_2)$. The model gives rise to three sets of equilibrium conditions:

1. Demand in each region equals trade flows to the region, i.e., $q^d_1 = q_{11}$ and $q^d_2 = q_{12} + q_{22}$,

2. Production in a region equals trade flows from the regions, i.e., $q^s_1 = q_{11} + q_{12}$ and $q^s_2 = q_{22}$, and

3. There is an implied condition that the equilibrium prices and quantities must lie on the supply and demand functions.

There is also an effect on community welfare when trade is allowed. For region 1, as price increases from P^e_1 to P_1, producers gain $(a_1 + b_1 + c_1)$ producer surplus, but consumers lose $(a_1 + b_1)$ consumer surplus. In this connection, it may be mentioned that producers' surplus is defined as the revenue received in excess of the amount that the producer would have been willing to accept for each unit produced. Consumers' surplus is defined as the area between the demand curve and the price line. Hence, region 1 has a net gain of c_1 in welfare. Since the excess supply function is derived by subtracting quantity demanded from the quantity supplied at prices higher than P^e_1, i.e., $q_{12} = q^s_1 - q^d_1$, then by construction $c_1 = z_1$ in the center graph of Figure 1. In region 2, as price falls from P^e_2 to P_2, the consumers gain $(a_2 + b_2 + c_2)$ consumer surplus, but producers lose (a_2) producer surplus. Thus, region 2 experiences a net gain in welfare of $(b_2 + c_2)$ which is equal to z_2. Hence, at equilibrium, the community defined by regions 1 and 2 experiences a net gain in community welfare of $(z_1 + z_2)$. Furthermore, equilibrium exists where $(z_1 + z_2)$ is maximized. It is the area under the excess demand function from zero trade to the optimum level of trade (q_{12}) less the area under excess supply function from zero trade to the optimum level. Simultaneously, the conditions regarding prices, demands and inflows, supplies and outflows, as well as

Figure 1. A graphical approach to spatial equilibrium.

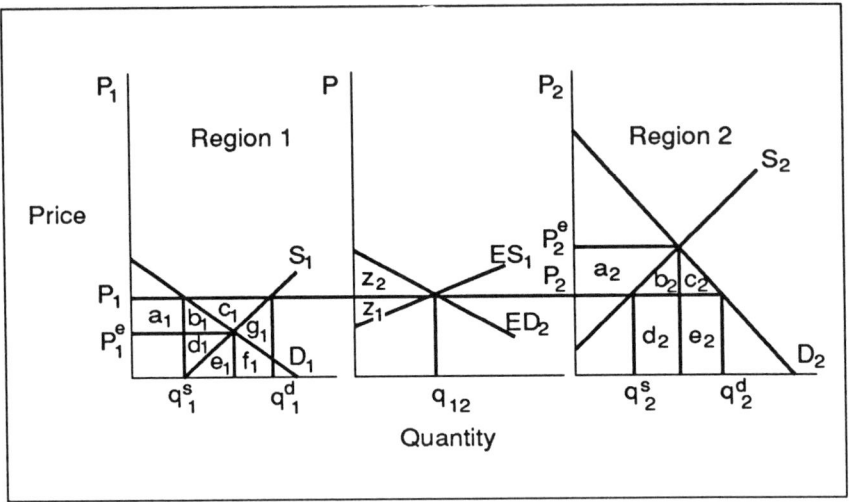

Figure 2. Two-region model.

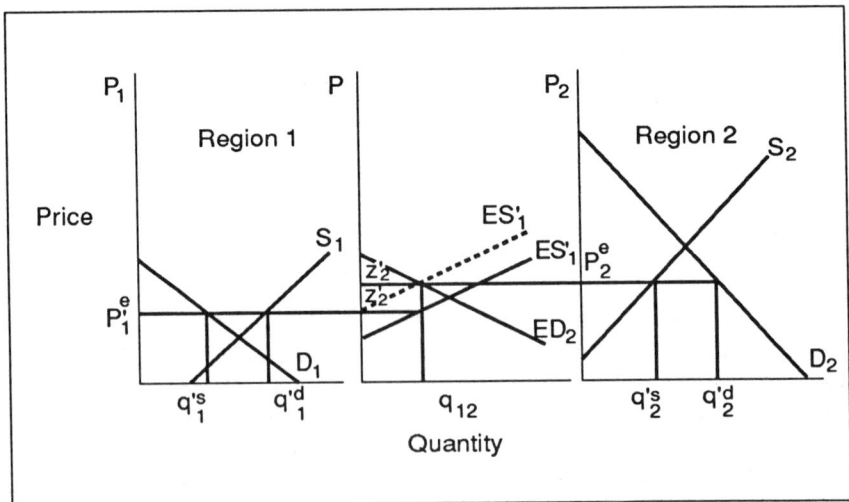

equilibrium prices and quantities which lie on the respective supply and demand functions are met.

Figure 2 presents the two-region model with a transport cost of t_{12}. This is done by shifting ES_1 upward by t_{12} (since it represents an additional cost) to ES'_1. Equilibrium is reached for region 2 at P^e_2, q^s_2, and q^d_2, and for region 1 at P^e_1, q^s_1, q^d_1. Now, equilibrium exists where $z'_1 + z'_2$ is maximized. It is possible that equilibrium may occur with no trade, in which case regional prices may differ by less than transport costs, i.e., $P_2 - P_1 < t_{12}$.

Mathematical model

There are two approaches to the mathematical model: the arithmetic approach and the programming approach. When there is a single commodity involved and there are two trading regions, a simple arithmetic approach will be followed.

Arithmetic approach

This approach can be conveniently employed in situations both with and without trade. The following step-by-step procedure can be followed for the two situations.

Case 1. Without trade:

1. Calculate excess supply in each region ($E_s = q_s - q_d$).
2. Find the equilibrium price in each region in the absence of trade ($E_s = 0$).
3. Use these prices to calculate the quantity supplied and demanded in each region.
4. Identify the potential exporting region and the potential importing region.

Case 2. With trade:

In a perfect market, prices in two regions will differ exactly by transport cost. In this example, since the no-trade price in region 2 is higher than that in region 1, it follows that $P_2 - P_1 = t_{12}$. If transport cost is greater than $P_2 - P_1$, no trade will take place. Thus, it is more accurate to write $P_2 - P_1 = t_{12}$, where no trade is done.

1. Define as quantity traded the excess supply in the exporting region which equals the negative of the excess supply in the importing region. That is, $Es_1 = E^*s_2 = q_{12}$ where $E^*s_2 = -Es_2$. Calculate Es_2.
2. Use the excess supply functions to write $P_2 - P_1 = t_{12}$, replacing Es_1 and E^*s_2 with the value q_{12}. Find q_{12} for desired level by t_{12}.

3. Find P_1 and P_2 for these values of q_{12}.
4. Calculate the quantity supplied and demanded in each region at these prices.

Illustrative example. The following is an illustration of a simple spatial equilibrium model using the arithmetic approach.

Let the supply and demand functions be as follows:

	Region 1	Region 2
Supply	$q_1^s = 2.00 + p_1$	$q_2^s = 1.75 + 0.25\, p_2$
Demand	$q_1^d = 5 - 0.5\, p_1$	$q_2^d = 5.50 - 0.50\, p_2$

Solution:

$q_1^s = 2 + P_1, \; q_1^d = 5 - 0.5 P_1, \; E_1^s = q_1^s - q_1^d = -3 + 1.5\, P_1$

$E_2^s = q_2^s - q_2^d = (1.75 + 0.25\, P_2) - (5.50 - 0.50\, P_2)$

$\qquad = -3.75 + 0.75\, P_2$

$E^*s_2 = -Es_2 = Es_1 = -3.00 + 1.50\, P_1 = -(-3.75 + 0.75\, P_2)$

If $\quad T_{12} = 0$, then $P_2 - P_1 = 0$ or $P_2 = P_1$

So $\quad -3 + 1.5\, P = 3.75 - 0.75\, P$

$\therefore 2.25 p = 6.75 \therefore P = \dfrac{6.75}{2.25} = 3$

$\therefore P_1 = P_2 = 3$

Quantity traded $(q_{12}) = 1.5$

$\qquad q_1^s = 5, \; q_1^d = 3.5$
$\qquad q_2^s = 2.5, \; q_2^d = 4$

If $\quad t_{12} = \text{Rs } 1$

Then $\quad P_2 - P_1 = t_{12}$

$\quad \therefore P_2 - P_1 = 1$
$\quad \therefore P_2 = 1 + P_1$
$\quad -3 + 1.5\, P_1 = 3.75 - 0.75\, (P_1 + 1)$
$\quad 1.5\, P_1 + 0.75\, P_1 = 3.75 + 3.0 - 0.75 = 6$

$\therefore 2.25 P_1 = 6 \therefore P_1 = \dfrac{6}{2.25} = 2.67$

$P_2 = 2.67 + 1 = 3.67$
$q_{12} = -3.00 + 1.50\, (2.67) = -3 + 4 = 1$
$\quad \therefore q_1^s = 4.67 \qquad\qquad q_2^s = 2.67$
$\qquad q_1^d = 0.67 \qquad\qquad q_2^d = 3.67$

Programming approach

When the regions and commodities involved in trade are more than one, neither a geometric model nor an arithmetic approach can be applied for a solution to the spatial equilibrium problem. In such cases, the mathematical programming approach is useful. The programming approach again depends on the objective function. If it is a linear function of the decision variables, a linear programming (LP) approach is appropriate. On the other hand, if the objective function contains a quadratic term, then the quadratic programming (QP) approach would be an appropriate tool.

Application of the linear programming technique to SEM

Samuelson (1952) first pointed out that a class of single commodity spatial price equilibrium problems such as those posed by Enke (1951) can be solved by using such mathematical programming methods as gradient methods. Special single as well as multi-product cases when (a) the demand functions and the supply functions are both linear, and (b) the demand functions are linear and supplies are generated by an activity analysis format were developed by Takayama and Judge (1964 a, 1964b). Later, LP found wide applicability. Von Oppen and Scott (1976); Randhawa and Heady (1964); Kanbur (1969); Onyenwaku, Ogunfowora, and Falusi (1982); Baumes and McCarl (1978) are some of those researchers who applied LP.

Drawbacks of the LP approach

SEMs based on LP, however, have certain disadvantages. In the linear activity analysis model, the prices, and therefore, the demand quantities are assumed known. In real world situations, prices and quantities are decision variables. Within the framework of LP formulation, the competitive spatial equilibrium prices are derived as a result of optimum production and flows. A new set of equilibrium prices might be derived by adding a constant to all regional prices and the production and the flow solution might still remain optimal. This arbitrariness of equilibrium prices, therefore, limits their valuation in the determination of the absolute price level.

Why QP in spatial equilibrium modelling?

QP would determine production and regional flows through primal and optimal prices through dual. While the primary problem ensures that the required quantity conditions are met, its duality ensures that the optimum consumption, production, and price conditions are satisfied.

Development of the QP approach

Kuhn and Tucker in 1950 published their important article on non-linear programming and laid the groundwork for developments in this area. The book by Arrow et al. which appeared in 1958, was an important addition to the non-linear programming literature. Articles by Wolfe (1959) and Barankin and Dorfman (1958) are important foundations in developing solution algorithms for the QP problem.

Following Wolfe's procedure, Takayama and Judge (1964c) indicated how a spatial equilibrium formulation in the case of linear, well-behaved regional demand and supply functions could be converted to a QP problem. This work was followed by Plessner and Heady (1965); Yaron et al. (1965); and Plessner (1967), which contributed to the formulation of the QP model and investigated ways of handling the problem when the market demand functions do not satisfy the integrability condition (asymmetric). Later QP found wide applicability. Martin (1972, 1981); Hardaker (1983); and Fuchs et al. (1974) applied QP with refinements in the analytical approach. A number of spatial models with government intervention in the form of trade restrictions and price controls have come up. Some of these include Abbot (1979); Von Oppen (1978); Krishnaiah and Krishnamoorthy (1988); Zwart and Meilke (1979); Zwart and Blandford (1989); and Devadoss (1992).

Empirical Application of SEM to Agricultural Marketing Research

The major objective of this chapter is to illustrate the application of SEM in agricultural marketing research. For this purpose, a three-commodity, three-region, spatial price equilibrium and area allocation model was developed for empirical application to the food grain sector in Andhra Pradesh. It was intended to determine the optimal pattern of crop allocation, commodity flows, and price outcomes consistent with optimal spatial allocation of selected food grains.

Materials and methods

Coastal Andhra, Rayalaseema, and Telangana are the regions, and rice, sorghum, and pulses the crops considered for empirical study. The relevant data are drawn from secondary sources. Since spatial equilibrium analysis requires supply and demand functions of selected crops and their transportation costs between trading regions, these were estimated using the necessary data and appropriate methodology.

The objective function is the maximization of net social welfare (NSW) in Andhra Pradesh measured as producers' surplus and consumers' surplus minus transportation costs.

Spatial equilibrium models in agricultural marketing research

The objective function is given by

$$\text{Max. NSW} = \sum_{I=i}^{3} \sum_{j=1}^{3} \alpha_j Q^d_{ij} - 1/2 Q'^d_{ij} \beta_{ij} Q^d_{ij} - V_{ij} Q^S_{ij} - 1/2 Q'^S_{ij} H_{ij} Q^S_{ij} - \sum_{k=1}^{3} \sum_{j=1}^{3} t_{ikj} X_{ikj}$$

Subject to

$$\sum_{j=1}^{3} l_{ij} Q^s_{ij} \quad < L_i \text{ for all i, i = 1, 2, 3}$$

$$e_{ijp} Q^s_{ijp} \quad < IR_{ijp} \text{ for all i, i = 1, 2, 3}$$

where,

- Q^d_{ij} = quantity demanded of commodity j in region i,
- Q^s_{ij} = quantity supplied of commodity j in region i,
- P^d_{ij} = demand price of commodity j in region i,
- P^s_{ij} = supply price of commodity j in region i,
- l_{ij} = reciprocal of yield per unit area of crop j in region i,
- L_{ij} = land available in region i that can be put under crop j,
- e_{ijp} = reciprocal of yield per unit of irrigated area of paddy in region i,
- Q^s_{ijp} = quantity produced of commodity paddy in region i,
- Ir_{ijp} = irrigated land that can be put under crop paddy in region i,
- α_{ij} = a_{ij}/b_{ij} and $\beta_{ij} = 1/b_{ij}$,
- V_{ij} = $-c_{ij}/d_{ij}$ and $H_{ij} = 1/d_{ij}$,
- a_{ij} = intercept of demand function for commodity j in region 1,
- b_{ij} = slope coefficient of the demand function for commodity j in region 1,
- c_{ij} = intercept of supply function for commodity j in region i,
- d_{ij} = slope coefficient of the supply function for commodity j in region 1,
- t_{ik} = the unit transport cost between each pair of regions i and k of commodity j,
- X_{ikj} = the quantity of commodity j flowing from region i to k,
- i,k = 1, 2, 3 represent regions, for i ≠ k,
- j = 1, 2, 3 represent commodities.

The spatial equilibrium model applied in this study requires that the supply and demand functions be linear. If the appropriate Kuhn-Tucker necessary conditions and the Lagrangean are formed, it would yield the following equations that are to be solved for optimal solution.

(1) $Q^d_{ij} = a_{ij} - b_{ij} P^d_{ij}$
(2) $Q^s_{ij} = c_{ij} + d_{ij} P^s_{ij}$
(3) $P_{ij} - P_{kj} < t_{ikj}$ for all i, k and j for i, k, j = 1, 2, 3

(4) $$Q_{ij}^d - Q_{ij}^s + \sum_{k=1}^{3} X_{ikj} - \sum_{k=1}^{3} X_{kij} = 0$$

Land constraint

The average area under rice, sorghum, and pulses during the recent past three years in different regions was taken as the total availability of land. Similarly, the average area under irrigated paddy was taken as the area restriction for rice.

Crop yields

The average yield per hectare of paddy, sorghum, and pulses during the recent past three years were considered as the productivity levels to be used in the programming.

Andhra Pradesh is considered an open economy where commodity flow out of/into the State is also permitted within previously assigned limits. The approach of programming for spatial equilibrium is to express prices as the dependent variables. After obtaining the inverted matrices of price coefficients of supply and demand and multiplying them by their respective vectors, the objective values are obtained. Then, the land constraints and trade restrictions were imposed in the model.

Results

Table 1 shows the optimal demand, supply, and commodity flows of rice, sorghum, and pulses in different regions of Andhra Pradesh in relation to the rest of the India. From the table it is evident that Telangana is self-sufficient in rice, but deficient in sorghum and pulses. Rayalaseema is deficient in rice, but has a surplus in sorghum and pulses. Coastal Andhra has surpluses in rice and sorghum, but is deficient in pulses.

Optimal area allocation, production, and prices in different regions of Andhra Pradesh and its comparison with the existing situation is presented in Table 2. From the table, it can be observed that the optimal situation results in an increased area allocation of 23% in Telangana, 16% in Rayalaseema, 20% in Coastal Andhra, and 21% in the state as a whole. Thus, viewed from this angle, production of rice may be concentrated in Coastal Andhra, while sorghum may be concentrated in Rayalaseema because it is comparatively advantageous for those regions to do so.

Table 1. Optimal demand, supply and commodity flows of rice, sorghum, and pulses (000 t) in different regions of Andhra Pradesh in relation to rest of India.

	Region			
	Telangana	Rayalaseema	Coastal Andhra	Rest of India
Demand				
Rice	1446.68	955.08	2727.47	-
Sorghum	1060.91	81.04	26.97	-
Pulses	230.11	29.79	264.38	-
Supply				
Rice	1753.67	453.53	3541.04	-
Sorghum	733.50	317.84	609.71	-
Pulses	209.38	50.51	178.24	-
Commodity flows				
Rice			619 - - - - - - - - - - >	
		<- - - - - - - - - - - - 194.57		
	306.99 - - - - - - - - - - >			
Sorghum	<- -327.41			
			236.80 - >	
			255.32 - - - - - - - - - >	
Pulses			<- - - - - - - - - - 86.14	
	<- - - - - - - - - - - - 20.73			

Evaluating social gains through inter-regional trade

This study is intended to determine whether the overall welfare (Marshall 1959) of the society is improved due to a deliberate policy change. Changes in producers' and consumers' surpluses are calculated using the following formulae (Hardakar 1983).

$$\text{Consumers' surplus} = (\alpha - P^e)Q^d - 1/2\, Q^{'d}\, \beta\, Q^d$$

$$\text{Producers' surplus} = (P^e - V)Q^s - 1/2\, Q^{'s}\, H\, Q^s$$

where the notations are the same as explained previously.

When the producer, consumer, and aggregate economic surplus across products in each region and also across products and regions are presented in Table 3, it may be seen that the producer surplus is higher in magnitude than the consumer surplus.

Table 2. Optimal allocation of area and production and equilibrium prices of rice, sorghum, and pulses in different regions of Andhra Pradesh under optimal and existing situations (area (000 ha); production (000 t); and prices (million Rps/000 t)).

	Region							
	Telengana		Rayalaseema		Coastal Andhra		Andhra Pradesh	
	Optimal	Existing	Optimal	Existing	Optimal	Existing	Optimal	Existing
Area								
Rice	1042 (34%)	1411 (46%)	295 (41%)	3178 (44%)	2038 (63%)	2424 (74%)	3376 (48%)	4153 (59%)
Sorghum	1550 (51%)	928 (31%)	369 (51%)	236 (32%)	1277 (39%)	108 (3%)	3197 (46%)	1272 (18%)
Pulses	1134 (37%)	696 (23%)	180.46 (25%)	174 (24%)	580 (18%)	726 (22%)	1895 (27%)	1559 (22%)
Total	3727 (123%)	3036 (100%)	845 (116%)	727 (100%)	3896 (120%)	3258 (100%)	8468 (121%)	6984 (100%)
Production								
Rice	1754	1988	454	424	3541	3367	5748	5779
Sorghum	734	436	318	204	610	51	1661	690
Pulses	209	128	51	193	178	297	438	476
Total	2508	2552	822	821	4329	3628	7847	7898
Prices								
Rice	6.24	5.80	5.44	4.50	5.50	4.50	7.54[a]	4.10
Sorghum	2.43	3.25	3.22	3.30	3.16	3.90	2.85[a]	2.16
Pulses	4.44	4.62	5.00	4.33	4.07	4.51	4.35[a]	3.70

[a] Weighted average prices with quantities produced as the weights.
Figures in parentheses are percentages of figures to existing situations.

Implications for Future Use of SEM in Agricultural Marketing Research

The SEM illustrated in this chapter specified linear supply and demand functions and ignored the cross-price effects of supply due to technical and data limitations. It has also used an arbitrary price at which exports and imports take place. Therefore, future research efforts in the use of such models should incorporate cross-price effects and accommodate export or import price flexibility.

Table 3. Producers' surplus, consumers' surplus, and economic surplus (million Rps) under an optimal situation in different regions of Andra Pradesh.

	Region					At the aggregate level
	Telangana	Rayalasema	Coastal Andhra	Andhra Pradesh	Rest of India	
Producers' surplus	47,158	5,362	15,706	68,225	6,070	74,295
Consumers' surplus	9,153	3,551	9,958	22,663	-375	22,288
Economic surplus	56,311	8,913	25,664	90,888	5,695	96,583
Share of producers' surplus in regional economic surplus	84%	60%	61%	75%		77%
Share of consumers' surplus in regional economic surplus	16%	40%	39%	25%		23%

Under an optimal situation, the surpluses resulting from trade with the rest of India are evaluated considering weighted average prices of rice, sorghum, and pulses.

References

Abbot, P.C. 1979. Modelling international grain trade with government controlled markets. *American Journal of Agricultural Economics* 61(1):22-31.

Arrow, K.J., L. Hurwicz, and H. Uzawa. 1958. *Studies in linear and non-linear programming*. Stanford, CA, USA: Stanford University Press.

Barankin, E.W. and R. Dorfman. 1958. On quadratic programming. *University of California Publications in Statistics* 2:285-318.

Baumes, H.S. and B.A. McCarl. 1978. Linear programming and social welfare: Model formulation and objective function alternatives. *Canadian Journal of Agricultural Economics* 26(3):53-60.

Devadoss, S. 1992. Market interventions, international price stabilization, and welfare implications. *American Journal of Agricultural Economics* 74(2):281-290.

Enke, S.A. 1951. Equilibrium among spatially separated markets: Solution by electric analogne. *Econometrica* 19(1):40-47.

Fuchs, H.W., R.O.P. Farrish, and R. W. Bohall. 1974. A model of the US apple industry: A quadratic interregional intertemporal activity analysis formulation. *American Journal of Agricultural Economics* 56(3):739-750.

Hardaker, J.B. 1983. *Some models for assessing the economic consequences of a supply shift*. Progress Report No. 54, Economic Program,

International Crops Research Institute for Semi-Arid Tropics, Patancheru, Hyderabad, India.

Kanbur, M.G. 1969. Spatial equilibrium analysis of rice economy of South India. *Indian Journal of Agricultural Economics* 24(2):13-34.

Krishnaiah, J. and S. Krishnamoorthy. 1988. Interrelational allocation of major foodgrains in Andhra Pradesh: An application of spatial equilibrium model. *Indian Journal of Agricultural Economics* 43(1):35-43.

Kuhn H.W. and A.W. Tucker. 1950. Non-linear programming. In *Proceedings of the Second Barkeley Symposium on Mathematical Statistics and Probability* (J. Neyman, ed.). Berkeley, CA, USA: University of California Press.

Marshall, A. 1959. *Principles of economics*. London, UK: Macmillan.

Martin, L.J. 1972. *The impact of improved technology on regional production and prices of major food commodities in Uttar Pradesh*. Ann Arbor, MI, USA: University Microfilms International.

———. 1981. Quadratic single and multi-commodity models of spatial equilibrium: A simplified exposition. *Canadian Journal of Agricultural Economics* 29(1):21-48.

Onyenwaku, C.E., O. Ogunfowora, and A.O. Falusi. 1982. An interregional programming model for agricultural planning in Nigeria. *Indian Journal of Agricultural Economics* 37(1):483-493.

Plessner, Y. 1967. Activity analysis, quadratic programming and general equilibrium. *International Economic Review* 8(2):168-179.

Plessner, Y. and E.O. Heady. 1965. Competitive equilibrium solutions with quadratic programming. *Meteroeconomica* 17(2):117-130.

Randhawa, N.S. and E.O. Heady. 1964. An international programming model for agricultural planning in India. *Journal of Farm Economics* 46(1):137-149.

Samuelson, P.A. 1952. Spatial price equilibrium and linear programming. *American Economic Review* 42(3):283-303.

Takayama, T. and G.G. Judge. 1964a. Equilibrium among spatially separated markets, a reformulation. *Econometrica* 32(4):510-524.

Takayama T. and G.G. Judge. 1964b. An interregional activity analysis model of the agricultural sector. *Journal of Farm Economics* 46(2):349-365.

Takayama T. and G.G. Judge. 1964c. Spatial equilibrium and quadratic programming. *Journal of Farm Economics* 46 (1):67-93.

Von Oppen, M. and J. T. Scott. 1976. A spatial equilibrium model for plant location and inter-regional trade. *American Journal of Agricultural Economics* 58(3):437-445.

Von Oppen, M. 1978. *Agricultural marketing and aggregate productivity: A dimension to be added to agricultural market research*. Discussion paper No. 3, Economics program, International Crops Research Institute for Semi-Arid Tropics, Patancheru, Hyderabad, India.

Wolfe, P. 1959. The simplex method for quadratic programming. *Econometrica* 27(3):282-298.

Yaron, D., Y. Plessner, and E.O. Heady. 1965. Competitive equilibrium–application of mathematical programming. *Canadian Journal of Agricultural Economics* 13(1):65-79.

Zwart, A.C. and K.D. Meilke. 1979. The influence of domestic pricing policies and buffer stocks on price stability in the world wheat industry. *American Journal of Agricultural Economics* 61(3):434-447.

Zwart, A.C and D. Blandford. 1989. Market intervention and international price stability. *American Journal of Agricultural Economics* 71(3):379-388.

20

Programming Models: Potential Applications to Agricultural Marketing Research

Scott R. Jeffrey and Merle D. Faminow[1]

Abstract

This paper discusses a mathematical programming technique, Modelling to Generate Alternatives (MGA), that can be used in conjunction with linear programming to evaluate "nearly optimal" solutions for marketing problems. MGA allows planners to incorporate important objectives that are difficult to include in a mathematical model by identifying and evaluating alternative, nearly optimal solutions. Some of these solutions may better reflect the goals of decision makers. An empirical application is provided to demonstrate the potential usefulness of this technique. Other previous MGA applications are also summarized to demonstrate the relevance of MGA in addressing marketing research problems. The use of MGA to complement and enhance other forms of mathematical programming analysis is also discussed.

Key words: Sensitivity analysis, modelling to generate alternatives, Hop Skip Jump method, nearly optimal solutions.

Introduction

The study of agricultural marketing problems is an important part of applied agricultural economics research. Agricultural marketing encompasses a wide range of issues, including analysis of firm-level marketing strategies, input and output demand relationships, and optimal location and transportation studies. Typically, empirical analysis using mathematical programming is based on objective economic criteria, such as utility or profit maximization or cost minimization. However, the study of agricultural marketing problems is often

---

[1] Department of Rural Economy, University of Alberta, Edmonton, Alberta, Canada T6G 2H1; and Department of Agricultural Economics and Farm Management, University of Manitoba, Winnipeg, Manitoba, Canada R3T 2N2.

a difficult process. Actual decisions and behavior for market participants are not solely based on economic criteria, but also reflect non-economic considerations. Furthermore, data limitations tend to be serious in some circumstances; that is, consistent time series of agricultural and economic variables are frequently not available.

Linear programming has a long history of use in the study of agricultural economic problems (Heady 1954; King 1953). In the past several decades, considerable attention has been devoted to the application of linear programming and other more complicated mathematical programming techniques to agricultural problems, including issues related to agricultural marketing (e.g., Faminow and Sarhan 1983; Kaiser and Apland 1989; Frank et al. 1989). Specific benefits of using mathematical programming in the context of applied research are well-known, and include (1) long time series of data are not needed; (2) specific guidelines for achieving the "optimal" solution are provided; and (3) opportunity costs for alternative uses of resources can be deduced through analysis of the dual solution.

Also well-known are the limitations of mathematical programming. Typically, linear programming and other mathematical programming techniques involve the use of a very structured model, requiring restrictive assumptions such as linear relationships and certainty of parameters. Some of the restrictions inherent in linear programming can be overcome through the use of techniques such as separable programming, stochastic programming, goal programming, and MOTAD.[2] However, there are other limitations which tend to affect the applicability of all mathematical programming approaches to a greater or lesser extent. For example, all mathematical programming models require the assumption of complete knowledge of parameters. Furthermore, because functional formulation is predetermined, the usefulness of solutions is dependent upon an accurate representation of the objective function and constraints facing decision makers. This can create inaccuracies because the reliability of optimal solutions is reduced if the system is not completely and/or accurately modelled.

This paper presents a mathematical programming technique that provides agricultural marketing researchers with a more flexible modelling strategy through the identification and evaluation of "nearly optimal" feasible solutions. The technique, referred to as nearly optimal linear programming or Modelling to Generate Alternatives (MGA), may be implemented using commercial computer software. The philosophy of MGA is based on the fact that mathematical programming models are usually imperfect representations of the real problem; and that many agricultural economic issues involve factors or concerns that are difficult to directly quantify.

---

[2] Hazell and Norton (1986) provide a discussion of these techniques.

The MGA approach deals explicitly with the fact that there are important objectives and/or constraints that cannot be fully reflected mathematically. MGA recognizes that the goals and constraints faced by different decision makers using any given model may vary considerably. In many cases, there may be many alternative solutions within a tolerable distance of the optimal solution. Decision makers could choose one of these alternatives that is "nearly optimal" in a narrow economic sense, in order to achieve broader objectives. The MGA technique described and demonstrated below provides a methodology that allows researchers to systematically search out these nearly optimal solutions and provide decision makers with a range of alternatives.

Rational and Quasi-Rational Behavior

Economics is primarily concerned with rational decision making. Rationality is the situation in which individuals make decisions that are consistent with improving their well-being. Economists often define rationality in terms of a constrained optimization problem, with the objective to be optimized being a measure such as utility or profit. Any behavior not consistent with the solution to this type of problem would be defined as nonrational.

Mathematical programming models based on rational decision making are used for both descriptive and prescriptive purposes in agriculture.[3] These models are typically used to identify a single "optimal" solution or a limited set of alternative "baseline" solutions to a problem. These solutions are based on and apply to rational individuals, as defined earlier, and thus do not typically allow for mistakes, alternative goals, or different information sets among decision makers.

The assumption of rationality is defended by economists from two perspectives. For descriptive modelling, it is argued that nonrational decision makers will be disciplined by market forces and cannot survive in the long run, so that optimal solutions provide a long-run view of decision making. When prescribing optimal behavior, economic models are defended as a method of modelling complex choices and providing guidance to decision makers. In some cases, the model is solved and then it is assumed that decision makers in the real world act accordingly, a blend of both the descriptive and prescriptive defense.

---

[3] A descriptive use is one that focuses on explaining or predicting behavior while a prescriptive use provides a normative judgement on what decision makers ought to do. In practice, most empirical applications of mathematical programming to agriculture involve simultaneous consideration of both description and prescription.

All three arguments are subject to criticism. Russell and Thaler (1985) demonstrate that nonrational behavior is prevalent and can persist in an economy, thus disputing the first defense for assuming rationality. The second argument can also be criticized for reasons discussed earlier. Given the inflexible assumptions required in constructing and using mathematical programming models, it is less than certain that they reflect the true economic circumstances underlying decisions in the real world (i.e., the true underlying objective function and constraints). Since the third defense involves simply a combination of the first two, it is subject to both criticisms.

The validity of "optimal" mathematical programming solutions is limited by these criticisms. In particular, mathematical programming solutions and actual behavior in agricultural markets often differ substantially, suggesting that: (1) the optimal solution is wrong; (2) market discipline does not guarantee that inefficient agents are eliminated; or (3) persistent mistakes may not be fatal because divergences from "optimal" behavior are not sufficiently large to be significant. Both (2) and (3) suggest the presence of quasi-rational behavior (Russell and Thaler 1985). Quasi-rationality, as discussed by Russell and Thaler (1985), is a term used to classify systematic deviations from optimal behavior, and captures common behavior such as following "rules of thumb," which often result in nonoptimal decisions.

One suggested precaution in applied research to account for the possibility of quasi-rational behavior "is to do the estimates in an unconstrained fashion whenever it is possible" (Russell and Thaler 1985, p. 1081). Standard sensitivity analysis is one appropriate technique to address these concerns. However, because the objective function and constraints are often an imperfect representation of the relevant decision process, sensitivity analysis may not be sufficient to provide insights into quasi-rational behavior.

Modelling to Generate Alternatives (MGA)

In response to these criticisms of mathematical programming, alternative modelling techniques have been developed to generate solutions that deviate from the global optimum within an acceptable range. These techniques have not been widely used in marketing studies. Early applications of the MGA approach, discussed below, included its use by civil engineers in water resource planning problems (Chang, Brill, and Hopkins 1982; Harrington and Gidley 1985) and by economists in a farm management application (Burton et al. 1987).

MGA is based on the premise that modelling should be a tool of the decision maker and allow a range of possible solutions rather than replacing decision makers with a single "answer" to the problem (Gidley and Bari 1986). Traditional optimization techniques reject all nonoptimal solutions in search of the optimal. An alternative is to generate a set of solutions that are significantly different from each other but which are optimal or nearly optimal with respect to the modelled objective(s). The basic MGA concept may be modified and extended to target results that are of direct interest to the decision maker. Unlike goal programming, this approach does not require that quantitative weights or priorities be assigned to individual objectives. MGA also provides information to the decision maker that is not available from sensitivity analysis. MGA can therefore be used to augment traditional post-optimality analyses common to mathematical programming applications.

In the MGA approach, solutions are generated that fall within an acceptable range of the optimal solution. A number of enumeration algorithms have been developed to identify these alternative solutions (Dyer and Proll 1977; Dyer 1983). Burton et al. (1987) also provide a method of computing the number of possible extreme points for a given problem. An enormous number of alternative solutions can be generated for most empirical problems using these types of procedures.

MGA can be implemented with one-phase or two-phase techniques. One-phase techniques generate a small number of solutions that differ significantly from each other, or target the key activities of interest to the decision maker. The use of two-phase techniques involves generating a large number of alternatives in the first phase and then selecting a sub-set or presentation set in the second phase. The selection of the presentation set can be accomplished with various techniques, including cluster analysis or simple ad hoc inspection.[4] Because of the computational burden of this approach, two-phase techniques are typically appropriate only for relatively small problems. A survey of one-phase and two-phase techniques is provided by Gidley and Bari (1986).

The MGA technique described and used in the application provided by this paper is the HSJ (Hop-Skip-Jump) method (Brill 1979; Chang, Brill, and Hopkins 1982). HSJ is a straightforward form of MGA that can be implemented using any commercially available mathematical programming software. It has the additional advantage of being a one-phase technique, thus avoiding the need for determining the relevant presentation set from a large number of alternative solutions. Gidley and Bari (1986) conclude that the HSJ method is the most practical MGA technique.

Implementation of the HSJ method begins with standard linear programming analysis. The first step is to determine the optimal solution and objective function value for the original problem. Once this is done, the original objective function is converted into a constraint. In particular, the

---

[4] The basic procedure involved in cluster analysis is the partitioning of a set of vectors into homogeneous subsets.

original objective function is constrained to take on a value within a certain tolerable deviation, or tolerance level, from the optimal value. For example, if the tolerance level is 1%, the value of the original objective function is constrained to deviate from the optimal value by no more than 1%.

Solutions that fall within this tolerable deviation from the optimal solution are then examined and evaluated through the appropriate definition and construction of a new objective function. As described by Gidley and Bari (1986), the HSJ technique involves minimization of the sum of the decision variables that are non-zero in the original optimal solution, subject to the new constraint set. The new objective function forces variables into the basis that were non-basic in the previous solution, thereby producing a solution that differs significantly from the original. In the extreme case, this approach would force all of the non-zero variables in the previous solution to zero, thus producing a solution that is completely different from the original optimal solution while still satisfying the objective function target value. The analysis continues in this manner, each time minimizing the sum of decision variables that were non-zero in the previous solutions. The procedure is stopped when

Figure 1. Graphical representation of resource sensitivity analysis.

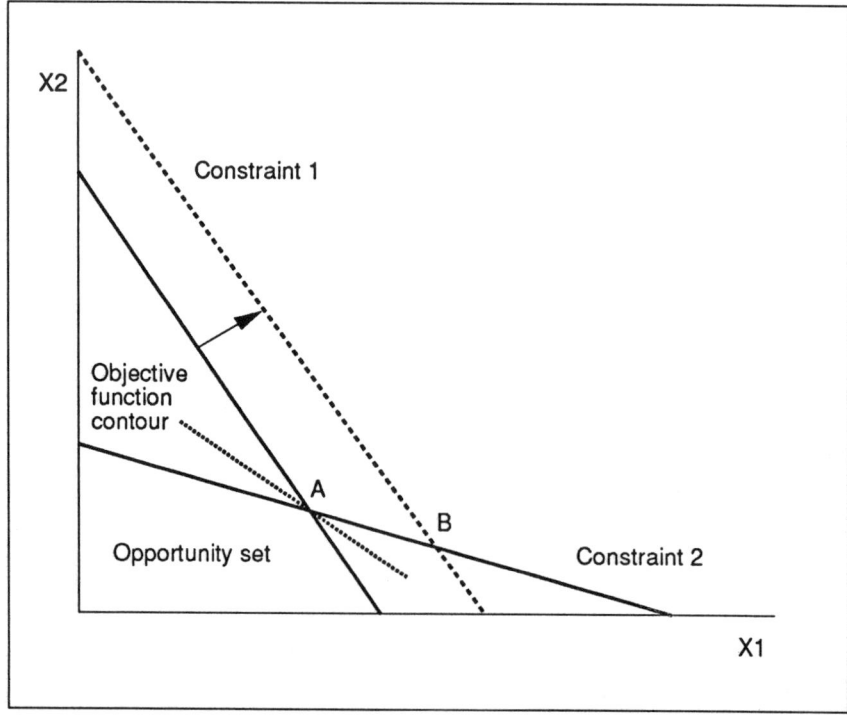

the MGA solutions stabilize (i.e., the set of non-zero decision variables does not change), or when a sufficient number of alternative solutions have been generated. Appendix 1 provides a mathematical presentation of the basic HSJ method.

The basic HSJ technique may be extended in one of two ways. Additional solutions can be generated by varying the tolerance level while maintaining the same objective function. A further extension of the HSJ technique is to structure the objective function in an attempt to force certain results that are of direct interest to the decision maker. In general, the objective function becomes one of maximizing or minimizing the sum of a set of target decision variables. While the HSJ method will not identify the complete set of nearly optimal solutions within the tolerance level, it does provide a wide range of alternative solutions that may be of interest to the decision maker.

Figures 1 to 3 illustrate the basic concept of MGA, relative to traditional sensitivity analysis. The original linear programming problem is a maximization problem, subject to two constraints on maximum resource availability (i.e., $\leq$ constraints). Sensitivity analysis addresses the hypothetical issues of what happens if resource availability or objective function coefficients

Figure 2. Graphical representation of objective function coefficient sensitivity analysis.

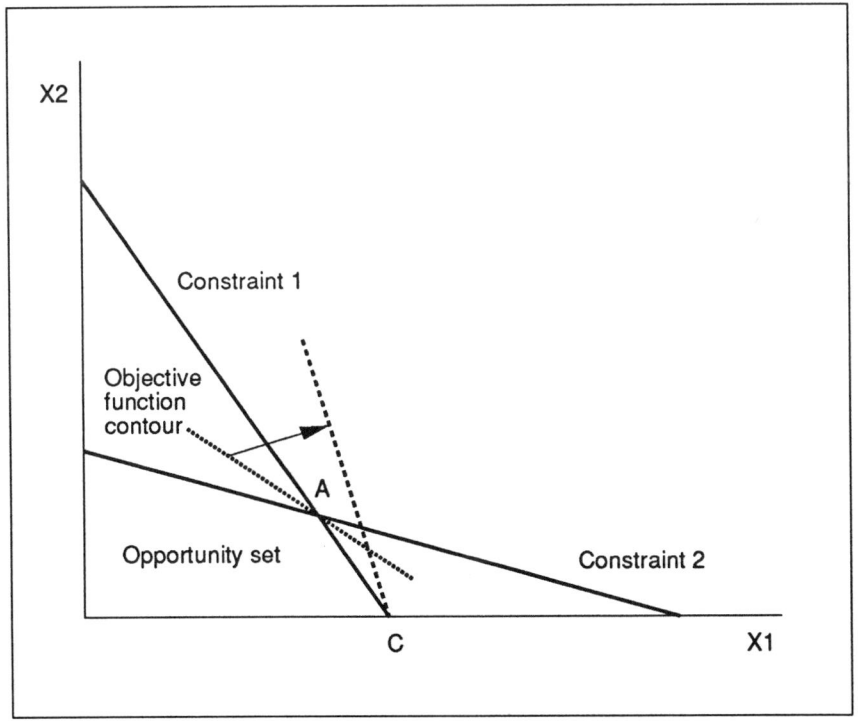

Figure 3. Graphical representation of MGA.

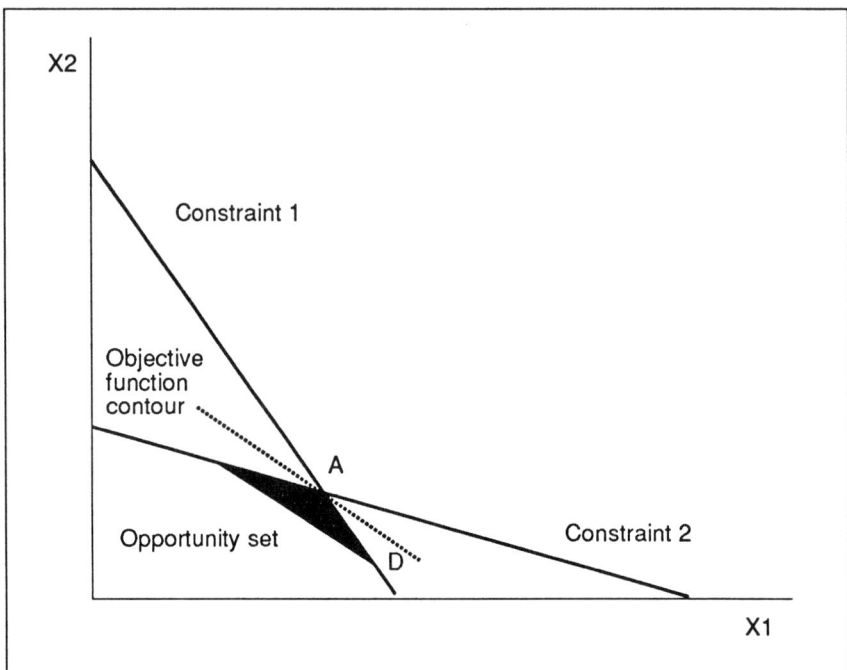

are altered. Resource sensitivity analysis is illustrated in Figure 1. The original linear programming solution, given the objective function contour, is point A. The sensitivity of the optimal solution to adjustments in the availability of resource 1 may be examined by shifting constraint 1. In this case, the solution changes from A to B.

Sensitivity analysis with respect to objective function coefficients is illustrated in Figure 2. The sensitivity of the optimal solution to adjustments in objective function coefficients (e.g., product prices) for activity 1 (X1) may be examined by shifting the slope of the objective function contour. In this case, the solution changes from A to C.

The basic concept underlying MGA is considerably different, as illustrated in Figure 3. Specifically, the interior region of the opportunity set is examined within some particular tolerance from the optimal solution, given current resource availability and objective function coefficients. In many cases this may be a more realistic portrayal of the circumstances that are dictating the choices available to decision makers. These interior solutions are shown in Figure 3 as the shaded area within the opportunity set. Note that point D may be revealed as an alternative solution when the set of tolerable deviations is examined. It is unlikely that this point would be revealed by sensitivity analysis of either the resource vectors or the objective function coefficients.

The HSJ technique, as described above, is straightforward in its use, both conceptually and empirically. As noted earlier, however, the methodology has received little usage in empirical agricultural research. One possible explanation is that some previous MGA applications have relied on unique solution algorithms. For example, Burton et al. (1987) utilize a more complex form of MGA which cannot be used with commonly available mathematical programming software packages.

The application presented in this paper provides an example of the ease with which the HSJ technique may be used as a tool to assist in assessing firm-level management decision-making in response to a change in marketing policy. The specific case examined here is a dairy ration formulation problem. The application, solved using a commercial microcomputer software package called GAMS, demonstrates the potential applicability of MGA to agricultural problems, including issues relating to agricultural marketing. [5]

An Agricultural Marketing Application of MGA: Dairy Ration Formulation[6]

The empirical application presented in this section illustrates the potential role of MGA in the analysis of agricultural issues. The issue addressed in this example is the possible effect of policy change on the marketing strategies and potential sales for a company that produces and markets a specific agricultural input: feed for livestock rations. Current transportation policy in western Canada involves subsidization of rail freight rates for grains and oilseeds, in support of export activities. Proposals have been made that would eliminate this subsidy, raising the cost of transporting grain and making it more expensive to export. One possible effect of this adjustment would be to reduce grain prices in the region. This would, in turn, affect the market (i.e., demand) for grains and forages in livestock rations in western Canada.

The specific example relates to the marketing strategies for a feed mill in western Canada. This business markets a number of products that are used as inputs in agricultural production. These include specific ration inputs, cereal grains, protein/vitamin/mineral supplements, as well as commercially

---

[5] GAMS is a mathematical programming package designed to handle a wide range of problems on the microcomputer. It is capable of solving large and complex problems for linear, nonlinear, and integer programming formulations. Additional information is provided by Brooke, Kendrick, and Meeraus (1988).

[6] This example is based on the application provided in Jeffrey, Gibson, and Faminow (1992).

mixed rations. The firm also markets a ration analysis service which provides recommendations with respect to livestock rations tailored to individual producer needs.

The objectives of the feed company are varied. They include maximizing the sale of feedstuffs and rations to local livestock producers. The firm also wishes to maximize the use of its ration analysis service. In order to do so, it must consider producer objectives in providing recommendations. In some cases, these producer objectives may not be consistent with the feed company's objectives.

Ration formulations and recommendations can be identified through the use of a linear programming model. Ration formulation is one of the more common agricultural applications of linear programming (e.g., Freeze and Hironaka 1990; Klein et al. 1988). This type of problem is typically well-defined, with the objective being to minimize the total ration cost. The minimization problem is subject to a set of constraints, defined by factors relating to nutrient requirements and nutrient balance. While nutrient relationships are not strictly linear, they may be approximated as linear with little loss of accuracy. As a result, linear programming provides a useful method of determining economically optimal rations.

While linear programming is a useful tool for this application, there are shortcomings arising from the required assumptions. For example, an implicit assumption in this type of ration model is that all feeds are of uniform quality and nutrient content. In reality, while purchased commercial ration mixes may have a guaranteed nutrient analysis, other feeds such as home-grown forage will not.

Another potentially restrictive assumption is that of cost minimization being the single objective of the decision maker. Typically, decision makers may have other goals or objectives in formulating a ration. For example, a farmer may wish to minimize cost, but also minimize the potential variability in nutrient content of the ration. The feed company, in formulating rations and making ration recommendations, however, may wish to maximize the use of feedstuffs that it currently markets. While traditional least-cost ration models cannot incorporate these alternative objectives, MGA may be a useful tool in addressing these concerns.[7]

To examine the potential effects of the policy change on product marketing strategies, the feed company uses MGA to identify and analyze nearly optimal rations for a "typical" customer; specifically, a local dairy farm operation. The farm is assumed to have a herd average annual production level

---

[7] There are other ways to address these shortcomings. Techniques such as stochastic programming or goal programming may be used to incorporate stochastic feedstuff quality and multiple objectives, respectively (e.g., D'Alfonso and Roush 1990).

equal to 8,160 kg of 3.5% butterfat milk. The herd has a calving interval of 12 months, with an average lactation period of 300 days. The farmer has three specific objectives: ensuring that the ration provides the minimum nutrient requirements for the dairy herd, minimization of ration cost, and minimization of the variability of nutrient quality (i.e., feed composition). As noted earlier, the feed company wishes to accommodate the farmer's objectives, while also meeting the firm's objectives of maximizing sales of its product.

The objective of this analysis is to assess the effect of the proposed policy change on the market for the feed company's products; specifically feedstuffs and commercially mixed rations. The empirical model used in the analysis is a least-cost linear programming formulation. Separate daily rations are formulated for each 100-day trimester of lactation, along with a daily ration for the dry period. The mathematical model is defined so as to minimize total annual ration cost, subject to nutritional requirements. Nutrient requirements and balance provide the structure for the constraints of this problem, and are determined by National Research Council (NRC) guidelines (1978), based on body weight and milk production.[8] The basic linear programming model is presented and discussed in Appendix 2.

Several potential feeds are assumed to be available for use in ration formulation. These include home-grown forages (i.e., alfalfa hay, corn for silage, and brome/timothy mix grass hay), as these represent crops that the farmer currently grows or would consider growing if economical and appropriate for use in the dairy rations. Purchased cereal grains (i.e., barley, corn, oats, and wheat), protein supplement (i.e., canola meal), commercial dairy ration, and vitamin/mineral supplement are included, as these are feedstuffs that are marketed by the feed company. Nutrient content for most feeds is based on NRC estimates.[9] Initial feed costs (i.e., objective function coefficients) are based on typical 1990 market prices, with the exception of the forage crops, for which variable production costs are used.[10] All values are determined on a 100% dry matter basis. Feed quantities are expressed in kg of dry matter.

The solution for the base model, given initial prices, is presented in Table 1. The least-cost ration includes alfalfa hay, grass hay, barley, and

---

[8] Average daily production levels in the first, second, and third lactation trimesters are 34.5 kg., 28.0 kg., and 18.6 kg., respectively.

[9] The only exception to this is the commercial dairy ration. The guaranteed analysis for a typical 16% crude protein ration is used to represent the nutrient content for this feedstuff.

[10] Market prices are used to represent opportunity costs for the various feeds. Costs of production are used for the forage crops because stable markets for these feeds do not exist in western Canada.

Table 1. Initial solution for the least-cost dairy ration problem (initial prices).

Feed	Annual dairy ration (kg)[a]
Commercial ration	-
Alfalfa hay	1,994.23
Grass hay	509.25
Barley	3,149.65
Oats	-
Wheat	-
Corn silage	-
Corn	-
Canola meal	-
Vitamins/mineral	7.83
Ration cost ($)	437.87

[a] All quantities are expressed on a 100% dry matter basis.

vitamin/mineral supplement. The total annual cost per dairy cow of this ration is $437.87.

With the elimination of the transportation subsidy, relative prices for alternative feeds will change. Management of the feed mill estimates that a 10% decrease in non-forage feed prices will occur as a result of the policy change.[11] The coefficients in the least-cost ration model are adjusted accordingly, and the model is re-solved. The resulting annual least-cost ration is presented in the first column of Table 2.

A comparison of the two "optimal" rations before and after the price adjustment shows that a 10% decrease in non-forage feed prices has no effect on the least-cost ration. While the ration cost decreases from $437.87 to $412.99, the optimal ration still consists of alfalfa and grass hay and barley. These results suggest that the policy change would have no effect on feed demand in dairy rations. This could be interpreted to mean that there should be no change in the marketing strategies for the feed company.

While this analysis incorporates the cost minimizing objective for producers, the alternative objectives are not considered. For example, if feed grain prices fall relative to forage prices, farmers may choose to substitute grain for forage to reduce nutrient content variability. The feed company may be able to increase sales of purchased feed for dairy rations (or the use of its feedstuffs in commercially mixed rations), while still reducing farmers' ration costs (i.e., maintaining an element of cost minimization). The basic linear programming analysis does not consider the possibility that other objectives may be important.[12] As a result of these factors, the original linear programming

---

[11] Forages are not presently eligible for the subsidized rates.
[12] Goal programming could be used to address this issue, but would require identification of specific weights for each objective.

Table 2. Alternative solutions for the least-cost dairy ration problem–basic MGA approach (adjusted prices).

Feed	Annual Dairy Rations (kg)^{a,b}			
	Least Cost	MGA1	MGA2	MGA3
Commercial ration	-	-	-	-
Alfalfa hay	1,994.23	953.67	2,035.04	2,068.83
Grass hay	509.25	-	630.62	557.96
Barley	3,149.65	-	1,388.17	2,045.30
Oats	-	4,234.49	-	-
Wheat	-	-	1,541.32	708.06
Corn silage	-	347.94	-	-
Corn	-	-	-	244.29
Canola meal	-	217.66	-	-
Vitamins/mineral	7.83	3.81	4.61	7.15
Ration cost ($)	412.99	437.77	437.77	437.77

^{a} All quantities are expressed on a 100% dry matter basis. Dashes (-) represent zero values.

^{b} The nearly optimal rations (MGA1 to MGA3) are obtained by minimizing the sum of activities that were basic in any previous solution, assuming a 6% tolerance from the minimum ration cost ($412.99). For example, MGA1 is obtained by minimizing the sum of alfalfa hay, grass hay, and barley in each time period.

model does not furnish complete information for providing ration recommendations to producers.

The HSJ form of MGA is used to generate "nearly optimal" solutions. The original linear programming formulation is further constrained by requiring that the annual ration cost be no more than 6% greater than the minimum cost; in other words, no greater than $437.77 per cow.[13] This 6% is the allowable tolerance from the original solution, and represents $24.78 per cow per year. This represents a deviation from the minimum cost, but it may be justified if the resulting ration is optimal with respect to alternative decision maker objectives. It is also slightly less than the cost of the original least-cost ration.

Table 2 shows three alternative rations (MGA1, MGA2, and MGA3) that were generated using the basic HSJ technique.[14] These rations are obtained by minimizing the sum of activities that are basic in any previous solution. For example, MGA1 is obtained by minimizing the sum of basic

---

[13] The tolerance value of 6% was chosen, somewhat arbitrarily, in order to demonstrate the HSJ technique. This value does result in nearly optimal solutions that are significantly different from the original optimal solution, and does provide slight cost savings, relative to the original least-cost ration.

[14] A total of nine unique nearly optimal rations, excluding the original least-cost ration, can be generated using this formulation and a 6% tolerable deviation. Only the first three are presented in this table.

activities from the original least-cost solution. MGA2 is obtained by minimizing the sum of basic variables from the original least-cost solution and the MGA1 solution. All three alternative rations meet the nutritional requirements specified in the original model and are within the allowable tolerance for cost. As may be noted from Table 2, the alternative rations utilize a wide variety of alternative feeds in various combinations.

The MGA results indicate that there is some degree of potential substitutability between forages, and a significant degree of substitutability between non-forage feeds. For example, the primary forages in the least-cost ration are alfalfa hay and grass hay. In MGA1, however, corn silage substitutes for grass hay. Also, oats and wheat are substitutes for barley in some MGA rations. However, with the exception of MGA1, there is considerable stability in all of the rations with respect to the overall forage content (approximately 45% of total dry matter). In MGA1, the forage content is less than 25% of total dry matter.

The MGA analysis may be of value in providing ration recommendations to farmers, as well as guiding the formulation of commercially mixed dairy rations by the feed company. The results in Table 2 provide a least-cost ration, along with several nearly optimal alternative rations. Each ration achieves, to a certain extent, the objectives outlined earlier. The least cost ration utilizes primarily alfalfa and barley (minimum number of feeds), and meets the criterion of least cost. MGA1 uses the least amount of home-grown forage, thus meeting the feed company's criterion of maximizing the use of its products. All of the rations (including the least-cost ration) achieve cost efficiency, to a certain degree. In terms of providing recommendations for farmers then, the use of MGA provides options from which the producer may choose, rather than have a single "correct" ration. [15]

The targeting form of the HSJ technique may also be used to optimize specific objectives. This formulation may be useful in identifying nearly optimal solutions that are of particular interest to decision makers, in this case the feed company. Table 3 provides three nearly optimal rations (MGA4 to MGA6) that are obtained in this manner, again allowing a 6% tolerance from the minimum cost. MGA4 is obtained by minimizing the overall use of forages in the rations, MGA5 is obtained by maximizing the use of cereal grains (i.e., barley, oats, wheat, and corn) and MGA6 is obtained by maximizing the use of commercial 16% ration. The resulting rations achieve a degree of cost efficiency while maximizing the use of feeds that are marketed by the feed company. These rations are also somewhat optimal in terms of reduced variability in nutrient content. As with the earlier MGA solutions, these rations utilize a variety of feeds in various combinations.

---

[15] In fact, this is consistent with the management practices of many feed milling companies, which offer alternative rations within a general class (e.g., dairy rations).

Table 3. Alternative solutions for the least-cost dairy ration problem–MGA approach with specific objectives (adjusted prices).

Feed	Annual Dairy Rations (kg)[a,b]		
	MGA4	MGA5	MGA6
Commercial ration	-	-	226.99
Alfalfa hay	859.52	1354.76	1891.72
Grass hay	420.31	115.35	571.39
Barley	-	-	2957.10
Oats	4255.82	4640.69	-
Wheat	-	-	-
Corn silage	-	-	-
Corn	-	-	-
Canola meal	210.22	-	-
Vitamins/mineral	7.65	0.40	3.62
Ration cost ($)	437.77	437.77	437.77

[a] All quantities are expressed on a 100% dry matter basis. Dashes (-) represent zero values.
[b] The nearly optimal rations (MGA4 to MGA6) are obtained by minimizing or maximizing total use of specific feeds in the annual ration, assuming a 6% tolerance from the minimum ration cost ($412.99). MGA4 is obtained by minimizing total use of all forages, MGA5 is obtained by maximizing total use of all cereal grains, and MGA6 is obtained by maximizing total use of commercial dairy ration.

The MGA solutions provide potentially useful information for both sets of decision makers. The results may give the feed company insights concerning the possible effects of the proposed policy change on the demand for their products, and possible product marketing strategies. If the objective of this modelling procedure is to provide ration recommendations to dairy farmers, the analysis provides a least-cost ration, along with several nearly optimal alternatives. All of the rations may achieve one or more of the previously stated objectives, while also ensuring that the ration meets the necessary criteria, including economic and non-economic considerations.

Other Marketing Applications of MGA

While not receiving widespread use, the MGA technique has been used in some recent studies to address marketing related issues. Burton et al. (1987) used a two-phase form of MGA in a firm-level setting to examine and evaluate marketing strategies for beef calves in West Virginia. A linear programming model was constructed and solved, maximizing returns to fixed assets, subject to resource constraints. A FORTRAN program was then used to generate all extreme points in the feasible set and to identify those feasible solutions that fell within a specified percentage of the original "optimal" solution. Selection of the presentation set was then done using ad hoc procedures. The nearly optimal strategies in the presentation set were then provided as possible options for decision makers. As noted earlier, this form of MGA cannot be directly used in conjunction with standard commercial linear programming solvers.

Linear programming is also used to address macro- or sector-level marketing issues. These include analyses related to optimal transportation patterns, aggregate demand and trade problems, etc. MGA also has a role in complementing the linear programming results from these types of studies. An example of this type of analysis is provided by Gibson, Faminow, and Jeffrey (1991). This study evaluates the impact of the Canada-United States Free Trade Agreement (CUSFTA) on the competitiveness of the Canadian flour milling industry. A spatial equilibrium model was constructed and solved, minimizing the cost of milling and transportation, subject to fixed regional milling capacities, supplies of wheat, and demands for flour. The model solution provided "optimal" regional flour milling volumes, as well as flows of wheat and flour, both pre- and post-CUSFTA. The HSJ form of MGA was then used to identify and evaluate alternative nearly optimal solutions within a specified tolerance of the original optimal solution.

While the least-cost solutions suggested that the flour milling industry in Canada would likely not survive free trade with the United States, evaluation using MGA indicated a wide range of nearly optimal solutions that included substantial milling in Canada. Analysis of these alternative solutions resulted in the conclusion that the Canadian milling industry could survive under the terms of CUSFTA.

The MGA technique is not limited to use in these types of applications. Mathematical programming has been used in a variety of studies related to marketing issues, both firm-level and sector-level in nature. Examples include papers by Faminow and Sarhan (1983), Frank et al. (1989), Kaiser and Apland (1989), and McMullen, Martin, and Cabeza (1989). The empirical models in these studies involve the use of stochastic programming, MOTAD, integer programming, etc. MGA is a complementary technique, and can be used in conjunction with these models and procedures, rather than replacing them.

Concluding Remarks

Economic models applied to agricultural marketing problems are typically based upon the assumption of rationality, defined in a narrow sense to mean agreement with the objective function in an optimizing framework. Quite often, this framework does not allow for divergence of objectives, or defines objectives in a rigid manner. Mathematical programming techniques based on this framework can be quite useful in addressing agricultural marketing issues, but they often fail to describe actual behavior accurately or result in recommendations that may not achieve other objectives. Techniques such as goal programming have been devised to address this concern but they also suffer from rigidity because of the necessity to predetermine the weighting of preferences.

This paper has suggested Modelling to Generate Alternatives as a technique to address the criticisms and limitations associated with mathematical programming. The approach provides a way to allow for the existence of quasi-rational behavior and alternative decision criteria. This technique permits a greater congruence between economic models and decisions in the real world. Furthermore, the solution technique proposed in this paper is extremely simple, can be solved using any commercially available mathematical programming software package, and requires no special computer skills. The information resulting from MGA complements the results from optimal baseline solutions and standard sensitivity analysis.

The use of this technique was demonstrated with a straightforward problem (ration formulation). As discussed in this paper, however, MGA has potential applications in a wide range of agricultural marketing issues. Thus, it is recommended as a possible methodology for analysts interested in the study of marketing problems at both the micro- and macro-levels.

References

Brill, E.D., Jr. 1979. The use of optimization models in public-sector planning. *Management Science* 25:413-22.

Brooke, A., D. Kendrick and A. Meeraus. 1988. *GAMS. A user's guide.* Redwood City, CA: The Scientific Press.

Burton, R.O., Jr., J.S. Gidley, B.S. Baker, and K.J. Reda-Wilson. 1987. Nearly optimal linear programming solutions: Some conceptual issues and a farm management application. *American Journal of Agricultural Economics* 69:813-818.

Chang, S., E.D. Brill, Jr., and L.D. Hopkins. 1982. Use of mathematical models to generate alternative solutions to water resource planning programs. *Water Resource Research* 18:58-64.

D'Alfonso, T.H. and W.B. Roush. 1990. A comparison of stochastic programming, linear programming, and linear programming with a margin of safety for least cost poultry rations. *Poultry Science Journal* 69:39.

Dyer, M.E. 1983. The complexity of vertex enumeration methods. *Mathematical Operations Research* 8:381-402.

Dyer, M.E. and L.G. Proll. 1977. An algorithm for determining all extreme points of a convex polytope. *Mathematical Programming* 12:81-96.

Faminow, M.D. and M.E. Sarhan. 1983. The location of feed cattle slaughtering and processing in the United States: An application of mixed integer programming. *Canadian Journal of Agricultural Economics* 31:425-36.

Frank, S.D., S.H. Irwin, G.H. Pfeiffer, and C.E. Curtis. 1989. Further evaluation on soybean marketing strategies: The role of options. *North Central Journal of Agricultural Economics* 11:213-9.

Freeze, B.S. and R. Hironaka. 1990. Effect of form of hay and carcass quality on the economics of concentrate: Hay substitution in cattle feedlot diets. *Western Journal of Agricultural Economics* 15:163-74.

Gibson, R.R., M.D. Faminow, and S.R. Jeffrey. 1991. The North American hard wheat milling industry under free trade: Spatial equilibrium and nearly optimal solutions. *Canadian Journal of Agricultural Economics* 39:35-53.

Gidley, J.S. and M.F. Bari. 1986. Modelling to generate alternatives. In *Water forum '86*. (M. Karamouz, F.R. Baumli, and W.J. Brick, eds.) New York, NY, USA: American Society of Civil Engineers.

Harrington, J.J. and J.S. Gidley. 1985. The variability of alternative decisions in a water resources planning problem. *Water Resource Research* 21:1831-40.

Hazell, P.B.R. and R.D. Norton. 1986. *Mathematical programming for economic analysis in agriculture.* New York, NY, USA: Macmillan.

Heady, E.O. 1954. Simplified presentation and logical aspects of linear programming technique. *Journal of Farm Economics* 36:1035-50.

Jeffrey, S.R., R.R. Gibson, and M.D. Faminow. 1992. Nearly optimal linear programming as a guide to agricultural planning. *Agricultural Economics* 8:1-19.

Kaiser, H.M. and J. Apland. 1989. DSSP: A model of production and marketing decisions on a Midwestern crop farm. *North Central Journal of Agricultural Economics* 11:157-69.

King, R.A. 1953. Some applications of activity analysis in agricultural economics. *Journal of Farm Economics* 35:823-33.

Klein, K.K., E.G. Smith, S. Dubetz, and E.E. Gardiner. 1988. A bioeconomic evaluation of fababeans in broiler chick diets. *Canadian Journal of Agricultural Economics* 36:337-47.

McMullen, B.S., M.V. Martin, and F. Cabeza. 1989. The impacts of transportation deregulation on wheat shipments in the Pacific Northwest. *Western Journal of Agricultural Economics* 14:253-60.

National Research Council, Subcommittee on Dairy Cattle Nutrition. 1978. *Nutrient Requirements of Dairy Cattle.* Fifth Revised Edition. Washington, D.C., USA: National Academy of Sciences.

Russell, T. and R. Thaler. 1985. The relevance of quasi rationality in competitive markets. *American Economic Review* 75:1071-82.

Appendix 1

Mathematical formulation of the HSJ technique

As discussed, the HSJ method is initiated by solving the original linear programming problem. For example, suppose that the original linear programming model formulation is as follows:

(1.1)   Maximize: $z = c'x$

   Subject to: $Ax \leq b$

   $x \leq 0$

where z is the objective function value, c is the vector of objective function coefficients, x is the activity vector, A is the constraint coefficient matrix, and b is the resource vector. Once the optimal solution has been generated, the objective function in (1.1) is converted into a constraint, as follows:

(1.2) $c'x \geq (1 - j)z^*$

where z^* is the optimal objective function value obtained from solving (1.1) and j is the tolerable deviation, or tolerance level, from the optimal objective function value. For example, if $j = 0.01$, the value of the original objective function is constrained to deviate from the optimal value by no more than 1%.[a] This yields a new linear programming problem, as follows:

(1.3)   Minimize: Σx_j^*

   Subject to: $c'x \geq (1 - j)z^*$

   $Ax \leq b$

   $x \geq 0$

where the new objective function involves the minimization of the sum of decision variables that were non-zero in the original optimal solution (i.e., x_j^*). This new formulation defined by (1.3) is solved to obtain a solution that differs from the original. This procedure can be repeated, each time adjusting the

---

[a] If the original problem involved minimization of $z = c'x$, the constraint in (1.2) would take the form $c'x \leq (1 + j)z^*$.

objective function in (1.3) to include all decision variables that were non-zero in previous solutions. This continues until the solutions stabilize, or a sufficient number of alternative solutions have been generated.

Appendix 2

Dairy ration model formulation

The linear programming ration model used in the empirical application may be stated as follows:

Minimize:

(2.1) $$Z = \sum_i \sum_j X_{ij} \, CST_j \, Days_i$$

Subject to:

(2.2) $$\sum_j X_{ij} \, Nut_{jk} \geq NUTREQ_{ik} \; \forall \, i \; \forall \, k$$

(2.3) $$\sum_j X_{ij} \leq Max_i \; \forall \, i$$

(2.4) $$\sum_j X_{ij} FIB_j - FIBREQ_i \sum_j X_{ij} \geq 0 \; \forall \, i$$

(2.5) $$\sum_j X_{ij} Ca_j - 3.0 \sum_j X_{ij} Phos_j \leq 0 \; \forall \, i$$

(2.6) $$\sum_j X_{ij} Ca_j - \sum_j X_{ij} Phos_j \geq 0 \; \forall \, i$$

(2.7) $$X_{ij} \geq 0 \; \forall \, i \; \forall \, j$$

where subscripts are used to indicate the individual rations for each stage of lactation (i), type of feed (j) and type of nutrient (k). The activities, z and X_{ij}, represent total annual cost and kilograms of feed j in ration i, respectively. The following constants refer to the fixed coefficients that are used in the model. They represent nutrient content and requirements, feed costs, and maximum feed intake for each ration.

CST_j = cost per kg for feed j

$Days_i$ = number of days over which ration i is fed

Nut_{jk} = kg of nutrient k per kilogram of feed j

$NUTREQ_{ik}$ = daily requirement (kg) for nutrient k in ration i

Max_i = maximum dry matter intake for ration i

FIB_j = fiber content of feed j

$FIBREQ_i$ = fiber requirement for ration i

$Phos_j$ = kg of phosphorus per kilogram of feed j

Ca_j = kg of calcium per kg of feed j

All coefficients, constants, and activities are expressed on a 100% dry matter (DM) basis.

Equation (2.1) is the objective function, which represents the total annual cost of the dairy ration. Equation (2.2) ensures that nutrient requirements are met by each ration. Included in this set of constraints are minimum requirements for net energy (NE_1), crude protein, calcium, phosphorus and Vitamin A.[a] Equation (2.3) ensures that the total ration in each period will not exceed the maximum dry matter intake for the dairy cow. Equation (2.4) requires each ration to meet the minimum fibre content, defined in percentage terms. The next two constraints require the ratio of calcium to phosphorus in each ration to be within a lower (equation (2.5)) and upper (equation (2.6)) limit, respectively. Finally, equation (2.7) ensures that all activities are non-negative.

---

[a] Within this set of constraints is an additional constraint limiting whe at to be no more than 40% of the non-forage portion of each ration. This constraint is required because of the digestive problems for ruminants associated with high concentrations of wheat in the diet.

21

Equilibrium Displacement Modelling: An Application to Indonesian Food Price Policy

Roley Piggott [1]

Abstract

Econometric modelling for the purpose of addressing issues in agricultural marketing can be time consuming, expensive in terms of research resources, and limited by lack of reliable data, especially in developing countries. Increasingly, equilibrium displacement modelling (EDM), a form of comparative static analysis, is being used to address real-world policy issues in agricultural marketing. In this paper, the method of EDM is outlined and its limitations discussed. Then follows an application dealing with price policy for food crops in Indonesia. The general conclusion reached is that EDM is a method that is a useful alternative to econometric modelling when research resources are limited and/or answers to agricultural marketing problems are needed quickly.

Key words: Parameter estimates, comparative static analysis, general equilibrium elasticities.

Introduction

Substantial research resources are used in the development and estimation of econometric models for use in agricultural marketing cum price analysis problems. This is especially the case in developing countries where often a precursory step to model estimation is the gathering of primary data, a step that is usually time consuming, and which therefore has the capacity to be a heavy drain on limited research budgets. Resources used in econometric modelling are resources that are not available for other analytical work that might ultimately have a greater payoff in terms of addressing the problem at hand.

---

[1] Department of Agricultural Economics and Business Management, University of New England-Armidale, 2351 Australia.

The author appreciates the importance of econometric modelling when values for key parameters in an agricultural marketing problem are needed. Economic theory alone is insufficiently powerful to allow one to determine parameter values, although it can be a useful guide. But it is also the case that econometric modelling provides only estimates of parameters. True values are never known. It is at least conceivable that informed judgement about parameter values, perhaps based in part on previous econometric work, will serve the purpose of a current research problem equally as well as parameter estimates obtained from an econometric model built specifically for the problem at hand.

Recently the author was involved in research on Indonesian price policy for rice and secondary food crops. Questions such as the mixture of rice price support and fertilizer subsidy needed to attain various levels of rice self-sufficiency were central to the investigation. Because of relationships between rice and other food crops—both on the supply side through competition for resources and on the demand side through substitutability in consumption, addressing questions in relation to self-sufficiency policies required taking account of cross-commodity relationships. Had there been sufficient research resources available, an econometric model specifically for the problem at hand could have been specified, the necessary data collected, and estimation undertaken. In this circumstance, it was necessary to look to alternatives. The alternative chosen was equilibrium displacement modelling (EDM), the tool that is outlined in this paper. Basically, it allowed the research team to address policy questions by making use of informed judgements about key parameters rather than embarking on the expensive exercise of building and estimating an econometric model.

The EDM approach is a form of comparative static analysis (see for example, Chiang 1984, Ch. 8) so it is by no means a new tool. It has been used in some important papers in the agricultural marketing and price analysis area over the last several years. An early example in relation to agricultural marketing theory is provided by Gardner (1975). Recent examples include Wohlgenant and Haidacher (1989), Alston (1991), Hertel (1991), and Holloway (1991). Some people refer to the procedure as "Muth modelling", since it was the procedure used in the seminal Muth (1964) paper. One can usually make useful qualitative statements about the effects of policy initiatives and, provided one is content to confine analyses to small (say, 10% or less) changes about an initial equilibrium and provided one is prepared to make judgements about elasticity values, one can make reasonably accurate quantitative estimates of responses to changes in exogenous variables. No assumptions have to be made about functional forms. The procedure provides first-order approximations to quantitative effects irrespective of underlying functional forms.

The procedure is outlined in the next section and a simple numerical example is provided. In subsequent sections it is demonstrated how EDM was used in analyzing questions about Indonesian price policy for food crops. Some strengths and weaknesses of the procedure are outlined in the final section.

The Procedure

Consider the following market model for two commodities, 1 and 2:

(1) $D_1 = D_1(P_1, P_2, W)$ (demand for commodity 1)

$S_1 = S_1(P_1, P_2, X)$ (supply of commodity 1)

$D_2 = D_2(P_1, P_2, Y)$ (demand for commodity 2)

$S_2 = S_2(P_1, P_2, Z)$ (supply of commodity 2)

$D_1 = S_1 = Q_1$ (commodity 1 market clearance)

$D_2 = S_2 = Q_2$ (commodity 2 market clearance)

where:

D = quantity demanded;
S = quantity supplied;
P = price;
Q = equilibrium quantity; and
W, X, Y, Z = exogenous influences on supply and demand.

The model defined by equations (1) is a "general function" model in that no explicit functional forms have been assumed. Too, although there is a unique exogenous variable in each equation, this is merely for convenience and there could in fact be several exogenous variables in each equation, with particular exogenous variables entering into more than one equation.

In equilibrium:

(2) $Q_1 = D_1(P_1, P_2, W)$

$Q_1 = S_1(P_1, P_2, X)$

$Q_2 = D_2(P_1, P_2, Y)$

$Q_2 = S_2(P_1, P_2, Z)$

The system of equations (2) contains four equations and four endogenous variables (Q_1, Q_2, P_1, and P_2), with the endogenous variables assuming their equilibrium values.

EDM allows one to examine how changes in exogenous variables affect each endogenous variable after the system has fully adjusted to the changes. In other words, the interest is in general equilibrium impacts. A convenient way of measuring these impacts when only a single exogenous variable changes is through *general equilibrium elasticities*. These elasticities show the percentage change in an endogenous variable associated with a 1% change in an exogenous variable after full adjustment has occurred. They are to be distinguished from Marshallian elasticities which show the percentage change in an endogenous variable associated with a 1% change in an exogenous variable assuming the values of all other variables do not change.

After total differentiation of (2) the following system is obtained:

$$(3) \quad \begin{aligned} dQ_1 &= (\partial D_1 / \partial P_1)dP_1 + (\partial D_1 / \partial P_2)dP_2 + (\partial D_1 / \partial W)dW \\ dQ_1 &= (\partial S_1 / \partial P_1)dP_1 + (\partial S_1 / \partial P_2)dP_2 + (\partial D_1 / \partial X)dX \\ dQ_2 &= (\partial D_2 / P_1)dP_1 + (\partial D_2 / \partial P_2)dP_2 + (\partial D_2 / \partial Y)dY \\ dQ_2 &= (\partial S_2 / \partial P_1)dP_1 + (\partial S_2 / \partial P_2)dP_2 + (\partial S_2 / \partial Z)dZ \end{aligned}$$

Using the relationship that $dQ_1 = Q_1 \, d \ln Q_1$, etc. (i.e., the "ordinary" differential of a variable equals the value of the variable times its log differential), the system can be rewritten as:

(4)

$Q_1 d \ln Q_1 = (\partial D_1/\partial P_1) \, P_1 d \ln P_1 + (\partial D_1/\partial P_2) \, P_2 d \ln P_2 + (\partial D_1/\partial W) \, W d \ln W$

$Q_1 d \ln Q_1 = (\partial S_1/\partial P_1) \, P_1 d \ln P_1 + (\partial S_1/\partial P_2) \, P_2 d \ln P_2 + (\partial S_1/\partial X) \, X d \ln X$

$Q_2 d \ln Q_2 = (\partial D_2/\partial P_1) \, P_1 d \ln P_1 + (\partial D_2/\partial P_2) \, P_2 d \ln P_2 + (\partial D_1/\partial Y) \, Y d \ln Y$

$Q_2 d \ln Q_2 = (\partial S_2/\partial P_1) \, P_1 d \ln P_1 + (\partial S_2/\partial P_2) \, P_2 d \ln P_2 + (\partial S_2/\partial Z) \, Z d \ln Z$

Dividing each equation by the Q_i appearing on the LHS and bearing in mind that $(\partial D_i/\partial P_i) \, (P_i/Q_i)$ and $(\partial S_i/\partial P_i) \, (P_i/Q_i)$ are Marshallian demand and supply elasticities, respectively, the system becomes:

(5) $\quad d \ln Q_1 = \eta_{11} \, d \ln P_1 + \eta_{12} \, d \ln P_2 + \eta_{1w} \, d \ln W$

$\quad d \ln Q_1 = \varepsilon_{11} \, d \ln P_1 + \varepsilon_{12} \, d \ln P_2 + \varepsilon_{1X} \, d \ln X$

$$d \ln Q_2 = \eta_{21} d \ln P_1 + \eta_{22} d \ln P_2 + \eta_{2Y} d \ln Y$$

$$d \ln Q_2 = \varepsilon_{21} d \ln P_1 + \varepsilon_{22} d \ln P_2 + \varepsilon_{2Z} d \ln Z$$

where:

η_{ij} (ε_{ij}) = price elasticity of demand (supply) for commodity i with respect to commodity j (i, j = 1, 2);

η_{ik} (ε_{ik}) = price elasticity of demand (supply) for commodity i with respect to exogenous variable k (i = 1,2; k = W, X, Y, Z).

In matrix form, the system is:

(6)
$$\begin{bmatrix} \eta_{11} & \eta_{11} & -1 & 0 \\ \varepsilon_{11} & \varepsilon_{12} & -1 & 0 \\ \eta_{21} & \eta_{22} & 0 & -1 \\ \varepsilon_{21} & \varepsilon_{22} & 0 & -1 \end{bmatrix} \begin{bmatrix} d\ln P_1 \\ d\ln P_2 \\ d\ln Q_1 \\ d\ln Q_2 \end{bmatrix} = \begin{bmatrix} -\eta_{1W} d\ln W \\ -\varepsilon_{1X} d\ln X \\ -\eta_{2Y} d\ln Y \\ -\varepsilon_{2Z} d\ln Z \end{bmatrix}$$

Upon post-multiplying both sides of matrix equation (6) by the vector

[1/d ln W   1/d ln X   1/d ln Y   1/d ln Z]

and setting the ratios of log differentials of any two different exogenous variables to zero (e.g., d ln W/d ln X = 0), one obtains

(7)   **E G = D**

where:

$$E = \begin{bmatrix} \eta_{11} & \eta_{12} & -1 & 0 \\ \varepsilon_{11} & \varepsilon_{12} & -1 & 0 \\ \eta_{21} & \eta_{22} & 0 & -1 \\ \varepsilon_{21} & \varepsilon_{22} & 0 & -1 \end{bmatrix}$$

$$G = \begin{bmatrix} d \ln P_1/d \ln W & d \ln P_1/d \ln X & d \ln P_1/d \ln Y & d \ln P_1/d \ln Z \\ d \ln P_2/d \ln W & d \ln P_2/d \ln X & d \ln P_2/d \ln Y & d \ln P_2/d \ln Z \\ d \ln Q_1/d \ln W & d \ln Q_1/d \ln X & d \ln Q_1/d \ln Y & d \ln Q_1/d \ln X \\ d \ln Q_2/d \ln W & d \ln Q_2/d \ln X & d \ln Q_2/d \ln Y & d \ln Q_2/d \ln Z \end{bmatrix}$$

$$D = \begin{bmatrix} -\eta_{1w} & 0 & 0 & 0 \\ 0 & -\varepsilon_{1x} & 0 & 0 \\ 0 & 0 & -\eta_{2y} & 0 \\ 0 & 0 & 0 & -\varepsilon_{2z} \end{bmatrix}$$

The elements of matrix **G** are general equilibrium elasticities (recall, for example, that $d \ln P_1/d \ln W = (dP_1/P_1)/(dW/W)$). The first row contains the general equilibrium elasticities of P_1 with respect to each of the exogenous variables, where only one exogenous variable changes at a time. Similar interpretations are placed on the elements in the other rows. These general equilibrium elasticities are obtained as:

(8) $\quad G = E^{-1}D$

where E^{-1} is the inverse of **E**.

As an example, suppose the explicit form of the model with equilibrium (market clearing) conditions imposed is:

(9) $\quad Q_1 \quad = \quad -0.8\ P_1 + 0.4\ P_2 + 1.4W$

$\quad\quad\quad Q_1 \quad = \quad 0.5\ P_1 - 0.2\ P_2 + 0.7X$

$\quad\quad\quad Q_2 \quad = \quad 0.3\ P_1 - 0.7\ P_2 + 1.4Y$

$\quad\quad\quad Q_2 \quad = \quad -0.4\ P_1 + 0.8\ P_2 + 0.6Z$

If the initial values of W, X, Y and Z are each 1.0, then in the solution each endogenous variable has a value of 1.0. The Marshallian elasticities computed at the equilibrium values of the endogenous variables and the base values of the exogenous variables are:

$\eta_{11} = -0.8, \quad \eta_{12} = 0.4, \quad \eta_{1w} = 1.4;$

$\varepsilon_{11} = 0.5, \quad \varepsilon_{12} = -0.2, \quad \varepsilon_{1x} = 0.7;$

$\eta_{21} = 0.3, \quad \eta_{22} = -0.7, \quad \eta_{2y} = 1.4;$ and

$\varepsilon_{21} = -0.4, \quad \varepsilon_{22} = 0.8, \quad \varepsilon_{2z} = 0.6.$

Equilibrium displacement modelling

One could now assume a change in the value of one of the exogenous variables, compute new equilibrium values for the endogenous variables and then compute the general equilibrium elasticity of each endogenous variable with respect to the exogenous variable whose value changed. For example, if W changes from 1.0 to 1.01 (i.e., by 1%) the new solution is:

$$Q_1 = 1.0056, Q_2 = 0.9996; \text{ and}$$

$$P_1 = 1.0137, P_2 = 1.0064$$

The general equilibrium elasticities are therefore:

$$G(P_1,W) = 1.37, G(P_2,W) = 0.64; \text{ and}$$

$$G(Q_1,W) = 0.56, G(Q_2,W) = 0.04$$

This exercise could be repeated for changes in X, Y, and Z to build up a complete set of general equilibrium elasticities.

An alternative is to use the comparative static methods outlined previously. By direct substitution of the initial Marshallian elasticities into matrices **E** and **D**:

$$\mathbf{E} = \begin{bmatrix} -0.8 & 0.4 & -1 & 0 \\ 0.5 & -0.2 & -1 & 0 \\ 0.3 & -0.7 & 0 & -1 \\ -0.4 & 0.8 & 0 & -1 \end{bmatrix}$$

and

$$\mathbf{D} = \begin{bmatrix} -1.04 & 0.0 & 0.0 & 0.0 \\ 0.0 & -0.7 & 0.0 & 0.0 \\ 0.0 & 0.0 & -1.4 & 0.0 \\ 0.0 & 0.0 & 0.0 & -0.6 \end{bmatrix}$$

Therefore:

$$\mathbf{G} = \begin{bmatrix} 1.3725 & -0.6893 & 0.5490 & 0.2353 \\ 0.6405 & -0.3203 & 1.1995 & -0.5098 \\ 0.5582 & 0.4209 & 0.0366 & 0.0157 \\ 0.0366 & 0.0183 & 0.7320 & 0.2863 \end{bmatrix}$$

$$= \begin{matrix} G(P_1,W) & G(P_1,X) & G(P_1,Y) & G(P_1,Z) \\ G(P_2,W) & G(P_2,X) & G(P_2,Y) & G(P_2,Z) \\ G(Q_1,W) & G(Q_1,X) & G(Q_1,Y) & G(Q_1,Z) \\ G(Q_2,W) & G(Q_2,X) & G(Q_2,Y) & G(Q_2,Z) \end{matrix}$$

In practice one may need to estimate the change in endogenous variables when several exogenous variables change simultaneously, allowing for general equilibrium effects to occur. For example, how does P_1 change when both W and Y change? In this case it is inappropriate to measure the change in P_1 as an elasticity because more than one exogenous variable is changing. The alternative is to measure the proportionate change in P_1 (i.e., d ln P_1 or dP_1/P_1) associated with simultaneous proportionate changes in W and Y. This can be approximated as:

(10) $\quad dP_1/P_1 = G(P_1,W)(dW/W) + G(P_1,Y)(dY/Y)$

Returning to the numerical example, suppose the proportionate change in W is .01 and the proportionate change in Y is .03. Setting the value of W at 1.01 and the value of Y at 1.03 in equations (9) and solving the system simultaneously yields a solution set $Q_1 = 1.0067$; $Q_2 = 1.0216$; $P_1 = 1.0302$; and $P_2 = 1.0421$. Hence, the proportionate change in $P_1 = 0.0302$. Alternatively, working with equation (10), set $dW/W = 0.01$, $dY/Y = 0.03$, $G(P_1,W) = 1.3725$ and $G(P_1,Y) = 0.5490$ (the latter two values being chosen from matrix **G** above) to obtain a value of 0.0302 for dP_1/P_1. It can easily be verified that the proportionate changes in the other endogenous variables can be obtained as the sum of products of total elasticities with proportionate changes (i.e., an equation corresponding to (10) above).

The Indonesian Food Crop Model

The model

The food crop model used in the Indonesia study consisted of eight demand functions and seven supply functions as follows:

(11) $\quad D_1 = D_1(P_{1c}, P_2, \ldots, P_8, Y)$
$\quad\quad\quad S_1 = S_1(P_{1p}, P_2, \ldots, P_7, P_9)$
$\quad\quad\quad D_2 = D_2(P_{1c}, P_2, \ldots, P_8, Y)$
$\quad\quad\quad S_2 = S_2(P_{1p}, P_2, \ldots, P_7, P_9)$
$\quad\quad\quad D_3 = D_3(P_{1c}, P_2, \ldots, P_8, Y)$
$\quad\quad\quad S_3 = S_3(P_{1p}, P_2, \ldots, P_7, P_9)$
$\quad\quad\quad D_4 = D_4(P_{1c}, P_2, \ldots, P_8, Y)$
$\quad\quad\quad S_4 = S_4(P_{1p}, P_2, \ldots, P_7, P_9)$
$\quad\quad\quad D_5 = D_5(P_{1c}, P_2, \ldots, P_8, Y)$
$\quad\quad\quad S_5 = S_5(P_{1p}, P_2, \ldots, P_7, P_9)$
$\quad\quad\quad D_6 = D_6(P_{1c}, P_2, \ldots, P_8, Y)$
$\quad\quad\quad S_6 = S_6(P_{1p}, P_2, \ldots, P_7, P_9)$

Equilibrium displacement modelling

$$D_7 = D_7(P_{1c}, P_2, \ldots, P_8, Y)$$
$$S_7 = S_7(P_{1p}, P_2, \ldots, P_7, P_9)$$
$$D_8 = D_8(P_{1c}, P_2, \ldots, P_8, Y)$$

where:

D = quantity demanded;
S = quantity supplied;
Y = income;
P = price; and

subscripts 1 to 9 denote commodities (1 = rice; 2 = corn; 3 = cassava; 4 = sugar; 5 = groundnut; 6 = soybean; 7 = sweetpotato; 8 = wheat; and 9 = fertilizer).

There are two rice prices: the consumer price (P_{1c}) and the producer price (P_{1p}). Quantities demanded and supplied are determined endogenously, as are the prices of sugar, groundnut, and sweetpotato. All other variables are treated as being determined exogenously.

The model is closed with the following identities:

(12) $D_4 = S_4 = Q_4$
       $D_5 = S_5 = Q_5$
       $D_7 = S_7 = Q_7$

The aim is to generate a set of general equilibrium elasticities showing how each endogenous variable responds to a 1% change in each exogenous variable, allowing for general equilibrium effects to occur. The endogenous variables are D_1, S_1, D_2, S_2, D_3, S_3, Q_4, Q_5, D_6, S_6, Q_7, Q_8, P_4, P_5, and P_7 (15 in total) and the exogenous variables are P_{1c}, P_{1p}, P_2, P_3, P_6, P_8, P_9, and Y (8 in total). Having obtained these general equilibrium elasticities, it is a simple matter to derive general equilibrium elasticities for other variables of interest, such as imports and revenues, by appropriate differentiation of identities.

After imposing the equilibrium conditions (12) on (11), total differentiation and conversion to log differentials, the Indonesian food crop model can be expressed as :

(13)   **RS = TU**

where **R** (15x15), **S** (15x1), **T** (15x8), and **U** (8x1) are shown in Figures 1 to 4, respectively. Now post-multiply both sides of (13) by**V** (1x8), where **V** is as shown in Figure 5, to obtain:

(14)   **R(SV) = T(UV)**.

Figure 1. Matrix R (15 x 15) of equation (13).

$$\begin{bmatrix} 1 & 0 & 0 & 0 & 0 & 0 & 0 & 0 & 0 & 0 & 0 & 0 & -\eta_{14} & -\eta_{15} & -\eta_{17} \\ 0 & 1 & 0 & 0 & 0 & 0 & 0 & 0 & 0 & 0 & 0 & 0 & -\varepsilon_{14} & -\varepsilon_{15} & -\varepsilon_{17} \\ 0 & 0 & 1 & 0 & 0 & 0 & 0 & 0 & 0 & 0 & 0 & 0 & -\eta_{24} & -\eta_{25} & -\eta_{27} \\ 0 & 0 & 0 & 1 & 0 & 0 & 0 & 0 & 0 & 0 & 0 & 0 & -\varepsilon_{24} & -\varepsilon_{25} & -\varepsilon_{27} \\ 0 & 0 & 0 & 0 & 1 & 0 & 0 & 0 & 0 & 0 & 0 & 0 & -\eta_{34} & -\eta_{35} & -\eta_{37} \\ 0 & 0 & 0 & 0 & 0 & 1 & 0 & 0 & 0 & 0 & 0 & 0 & -\varepsilon_{34} & -\varepsilon_{35} & -\varepsilon_{37} \\ 0 & 0 & 0 & 0 & 0 & 0 & 1 & 0 & 0 & 0 & 0 & 0 & -\eta_{44} & -\eta_{45} & -\eta_{47} \\ 0 & 0 & 0 & 0 & 0 & 0 & 1 & 0 & 0 & 0 & 0 & 0 & -\varepsilon_{44} & -\varepsilon_{45} & -\varepsilon_{47} \\ 0 & 0 & 0 & 0 & 0 & 0 & 0 & 1 & 0 & 0 & 0 & 0 & -\eta_{54} & -\eta_{55} & -\eta_{57} \\ 0 & 0 & 0 & 0 & 0 & 0 & 0 & 1 & 0 & 0 & 0 & 0 & -\varepsilon_{54} & -\varepsilon_{55} & -\varepsilon_{57} \\ 0 & 0 & 0 & 0 & 0 & 0 & 0 & 0 & 1 & 0 & 0 & 0 & -\eta_{64} & -\eta_{65} & -\eta_{67} \\ 0 & 0 & 0 & 0 & 0 & 0 & 0 & 0 & 0 & 1 & 0 & 0 & -\varepsilon_{64} & -\varepsilon_{65} & -\varepsilon_{67} \\ 0 & 0 & 0 & 0 & 0 & 0 & 0 & 0 & 0 & 0 & 1 & 0 & -\eta_{74} & -\eta_{75} & -\eta_{77} \\ 0 & 0 & 0 & 0 & 0 & 0 & 0 & 0 & 0 & 0 & 1 & 0 & -\varepsilon_{74} & -\varepsilon_{75} & -\varepsilon_{77} \\ 0 & 0 & 0 & 0 & 0 & 0 & 0 & 0 & 0 & 0 & 0 & 1 & -\eta_{84} & -\eta_{85} & -\eta_{87} \end{bmatrix}$$

Figure 2. Matrix S (15 x 1) of equation (13).

$$\begin{bmatrix} d\ln D_1 \\ d\ln S_1 \\ d\ln D_2 \\ d\ln S_2 \\ d\ln D_3 \\ d\ln S_3 \\ d\ln Q_4 \\ d\ln Q_5 \\ d\ln D_6 \\ d\ln S_6 \\ d\ln Q_7 \\ d\ln D_8 \\ d\ln P_4 \\ d\ln P_5 \\ d\ln P_7 \end{bmatrix}$$

Equilibrium displacement modelling 471

Figure 3. Matrix T (15 x 8) of equation (13).

$$\begin{bmatrix} \eta_{11} & 0 & \eta_{12} & \eta_{13} & \eta_{16} & \eta_{18} & \eta_{1y} & 0 \\ 0 & \varepsilon_{11} & \varepsilon_{12} & \varepsilon_{13} & \varepsilon_{16} & 0 & 0 & \varepsilon_{19} \\ \eta_{21} & 0 & \eta_{22} & \eta_{23} & \eta_{26} & \eta_{28} & \eta_{2y} & 0 \\ 0 & \varepsilon_{21} & \varepsilon_{22} & \varepsilon_{23} & \varepsilon_{26} & 0 & 0 & \varepsilon_{29} \\ \eta_{31} & 0 & \eta_{32} & \eta_{33} & \eta_{36} & \eta_{38} & \eta_{3y} & 0 \\ 0 & \varepsilon_{31} & \varepsilon_{32} & \varepsilon_{33} & \varepsilon_{36} & 0 & 0 & \varepsilon_{39} \\ \eta_{41} & 0 & \eta_{42} & \eta_{43} & \eta_{46} & \eta_{48} & \eta_{4y} & 0 \\ 0 & \varepsilon_{41} & \varepsilon_{42} & \varepsilon_{43} & \varepsilon_{46} & 0 & 0 & \varepsilon_{49} \\ \eta_{51} & 0 & \eta_{52} & \eta_{53} & \eta_{56} & \eta_{58} & \eta_{5y} & 0 \\ 0 & \varepsilon_{51} & \varepsilon_{52} & \varepsilon_{53} & \varepsilon_{56} & 0 & 0 & \varepsilon_{59} \\ \eta_{61} & 0 & \eta_{62} & \eta_{63} & \eta_{66} & \eta_{68} & \eta_{6y} & 0 \\ 0 & \varepsilon_{61} & \varepsilon_{62} & \varepsilon_{63} & \varepsilon_{66} & 0 & 0 & \varepsilon_{69} \\ \eta_{71} & 0 & \eta_{72} & \eta_{73} & \eta_{76} & \eta_{78} & \eta_{7y} & 0 \\ 0 & \varepsilon_{71} & \varepsilon_{72} & \varepsilon_{73} & \varepsilon_{76} & 0 & 0 & \varepsilon_{79} \\ \eta_{81} & 0 & \eta_{82} & \eta_{83} & \eta_{86} & \eta_{88} & \eta_{8y} & 0 \end{bmatrix}$$

Figure 4. Matrix U (8 x 1) of equation (13).

$$\begin{bmatrix} d\ln P_{1c} \\ d\ln P_{1p} \\ d\ln P_2 \\ d\ln P_3 \\ d\ln P_6 \\ d\ln P_8 \\ d\ln Y \\ d\ln P_9 \end{bmatrix}$$

Figure 5. Matrix V (1 x 8).

$$\begin{bmatrix} 1/(d\ln P_{1c}) & 1/(d\ln P_{1p}) & 1/(d\ln P_2) & 1/(d\ln P_3) & 1/(d\ln P_6) & 1/(d\ln P_8) & 1/(d\ln Y) & 1/(d\ln P_9) \end{bmatrix}$$

After setting the ratio of log differentials of any two different exogenous variables equal to zero, the matrix **UV** becomes the (8x8) identity matrix. Relative to equation (7), matrix **R** corresponds to matrix **E**, matrix **SV** (15x8) corresponds to matrix **G**, and matrix **T** corresponds to matrix **D**. In other words, equation (14) is of the form of equation (7) where **E** is of dimension (15x15), **G** is of dimension (15x8), and **D** is of dimension (15x8).

Values of the Marshallian elasticities needed for equation (14) were obtained by scanning the literature and exercising judgement. There is much uncertainty regarding these parameters. Previous econometric work was helpful in choosing elasticity values although different studies contain widely differing estimates for some elasticities. Economic theory is of assistance insofar as it provides theoretical relationships among elasticities (e.g., the homogeneity condition relating own-price, cross-price, and income elasticities of demand). The elasticities chosen are reported in Tables 1 and 2.

Table 1. Demand elasticities used for the Indonesian model.[a]

	Rice	Corn	Cassava	Sugar	Groundnut	Soybean	Sweetpotato	Wheat	Income
Rice	-0.60	0.04	0.03	0.02	0.03	0.03	0.02	0.04	0.36
Corn	0.34	-0.80	0.28	0.02	0.02	0.03	0.03	0.04	0.01
Cassava	0.10	0.15	-0.55	0.02	0.05	0.04	0.14	0.02	0.01
Sugar	0.04	0.02	0.02	-0.70	0.02	0.04	0.02	0.02	0.50
Groundnut	0.05	0.05	0.05	0.02	-1.00	0.10	0.03	0.02	0.65
Soybean	0.08	0.04	0.04	0.03	0.12	-0.90	0.02	0.03	0.50
Sweetpotato	0.01	0.05	0.10	0.01	0.02	0.01	-0.25	0.01	0.01
Wheat	0.12	0.04	0.01	0.02	0.01	0.02	0.01	-0.80	0.55

[a] The number in any cell shows the response in quantity demanded of the commodity given by the row heading to a 1% change in the price of the commodity given by the column heading.

Table 2. Supply elasticities used for the Indonesian model.[a]

	Rice	Corn	Cassava	Sugar	Groundnut	Soybean	Sweetpotato	Fertilizer
Rice	0.30	–0.05	–0.01	–0.02	–0.01	–0.02	–0.01	–0.15
Corn	–0.12	0.50	–0.02	–0.02	–0.02	–0.02	–0.02	–0.20
Cassava	–0.08	–0.01	0.20	0.00	0.00	0.00	–0.02	–0.05
Sugar	–0.02	–0.02	0.00	0.30	0.00	0.00	0.00	–0.15
Groundnut	–0.01	–0.02	0.00	0.00	0.40	–0.02	0.00	–0.10
Soybean	–0.02	–0.02	0.00	0.00	–0.02	0.40	0.00	–0.15
Sweetpotato	–0.01	–0.02	–0.02	0.00	0.00	0.00	0.25	–0.05

[a] The number in any cell shows the response in quantity supplied of the commodity given by the row heading to a 1% change in the price of the commodity given by the column heading.

Some Policy Experiments

Suppose one wanted to determine the proportionate change in the producer price of rice that would be necessary following some proportionate change in the price of fertilizer assuming the government wished to maintain the same level of rice self-sufficiency, defined as the ratio S_1/D_1 (i.e., the ratio of rice supply to rice demand).

For the self-sufficiency ratio to remain constant, the proportionate changes in rice supply and demand, following changes in producer prices for rice and fertilizer, would need to be equal. That is:

(15) $\quad dS_1/S_1 \quad = \quad dD_1/D_1$

where:

(16) $\quad dS_1/S_1 \quad = \quad G(S_1, P_{1p})\,(dP_{1p}/P_{1p}) + G(S_1,P_9)\,(dP_9/P_9)$

and

(17) $\quad dD_1/D_1 \quad = \quad G(D_1, P_{1p})\,(dP_{1p}/P_{1p}) + G(D_1,P_9)\,(dP_9/P_9).$

After substituting (16) and (17) into (15) and a little manipulation one obtains:

(18) $\quad dP_{1p}/P_{1p} \quad = \quad [[G(D_1,P_9) - G(S_1,P_9)] / [GS_1, P_{1p}) -$
$G(D_1, P_{1p})]]\,(d_P/P_9)$

Equation (18) gives the proportionate change in the producer price of rice that is necessary for any proportionate change in the price of fertilizer. From Figure 6:

$G(S_1, P_{1p}) \quad = \quad 0.29930$

$G(S_1, P_9) \quad = \quad -0.15489$

$G(D_1, P_{1p}) \quad = \quad 0.00106;$ and

$G(D_1, P_9) \quad = \quad 0.00747$

Substituting into (18):

(19) $\quad dP_{1p}/P_{1p} = \quad 0.54439\,(dP_9/P_9)$

For example, if the government increased the price of fertilizer by 5%, it would have to increase the producer price of rice by 2.72% ($= 0.54439 \times 0.05 \times 100$) in order to maintain the existing self-sufficiency ratio.

To acknowledge the uncertainty surrounding the Marshallian demand and supply elasticities, the experiment can be repeated for alternative values for these parameters. Although all the Marshallian elasticities reported in Tables 1 and 2 play a part in determining the answer to the policy question that has been posed, two that are crucial in that regard are the elasticities of rice supply with respect to the producer rice price and the price of fertilizer. Sensitivity analysis with respect to these parameters (with other elasticities fixed at the values reported in Tables 1 and 2) is reported in Table 3.

At first thought, the range covered by the extreme values in Table 3 is alarming (from 0.97% to 8.01%). However, the range over which the two supply elasticities has been varied is also large (50% either side of the base values). More importantly though, the extreme results correspond to the lowest value of one elasticity and the highest value of the other. One would expect that the higher the true value for one elasticity, the higher the true value for the other. This would lead one to consider 2.65% to 2.95% as the range of outcomes for the extent to which the producer price of rice would have to be increased in response to a 5% increase in the price of fertilizer in order for the self-sufficiency ratio to remain constant. The narrowness of this range suggests to this author that there would not be much payoff from investing a large volume of research resources in "fine-tuning" the two crucial supply elasticity estimates provided one is reasonably confident that the true values are in the ranges used in Table 3.

A slightly more complicated question that one might wish to address with the model is as follows: if there was a 1% increase in income, what is the nature of the tradeoff between changes in the producer price of rice and changes in the price of fertilizer that would maintain the rice self-sufficiency ratio? To answer this question, write the proportionate increases in rice supply and demand, respectively, as:

(20) $dS_1/S_1 = G(S_1,P_{1p}) (dP_{1p}/P_{1p}) + G(S_1,P_9) (dP_9/P_9)$
    $+ G(S_1,Y) (dY/Y)$

Table 3. Percentage changes in the producer price of rice consistent with maintaining the rice self-sufficiency ratio following a 5% increase in the price of fertilizer.[a]

	ε_{11}[b]		
ε_{19}[c]	0.15	0.30	0.45
−0.075	2.95	1.46	0.97
−0.15	5.48	2.72	1.81
−0.225	8.01	3.98	2.65

[a] Elasticities other than ε_{11} and ε_{19} have been set at the values shown in Tables 1 and 2.
[b] Elasticity of rice supply with respect to the producer price of rice.
[c] Elasticity of rice supply with respect to the price of fertilizer.

and

(21) $dD_1/D_1 = G(D_1,P_{1p}) (dP_{1p}/P_{1p}) + G(D_1,P_9) (dP_9/P_9)$
$+ G(D_1,Y) (dY/Y)$

Again, the proportionate changes in rice supply and demand need to be equal in order to maintain the same rice self-sufficiency ratio. After some manipulation, the following equation provides the proportionate change in the price of fertilizer necessary to maintain the self-sufficiency ratio following changes in income and the producer price of rice:

(22) $dP_9/P_9 = \left[\left[(G(D_1,P_{1p}) - G(S_1,P_{1p})\right) (dP_{1p}/P_{1p})\right.$
$\left.+ (G(D_1,P_9) - G(S_1,P_9)) (dP_9 P_9)\right]\right]$
$\div [G(S_1,Y) - G(D_1,Y)]$

Following substitution into (22) from the general equilibrium elasticities presented in Figure 6 and setting $dY/Y = 0.01$, the numerical form of equation (22) is:

(23) $dP_9/P_9 = -0.0247 + 1.8369 \, dP_{1p}/P_{1p}$

Hence, if incomes increased by 1%, an increase in the producer price of rice of 1% and a reduction in the fertilizer price of 0.6% would keep the rice self-sufficiency ratio constant. Alternatively, if the producer price of rice was increased by 5%, the price of fertilizer could be increased by 6.7% while maintaining the rice-self sufficiency ratio at its existing level.

Table 4 shows the values for the percentage change in fertilizer price necessary to maintain the rice self-sufficiency ratio at its existing level, given a 1% increase in the producer price of rice and income, and allowing for different

Table 4. Percentage changes in the price of fertilizer consistent with maintaining the rice self-sufficiency ratio following 1% increases in incomes and producer rice prices.[a]

	$\eta_{1y}{}^a$		
$\varepsilon_{11}{}^b, \varepsilon_{19}{}^c$	0.18	0.36	0.54
0.15, –0.075	–0.83	–2.89	–4.95
0.3, –0.15	0.48	–0.63	–1.74
0.45, –0.225	0.96	0.20	–0.56

[a] Elasticities other than η_{1y}, ε_{11} and ε_{19} have been set at the values shown in Tables 1 and 2.
[b] Elasticity of rice supply with respect to the producer price of rice.
[c] Elasticity of rice supply with respect to the price of fertilizer.

income elasticities of demand for rice and different rice supply elasticities. In this example, the supply elasticities have been parameterized, holding their ratio constant.

The extreme values shown in Table 4 are -4.95% (corresponding to the highest income elasticity and lowest supply elasticities) and 0.96% (corresponding to the lowest income elasticity and highest supply elasticities). Since the income elasticity of demand can be high (low) when the supply elasticities are low (high), the range of results shown in Table 4 has to be regarded as feasible. This is a case where better knowledge of Marshallian elasticities would be important in answering the policy question posed. In the absence of better information, it is incumbent upon the analyst to present the type of information shown in Table 4 to policy makers in order to highlight the uncertainty surrounding the answer. Of course, even where Marshallian elasticities have been estimated using an econometric model specifically designed for the problem at hand, the analyst has a responsibility to acknowledge uncertainty surrounding parameter values by presenting sensitivity analysis, rather than treating parameter estimates as if they were buried in cement.

Clearly, many other policy experiments could be conducted using the general equilibrium elasticities provided in Figure 6.

Strengths and Weaknesses

EDM is clearly a useful analytical tool that allows the analyst to explore the impacts of changes in exogenous variables. At times the analyst might only be concerned with making qualitative statements about impacts, such as the direction of change in endogenous variables. Sometimes this will be possible just with the usual assumptions about the signs of Marshallian own- and cross-price elasticities and the assumption that Marshallian own-price elasticities exceed (in absolute value) Marshallian cross-price elasticities. Sometimes it will be necessary to make assumptions about the relative sizes of demand and supply elasticities.

To demonstrate, consider applying Cramer's rule to matrix equation (6) assuming W increases (d ln W is positive) while other exogenous variables remain constant (d ln X, d ln Y, and d ln Z = 0). It can be easily verified that the solution to d ln P_1 is unambiguously positive assuming η_{1w} is positive, but the sign of d ln Q_1 will be ambiguous unless assumptions are made about the relative sizes of demand and supply elasticities.

EDM can also be used to make quantitative predictions about the impacts of finite changes in exogenous variables in the manner demonstrated in this chapter. Because it is a procedure based on differential calculus, the degree

Figure 6. General equilibrium elasticities matrix G (15 × 8) for the Indonesian model.

Endogenous variable	Exogenous variable							
	P_{1c}	P_{1p}	P_2	P_3	P_6	P_8	Y	P_9
D_1	-0.59763	0.00106	0.04535	0.03659	0.03394	0.04129	0.38537	0.00747
S_1	-0.00141	0.29930	-0.05285	-0.01335	-0.02196	-0.00077	-0.01543	-0.15489
D_2	0.34223	0.00119	-0.79376	0.28860	0.03331	0.04135	0.03113	0.00777
S_2	-0.00201	-0.12098	0.49519	-0.02618	-0.02307	-0.00114	-0.02064	-0.20671
D_3	0.10578	0.00371	0.17359	-0.51352	0.04859	0.02411	0.05072	0.02172
S_3	-0.00045	-0.08041	-0.01286	0.19516	-0.00049	-0.00042	-0.00098	-0.05212
Q_4	0.01235	-0.01383	-0.00682	0.00770	0.01267	0.00622	0.15313	-0.10391
Q_5	0.01471	-0.00685	0.00148	0.01651	0.01474	0.00601	0.18905	-0.06964
D_6	0.08609	0.00198	0.05062	0.05057	-0.88783	0.03285	0.57301	0.01584
S_6	-0.00074	-0.02016	-0.02107	-0.00083	0.39826	-0.00030	-0.00945	-0.15152
Q_7	0.00557	-0.00482	0.01576	0.04054	0.00608	0.00525	0.01228	-0.02347
D_8	0.12141	0.00070	0.04285	0.01335	0.02196	-0.79923	0.56543	0.00489
P_4	0.04118	0.02057	0.04393	0.02567	0.04222	1.02072	0.51043	0.15364
P_5	0.03678	0.00788	0.05369	0.04127	0.08684	0.01503	0.47263	0.07590
P_7	0.02229	0.02073	0.14303	0.24216	0.02432	0.02102	0.04911	0.10611

of accuracy of the predictions is inversely related to the size of the exogenous changes being considered. (The same is likely to be true of structural econometric models.) Research by Alston and Wohlgenant (1990) suggests that the predictions will be quite accurate for changes in exogenous variables of 10% or less. If the underlying functional forms are indeed linear, then the procedure is exact provided proportionate changes in any exogenous variable x are measured as $(x_1 - x_0)/x_0$ where the subscripts 0 and 1 indicate initial and new values, respectively. If proportionate changes are measured as $d \ln x$ (= $\ln x - \ln x_0$) then the procedure will be exact for functional forms that are linear in logs (B. Hurd, pers. comm., 1992).

The author believes that, given the severity of problems normally encountered in estimating structural econometric models in developing countries, EDM provides a convenient alternative which is economical (relative to econometric modelling) in terms of research resources. While it only provides approximations, the same is true for econometric modelling. For example, one never knows the "true" functional forms to use in an econometric model, although one can choose those which appear most appropriate based on any a priori information available and statistical tests. The procedures outlined in this chapter provide first-order approximations for any underlying functional form.

Because EDM is a form of comparative statistics, it can be criticized on the grounds that adjustment paths from one equilibrium to another are ignored. Of course static econometric models also suffer this criticism. The criticism could be overcome to some extent by repeated applications of EDM using Marshallian elasticities corresponding to different lengths of run.

References

Alston, J. M. 1991. Research benefits in a multi-market setting: A review. *Review of Marketing and Agricultural Economics* 59(1):23-52.

Alston, J.M. and M.K. Wohlgenant. 1990. Measuring research benefits using linear elasticity equilibrium displacement models. In *Returns to the Australian wool industry from investment in R & D* (J.D. Mullen and J.M. Alston, eds.). Rural and Resource Economics Report No. 10, NSW Agriculture and Fisheries, Sydney, 99-111, Australia.

Chiang, A.C. 1984. *Fundamental methods of mathematical economics*. Third Edition. Singapore: McGraw-Hill.

Gardner, B.L. 1975. The farm-retail price spread in a competitive food industry. *American Journal of Agricultural Economics* 57(3):399-409.

Hertel, T.W. 1991. Factor market incidence of agricultural trade liberalization: Some additonal results. *Australian Journal of Agricultural Economics* 35(1): 77-107.

Holloway, G.J. 1991. The farm-retail price spread in an imperfectly competitive food industry. *American Journal of Agricultural Economics* 73(4):979-89.

Muth, R.F. 1964. The derived demand for a productive factor and the industry supply curve. *Oxford Economic Papers* 16(2):221-34.

Wohlgenant, M.K. and R.C. Haidacher. 1989. *Retail to farm linkage for a complete demand system of food commodities.* Technical Bulletin Number 1775, Economic Research Service, United States Department of Agriculture, Washington D.C.

Index

—A—

Abbot, P. C., 125, 430, 435
Abbott, J. C., 4, 13, 61, 134
Abbott, R., 134
Activity analysis models, 423
Agricultural commercialization, 187, 188, 189, 191, 212
Agricultural marketing, 3, 14, 17, 43, 54, 134, 211, 237, 324, 403, 437, 439
Ahmed, R., 327, 341
Akaike, H., 332, 341, 348, 356
Alberti, A. M., 190, 212
Aldenderfer, M. S., 208, 212
Alston, J. M., 404, 408, 418, 462, 478
Alvarez, M., 16, 125, 134, 136
Amemiya, T., 203, 212
Analysis of dynamic adjustments, composite index, 333
Analysis of prices, seasonal index, 277, 280-81, 283, 285, 288, 290-91, 296-97
Analysis of variance, 204
Analysis,
    comparative static, 461-62
    Hop Skip Jump method, 439
    temporal, 283, 285, 286, 294, 297, 298
Anderberg, M. R., 208, 212
Apland, J., 440, 454, 456
Aranda, J., 190, 212
Ardeni, P. G., 329, 341
Argentina, 7, 10, 239, 240, 248, 251, 252
Arizpe, L., 190, 212
Arrow, K. J., 430, 435

Asian Productivity Organization, 13
Atkin, R., 323
Austin, J. E. II., 5, 13, 116, 118, 123, 130, 132, 134

—B—

Babu, S., 337, 340, 341
Bagayoko, B., 46, 61
Bain, J. S., 219, 221, 224, 226-27, 230, 236, 310, 323-24
Baker, B. S., 455
Baker, D., 4, 14
Bale, M. D., 74, 97
Bangladesh, 7, 152, 171, 174, 185, 325-26, 336-39, 341
Barankin, E. W., 430, 435
Bari, M. F., 442, 443, 444, 456
Barkin, D., 213
Barriers to entry, 217, 225, 227, 228, 232, 235
Bashfield, R. K., 208, 212
Bateman, D. I., 4, 13, 323, 324
Baumes, H. S., 429, 435
Beltran, N., 135
Ben Salah, H., 413, 418
Ben Temime, A., 418, 419
Benavides, M., 134
Benson, B., 348, 356
Bessler, D., 349, 356
Best, R. A., 136, 362, 363, 376, 377
Blandford, D., 430
Blanken, J., 189, 212
Blumberg, R. L., 190, 212
Blyn, G., 329, 341
Bohall, R. W., 435
Bogatay, A., 17

Booth, R., 135
Booth, R. H., 419
Bongarts, 2, 13
Boughton, D., 44, 60, 62
Bouis, H. E., 189, 190, 212, 214
Boyd, M., 331, 341, 348, 356
Breimyer, H. F., 4, 14
Brennen, M. J., 405, 418
Bressler, R. G., 6, 14, 218, 230, 236
Brieva, S., 7, 10, 250
Briggs, C. L., 151, 163
Brill, E. D., Jr., 442, 443, 455
Bromley, R. J., 4, 8, 14, 143, 144, 156, 163
Brooke, A., 447, 455
Brorsen, B. W., 331, 341, 347-48, 356
Brown, J., 153, 165
Brown, M., 88, 97
Bucklin, L., 4, 14
Bulmer, M., 5, 14
Bunster, X. B., 157, 163
Burgess, R. G., 145, 148, 157, 163
Burton, R. O., Jr., 442, 443, 447, 453, 455
Byerlee, D., 117, 134

—C—

Caballero, R., 190, 215
Cabeza, F., 454, 456
Casley, D. J., 184
Cassava, 12, 22, 25, 30, 31, 36, 37, 41, 67, 100, 135, 361-79, 469
  financial profitability analysis for, 378
  flour, 176
  processing plants, 346, 365, 373
  project pilot phase, 368, 375
Castañeda, J., 190, 215
Caves, R., 219, 236
Censored variables, 383-85

Centro Internacional de Agricultura Tropical, 136, 361, 362, 363, 366, 368, 376, 377
Centro Internacional de la Papa, 40, 133, 135, 136, 178, 185, 239, 240, 242, 251, 361, 414, 418
Chambers, R., 151, 163
Chang, S., 442, 443, 455
Chapman, G. P., 318, 323, 324
Chavas, J., 416, 418
Chavez, A., 213
Cheikh, M., 418, 419
Chiang, A. C., 462, 478
Chuzel, G., 376
Clarete, R., 351, 356
Claypoole, K., 214
Cluster analysis, 208
Coarse grain, 43, 45, 48, 393-97, 401, 402
Coefficient of variation, 205, 351
Cogill, B., 2, 15
Collins, J., 190, 214
Collusive practices, pricing, 230
Colman, D., 4, 14
Concentration indices, 223, 224
Consumer price index, 52, 413
Copra markets in the Philippines, 12, 343-55
Coursey, D. G., 115, 121, 134
Crop diversification, 193
Crop losses in storage, 114, 403-17
Crop storage,
  conceptual model of, 405
Cross disciplinary approaches, 145
Crow, B., 152, 163
Curtis, C. E., 456

—D—

D'Alfonso, T. H., 448, 455
Dairy marketing, 7, 73
  social values, 73, 77, 78, 82, 89, 91, 93

Dairy,
  production, 86
  ration formulation, 447
Daniell, W., 214
Darrah, L. B., 273, 274
Data collection (see fieldwork), 1, 6, 9, 21, 22, 26, 51, 54, 84, 99, 103, 125, 127, 169, 170, 172, 173, 174, 179, 181, 182-84, 192, 194, 195, 201, 229
  library research, 148
  on consumption, 3, 16, 23-25, 34, 39, 43-48, 55, 57-62, 109, 112, 118-19, 122-24, 135, 137, 148, 150, 163, 167-68, 174-77, 180, 193, 200, 213, 257, 259, 262, 276, 279, 316-17, 344, 362, 366, 376, 392, 410, 411, 417, 422-25, 462
  on food marketing, 164, 172, 274, 342
David, V., 277, 346, 356
Davidson, S., 365, 376
Davis, J. S., 404, 419
Decision making, preliminary decisions, 365
Decomposition analysis, 205
Delgado, C. L., 101, 113, 294, 298
Della Vedova, O., 7, 10, 239, 241, 250
Denen, H., 124, 134
Devadoss, S., 430, 435
Devine, P. J., 222, 236
DeWalt, B. R., 213
DeWalt, K. M., 189, 213
Dewey, K. G., 190, 213
Dickey, D. A., 329, 330, 341
Distributive margins, dynamic analysis of, 304
Domestic resources costs, 73
Dorfman, R., 430, 435
Dubetz, S., 456
Dutt, A. K., 2, 14
Dyer, M. E., 443, 455

—E—

Economic anthropology, 144
Economic development, 14, 99, 356, 383, 398, 419
  selectivity models, 383, 393
Economic performance, 219, 237, 356
Ecuador, 7, 11, 144, 277-99, 362
EDM (Equilibrium Displacement Modelling), 461-64, 476, 478
  physical functions, 257, 265
  policy experiments in, 473
Edwards, M., 211, 213
Edwardson, W., 116, 135
Efficiency studies, commonly available data, 302
Eicher, C., 4, 14
Elz, D., 4, 14
Engle, R. F. C., 329, 330, 341
Enke, S. A., 429, 435
ERR (Economic Rate of Return), 363-65
Escudero, J. C., 213
Essamet, M., 418, 419
Everitt, B., 208, 213
Ewell, P. T., 419
Export vegetables, 191
Eyles, J., 145, 163

—F—

Factor analysis, 202, 203
Falcon, W. P., 17, 185, 238
Falusi, A. O., 429, 436
Fama, E. F., 347, 356
Faminow, M. D., 7, 13, 348, 356, 439, 440, 447, 454, 455, 456
Farace, V., 17
Farid, N., 327, 337, 338, 341
Farmer food purchases, 99
Farris, P. L., 16, 348, 356
Farrish, R. O. P., 435
Farruk, M. O., 341
Fei, J. C. H., 205, 213, 214

Ferguson, C. E., 135, 136, 228, 236
Field studies,
  research strategies for, 196
  design, 196
Fieldwork (see also data collection) 46, 84, 85, 146, 148, 149, 150, 151, 153, 155, 162, 164, 165, 167, 179
Finan, T., 97
Finlayson, M., 189, 213
Fischer, D., 44, 59, 60
Fleming, E. M., 4, 5, 14
Fleuret, A., 213
Fleuret, P., 190, 213
Food production, 170
Food system interrelationships, 22
  dietary, 190
Foote, R. J., 273, 275
Ford, S., 349, 356
Forker, O. D., 334, 335, 342
Fox, R., 79, 97
Frank, S. D., 440, 454, 456
Freeze, B. S., 448, 456
FRR (Financial Rate of Return), 361, 363-74, 381
Fuchs, H. W., 430, 435
Fuglie, K. O., 7, 12, 403, 404, 414, 416, 418
Fuller, W. A., 150, 329, 330, 341

—G—

Gana, J. A., 149, 163
Gardiner, E. E., 456
Gardner, B. L., 414, 418, 462, 478
Gender patterns of trade, 159
General equilibrium elasticities, 461, 464, 466, 467, 469, 475, 476
Geographical research, 7, 143, 144, 163-65
Gibson, R. R., 447, 454, 456
Gidley, J. S., 442, 443, 444, 455, 456

Gittinger, J., 363, 364, 377
Glover, D., 190, 213
Goddard, E., 16
Goetz, S., 5, 7, 12, 168, 174, 179, 184, 279, 283, 298, 383, 392, 396, 397, 398
Gómez, R., 135
Goodwin, B. K., 101, 113, 329, 341
Goueder, J., 419
Goueder, M., 419
Gould, J. P., 228, 236
Government policy, 2, 236, 325, 327
Grand Seasonal Index (GSI), 290
Granger, C. W. J., 329, 330, 341, 349, 356
Greene, W. H., 388, 390, 398
Griffiths, W. E., 342, 398
Gross, D., 190, 213, 379
Guatemala, 7, 10, 17, 187, 188, 191-93, 203, 204, 210-15
Gutiérrez, E., 190, 215

—H—

Habito, C., 351, 356
Haddad, L. J., 189, 190, 212
Haidacher, R. C., 462, 479
Handwerker, W. P., 145, 163
Hardaker, B., 213
Hardaker, J. B., 430, 435
Harman, H. H., 202, 213
Harrington, J. J., 442, 456
Harrington, L., 134
Harrison, K., 4, 15, 17
Harriss, B., 7, 11, 15, 101, 113, 294, 298, 301, 304, 305, 316, 317, 323, 324, 326, 329, 342
Hartog, A. P., 122, 135
Hazell, P. B. R., 440, 456
Heady, E. O., 429, 430, 436, 437, 440, 456
Henley, D., 15
Henry, W. R., 218

Herfindahl Index, 223, 225
Hernández, J. R., 213
Hernández, M., 190, 213
Herrera, E. J., 21, 40, 239, 251, 257, 277
Hertel, T. W., 462, 479
Heytens, P. J., 348, 356
Heywood, P., 213
Hidalgo, C. P., 213
Hill, C., 398
Hill, P., 145, 150, 153, 163, 164
Hill, R. C., 342
Hironaka, R., 448, 456
Hoisington, C., 4, 14
Hollier, G., 143, 145, 152, 164
Holloway, G. J., 462, 479
Holtzman, J. S., 5, 7, 8, 15, 40, 43, 44, 46, 47, 55, 60, 61, 121, 135, 168, 169, 173, 184
Hopkins, L. D., 13, 17, 97, 134, 163, 185, 212, 238, 377, 419, 442, 443, 455
Hoppin, P., 190, 214
Horton, D. E., 127, 135, 175, 184, 415, 419
Hotchkiss, D., 17, 189, 190, 191, 212
Household,
  food availability, 190, 192
  income, 187, 191, 192, 198
  resource allocation, 187, 191, 212
  resources, 189, 192
Howard, W., 16
HSJ (Hop Skip Jump Method), 443, 444, 445, 447, 451, 452, 454, 457
Humphreys, C., 74, 97
Hurtado, E., 214
Hurwicz, L., 435

—I—

Idaikkadar, N. M., 184

Immink, M., 7, 10, 17, 187, 189, 190, 191, 203, 204, 212, 213
India, 3, 7, 10, 11, 13, 15, 17, 120, 129, 135, 136, 139, 303, 307, 316, 319, 320, 321, 322, 324, 342, 421, 432, 433, 435, 436, 437
Indonesia, 299, 324, 361, 461, 468
Indonesian food price policy, 461
Instituto Colombiano Agropecuario, 126, 135
Internal Rate of Return (IRR), 363
International Crops Research Institute for the Semi-Arid Tropics, 4, 15, 17, 324
Interviews, informal, 9, 21, 26, 27, 28, 42, 43, 44, 46, 47, 54, 55, 56, 57, 115, 122, 127, 133
Interviews of traders, 148
Irwin, S. H., 236, 456
Ishak, H. O., 220, 224, 225, 226, 227, 228, 230, 236

—J—

Jabara, C. L., 4, 17
Jaeger, W., 74, 97
Jarrett, F. G., 408, 419
Jeffrey, S. R., 7, 13, 439, 447, 454, 456
Jones, C., 403, 419
Jones, R. M., 3, 4, 15, 16, 236
Jones, W. O., 101, 113, 168, 184, 328, 342, 403, 419
Judge, G. G., 331, 332, 342, 385, 398, 429, 430, 436

—K—

Kaiser, H. F., 202, 214
Kaiser, H. M., 440, 454, 456
Kanbur, M. G., 429, 436
Kaynak, E., 15
Kaysen, C., 226, 236
Keane, P., 135
Keifer, M., 214

Kendrick, D., 447, 455
Kennedy, E., 2, 15, 189, 190, 199, 212, 214
Kenya, 3, 7, 9, 15, 73, 86, 87, 90, 95, 97, 214
Khon Kaen University, 135
Kim, K. S., 2, 14
Kindra, G. S., 3, 15
King, R. A., 6, 14, 218, 230, 236, 440, 456
Kinnucan, H. W., 334, 335, 342
Kinsey, J., 3, 15
Kirk, R., 204, 214
Klein, K. K., 448, 456
Koch, J. V., 218, 222, 223, 237
Kotler, P., 130, 135
Krishnaiah, J., 7, 12, 421, 430, 436
Kuhn, H. W., 430, 431, 436
Kuo, S. W. Y., 205, 213
Kydd, J., 2, 5, 16

—L—

Lappé, F. M., 190, 214
Larson, D., 17
Lee, L. F., 395, 398, 401, 402
Lee, N., 236, 395, 398, 401, 402
Lee, T., 342, 398
Lele, U. J., 304, 324, 342
Lerner's Index, 223
Lerner, A. P., 223, 237
Librero, A. R., 228, 237
Lichte, J. A., 8, 43, 46, 55, 60, 61
Lin, T. F., 390, 398
Lindgren, B. W., 342
Lindner, R. J., 408, 419
Lipton, M., 415, 419
Logarithmic trend, formula for, 300
Loizos, P., 5, 15
Loveridge, S., 7, 9, 99, 100, 108, 111, 113
Lowdermilk, M. L., 44, 62
Lunven, P., 190, 214
Lury, D. A., 184

Lutkepohl, H., 398
Lutz, E., 74, 97
Lynam, J., 135

—M—

Maddala, G. S., 388, 395, 398, 402
Madrigal, H., 213
Magrath, P., 5, 15
Maize, 7, 21, 22, 23, 24, 32, 33, 34, 36, 37, 38, 39, 58, 61, 62, 108, 178, 277
  evaluation of export possibilities, 38
  net returns per hectare, 21, 36
  production technology, 21, 34, 116, 242, 407
  profitability analysis, 34, 378
Makeham, J. P., 4, 13
Malawi, 7, 325, 326, 336, 337, 340, 341
Mali, 7, 8, 43, 44, 45, 46, 47, 48, 50, 58, 59, 60, 61, 62, 163
Mann, H. M., 226, 237
Margins, static analysis of, 304
Market analysis, 6, 117, 124, 127, 217, 218, 220, 227, 235, 355
Market concentration, 222, 223, 224, 226, 232, 235, 343
Market conduct, 217, 219, 221, 227, 228, 230, 232, 236
Market coordination,
  efficiency of, 9, 44, 74, 76, 79, 96, 111, 199, 217, 218, 219, 220, 221, 232, 233, 237, 278, 281, 301, 302, 303, 304, 307, 310, 323, 325, 333, 339, 347, 356, 373, 374, 403, 422, 452
  price correlation in, 294
Market enterprises, profits of, 301
Market integration model, 334, 373
Market integration,
  analytical framework for, 188, 327

Index

analyzing, 325, 340
applications of, 144, 202, 336, 340, 418, 419, 439, 453
cointegration coefficients, 325, 328, 329, 337, 338, 339
conceptual framework, 326
degree of, 173, 336, 340
determinants of, 326, 328, 341
dynamic adjustments in, 331
effects on, 336, 338, 339
factors affecting, 328
factors of integration, 335
framework of, 334
horizontal, 325, 334
knowledge of, 326
market network, 328
measuring, 326, 328, 335, 340
monopoly and, 222, 228, 236, 237, 305, 351
price competition, 6, 42, 53, 60, 76, 78, 86, 101, 131, 221, 222, 223, 224, 226, 228, 233, 236, 273, 297, 302, 331, 345, 423, 462
price rigidities, 333, 337
structural factors affecting integration, 337
time series analysis, 325
Market participation, conditional, 383
Market performance and systems, data requirements for, 9, 12, 25, 41, 75, 84, 221, 320, 343, 344, 355
Market performance, 22, 73, 101, 113, 217, 219, 227, 228, 230, 232, 298, 343, 352
Market structure, 217, 219, 221, 222, 227, 228, 232, 233, 234, 235, 236, 237, 294
Market, transaction costs, 12, 301, 327, 383, 384, 385, 386, 394, 395

Markets
data requirements for analyzing, 9, 12, 25, 41, 75, 84, 221, 320, 343, 344, 355
Distributive margins in, 301, 304
input, 239
periodic, 143
Marketing and production cooperative, 29, 88, 89, 91, 192, 194, 195, 199, 204, 205, 276, 348, 353, 361, 362, 376
Marketing channels, 28, 33, 34, 35, 39, 79, 80, 85, 96, 125, 130, 132, 133, 257, 258, 261, 262, 265, 266, 270, 274, 283, 334
analysis of, 257, 258, 262, 274
basic concepts, 258
maize, 33
study of, 274
Marketing costs, 53, 56, 74, 168, 173, 218, 219, 221, 227, 228, 232, 233, 234, 235, 267, 268, 273, 328, 376
Marketing,
agents, 259
calculating margins, 267
estimates, 105
exchange functions, 257
price estimates of, 107
Marketing margins, 8, 11, 21, 34, 36, 167, 173, 217, 230, 232, 233, 234, 258, 261, 265, 267, 269, 270, 273, 274, 279, 301, 324, 342, 403
stability of, 270
Marketing systems, 3, 4, 8, 15, 16, 17, 22, 47, 61, 113, 266, 301, 302, 316, 320, 321, 323, 327, 340
comparability of firms, 317
returns to trading firms, 316
Marshall, A., 433, 436
Martin, J., 61

Martin, L. J., 430, 436
Martin, M. V., 454, 456
Massel, B. E., 404, 419
McCarl, B. A., 429, 435
McComb, J., 213
McConnell, R., 214
McDonald, J. F., 398, 400
McMullen, B. S., 454, 456
Meeraus, A., 447, 455
Meilke, K. D., 430, 437
Mejicanos, P., 214
Mello, L. E., 133, 135
Mendoza, G., 7, 11, 233, 243, 245, 246, 248, 252, 254, 257, 260, 274, 336, 342, 343, 348, 356
Mendoza, M. S., 7, 12, 149, 164, 233, 243, 245, 246, 248, 252, 254, 257, 260, 274, 336, 342, 343, 348, 356
Model
  crop storage and food supply, 405
  financial components of a cassava, 361, 366
Modelling,
  equilibrium displacement, 461
  to generate alternatives, 456
Models, (PAM), sensitivity analysis, 8, 36, 73, 80, 94, 95, 208, 367, 368, 415, 416, 439, 442, 443, 444, 445, 446, 447, 455, 474, 476
Mathematical programming models,
  using nearly optimal solutions, 439, 441, 445, 451, 452, 454, 456
  sensitivity analysis in, 36, 80, 94, 95, 416, 439, 446, 474
Moffitt, R. A., 398
Monares, A., 242, 248, 251
Monke, E. A., 15, 74-79, 81, 84, 86, 96, 97, 101, 113
Morris, M., 7, 8, 21, 40
Mudiantono, 219, 234, 237

Murphy, K. M., 399, 402
Murray, D., 190, 214
Muth, R. F., 408, 419, 462, 479

—N—
Nason, R., 17
National Economic Development Authority, 345, 346, 356
National Research Council, 449, 456
National Statistics Institute, 413, 414, 419
Nave, R. W., 120, 129, 135, 139, 140
Netting, R. M., 190, 214, 317
Neves, F., 17
Newbery, D. M. G., 331, 342
Nichols, P., 5, 16
Nigeria, 7, 9, 113, 134, 143, 146, 147, 149, 150, 151, 156, 163, 164, 298, 420, 436
Norton, G. W., 404, 419
Norton, R. D., 440, 456

—O—
Ogunfowora, O., 429, 436
Onyenwaku, C. E., 429, 436
Organization for Economic Cooperation and Development, 237
Ospina, B., 362, 377
Ostertag, C., 7, 12, 361, 363, 366, 377

—P—
Pabuayon, I. M., 238
Palacios, M., 419
Palaskas, T. B., 304, 323, 324, 326, 329, 342
PAM (Policy Analysis Matrix), 7, 8, 73-97, 461
  advantages of, 80

Index

agricultural commodity markets in relation to, 73
calculation of coefficients, 82
calculations for activity budget, 82, 87
indicators, 95, 174, 199, 200
limitations, 81
use for policy analysis, 78
Papandreou, A. G., 224, 237
Paraguay, 7, 8, 21, 22, 23, 24, 25, 26, 27, 28, 30, 31, 32, 33, 34, 36, 38, 39, 40
Patai, D., 162, 164
Pearson, S. R., 15, 17, 74, 75, 76, 77, 78, 79, 81, 84, 86, 96, 97, 185, 238
Peck, A. E., 297, 298
Peil, M., 149, 151, 152, 164
Petzel, T. E., 101, 113
Pfeiffer, G. H., 456
Philippine Coconut Authority (PHILCOA), 346, 356
Philippine copra market, 345
Philippines, 3, 7, 167, 212, 217, 220, 224, 228, 235, 237, 238, 342, 345, 346, 352, 356, 357
Pindyck, R., 279, 299
Pinto, I., 195, 214
Plate, R., 273, 275
Plattner, S., 145, 164
Plessner, Y., 430, 436, 437
Policy, marketing agricultural commodities, 75
Pomeroy, R. S., 7, 9, 217, 219, 220, 224, 225, 227, 228, 230, 232, 234, 235, 237
Popkin, B. M., 190, 214
Porter, G., 7, 9, 143, 148, 159, 161, 164
Potato, 7, 11, 16, 103, 120, 126, 133, 136, 140, 170, 185, 193, 240, 242, 243, 244, 247, 252, 253, 262, 269, 270, 275, 403, 412, 416, 418

seed, 10, 239, 240, 241, 246, 248, 249, 252, 253, 254
seed renewal rate, 240
Potato storage, 403 (see also Storage)
Pratt, B., 5, 15
Prebish, R., 1, 16
Price analyses,
price trends, 278
price variation, 52, 53, 267, 273, 278, 302, 309, 350
Price collusion, 343
Price correlation coefficient, 11, 30, 32, 47, 48, 51, 53, 84, 101, 169, 173, 219, 221, 277, 303, 310, 327, 328, 336, 349, 350, 414, 415
Price data analysis, 30, 47, 51
Price formation, 246, 248, 259, 294, 295, 305, 342, 355, 407
Pricing,
price correlation coefficient, 11, 102, 293, 294, 295, 296, 297, 328, 329, 336
Primary data collection,
informal interviews, 9, 21, 26, 27, 28, 42, 43, 44, 46, 47, 54, 55, 56, 57, 115, 122, 127, 133
interviews, 9, 10, 21, 26, 27, 28, 29, 42, 43, 44, 46, 47, 54, 55, 56, 57, 85, 102, 103, 115, 119, 122, 123, 124, 127, 133, 144, 145, 146, 148, 150, 152, 153, 155, 156, 157, 175, 194, 195, 198, 244, 265, 266, 270
Priscilla, M., 190, 214
Probit, 203, 204, 383, 389, 390, 392, 393, 396, 397, 398, 400
Product development, 135, 136, 361
Production cycle, 32, 115, 192, 276, 280, 282, 283

Production,
   agricultural, 44, 105, 109, 178, 191, 192, 199, 317, 318, 323, 447
   crop, 119, 125, 188, 189, 190, 194, 195, 198, 200, 208, 209, 213, 214, 392, 407, 409, 424
   export crop, 194, 195, 208, 209
   farm, 78, 126, 187, 191, 193, 195, 197, 199, 200, 405
   household, 208, 213
   market, 199
Profit seeking, and dynamic analysis of firms, 307
Proll, L. G., 443, 455
Puetz, D., 189, 213
Punch, M., 164
Puzon, M. Y., 228, 237
Pyatt, G., 205, 214

—Q—

QP (quadratic programming), 421, 429, 430, 435, 436, 437

—R—

Rahmouni, A., 418
Raman, K. V., 419
Ramos, H., 283, 299
Randhawa, N. S., 429, 436
Ranis, G., 205, 213
Rapid appraisal, 8, 21, 22, 26, 40, 43, 44, 45, 46, 47, 51, 54, 56, 58, 60, 61, 129, 266, 328
   a list of data requirements, 41
   data analysis techniques, 30
   devising structured informal interview guidelines for, 54
   information gathering in, 47
   problems in conducting, 56
   study focus and key informants, 46
   survey of input prices, 29
   survey interviews, 28
   verification survey of maize production practices, 29
Ravallion, M., 101, 113, 299, 331, 342, 348, 356
Rayo, M., 214
Reeves, E., 5, 16
Renkow, M., 405, 419
Rhoades, R., 127, 134, 136, 226, 237
Rice, 7, 45, 178, 277, 283, 346, 433, 434, 472
Riley, H. M., 4, 15, 16, 17
Rimmer, D., 164
Robinson, K. L., 222, 233, 238, 279, 280, 282, 299
Roemer, M., 3, 16
Rogers, B. L., 44, 62
Rosegrant, M., 7, 12, 336, 342, 343
Rosenstock, L., 190, 214
Rothschild, K. W., 223, 237
Roumasset, J. A., 351, 356
Roush, W. B., 455
Rubinfeld, D., 299
Russell, T., 442
Ruttan, V. W., 403, 419
Rwanda, 7, 9, 99, 100, 101, 103, 105, 106, 108, 110, 112, 113, 185, 212

—S—

Salayo, N. D., 235, 238
Samples, selecting the research, 243
Samuelson, P. A., 429, 436
Santos, O. F., 2, 16, 346, 357
Sarhan, M. E., 440, 454, 455
Savit, R., 323, 324
Scarborough, V., 2, 5, 16
Scheid, A. C., 219, 220, 224, 225, 230, 233, 234, 235, 237
Schell, G., 214
Scherer, F. M., 219, 222, 223, 224, 226, 237

Schindler, J. S., 376
Schlesinger, L. E., 145, 165
Schmidt, P., 390, 398
Schoepfle, G. M., 145, 148, 151, 152, 165
Schoonmaker, K., 60
Schroeder, T. C., 101, 113, 329, 341
Scobie, G., 408, 418
Scott, G. J., 1, 7, 9, 10, 16, 21, 40, 99, 115, 116, 120, 122, 129, 132, 133, 135, 136, 138, 139, 167, 168, 185, 239, 251, 257, 277, 377, 403, 418, 419
Scott, J. T., 429, 437
Scrimshaw, S. C. M., 214, 419
Seasonal factors,
  fluctuations, 281, 327
  index, 277, 280, 281, 283, 285, 288, 290, 291, 296, 297
  patterns, 279, 294, 298
  prices, 103, 280, 281, 285, 288, 403, 407, 409, 414, 415
  supply variations, 281
Secondary data,
  analysis of, 47
  how to present, 183
  how to procure, 179, 181
  multilateral and bilateral agencies, 178
  research methods, 15, 40, 97, 111, 164, 167, 236
  where to find, public sector, 177
Seed potato,
  demand for, 118, 137, 240, 280, 416, 425, 428, 433, 472
Sellen, D., 16, 97
SEM (see Spatial Equilibrium Models)
Service National de Recensement, 100, 113

Shaffer, J. D., 6, 15, 16, 22, 40, 99, 113
Shwedel, K. J., 17
Siddle, D. J., 145, 164
Sikka, B. K., 136
Simulation models, 424
Singh, A., 2, 14, 405, 419
Singh, R. P., 405, 419
Size distribution of sellers, 222
Slater, C., 6, 17
Small-scale agro-enterprise
  rate of return, 317, 361
  financial model for, 361, 363, 365
Smith, C. A., 145, 150, 164
Smith, D. M., 163
Smith, E. D., 219, 220
Smith, E. G., 219, 220, 237, 456
Smith, R. H. T., 144, 145, 150, 164, 165
Socioeconomic methods, 239
South Asia, 2, 301, 302, 305, 317, 318
Spatial analysis, 144, 277, 293, 297, 298
Spatial Equilibrium Model (SEM), 12, 421, 423, 424, 428-29, 430-31, 434, 436, 437, 454
  an empirical application, 430
  purpose of, 424
  spatial price equilibrium, 422
  using microcomputer spreadsheets for, 277
Spatial equilibrium, general competitive, 422
Spatial integration, 293
Spatial perspectives, 143
Spatially differentiated markets, 347
  hypothesized pricing behavior, 348
  modelling spatial pricing behavior, 344
  price discovery, 343

price discrimination, 302, 343, 345, 348, 352
price series, 349
using the bivariate autoregressive model, 343, 352, 353
Squire, L., 405, 419
Srivastava, B. N., 120, 136
Staatz, J. M., 4, 16, 44, 60
Statistical methods, 383, 384
Statistical procedures, 202
Stevens, R. D., 4, 17
Stickney, C. P., 376
Stigler, G. J., 237
Stiglitz, J., 331, 342
Stone, G. D., 190, 214
Storage,
    potato storage model, 404
    reduced costs, 404
Strauss, J., 405, 419
Strickland, D. A., 145, 165
Survey design, 10, 112, 143, 244
Survey tools, archives, 148, 149
Surveys,
    analysis of, 8, 9, 11, 12, 30, 34, 62, 73, 74, 76, 86, 87, 95, 97, 107, 124, 127, 159, 204, 208, 210, 211, 217, 234, 277, 283, 290, 293, 296, 304, 307, 318, 320, 342, 378, 454
    conducting a, 154, 246
    data processing of, 247
    field methods, 1, 6, 8, 9, 143, 188, 316
    field procedures, 201
    fieldwork, 6, 148, 152, 153, 165, 167, 324
    interview procedures, 143
    interview schedules, 151
    preliminary stage, 153
    questionnaire, 10, 11, 54, 55, 103, 112, 122, 127, 133, 144, 151, 154, 156, 157, 158, 173, 240, 244, 250, 252, 265
    recording data, 51, 143
    revision of, 154, 158
    sample design, 103, 240, 250
    sample determination, 243
    sample questionnaire, 252
    sample size, 243, 266
    sampling methods, 99
    sampling method, household, 103
    locating markets, 150
    maps in, 149, 160, 180
    market level, 99
    obtaining local permission, 150
    of markets, 100
    recruitment of field assistants, 152
    research permission, 149
Sutinen, J. G., 219, 220, 224, 225, 230, 233, 234, 235, 237
Swindell, K., 145, 164
Symanski, R., 4, 8, 14

—T—

Takayama, T., 331, 342, 429, 430, 436
Tefft, J. F., 8, 43, 46, 55, 60, 61
Témé, B., 44, 60, 62
Thaler, R., 442
Thomsen, F. L., 273, 275
Thorpe, J. K., 144, 165
Timmer, C. P., 4, 17, 106, 113, 173, 185, 238, 294, 295, 296, 299, 305, 324 , 329, 342
Tobin, J., 388, 399
Tobit, 383, 384, 387, 388, 390, 391, 392, 393, 394, 398, 400
    and truncated estimation, 388
Tomek, W. G., 222, 233, 238, 279, 280, 282, 299
Topel, R. H., 399, 402
Torres, E. B., 219, 220, 224, 225, 230, 234, 235, 236, 238
Trager, L., 144, 165

Trends, policy and development, 169
Trotter, B. W., 5, 17
Trost, R. P., 395, 398, 401, 402
Tucker, A. W., 430, 431, 436
Tucker, S. K., 190, 215
Tunisia, 7, 12, 403, 404, 412, 414, 415, 416, 417, 418, 419
Turner, D. F., 226, 236
Turner, G., 310, 324
Tyson, W. J., 236

—U—

Underwood, B., 190, 213
Uzawa, H., 435

—V—

Van Horne, J. C., 367, 377
Vaus, D. A., 151, 165
Verkoren, O., 159, 163
Vertical integration, vertical dimension of, 22
Viera, M. A., 366, 376, 377
Von Oppen, M., 324, 429, 430, 437

—W—

Warwick, D. P., 5, 14
Webb, T., 17
Weber, M. T., 4, 5, 16, 168, 174, 179, 184, 279, 283, 298
Weil, R., 376
Welfare benefits,
    measuring, 403
    technical change and, 403, 404, 410, 411, 412
Werge, R., 136
Werner, O., 145, 148, 151, 152, 165
Westlake, M. J., 74, 97
Wheatley, C. C., 7, 12, 116, 136, 138, 361, 362, 363, 376, 377
Whitehead, T. L., 153, 165

Whyte, W. F., 156, 165
Wiersema, S., 135, 136
Williams, T. O., 74, 97
Wilson, K., 162, 165, 455
Winkelmann, D., 134
Wohlgenant, M. K., 405, 420, 462, 478, 479
Wolfe, P., 430, 437
Wollen, G. H., 310, 324
Wong, D., 16, 123, 133, 135, 136
World Bank, 4, 14, 17, 45, 60, 97, 178, 180, 185

—Y—

Yaron, D., 430, 437
Youdeowei, A., 415, 420
Young, R. H., 4, 14, 17, 121, 136

—Z—

Zwart, A. C., 430, 437

About the Book and Editor

Markets for agricultural commodities in developing countries are changing rapidly. Population growth, rural-urban migration, technological innovation, environmental concerns, and policy shifts—both domestic and international—are but a few of the more prominent factors introducing new pressures to which markets must respond. This book addresses the critical task of understanding these ongoing changes and responding with effective marketing arrangements.

The authors go beyond the traditional presentation of economic principles, offering instead a series of applied methods for data collection and analysis. Drawing on extensive experience in Africa, Asia, and Latin America, they not only describe specific procedures, but also provide a wealth of illustrative research results. The book will be particularly useful to teaching professionals, development specialists, and applied researchers working in developing countries.

Gregory J. Scott is an economist in the Social Science Department of the International Potato Center (Lima, Peru).